MW00989116

Cosmic Astrology

An East-West Guide to Your Internal Energy Persona

Mantak Chia
and
William U. Wei

Destiny Books
Rochester, Vermont • Toronto, Canada

Destiny Books
One Park Street
Rochester, Vermont 05767
www.DestinyBooks.com

Destiny Books is a division of Inner Traditions International

Originally published in Thailand in 2011 by Universal Tao Publications under the title *Magical Persona Astrology: Guide to Everyone's Internal Energy Persona*

Library of Congress Cataloging-in-Publication Data
Chia, Mantak, 1944–
  Cosmic astrology : an East-West guide to your internal energy persona / Mantak Chia and William U. Wei.
    p. cm.
  Rev. ed. of: Magical persona astrology.
  Includes bibliographical references (p.   ) and index.
  ISBN 978-1-59477-450-8 (pbk.) — ISBN 978-1-59477-699-1 (e-book)
  1. Astrology. I. Wei, William U. II. Chia, Mantak, 1944– Magical persona astrology. III. Title.
  BF1711.C43 2012
  133.5—dc23

                                                                    2012008245

Printed and bound in India by Replika Press Pvt. Ltd.

10 9 8 7 6 5 4 3 2 1

Text design and layout by Priscilla Baker
This book was typeset in Janson, with Futura and Present used as display typefaces

Contents

Acknowledgments

The Universal Tao Publications staff involved in the preparation and production of *Cosmic Astrology* extend our gratitude to the many generations of Taoist Masters who have passed on their special lineage, in the form of an unbroken oral transmission, over thousands of years. We thank Taoist Master I Yun (Yi Eng) for his openness in transmitting the formulas of Taoist Inner Alchemy.

Thanks to Juan Li for the use of his beautiful and visionary paintings, illustrating Taoist esoteric practices.

We offer our eternal gratitude to our parents and teachers for their many gifts to us. Remembering them brings joy and satisfaction to our continued efforts in presenting the Universal Healing Tao System. For their gifts, we offer our eternal gratitude and love. As always, their contribution has been crucial in presenting the concepts and techniques of the Universal Healing Tao.

We wish to thank the thousands of unknown men and women of the Chinese healing arts who developed many of the methods and ideas presented in this book. We offer our gratitude to Bob Zuraw for sharing his kindness, healing techniques, and Taoist understandings.

We wish to thank Colin Drown for his editorial work and writing contributions, as well as his ideas for the cover. We appreciate his research and great labor. We wish to thank Udon Jandee for his artistic contributions to the revised edition of this book, as well as thank our senior instructor, Wilbert Wils, for his insightful contributions to the revised edition. Special thanks to Ted Ross for editing and resourcing the book; without him, the book would not have come to be.

A special thanks goes to our Thai production team for their cover illustration and book design and layout: Hirunyathorn Punsan, computer graphics; Sopitnapa Promnon, photographer; Udon Jandee, illustrator; and Suthisa Chaisarn, production designer.

Introduction

The Five Systems of Astrology

With your first breath, you take in the energy pattern of the universe at that particular time and place. This is the alignment of the stars, planets, and constellations at that exact moment. As you breathe in, your internal energy pattern is formed from energy vibrations radiating from the stars in their alignment and position in the cosmos. This is the Five Element Theory of the Tao, which applies to Chinese, Western, and Birth card astrology.

When you breathe in the energy pattern from the cosmos, at that moment it is the same energy in the trees (wood) and the planet Jupiter that is in your liver, the same energy in the sun (fire) and the planet Mars that is in your heart, the same energy in the ground (earth) and the planet Saturn that is in your spleen and stomach, and the same energy in the mountains (metal) and the planet Venus that is in your lungs, the same energy in the rivers and lakes (water) and the planet Mercury that is in your kidneys. The Taoists know as above, so within. This is the Taoist Five Element Theory, and your internal energy pattern is formed at that moment in time and space for your life.

To change this pattern to balance and transform it into your immortal being, one must first discover it. This is the purpose of this book: to discover your internal pattern so you balance and transform it through these five systems of astrology. Each system gives you a different look or perspective to formulate your own persona. The Taoist leave nothing to chance, and five different angles to view your persona should give you the perspective necessary to develop the correct idea. The five systems described here are the twelve Chinese animal signs, the twelve Western astrology signs, the Western Sun and Moon Sign combinations, the Chinese animal and

Western sign combinations, and the Birth Personality and Destiny cards.

These are five different astrological systems combined together to give you your complete persona—the internal energy pattern adopted by each individual. Describing the persona is like five blind men trying to describe an elephant. Each blind man smells, tastes, hears, and touches the elephant. They all detect the same smell, taste, noise of the elephant, but they all touch it in different areas. The first blind man touches the elephant's ear and describes the elephant as thin and floppy; the second blind man touches the elephant's trunk and describes the elephant as a thick hose; the third blind man touches the elephant's tail and describes the elephant as skinny and flexible; the fourth blind man touches the elephant's foot and describes the elephant as a tree trunk; and the fifth blind man touches the elephant's belly and describes the elephant as an elephant's belly. Each blind man has one perception of the elephant but not the whole elephant; this is the concept of this book. When you combine all five perceptions together you will see the whole elephant.

The results of combining five different but similar and connected astrology systems for your whole persona are amazing. With very simple charts and analysis and explanation, you will discover your persona that you took in with your first breath so many years ago. Once you know your persona then you can balance and transform it to become your real self, and discover divinity through Taoist immortal practices.

Especially note that because of the way the book is designed, you will be able to discover not only your persona but also the persona of your spouse, relatives, business associates, and colleagues, plus people admired through-out history in the arts, politics, business, and sports. Once you know their persona, you will understand why and how they did the things they did based on their internal energy patterns.

This is why this is such a fun book to work with; not only will it help you discover your complete persona, but it will also connect you with people you admire and provide context and understanding of their accomplishments in their fields.

This is your energy journey of self-discovery, giving you the patterns of the universe and how they repeat themselves through different combinations, finally revealing to you the secrets of yourself and the people you admire the most.

YOUR FRIEND IN THE TAO,
WILLIAM U. WEI (WEI TZU)

It's All in the Stars

THEORY AND CONCEPT

In deep meditation the Taoist sages of old could see the molecular sea in which we live, with its repeated patterns in spiraling motions. As these sages started to analyze these patterns of molecular streams, they could detect certain vibrations in repeated patterns. These patterns evolve over centuries into the Five Element Theory. From the cosmos (planets), to the Earth (elements), to the human body (organs), and to its senses (hearing, speech, sight, smells, and taste), the Taoist sages can sense the whole flow of universe from the cosmos to their inner being, all in repeated patterns in this molecular sea.

The difficulty came when they tried to explain this phenomenon to others who did not meditate or understand this system of molecular repeated patterns. This dilemma brought on a major breakthrough for the Taoist sages: they discovered that these molecular patterns were similar to the behavior of particular animals in nature. People could identify with these animals—the rat, buffalo, tiger, rabbit, dragon, snake, horse, monkey, rooster, dog, and boar—more easily than they could with the repeating patterns. The sages also discovered twelve different energy patterns that repeated every twelve years, which corresponded to the behavior patterns of the animals. They further discovered that these animals combined with the elements of the Earth—Metal (rocks and the mountain), Water (rivers and the sea), Wood (trees and the forest), Fire (sun and the stars), and Earth (ground and dirt)—gave each animal a different phase of energy, based on the frequency of the Earth plane that a person was born in. This gave birth to the Taoist Five Element Theory and Chinese Twelve Animal Astrology.

The sages wanted to spread this wisdom to the common people. There-fore, instead of trying to explain the molecular energy pattern of the moment of a person's birth—when a common person of that era had no knowledge of energy or how it moved and repeated itself—the sages achieved their goal by explaining that a person was born in the year of the Horse, which has the behavior pattern of a horse and wood (1954), with its year in the element cycle. Today we have electricity, television, and the Internet so we can easily understand a molecular sea and how energy moves and interacts, because we live in a world that uses it daily. However, we can still benefit from this animal/element system of energy patterns, and the Five Element Astrology of today, with its complete repeating cycle of sixty years.

Western zodiac astrology has evolved over the centuries as well, based on astronomy and the movement of the stars. This is a little more complicated to the common person, as it contains different angles to the energy patterns rather than simply identifying with an animal and element as in the Chinese system. Both have different approaches with similar and linked results. The Western approach deals with a twelve sign zodiac (Aries the Ram, Taurus the Bull, Gemini the Twins, Cancer the Crab, Leo the Lion, Virgo the Virgin, Libra the Scales, Scorpio the Scorpion, Sagittarius the Archer, Capricorn the Goat, Aquarius the Water Bearer, and Pisces the Fish) with the sun, stars, moon, and planets. Again, that is a different angle from the twelve animals but can lead to very effective findings with its combinations.

The third angle, the Birth card, gives you insight and direction in your life based on the day you were born, and also for your intimate relationships. It will give you a new language to communicate and relate with others in your life. This system uses all fifty-three cards in a deck, including the Joker, to describe personality traits and destinies based on the particular day in the year you were born. This important aspect, and the specific meanings for each card, will be discussed in chapter 4.

These three approaches and their combinations give you a broad understanding and explanation of your persona with clarity, perception, insight, and completeness for your life's journey into the great beyond. Please enjoy discovering your persona from this book. It seems like magic as the charts and analysis pages reveal your internal energy pattern from your first breath. It is a simple and complete way to understand why you do the things you do and how you do them, and how this is different from others' approaches to similar issues.

The reason we are all unique is because of all the different energy patterns within us, and their different frequencies at that particular time in space when we formed our pattern. Utilize these five different perspectives in this book, and obtain this information to formulate your own unique persona. The goal of the book is to connect with your own uniqueness, so you can proceed to balance and transform your energy into the next realm.

This next section gives an overview of each of the twelve Chinese animals, five Chinese elements, and the twelve signs of the Western zodiac. These animals, elements, and signs will be discussed and combined in more specific, personal detail later in this book, but before doing that it is helpful to understand their broad properties, patterns, and energies.

The patterns are all in the stars.

TWELVE CHINESE ANIMALS

Rat

Years: 1900, 1912, 1924, 1936, 1948, 1960, 1972, 1984, 1996, 2008, 2020, 2032, 2044, 2056, 2068, 2080

Rat is yin and the first sign of the Chinese horoscope.

Positive Traits: Intellect, Charisma, Thrift, Appeal, Skill, Sociability, Influence

Shortcomings: Meddling, Guile, Acquisitiveness, Dirty, Verbosity, Nervous, Powerful

The popular notions about Rats are anything but positive. They are seen only as dirty, thieving disease-carriers. When we consider the natural inclinations of the Rat out in the world, we must set aside our biases that name the rodent an "enemy" of humankind. Rats take care of their own families and are tireless and tenacious when it comes to caring for their young. Here is an example of an elevated Rat position in history: When we see statues of the Indian elephant god Ganesh, it is not unusual to see a Rat in attendance. Rats are seen as special because they are bound to be reincarnated as Hindu holy people. This is certainly different from the commonly held viewpoint. Rats are masters of "chit-chat-ananda"; they will talk your ear off. The positive side is that they are great communicators. Plato and Tolstoy are Rats. The wonderful creators Haydn, Mozart, and Tchaikovsky are also musical members of the "Rat Pack." Rats are ambitious and smart and very family oriented. They make terrific friends and are a veritable force of nature when it comes to providing for the family and tribal companions. They are also busy, busy, busy. The story goes that Buddha himself once summoned all of the animal kingdom to a super-important get-together. This was a very big deal at the time: the Buddha was calling on line one, and there were a lot of animals on planet Earth. Only twelve of the countless creatures showed up, and who was the first among the many who were called? Why, our friend Rat, naturally. Rat wants to get ahead in the world and recognizes the value of powerful associations. The Buddha understood the positive nature of Rat and assigned the smallest of the zodiac beasts the head of the calendar, the first year of the Chinese astrological configuration. Kenneth Grahame's famous story *Wind in the Willows* features the character Ratty, who is a warm and loyal friend. He demonstrates those characteristics that shine like the warmth of the sun on his companions. Rat is a natural leader and is not above using whatever tactics are necessary to achieve a goal. Rat gets along best with Dragon, Monkey, and Buffalo. Like the Buffalo, Rat is a deep thinker. Further, Rats will do their best to get along with all if it will support their goals. Rats are happiest when they are taking care of business, when they are doing what needs to be done to reach what they want and what will serve their communities of family and friends. Rat people contemplate the many virtues of Rats. Use the Inner Smile and Six Healing Sounds to transform the negative qualities that the Universe has bestowed into positive Rat energy. Rats go forth and rule.

Buffalo

Years: 1901, 1913, 1925, 1937, 1949, 1961, 1973, 1985, 1997, 2009, 2021, 2033, 2045, 2057, 2069, 2081

Buffalo is yin and the second sign of the Chinese horoscope.

Positive Traits: Stability, Innovation, Integrity, Eloquence, Diligence, Strength of Purpose

Shortcomings: Plodding, Stubbornness, Bigotry, Bias, Vindictiveness, Standoffishness

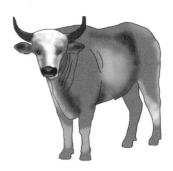

In some cultures the Buffalo is seen as hardworking but possessing very little intelligence. The Buffalo is hardworking. You bet. Just watch this beast of burden hauling the heavy load, whether it be plowing the rice field or drawing a heavily laden wagon. The Buffalo is a dullard. Here are some noted names of world renowned artists famous for their clever creativity: Bach, Handel, and Dvorak in the musical sphere; as well as Vincent Van Gogh, Walt Disney, and Charlie Chaplin. These are extraordinary Buffalos. The danger with citing the famous is that one must also cite the infamous: Napoleon Bonaparte and Adolf Hitler were also hardworking and diligent in their perseverance and laboring toward their goals. Buffalos are not known for being romantic; however, they can be quite affectionate. They are loyal and faithful to a fault. They care deeply for family and close friends. They have self-imposed high standards and expect those in their inner circle to adhere to and meet those lofty expectations. Buffalos are pretty serious beings. Sex is not high on their list of priorities; the Rooster, Rat, or Snake can seduce the Buffalo with patience and creative wiles. Buffalos are faithful to the family, but sometimes they do stray so as to break out of the rigorous discipline and schedule they have set for themselves. Buffalos like to relax at home;

they are not social animals, and you have your work cut out for you if you want to pry them out of the home garden and go to a party. Buffalos have fiery tempers and are easily provoked. Others can be inspired by the self-confidence demonstrated by Buffalo people. Some people call Buffalos stubborn; it is only because Buffalos are following their way, which they know to be The Way. Buffalo virtues include tranquillity, patience, honesty, modesty, and responsibility. Use the Inner Smile and Six Healing Sounds to transform Buffalo's negativity, which includes possessiveness, intolerance, materialism, and inflexibility. The Buffalo makes a great couple with Rooster, Snake, or Rat. Buffalos have the reputation of being in charge of human nature through reflection and meditation. The problem is that some folks view the Buffalo as aloof or antisocial. For the Buffalo, it is obvious that thoughtful contemplation benefits all. Buffalo is a deep thinker. Our hardworking, deep-thinking Buffalo oftentimes has an interior polar opposite that can be manifested in tomfoolery. When this creature wants to get up to some mischief it's difficult to see it coming. Such nonsense is totally unexpected from Buffalos. Listen with respectful attention when Buffalo begins a recounting of a family drama. Buffalo can speak with such gravity and involvement that his reporting can seem like historical fact or highly refined entertainment. If a Buffalo were writing this we would have a book-length exposition of the subject and it would never be boring. The Buffalo is quite willing to be the center of attention, especially if it serves the enlightenment of the immediate audience. With all of the thoughtfulness Buffalo inserts into any endeavor, success cannot elude this hardworking, stable creature.

Tiger

Years: 1902, 1914, 1926, 1938, 1950, 1962, 1974, 1986, 1998, 2010, 2022, 2034, 2046, 2058, 2070, 2082

Tiger is yang and the third sign of the Chinese horoscope.

Positive Traits: Magnetism, Bravery, Benevolence, Authority, Lucky

Shortcomings: Swagger, Impatience, Hotheaded, Intemperance, Itinerancy, Disobedience, Impetuosity

The song goes: "Everybody wants to be a cat, 'cause the cat's the only cat who knows where it's at. Everybody's pickin' up on that feline beat, 'cause everything else is obsolete."* Now, substitute Tiger for cat; Tiger does not rhyme so well, but the lyrics suggest Tiger's

*"Everybody Wants to Be a Cat," from Disney's *Aristocats*

self-image. Tiger knows that practically everyone who counts is a Tiger . . . or wants to be. Sometimes Tiger is seen as quick-tempered and rebellious. Authority figures had best refigure the rules when faced with a Tiger on the move. The rest of us just don't get that Tiger is the entrepreneur, and to achieve the goals all is permitted to Tiger; there are no limits. As you might imagine, this behavior can land a fearless Tiger in a heap of trouble. Here again instincts serve, and the Tiger can spring away to do battle again another day. What an ally the Tiger can be with the right partner—one who believes that the world is a playground for the courageous and dedicated. The best relationship can be made with Horse; also an association with another Tiger can be fruitful. Dog is a good match for Tiger, because Tiger admires Dogs heroic quality. Horse, Dog, and Tiger are freedom-loving, self-centered beings, which help them to comprehend each others' natures.

Tigers laugh at the law as they adhere to the "law of the jungle"; the strong survive. Tigers will steamroll over whatever is between them and their objectives. Tigers are very opinionated and will dominate any debate or discussion using their authority and magnetism. It doesn't matter that their positions may actually be untenable, on shaky ground. Tiger places the body in a rooted chi kung stance, and that root will not be budged. Brave, benevolent Tiger, for your health and well-being please: Root yourself, smile, and tune that roar into the "shh" sound, for the sake of your precious liver. The Inner Smile and Six Healing Sounds have no laws governing the practitioner so go, Tiger, go. Tigers are powerful and passionate creatures, and these attributes can cause a big commotion at times. Their unpredictable impulsiveness should not be underestimated. Watch out for these cats. When a Tiger is in attendance at a gathering there is no missing their presence; everyone knows and is keeping a watchful eye. Tiger, pay more attention to your future and don't burn out before your time. A wonderful quality of Tiger is the ability to weather the storm; Tiger can always revert to housecat ways, licking the paws and carefully grooming the fur, head to tail. Unflappable and cool as a cucumber is Tiger when he needs to be. Because of Tiger's disdain of convention and law and the tendency to bend or break laws and conventions, Tiger can find himself at odds with authority and be branded an outlaw. Even in such a predicament Tiger has the possibility to emerge unscathed thanks to fruitful cultivation of friends of influence. Tiger is known also as a kindly and generous sort, and by association Tiger's good luck has been known to rub off on friends and associates. A Tiger is to be cautiously observed.

Rabbit

Years: 1903, 1915, 1927, 1939, 1951, 1963, 1975, 1987, 1999, 2011, 2023, 2035, 2047, 2059, 2071, 2083

Rabbit is yin and the fourth sign of the Chinese horoscope.

Positive Traits: Ambition, Longevity, Finesse, Tact, Virtue, Prudence

Shortcomings: Complexity, Secretiveness, Pedantry, Dilettantism, Hypochondria, Squeamishness

Rabbits are thrifty, and if they loan out money they are sure to collect what's due with interest: not a penny more and not a penny less. "Waste not; want not" may be the motto of some Rabbits. Others may go to the extreme: do with or do without. Rabbits are not seeking wealth; they do take good care of what they've acquired through ambition and prudence. They are the detail people. They also make warm friends with their kind ways and discretion. Rabbit understands nature ensures firm bonds, especially with Ram and Boar. Rabbit appreciates fully their good manners and gallantry. Rabbits avoid stress and conflict, preferring peace and quiet. This makes them a natural for meditation; they were born with knowing Inner Smiles. The Healing Heart Sound "haww" is an effective method for encouraging those qualities of love and joy that Rabbit so delights in others. Rabbit's own heart would benefit mightily from the physical practice of Spinal Cord Breathing as taught in the Universal Healing Tao chi kung curriculum. Rabbits are generous with what they have and can be personable when not lecturing. Rabbits can be elegant and refined. Because of their ambition and diplomacy, Rabbits can become successful leaders. Although Rabbits can sit a long, quiet time, they are also nimble and quick, and can be on the other side of the garden in a flash. Peter Rabbit found himself in a sticky dilemma with the farmer, but with finesse (and not a little luck) he made his way back to his forest home (and the trouble waiting there). Rabbit's predisposition to evasiveness and secrecy can be overcome by patient understanding and love, love, love. We should say that is Rabbit's patient understanding and love for Rabbit's own self that needs be put in action. Have the pleasure of observing a Rabbit out in the woods, it is its home territory. A Rabbit characteristic is prudence; Rabbit has the good sense to quietly assess its surroundings and situation before making a move. After all, Rabbit in the forest is often the prey not the predator. Its yin character serves Rabbit well, as whatever it needs seems to manifest, especially when Rabbit follows the plain dictum: simplify, simplify, simplify. Rabbit tends to complicate the scene with too many useless details, which become like a web and stifle Rabbit's latent imagination. Rabbit, be less serious and more open to humor. Before the Inner Smile Meditation, sit with closed eyes and begin laughing, laughing, and laugh some more. This can be very effective when done in front of the mirror. In fact laughter has been known to heal, so Rabbit's hypochondria stands a good chance of being laughed right down into Mother Earth to be transformed into that sense of well-being so necessary to Rabbit's longevity. Pedantry or lack of imagination can slow Rabbit's spiritual growth. The Fusion of the Five Elements Meditation will support Rabbit's transformative capacity, and he will soon be hopping down the bunny trail of peace and tranquillity.

Dragon

Years: 1904, 1916, 1928, 1940, 1952, 1964, 1976, 1988, 2000, 2012, 2024, 2036, 2048, 2060, 2072, 2084

Dragon is yang and the fifth sign of the Chinese horoscope.

Positive Traits: Enthusiasm, Sentimentality, Strength, Pluck, Success, Good Health

Shortcomings: Braggadocio, Rigidity, Volubility, Mistrust, Infatuation, Dissatisfaction

It is strange that the other eleven animals in the Chinese zodiac can be observed in nature, or at least in the zoo or on the Nature Channel. This creature must be very special, and Dragon people know that they are indeed very special. What a proud, self-assured personage is the Dragon. Just think of Tolkien's Dragon Smaug from his famous book *The Hobbit*. The trouble is that the Dragons' sometimes violent and tyrannical side can be their downfall. Like the Tiger, Dragon is born with an innate authority, and like the Tiger, Dragon can be brought down by authority's double-edged sword. Authority, even inborn authority, must be used judicially. Dragon people can find an equal intelligence in match-ups with Monkey people or Rat People. In the West, Dragons are generally seen to be evil worms bent on destruction and murder. In the East, Dragons are divine bearers of good fortune; they are fierce and steadfast guardians. It's not unusual to see Dragons wrapped around the pillars of a Kuan Yin chapel or temple. In Michael Ende's fascinating book, *The Neverending Story*, one of the protagonists is Falkor, a genial luck Dragon who devotes himself to the young hero Atreyu. Falkor lives those strong Dragon traits of enthusiasm, pluck, and bravery. In the Chinese New Year parades, the Dragon is the leader because he leaves a trail of wealth, virtue, harmony, and long life. Let's join the parade. Dragons are natural show-offs and with good reason: they have a lot to show. And they are veritable energy sources. So much energy must be managed wisely to benefit Dragon's magnificent body, challenging intellect, and soaring spirit. The Inner Smile and Six Healing Sounds prepare Dragon to circulate this formidable energy in the micro- and macrocosmic orbits. If you are at a large gathering you'll spot the Dragon people right away by their elegance and flamboyance and splendor. Rat people, Boar people, and Rabbit people are good partners for the fiery, passionate Dragon people. In China, Dragon was a symbol for the all-powerful emperor. What can really do a Dragon in is the predilection for bragging, born out of a morbid and deep self-absorption. This vanity is a clear indication for Dragon people to take some distance and to make a huge leap and smile and laugh at the absurdity of such narcissistic self-admiration. The Dragon is a ready candidate for the Universal Healing Tao's advanced practices of Kan and Li. In popular fantasy, representations of Dragons are known to inhabit dark, treasure-laden caves deep in remote mountains. The Tao Garden in northern Thailand offers Dark Room Retreats led by Master Mantak Chia. In the days and weeks of total darkness and silence, Dragon people can enrich body, mind, and spirit with the Three True Treasures as revealed by Lao-tzu's *Tao Te Ching*: compassion, frugality, and humility. All is possible with these indisputably wonderful monarchs of the Chinese zodiac.

Snake

Years: 1905, 1917, 1929, 1941, 1953, 1965, 1977, 1989, 2001, 2013, 2025, 2037, 2049, 2061, 2073, 2085

Snake is yang and the sixth sign of the Chinese horoscope.

Positive Traits: Discretion, Intuition, Compassion, Clairvoyance, Sagacity, Attractiveness

Shortcomings: Extravagance, Dissimulation, Laziness, Presumption, Exclusiveness, Cupidity

Snake people can find accomplishment in elected offices. They are effective negotiators, which is an essential skill for political success. Snakes are able to distance themselves when there is a predicament in which everyone is very tragically and seriously involved. Snake is not easily upset in such a state. With this posture of detachment, the Snake supports others to lighten up and see the situation more clearly. This quality, coupled with Snake's ability to slither below the surface and get to the core, makes friendships both romantic and professional with Buffalo people and Rooster people most propitious. Some Snakes are seen as the most intuitive, introspective, refined, and collected of all the creatures in the Chinese zodiac. The difficulty for Snake is the popular image of Snakes in the West: Eve and Adam's banishment from the garden or Eden, as orchestrated by the evil Snake, is a Christian image formed at an early age. The pejorative snake in the grass brands the person a betrayer of trust. In China, a snake living in a human abode is seen as a good sign that the family will not want for food. In the Chinese language, to call a woman "a real snake" is high compliment. Snake people are quick and sharp-witted and become very good with the family or business economics. They do not have to work too hard to maintain a healthy cash flow. They are natural leaders and attract the right people around them, especially the people who can help with the daily chores in order that Snake be able to concentrate on what is truly important: more beautiful things. Mysterious and attractive, Snake people can be very seductive. Do not cross a Snake; he will plot a delicious revenge. Snakes can be lazy, especially after a victory. Snakes can be jealous and unforgiving. They are not especially communicative, and Snakes can be quite possessive when they've decided on a course of action to achieve a business or personal goal. Snakes can be intelligent advisors and have excellent instincts. Snake is a thinker who also likes to live well and is seriously concerned with affluence. Snakes love the arts, fancy adornment, and gourmet meals and drink; however, their inborn poise and taste bequeaths a disdain of trivialities, narrow thinkers, and chit-chat-ananda. In times of confusion and trouble, the Snake is a pillar of strength because he maintains a presence of mind. The Snake can manage bad news and calamity with self-composure. Snake people have a weighty idea of what responsibility entails and keep all eyes on the goal. It will be this constancy of purpose coupled with a natural hypnotic charisma that could carry a Snake to the highest realms of power. Snakes emanate calmness and they understand other people, but they themselves sometimes are hard to predict. They find it easy to attain success and fame. They are selfish and would not mind using other people to get what they want. Snakes are very superstitious. Snakes have beautiful skin, and Snake people should be sharp dressers.

Horse

Years: 1906, 1918, 1930, 1942, 1954, 1966, 1978, 1990, 2002, 2014, 2026, 2038, 2050, 2062, 2074, 2086

Horse is yang and the seventh sign of the Chinese horoscope.

Positive Traits: Persuasiveness, Style, Autonomy, Dexterity, Popularity, Accomplishment

Shortcomings: Selfishness, Haste, Unscrupulousness, Anxiety, Rebellion, Pragmatism

Black Beauty is one of the most popular Horses to come to mind in the English-speaking world. Black Beauty, from the cherished novel of the same name, is cheerful, quick-witted, and intelligent. These qualities are also shared with Tiger and Dog, which makes for good possibilities for successful alliances among these three. Horse people are known as honest folk. They have a very friendly nature and are broad minded enough to accept different-natured people and their points of view. It's said that to truly understand another person it is necessary to walk a mile in that person's moccasins. Horse people understand that and put it into practice in life's daily situations. Sometimes Horses are seen as being too fond of themselves and will pitch a fit when things don't go in their favor. Horse people are extremely vigorous and physically powerful. Horse people have a witty, extroverted way about them that is accented by a muscular poise. Horses are the action figures of the Chinese zodiac, which always makes them the center of attention, especially in competition. Think of the famous American racehorse Seabiscuit. And if that's not enough, they are renowned for their wisdom and keen sense of humor. Horse people demonstrate "horse sense," which is manifested in their endeavors whether they are personal business, competition, or work related. In the professional world you will find Horse people to be efficient and genial in positions that require them to cooperate with other people. The routine job is not one for which Horse is particularly suited. Horse's special characteristics empower Horse people to accept almost any task and excel in its successful completion. Horse people tend to fall deeply in love at first sight. Horse does not understand that falling fast and hard is wishful thinking in action, minus the thinking part. This new love object will fulfill Horse's deepest needs and desires. Stay tuned for the next edition in the never-ending series of "How the Horse Learned to Discern Lust and Longing from True Caring and Sincerity." Horse people are fonts of innovative techniques for solving tricky and sticky problems. When they have an idea, they want to put it in action this moment. Horse people work around the clock until they are satisfied with a job well done. Horse wants you to cut to the chase quickly, because although time is on their side they don't have time to waste. They'll respect your input, but time is precious so be succinct. Horses have got to learn to live out their emotions appropriately. They are hot-tempered and impatient. They are perfect candidates for the Inner Smile and Six Healing Sounds. When Horse people sincerely put those meditations, movements, and sounds together and live the results, they will become Taoists and urge their inner circle to get with the program. Horses like being the hub of the wheel and have the Universe spiraling about them. In return, they work hard and share with everyone. Horse people do not mind starting over. They persevere in their determination and relish fresh challenges.

Ram

Years: 1907, 1919, 1931, 1943, 1955, 1967, 1979, 1991, 2003, 2015, 2027, 2039, 2051, 2063, 2075, 2087

Ram is yang and the eighth sign of the Chinese horoscope.

Positive Traits: Good Manners, Sensitivity, Invention, Taste, Whimsy, Perseverance

Shortcomings: Tardiness, Parasitism, Lack of Foresight, Pessimism, Worry, Impracticality

Rams are considerate; they reflect before action and try not to hurt somebody else's feelings. If Ram inadvertently emotionally wounded someone, most likely Ram would 'fess up and do the best to achieve atonement. This is a characteristic that sees Ram through the daily challenges that life offers. Empathy is very important to Ram people, and they cherish the approval of people they respect. But Rams sometimes demand too much attention and force too much attention on those with whom they are close. Oftentimes their sensitivity is just too delicate for this world, and its not unusual for a Ram to misread a situation. This produces a sense of insecurity that fills them with the need for love and the desire for being held and protected. Rams can simply walk into an intricate predicament in which they can easily become bogged down, with the result being that they begin to shy away from confrontation. They shudder at the possibility of being identified with an unpopular position. Ram people are very romantic, sweet, and lovable, and these traits combined with their gentle and caring nature make them very attractive to the opposite sex. Because of a tendency to be in charge and knowing what's best for the loved one, Rams and their partners will find particular benefit in the chi kung posture the Golden Turtle. When Ram discovers the rootedness of his physical being while being pushed, it will be much easier to let go of the emotional baggage that has been weighing so heavily on Ram's spirit. Ram people are very creative, and this should not be suppressed. They love beautiful objects and find great satisfaction in crafting harmonious works of art. Family and colleagues may view their absentmindedness as thoughtlessness, but Ram people would never intentionally try to hurt a loved one or friend. Ram's compassionate, mothering nature strengthens the family ties. Boars and Rabbits make good match-ups for Ram people. Because of Ram's emotional vulnerability, the Inner Smile and Six Healing Sounds are *required*, not suggested. Another view of people born under the Year of the Ram suggests that they simply want to be left alone to live out their lives in peace and harmony. Ram people are calm and tranquil, doing their best to avoid drama at every turn. These relaxed people are content to go with the flow and will avoid creating an upsetting scene whether at work or at home. While being easygoing is admirable, striving to evade conflict at all costs can be costly. Here's what a thumbnail sketch of Ram might look like: Ram people are elegant, charming, artistic, gifted, and fond of nature. Ram people are also very delicate and very creative but often insecure. Ram people are often dreamers and sometimes can be very pessimistic and become overanxious worriers. Sometimes Ram people are seen as lazy. Due to their indecisive nature, Ram people enjoy studying the esoteric and always want to know more about the unknown. Therefore Rams are good at being astrologers or fortune-tellers. Ram people are very romantic, sensitive, sweet, and darling. In a relationship they can be overbearing and lazy, but with their gentle and caring nature, it is difficult for others to resist Rams.

Monkey

Years: 1908, 1920, 1932, 1944, 1956, 1968, 1980, 1992, 2004, 2016, 2028, 2040, 2052, 2064, 2076, 2088

Monkey is yin and the ninth sign of the Chinese horoscope.

Positive Traits: Wit, Zeal, Improvisation, Cunning, Leadership, Stability

Shortcomings: Opportunism, Deceit, Self-involvement, Loquacity, Ruse, Silliness

Here follows a modern observation of domesticated Monkey. On an island in the Gulf of Siam there are extensive coconut plantations, and when the crop is ready for collection the farmers attach a rope around the neck of their trained Monkeys. It's a long rope allowing the Monkey plenty of slack as it scampers up the coconut palm tree. The Monkey grabs a coconut and hurls it to the Earth far below. Sometimes Monkey gets distracted by something interesting like an ear itch or rectum scratching, and the farmer beneath is quick to give some firm tugs on the rope. Sure enough Monkey gets back to the business of picking that coconut off the stem and throwing it where it belongs. This is not to suggest a treebound career for Monkey people, oh no. It is to point out that it's very easy for Monkey people to turn their attention to details that distract from the task at hand. Monkey people tend to be in the vanguard of their chosen fields. Monkey people think creatively and with imagination, discovering fresh and inspiring ways to achieve business goals. Monkey people are good at sales or positions that require dealing with numbers and money. They are meticulous in record keeping and driven to become even more efficient. Persuasive and intelligent, Monkeys do their utmost to excel. Their extraordinary natures and magnetic personalities are always well liked. Their charm and humor are the reasons for their popularity. Monkey people are very good at problem solving, and they know how to listen to colleagues and arrive at solutions at the same time. Along with Monkey's curiosity there is a steady striving for knowledge. Monkey people have a good chance of becoming famous or well known at whatever they do. Monkeys are full of chi and generally cheerful in nature. Because of this abundance of energy, Monkey people need to find healthy outlets. The Universal Healing Tao's Macrocosmic Orbit is an excellent practice for Monkey people, promoting vigorous health and longevity. Monkeys keep their secrets close to their chest and use their love of competition to keep themselves stimulated in their occupations. Monkey people do best when allowed to excel in things that showcase their strategic planning or money skills. Financial planning, accounting, stock broker, or banking positions are excellent opportunities for them. Monkey is most compatible with Rat and Dragon. Either of these will make strong unions in friendship, love, or business. Rat, Dragon, and Monkey make fine companions in adventures. Boar is also fairly good if there are specific areas of common interest. Monkey people should, however, avoid any type of long-term relationship with Tiger people as there are few, if any, common areas of interest. The Chinese classic novel *Journey to the West*, by Wu Cheng'en, or its stage adaptation, *Monkey: Journey to the West*, by Shi-zheng Chen, Damon Albarn, and Jamie Hewlett, is assigned reading for anyone wishing to understand the Eastern view and origin of Monkey people characteristics. Monkey people love children and may go playing outside of the home but will always return to the family.

Rooster

Years: 1909, 1921, 1933, 1945, 1957, 1969, 1981, 1993, 2005, 2017, 2029, 2041, 2053, 2065, 2077, 2089

Rooster is yang and the tenth sign of the Chinese horoscope.

Positive Traits: Intellect, Enthusiasm, Humor, Resilience, Candor, Chic, Conservatism

Shortcomings: Boastfulness, Blind Faith, Cockiness, Bossiness, Pedantry, Dissipation

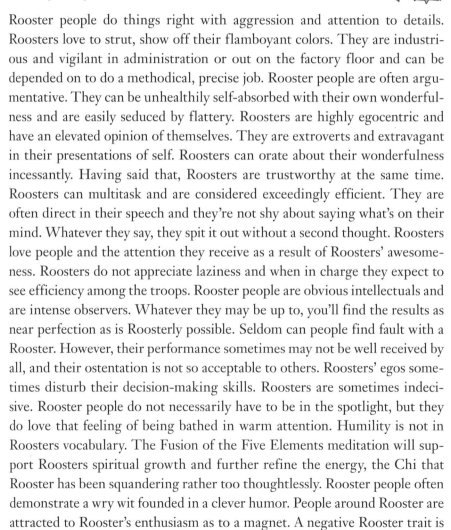

Rooster people do things right with aggression and attention to details. Roosters love to strut, show off their flamboyant colors. They are industrious and vigilant in administration or out on the factory floor and can be depended on to do a methodical, precise job. Rooster people are often argumentative. They can be unhealthily self-absorbed with their own wonderfulness and are easily seduced by flattery. Roosters are highly egocentric and have an elevated opinion of themselves. They are extroverts and extravagant in their presentations of self. Roosters can orate about their wonderfulness incessantly. Having said that, Roosters are trustworthy at the same time. Roosters can multitask and are considered exceedingly efficient. They are often direct in their speech and they're not shy about saying what's on their mind. Whatever they say, they spit it out without a second thought. Roosters love people and the attention they receive as a result of Roosters' awesomeness. Roosters do not appreciate laziness and when in charge they expect to see efficiency among the troops. Rooster people are obvious intellectuals and are intense observers. Whatever they may be up to, you'll find the results as near perfection as is Roosterly possible. Seldom can people find fault with a Rooster. However, their performance sometimes may not be well received by all, and their ostentation is not so acceptable to others. Roosters' egos sometimes disturb their decision-making skills. Roosters are sometimes indecisive. Rooster people do not necessarily have to be in the spotlight, but they do love that feeling of being bathed in warm attention. Humility is not in Roosters vocabulary. The Fusion of the Five Elements meditation will support Roosters spiritual growth and further refine the energy, the Chi that Rooster has been squandering rather too thoughtlessly. Rooster people often demonstrate a wry wit founded in a clever humor. People around Rooster are attracted to Rooster's enthusiasm as to a magnet. A negative Rooster trait is nagging; Rooster, observe that the constant pounding away at whatever you see as wrong does not produce the desired result. The same is true of bragging: What is the result you desire, and does vain immodesty support you to achieve your aim? Your attention to detail will help you not only in your professional life but also in your loving relationships. Apply the same respect you expect to those you are close to. Anticipate and fulfill their needs and desires and watch your results.

Dog

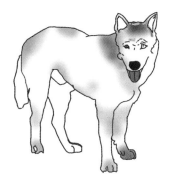

Years: 1910, 1922, 1934, 1946, 1958, 1970, 1982, 1994, 2006, 2018, 2030, 2042, 2054, 2066, 2078, 2090

Dog is yin and the eleventh sign of the Chinese horoscope.

Positive Traits: Loyalty, Duty, Constancy, Intelligence, Heroism, Morality, Respectability

Shortcomings: Tactlessness, Uneasiness, Criticism, Cynicism, Self-righteousness, Unsociability

Dog people show integrity and a strong moral sense, seeking out justice. Dog is honorable and will speak out about wrongs in the world and demand fairness. Dog people have a strong sense of fair play and are usually straightforward and candid. Dog people are the perfect spokespersons for those who can't or won't speak for themselves. Dog people are most likely an esteemed component of the family as well as the community. Dog people are protective of family members and are apt to enjoy celebrating the country's Independence Day with family. Loyalty and patriotism are near and dear to the Doggy heart. They respect the flag and respond to the national anthem with patriotic zeal. Dog people can keep a confidence. Pessimism can do a Dog in. If not checked, Dog will emphasize the negative, which feeds anxiety and fear. Dog people, learn and do the Six Healing Sounds especially the Kidney Sound. The Six Healing Sounds are very effective with worrywarts. Certain Dog people are prone to not fall asleep easily, but lie in bed stewing in their own juices, gnawing on the bare bones of their concerns. The Inner Smile is the best remedy for those useless worries. Dog's loyalty, sincerity, and kindness make for a most desirable friend and comrade. Dog's friends become part of the family as Dog extends concern and protection. Dog people are not materialists, but they derive the most pleasure from love and family. Their concern extends to all humanity, and Dog people are altruistic by nature. Dog people choose to use material gains to help others. Dog's gentler qualities include the fact that most often Dog is slow to anger, yet quick to recover. Unlike Rooster, Dog is not one to badger and carp. Dog is in control of the emotions. Dog also has fine powers of judgment. Dog chooses the battles thoughtfully. Dog people are easy to get along with on a day-to-day basis and are valued professionally and at play. The Dog is generous and compassionate. Dog people use friendly words and give support and advice to friends and family. Dog is a good listener, always available to offer support to friend in need. It's not unusual for Dogs to know a lot about their friends. Often Dogs surprise, in a happy way, a friend with just how much they do know about them. Dogs can be so attentive. Sometimes that attentiveness is way too intense for friends and family. Dog, find the balance of not too much, not too little. Dog people should pay more attention to their own needs. In private, many Dog people worry a lot. Dog people get along really well with Tiger people and Horse people. They are intelligent, alert, and aware. All three really value their freedom and understand and accept that in one another. The positive attributes of Dog people are excellent: smart, heroic, and respected by all for their loyalty and devotion to duty. Dog is not particularly drawn to wealth and fame; Dog is much more concerned with the well-being of family and friends. Before setting off on a new venture, Dog gets informed and studies up on the subject before leaping in to the activity. Dog finds great satisfaction in completing a job well done.

Boar

Years: 1911, 1923, 1935, 1947, 1959, 1971, 1983, 1995, 2007, 2019, 2031, 2043, 2055, 2067, 2079, 2091

Boar is yin and the twelfth sign of the Chinese horoscope.

Positive Traits: Honesty, Scrupulousness, Gallantry, Voluptuousness, Sincerity, Culture

Shortcomings: Boar-headedness, Materialism, Wrath, Gourmandize, Credulity, Hesitation

Boar symbolizes virility and fertility. Boar people believe all fellow humans are basically good and have one another's welfare in mind and heart. This is because Boar people have all of these traits; they are pure of heart and wouldn't dream of cheating anyone for their own gain. They are honest to a fault and can be trusted with the keys to the kingdom. Boar people are such steady and loyal friends you can be sure that they'd never disappoint you. Boar people are not so excited about love and romance at the beginning, but once they've connected and commenced they get the hang of it and they're ready to give their all to the relationship. They cherish heartfelt expression of emotions and ideas, and are more than tolerant of their partners' opinions and feelings. For the Boar patience truly is a virtue, and Boar puts the virtue into action when listening to others' tales of woe. Boar people will work at a friendship so as to gain confidence to bestow the best part of themselves onto their loved ones. Boar people can be quick-tempered, but they'll do anything to avoid arguing or fighting. They've been described as knights in shining armor because of their gallantry, sincerity, and honesty. If you have a Boar as a friend and that Boar takes up your cause, you can be sure he will not abandon you and will defend your position in the best way possible. No retreat and no surrender. Boar people are brave and giving; they thrive on commitment and are reliable, strong, and do not hold on to anger. Boar people are born under lucky stars, and they are receivers of good fortune. Boar people are basically happy and because of their shyness are sometimes taken for granted. Boar can be naive to the point of gullibility and can be taken advantage of by the person who is not-so-decent at heart and not so admirable. Boar people are so well mannered that some folks see them as snobbish; nothing could be further from the truth. It's just an example of Boar living up to its own high standards. Boar people have an enviable and excellent purpose in life. "To serve, to strive, and not to yield," is the motto of the Outward Bound program and could just as well grace the Boar banner; to serve is Boar's reason for being. Boar people love to read and soak up new knowledge. If they are with others with similar interests, Boar can come out of the background and speak well and knowingly. Rabbits and Rams make good companions and match-ups with Boars. Oddly enough, Boars should not get involved with other Boars. Other Boars are likely to lecture about how to be a model Boar, and this is not going to be accepted with Boar's usual grace. In most cases, no matter how old they get, Boar people still only see and believe that all humankind is basically good. Boar people constantly sacrifice their own happiness and comfort for the sake of their loved ones.

THE FIVE ELEMENTS

Metal Element (Axe, Rock, Mountain)

Movement: Chopping

Patterns: Decision Maker, Orderly, Inflexible, Organized, Systematic

There is very little flexibility in Metals. They reject other people's points, disputing their views and ways of doing things. If things are not done their way, they are unable to enjoy them. Metals have a specific program for everything, and they must be in accord with their vision. They are almost never distracted from their ends. Their home must be totally scrubbed and absolutely organized, or they find it difficult to function. They are distracted from their work if anything is even a little bit out of place. Classification is something that Metals enjoy, and they categorize as they organize their closet or desk. Metals are very autocratic and love being managers of things and appreciate those who respect their decisions and dictates. They are so proficient at organizing; preparing, and assisting others that people often ask them for aid or advice. In such cases, they feel really gratified about it, and their feeling of self-worth grows. Metals have a fondness for sour things and they love eating raw limes, cranberries, pickles, sour candies, and sour cream. Metals dislike it when people cry or break down emotionally. They have an urge to run out of the house and allow the person to cry to their heart's content and then come back when they have regained their composure. They cannot sit still while others whine and complain. Metal's clothes are best when they have symmetrical patterns and matching colors because they provide them with a sense of security in their surroundings. Light colored tops and dark bottoms are favorites with all Metals. Metals are competitive when they know they can win, or they will not participate. They dislike losing and let others stick to a cause without hope of winning. Justice is important to Metals, and they think of themselves as always being correct. When they argue, it is not about whether what a person says makes sense or not; rather it is something that is deeper and consequently harder to change. If one understands the elementary fact that knives get sharper when they are clashed against each other, it is understandable why Metals like debating so much. Because they believe they are right, others are wrong and require correction. Metals are unaware of the fact that those who they argue with are in psychological pain and are looking for ways to avoid discord. Metals abide by laws, rules, and regulations, but from time to time, when they break the rules, they justify it as being essential for an important principle. It is easy for them to follow instructions of any type as well as to obey the law. At times, Metals can be too obsessed with laws and ordinances, missing more crucial facets of a relationship or state of affairs. However, Metals are able to go against the rules when confident something is not right. Metals like the fact that they have personal strength and enjoy displaying it, especially with brawniness and physical fitness. Metals need to feel the strength and tautness of their muscles and have a sense of well-being. Metals can spend several hours a day just building up and exhibiting their muscles. They are able to save money no matter whether they earn a lot or a little. Metal youngsters ask their mother or father for additional chores to earn a larger allowance, and sometimes they start working for their neighbors. These children just sense how to put money aside and forego the temptation to buy something. Metals value a scientific view of the world rather than a religious, non-physical perspective and really enjoy empirical studies. Measuring and comparing results of experiments are tasks they love, which is the pillar of scientific thinking. If something cannot be observed or assessed by an instrument, it is not real. Metals frequently live according to a timetable, are always on time, and arrive at the appointed hour or a few minutes ahead of time. They despise being late. They strictly live up to their promises and agreements and have no tolerance for those who are tardy, forget about their promises, or make promises that they do not keep. Competition is a form of achieving things, and it also creates the exact challenge Metals might need to commit their time entirely to one goal. Metals are known to motivate themselves by setting up a deadline for their own project, which puts even more pressure on them, so they are prompted to work even harder. Metals apply all their energy toward finishing the plan on time and delivering the goods when others might have failed. Metals are list-makers. That is their way of organizing the universe to their liking, and creating more useful lives simultaneously. They create long lists of things they do daily, checking them off one by one. This gives them a sense of relief and a feeling of accomplishment. Metals love creating lists for each and every month of the year and every single year of their lives. Nothing is more upsetting to a Metal than a totally impossible task on their to-do list that they are unable to complete on time. The flipside of Metals' built-in intolerance for personal losses is their desire to celebrate all their triumphs. This is done with serious commitment as they accumulate and exhibit all marks of personal distinction for others to see; this includes diplomas, honors, trophies, medals, prizes, and credentials. This gives Metals a sense of pride, and they share this information with their relatives and friends. They are not timid or easy to intimidate. Metals' militancy expands when they are on the side of a just cause, when protecting their own interests or the interests of those they care about. Metals lack the empathy that allows them the ability to experience the suffering and defeat of other people. Metals are stoic about other individuals' trouble and suffering. They learn to love and value others but do not develop intellectual and emotional attachments. Most often it is romance or friendships where one first experiences hurt from the sharp edges and bossy demeanor of Metals. For Metals the power-color is plain white for its purity, honesty, and integrity. Metals also love colors that have contrast, and they are invigorated by them. They enjoy wearing white shirts and blue jeans, or for women, black skirts with red blouses. Metals enjoy contrast in food, but it should be neutral as well as flavorful. Autumn is the season for Metals. They love the profusion of contrast in bright autumn foliage. They enjoy autumn's early morning chill with the warmer temperatures during daylight combined with freezing temperatures in the darkness. The late afternoon and evening give Metal copiousness amounts of their element. Of course, when business is finished and the to-do list is put away, Metals can start to unwind according to their own plan of relaxation, which is scheduled for self-improvement. This can be an exercise program, art lessons, or neighborhood projects. Metals totally despise loafing, uselessness, and overflowing emotional entanglements with others. When the workday is over, they like to be active, and focused on goals. They only enjoy parties and recreational activities that are in accord with their own schedules and interests. Metals are the happiest when all their work is complete when the sun goes down. Traditionally, Metals are linked with the West. A lot of access to light from the west through windows, porches, or other locations provides a significant power boost to Metals. Metals sometimes have difficulty with their breathing, and often, when under stress, their muscles tighten, and they breathe in a shallow manner. Simple exercises done at home or at work are good, as is singing so that the lungs and lower sections of the body benefit. Metals relax when swimming or dancing as long as it is not competitive. Breathing slowly along with meditation are excellent for Metals, because frequently it is difficult for them to stop thinking so much.

Water Element (River, Lake, Ocean)
Movement: Flowing
Patterns: Stable, Shy, Predictable, Polite, Pleasant, Non-Confrontational

The personality of Waters is stable. They are creatures of habit who go to the same restaurant and order the same food for breakfast and dinner. They want an organized and stress-free environment. Waters do like to say no but they are not always good about following through on what they say they will do. Waters do not like to express their opinions. Debates or efforts to convince them of something they do not want to do are essentially futile. If they choose to avoid a request, they are basically polite, good humored, and avoid confrontations. Waters seldom yield to social pressure. They do not like friction, arguing, or giving explanations for their decisions. They tend to hold on to things and dislike throwing the old, broken, or even useless away. Waters believe everything might have some use in the future. They do not like to relocate to new environments and are fearful of it. Their friends tend to remain the same for long periods. While they are extremely loyal and dedicated as friends, their shyness often gets in the way of establishing new friends. There is a kind of passivity in Waters, and it is very difficult for them to start a new relationship. Frequently they are very quiet and aggression of any type is not possible for them. They will put up with the negative behavior of others because they are afraid to be confrontational. Sometimes they can change their fears into an enormous ability to be tolerant and forgiving. However, in its lower form, fear holds back the Waters' life. They are patient and supportive individuals who speak softly and pause to ponder their words. Fear is their defining emotion, so by watching horror movies, reading books, and playing computer games based on fear, they can connect to this emotion safely. Waters feel tired and fatigued more than average. Waters often are bored by others because people frequently seem to have nothing to say, or they simply have no interest. Waters have no interest in controlling people. They tend to be spiritual or philosophical relative to their pursuits and conversation. Waters develop their own areas of involvement where they are at liberty to do what they truly like. They might like the Internet where they can participate in a non-physical manner, and their timid personalities can catch the attention of the rest of the world. In some situations things might be totally out of control, but Waters will be right in the center of the conflict in one way but completely outside simultaneously. Waters simply do not show emotions one way or another, but just walk away from loud, opposing individuals. This frequently makes Waters excellent peacemakers. They can accomplish this by simply being there during conflict because they judge no one, do not take sides, and patiently bide their time while the fight slowly cools down. Waters like to collect things, and they are pack rats tending to never throw anything away and constantly accumulate new things. Among their favorite things are those related to sports cards, beads, animal statues, and items pertaining to their secret fantasy world. Boxes are one of the Waters' favorite items, oddly enough, and they do not like it when people touch or discard them. One reason why they do not share their views is that people always twist what they say. Waters often do not like to talk to others at all. They think that others do not listen carefully. They talk to themselves. Waters tend to be the wisest individuals, and this includes knowing other people's strengths and weaknesses; perhaps better than they know their own. Waters can reflect on others but find it difficult to reflect upon themselves. Waters eat their food or drink their tea at room temperature and enjoy raw salads and fruits. They will stay in a relationship with a partner even if they are aware that the partner is not faithful, and they usually do not complain or do anything about it. They like to maintain the status quo and resist pressure to change most situations. They tend to be sentimental especially about things such as their old houses, family, school, and friends. Waters are frequently tightlipped and have an ability to keep secrets. Waters usually conceal their love, affection, and other significant psychological needs and wants very deeply. Waters have intense dreams routinely. Sometimes, when they wake up, it is hard for them to separate their dreams from real life. Shades of blue are Waters' colors wearing them in their clothes, and they are akin to lakes, rivers, oceans, and rain. Waters never tire of the same things. Food for Waters is eaten to sustain life, not for celebration. They do not like to eat in large groups. They are very pokey and picky eaters and eat as though they do not enjoy their food. Waters need to do things while eating. They do not look at their food but toward the other individuals at the table, or anything except what they are eating. Waters have a list of foods they will not eat under any circumstance. Waters have few favorite dishes that they really enjoy, and they will stay with those for a very long time. Waters are heavy users of salt because it supports their kidney functions and helps them feel more energetic. Winter is generally better for their constitution and gives them a built-in reason to withdraw, and go slow. Waters do not like to search for jobs, or anything for that matter (other than on the Internet, which is their most important form of entertainment). Winter seems to have a positive influence on them and boosts their creativity, but Waters do not do well when the weather reaches bitter arctic temperature, or when they are cold over a long period of time. A climate where a coat or jacket is needed seems appropriate. The only time Waters can actually enjoy eating is a very late dinner or snacks around midnight, but unfortunately, this can possibly give them digestive problems. They have a tendency to suffer from a slower digestive system, and this indicates that they should never eat near their bedtime. Waters also seem to be night people, because they transform from the dispassionate and disengaged daytime person, to a more animated individual during the night hours. At night they can actually become intense and very interesting, adventuresome, stimulating, and even risk-taking individuals. The moon governs the dark universe and that is what Waters prefer. The dark of night finds Waters winning video games, writing fantastic stories or songs, or mysteriously becoming a seductive and skillful lover. Since the night is a special time for Waters, they should pay careful attention to their visions, thoughts, and dreams. Nighttime is when reflecting on the nature of things generally works out at a peak, and decisions facilitate their minds. For self-employed Waters who work in creative or business areas, the night is a good time for fruitful work, sending significant messages and e-mails, and even making phone calls. Waters who are not very garrulous during daylight hours, suddenly want to talk during the night when their language becomes perfect and their thoughts absolutely clear. Waters are linked to the north. Even in a garden, the northern side is best. They appreciate firs, ferns, pines, and other cold-loving trees and plants. Waters' bodily organ is the kidney. It is not uncommon for young Waters to be bedwetters. Waters procrastinate on going to the bathroom, partly because the urge takes place during the hours when they should be sleeping. The fundamental life-force of Waters remains awake and active at night. When the body's biorhythms are thrown off, they may have issues with their bowels or urinary systems. Constipation and other problems related to cleaning the body's waste could become a problem. Another issue is that Waters are very shy people. They feel self-conscious using unfamiliar bathrooms. Massaging and soaking their feet in warm water morning and night help their kidneys.

Wood Element (Flower, Tree, Forest)
Movement: Sprouting
Patterns: Kindness, Sensitive, Gentle,
Criers, Worriers, Caring

Woods have a sweet tooth and especially like to eat chocolate, candies, cakes, and ice cream. They are aware that eating sugar is not healthy but sweets make them feel a lot better, and they cannot resist. However, when friends say sweet words their craving is diminished, and they can also mentally record and play their positive statements in the morning and evening. Woods are prone to crying and cry a few times a week. When they are at home alone, they cry often and actually like the feeling, which is normal for them and should be expected. They have a strong sense of justice and take it personally when people, animals, or even plants are victimized. Their sympathy brings on tears. Heartlessness is practically beyond their comprehension as is why others hide their feelings and never cry. Woods are extremely kind to others even though some Woods know how to alter that kindness. Woods that have discovered the real power of kindness start by producing kindness toward themselves. Others cannot be as sweet and naturally kind while being as unrelenting and firm in the nonviolent fashion of persuasion and discipline as Woods. Those in trouble, especially deep emotional difficulty, naturally turn to Woods for help. People telephone them or sit with them and reveal their souls. Woods are fantastic listeners and let people pour out the negative thoughts and emotions from their hearts. After they tend to people's needs, Woods can start to feel quite badly unless they have learned to practice kindness toward themselves. They absorb the pain of others and put it into themselves. Woods are romantically inclined, and love is food for their soul. Woods can lose their vital force easily, but are able to get it back without effort. The beautiful, loving, kind, and romantic heal and restore them quickly, and they can resume their visions or fantasies. They are simply moved by anything filled with love and sweetness. Nature is dear to their hearts, and they enjoy taking care of plants, children, and animals. Woods have green thumbs and are able to cultivate plants even in harsh environments. Woods love the underdog and the downtrodden much more than the victorious. They feel the pain of the injured and support them over those who precipitated the injury. They feel unworthy of the good things they have because so many on the planet do not even have basic necessities. Woods are unaware; they think they are responsible for suffering and therefore want to take it on themselves. Woods constantly look for ways to assist others. Woods are not good at fighting for their own interests, but their power grows when they have to defend other people. When attacked they never have the strength or desire to defend themselves. They can even sympathize with the individual who tries to verbally attack them or do harm to them. When others are attacked something changes in them and they immediately start defending their friends and frequently regret what they say later and usually apologize to those to whom they have spoken in an abrasive manner. Woods are very sensitive to verbal attacks by others, and even signs of indifference and general lack of gratitude can hurt them. Like a small ax to a large tree, Woods can be hurt by a quick exchange of words or looks. Vulgarity, dirty looks; everything that is unclean and not courteous is disturbing to Woods. Woods are insecure about themselves and are usually not sure if they are doing the right thing. They are worriers and are constantly thinking. They are mixed with fears and notions produced by lack of confidence. Making a decision does not stop Woods from continuing their doubt and worry; it seems to never shut down. They seek metaphysical help and guidance by praying, and sometimes visions provide answers to their questions. In addition they make a lot of hand-and-arm gestures and frequently touch their hair or something else near their head. It is like a sign indicating a lot of difficulty in thinking correctly. Finances can be a problem with Woods, and they often struggle with money. This does not prevent them from having visionary ideas about a business worth billions of dollars, but they are unable to stick to a budget and usually spend more than they make. Woods can be untidy with their rooms or houses, but everyone feels welcome wherever they are because a person can relax, be themselves, and not worry about messing things up. Woods are constantly engaged in taking care of other people, so they have little time or energy to take care of themselves. Frequently Woods become vegetarians because of compassion, as well as not being able to stand the idea of hurting another living being for food. They seem unable to harm any living creature or plant. Woods will sometimes lie or mislead people in order to not hurt their feelings. This sometimes has a short-term benefit, but in the long term it repeatedly gets them into trouble. Like a tree in the neighborhood, they provide shade and shelter from the sun. The air is purified and neighborhoods look better but branches and leaves fall onto roofs causing damage. Many Woods report that the reactions of others to their offers to help made them cry. Being called nut cases, degenerates, or other unkind names is often the result when they only wanted to offer sincere assistance. Woods have a difficult time being resentful against a person who has done them wrong. It is worse for them psychologically to feel badly about a person than to release the entire thing and act as if nothing has taken place. Candles, cookies, or essential oils with fragrant smells like flowers aid Woods in their lives. Unpleasant odors cause Woods to get strong headaches, allergies, or sinusitis. Woods have reactions to cold and lose their good temperament the minute the sun goes down and it gets cold. Woods find motivation difficult to acquire unless they believe that they are assisting others. Aiding others gives them happiness and a reason to work very hard. Green is a good color for Woods because they are strengthened by the vibrations. Their body and soul are simply fortified by this color. Woods tend to be artists, interior designers, or jewelers and are good at working with gems, beads, fabrics, flowers, light stones, and wood. They should eat only good quality sweets and get sweet feelings from romance or family life. Dancing is a good activity for them. Doing what they love prevents sweet food from becoming an addiction and helps them stay in shape as well as be psychologically happy. Woods love to hear pleasing, genial, loving, and caring words or they will become pitiful and perhaps ill with depression. Spring is the perfect period for Woods to find their ideal mate, move to a new house, buy a new car, or find another career and is excellent for taking a holiday for renewal and general revitalization. Breakfast is probably the favorite meal for Woods, and they are usually in a better frame of mind during the first portion of the day. Woods are connected to the liver. The liver takes care of cleaning the blood, and giving lovely silky, bright skin to Woods when they are in good health. However, when they have a poor diet, too much stress, grief, or drinking, they can have skin issues. Woods will develop terrible skin rashes on their face, hands, or entire body if they are under too much stress. Woods need to learn to laugh and smile a great deal because it will make their liver healthier. They will be happier if they drink a lot of herbal teas such as chamomile, mint, rosehip, and dandelion. Woods need to practice breathing techniques while imagining emerald green light passing through the liver. This keeps it bright and happy and is a great facilitator of happiness and health. They should have an internal conversation with the liver urging it to be happy and thanking it for all the work it does.

Fire Element (Flame, Bonfire, Volcano)

Movement: Blazing

Patterns: Impatient, Narcissism, Impulsive, Quick, Passionate

Fires enjoy being busy all the time and are often quite impatient and dislike waiting because they must always be active. Fires enjoy risks, and, beginning when they were young, they invariably did what other kids were fearful of doing. They did things like drive too fast in bad conditions, whether on ice or a narrow winding mountain road. Fires have a passion for the adrenaline rush. They can rapidly get enthusiastic about someone or something; however the passion often does not endure. They often feel a longing or pain with separation from individuals and things that attract them right after they see them. Fires engage very quickly and in a passionate and unplanned way with everything happening at once. They find out that attempting to change individuals and situations is what they delight in the most. They are like fireplaces that have a need for the flow of oxygen in order to burn. Fires need to be outdoors daily just to keep their energy at a high and healthy level. Sometimes they even prefer to sleep outdoors. A permanent employment situation is hard for them because they cannot tolerate being in an office all day. Fires need challenges, a great deal of help and persuasion, or a good portion of mental discipline in order to complete what they started. They crave attention and the spotlight. They love being watched by the public and enjoy being the center of everyone's attention, whether it is fantasy or reality. They have no problem walking into a room full of people and having everyone stare at them. Fires dance without inhibition even if they are poor dancers. They tend to break or damage things easily just as fire in the natural world does. Fires never close drawers and doors even though they know how to, and when they finish the room looks like it was hit by a cyclone. Doors are wide open, and all rugs are twisted. They abuse and destroy their clothes and shoes, and their homes are always in the need of repair. They touch something and it seems to burn. Fires love to play and are really into sports. They fight boredom at work by developing their own games, playing them alone or with others. During business meetings, they may do or say something truly humorous just to disrupt the routine, making themselves and others laugh. Many athletes are Fires because they love a challenge against others and can get seriously dedicated to sports. Strength, speed, and agility are all part of Fires. Fires have big appetites for food and get very hungry abruptly; if they do not eat immediately they can become temperamental or annoyed. They sometimes think that when they do not eat for a period their stomach starts devouring itself because of an unusual metabolism. This can happen even after having just eaten, and they can eat again in half an hour or so. In the same manner that natural fire devours wood and other fuel in a very fast manner, the Fire element requires more and more energy to sustain its flames. This is due to Fires utilizing more energy than other elements because of their ceaseless actions while existing in an endless manner of aggression and persuasion with others. Fires travel a lot because they are passionate about escaping their normal routine. They travel inexpensively, go without hotels, and sleep in cars or in tiny tents; none of that matters. They just need to pack a bag and drive away from their daily routine lives. Fires do not like to be alone, and they find ways to manipulate people into keeping them company. Fires like to read or write, sometimes online, but they savor it more in a café or some other public place where there is a group, and they are not alone. Fires frequently speak loudly and have no difficulty cutting off other people when they speak. Fires enjoy speed and are the type who does things fast; that means everything. Whatever they do has to be done quickly. They are able to complete all their work while their colleagues are still figuring out to how get started. They learn things more quickly than the teacher puts them into words. Unfortunately, they often remember nothing by their next class. This is due to the vast array of new things that have happened to them during that time. The same concept involved with burning things quickly applies to every single aspect of the Fire's life. Fires can become angry quickly and easily and possibly even get enraged. This is just one reason why Fires usually get what they want. Losing psychological control of themselves can make Fires do dreadful things. When the rage burns out, they attempt to apologize to the individual they hurt and believe that what they did is not a big problem. They think everything can go back to normal. There is essentially no respect for rules, and Fires do not believe that others should have any authority over people. They have powerful personal magnetism and can overcome in most situations with others. They believe the social structure is against them. Fires are in search of the freedom to be themselves, and they experience intense unhappiness when they become aware that society does not permit their physical ability and mental courage. Fires are forgetful and might require reminders of their promises and responsibilities. Memory for the past is not particularly good with Fires. At a certain age remembering past excitement is not easy. It is therefore wise for Fires to keep diaries throughout their lives or else record events on audio and video. Animals make Fires happy because they can be animalistic without the sanctions of society. Healthy Fires who are not suppressed love to play crazily and sometimes growl, kick, jump, and run quickly. Fires tend to think like animals themselves and that they can never be completely tamed. Playing with children is something they enjoy doing as long as they do not have the daily responsibility of taking care of them. They do not want rules or regulations and sometimes fail as parents because when they stop having fun with children, and the time comes for their grown-up function, boredom has become part of their lives. Fires sometimes talk back and disagree with people. It is easy for them to hurt people's feelings when this happens. Fires do not listen well to what others are saying to them, and everything they hear is thought of as a command of sorts. Hot and spicy foods are a culinary favorite of Fires, and addiction to drugs, alcohol, and coffee are possibilities, but they are capable of stopping if things get out of hand. In terms of colors, bright orange, red, and yellow invariably affirm Fires, because they animate their inner fire. Food that is hot is a favorite of Fires. All things novel and unusual energize Fires, and eating the same dishes for three days in a row is torture for them. Experimenting with new and stimulating combinations of food and drink each time gives them a sense of power. Summer is the Fires' best season, and their most important projects should be done then. Sunlight and outdoor activities, especially in the summer, but throughout the whole year, uplift their mood and energy level. Fires enjoy being nude and dancing naked to a torrid song is something they love. Fires are affirmed by the everyday rhythm of the sun as it arrives at its highest level on the horizon and enjoy lunch or brunch as their favorite meal. Noon is a time for their sexual hunger too. Fires work during the day, and their energy level can drop toward the evening, removing their sexual drive. Fires like warm climates as found in the South. Fires should have easy access to southern, sunny walls and sit there as much as possible during the cold days of winter. Fires' internal organ is their heart and Fires must take care of their hearts regardless of their age. Fires burn up their heart Chi by working too hard and leading stressful lives. They need a diet that is good for the heart.

Earth Element (Dust, Soil, Ground)
Movement: Grounding
Patterns: Balance Keepers, Peacemakers, Communicators, Supporters

Earths delight in all things sweet and are capable of being very organized if they need to be, but they do not go to extremes. Earths are the balance keepers that provide peace and harmony between people, but have a hard time reaching their own goals. They do not get enthusiastic about one specific thing. They patiently wait to see what the cosmos will send their way. Earth's acceptance is notorious, but they frequently beat themselves up for being lazy or not achieving enough in their lives. Earths do not appreciate excesses and extremes. Of course they attempt to stop their screwball friends from leaping from tall buildings and are intelligent enough to avoid the danger themselves, but on occasion they have to go to extremes to get things done. There is a kind of sadness in the hearts of Earths for this reason. They need to keep in mind that they are important to the community, even if they do not attain any high-powered goals. Earths are superb members of any team. Because they support others, they shine, becoming quite magnificent. Earths are inclined toward a bland, neutral taste in virtually everything, including foods and styles. They do not want to have clothing that makes them stand out in a crowd. They might wear baggy clothing in strange brown colors and think only in terms of comfort. Earths have a talent for procrastination, but they have enough social awareness to remember what their family and friends asked of them and truly want to help. This long delay eventually leaves whoever has to deal with Earths worn out, but with a distinct and living memory of dilatoriness. Earths are very agreeable. If they are presented with a new and perhaps unpleasant situation, Earths are able to reach beyond their natural preferences and find grains of truth in nearly everything from actions to ideological platforms. They are capable of relating to different ideas and concepts, but they feel no obligation to follow them in their lives or actively support them. Earths like dirt, mud, clay, and actually enjoy digging in the ground, planting trees, making pottery, and sculpting. This is healing for them. Earths tend to find a way to get dirty. They enjoy being in the middle of things, as long as it is not too involved or committed. Earths enjoy a good chat, even with people they do not know, but only if they are not the ones who initiate it, and it requires no commitment on their part. Earths listen to everybody complain, know everyone's position, but manage to stay away from forming moral judgment or taking sides. Earths seem skilled at locating a special, comfortable place in a chair or bed and remain in a relaxed, meditative-like posture for a long time each day reading, watching TV, or playing on the computer. Even though they can get bored, they are experts at slowing down. A favorite food of Earths is potato dishes like French fries, potato chips, or mashed potatoes. They are completely capable of eating potatoes in some form or another every day of the year and also like rice and bread. They avoid food that is too spicy, sour, or bitter. Their personal hygiene is not always great. Earths have a natural resistance to two showers a day, washing their hair every day, and changing into clean clothes every day. They like wearing the same clothes for two days or more. Many odors do not offend them, but they use deodorant if they care enough about a special person. They get involved with anyone who is conveniently available and become involved with person living on their floor in an apartment or are just minutes away. Competition in nearly all forms is avoided. Earths often have no concern about promotions, pay raises, or striving for educational or professional awards. They do not like conflict or conquest so they settle for less, and often accept a position lower than they have earned. Things come easily for them because they are gifted beginning at an early age and talented in almost everything they try. They are oblivious to fighting for something and can relate to everything. Earths are the balancers, consequently they have difficulty developing the needed judgment, which results in them becoming stuck in some unpleasant situation. Sometimes they choose friends who are not especially moral. Earths frequently feel uncomfortable in high places and often suffer from acrophobia. When they are significantly elevated above the Earth, they can experience a great psychological and physiological discomfort. Earths enjoy hiking or even mountain climbing when it is done their own way and according to their own speed. They have a knack for getting their basic needs taken care of. There is something almost magical about the way the universe reaches out to them when they need assistance. It is as if Earths are being repaid for all the peace and harmony they have brought to others. Earths view themselves as rationalist, but it is very clear that emotions play a significant role in how they approach life. Earths have a special dual capacity for intelligence; one gained from the emotional connections they make with people and the other one from logic and reason. They have an ability to help people understand themselves better. Like all people, Earths have their own distinct characteristics, but they are quite subtle sometimes and difficult to detect. Earths have a lot of stamina, and their Chi is not often exhausted. Colors that are brown, brown-green, brown-black, and brown-purple provide energy for them because they are similar to earth's own colors. Earths are by nature attracted to yellow and gold: gold jewelry and clothes in gold and yellow colors elevate their Chi. They also like 100 percent natural fabrics because it gives them a pleasant tactile sensation and relieves stress. A variant of flavors give Earths energy, but they should not be over-consumed. A bit of sour in the diet is suggested. A bland and neutral diet is best for Earths because it keeps everything in order. Indian summer is the best time of year for Earths' power. Throughout between-season days, individuals from the other elements will be much more giving to the necessities of Earths and pay more attention to their communication. Lukewarm temperatures are a favorite of Earths along with a slight breeze and clouds. They do not like extremes. On good days Earths can feel their vibrations and the universe being more open and a good time to make very important decisions. Earths' best time is the early afternoon when they can recharge themselves. Their energy can shift noticeably, and the result is a total recharge. They will be ready to go out, study, or do projects at home. It is possible that Earths will learn that they have more energy and their lives are easier if they live toward the center of a country like America's Midwest. Daydreaming is also a way Earths can be reenergized. Anything that affects the function of the stomach or spleen also activates and heightens the flow of Chi in Earths. They enjoy food and may have a disposition toward accumulating extra weight. Activities and exercises intended to move energy in the mid-section are recommended for Earths. Tennis, Ping-Pong, swimming, hula-hoop, gentle yoga, breathing exercises, and Chi Kung, or being rooted to the ground are good for Earths. They do not like competitive sports, and if they get involved in activities, which bring about losing self-respect, heated arguments, or hurt feelings; the exercises are of no use. Regularly drinking herbal tea is good for Earths, which increase the health of the stomach, such as chamomile, peppermint, or a mild ginger.

Five Elements in your first Sixty-Year Cycle: According to Five Element Astrology tradition you are also under the influence of one element every 12 years of your life as follows: *Wood Energy (Spring) 1–12 years old; Fire Energy (Summer) 13–24 years old; Earth Energy (Indian Summer) 24–36 years old; Metal Energy (Fall) 36–48 years old; Water Energy (Winter) 48–60 years old;* and then it repeats itself for a second cycle, then third, or fourth time. You also have other secondary element influences in your energy pattern but your birth-year element is your primary influence having the most impact on your persona.

TWELVE WESTERN ASTROLOGY SIGNS

Aries (Dragon) the Ram
March 21 to April 20

Ruler: Mars

Element: Fire

Quality: Cardinal

Aries is the first sign of the Western zodiac.

Positive Traits: Drive, Enterprise, Heartiness, Courage, Talent, Affability

Shortcomings: Sanctimony, Naïveté, Excess, Ostentation, Willfulness

Aries people are seen as rebels; independent mavericks who do not take orders well. Aries want to give orders, not take them. Aries will fight at the drop of a hat and are not easily beaten.

Aries are known to lie and oh, what a tangled web we weave, when first we practice to deceive. Aries is often caught in that web because Aries is not well skilled at lying. They are not so tactful at times, but even so, Aries people are not out to injure anyone on purpose. Aries people are vigorous and exciting leaders inspiring their followers with novel ideas. Aries enthusiasm fires these inspirations with a positive outlook and expectations of success. Aries is quick to anger and can get bogged down in a destructive brooding moodiness. The Inner Smile Meditation and Six Healing Sounds were tailor-made for these negative tendencies. Aries people feel the results of these practices almost immediately, and they are rapidly back on their game. Moving Iron Shirt chi kung, known as t'ai chi, can benefit Aries people immensely. The centered breaths and movements help to control Aries' inner fire and fiery outward nature. The important challenge for Aries will be to follow t'ai chi's precise instructions and movements. Another plus in doing t'ai chi is that Aries must complete the pattern of movements and not quit suddenly and jump into some other activity. Aries knows the value of money, but it's usually burning a hole in Aries' pocket. Aries people have such a sense of pride that they abhor being beholden to others, and so they pay their own way and repay debts as timely as can be. Aries are helpful when a friend is in need and expect to be thanked and recognized for the good work. Aries people can be inspiring speakers but sometimes overpower other voices. Aries people are usually well liked by others although their bluntness can put the recipient off. Aries people are quite respectful of their elders and make frequent visits to their parents. The Aries color is red.

Taurus (Snake) the Bull
April 21 to May 21

Ruler: Venus

Element: Earth

Quality: Fixed

Taurus is the second sign of the Western zodiac.

Positive Traits: Determination, Sensuality, Logic, Patience, Industry, Ardor

Shortcomings: Jealousy, Complacency, Gluttony, Languor, Prejudice, Intractability

Taurus is of the Earth and as such is warm and sensuous. Taurus people want to be rooted in their families. They value stability, balance, and wholesomeness. Let's recognize up front that Taurus people can be jealous in relationships and can retreat into laziness. They can be narrow-minded and indeed appear hypocritical. The Six Healing Sounds, especially the Spleen Sound, will be of immense help to open that Taurus mind into fairness and a broader perspective. With the Inner Smile meditation, the Taurus will be bound to discover a spiritual dimension of self that is very fulfilling. Taurus people admire beautiful objects. The meditations will expand that sense of beauty to include the wonder of the inner universe and the outer universe. Taurus makes for a true and loyal friend who will share generously of what is needed or desired. Watch out if Taurus gets angry. Taurus people's tempers are slow to ignite, but when they do there can be fierce and explosive confrontations. You will wonder where went the peace-loving, argument-avoider. In the end the Taurus makes peace after having vented. Taurus rootedness can be a strong support in a potentially explosive situation. The Bull posture and movement in Tan Tien chi kung can help Taurus vent in a safe, healthy way that will let Taurus steer clear of unproductive outbursts. Taurus people are sensualists and can be very sensual in their sexuality (Taurus, see our book *Sexual Reflexology*). Taurus people can be gourmets and must learn to control the appetite for good food and drink and to not overindulge. Mentally, Taurus people are sharp and pragmatic rather than intellectual; however, they can become rigid in their thinking and attitude. They are dependable and will persevere in spite of the difficulties that may arise. As they have materialistic values and physical possessions, respect for ownership and a terror of falling into debt, they will do everything in their power to maintain the security of the status quo and be somewhat hostile to change. To the point: never try to physically move a bull. They can be stubborn to the point of being seen as more mulish than bullish. To sum up and to illustrate the drive and thrust of the Taurus people: "At the age of six I wanted to be a cook. At seven I wanted to be Napoleon. And my ambition has been growing steadily ever since." So stated Salvador Dali, Taurus extraordinaire. The Taurus colors are blue and violet.

Gemini (Horse) the Twins
May 22 to June 21

Ruler: Mercury

Element: Air

Quality: Mutable

Gemini is the third sign of the Western zodiac.

Positive Traits: Dexterity, Quick-Wittedness, Perspicacity, Flexibility, Versatility, Performance

Shortcomings: Inconstancy, Self-deception, Impatience, Superficiality, Glibness, Indecisiveness

Gemini people are always looking at the bright side of whatever life is presenting. They see every sunrise as beautiful and presenting a fresh start. If it's a rainy dawn they see the beauty in that and will declare, "The earth needs this rain. Let it pour!" Gemini people can respond to the rain in a childlike manner, running out with face upturned. To complain is boring, and boring is a no-no. Everything and everyone is full of possibilities for the Gemini. They love to know the whys and hows and the inner workings of situations and people that they encounter. And they enjoy the company of like-minded friends and family. They have a gift for languages plus a gift for attention-grabbing storytelling. Clever, Gemini people have an ability to change to fit the new situation. They have no problem keeping up with more than one situation. They thrive on the "busyness" they create. Gemini people are affectionate, generous, and forgiving. When there's a party going on the Gemini will be enthusiastic participants as raconteurs and "spark plugs." Because of Gemini's intellectual activity, relaxation and quiet time are necessary, and it behooves the needful Gemini to learn and practice Fusion of the Five Elements. The results will assist in negating the effects of the Gemini mood swings. Further, this meditation will also satisfy the intellectual curiosity of the

Gemini, thanks to the Taoist view of heaven, human, and Earth. Gemini people crave respect, and with their charm and attentiveness they will have what they desire. The Twins are great communicators thanks to their intelligence and bright and outgoing personality. The Gemini color is yellow.

Cancer (Ram) the Crab
June 22 to July 23

Ruler: Moon

Element: Water

Quality: Cardinal

Cancer is the fourth sign of the Western zodiac.

Positive Traits: Caring, Caution, Imagination, Insight, Affection, Tenacity

Shortcomings: Hypersensitivity, Possessiveness, Moodiness, Irritability, Avarice, Despondency

Cancer people love their freedom and achieve this quest with courage and a pioneering way of life. Cancer has so much energy that it obliges them to learn and practice the Microcosmic Orbit so that they may continue in a healthy way. Because Cancer people are so given to extremes in the emotional department, they simply are required to do the Six Healing Sounds.

These precious movements, sounds, and meditations are just what the doctor ordered to aid Cancer people in letting go of what needs to go. These meditations should come naturally to Cancer because of their ease of going deep inside to contemplate. The Universal Healing Tao's active meditations will be a natural outgrowth of contemplation. The Cancer personality is full of compassion when its lineup of virtues is shining. Cancer people are family people, and indeed family life is perhaps highest on their list of priorities. They are at their most comfortable snug in the family and friendship circles. They are great learners, and when they've decided on a course of acquiring new knowledge they are successful. Cancer people are clever and have good instincts; they are imaginative and capable but know when to ask for aid. They are adventurers; however, their exploits are well thought out in advance so that risks are minimized whether the adventure is an overnight mountain trek or a financial undertaking. Because of their contradictory natures, Cancer people may be found at one end of the spectrum or the other; for example, they can be extremely dependent on others or independent in the extreme. Cancer has to have family and friends around who truly need him or her. They have a tendency to take things too personally and are prone to moan and complain about real or imagined slights. This gives rise to a morbid dwelling on the past. The Crab is an apt animal for Cancer: one may emerge from the shell or hide within. One may be grabby and crabby or generous and in good humor. Its a personal choice. Cancer colors are violet and blue.

Leo (Monkey) the Lion
July 24 to August 23

Ruler: Sun
Element: Fire
Quality: Fixed
Leo is the fifth sign of the Western zodiac.
Positive Traits: Philanthropy, Warmth, Nobility, Loyalty, Protective, Powerful
Shortcomings: Immodesty, Promiscuity, Vanity, Self-satisfaction, Tyranny, Arrogance

Leo people are brave and courageous. Leo people are determined, self-assured, self-governing, devoted, and giving. They are alluring and prominent people who are right at home when they are in the front of the room before a grateful audience. Leo is thought of as a regal sign because of their symbol, the lion, the king of the jungle, endowed with authority and substance. Leo is intelligent and distinguished; however, the flip side of their personality is that they are somewhat vain and pompous. Leo people at their best are a bright, shining light that naturally keeps all its subjects within a safe and sound range around themselves. They are affectionate, compassionate, benevolent people who will make it their undertaking to ensure that the lives of those around them are very comfortable, as long as they feel appreciated for their efforts. However, without enough gratitude, Leo people can become heavy-handed, officious, and obstinate, knowing that they are right and everyone else is wrong. They can be unforgiving and take even the slightest criticism personally. Leo people need to work on forgiveness; the Liver Sound in particular of all the Six Healing Sounds is called for. Resentment will eat away at the liver and the spirit. By going directly to the source, Leo people can do themselves a world of good. Leo people love the spotlight and make sure that its centered on themselves and their endeavors. Leos are tough, smart, motivated leaders who will sort out and inspire others. Leos assume responsibility and can make a significant contribution in their chosen professions, so long as their inclination to become bossy is kept in check. Leos love status, and positions with high-status titles are very alluring to them. Decision-making positions in education, medicine, and law are the Leo's meat and potatoes—if the limelight is focused on them, naturally. Leo people lead also in love in that they expect to be in charge. Their gratitude and attention will flow as long as the partner is appreciative and attentive. Do not try to take over unless you are a strong Aries or another Leo; oh no, two lions are equal to a fierce cat fight. The Leo color is golden-yellow.

Virgo (Rooster) the Virgin
August 24 to September 23

Ruler: Mercury

Element: Earth

Quality: Mutable

Virgo is the sixth sign of the Western zodiac.

Positive Traits: Practicality, Service, Discrimination, Decorum, Lucidity, Courtesy

Shortcomings: Snobbery, Nit-picky, Crankiness, Negativism, Meticulousness, Reserved

Virgo people are very devoted to their families. Virgo is a clear thinker but also a worrywart. Virgo people are the detail people; in fact it has been said only half in jest that the world keeps spinning thanks to the attention of Virgos. They are not big talkers and do not seek to stand out in a crowd. However, they will be noticing every little thing down to the last detail. Perfectionism is considered a strong Virgo personality trait. Everything around Virgo people has to be just perfect or else the situation has to be put right by a Virgo. Virgo people do not like crowds and rather than attending the party would sooner be helping the children put the finishing touches on their nearly perfect school homework. Virgo people have a mysterious knack to see in to the essence of a particular situation or to the core of a person. Virgos are meticulous in their work habits and also in personal hygiene. Because of their tendency to fret and worry over the details and how the world is going to hell in a hand basket and how this Virgo is needed to set the world right, the Spleen Sound of the Six Healing Sounds is prescribed. When the Virgo discovers and lives the beneficent results of these movements, sounds, and meditations, the sounds will be a fixture of the Virgos bedtime routine, right after flossing. Virgo people base their actions on what is real, not what is imagined. Sensation is prized over thoughts or feelings. Virgo people live with their feet rooted in the Earth. Once they discover Iron Shirt chi kung they understand that Virgo really is the connection between heaven and Earth. Virgos—just like doubting Saint Thomas—must see or experience to believe. Although Virgos are popularly held to be aloof or distant regarding physical love, when they focus their loving attention they become passionate paramours. Virgo people are quite efficient at sorting through things or people or situations to draw out what is important and what is a waste of time. They look for the best and flush the rest. Virgo people feel complete when they are helping, when they are in service. The Virgo color is blue.

Libra (Dog) the Scales
September 24 to October 23

Ruler: Venus

Element: Air

Quality: Cardinal

Libra is the seventh sign of the Western zodiac.

Positive Traits: Aesthetics, Idealism, Justice, Equilibrium, Gentility, Charm

Shortcomings: Manipulation, Quarrelsomeness, Procrastination, Talkativeness, Indecision, Self-indulgence

Libra people are charismatic and stylish. They are loquacious and classy public speakers. Libras are good looking, graceful, and sincerely admired. Libra people are the spokespeople for equilibrium, evenhandedness, and teamwork, especially in relationships. Libras are romantic and delightful, good company, and enjoy social outings to the max. They are on occasion interfering perfectionists, and this is not so charming. It's good to love oneself but not to the point of obsession. Libra people live to be in positions of public service, especially if it increases their popularity. Libras love being adorned in the height of fashion. Libras don't function well under pressure; unhurried and intelligent planning keeps the scales level. Libras bask in attention and are favorably recognized in debates be they social or formal public encounters. Libra people do not appreciate criticism of their work or presentations. Equilibrium, balance of yin and yang, are the hallmarks of Libra. Libra people are experts at hiding their frustration and anger. However, eventually there can be such an accumulation that one day there is an explosive outburst way out of proportion (not in balance), and stunning to the people around, who are accustomed to Libras' balance and grace under pressure. Libra people are so attuned to the balance of yin and yang that they take to t'ai chi as if it were the ultimate, and in a way t'ai chi is the ultimate. Each movement connected with each breath has its yin phase and its yang phase. Nowhere is this more evident than in Mantak Chia's Universal Healing Tao teaching of t'ai chi. Libra people appreciate beauty in all that surrounds them. Venus, the goddess of love, rules the Libra sign, and that's why Libras value and admire beauty in people and the arts. Libras are compassionate and loving, and they are remembered for their kindness and grace. Libras are great charmers and have an ability to make everyone feel at ease with them. Libra is a respectful listener and can offer keen insight into the event or person under consideration. Libra people never want to hurt anyone and are tactful in managing sensitive situations. Libra people treat others with fairness and expect to be treated the same. Libra can give and take both publicly and in intimate relationships. They make for warm friends and love to be in a circle of friends after they've made sure everyone is comfy and included. The Libra color is pink.

Scorpio (Boar) the Scorpion
October 24 to November 22

Ruler: Mars

Element: Water

Quality: Fixed

Scorpio is the eighth sign of the Western zodiac.

Positive Traits: Magnetism, Inspiration, Discipline, Sovereignty, Tenderness, Dedication

Shortcomings: Suspicion, Mercilessness, Revenge, Fanaticism, Intransigence, Sadism

Scorpio people carry an air of mystery to accompany their exceptional good looks, and this combination functions like a magnet to attract followers. Scorpios are passionate in whatever they are doing: no half-measures for them. An unfortunate feature of Scorpio is resentment leading to revenge; their nature is unforgiving and for this the Six Healing Sounds are especially called for. Unforgiveness (resentment) eats away at the liver and the spirit. Forgiveness nurtures kindness and compassion. Scorpio has so much energy and this energy goes to feed what is present in Scorpio's heart and mind. If the thoughts are resentful and the intentions are aimed at revenge, then the Scorpio person will probably taste the bitterness in the liver. In the long run Scorpio risks great harm to Scorpio, to oneself. The alchemy of Fusion of the Five Elements and Kan and Li is the life force tailored for the dedicated Scorpio. The result will be a refined energy feeding the highest qualities of Scorpio: loyalty, courage, discipline, and inspiration. Scorpio people are known to lead double lives, one for the public self and a secret life where they dedicate their true intentions to their true goals be they life-affirming or of a dark and hurtful sort. Scorpio people tend to bring a cool and determined posture to critical or dangerous situations. They work themselves very hard and expect that others will also toil tirelessly. They abhor failings in themselves or in those around them. Scorpio people are extremists; they are very protective and caring for their loved ones and can be ferocious in the face of someone who has wronged them. They respond with generous praise for those who are kind and loving. Scorpio people are very emotional; if jealousy comes into play, watch out. Scorpio people generally are intuitive, and they are quite observant and understanding of an individual's purpose and what frame of mind he is in. They are loving and possessive but are often misunderstood. Scorpio people are daring and have the capabilities to successfully manage large, complex ventures with magnificent self-confidence and control. When they've decided on a path of action their focus is unshakable. They are especially observant: no good work goes unrewarded, and no slight goes unnoticed or unpunished. Scorpio people relish a healthy challenge and are more apt to come out on top than not. The Scorpio color is red.

Sagittarius (Rat) the Archer
November 23 to December 21

Ruler: Jupiter
Element: Fire
Quality: Mutable
Sagittarius is the ninth sign of the Western zodiac.
Positive Traits: Reasonable, Solicitude, Cheerfulness, Honor, Valor, Openhandedness
Shortcomings: Contradiction, Vacillation, Outspokenness, Bad Manners, Carelessness, Recklessness

Sagittarius people face life with a naturally philosophical point of view, and they can make very good friendships. We can say they have a positive outlook on life. They are full of vim and vigor, and because of their love of travel they are known as adventurers. They love to selflessly focus their considerable energies on a project that will serve humanity in some way. This they generally do with a happy, engaging manner and a desire to support the best in everyone. They are strongly determined and efficient organizers. Sagittarius people are world travelers and are sincere seekers of the essences of spiritual beliefs and religious faiths. The negative side is that they can find themselves enmeshed in the religious rites and form, forgetting the why of their practice. They seek not only to expand their knowledge but also to discover the heart in the objects of their researches. When they understand what they have been after and they have this in their minds and bodies, they become teachers of the best sort. Sagittarius people are thought to possess a good sense of humor and to be compassionate and openhearted. Sometimes they grow to be too proud and act out with impulsive silliness. They are not particularly suited for homebound family life because of that innate restlessness and "traveling bone" that sends them seeking the profound and the true nature of humanity. Even when Sagittarius people find themselves in situations that bring most of us down, they resolutely maintain an optimism that oftentimes is not easy. When that darkest hour just before dawn is on their part of the world, Sagittarius people are apt to raise their chins and ask their friends to forge ahead. They have a passion for justice, the evenhanded treatment of all. They can rebel against an unjust law and will take the part of the weak and downtrodden. Sagittarius people are honorable in their friendships and not likely to hurt a companion; however, they know precisely how to injure an adversary with just the right cutting remark. They are forgiving in nature, and this is no small matter. They are very responsible when it comes to caring for their elders. Sagittarius people crave the liberty of the open road, the active life, and there can arise the conflict of career or seeking versus home and family. The Sagittarius color is purple.

Capricorn (Buffalo) the Goat
December 22 to January 20

Ruler: Saturn

Element: Earth

Quality: Cardinal

Capricorn is the tenth sign of the Western zodiac.

Positive Traits: Dependability, Resolve, Ambition, Superiority, Generosity, Wisdom

Shortcomings: Self-doubt, Stiffness, Pretension, Clumsiness, Loneliness, Epicureanism

Capricorn people are serious, pleasant, and reassuring in their quiet manner. If you have ever seen the 1983 Woody Allen film *Zelig*, the title character becomes a member of whatever culture or religion he finds himself in by absorbing the language and customs and even taking on the physical characteristics of the group. He is like a chameleon. The Capricorn personality is not unlike Zelig. Capricorn becomes part of the group it is with to the point that it appears to be a founding member. Acquiescence and personal adjustment are qualities that allow Capricorn to blend in and help out. Capricorn people are not given to emotional outbursts; they understand that such venting is not healthy and that they distract energies and attention from the objective, the goal. They are practical and keep their eyes out for what supports their aim. Capricorn people give age and experience the respect they merit. They tend to not offer advice unless asked directly, and when they make suggestions they expect them to be accepted and put into real life; otherwise don't ask. Capricorn people are worthy of your trust and they are dependable. They will comfort you when necessary and take care of you when needed. Capricorn people seem to be cool, tranquil, and possess great inner reserves of strength and confidence. They enjoy power and authority and the respect these bring. They know the customs and rules of life's games and follow them to the point of conformity. Capricorn people are given to rigid thinking and pessimism. The Iron Shirt chi kung practices of Embracing the Tree and Holding the Golden Urn (yang and yin positions) combined with the Inner Smile Meditation will help Capricorns' strength and rootedness to overcome the stiffness and narrow-minded pessimism. Capricorn people can carry heavy workloads in their professions and are as devoted to their chosen jobs as they are devoted to their loved ones. They are not much for socializing, mainly because socializing does not get the job done. In loving relationships Capricorn people are stable and loyal, which does not sound overly romantic, but that's Capricorn. They are not so imaginative but are down-to-earth types who will be there for you in your time of need. The Capricorn color is deep red.

Aquarius (Tiger) the Water Bearer
January 21 to February 19

Ruler: Saturn/Uranus

Element: Air

Quality: Fixed

Aquarius is the eleventh sign of the Western zodiac.

Positive Traits: Originality, Individuality, Independence, Tolerance, Charity, Vision

Shortcomings: Neurosis, Disobedience, Thoughtlessness, Eccentricity, Cruelty, Separateness

Aquarius people have a Broadway show tune written for their sign. From the musical *Hair:*

> *Harmony and understanding*
> *Sympathy and trust abounding*
> *No more falsehoods or derisions*
> *Golden living dreams of visions*
> *Mystic crystal revelation*
> *And the mind's true liberation*
> *Aquarius! Aquarius!*

Aquarius people are compassionate and kind and love all of humanity. They have a lovely quality of acceptance that allows them to travel and visit and be well received. They think creatively about humankind's spiritual growth and how that creativity is powerful and needs to be encouraged. Aquarius people know a lot of people but are close with relatively few. And those few intimate companions will not see or hear emotional scenes where one lets one's hair down. Sympathy and trust abounding, yes; poems of love, no. They are keen, entertaining, and avant-garde, and someone that everyone will remember with a smile. They enjoy being in groups where they use their vision and inherent sense of fairness to further the group's purpose. Aquarius people also are lone rangers, pioneers who are outsiders as far as society's niceties are concerned. They sometimes affect changes just for the sake of changing. Jack of all trades, master of none describes many Aquarius people. They will linger in any work or profession but not long enough to gain proficiency. If you have them as supervisors, you are lucky because although they can be erratic, they give praise where praise is due and are evenhanded in their treatment of their underlings and colleagues. Aquarius maintains a very interesting office, more like a gallery cum workshop with intriguing objects. "Do not fence me in" could be an Aquarius motto in the romance section of life. Some love objects of Aquarius complain of a dearth of emotional outpourings, but not to be concerned, it's just in their nature to work it out inside. It's like Aquarius people were born doing the Fusion of the Five Elements meditation, transforming and refining their negative energies through the neutralizing and purifying techniques of Internal Alchemy. The resulting transformation of destructiveness into creative energy fuels Aquarius' desire to solve all that is wrong with humanity. The Aquarius color is deep red.

Pisces (Rabbit) the Fish
February 21 to March 20

Ruler: Neptune

Element: Water

Quality: Mutable

Pisces is the twelfth sign of the Western zodiac.

Positive Traits: Spirituality, Understanding, Creativity, Perception, Awareness, Compatibility

Shortcomings: Indecision, Rage, Diffidence, Fearfulness, Lack of Will, Smugness

Pisces people are so sensitive that as princesses they would notice the bump of the pea under all those mattresses. They are so sensitive that its best they not watch the evening news programs, because they would be reduced to trembling, sobbing wrecks before the end of the broadcasts of the world's woes for that day. They are so sensitive that when the leader of their country states we must tighten our belts and double production, they take it personally and indeed tighten their belts and leave home to return to the workplace. When they overcome this sensitivity, their power of determination and intention will come to the fore in strong way. Pisces people sometimes have a weakness about them; its dangerous for them and those around them because these limitations can pull themselves and others into despair and inaction. Action is the key here; healthy action such as that demanded by t'ai chi chi kung. By activating the Universal, Cosmic, and Earth Forces, Pisces will find the energy and will to get back in the swing of things instead of staying stuck in depression. Pisces people take friendships seriously and are loyal to the people who trust and admire them. They are dependable, and their support may be counted on. Pisces people are broad-minded and are open to learning, especially through travel and personal experience. They have to be careful of being overly concerned about their future. Diligent and determined practice of the Six Healing Sounds will help Pisces to be more serene and rooted. Pisces people need this rootedness and open-mindedness to support their highest qualities: awareness and compassion. They must smile and let go of that confusion that sometimes stymies their creativity and spirituality. Pisces people are given to strong emotions and must be aware and not let themselves be swayed by phony friends or shaky situations with which life presents them. The beautiful objects a culture can produce attract Pisces; music, art in many forms, and harmonious and lovely furnishings in the home are important to their sense of refinement. Pisces people are born to serve, and with their wise, compassionate nature they can find self-fulfillment in service to humanity. The Pisces color is lilac.

Sun and Moon Signs

THEORY AND CONCEPT

Almost everyone knows something about his or her astrological Sun Sign. But what they know is often incomplete or misleading. Because of the distortions and generalizations common to Sun Sign astrology, people frequently feel strangers to their own signs. They may strongly identify with some of their Sun Sign characteristics but feel that something is missing. This analysis combines the personal messages of your Sun and Moon Signs for a complete astrological portrait of your emotional nature, hidden drives, and richest potentials. It has been said that a little knowledge is a dangerous thing. Today people who have picked up only a smattering of astrological knowledge at cocktail parties can say with confidence that Scorpios are sex fiends, Librans are lazy, Taureans are money crazy, Aquarians are crazy, and Virgos lose their virginity somewhere around middle age. Although the above common fallacies are humorous, they are for the most part distortions and exaggerations of astrological truth. The practitioners of popular astrology are often to blame for the very misunderstandings they try so hard to avoid. Everyone knows his Sun Sign, and knows something about it. Scorpios have read time and again about how "intense" they are. Taureans are tired of the sensual, stubborn, and comfort-loving routine. Virgos are fed up with words like *fussy, conservative,* and *frugal.* Cancers are becoming defensive about being labeled "defensive." And poor Geminis are no longer sure who they are. Because of the distortions and generalizations common to Sun Sign astrology, it's no wonder that people so often feel strangers to their own signs. Most Librans will identify with the need for harmony and tranquillity, as most Capricorns will identify with the need to prove themselves to the world. But what about the characteristics of your sign that you do not agree with, the characteristics that just don't fit? For example, many Virgos spend money without a care in the world, many Sagittarians are practical and down-to-earth, many Scorpios are not controlled by their libidos, and even a few Aquarians are neither revolutionaries nor eccentrics. It is obvious that your Sun Sign does not fully convey the complexities of your personality. Something is missing. What is missing is the Moon Sign.

The Moon Sign is simply the sign the Moon was in at the time of your birth. The Sun changes signs once each month. The Moon also changes signs, but much faster than the Sun, taking only a couple of days to go through a sign. A sign is a change of position in the universe. Finding your Moon Sign is simple. Using your year, month, and date of birth, you can locate it by referring to the tables at the end of this chapter. In traditional astrology, the Moon represents the emotional facet of your personality. It is the underlying force that determines your hidden drives, desires, and motivations. It represents your deepest dreams and aspirations. The Sun Sign, on the other hand, represents your revealed drives and motivations. The Sun Sign is your ego. It is what you expect of yourself in terms of achievement and potential. It is also how you think of yourself and the way in which you deal with others. By combining the Sun and Moon Signs, a much more in-depth portrait of astrological identity emerges. If you are a Gemini, you will probably have many traits common to Geminis. You may be talkative, high-strung, and mobile. Others may find you somewhat inconsistent and quick-changing. You will probably pursue an active life, and your quest will be geared toward the pursuit of variety and excitement. If, however, you are a Gemini with the Moon in Taurus, or a Gemini-Taurus, you will have an underlying emotional stability and thus will appear much more consistent than your fellow Geminis. You will also be a lot more stubborn, and you will hold on to impressions and beliefs with fixed intensity. In addition, your life-long quest will be geared toward the pursuit of luxury, comfort, and material security rather than constant novelty and excitement.

Let us take an actual example: Former president Jimmy Carter is a Libra with the Moon in Scorpio. His Libran nature is very evident in his style, mannerisms, and tactics. We know that Librans are concerned with establishing peace, harmony, and happiness for those around them. Jimmy Carter's campaign rhetoric, true to his Libran nature, was filled with references to love, the politics of joy, and the importance of bringing the country together again. His appeal was populist, also very Libran. Librans are fond of partnership and cooperation. They generally do not make decisions without first consulting others. In Carter's inaugural address he stressed the limitations of power, the need to have an open administration, and the vital importance of partnership and cooperation. Librans favor compromise over combat. True to form, Carter is in favor of compromise, avoiding extremes, and walking the middle path. Librans are also known for their vanity and perhaps this is why Carter is so concerned with the image he presents to the world. But what about the other side of Jimmy Carter, the side that is not so apparent? The side that is represented by his Scorpio Moon. Scorpios are very much the opposite of Librans. They are confident, bold, ambitious, stubborn, and decisive. Carter's intense ambition and self-confidence attests to this Scorpio facet. He has at times proved himself to be very decisive and unafraid of initiating bold actions, all very Scorpion attributes. Many have observed an underlying self-righteousness and egotism in Carter that may bring about tyrannical behavior (especially in times of crisis). In Carter's Sun-Moon combinations we see an apparent disparity or contradiction between the two sides of his nature. On one hand, we have the peace-loving Libran and, on the other hand, the aggressive Scorpio. Although his Sun Sign nature (Libra) seems to be at odds with his Moon Sign, or emotional, nature (Scorpio), both actually work in harmony. His Libran nature balances his Scorpio nature, so the portrait of a leader emerges: one who is decisive yet willing to compromise; one who is intensely shrewd and ambitious yet considerate and compassionate toward others. Judging President Carter by his Sun Sign alone is insufficient. By adding his Moon Sign, a much more accurate appraisal of his personality emerges.

In another example, Jacqueline Kennedy Onassis was a Leo with the Moon in Aries, or a Leo-Aries. Both signs of her combination are fire signs, and the two work together harmoniously. Her Leo nature gave her a regal, queenlike bearing and a desire to be in the spotlight. Her Aries inner nature was impulsive, ardent, and adventuresome. Both signs are egotistical and self-centered. When we combine the two we can understand why her attitude toward others was somewhat condescending and aristocratic. For Onassis the self always came first. Her Sun-Moon combination, being harmonious, would also indicate good health, high intelligence, courage, and strong creative drives.

Now let's look at Mahatma Gandhi, who was a Libra with the Moon in Leo. His Libran nature gave him a peace-loving outlook, amazing diplomatic skills, and the charm necessary to win the hearts of millions. His Leo emotional nature gave him the courage and determination to put his lofty ideals into practice.

These are just a few examples of how the Sun-Moon combination gives a more complete portrait of character. No combination can be labeled good or bad, strong or weak. It is clear that, in each, there are potential strengths and talents, as well as potential weaknesses and limitations. But it is important to remember that these are only potentials, and it is ultimately our responsibility as individuals to recognize and develop our unique talents and skills and to apply them in a positive, creative, and self-affirmative manner. Your Sun-Moon combination is only part of the story. Your individual persona has other factors that can significantly modify your Sun-Moon combination. This is just another look or angle to discover your persona and the personas of others. The important thing to remember is that the Sun-Moon combination forms the core of your personality: your ego and your emotional nature. Other factors go into shaping your persona as well, such as your Chinese animal, Birth card, childhood environment, cultural background, and education.

The Sun-Moon combinations that follow are based on the traditional astrological method of combining or synthesizing the most important elements of an individual's chart. They are drawn from insights gained from astrologer Jefferson Anderson's book, *Sun Sign Moon Sign*, and observation of many different individuals. Astrology never denies the power of free will or the ability to change. By recognizing and identifying our strengths and weaknesses we are better able to deal with them. But we cannot begin to solve the riddle of our personalities or deal with our problems until we first understand them. This book gives the individual a chance to travel the road to self-discovery independently. Through Western astrology we can learn about our strengths and our weaknesses from the foundation of true self-knowledge. We can become confident individuals, ready to embark on other paths toward full self-improvement and self-realization. In short, to know thyself. In each description there is also a place for you to record the names of friends who fit that persona.

SUN IN ARIES/MOON IN ARIES
Swashbuckler

A bright fresh charm attracts others to you, as does your love of life. On the other hand, your insensitive nature can keep people from getting too close. Making time to listen to your friends' problems or to help them with advice is difficult for you. You have the highest degree of intuition as well as intelligence. There is some selfishness and acting without reflection on the part of the Aries-Aries combination. This is coupled with impatience; all of which is left over from childhood. A store of energy that cannot be depleted drives them. A full life of experience is what you strive for, and you hold that there is nothing that can replace this. Like a daredevil, there is foolhardiness and recklessness in your character. Essentially, it is challenge you seek, whether on the job, in love, or just life itself. You need to listen more carefully to what others say, because you are not infallible. Think things over prior to acting and do not be so impatient to do something. There is a tendency for Aries-Aries natives to forget things quickly and live in the present. Behaving like this can lead to the repetition of mistakes. There is no substitute for the best teacher, which is experience. You also need to find an outlet for all that store of energy. In order to succeed in various parts of your life, it is necessary to have physical activity of some sort. This is also significant for physical well-being. You need to work on being a bit more sensitive in your relationships with others, particularly your romantic partner. Their needs, desires, and emotions are of importance for a good relationship. You have a fundamental selfishness under your passion and enthusiasm, as you seek out love. You are prone to see love as a sport and, in addition, you have a strong sex drive. A closed and strict routine would certainly never permit happiness for you, because variation and challenges are what your inner motivation needs. A career that has a lot of responsibility and stiff competition brings out your best work, but you need to have something that does not enclose you in boredom and frustration. Positions of this nature could actually damage or destroy your sense of self. Working for progress and change brings out your pioneer spirit, and you are the pathfinder in that regard. Aries-Aries individuals are often successful in the areas of medicine and science. Surgery is a good choice, as is social activism.

SUN IN ARIES/MOON IN TAURUS
Speculator

You have a golden voice, and you choose your words gracefully. This can help you with a career. You have a great ability to persuade people carefully, and this will assist you with your ambitions. There is a need for security in your makeup. You are dedicated to the work ethic. Pleasure is high on your list of priorities, and this includes sensual and natural pursuits as well as comfort, food, and other pleasures important to you. You have a sense for money. Good things will come your way because of your excellent skills in management. This interest in material possessions is capable of getting out of hand and becoming all-powerful. Because you are fundamentally a kind person there is no hint of cruelty and ill-mannered behavior in you. Dedication is a part of your character, though. It is this stubbornness, stemming from your Moon in Taurus, that can get in your way. Your Aries Sun Sign is in tune and focused. You are an enthusiastic and energetic person. You even put out a feeling of confidence and calmness. You are different from other Aries because of your patience. You are careful and have a lot of sense, and that will guarantee success even though you are not as energetic as others of your sign. Strong biases sometimes come to get in the way of your fundamental good sense. Being flexible and compromising relative to different viewpoints would be wise. Creativity needs freedom, and that cannot be found in an environment of materialism. You need satisfaction in terms of your sensual side, but you are not inclined to experimentation. You want a stable relationship. A problem with jealously can exist because of the inflexible approach you take to romance. You can hold your feelings inside without communicating, but communication is something you do well. You should learn to be freer with expression of your thoughts in general. There is a master artist or other creative person in a lot of Aries-Taureans. Being an artist or working in another creative area is a secret desire even though you are so good at business. Even if the result leads to a more satisfying and meaningful life, you would never start down an uncertain path that could put your security at risk. You should not fret and worry so much about finances, because you will always have the security you want.

SUN IN ARIES/MOON IN GEMINI
Hustler

Your presence is always felt by others, partly because of your talkative nature but also because of your movements, which are nonstop. If something comes into your mind, whether it is an idea, emotion, or thought, you talk about it and sometimes very emphatically. Furthermore, you have an authority figure mentality and believe that you are always correct. The easily excited Gemini is tense and superior at communication, while Aries is speedy, driven, and flexible. A golden-tongued, fast-acting individual with tons of energy and motivation is the result. You have a very strong sense of freedom about you and are a unique individual. Solutions as well as answers come easily for you, and you have a steady mind. This tendency to communicate everything can tire you out as well as those around you. Another caution is that your sense of humor can be mean and direct sometimes. Others might very well think you are aggressive if you are not careful. Allow others their chance to speak and give up dominating a conversation. Relax, think a bit, and refrain from being so self-directed and stubborn. You are a very popular person in spite of all of this, and the reason is the confidence and knowledge that you wear on your sleeve. People cannot help but respect and look up to you. If you are ignored or unappreciated, that is about the only time that you will brood. This is one of the rare occasions where you will get exceptionally and memorably angry. Being edgy is one of your traits, and as a result you need to have meaning-ful places to release your strength and energy. You have a natural talent for grasping everything around you quickly. An open-minded and flexible part-ner is best for you, but you need to learn how to appreciate such a partner just as you do yourself. You need a partner who is tolerant and receptive to that constant flow of ideas. You do not miss anything in your environment. You let a fake person know immediately what you think because of your ability to spot them and your desire to communicate. On occasions you put people off, because you do not beat around the bush. Keeping some things to yourself is something you need to do sometimes. Work is an excellent outlet for you, but the key is to stay busy and put your inventive, original talents to use. These talents are wide ranging and there is very little that you are not good at. The Aries-Gemini personality can be excellent at everything from science and engineering to investigative reporting and law.

SUN IN ARIES/MOON IN CANCER
Faint of Heart

This combination is something of a mismatch, because the Aries part is rest-less, driven, and fearless, but the Cancer personality is careful, cautious, and security driven; someone who is fluctuating and lacks in security. The result is an emotional side that wants to be careful and have a solid sense of security, but at the same time, an ego that wants excitement, challenge, and risks. You are crafty and emotionally deep like a Cancer but also have a fire driving you like an Aries. Security in the areas of home, money, and emotions are a very important part of you and something that will be in charge of a large portion of your life choices. This mismatch will result in some of the issues you face in life, because your situation is practically impossible. After this split is dealt with, there are a lot of possibilities for the Aries-Cancer. Your total potential can be released if you set up a strong emotional foundation for yourself. The combination of a powerful and creative Cancer with an Aries, who is so dynamic, clever, and aware, can not only overcome childhood issues but also can be very successful in life. Be careful, however, with swift mood changes stemming from the highly sentimental and emotional person deep inside, mixing with the dictator part of your personality. An explosion is possible, because you tend to stuff your anger down for a long period of time until you decide to release it. This is another one of the challenges you face in life. You need to refrain from being upset with your natural feeling of being courageous and certain about your talents. Possibly your early home situation was not a happy one in some way or was even disrupted, bringing about a conflict with your Sun and Moon. Your childhood is almost certainly the source of this fixation with security and making it such a high priority. You crave a home environment different from what you had in your youth, because you want to compensate for the situation you were in. You need to be cautious that you do not overdo things in this department and arrest your leadership skills and talents for being innovative.

SUN IN ARIES/MOON IN LEO
Eager Beaver

You are someone who needs attention, and sometimes you go a bit overboard being dramatic in order to get it. You have a clear presence that gets you attention; however, you still use your clothing and behavior to acquire it. A condescending attitude toward others is possible, but you laugh easily and are generous, and this essentially compensates for that. You have a strong loyalty that makes up for your lofty persona, and your intuition is generally reliable. That means that you generally know who to be loyal to and how to go about it. One of the main features that you have is being yourself, which is very much an individual who marches to the beat of your own drummer. You have the courage of spirit to be real, to be creative, coupled with an ambition and assertiveness that makes you a unique individual. This results in a person who is the paradigm example of an Aries; one who strives to attain power as well as status along with creativity. Defensiveness and self-justification are foreign as far as your character is concerned, thanks to your inborn confidence deep within you. Generally, you know that you are right and do not feel the need to justify your concepts or opinions. You are someone who attracts other people to you with your determined spirit and bold personality, and this makes you a confident leader. As frequently as not, your inclinations are correct, but your judgment is sometimes a bit lacking. Professionally, you are best suited for any career in which your executive and creative strengths can be put to use. The creative strength can be combined with your innovation and decision making and bring you success. You must, however, try to be less biased. A role that some associate with being for males is fine for you. You should not be intimidated by your own assertiveness. When you are young this is especially true. It is very likely that you will seek a professional career. Self-deception is always a possibility for you, particularly relative to trusting others. Others do not always live up to your expectations, and often this surprises you. Caution needs to be used to protect against immoral people who take advantage of your trust. Most often this is simply a matter of putting your antenna up and using your excellent intuition. You are somewhat fixed in your opinion in spite of the fact that you are a pathfinder in many ways. You seem to have fixed ideas and beliefs in your mind and often do not want to give them up.

SUN IN ARIES/MOON IN VIRGO
Griper

You are a thoughtful and precise person who resists mistakes. This makes you a bit of a perfectionist. Obtaining a complete knowledge of something comes about because of your attention to details. Your conservative perspective on life is not like most Aries. Rather, it is the result of both reason and experience. There is a special calmness about you. This might be because of the interacting opposites in you; confidence comes from Aries, and shyness comes from Virgo. You are not that impulsive and daring, and, in general, you tend to be more careful than other Aries people. The main reason for this is because your Virgo nature will restrain you a bit even though you have plenty of energy and are excited about many things in your life. You usually choose an occupation that uses your fine intellect and great ability to analyze, and that is where your directness and power generally are focused. You are torn between your basic shy personality and the part of you that wants to be daring and flashy. This often results in an irreconcilable conflict in your personality. Again, you are faced with the possibility of disappointment. You can easily have a career as a doctor, lawyer, or engineer because of your intelligence, attention to detail, and concentration. Admired for their sincerity, Aries-Virgos usually discover true success through their occupation. Your lofty standards are something you try to live up to. You should guard against overdoing things to reach impossible goals. Furthermore, a caution is also in order because you are inclined to be a faultfinder in the business place as well. Problems come about when people disagree with your ideas, because you think you are always right and the best informed. More tolerance pertaining to other views and lifestyles is needed. Your mind, simply put, needs to be more open. You should not be so judgmental. You might be nervous, agitated, and stressed like a lot of people with a Moon in Virgo alignment. Problems at work will almost surely bring this out. You need to be careful to not take things out on those you love, who can be victims of these moods. The combination can make your Aries side feel let down and frustrated. The problem created here is that you need more self-acceptance in order to move on.

SUN IN ARIES/MOON IN LIBRA
Rebellious without Cause

You are the type of person who rejects reason and even good advice in favor of intuition and impulse. If romance or adventure comes your way, you may very well drop everything and pursue it. You have a three-dimensional personality that attracts others because you are quite intelligent and have so much vitality. In many ways you are precisely the adventurer and pathfinder that you believe yourself to be. You are the type who actually does go out and discover what you want, rather than sitting and dreaming. It does not matter if others have discovered things before you, your natural curiosity drives you to make your own map and discover them for yourself. You probably have, as an Aries-Libra, a million projects going at the same time in order to placate your independent spirit. You are an extreme individualist, and you want to find out about life and yourself—but on your own terms and in your own peculiar way. In that quest, you will leave no stone unturned. Sometimes you seem insensitive, but the fact is that you are not. It is simply a matter of you having difficulty cooperating with others sometimes because you prefer your own vision and your own way. A sedentary job behind a desk is not for you because, in spite of your intelligence, you usually have trouble concentrating. Real accomplishment might be difficult, because your determination can get you into trouble. Despite your desire for challengers, dissatisfaction can set in along with anxiety. Aries-Libra people have an excellent sense of aesthetics and, therefore, something in the field of art, design, or other visual media might be worthwhile. Such a vocation is practically perfect because it can satisfy your need for change in terms of art itself, and also for travel and challenges. You have difficulty focusing, and this leads to an anxiety and restlessness that make it hard for you to see things through. Consequently, responsibility can be an issue. Your wanderlust is a disguise for shying away from your responsibilities and even yourself. The solution is simple. Seek out an occupation that gives you the excitement and change you need. A careful and astute partner who keeps your impulses checked is best, but working alone is possible.

SUN IN ARIES/MOON IN SCORPIO
Self-Directed

Excitement and thrill are always a part of your life. You move ahead in the world because of great concentration and ambition. As a result, you love competition. You are defiant and independent, and at times this can be your undoing. It is hard for you to restrain your aggression, and you do not accept compromise well. Those who stand in your way get no sympathy. You have a drive for life that includes the entire spectrum of the spiritual, emotional, and sensual. Mars rules both of these signs, and according to mythology Mars also rules passion and war. The result is an aggressive person. Regardless of what you do, fun generally involves a fight. This includes business, love, and life itself. You are an extremist in spirit and thought, so doing something partway is not part of your character. As a result, when you fail it is a complete tragedy and when you succeed a total victory. Advice should be listened to at times though, so the next time there is a disagreement, do not be so resistant and prepare for battle, but rather listen carefully. You might learn something. Others might have something helpful to say so compromise sometimes. You are very creative and have an enormous amount of willpower, but you cannot really succeed until you learn to work in cooperation with other people. Constructive and positive outlets need to be found for your aggression so they can be channeled for success. Your concentration is good, and you have an excellent intellect. You want to dig deep with your pursuits and are not happy just to get superficial impressions. There are Aries-Scorpio social activists, scientists, and scholars. You have the power of self-rejuvenation as do all Moon in Scorpio people. You may get in trouble at times or even fail, but you always have the ability to bounce back. You are a courageous and freedom-loving person. Sports like swimming, jogging, or tennis as well as creative endeavors like art can release anger better than getting upset with your spouse, coworker, or children. There is a pioneer inside you and great accomplishments are possible with your ambition and enthusiasm. It is very likely you will explore the world and seek adventure when you are young. You can be very hard to control early in life though, so some professional training is a good idea. Great success later in life is attainable if you are guided properly.

SUN IN ARIES/MOON IN SAGITTARIUS
Inquisitor

You have a deep and real sense of loyalty, and you automatically assume others are like that. Unfortunately, your good nature around this issue can get you in trouble with ill-intentioned individuals who want to take advantage of you. Consequently, be careful in trusting others, but don't become cynical and lose that wonderful naive persona that you radiate. You are acutely aware of your surroundings and, because of your curiosity, always have your eyes open for something new everywhere you go. You do not want to miss out on anything. There is, however, superficiality about you relative to what you are interested in and your pursuits. In addition, your inability to focus for long means that you easily lose interest and move on to something new. The issue here is a lack of concentration. Here we have a Sagittarius, an idealistic person who loves philosophy and spiritual things, combined with the impulse-driven and energetic Aries. You have a distinct innocent curiosity in your approach to everything, as well as a sincerity that is appealing. You are so charming as to be almost irresistible, and people are naturally drawn to you. What you need is a heavy dose of realism if you want to attain your dreams and those high goals you have established. Because you often drift from project to project, you might never find your purpose in life, though you know intuitively that you have one. You might, if you are not careful, actually become a lifelong hippie as some Aries-Sagittarians do. The good news is that when you find your purpose or mission in life, you are very capable of being a dedicated and focused individual. You can become a fantastic leader in the areas of management and creativity because of your intelligence combined with your winning personality. You always have the courage of your convictions. Excellent examples are Charles de Gaulle and Thomas Jefferson. Because of your contagious enthusiasm, you would also make an excellent educator and be very inspiring to your students. You are so good at this you even liven up boring topics. You are open about your feelings and do not repress them. This probably stems from your honesty. While some may see you as tactless, the fact is that you harbor no ill feelings toward people and are not a hypocrite.

SUN IN ARIES/MOON IN CAPRICORN
Name Dropper

For the most part, your desire for respect will be fulfilled because you have the necessary qualities to earn it. You possess the mental framework and are practical enough to balance your natural Aries' zeal and desire to initiate things. Internally you are careful, calculating, and detail oriented, and that goes together with your strong motivation. Work is important, but less out of duty than out of boundless ambition. Unfortunately, you can be merciless, opportunistic, and even cruel in your pursuit of a goal; this is possible because often the end justifies the means for you. The top items on your priority list are your financial goals, and they can dominate you. Your desire is to be powerful and have a high position. This is your primary interest, even though you are a friendly and generally kind individual. These individuals can ride the road to success with you after they have acquired your friendship. By the same token, those who help you are not forgotten because you are a very loyal person. You can, however, be a serious opponent if you are challenged or menaced in any way. Perhaps because of personal reasons, you had to assume a lot of responsibility when you were quite young. There was not much time for play, socializing, and fun then, but it was good training for adulthood and the goals you seek. Your ambition in this regard might stem from this early responsibility. You are probably motivated to prove yourself again and again, in spite of your dynamic personality and decisive character, because of a deep-seated insecurity. Relentless anxiety or depression might be the result of this. More self-respect and acceptance could help you remember that being on top is not everything in life. Management and administrative positions are probably your best areas for a career. As you move up the ladder of success, you will be challenged to be more understanding and tolerant of others. Activities such as reading and meditating are recommended. Seeing a wider picture of your world and noticing the emotional and academic side of things can help round out your character. Your personality is magnetic as well as dynamic, and other people respond to you as a mature and responsible individual. Respect from your colleagues is sure to come your way. In a strange twist, your manipulation of others to suit you is to their benefit.

SUN IN ARIES/MOON IN AQUARIUS
Innovator

Management of your life is easy because of your sense of what will happen. Essentially, you have a fairly clear vision of tomorrow before you at all times. This gives you a feeling of confidence. Being human, however, there are certain issues you must deal with. In your case, they are inflexibility and self-importance. Your personal relationships tend to suffer because you are uncompromising and believe you are right. You are speedy in everything and go all out all the time. Unfortunately, you are always wondering why others cannot keep up with this superhuman pace. You are independent, moody, and anxious a lot of the time. The Aries combined with Aquarius reveals an individual who is a pathfinder and in search of adventure. The new, the novel, and the interesting are what you seek. You are very decisive and filled with tremendous energy. On the Aquarius side, there is an imaginative person trained on the future. Your main feature is a tuned intuition. On the intellectual front, you are fine because you are a tolerant humanitarian. Sometimes you are unaware of other people's feelings because you are assertive in your individuality. This blindness may cause you to appear arrogant. The thoughts, feelings, and ideas of others need to be heard. You may be excited about some idea you have, but patience regarding the pace of others should be taken into account. There is unpredictability in you under your charming facade. Your individual autonomy is something you guard carefully, and this means you do not like to get involved with individuals or groups. You can allow this to be almost a phobia if you let it go unchecked; from romance to the job you need to allow some freedom of movement for things to work. In order to be happy in your job and be successful, you must have as much liberty as possible. The unexamined, the new, and the radical appeal to the inventive side of you. You are fun to be with, but you are also subject to temper tantrums and emotional explosions. A shotgun blast of anger does burn itself out quickly, but you must learn to manage these flare-ups. Some of this needs to find a constructive means of release. Your Moon in Aquarius means you can be grumpy. To avoid some of these stumbling blocks, you would be wise to make an effort to avoid stressful and tense situations.

SUN IN ARIES/MOON IN PISCES
Seer

A busy and aggressive adventurer is the personality of your Aries. On the Pisces side, there is almost a passive and timid character and a very sensitive individual. All of this makes it hard to actually be the dynamo that so many people think they see. Your challenges are sometimes met with fear because insecurity stops you. Fear often keeps you from confronting the challenges you encounter. The Aries-Pisces mixture results in emotional conflict combined with excellent creativity. Your spiritual journey from the Pisces side might lift your Aries such that great ideas can get a start. Lack of certainty and a less than secure mind-set can block the road to success and fulfillment. There are two extremely different natures in one being here. Due to childhood experiences, you get a deep sense of inferiority. This prevents your natural decisive nature from opening up because you do not perceive things clearly. It is critical for you to accept yourself. A careful self-examination will show your powers and talents. There is nothing lost in power with a sensitive individual. Do not succumb to self-doubt, but rather work to understand your anxieties. You have a great sense of fantasy and imagination, which can be either good or bad depending on how it is put to use. In businesses involving speculation, you can employ your extremely sensitive skills of intuition and be successful. A single dream led publisher Hugh Hefner, an Aries-Pisces, to establish a worldwide brand as a reality. As for your sexual needs, your sensitivity and creativity are significant elements. You can be the master of your fate by rising above insecurity. Only after you have done so, will you conquer fear and become the master of your life. You are a mirror for those around you; you reflect back their general mood of things. This comes from your sensitive nature. Psychological support from friends and family is important. Choose carefully who you spend your time with. Keep your lines of communication free; otherwise there is a chance of loneliness and isolation. Maintain a level of social activity. Keep in mind that you can successfully deal with things you see as weaknesses by discussing them. In terms of a career, possibilities are something in the creative fields of art, design, drama, or even music.

SUN IN TAURUS/MOON IN ARIES
Self-Absorbed

You are intense in your pursuit of a goal once you are clear that it is what you want. You seek it out directly. You set out to get your way and nothing, not even most scrupulous people, can stop you. They dare not even try. If you want it, then it is right. That is the nature of a Taurus-Aries. You could, theoretically, have destructive tendencies, but they are held back by your natural caution. If you can find a way to justify your self-interest, you can make allowances for others and compromise. Controlling your own life path and being in charge of your destiny is what you really desire. You are basically a worldly person who wants to have a secure, comfortable, and pleasurable life. Under your confident and controlled exterior, you are masking your irrationality and unruliness. To satisfy your desires you need to struggle. You have some strong desires, and you must work very hard. Yes, you might be caring, polite, and gentle to people, but you are your own main concern. Your basic nature is one of being determined and controlled. You do not think of spiritual issues. You take an inventory of what you have, and after that you proceed to collect everything possible and acquire all the power and status you can. As with many things, anxiety and hostility can be dealt with through constructive means such as sports, tennis for example. This does not mean you should try to be more competitive. A little competition is fine, but coming out on top is not the meaning of life. Go exploring for other realms such as the spiritual, psychological, and academic. Find out what life is really about by expanding your perspectives. It is not merely about possessions. Do not let prejudice and impulsive behavior be your guide. Loosen up and open your mind and your heart to the others' views and feelings. Furthermore, it is possible for you to achieve this because of your firmness and ability. You have a great aptitude to persuade people of things, and it comes naturally for you. Your presence sometimes intimidates others. Temper is among the faults that can get in your way. Suppressing feelings comes easily for most Taureans, but not for you. You sometimes quickly get angry and are subject to anxiety, neither of which can be ignored for long. Working together with others and being patient and tolerant are things you must learn.

SUN IN TAURUS/MOON IN TAURUS
Cornerstone

Your thought out comments, although infrequent, are almost always heeded because of your directness. You have an uncanny ability to be accurate, truthful, and frank. Beneath your calm exterior you are totally confident and do not lack for ambition. Once you undertake something, you do not stop until it is clear to all that you have mastered it to your own satisfaction. Bumps in the road are dealt with in a calm and patient fashion, and you are not moved if you encounter a roadblock. Your self-respect translates into respect from others. You have a built-in self-confidence but are real about it, and that presence speaks volumes. You know you have ability, and there is no need to broadcast it. You are skeptical about things that are not your own ideas. Your worldly success is guaranteed by confidence as well as your patience. If anyone mistakes you for being slow, they are fooling themselves. Your distaste for the superficial and trivial makes you seem antisocial, but you are just a good observer. Your ultimate place in the scheme of life is to be your own boss, and this will happen slowly but surely. You love to have a lot of responsibility, and you gain great joy and purpose in life from your work. Open expression of your feelings is also suggested as a release valve. Talking about your feelings and not being so inhibited does not mean that we should never be controlled in our approach. But everyone needs to let go sometimes. Common sense is also one of your good qualities, and this results in a practical and easy solution to many of the dilemmas in life that baffle people sometimes. Occasionally everyone gets fed up, and this is true of you as well, especially relative to your friends' faults. Complete determination and dedication are the only ways you know in terms of approaching a challenge. It is likely that you feel a connection with nature, because both of your signs are earth signs. You are satisfied living most places, but you are a natural-type person and you would, at the very least, need to visit natural areas for peace of mind. Like most Taurus people you almost never get angry, but this is sometimes because you stuff your anger down. Unfortunately, this can result in assorted psychological issues. Tension always needs to be released through positive avenues to vent the steam.

SUN IN TAURUS/MOON IN GEMINI
Buttinsky

You need to share your opinions and emotions with other people, and this means that you are a very sociable person who enjoys the company of others. The fascination with the world around you, oddly enough, is something you may actually be too aware of. You are a born problem solver. When a problem appears, you are ready to deal with it. This combination of signs is pragmatic, worldly, and energetic from Taurus, and logical, adaptable, and humorous from Gemini. There exists within you an intuitive vision that is excellent, and you do not let things slip by you. Your acute observation skills allow you to recognize the fake and deceitful. The new and the exotic are among the things that catch your wide-ranging interests. It is not easy, however, for you to settle on something, whether it is a job, a romance, or even a way of life, that permanently satisfies you. Popularity, in most cases, is guaranteed: a Taurus-Gemini has a charming and vibrant personality. The areas you know well enough to contribute to and provide innovations to are wide ranging. Psychology, because of your ability to analyze and understand things, is a possible profession. Sigmund Freud, the founder of modern psychology, was a Taurus-Gemini. In addition, technical professions, research, or even being a writer are also very real possibilities. Focus is what you need, because of your numerous opportunities. You are a bit moody and perhaps aggressive in your relationships. Your current projects are often left behind the minute you find something new. Errors and behavior patterns, in a somewhat childlike approach to the world, are often repeated and lessons learned slowly. Taking a close inventory of your past behavior and trying to discern when you have been at fault or gone wrong is a good idea. Instead of allowing impulses and momentary fancies to control your life, learn from the past. Even though you are a Taurus, you know how to release your emotions and express yourself. This can lead to some issues in your life. For example, you can be rebellious, find fault, and stir up trouble. You can become a complainer if all you do is examine your environment for the purpose of finding things that you do not like or want to change. This world is an imperfect place and to not realize that can bring nothing but disappointment.

SUN IN TAURUS/MOON IN CANCER
Provider

There is an insecurity and restraint about you. This results in a person who shows an exterior that is stable, while internally there is insecurity. There is a gentle kindness in you that attracts others. You also have a charming and tactful nature to go with it. You realize that aggression does not work nearly as well as diplomacy. Handling people well is an inborn trait, as is your almost instant adaptability to situations. You seem to be on everyone's side at the same time. You carry yourself with an air of confidence. You are controlled in your approach to life, and this makes you seem secure. This combination has a Taurus side that is dedicated, motivated, and sensual. The Cancer aspect shows sensitivity along with imagination. Caution is necessary if you do not want to lose your own identity in this process of trying to please everyone. As you move on in age, do not allow yourself to become self-satisfied and smug, because a big part of you is easily satisfied with your life. Push yourself beyond what you see as your limitations, and this will surely help round out your life. It would be a shame to waste your numerous strong points and talents. Creativity in design or architecture are places you can showcase your wonderful imagination and artistic talents. However, professions that provide more financial security because of your Moon in Cancer attract you. Undertaking a career that is a gamble is unlikely because it goes against your basic nature. The Taurus powers of concentration and the Cancer Moon provide an ability to understand and remember what you have learned. However, you also keep a ledger grounded in emotions such that you remember every insult, rejection, threat, or other circumstance for a very long time. You prefer to pout rather than discuss your feelings of hurt or anger. You can become a cynical and sluggish person if you experience a serious emotional setback in the form of rejection. Obviously, releasing negative feelings like anger is best for you, and this means expressing them openly. Aggression is almost unknown to you because you are a peaceful person. Luckily, the vast majority of people respond to you kindly, because you will probably not come to your own defense. Occasionally though, it is imperative to state your views.

SUN IN TAURUS/MOON IN LEO
Performer

You care deeply about the less fortunate, and even though you have a runaway ego, your spirit is so three-dimensional that you can make the most depressed people come alive. Your own self-respect translates into respect coming from others. Because you believe in yourself and have confidence, you want to show others how valuing themselves can help them. You are uniquely outgoing and have a powerful character, probably more so than anyone you know. The admiration you get from others and the fact that they are in your social sphere is, you believe, something they are fortunate to share. You exude optimism and excitement even though you might be eccentric, self-righteous, and opinionated. One thing you are not is boring. You see things for yourself and have an ambitious and independent character. You are not in need of verification from others because of your belief in yourself. You stick to things, and that includes your opinions. Intuition is often your guide, and it is generally correct. If you have decided on something, you refuse to change your mind. This can lead to inflexibility if you are not careful. An effort to keep an open mind is required. Your judgment and actions must not be impaired by prejudices.

Open your ears and listen to others. Attempt to be a little more humble and restrain your pride. In addition, you are very practical. Fun for you entails at least a measure of showmanship and drama. This can take the most mundane activity and turn it into a Broadway play. Being noticed is the name of the game, and you behave accordingly, replete with dress and the appropriate actions. While you have an inborn feeling of superiority, you are, at the same time, very compassionate, kind, and generous to others. You have a lot of determination and the motivation to follow through and reach your goals, because both your Sun and Moon Signs are fixed. Compromising is another matter, and that is very difficult for you. Plainly put, it is your way or no way. Frustration brings your temper to a boil when you do not get what you want. Cooperation is always helpful, no matter how independent you are. A sense of conviviality when you work can bring out the tremendous creative power within you. And Taurus-Leo definitely has the potential for great innovation. There is a born show person in you, and you love to utilize it.

SUN IN TAURUS/MOON IN VIRGO
Practical Experience

You have a worldly mental framework that is filled with wisdom and experience. This means that others frequently want you to advise them because you are so good at it. Unfailingly, your counsel is logical and well thought out. It is based on logical principles combined with pragmatism. You have an acute method of thinking that can analyze and penetrate to the core of issues. You can readily put your plans into action because you are a perfectionist who insists on preciseness in quality. Taurus-Virgo individuals are superb planners. You are smooth and easygoing in all things. You have a character that is even-tempered and self-confident. Your dedication and ability to use the resources at hand mean others admire you and they are drawn to you. The result is that you have a clear path through life stemming from your significant balance of pragmatism and dedication to the tasks you face. Plainly put, you know what you are doing. Wasting your time on fantasies or daydreams is not something you do. Simply contemplating action does not work. You would rather act on your ideas, seeing that as the only way to accomplish your goals. You are a supremely serene person and recognize that life is not always smooth sailing. You ride the waves and never get upset with the routine workings of events. You easily move beyond the few barriers that life puts in your way, because you are a determined person with a lot of self-control. Passivity will only lead to lethargy and laziness. Big responsibility and stiff competition are where you are at your very best. Management and administration are quite suited to your character. Verbally, you are well spoken, extremely persuasive, and destined to produce results. Organization and long-term planning are among your numerous abilities. If there is a weakness in this area, it would be a lack of imagination and creativity. Self-satisfaction is one of the few challenges you will face. Coupled with this is the fact that you might sit by and observe the world and all its problems and be tempted to not use your strength to accomplish what you are capable of. Who you associate with can have an influence on your life choices, and that only increases the temptation to be complacent. You need to be alive and active in your surroundings.

SUN IN TAURUS/MOON IN LIBRA
Good Guy

People are drawn to your charismatic personality, worldly common sense, and sensitivity. Respect and equality are things that you give to all. Your signs show a just and fair individual on the Libra side and a wise person on the Taurus side. All Taurus-Libra people are thought of as being kind and decent. If you have difficulties, often the best way for you to handle them is by relaxing in natural surroundings. A beguiling and even-tempered person is the result of this double Venus sign combination. There is a special calmness about you that suggests serenity as well as peace. Stress and anxiety are essentially unknown to you and this results in an elegant and extroverted personal magnetism. Hidden behind the smile is an uneasy tension. Socializing is of great significance to you, because, as a native of the Moon in Libra, your vision of yourself is a result of how others perceive you. Fresh air and a country environment are just what you need when the tension and confusion of life become overwhelming. Due to your low threshold for tension, you require more relaxation and recreation than most people. Your peer group has a significant influence on you, so it is very helpful to befriend those who work at success and fulfillment. Virgos and Capricorns are known for being ambitious types and being around them would be great. Stick to your goals and objectives, and do not take the easy way out. You have a fantastic imagination and are very talented. Design, drama, and the arts are real possibilities for excelling. Endless diversionary activities and entertainment are needed, because you have an internal uneasiness that keeps you on the move. The problem is that you do not have a good sense of direction in this regard. You need to establish priorities and goals that you stick to. The easygoing and pleasurable are your preference over the stress and tension in the modern and competitive world. This is true of all those ruled by Venus, but eliminating the challenging also diminishes the rewards. Your urge for the easy life often wins out over true self-fulfillment. A more assertive mind-set is needed if you want to be successful in your profession.

SUN IN TAURUS/MOON IN SCORPIO
Killjoy

When you were young you were probably an explorer, investigating your surroundings, because you are a courageous and sensual mixture. Over the years a feeling of incertitude began to influence you, and you became lethargic. Expressing your feelings is somewhat difficult for you. You have a powerful need to let go of your passions at times, but you fear that if you do they would become all consuming. You are a very sober-minded individual even by Taurus standards. Everything around you is viewed with an acute and gravely serious eye. You are a loner and do not want others involved too much in your life, because you are mistrustful and tight-lipped. There is a high level of suspicion in you, and this can reach paranoid levels when you start thinking that others have a plot against you. You walk around at times as though there was a very serious and dire concern on your mind. You have a profoundly negative view of humanity and virtually smirk when you read something unfortunate in the newspaper that confirms your notion that our planet is evil. Essentially you try to conceal your inner being. There are a handful of manifestations that result from stifling your emotions. Application of your energy can be utilized in numerous areas. You have a wonderfully creative vision, and art, either as an avocation or even a profession, is possible. In the realm of business you are very clever and can be successful there too. Furthermore, you can spot misrepresentation and shallowness because of your excellent intuition. As with most Taurus people, you have an emphatic personality that makes you known and frequently dreaded. Going about your life in a contemptuous, sulking fashion and being fundamentally inarticulate can be the result. Another possibility is that you become tempestuous and turn to damaging habits. There is a prospect that you will take out your belligerency on others. These things are only possibilities. Release is important, and that means being more believing, as well as expressing yourself without censorship. Opening up to others is not something to fear because you are a friendly, giving person who can be forthright with others. Having made a decision, you have a great deal of self-command and resoluteness along with the ability to surmount most problems or obstacles.

SUN IN TAURUS/MOON IN SAGITTARIUS
High Roller

This combination combines the common sense and worldly wisdom of Taurus with the spiritual understanding, imagination, and philosophical nature of the Sagittarian. You are at once idealistic and practical, possessing the resolve and determination to see your many dreams through. You have a broad, far reaching, and perceptive mind, and you are never without a buoyant faith in the future. Yours is a gifted combination. If you have one flaw, it is that concentration and dedication do not come easily to you. A freedom lover, you resent any form of restraint of limitation. Though just as industrious as your fellow Taurians, you prefer making your own rules and setting your own schedule. Impulse often rules your actions and undermines your efforts. You have a constant craving for novelty and excitement, so when you become bored with your current activity, which does not take long, you are ready to pack your bags and run off to find something new. It is your refusal to take advice or submit to professional guidance that so often leaves you without any sense of purpose or feeling of accomplishment. And that inner restlessness and caprice often thwart the lofty goals you set for yourself. Financial security can be an eternal quest for the Taurus-Sagittarius. Like all Taureans, you crave comfort and luxury. But no matter how hard you work to satisfy those expensive tastes, your extravagance and generosity will often leave you in debt. You must learn to control that impulsive spending. Even though generosity wins you lots of friends, sometimes it is better to look after yourself first. Your inherent kindness and charm will assure you popularity and respect. Intuition is your best guide, because your hunches often prove astonishingly accurate. You need to settle on a field or pursuit, which gives you a chance to express your far out imagination, but at the same time gives you plenty of breathing space. Once you have found that interest there will be no end to your determination. All sorts of creative activities will be open to you. Your Taurean sense of form and taste is enhanced by your Sagittarian imagination and understanding of the abstract. You have a strong scholarly bent and you can succeed at intellectual endeavors. Open-minded and uninhibited in love, you have probably had many exciting affairs. But though you may not readily admit it, what you are really after is one stable, fulfilling relationship. Try to steer clear of domineering partners. Find someone who shares your expansive, freedom-loving nature.

SUN IN TAURUS/MOON IN CAPRICORN
Nervous Nellie

You do not allow your personal doubt and worry to take over, but it is there in spite of your many strong points. This can keep you from putting your talents to good use. The things you are probably most fearful of are being poor and losing control. Your strong need for security combined with your need for material things can easily rule your life. This is quite unnecessary, because you are able to take care of everything you desire and you have the power to do that. Consequently, your worries are unfounded. You are a calm person who is kindhearted, sensual, and a fun-loving spirit, like most Taurus individuals. However, there is a strong purpose and strength in your attractive appeal. You know where you are headed, and that is your purpose in life. You are very witty and can add joy to any conversation. Unfortunately, deep inside of you is a sadness that almost never comes to the surface. Leading a more spontaneous life would help you to rid yourself of your fears. What you really want is inside you and not in mutual funds, bank accounts, or a house. Your varied and appreciated talents and abilities are what you should value. Becoming psychoneurotic and tyrannical can result from frustration in a Taurus-Capricorn. The most serious example of such a maladjusted individual was Adolph Hitler. Saying what you feel is not something you should fear. It is better to deal with stress or aggression honestly and openly. You can easily turn this problem around, because you are capable of great organizational feats in this area and others. As a Taurus-Capricorn, you might want to concentrate more on some of your artistic abilities such as music. Your personality is also absolutely charming, and that is an asset. You are able to deal with the most difficult types of people because of your very persuasive nature. You have good common sense coupled with stability and wisdom, and this draws people to you for advice. You stand fast with your friends. You are truehearted and giving. Feelings of frustration and anger are often bottled up in you because you hold on to them rather than release them. Talking about these buried emotions can help prevent later problems, such as depression, anxiousness, paranoia, and other psychological issues.

SUN IN TAURUS/MOON IN AQUARIUS
Reactionary

Adaptability and originality moderate everything that you approach. You have a hard time making firm emotional ties with others. You try to stay uninvolved and objective about everything all the time so you can appear to be different from others. You are never considered self-important because you are kind, generous, and thoughtful to others. You might feel that you have a special purpose in life like other Taurus-Aquarians do. You look almost like a visionary or prophet and seem to have a special soul. This look is in addition to your Taurus look of the strong, determined, and sensual type. You do not merely dream of doing things. You do them. You know yourself well because of self-contemplation, so you are able to communicate well with others. It is a situation of the proverbial "Know Thyself" that was made famous by Socrates and others. Psychology, sociology, and politics are just a few of the many areas where your solid knowledge of your own essence can be applied. Social scientists as well as members of the scientific community at large have individuals of this combination. You generally work inside the system because you are, in reality, a mainstream person at heart, even though you see yourself as a maverick. For the most part this is a pragmatic decision, because it works as a rule. Before undertaking a project of any kind you have a tendency to do things like take care of monetary resources, because you are ever security conscious like most Taurus people. A gift or legacy to the human race is actually something many Taurus-Aquarius people worry about and hope to accomplish. Examples of this going badly are Nikolai Lenin and Machiavelli. You are very flexible and accepting of your romantic partner in spite of being a bit possessive. You are inventive and imaginative in your love life as with life in general. You tend to have a large sense of your own importance because both of your signs are fixed, and this means you are determined and confident. When things do not go as you planned you can become temperamental and difficult, again because of your fixed sign aspect. Angry explosions are possible and often irregular and uncalled for, even though you put forward this appearance of being in command most of the time.

SUN IN TAURUS/MOON IN PISCES
Shy Person

Your sensitive nature pertaining to stressful states of affairs means it is hard for you to learn from others, even though you are very capable. Your persona is goal directed, courageous, and abiding, but you find it extremely difficult to live up to that perspective. You are tempted to bury your head in the sand when people actually expect you to live up to that view of you. This is because you have a fear of failure. The first thing to learn is to accept yourself. You have a gentle approach to life for a Taurus, a great deal of depth. This combination wins admiration. The spiritual and artistic are in your realm, and you are the most imaginative of all the Taurus combinations. This is an interesting combination of the tender and poetic inspiration of a Pisces along with the experience and wisdom of the Taurus. The thought of hurting others is painful to you. Your primary challenge in life will be to overcome your self-consciousness. You should see it as an asset that you have such a sensitive emotional nature, and develop a compassion for yourself. Disapproval and frustration with yourself will not do any good. Choosing your friends is quite important, because you are a highly malleable person who is easily influenced. Romantic areas make this all the more the case, because it would be unfortunate to be dominated by a highly aggressive individual who insists on pushing you around. Long-term happiness is quite important, and the Taurus-Pisces woman should be especially careful about marrying too young. Be certain that whomever you marry can understand your sensitive, kind, and gentle being and treat you accordingly. Lastly, leave fantasyland behind and take a journey to the real world. Open up and communicate freely with those around you in order to release your smothered feelings. You have so much to offer, why keep it inside yourself? Self-renewal is always available to you, and you have the usual perseverance of a Taurus. Faith is renewing for natives of the Pisces Moon, and they can acquire strength that way. Rather than denying your spiritual assets, improve them. A beautiful unfolding of your creative abilities will take place when you toss aside your prohibitions. A famous Taurus-Pisces native is Leonardo da Vinci. He is a remarkable, artistic, and spiritual person who exemplifies the possibilities of this combination.

SUN IN GEMINI/MOON IN ARIES
Reckless Abandon

When something comes your way you discern an opportunity or benefit and grasp it. You enjoy multitasking, because your mind is always in a spin and you do not like being idle. Most people would be exhausted just relaxing in your fashion. Your personality demands stimulation and exploration, and you are drawn to it. It is not beyond you to stir up some trouble if things are not hectic enough for you. Your world is an endless source of things you are terrifically interested in, but you put yourself first. An excitable, savvy, and nervous person is what you find in a Gemini. Energy is what the Aries mixes in along with quick thinking and a combative spirit. Organized confusion is the result of the combination. Gemini-Aries people are great at acquiring information fast, but they frequently forget about it just as fast. Your memory is not the best, although you are intelligent and insightful. Maybe this is why you have a behavior pattern that is repetitious, repeating the same things again and again. Gemini-Aries' main assets are good comprehension, versatility, and speed. Getting what you want is a priority, and you expect double payment for what you give. For some reason you find yourself in nerve-wracking situations, and this is hard for an excitable person like you. Social activities and athletics are outlets for your skittish personality. You make even big decisions, like marriage or your future, quickly because of your speedy thought process. Disaster can frequently result with your speedy decision making. When you are asked to listen to a viewpoint not your own, you generally are not interested. You are, however, well spoken and passionate about your own ideas, which, by the way, change frequently. Instant satisfaction and impulse do not always work, and you need to learn this. Patience would help a lot in getting what you desire. It would also be good to limit your numerous interests and activities to a reasonable extent. The communication profession is a good choice, or even being a detective or critic is also possible because of your excellent perception. You come up with original solutions, and this makes you a good problem solver. A big issue is your ability to cope with stress.

SUN IN GEMINI/MOON IN TAURUS
Instigator

You can have a problem getting rid of a youthful mind-set because, even in looks and mannerisms, you are youthful. The combination here is a little in opposition because of Gemini's adventurous spirit and Taurus's need for security. This might result in needing something different right after you have found the security of a job, spouse, and home. Satisfaction is something that eludes you. The Taurus Moon balances out the whimsy of Gemini. Your emotional foundation and centering is maintained even if you get kind of far-out. Your Taurus nature helps you bounce back from the most absurd situations that you manage to get into. You return for new challenges ready and refreshed. Innovation is the ideal goal for a combination that is so original. Past mistakes are not learned from in many cases though. Youthful patterns of behavior are hard to let go of for this combination of two Spring signs. You often work hard to get something in place, only to allow curiosity to get you to leave it once you have accomplished your purpose. Try to be less impulsive. The Gemini-Taurus is pragmatic and experienced in life, and makes an excellent unpaid psychologist and adviser. Numerous fields could benefits from your skillfulness and intelligence. Fields such as writing, music, and architecture are possible because of your aesthetic and structural sense. Bob Dylan and Frank Lloyd Wright are two examples of Gemini-Taurus, and notice the fact that these people need to communicate. Form, aesthetics, and structure are things they naturally understand. A life with little to look back on will come about if you give in to the constant desire for adventure and challenge. Also, learn to respect your own achievements, even if they seem to come quickly and easily. Personality is one of your strong points. Your quick humor and joyful spirit are an inspiration that allows you to melt the coldest heart of those you encounter. Regardless of your background, you can rise above it and are probably headed upward on the ladder of success and sophistication. You have a certain dignity and pride that make you stand out from the masses. You have a composition and emotional element to you that goes nicely with your analytical Gemini mind.

SUN IN GEMINI/MOON IN GEMINI
Whirlwind

You are totally unpredictable and might as well be several people as one. You are very inventive though, and that is a big help in your life. Quick, practical, and logical solutions come from you in the persona of being a problem solver. You are a walking encyclopedia, know everything, and are extremely well-read. It is hard for others to keep up with you because you retain information so well and do it so quickly. You want a world that rotates faster on its axis. You love the new and the excitement of seeing it unfold. Your own nervous energy keeps you going. You frequently end up consuming your resources and possibilities because you drift from place to place, checking things out and exploring everything. You are enthusiastic about things for a short time, because it is born of nerves rather than energy. You are never sure which side you are on or whom you want to be with because you change often. You are a combination of Einstein's originality,

Jonathan Swift's humor, and Immanuel Kant's intelligence. The challenge is to master the substance, discernment, and self-control needed to use these abilities. Assuming that you have not misused your ability already, there is hope. The difficult part is that you have the ability of a mastermind of crime who is always in trouble; a mentality looking for a fast buck and quick advantage is your problem, not an evil or ill-intentioned mind. You are a psychic sponge and read the people around you with ease. Sometimes you do not know if an idea is yours or someone else's. If they can acquire the patience, some double Gemini are very skillful and can make excellent craftsmen and artisans. Relationships come easily for you, and you probably have several at once. This leads to the problem of narrowing down your choices and focusing in order to attain real closeness. Developing ingenious schemes to rob a museum or gain the profits of investors for yourself rather than work is what you want. Your undoing is that you forget some small point, which gets you caught in spite of your genius. You have several selves at a minimum, so it is not a matter of self-discovery. You can easily play any role necessary depending on the situation. You have the gift of gab and can out-talk anyone. Therein lies a problem of hurting others, because while you do not mean to, your tongue is faster than your mind.

SUN IN GEMINI/MOON IN CANCER
Timekeeper

Success is practically guaranteed because of intuition, intelligence, and skillfulness. Franz Kafka, Jean-Paul Sartre, and Igor Stravinsky are a few examples of this combination. Liabilities are exceeded by positives, but as a very emotional person you need to learn to deal with some difficult issues. The people around you, including your spouse, coworkers, and family, have an impact on your supersensitive and impressionable being, and you need to learn to reduce their impact on your feelings. Being prone to mental disturbance, including depression and mood swings, is one side of this combination, but a very high level of creativity is the other. An imaginative, very sensitive, and sympathetic aspect enhances the need for expression, novelty, and innovation. Removing stress, ill will, and discord from your environment is very important for personal growth. You become antisocial, glum, depressed, and withdrawn if you live in an emotionally charged environment. Your surroundings must be overcome to eliminate this issue. Do not totally blend into your surroundings like a chameleon would, but rather inform others of your desires. Sacrificing your own happiness for that of others is not necessary all the time. You occasionally get withdrawn because you are subject to mood swings. Long-term closing off of others is extremely bad for you, but like most people some private time to think and introspect can be useful. A degree of social activity is important for your happiness. You will surely be popular, especially with the opposite sex, because of your good sense of humor, charm, and good nature. You have a negative self-image in spite of being so high-spirited and playful in your approach to life. Instead of thinking of your sensitivity as a disadvantage, view it as a strong point. This can help you climb mountains. Gemini-Cancers are great at role-playing because of an ability to adapt to their environment. You can do great in the theater. When you choose friends or romantic partners, as well as business associates, use your intuition and discrimination in order to make sure you get some emotional support. There is no need to always accommodate people. Some people will just take advantage of your goodness if you always say yes. Be more assertive.

SUN IN GEMINI/MOON IN LEO
Headliner

You have a definitive nature that results from your slightly overblown sense of your own importance. You are relatively serious. You have a dual personality, so figuring you out is not easy for most. There is kind of an executive nature about you that holds forth with advice and opinions on the one hand, and a humorous and carefree person on the other hand. You make more of a show of being the boss than taking it seriously. Volatility, nervousness, and self-expression are what we find in the Gemini. On the other hand, showiness, lavishness, and drama are part of the Leo character. The combination is a running drama that is high-strung and almost absurd. What we have here is a melodrama of the outrageous that runs almost day and night. Fanfare and panache are your prime movers. Expressing your feelings is a need residing deep inside you. You are a magnet made of charm, optimism, and exuberance that is irresistible, and this makes you very popular. Others can hardly wait to hear the next episode of your soap opera. Be more open to the contributions of other individuals and not so prideful and stuck on your own opinions. You are creative in your professional goals and do well in business, because in the end you are actually down-to-earth. You have sales and promotion talents. You are loyal, responsible, and dedicated in everything you do. You search for the perfect partner because you are very much a romantic as well as an adventurer. You want someone who is enthusiastic about life and shares your interests. You love to play the role of boss though, and enjoy showing off that side of you. It might be wise to go a little easier in your act because you can intimidate others to a point you may not imagine, even though you do not mean to. You follow your own rules like most Moons in Leo natives, and this means you often ignore the opinions and advice of others. You feel you are always right even though you are open-minded and generally listen to others who are reasonable in their approach. The feeling that you know what you are doing can bring about an impulsive and dangerous set of actions, and, when combined with your stubbornness and need to prove others wrong, you can do damage.

SUN IN GEMINI/MOON IN VIRGO
Quibbler

You are wise and seek knowledge avidly. This gives you a confident appearance. Restricting yourself to one field is hard for you though, because you want to learn so much and feel like specialization is a waste of time. You have a lighthearted presence that is also urbane, but you are discontented. Mythology tells us that Mercury governs both Gemini and Virgo, and it is the messenger of the gods. Communicating in the form of storytelling, writing, deliberating, or talking is all self-expression, which is one of your strongest necessities in life. For you, deep feelings and hidden ideas need to be communicated in an ongoing fashion. You always need an audience to do this because you are a very expressive person who wants to air your opinions, display your humor, and show off your sophistication. Agitation and moodiness result if you are prevented from doing this. You are generally guaranteed the audience you desire because you are high-strung, extravagant, and charming as well as extremely intelligent. Despite your polished, playful manner, you are often not happy. Living up to the high goals you set is nearly impossible, but that is what you strive for. You may experience pessimism, anxiousness, and confusion because you are not satisfied with your projects for much of your life. You have very good perception, and your critiques as well as analysis are generally accurate. You give wise advice in a tactful and thoughtful way. You love to give it to help others. Preciseness and analysis might very well be the areas that assist in your profession. Also, the news media, promotion, or advertising might be good choices in the area of communication. Moodiness, restlessness, and criticism of others can come about when you experience this discontentment and lack of confidence. Self-destructive behavior patterns can come about including alcoholism if you get so frustrated you cannot bear it. Compassion for yourself is suggested as a way to combat this feeling of discontent. Do not beat up on yourself. See your own achievements and endowments and be forgiving of yourself. Patience is something you need to develop. You cannot always gain recognition and reward over night no matter how hard you work.

SUN IN GEMINI/MOON IN LIBRA
Arbitrator

You are not responsible for all the difficulties in the world, so there is certainly no obligation on your part to take care of those around you, humankind, or the universe itself. Your own happiness needs to be emphasized more in your case. You can set a positive example for others when, because of your restless spirit, it turns out that the world does not align with your ideals and vision for how it should be. You are a born peacemaker and are only happy if you feel that those around you are happy. Within yourself, you work toward quietude, concordance, and balance. Life, however, does not always operate like we want it to. Because the world is in tension and a constant flow, such equilibrium is essentially impossible emotionally. A sad and secluded Sun-Moon combination like yours is truly sad indeed. Nevertheless, you may feel the desire to surrender to isolation or fantasy when life is stressful and people are impossible for you to deal with. But this is only a temporary solution to the difficulties of such a situation, and, in fact, it will only make matters worse. Doing this only means the world will miss out on what you have to offer. Hold off that desire to run away from a world that does not always work the way you want it to. Be dynamic, brisk, and alive. While you could skate through life, you should resist that temptation just because you are so flexible, capable, and intelligent. Do not elude challenges, adventures, and responsibilities. Pushing your endowments to the boundaries is important for all Gemini-Libra people. You will travel far if you resist the temptation to just do the minimum. You will probably search for a perfect partner because you are a romantic at heart and a dreamer. Before you find the right person for you, there will be many affairs along the way. The mass media, social world, and politics are fields than can profit from your natural statesmanship, great perception, and insight. An artistic field is also a possibility because of your strong imagination. You are adaptable and can probably live almost anywhere. You have an extremely open mind about other cultures and lifestyles and probably like to read about faraway places. Your essence breaks down roadblocks and transcends cultures, faiths, political orientations, and all divisions. You do not lead a tiring life, because it is a harmonious combination.

SUN IN GEMINI/MOON IN SCORPIO
Allegorist

You are cautious when things concern you personally because you have a volatile, charged-up image that people can see. Because of your boldness and aggressive demeanor, people always notice you. Your skills in observation mean you notice them too. You always notice details that you can proceed to analyze, and you are proud of your ability to perceive things. When you are in a talkative mood you might tend to hyperbolize and dramatize things even though you have good insights and perceptions. Your personality is emphatic and magnetic. You are very aware of where you are going and are a more intense individual than other Geminis. There is an aura of mystery about you because you are secretive and do not show your entire being. You get carried away at these times with your vivid imagination and emotions, which is usually okay, but it can unintentionally result in harmful distortions when things get way out of proportion. Relating things with less exaggeration and learning to watch what you say is important. Your past relations with your parents and others should be carefully examined to decide whether some of your bad issues and destructive behaviors have been handed down from those who had a strong influence in your in life—especially your mother and father, or sisters and brothers. Because you cling to impressions and convictions so strongly, it is hard for you to let go of them even if they are the origin of your difficulties. It will help you if you can open up your thoughts and feelings to a good friend or a professional counselor. You are a sponge that assimilates the mood, ideas, and ends around you, even if not consciously. You are direct, strong-willed, and seem to be your own leader. But you often give in to insistence from friends, family, or lovers when making choices about your profession or romantic life. You need to make decisions based on your own true feelings even though it is important to open your mind to the opinions and ideas of other people. Going with your own true nature is always the best for you. Your psychological well-being is heavily molded by the emotional receptivity you have with those around you. You can easily take on the goals and perceptions of those in your circle because you absorb them so quickly. That includes their neuroses and behavioral forms.

SUN IN GEMINI/MOON IN SAGITTARIUS
Hired Gun

Your enthusiasm, perception, and creativity are awesome in scope. All of this would be terrific if it were not for the fact that it is so much work for you to keep yourself in tune. There to blow up your dreams is a lack of patience and good sense combined with needless rebellion and wastefulness. You hate to be restricted in any form because you love freedom. Classrooms, mundane jobs, and other things you regard as drudgery are avoided. You want to find out what life really is and experience everything, no matter what mistakes you have made before. You are an explorer and consequently can either be a genius who makes great discoveries, or be like a Fool in the tarot deck. There is an inspired person in you, but also someone who is impulsive and immature. At times, when you wake up, it is almost as though you are seeing your world with new eyes. You might experience extremely bad luck or even a personal disaster, but you always remain an optimist. Your glass is always at the very least half full. Part of this is because of your short memory. You are about twenty people in terms of your projects and interests. Conforming to anything or being a part of the establishment in not for you. You are a rebel. The exotic and exciting continue to call you, and because you are so impulsive you do not mind dropping something you were engrossed in and moving on. What you need to learn is to concentrate and develop self-discipline. An environment that is conducive to this would help you; one that is structured and organized. You can learn to direct your skill in a useful way and still be a vagabond. Try to be around organized and well-directed people to reduce your gullibility. Capricorns, Virgos, and Taurus people might be very good for you in that regard. Fellow Geminis and Sagittarians are not. You must ease up on restlessness and get organized. If you do not do this, you will have a life of disasters and the mishaps that go with them mixed in with all your adventures. Some like it that way, and maybe that is you. Philosophers, academics, and inventive scientists can come from this combination. If you mange to get some self-control and willpower, you can do anything.

SUN IN GEMINI/MOON IN CAPRICORN
Handshaker

You have well-established goals and you seldom have to reorganize your thoughts or perspectives. You are admired for being well spoken as well as efficient because of your discipline and self-control. Emotionally, you try to stay in control to the extent that you may not be aware that everything you say is designed to produce a result. The Capricorn inner self makes a more serious Gemini than most. The latter is usually exciting, has more interests, and is a communicator. Your mixture makes you cool and calm as well as strong, detached, and ambitious. You can talk people into almost anything because of your charm and magnetism. You direct yourself toward power and influence because you are aware of your attraction to others and put it to use very well. Your personality seems a bit above the fray because you do not reveal the feelings you have under your dynamic personality. You do not need to be aggressive in your desire for power because you possess an inborn sense of dignity and principled moral values. In spite of this, you usually get the best of a deal in business. The spiritual side of life should not be sacrificed because of competition, even though that has it proper place. The biggest challenge for you is to discover the side of life that has more meaning, because the material portion will take care of itself. You will recognize your mistakes later in life when you have time to contemplate them. So do not fail to recognize this facet as early on in life as possible. Sadness and bitterness in old age can result if you do this. Overcoming difficulties and barriers with your courage and unwillingness to quit shows that you have a lot of inner fortitude. You can use your well-developed power of persuasion to bend others to your will because you sense their vulnerabilities. You are a master of manipulation. Inside you are numerous personalities moving about trying to be the most influential and recognized. Your desire for power in the name of material possessions is done at the expense of other parts of your being.

SUN IN GEMINI/MOON IN AQUARIUS
Originator

You are refined, extroverted, and captivating. In addition, you are autonomous and independent, and this moves you to make some of your dreams become realities. One of your most important gifts is your intuition. You appear to know what people will desire in the future, what their thoughts are, and what they want right now. Your life seems to be led more for the future than the present. You have had an inquiring and investigative mind ever since you were a child. No doubt you used to love to fix broken things, put things together, and understand their inner workings. Your parents probably had to keep an eye on you so you did not blow fuses. You cannot satisfy your curiosity about the universe. You are endlessly intrigued by the strange and the unexplored, and you love science and change. The world, in your view, needs change, and it is your goal to do that using your imagination and intelligence to apply your ideas. Communication is something difficult for you because you appear to be way ahead of others in your mind. It is almost like you are living in another dimension. Approaching life optimistically, you are fundamentally detached and do not show your emotions. Others' unhappiness is hard for you to comprehend. Confusion and agitation sets in when you run in to a very emotional situation. You do not look inside yourself often enough because you are so busy with projects and other people that there is not enough time. Meditation or contemplation are good breaks. An exploration of your own inner workings would benefit you. You are not easy to deal with or understand because of erratic changes in mood ranging from serious to lively and fun loving. On a positive note, you are in total control of your temper. Anyone in your circle who appears to be unhappy or upset causes you to do everything you are able to help them improve their emotional state. Your charms as well as positive and humorous attitude usually work wonders. Sometimes you forget the beauty of the present because you are planning for the future. A pause and appreciation for what you have now is always good, because the world will wait for you. The invention or great discovery will be just as appreciated tomorrow.

SUN IN GEMINI/MOON IN PISCES
Dual Identity

Your early childhood may be causing you to be guarded and protective. You are, however, extremely emotional, perceptive, and sensitive. This sensitivity is often concealed by rationalization of issues that should be addressed directly as well as detachment and superiority. The danger here is never finding satisfaction because you lose contact with your emotions completely. Openly and honestly facing your feelings is something you should learn to do. Gemini is objective and analytical while, in juxtaposition, Pisces is understanding and very emotional. In any case, you are an intricate and versatile individual. Kindness can grip you completely at times even though you think you are distant and sophisticated. Perhaps you see yourself as cool and highly developed, but there are times when you can feel overwhelmed with compassion. You probably learned to hide your true feelings when you were young because you may have had a difficult time of things. The bad feelings, moods, and ideas of those around you are absorbed because you are quite impressionable. More emphatic types are to be kept at a distance so they do not gain control and influence over your life as they surely can do. Becoming aware of how to control your own destiny and environment should take precedence over going with the crowd of emotional impressions. You are dedicated and conscientious in all your undertakings along with having high principles. This makes an excellent professional of some type. Your humor and charm usually draws the opposite sex to you. Even though you need to be exceptionally careful in choosing a partner, you have an extremely romantic character. Finding someone would be easy. Finding the right one would probably not. You generally know what is best for you, so it should be quite easy to use your intuition. Listen to your sixth sense and keep your independence. A lot of Gemini-Pisces people find religion a good support system for them. The moon in Pisces allows Gemini, the communicator, to express things creatively. This opens doors for you. Because your intuition lets you know what people want, you can be strong as a business or marketing individual. Gemini-Pisces people are also good teachers and scholars.

SUN IN CANCER/MOON IN ARIES
Self-Righteous

You can feel misunderstood and let down because they do not place you on a pedestal. You run into problems because you sometimes do not accept yourself. You cannot be in the spotlight all the time. There is no need to live life as though you can save the world and run from place to place trying to meet all kinds of impossible goals. This can only result in ill health. Be happy and grateful for who you actually are, and do not worry about being superhuman. Self-acceptance is the key. There is a competition here between an aggressive and assertive Aries and a careful and sensitive Cancer. The fact is though, that it is quite difficult to live up to being a person who is all things to all people. The scenario might be that you believe yourself to be a leader, but the insecure and careful Cancer side stops you from enacting those fantasies and delusions of grandeur. Depression and moodiness can result if you do not keep up with the challenges of your dreams. You are a very talented person, and the Cancer-Aries is quite self-motivated. Careers that might suit you are in politics, engineering, or other things that involve projects emphasizing improvement. Academia is also a possibility because of your strong intellectual abilities. Discarding your idealistic image can open up several creative areas because of your abilities and talents. You might have an inclination to think you are superior to others even though you are generous and polite. This can cause serious problems for you. The road to your career is sometimes blocked by your lack of patience and pride, in spite of your gusto and ambition. You like to have attention and you can range from being the ham to the sophisticate. You are always trustworthy, truehearted, and steady in your close friendships. You are also a committed and tender partner who is extremely amorous. There is a need to always believe you have someone on your side who gives support. Your spirit and mind keep you ahead in school or work. When things do not go as planned, you can throw aside everything you have worked for. You do not take orders well, and this means that being the subordinate is not easy for you. You sometimes do not accept it and ruin your chance for advancement. A Cancer-Aries probably has the most difficult challenge in overcoming self-importance. You are high spirited, friendly, and outgoing in a social setting.

SUN IN CANCER/MOON IN TAURUS
Smorgasbord

You are excellent at figuring out and understanding others, and you have a good degree of self-knowledge. You have tested most of the defense and escape mechanisms that Cancers tend to use, but, in the end, you depend on your own tenaciousness and wisdom as a protective cover against the difficulties in life. You utilize these to permit you to feel more secure. Even though you are thoughtful of others, you do not often follow their advice or listen to their suggestions. The Taurus Moon gives you durability and determination that underlie your charm, innocence, and soft nature. You have an astuteness, strength, and assurance residing under that delicate and unsure outer layer. You almost always go around with your guard up, because you probably had a difficult time earlier in life and do not want to be taken advantage of like you were before. Adaptability is one of your strengths, but you do not lose sight of your own being. Intuition guides you in a stubborn and unrelenting fashion, and consequently it is hard for you to give up first impressions or forget previous transgressions. You hold grudges. This part of your personality might ruin you if you do not learn to put the past behind you. There is an original approach to what you do, and you have a wonderful imagination. This can serve you for good or for ill. This is true, because the same imagination can, unfortunately, cause irrational fears, doubts, and even paranoia. Be constructive with the use of your imagination, and you can succeed at nearly anything creative. A deep depression is possible if you spend too much time in your fantasy life, so you should try to stay based in reality. Criticism is hard for you to grasp, because you always think you are right. Admitting you are wrong is almost impossible. Shifting the blame for something to another is easy for you, and you do it frequently. If someone disputes what you say, you can get irritable and irrational with him or her. The same holds true if you are emotionally threatened, because you need to feel secure. Learning that some advice is sound and that not everyone is a threat to your security would be helpful, as would not being so vindictive. You have excellent potential for creativity because of your imagination and originality.

SUN IN CANCER/MOON IN GEMINI
Sky Wire

You have a lot of demands on you as well as assorted perceptions, and you find introspection hard because of your busy mental schedule. You tend to want to help everyone and adapt to everything, because you are kind and sensitive. No one can do this though. Try to fulfill your own dreams rather than worrying about fulfilling another person's dream. Your feelings at any given moment may just be a reflection of the environment. You have a lot going for you, including a great memory with the ability to learn a lot. In addition to intelligence, you are humorous and sophisticated. Furthermore, you are very perceptive and an excellent critic. Gemini is, of course, restless by nature and wants a lot of variety in addition to being curious. Sensitivity and intuition combined with being impressionable are hallmarks of a Cancer. This combination is not without its difficulties though. Yes, there is the friendly spirit and excellent mind. Belligerent and tense situations make you that way as do, on the positive side, peaceful and calm ones. You tend to take on the emotional situation you find yourself in, and it is difficult, accordingly, to discover what your real life situation and true goals are. Your intellect, imagination, and inventiveness can be an asset in your profession, but you are not decisive enough to be in management. A career in media or advertising is a possibility, or something in the arts would be a good choice. You are not great about keeping promises, and your loyalty is spread very thin. Very assertive and strong partners are a bit of a challenge for female Cancer-Gemini individuals, and they might lose themselves as a result. Someone who is freedom loving and open-minded like you is the best sort of partner for you. You cannot hear yourself because of the noise around you. A famous person who illustrates a lot about Cancer-Gemini people is Henry David Thoreau. His important work was done in an environment of quiet and solitude. Be more honest with yourself about what you want. Learn to be more self-assertive. Try to learn what it is that you really want, what your own goals are, and then, when you know, go after them. First impressions are generally the right ones for you, so trust them and depend on them. While it is true that Cancer-Gemini people work well in a structured and organized situation, you should make decisions for yourself.

SUN IN CANCER/MOON IN CANCER
Bodyguard

The emotional sensitivity and depth of the Cancer, along with your astuteness and ability to erect stronger barriers between you and your environment at the same time as you become more sensitive, combine with your resourcefulness, intelligence, and refinement. You either withdraw deep inside your fortress or utilize your natural ability in the face of the aggressive and hostile world. You saw and dealt with the uncongenial world around you in your youth, which was probably a test. Through careful examination, you ascertained the most dependable and certain way to move through a very irregular world at that time. You held on to this habit once it was set in motion. The double Cancer wants protection from the time of childhood until their old age. Nearly everything for them is self-protection. Building metaphorical castles to protect you and preparing your defenses occupies a lot of time. In dual points, this gives you huge weaknesses and terrific strengths. Your Cancer Sun is magnified along with the Cancer Moon. You keep a low profile and are humble in your lifestyle and interaction with others. You can have big swings of depression and high spirits, with ebbing and flowing feelings and responses. You can, on one hand, have a deep understanding of the mood of people close to you or, on the other hand, your overextended sensitivity may cause you to stave off people altogether. Phobias and fears of assorted varieties are also possible psychological results, but once dealt with you can be creative. You are astute at finance and have an excellent vision when it comes to business. A spiritual path may call you, because many Cancer-Cancer people are quite religious. You move through life adapting your strategy and personality to handle the moment, even though you are active all the time. Instinctively, you are aware of what others expect of you, and this makes you an excellent tactician and diplomat. There is nothing more fearful to you than vulnerability, so in a battle you never go at an opponent straight on, but rather circuitously. Total withdrawal is possible if your environment is truly hostile or threatening, favoring complete closing off with others. That others do not care much about what you are hiding would probably surprise you. Your ego is actually the cause of your serious paranoia.

SUN IN CANCER/MOON IN LEO
Party Pooper

You know yourself well so you do not mind expressing your feelings and thoughts. Your lack of inhibitions along with personal appeal, self-confidence, and magnetism add to your success. You want the applause, credit, and position that comes with success, because your Leo nature needs it. Here we have Cancer with the bravery to be creative and Leo with the imagination and sensitivity. The result is a gifted mixture. You succeed at anything you set out to accomplish as the result of your adeptness and talents, and this provides confidence. Unlike most Cancers, you do not feel the need to guard your emotions. You believe that you have earned esteem, appreciation, and sometimes adulation, and you will be content only when this is provided. You almost certainly have very powerful creative drives. The arts have probably called you at one time or another during your life. There is a wide variety of things that interest you in this area, including design, film, writing, music, and architecture. You are prone to taking setbacks so hard that you let a martyr complex consume you. It's possible you will sit back and moan about the world not acknowledging your genius because it is so blind and callous. Learning things from defeat is something you need to do. Experience and good advice can assist you, and you need to know this or you will lose a bright future. Others are often attracted to you because you have a strong need for credence, and thus your benevolence and magnetism draws them. Manipulation to gain an advantage from others is something to be cautious of. You are kind and generous, but you always put yourself first. A couple of issues for you are conceit and pride. Criticism is something you have difficulty dealing with, even though you are patient and strong-minded. Furthermore, you have problems taking the reversals or normal defeats that all talented people must run in to in moving toward success. Part of this stems from stubbornness. No one can deter you at times from the feeling that you are right. You often wonder how anyone can question you. Your downfall might just be a high-minded inflexibility in your attitude toward change or learning. Your first defeat, after a super quick start and strong gains, can be crushing for you. Recovery from wounded pride and conceit comes very slowly in your case.

SUN IN CANCER/MOON IN VIRGO
Attendant

At a young age you were wise because you matured faster than your peer group. You have, luckily, adaptability, and that helps with your high degree of sensitivity. You can overcome whatever barriers you encounter because of your perception, level-headedness, and experience. The mental perception of the Virgo Moon heightens the emotional sensitivity of the Cancer person. The antagonism and malevolence of the world is something you have had to deal with since you were very young, and this has a big impact on you. Super-sensitivity may be present in you because of the adversity, suffering, and indifference that has, at times, haunted you. Consequently you may be too shy, introspective, and even emotionally catatonic. A Virgo Moon that provides forbearance, inner strength, and ability for self-sacrifice also assists you. You are bighearted and kind as well as generous to everyone. That is your essence, and you are known and admired for it. You maintain your sympathy and compassion for others no matter how difficult your life is or what you might be going through. You often find your calling is working for others, because you want so much to feel needed. You are extremely frugal in terms of personal expenses but very generous, almost to a fault, with others. Be more generous to yourself and then you can enjoy life more and open up to the world around you. You love to give affection to others, but oddly you do not particularly like to get it in return. You want to feel needed in a relationship, but luckily your standards are very high. That helps keep away people who would drag you down. It is possible you will have a symbolic relationship of sorts. You might seek a religious or social ideal or enterprise. The merely physical is not adequate for you. Being a workaholic is the approach to life that many Cancer-Virgos take. Even considering all this, you never lose yourself while helping others. Your self-awareness is quite strong. You are a potential educator, counselor, physician, or clergyperson who uses your compassion, intellect, and strength to be of assistance. A number of Cancer-Virgo people are also excellent in the field of business. Your organizational skills are excellent, and you are intuitive and clever. A mainstream and organized work environment is best for you because you are careful by nature.

SUN IN CANCER/MOON IN LIBRA
Yes-Man

You often follow the road that your peers, parents, or authority figures have gone down, and a lot of your disarray comes from not doing what you feel. You can easily give in to self-consciousness, shyness, excessive self-examination, and maybe even closing yourself off when your desire to defend yourself or shield your feelings takes priority. Learn to control your surroundings, because your environment can often dictate to you. This is particularly true when you choose friends and associates. When combined with the Moon in Libra, the emotional anxieties and the shyness of Cancer are magnified. Your quest for internal peace and quiet is held back by your emotional vulnerability and high degree of sensitivity. How you perceive yourself often takes a backseat to how others see you. You sometimes lose your way in the attitudes and roles of those around you. This is because you are so busy watching what others are saying and doing. Somehow you believe you will find yourself there. A positive and supportive situation will result if you do. Your opinions are just as good as others, and you should learn to speak up more and be confident. Perils and occasionally daring are sometimes necessary to take advantage of opportunities. You are very romantic and long to be needed. The sexual aspect is not as important as the romantic and sentimental side of romance for you. You often completely ignore the bad traits in your partner and build up the good ones to almost unreachable heights. You need emotional support and encouragement at every turn, and you will practically worship a person who gives it to you. Your endowments are inside of you, and you need to search for various ways to express them. You can rid yourself of fears and meet larger challenges after you have acquired more self-confidence. You are extremely creative because of your powerful imagination. A Cancer-Libra has numerous artistic opportunities if they have gained enough confidence. You have a knack for singling out the sources of stress and conflict, and this would make you an excellent diplomat and a natural conciliator. You can apply you social skills in wide-ranging areas like psychology, sociology, law, or public relations once you achieve emotional balance and harmony.

SUN IN CANCER/MOON IN SCORPIO
Viper

Success in life is almost guaranteed because of your self-assurance and personal magnetism. Cancer-Scorpios seem to just get things easier than others because they are just plain lucky. You have both influence and respect because, no matter what you undertake, you just seem to be a winner. This gets noticed. You appear mysterious, and you intrigue people because of your Cancerian protective exterior. You do not want to share your inner thoughts so you are guarded about revealing feelings and reactions. The Cancer-Scorpio person is not the Cancer who most people think they know. They are not an insecure, timid, introvert that we usually read about. The real shrewd and tenacious self is difficult to spot under your modest and mild-mannered exterior. You may seem unprepossessing and even modest, but it's not hard to discern your true inner shrewdness and tenacity. Underneath that cool image of yours is a very intense, forceful, and determined individual. You are a very emotional person beyond your exterior. The situation you are dealing with or the person himself or herself determine your response and reaction to them. Intuition is your decision maker, and reason plays little or no role. Your shrewdness and perception mean that you are almost always right. You are always plotting your next move because you are so untrusting and suspicious. Wrongs are never forgotten, and you have a terrific memory. Betraying you is not a good idea, because you will take your time and get your revenge. You can be vengeful, vicious, and petty. You are up for experiencing anything like most competitive people. You can go after pleasure, self-indulgence, and sensuality as aggressively as you do professional enterprises. You take risks about whom you can trust, and your sense is reliable in most cases. Making fun of you is hazardous, because you are quite serious about yourself. You, on the other hand, can be cruel, sarcastic, and blunt about the weaknesses of others, which you can readily perceive. Honing your sense of humor and tact would be a good idea. Gloom and depression are things that you might suffer from, even more than other Cancers. Your emotions need to be dealt with candidly, and you should be less tight-lipped about your feelings, including hurt and enmity. Holding a grudge or pouting are not healthy. You think life is an endless struggle, and you are always on guard.

SUN IN CANCER/MOON IN SAGITTARIUS
Starry-Eyed

You have a nature that is two-sided and, like most Cancers, a personality that needs a home, vocation, and security. At the same time the Sagittarius side wants adventure, romance, and freedom in general. This dream will always be a part of you even though you might be more conventional with your profession and lifestyle. Your Sagittarius Moon gives you optimism, faith, and hope for the future so you are not the ordinary gloomy Cancer. You are open-minded and cheerful no matter how many difficulties you are encountering. You have a positive outlook on life. There is a spirituality about you, and this makes you idealistic and talkative. Your lifetime has been one filled with lofty goals and numerous dreams, and because you possess high standards, you do not settle for second best. You have an expansive vision and find it difficult to narrow things down. When you think of all the terrific things you are interested in, you can lose your sense of self. It is hard for you to choose only one. Your efforts can be sabotaged by these internal longings, particularly when you are overworked or have a lot of responsibility and drudgery in your life. Do you sometimes instantly leave what you are doing and chase after some far-fetched fantasy? Rather than abandoning your structure, projects, and responsibilities, you should be sure to allow time for contemplation, music, and travel. You appear carefree and free-spirited in your social life, and this implies an enthusiastic, outgoing, and trusting person. You are, however, a lot deeper than you generally seem to be. You are fascinated by new ideas and are philosophically minded. You dig deeper and are never satisfied with what is only on the surface. You want the real and true meaning of things. You find it hard to focus your affection, but you are very trustworthy and loyal when you love someone. Sticking with one partner might be difficult because you get bored easily. Things that fulfill your desire to be an adventurer should be allowed too. Get on a plane or train and permit your being to escape. You always speak your mind directly and candidly. You are fundamentally an emotional being, and your tastes are frequently grounded in gut reactions. You say things that are regretted later because your emotions are the boss and as a result you need to develop some tact or you will lose friends.

SUN IN CANCER/MOON IN CAPRICORN
Low Self-Esteem

Your insight into people is extraordinarily good because of your experience. This gives you prohibitions and conflicts even though it provides special perceptions for you. Unlike most Cancers, you do not feel fearful of a future that is not certain. Your goals are very high as the result of your ambitions and desire for recognition. Your Capricorn aspect is goal oriented, distant, and rugged while the Cancer part is benevolent, unsure, and emotional. This obviously puts the signs in some opposition. You have inner disputes trying to solve issues, and you need to build yourself up because of this. Inner firmness of purpose and determination have helped you over the early obstructions that in all likelihood you experienced in your childhood environment. This made you a self-examining and calculating person, especially for a Cancer individual. You are a quite serious person and learn things easily. Your strong Capricorn inner nature finds opposition from the gentler Cancer. You are in need of proving yourself for inner satisfaction as well as recognition from the world at large. You have a somewhat unique approach to life, and you are never happy with external impressions. You approach it with a view toward change and novelty no matter what you do. Galileo the astronomer and the writer Ernest Hemingway were both members of your combination, and their work shows the totally different nature of the Cancer-Capricorn perspective. Seclusion is something that you desire, but while that may be good in limited amounts, too much can bring about alienation from the world around you, and feelings of not being good enough. Depression, disappointment, and withdrawal can come about with your continual dissatisfaction. Even turning to drugs or alcohol are possible in severe cases. Try to recognize you have gifts and learn to appreciate yourself, while accepting you limitations. You have strengths that need to be acknowledged, and it is okay to be sensitive in life sometimes. You need to work on accepting yourself and loving yourself. You can accomplish anything after you have learned to make peace with your inner nature. Capricorn's realism, organization, and aspirations combined with Cancer's vision and intuition can give you an excellent business sense.

SUN IN CANCER/MOON IN AQUARIUS
Diehard

You have remarkably astute intuition and perception. Others may find you somewhat self-important and assuming because you always have a ready answer or belief. You are one or two steps ahead of everyone else. You become testy with those who fail to see things the way you do or who cannot understand the truth you may have just discovered. Searching for new frontiers is the focus in your combination because of Cancers' depth and sensitivity to their surroundings. It can also bring about the flaky crank or fanatic, but ideally the result is the interested and devoted politician, humanist, or researcher. You are different from other Cancers because of that offbeat and unusual imagination of yours. You are the first to experience something new and different, and there is nothing very careful about you. Your deep internal restless spirit pushes you on, as does your independent thought. Either that will result in lasting achievements or absurd rebellion. This impatience and intellectual arrogance can be your undoing. Your complete apathy toward the beliefs of others may cause you to lose out on much of what life can give. When young, you no doubt saw yourself as a white knight, righting wrongfulness. Eventually reality and recognizing your own limits either nurtured a more realistic viewpoint or led to a sense of disenchantment and, perhaps, acrimoniousness. Cynicism may have come about. Drowning yourself in some radical group that promises heaven is possible. Fanaticism or passionate dedication to a cause or political theory may be an alluring last resort for the disenchanted. That is not the case, fortunately, for most Cancer-Aquarians. You may very possibly seek a technical or scientific vocation with your scientific mind and wild imagination, but your strong social consciousness could lead you into humanistic endeavors, politics, or law. You are dedicated to pursuing your own unique path toward wisdom, accuracy, and self-realization. Many Cancer-Aquarians are haunted by mental disarray. Your mind inclines toward drifting in the classroom, on the job, or in discussions. You dream about some new concept or unfinished project and stare into space when you should be paying attention. Locating something absorbing enough to hold your attention for a time is difficult because your curiosity is interminable. You no doubt feel a strong sense of duty as all Moon in Aquarius natives do.

SUN IN CANCER/MOON IN PISCES
Charlatan

You have overpowering spiritual and selfless urges that the highly developed Cancer-Pisces often has. You feel the call for protection even though you may be a saint in essence. Like all impressionable, highly sensitive, and sharing individuals, you protect your emotions to avoid being harmed. The Cancer-Scorpio hides behind privacy and all Cancers have their special defense mechanisms; arrogance for Cancer-Leo, and using an offense as a defense for Cancer-Aries. Role-playing is your special defense. Yours is the most tenderhearted, sensitive, and sympathizing of all the Cancer signs. Needless pain, inhumane treatment, or unfairness automatically repulses you. You have a strong desire to reach out and assist others because you are authentically concerned and always ready to give of yourself. Worrying that his sensitivity is a form of helplessness, a male Cancer-Pisces may try to feign an aggressive persona. He is hoping to hide his feelings with an obvious show of manliness or machismo. In hopes of being swept off her feet and forever protected, a female Cancer-Pisces may utilize an excessively feminine role. So afraid are they of showing their true selves, both genders risk assuming roles that are completely at odds with their real natures. Continuous role-playing is a manner of self-deception and escapism, even though it is sometimes required in order to get along in life. You have a wonderful and unique personality, and if you learn to make good use of your talent to fantasize, it will be an excellent way of handling stress and anxiety. You may be successful as an artist or in other creative areas if you do not lose your hold on the actual world. Moreover, education, medicine, counseling, and law are ideally suited for you. You learn with amazing speed, and you have an excellent memory. You rely on others for centering and inspiration because you are essentially passive. You should associate with highly motivated individuals. Most of all be true to yourself. See sensitivity as a strength. You can cut yourself off from your happiness by denying part of yourself. It is not necessary for you to build a protective wall around yourself, because your combination shows constancy, wellness, and luck. Being who you actually are will let you feel far more satisfied and content.

SUN IN LEO/MOON IN ARIES
Barnstormer

For you life is not fun unless it involves a battle, and this includes political affairs, business, and love. You are a principled, loyal, and dependable person because you have an inborn code of morals. You might seem aggressive at times, but you still would never be disloyal to or hurt a friend. You simply are not someone who uses duplicity or dishonesty. Daydreaming about exploration or romance does not satisfy you, because you have the passion and vitality to go out and find it. Fantasy is not part of your life because you are so busy that you have basically no need for it. You are aggressive and self-assured, and when you say something people listen. You have a great asset in being courageous. You will speak your mind honestly about your thoughts and feelings with no inhibitions. You are most happy when you are in charge because you are a born leader. You get the attention your very large ego needs because you have both aspirations and vigor. As a Leo-Aries, you consider life a war. You are restless like most Leo-Aries people, and life is not boring. You probably have very few emotional issues because you are open and candid about nearly everything. You never suppress your inner drives, and you are self-confident. As an alternative, you direct your antagonistic impulses into helpful and constructive activities. As with all Leos, your profession is very significant because you seek standing, credit, and as much comfort and gratification in life as you can get. You are conceited in your views and assumptions and are a natural member of the aristocracy. You often overlook the feelings of others in your blunt and outspoken remarks. You can frequently express yourself harshly. Your principles demand honesty and openness, and you do not really mean to be tactless, you just always say precisely what you feel. Learn to value others in the same way you value yourself and control your egotistical bluntness a bit. You have the willpower to see your projects through, and very little stands in your way. There are three things you must keep in check: conceit, impetuosity, and impudence. Logic is very often blocked by passion, no matter how intelligent you may be. You are inclined to leap before you look. You hardly ever stop to examine those on-the-spot choices of yours, because you are so certain of your judgment. Learn to be modest from time to time because you cannot possibly be right in everything you do. Prior to starting on some doomed project, listen to the good advice of others.

SUN IN LEO/MOON IN TAURUS
Highfalutin

You are theatrical, forceful, and purposeful, and there is a heaviness to your being. There are a limited number of things you want in life, but they can become powerful in terms of your priorities. You go after power and position primarily for the comfort and lavishness they provide, because you are sensual and worldly. You are somewhat of an egoist as are most Leos. You try hard to accomplish your dreams and goals with confidence in your strengths and intuition. You are extremely motivated, and this goes with the fact that you have two fixed signs. That results in a strong resolve to achieve the high goals you have set for yourself. You can, however, thwart yourself in spite of your commendable qualities. You are very serious about yourself and your actions. You are also headstrong, obstinate, brave, and resolute. You tend to have a lot of common sense and wisdom. Most of the time you are calm, composed, and understanding. But you can be just the reverse. You will be unpredictable, morose, difficult, and even oppressive if you are in a demanding situation or things are just not the way you want them. Impudence and inflexibility often hinder your judgment and cause you to unconsciously chip away at your own efforts. It is not simple for you to admit defeat, and not having things your way can bring about states of depression and fits of temper.

You might also take out your fury on those around you. An extraordinary sense of pride and powerful ego bring this about. Success is not continuous for anyone unless they are very fortunate. Everyone must learn to handle dissatisfaction at times. Remove yourself a little more from your actions. Inner peace and contentment can only come from within, so the next time you feel let down or irritated, do not take it so seriously. Look from a distance instead. Your vision is far reaching, and you are practical. Furthermore you have a wide and sweeping vision, but the total faith you have in yourself often causes you to reject or ignore the opinions of other people. You have often ignored what others have said, only to find out your blunder later on. Only after you have learned to work together with people are you capable of incredible creativity. Open your mind to some advice, because you cannot be correct all the time. Learn to value and accept other points of view and lighten up in your confidence. Perhaps you were born to lead, but the finest leaders know full well to cooperate now and then.

SUN IN LEO/MOON IN GEMINI
Confidence Man

You express yourself with spectacular style as well as feeling, and you are outspoken. Your sarcasm and keen perception are widely known, and you can be a combination of speaker, comedian, speechwriter, or dramatist. George Bernard Shaw is a great example of a Leo-Gemini. Unfortunately, a con artist is also possible with this combination. You are no exception to the fact that Leos are lazy. Anything that requires order and concentration is strictly avoided, and you are great at delegating responsibility and thus avoiding work. You need to be the center of attention or you are not happy. All parts of you, from your humor to your hair to your ability to speak well, seek adoration and ego boosting. You do have, after all, a large ego. You often keep away from the very challenges that could give you some real self-esteem and recognition. Frequently, a heavy social calendar is actually your way of avoiding responsibility. You are quite removed even though people think you are understanding, compassionate, and sociable. It is amazing how readily you can end an affection or relationship without crying a tear. Your outbursts are more of a show than passion. You are a very discerning critic because of your aptitude to observe and evaluate others from afar, but this may cause your friends a lot of disappointment. You are never fearful to tell your partner how you feel because you are open and unrestrained in love. Due to your deep-seated need for variety and exhilaration, your romantic life is constantly in flux. The inner Gemini impatience repeatedly causes you to be irresponsible no matter how resolute and hardworking you may seem to others. Concentrating your energies on one area is not simple for you. Your curious mind is always seeking exploration, and your greatest happiness is constant diversity. Living for thrills and stimulation should be stopped, and you should focus more on lasting self-fulfillment. You will achieve much more in the end if you are patient. You can find incredible expression ideally via reporting, writing, or drama, so that the creative strengths of your Leo character can be fulfilled. Your combination has versatility and, actually, you can stand out in almost any field you choose. You can talk anyone into anything so you would be a wonderful salesperson. Gaining social distinction and recognition will probably use much of your time. This can become very strong for some Leo-Geminis.

SUN IN LEO/MOON IN CANCER
Gallant

You have a keen sensitivity and compassion for others. You are a creative, open-minded, and extremely emotional person, and you can achieve anything, if you have the proper ambition. The one thing you lack, unfortunately, is precisely that. You may very well settle for far less than you are able to accomplish because of your total self-acceptance and inability to question yourself. You do not feel the obligation to verify your importance to the world like most Leos. Your best gift is accepting yourself. People think well of you because you think well of yourself, and you are self-assured and confident. For your overall contentment, a tranquil and secure home life is very important. You need the reassurance and strength of a home base like all natives of the Moon in Cancer. You are very proud of your partner and children because you are family-oriented and they help validate your existence. You are aware of how to give and take in love, and you are very romantic and idealistic. Before you eventually select a partner and settle down, your inborn curiosity will no doubt lead you through many romantic affairs. You are in jeopardy of adopting a feeling of self-satisfied complacency, because your nature does not have the hang-ups and inner turmoil that curse so many others. That which is pleasant interests you more than that which is gratifying, and you are too easily contented. Therefore, your special abilities are unused, and your creative possibilities often lie undeveloped and are not available for you or for others to tap. A strength and a weakness about you is your pride, which helps overcome obstacles and self-esteem and reinforces your inner strength on the one hand, but it also leads to arrogance on the other hand. Your goals in life need reexamining, and you need to ask whether your talents are really being used. Do you have a career that will help bring about a good future? Your mind's eye and originality are more matched to creative endeavors, particularly in the area of theater and the visual arts. However, you have the allure, instinct, and subtlety to give you an excellent business aptitude. Religion also attracts many Leo-Cancers and some find themselves drawn to charitable work, spending a lot of time helping the handicapped or needy. Psychology, counseling, teaching, and running a charitable organization are excellent professions for Leo-Cancers.

SUN IN LEO/MOON IN LEO
King of the Barnyard

You think the world you live in is your realm and personal recreational area. You frequently mistake friends for serfs. You get mixed up, offended, or irritated when the world fails to be grateful for your heavenly despotism. You are open, positive, and playful. Your magnetic company repeatedly draws people to you. People ultimately realize that the only thing that you are interested is you. Even though you a have special brand of magnetism, you are not egotistical or self-serving, and your kindness, allegiance, and generosity are boundless. It is just a matter of you never getting over your attraction for the image that you have of yourself. You want everyone to go along with your view and your will. You are a compassionate egomaniac. They do not know that once they are your friends, they have little chance of staying the same. Behavior alteration is an area you are good at. Most are better than they were before getting to know you and, luckily, only a few experience permanent damage. Being noticed is often what your behavior is intended to do. Consider, for example, your clothing. Anything goes for the theatrical and colorful double Leo, who is never happy doing things halfway. You do have a cold aspect, and if you must be brutal in order to get what you want, you will, even though you are essentially kindly and protective. If necessary, you will be disloyal to your own high morality of honesty and faithfulness to fulfill your material requirements. You have to work hard in order to sustain those excessive tastes. You think you are above the law in many ways and need to answer only to yourself. You are engrossed in ceremony, glamour, spectacle, and anything that is dramatic and showy. You are an idealist but also astute and your piercing gaze can see through tastelessness and dishonesty. Your decisions are almost never based on reason. Your heart always has the final say. You just pick yourself up and make believe it never happened if some spontaneous decision causes you to get burned. Courage and will keep you forever bouncing back anew. Despite your flamboyance and casual air, you also have a very solemn side to your nature. Leo-Leos want the acknowledgment and status they know they deserve and are proud and dignified.

SUN IN LEO/MOON IN VIRGO
Incorruptible

You have a contradictory mixture in your character. Your Leo Sun desires recognition, standing, and influence, but your Virgo Moon needs the security and steadiness of a less dangerous role. The position of leadership you feel you merit is held in the background by your reserved nature. Your need to help others must contend with your desire for admiration and attention. But, both sides of your character work together pleasantly for the most part. Although you are still able to voice your views and use your organizational abilities to control authority from behind the scenes, you may not be a vibrant manager or supervisor. An internal nature that is timid and somewhat restrained is hidden by the incisive, analytical, and exacting external show of direction and certitude. You look for power through mental activities instead of getting the authority and status you crave through real leadership. Your pen rather than the sword is your preferred weapon of choice. If you have an issue, there are occasions when you can be very critical, even egotistical, in your views and suppositions. Although you are inclined to be a little too frank in verbalizing your interpretations, you are usually amazingly correct with them. It is little wonder you so frequently alienate people. Virgo's emotional conservatism restrains you socially to an extent. However, you are charismatic, outgoing, and friendly and want to be the life of the party. Maybe because of guilt about taking part too vigorously or permitting yourself too much pleasure, it is hard to completely let go of those inhibitions. Reporting and communications, in addition to endeavors that require mental depth and detailed analysis, are professionally good choices for this combination. An ordered and regimented framework is where you work the best. Living up to the stiff requirements of a Leo ego can make you overwork; you direct a lot of your Leo passion and interest into your occupation. You will find a way to lead others even if it is by outproducing them. You may push yourself too hard because you are a perfectionist. You will slip in to states of too much criticism, agitation, and severe nervousness if you are too hard on yourself. You may aim your aggravation at friends and associates. Inspire those around you instead using your stiff ethical code.

SUN IN LEO/MOON IN LIBRA
Grandstander

You are prevented from seeing the world as it actually is because of this overly optimistic vision. You become disoriented and nervous when actual reality interrupts. You expect everyone to be naturally kind, dependable, and compassionate like you are, and this interferes with your judgment. You have already learned, no doubt, that many people are not up to your personal standards. People are attracted to your friendly personality and even-tempered nature. You are sociable and pleasant. When you are in a position that requires tact or when you have center stage, you thrive. You help to settle problems and disagreement with grace and a calm manner, as do most Leos. Your view of life is dreamy and romantic. Fortunately, your naive innocence as well as good nature and charm usually brings out the best in others and works to your benefit as well. It is not easy for the Leo-Libra to be a person in charge, but they have strong leadership drives. You worry about hurting people's feelings, and you dislike infringing on anyone else's territory. Furthermore, you always want to be admired by everybody. You never do anything until you have heard everyone's opinion, so making decisions is also hard. You naturally dedicate a lot of time to recreation and sensual enjoyment, because both signs of this combination love comfort and leisure. However, idleness can become a way of life, particularly when you feel you are not getting all the acknowledgment you merit. You do well in professions that offer prestige. Excellent choices are cinema, the arts, marketing, and design. In addition, you would be good in all fields involving adjudicating conflicts or settling differences. You are perplexed when viewpoints conflict, as they always do. You just go with your Leo hunch most of the time. Pride is a very powerful aspect in your combination, and you often see yourself by the way others see you, instead of the way you really are. You can build up a very repressed and self-conscious attitude if you get too much criticism at some point in your life. Remembering that your view is just as correct as anyone else's helps maintain a sturdy and healthy self-image. Refrain from giving so much credence to what other people may be thinking. You assure yourself many friends with your natural charm, but your endless need for compliments and approval may drain them. You run the risk of backsliding into states of indecisiveness, anxiety, and, worst of all, weariness when you feel unacknowledged.

SUN IN LEO/MOON IN SCORPIO
Vacillator

You relish a good battle, and, in fact, if there is not a lot of competition you feel somewhat cheated and let down. You are very motivated and determined, even though you show a playful image to the world. You probably believe that if you ever revealed yourself you would give your enemies an advantage, even though most of your enemies exist solely in your mind. Consequently you are very secretive in order to protect yourself. You view yourself and humanity with the greatest importance, and you are a very intense Leo. Your approach is almost always a serious one. Jokes at your expense are not thought of kindly. You generally have a master plan for life, and you carefully follow it because you are purposeful, bold, and aggressive about everything. A kind of wall is built around you. You desire all the comfort, authority, and control you can get from life. You like material possessions and are sensual. Nothing can hold you back after you have set your sights on a job, toy, or romance. You go after your aims with quiet firmness, and your charisma, self-assurance, and ruthless willpower help you to get them. You have a lot of determination, fortitude, and a strong sense of purpose because both signs of your combination are fixed, but that also makes you obstinate and rigid, especially pertaining to your beliefs. It is very hard for you to accept the views or opinions of others. You are very independent, and you seldom compromise. You have a very low stress threshold thanks to your rigidity. Aggression, irritation, or injured pride cannot be held in for very long, and it is generally released quickly. You are obstinate and somewhat spirited. You are very insightful and astute to the ways of the world, unlike most Leos. Finance, management, and business attract you, as do most things involving competition. However, you have probably experienced strong creative desires. A Scorpio Moon can inspire and assist the creative needs of the Leo Sun. You rarely follow through on those artistic desires because you are so worried about instant gratification, including things such as when you might get your promotion or have your next sexual conquest. You might be the next van Gogh or Picasso if you would redirect some of those sensual drives and use some restraint. In this lifetime, when there is so much going on, your creative talents are not likely to find an outlet.

SUN IN LEO/MOON IN SAGITTARIUS
Globetrotter

You are generally moving but there are uncommon times when you are silent. This only shows that you are preparing some new action or venture. You do not just sit and dream about excitement, you actually go for it. You want respect and standing and set high goals for yourself like most Leos. Very often recklessness undermines those positive activities. You are an eternal child at heart regardless of how old you seem, how hardworking you are, or how responsible you may be. You have an affinity for exploration and romance that will last your entire life, and you are tolerant, enthusiastic, and playful. You are an eternal optimist and very active. You have no time for depression or self-pity. You never bottle up your feelings, and you are a bit naive. You are well known for your up-front views, frankness, and openness. Truthfulness and reliability are your principles. You are self-confident and spirited and have the assurance to put your magnificent ideas into practice. Action probably describes you better than any other word. Nearly everything in the world fascinates you. With so many new friends to make, so many new places yet to discover, and so many dreams to consider, it is not surprising you cannot find the time to conclude anything. A daily difficulty for you is controlling your impatience. You must learn to direct your abilities and energies in a more limited area of activities and interests for you to be actually creative and productive. Make sure that your position or other involvement handles your need for stimulation and diversity, because if monotony or drudgery starts, you are ready to leave. You are impatient when it comes to obeying someone's orders, and it is not simple for you to be in a low-level role. You must be the leader on the job and at home. You are totally independent. A certain amount of deference is needed in everyone's life, so learn to be humble now and then. You are sure to be your own boss eventually in any case. You will stay with things tenaciously once you have discovered something that keeps your attention. You are not going to have many psychological hang-ups because you are so open and unreserved. Being deceitful with yourself or with others is almost impossible for you. One of the few barriers to complete fulfillment is pride. Your manner is distinguished, at times a bit haughty and condescending, and you are a born aristocrat.

SUN IN LEO/MOON IN CAPRICORN
Crowned Head

You are a serious but cool person who is strong and self-sufficient in spite of your inborn charm. Remember that Napoleon Bonaparte was a Leo-Capricorn. This is not an easy combination unless you were born into privilege, however. You can be very intimidating as well as stubborn, self-important, and condescending. You present an impression of poise and good manners at all times. Your gaze alone can scare off some weaker individuals. Regardless of what you set out to do, you do it with drama and high style because your world consists of a stage of self-assurance. You are almost sure to get what you want once you set your sights on it, whether it be an occupation, a romance, or a special prize. Things always work out for you. You do not think you are right, you actually know you are, and this makes you capable of huge and almost scary superhuman efforts. No one who knows you would ever dare tease you, because you take yourself so seriously. You know your limitations and you have no need to be reminded, but, like all Capricorns, you are also well aware of your endowments and capabilities. Your managerial and leadership qualities are awesome. There are no limits to the great things you can achieve in life, as long as you restrict your big ego to a reasonable extent. You also have a very pragmatic and responsible side in spite of that extravagant showiness. You are able to assume a lot of responsibility, even with that absurd outfit you might have on. What you desire more than anything is just to be highly thought of and valued for the amazing person you know yourself to be. You are just seeking attention with your flamboyance, but luckily for them, most Leo-Capricorns do get plenty of respect. People actually worship and love you. You will always have more than enough admiration and respect for your ego demands, so it is best to tone down your performance a bit and step off your high horse. You think others should be as serious about things as you are because you are a severe judge. They need to always abide by your decisions. It can be difficult working for you because of your watchful, nearly dictatorial stare. You are a strong manager who makes workers shake in their boots. There is a very tender and frequently anxious person below that hard exterior and those big displays of magnificence.

SUN IN LEO/MOON IN AQUARIUS
Sponsor

The Sun and Moon in your combination are in conflict, designating that your early life was likely hard. A potent sense of independence and self-sufficiency in you came about as the result of that struggle to overcome those hardships. It also caused you to look far inside yourself. Unlike most Leos, you are self-examining and the realization you have acquired from looking within inspires you to reach out to help others. You have a very tender, almost naive presence and disposition that is relaxed but a bit aloof. The commonplace details of life do not perturb or confuse you, because your scope of imagination is wide, boundless, and abstract. Others would be very surprised if they saw the ambition, strength, and futuristic visions in your dreams. All this is kept shrouded under that effortless exterior. Your judgment is seldom fooled by self-centered views or superficial impressions, because you are able to acknowledge your limits and appreciate your many endowments. With your firm idealism and compassionate perspectives, you probably feel that you are destined to help others in life. You pursue that goal with silent and steadfast purpose, whatever that mission may be. All you need to do is see it once. You have noteworthy intuition and inherent aptitude that often controls your action even though you value reason. Your preferences and major choices are generally founded on what you feel about the individual or situation, rather than what you conceive. This total belief in your intuition can be dangerous at times, both for you and others. You can be led by your hunches to a point in managerial positions, but you have to also be aware of the facts. Being more adaptable to the pressures and opinions of others is something you should learn. Never ostentatious or arrogant, you treat people as peers, and you in all likelihood live in a humble, understated way, but there is something that sets you apart. Some people think you have a special insight because your unique manner of life gives you an effortless air of nonchalance, and people are attracted to you. A lot of Leo-Aquarians are natural leaders. Helping you to put some of those ambitions and sights into action is your resourcefulness and inner force. Your solution to an issue is often the cleverest, and you are inventive and forward thinking. One reason why you often seem so out of it and forgetful is you see things from a very wide and detached perspective. You favor the big picture and details slow you down.

SUN IN LEO/MOON IN PISCES
Sweet Talker

You are a very fascinating Leo for sure; your nobility of spirit and worldly charm make for a very interesting mixture. You possess self-regard, dash, and a magnetic presence that intrigues people without you needing to brag. Your Pisces inner being is a very kind, tender, and unselfish one, but your Leo personality is ambitious, emphatic, aggressive, and attracted to leadership. This is rather a remarkable difference of aspects. Most Leo-Pisces people will elect to meet the needs of their egos first if they are made to choose the spiritual or the materialistic. You are really very pragmatic, matter-of-fact, and shrewd in spite of your elevated ideals and humanitarian persuasions that are also present. While young, you were surely a romantic, affirmative, and distressingly sensitive person, but slowly, after seeing the world as cruel and exacting, your innocence wore off. You came to realize that if you could adjust you would prosper, and this had a basic appeal to you. By nature, you are still good-hearted and considerate of others, but you will work very hard to get material comfort and status too. Few would ever guess how strong-willed and ambitious you really are underneath, because you are usually easy going, and your way of persuasion is so elusive and indirect. Because of this, you can succeed in business with your excellent ability to charm and impress others when that soft approach is most effective. Your elegant and sensitive being may attract you to the arts, however, even though you are clever in the business world. You set exacting standards for yourself. Sometimes you may be afraid of your own power to frighten people, and you may feel guilty for using it. Your great imagination can make you tense. Many Leo-Pisces are bothered by imaginary sickness and fear of the unknown. Stay active socially, because too much solitude will only make your fears worse. Be creative instead, with your vivid imagination. You love the stage, design, and creativity in general. Most health fields, and even being a doctor, would be good choices. No matter how dedicated and motivated you are, you never lower your ethical standards—because in all of your activities, as is the case with all Leos, you value honesty, loyalty, and trust. You are very centered in that regard. You will aim your Leo fervency to assisting others and doing charitable work, after you feel totally satisfied with your accomplishments and have satisfied your desire for luxury and comfort. You will move on then. Some problems for Leo-Pisces are often unnecessary. You may not feel completely comfortable with all those ambitious goals.

SUN IN VIRGO/MOON IN ARIES
Adam West

For an easygoing and timid Virgo, or anyone else for that matter, to live up to that astonishing self-image is impossible. Self-acceptance is one of the first lessons you must learn in life. You are a lot of the great things you believe you are, but there is no need to be a fearless daredevil to prove yourself. There is no reason to get upset with yourself when carefulness or reasonable sense stop you from commencing whimsical and dangerous adventures. You are dapper and forceful in your dreams, but actually you are not really that certain or heroic. You were probably shocked when you first recognized you were not the champion you had always believed you were. When it was time to realize your fantasies, you may have had the courage and strength to plan, but you immediately hesitated and got insecure. The issue is always whether to relax and let whatever happens happen, or to just go ahead and do it. Aries has an inner character that is fervent, aggressive, and fearless, while Virgo is conservative, careful, and shy. There are plenty of more normal ways to find exhilaration. Because you are very perceptive and very astute, big business can be exciting for you. You gain great gratification and satisfaction from hard work, as do all Virgos. You are hardworking and honest and combine industrious enthusiasm with attention to detail and common sense. You do, however, need work that challenges you. Aries' inner being is always uneasy and rejects drudgery and boredom. You are never fearful of asserting yourself when your hunches tell you to grab an advantage or try a bold venture, even though your Virgo character will always be incisive and conservative. Exactitude and flawlessness are your goals, and respect and allegiance your standards. You are inclined to take personal matters very seriously, but you do have a sense of humor. Extreme anger and occasionally retaliation can come about with insults to your self-regard or pride. Your mood can be temperamental with cold assessments of others and, even though accurate, tend to be serious. Dealing with your moods is one of the most difficult aspects for you to know how to do. Sometimes, before you take the time to think about it, because you cannot restrain your anger, it is unleashed with lightning speed. Because you are mentally astute, even without realizing it, you soak up the stress and antagonism around you. Give yourself a chance to relax, have fun, and meditate if you want to stay more in control.

SUN IN VIRGO/MOON IN TAURUS
Mr. Reliable

Your value system is old-fashioned, conservative, and strong. Indeed, old-fashioned is frequently the best approach for the Virgo-Taurus. People often turn to you because the counsel you give out is always sensible and well thought out. They can feel your worldly understanding and experience. This might be the most well-rounded of all the Virgo combinations. You are tranquil, easygoing, but also determined. There is not much you cannot accomplish in life after making up your mind that you want to do it. You are a paradigm of resolve, character, and pragmatism with a nature that is accountable, genuine, and dependable. It is not very difficult to tell you have a soft heart, even though sometimes you try to seem severe, harsh, and demanding. Regrettably, you see your compassion as a flaw, and you always try to conceal it behind a seemingly uncaring exterior. Fortunately for you, most individuals know what you are doing. You are an individual that others imitate because of your commitment, sincerity, and honesty. Too much ease in doing things is the only thing you must be cautious about. A good thing for the cautious Virgo-Taurus is travel. Business and finance are good professions for you. What you are especially good at are long-term projects that require fortitude and practicality. You can be excellent at administration, finance, and management; and you are also a terrific organizer. You are reliable and consistent in love, and you look for those traits in a partner. Once you are married, you will most likely remain married. The ease and constancy of home life are very central to the Virgo-Taurus. This will always play a role in your self-identity. There are few serious barriers in your life because Virgo-Taurus is a very harmonious mixture. You take the chance of falling into self-satisfaction in spite of all your ingenuity and work ethic if you are not careful. You are inclined to resist any modifications or innovations due to that traditional approach of yours. Be aware of changing lifestyles and new concepts. New experiences help you gain insight, so learn to take a few chances. Try to expand your friendships and your social circles. You tend to play it safe here too, keeping your associations to those who are a lot like you. Occasionally, you should make an effort to open up a bit to new people.

SUN IN VIRGO/MOON IN GEMINI
Virtuoso

People do not realize just how sensitive you actually are. If you know mythology, you remember that Mercury controls communication and the intellect, and both of the signs of your mixture are ruled by Mercury. So you have a continuing need to articulate your latest—often ingenious—thoughts, as well as a brilliant mind. However, frequently you use your intelligence to rationalize your troubles and feelings. You strive to keep your emotions under control so you can avoid getting hurt, because you are sensitive and vulnerable. You are cool and collected as well as reserved. There is a perception of aloofness about you. It is not simple to stimulate your earnest feelings or bring out the passion you so cleverly hide behind your remote and intellectual exterior. Discontent and anxiety will just come about by divorcing yourself from your feelings. Openness is better for your well-being. Do not let your intelligence determine every step you take, no matter how very brilliant you may be. Let go of your cares and worries once in a while and allow enthusiasm and feelings to show themselves. Not much gets past your very observant eye or analytical mind. You set demanding values for yourself and strive for perfection in your life and work. You are rather direct in pointing out the flaws of others, and your need to articulate your thoughts and impressions makes you do just that. Virgo-Gemini can get overcritical when faced with those who do not meet their standards. You have got to become less of a cynic and to learn to be more open-minded. If it is helpfully given, others will be grateful for your criticism, because your observations on human nature can be astonishingly accurate. Plainly put, you are not particularly romantic, but you do enjoy companionship and a person to share your ideas with. You are usually attracted to those who can give you mental stimulation and physical love. You are more than likely working too hard to keep up with them. You are the one sitting in the front row in the classroom, taking profuse notes and asking the most relevant questions. At work, you are always on time and precise in carrying out your duties and responsibilities. You try to do the utmost of your capabilities and are dedicated and sincere, but at times you push yourself too hard. Nervous anxiety and edginess often bother the Virgo-Gemini. Do not set such unreachable standards for yourself and attempt to relax sometimes. It is too bad, with your exceptional perception, that you generally see error before you see merit.

SUN IN VIRGO/MOON IN CANCER
Loner

You are always in danger of falling into some fantasy and isolating yourself, and you are hurt easily and bothered by the tiniest tension around you. If you were raised in difficult or disagreeable surroundings, this is particularly true. You may have acquired unwarranted fears, neuroses, or paranoia that can be difficult to get rid of later in your life. You will be among those who inherit the Earth if it is true that the meek will be included. You are, however, an impatient person who will not wait long. You also happen to be very practical in your nature. Of all the Virgo combinations, yours is maybe the most sympathetic and gentle, and like all very giving and sensitive people, you have a lot of gifts and abilities that can find useful expression. Sadly, timidity, reserve, and self-consciousness are the most incapacitating obstructions you come across on the way to fulfillment. You can establish big walls of defense to protect yourself from a world you comprehend as uncaring. You can constantly guard your fragile feelings. The world, surely, is not as bad as you think it is. Most of your doubts and fears exist strictly in your mind or are left over from childhood, if you stop to think about it. It is not always simple for you to understand or tolerate dissonance with that mild, generous nature of yours. It is consequently important that you associate with people who brighten up your world and make it seem less menacing. After learning to be more assertive, more means of expression will be available to you. Virgo-Cancers can be good in medicine, the ministry, and service fields because they have compassionate desires. You can be clever and are an excellent organizer, so business is also open to you. Be careful in your love life. Do not allow yourself to get absorbed by a bossy partner who takes away your identity. You are kind and giving by nature, and this is appreciated by most. Learn to be assertive and less afraid of the unknown rather than running away from dangers and challenges. Eventually you should find it simple to purge yourself of your worries if you try to understand their cause. Determine whether your close relationships are allowing you to grow or not. You rely a lot on the views and moods of those around you because you are impressionable.

SUN IN VIRGO/MOON IN LEO
Simple Soul

You are deeply honest and are puzzled when you meet others who do not have your righteousness. Your supremely moral character is admired, but it will not bring success. Consequently, in life you have strength of mind and start out to prove your value and merit. It is you who always works extra and never asks for recompense. Virgos with a Leo Moon are dependable, moral, and idealistic; they are known for being compassionate, moral, and caring. The two combined result in fundamental goodness. You were a perfect child, and your mother never had to ask you to be a good girl or boy. You are innocent, charming, and always ready to help with the chores. You lead your life by a code that the modern world is leaving behind; one that is innocent, cheerful, and warm. By doing the most difficult and often least desirable projects, you are the one who shows loyalty. This helps you live up to your moral code without infringing on anyone's territory. You do not often take full credit for all the great things you achieve, and while you are dignified, you are also truly humble. You see others more cunning than you pass by and get all the honors, while you, innocent to the actual realities of life, watch speechlessly. Understanding the world better would help you. Demand the acknowledgment you deserve and stand up for yourself. Be a little less naive in your dealings with people and have a sense of reality. You love fun more than your other Virgos and are much more spontaneous. You need to be careful of your tendency to moralize. If you do not like the treatment you have been given, you may become bitter. Your sense of justice is almost self-righteous. There is actually no need for you to preach, because your many wonderful assets make you a person others admire. You are probably mixed up by quickly changing sexual morals, because you are as inexperienced in love as you are in other parts of your life. Your intuition is accurate and usually guides you well, but you are always ready to listen to others. Your Leo Moon gives you a strong creative motivation, and you have a powerful autonomous streak. Be sure that your abilities are not held back in a mundane job, even if you are drawn to a predictable and ordered working and living situation. Your virtue and charm attract people. You treat people with respect and acceptance because you are thoughtful, even-tempered, and forbearing.

SUN IN VIRGO/MOON IN VIRGO
Sharpshooter

You have unrivaled abilities to remember facts and analyze data. Sporadically you remove that humble appearance and argue or express a viewpoint that is so logical, clear, and precise that others do not even dare to disagree with you. Double Virgos often unnerve individuals with their piercing stares. Your comprehension and insight into other people is extremely accurate too. Practically nothing escapes your notice. From the reserved librarian to the genius analyst and administrator, there are many types of double Virgos, but they all share two qualities: they are far tougher than they appear to others, and they are quite insightful. Others can feel that core of resolve and purpose through the timid, reserved, and kind person you are on the outside. There is almost nothing you cannot do after you have made up your mind, because you are flexible, systematic, and vigorous. You also have an exceptionally gifted mental ability. You aim criticism most harshly at yourself, but like most Virgos you are inclined to see faults and errors nearly everywhere and in everyone. Do not stunt your emotional growth with self-criticism. Living up to the lofty standards you apply for yourself is almost impossible. Instead of getting upset about your faults and endlessly placing yourself under such scrutiny, learn to value your talents, strengths, and virtues. It would be wise to try to have a bit of self-love at times. Your need to help and assist others may attract you into social service areas such as the clergy, medicine, or political activisms. Self-fulfillment and happiness are found in work, as with all Virgos. It is critical that your career utilize your unique talents. Leo Tolstoy and Lyndon Johnson are good examples of natives of your combination. You are very flexible and always accept advice and reason, because both signs in your combination are mutable signs. Using your mind and your strong determination will take you where you want to go. You have a lot of difficulty dealing with betrayal and deceit because you are basically compassionate, kind, and thoughtful. Your bravery and perseverance helps you to live and prosper in a difficult world even with all your innocence. You think you can control anything with your intellect and the application of your inner strength. Relative to a profession, you have an aptitude in all areas that need thorough analysis, accuracy, and exactness. A lot of double Virgos are fine academics, writers, and journalists because of their powerful intellects.

SUN IN VIRGO/MOON IN LIBRA
Seductive

You are a natural diplomat because of your friendly good nature and tactful approach. Standing in your way is self-consciousness. It is hard for you to comprehend the aggressive approach of other people because you are not the pushy type. You are vulnerable to other individual's moods, as are all natives of a Moon in Libra. Therefore, if your work or living conditions are less than calm, you may withdraw into yourself or go into fantasies and castles in the air for quiet and peace of mind. You probably had a hideaway where you could think and be alone when you were young. Everyone appreciates your composed style and laid-back disposition. You are essentially a gentle, calm, and refined person. With skill, charm, and delicate persuasion you can convince anyone to come to your side. You have a truly unique manner with people. You have to understand, as an adult, that you need to deal with the starkness of reality. Running away all the time is not an option. Everyone needs serenity from time to time, so it might be a good idea for you to do yoga or meditation. Find peace in nature by taking country walks and simplifying your surroundings as much as you can. This will let you be able to make your own happiness in spite of the troubles in the world. You are romantic and possess a sharp artistic sense. When selecting a partner you place value on physical magnetism. Compatibility is something that needs to be emphasized in your selection too. Your romantic associations can easily be out of balance with you doing all the giving and your mate doing nothing but taking. Be certain that your partner understands you and can give you the emotional backup and boost you need. People may simply believe you are introverted and may not know your fears. However, being shy is frequently an excuse for not dealing with the opportunities and challenges that life offers. Do not refuse outlets for yourself and your talents. Use your willpower to alter and redesign your fate. Do not be so reliant on those around you, and make yourself do things. The hidden abilities you have may be a surprise to you. You are very perceptive and logical and have an understanding and insight that is extremely precise and can be profound. Your astuteness and penetration can assist people in the courtroom or hospital or in fields like counseling, social work, and management.

SUN IN VIRGO/MOON IN SCORPIO
Devious

You are essentially pretty hard-hitting, and you know your mind even though you might seem soft-spoken and mild to others. All your determination and confidence has a price because you are made to keep your emotions in check a lot of the time. You have sharp and often amazingly correct perceptions. Intuition is how you judge others, and that method is extremely accurate in your case. You prefer hiding your own being while you are going around judging your friends and coworkers. You possess a quiet intellectual approach to life that hides your true nature. You are mysterious, sensual, very passionate, and intense. Most of your decisions are grounded on your hunches and intuition, regardless of how calm and logical you try to seem. Favoritism and passion generally are the primary decision makers in your dealings, even if reason and logic are in the mix. You know and go after what you want in life. You are determined and a hard worker. Very few actually know whether you are troubled or ecstatic, because your persona almost always remains cool, removed, and unswerving. Not many appreciate your real sensitivity and depth because you are so good at presenting that detached facade. Try to express yourself with more vigor and be more forthright with your emotions. Refrain from being so supremely rational about everything, and let passion take you away from time to time. The Virgo-Scorpio combination is well suited to social service, medicine, and government. Business is also a possibility. Romantically, you are jealous and controlling and act as if you possess your partner. This can bring about endless problems. You often point out your lover's failings in a tactless manner, and therefore you may be inadvertently cruel, even with all the perception you have. You can be quite sensual and giving, however, if you are truly in love. You may reason yourself and your real feelings out of existence. Your satisfaction comes through work as with most Virgos. Frequently, it is everything to you and replaces relationships and recreation. Make sure you have some interests outside work, not involving what you do nine-to-five, if you want to avoid becoming a workaholic. You may have revolutionary concepts and secretly desire to apply change even though you are professionally drawn to the conservative and conventional. You are able to bring modernization and inventiveness to your work.

SUN IN VIRGO/MOON IN SAGITTARIUS
Dreaming Idealist

You can be either the rebellious adventurer who listens to the inner voice, or you can allow the Virgo to be the boss and settle for the devoted and responsible approach, but as a highly frustrated traditionalist. The balance of Virgo-Sagittarius people compromise by working in an integrated and formal framework, but keeping a bold, impulsive spirit. You have a strong autonomous aspect and high standards. Your Sagittarius Moon makes you a lover of freedom and a rebel, someone who is impulsive and adventurous. On the other hand, the Virgo Sun leads you to be careful, tolerant, quiet, and methodical. These are very diverse signs, which lead to a multifaceted and interesting person, but one who is mixed up. When setting your goals and defining your beliefs and lifestyle, you are never certain which part of your twin personality should be in charge. You believe you ought to be your own boss, and this is probably correct. Being an independent businessperson is a good choice for Virgo-Sagittarius. No matter what you choose for your profession, your work behavior always shows a Virgo's realism and administration, together with the Sagittarius fervor and nerve. At times, impulsiveness counteracts your best attempts. A full social life and a lot of outside interests are very important. You will surprise yourself and just move on one day if you let your attachment to your job make you feel restricted. You have a powerful need to express your feelings and beliefs and are very humorous, but there is also a leaning toward speaking out and being blunt with off-the-cuff comments. You may at times, because of this, disaffect those very close to you. You should attempt to think about the feelings of others before you speak. As wonderful as they may be, keeping your thoughts to yourself is sometimes better. Your success in life is helped by your persuasive, charming manner, which draws people to you. There are times when you fancy testing your luck, use intuition, or go with some amorous or daring notion even though you seem to be fairly unworried most of the time. If you feel you are somewhat restricted or controlled by work, marriage, or lifestyle, this yearning will overcome you. At the first sign of boredom or drudgery you get fidgety. By being sure your pursuits and work offer the exhilaration and variety you require, you can learn to manage that unpredictable nature of yours.

SUN IN VIRGO/MOON IN CAPRICORN
Individuality Accomplished

From a youthful age you knew exactly what you desired, and you went after it systematically and with complete self-assurance. Any difficulties, handicaps, or obstructions you may run in to, your strong mind and inner fortitude can deal with. You are a paradigm of independence and self-sufficiency. Pragmatic and sensible, you believe your future is squarely in your own hands. You hate whining and pessimism and have no patience for those who partake in it. While your combination is one of the most favorable to worldly achievement and status, it is one of the hardest of all Virgo combinations to live with. Your responsibility, determination, and dedication to duty are equal to your powers of management and concentration. The tunnel vision pursuit of authority and success are Virgo's aim, and exactness, accuracy, and administration are focused upon those goals. You need to be ready to survive and win because the world to you is a Darwinian battle for survival. In social situations you still seem as shy and benign as a lamb, even though you are far more outgoing than most Virgos. You are an intense observer and never miss a detail. When confronted, however, you can let go of your normal soft-spoken manner and become supremely furious. Your tolerance has very defined limitations even though you may think of yourself as calm. A real challenge is keeping your temper in control. You are drawn to managerial and administrative vocations where you can get the authority and status you want. Law and engineering are good, as well as professions that require more education. You are thoughtful, reserved, and quite tender, because the toughness so often apparent in Moon in Capricorn natives is dampened when combined with Virgo. But you are hard and very gung ho at home or at work. Your notion of justice may be another person's notion of totalitarianism. However, in your quest for power and rank, you will not be unjust or engage in cruel or unethical schemes. There is no understanding or lenience for anyone who fails to live up to your almost impossible expectations. Being less judgmental is something you need to learn. Try a little more compassion for human limitations. Keep in mind that not everyone has your strength and ability. Your mind is extremely powerful and incisive with the logic and organization you have. You are able to present a line of reasoning with such lucidity and logic that few can disagree.

SUN IN VIRGO/MOON IN AQUARIUS
Probing Mind

You have a passion for adventure and excitement. Your activities and interests are made for the scientific and the conceptual, as well as people and social campaigns, especially the uncharted and the unfamiliar. This is because the logical and careful Virgo has a humanitarian and visionary Aquarian Moon that is creative and curious. This means your dreams and ambitions are both extensive and offbeat. Mentally and spiritually you are a maverick and a pacesetter, but like most Virgos you might reside and work in a conformist setting. Your faraway look makes you different from other natives of your sign and suggests shenanigans and revolt, even though you may look in some ways like a mild-mannered Virgo. Your quick motions and gestures show your need for diversity, no matter how reserved and careful you may appear to some. You enjoy observing others from afar and are objective and quite insightful. Your feelings about people are amazingly on target and they fascinate you. There are occasions when those around you feel more like objects in a scientific test than real friends, because you are so objective and detached. You treat everyone with thoughtfulness and deference. Your real fondness is usually just for social causes, ideals, or scientific projects. You think that love embraces all of humanity, not just a few. You need a lot of freedom and autonomy on the job in order to stay content and concerned. Your combination is perfect for scientific success. Besides technological pursuits, you can do well in education, psychology, social activism, and unusual areas like astrology and the occult. Your talent of detaching yourself from things is perfect for humane pursuits such as nursing, medicine, and the clergy. You mostly feel a strong connection with charitable and humanitarian undertakings in general. As with all Virgos, work is extremely important to you, but enchantment is the key to your combination. You instantly become restless and perplexed if drudgery or boredom sets in. Specialization is the nature of this combination. You are primarily interested in mastering one thing, even though your pursuits and dreams involve a broad and creative spectrum. There is no stopping your dedication once you have discovered the area that interests you most, because you have the logical strengths and accuracy of the Virgo as well as the innovation and pioneering spirit of the Aquarian.

SUN IN VIRGO/MOON IN PISCES
Boy Scout

You interact with people openly, and they generally give the same in return. You are dependable, demonstrative, understanding, and sincere. You are not an antagonistic sort and are aware there is not much you can do to change things, even though your sensitivity makes you painfully aware of the evil and unfairness in the world. You adjust yourself to a difficult life and try to hold on to your principles. Subtle persuasion is one of your talents. You use your gifts of delicacy and tact to gain the comforts you enjoy so much, because you understand the importance of security. Your calm and sophisticated manner is hard for people to resist. You have an inner peace that others would love to have and are mild, soft-spoken, and very sensitive. Experience has most likely taught you that goodness, compassion, and honesty succeed where aggression and toughness fail. You are a good student in this regard. You find purpose in your work like most Virgos, and in your profession you are devoted and sincere. You run the risk of not doing what you are capable of, because your combination is essentially passive. You just cannot stand to be with aggressive people, because you have a quiet and tender nature. To keep your peace of mind and vision, it is vital for you to get away for contemplation regularly. Quiet kinds of recreation, study, and meditation are perfect for you. For a lot of Virgo-Pisces people, faith is a real means of self-renewal. You may have an artistic career because of your vision and aesthetic nature. Service-oriented areas like law, medicine, and social work are areas you can do well in. You have a powerful imagination and many cerebral and creative gifts that can find pragmatic expression, so do not let your talent lie sleeping. Learn to take a few gambles sometimes. You may give way to serious depression and nervousness if you do not learn to feel satisfied in your career. Some fear, which usually has no foundation in reality, is often the root cause. Your emotional well-being is affected by your environment. Your mood tends to subconsciously soak up the feelings of those near you. Be sure to give yourself a home and professional environment that is as free of strife as possible in order to have stability.

SUN IN LIBRA/MOON IN ARIES
Agitator

You love to play the devil's advocate and take the differing side in any conversation. If the discussion becomes slow, you will come up with some outrageous and contentious statement. Tomfoolery is your hobby. Some of that restive disquiet can be handled through self-discipline, which counteracts it. Centering your enthusiasm on a destination or interest is vital. Rather than wasting your vigor and talents in numerous directions, try focusing your activities and concentrating on one thing at a time. Disproportionate reliance on fantasy is one of the risks you face. You may appear to be the mild, passive, and laid-back Libran, but deep inside burns the scorching spirit of an Aries. All the exhilaration and motion immediately tells people that you are there. You find it hard just sitting quietly, and there is no time for silent meditation or relaxation. Nevertheless, like all Libras, you want peace of mind and emotional equilibrium. Your constant craving for originality upsets your Libra scales and brings about tension. You are fidgety and autonomous. Your unvarying enemy is boredom. Things never seem as lively as you like them, so you dream of worlds full of adventure and romance. Fantasy is good for you, but to an extreme it can be very hazardous. You will be in better shape if you keep your attention fixed on future ends instead of dwelling on passing upsets or defeats of the moment. Your sparkling vigor, used correctly, can also take you to wonderful heights, but Libra-Arians have to deal with anxiety. You are a little self-absorbed but also have a very romantic character. The Libra-Aries must have as many distractions as possible to battle that inclination to withdraw into illusion. Your two signs are so opposite in nature that you may find yourself the victim of repeated mood swings. Your Aries inner being is unruly and just plain bothersome; however, as with all Libras, you believe in peacekeeping and benevolence. The result is alternating between shyness and assertiveness as well as ecstasy and despair, cheerfulness and anguish. You should attempt to keep away from overly anxious situations that bring about these mood changes. It is imperative that you give your Libra side a chance too, by taking time out for meditation and contemplation, even though you may secretly flourish with stimulation and tension. Be careful also about morose self-pity.

SUN IN LIBRA/MOON IN TAURUS
Pleasure Seeker

Your personality combines the mature wisdom and logic of Taurus with the fairness and restraint of Libra. Nothing bothers you more than the idea of harming a person. You always have a fundamental quality of principle and stability, but externally you may appear to be on edge as well as excitable. You have an even approach to the world and are kind and forbearing. You give the benefit of the doubt at all times. You have a captivating personality and an amazingly even disposition because Venus, the planet of romance, harmony, and accord, rules both of your signs. You have an advantage in life because of your allure, tact, and compassion. If there is serious difficulty, or a terrible crisis, your tranquil and self-confident presence can prevent a disaster. You love lavishness and comfort and are quite sensual and acquisitive, but you should be cautious to keep pleasure from becoming an end in itself. You always have the possibility of falling into weariness or intemperance, even though you have many gifts to offer. You are able to assume a lot of responsibility, as are all Moons in Taurus people, and you have the willpower and inner tenacity to motivate yourself to the top. Still, you can be enticed into remaining in a soft, comfortable, and anxiety-free environment. This way you can avoid one that is high paced. You may settle for instant satisfaction in a vocation or an expedient marriage that provides safety and little risk but pass up a lot of demanding opportunities. You need to get out into natural surroundings at times because of your rustic spirit. This is especially true when pressures begin to rise. You might also get away momentarily into your vibrant imagination, but make sure you do not forget to return to reality. Libra-Tauruses often experience heartbreak. Sentimental feelings and emotions often take you away and warp your otherwise good judgment, and you are not as objective as other Librans. Attempt to put yourself in an objective mind-set and move back now and then. As with all Venus-ruled people, you have a visual intellect and a wonderful imagination. You can easily do well in music, art, and design. Business is an additional opening for the Libra-Taurus, because you also have a natural grasp for money and finance. Social work and public relations are good because your diplomatic nature would help you.

SUN IN LIBRA/MOON IN GEMINI
Academician

Expressiveness is one of your best talents. Because people feel your basic sincerity they react positively to your refined and easygoing manner, so you are able to convince others of almost anything. Most people like your frankness and know your intentions are always the best, even though you frequently alienate some with your keen wit. You have to struggle against tediousness and lack of interest. When joined with a Gemini Moon the social consciousness and mental strengths of Libra are finely tuned. Restlessness and inquisitiveness push you to discover the world, to seek answers and hidden truths. You are a real intellectual who stands apart and is objective, and it is hard for you to comprehend those who are satisfied with outside impressions or who choose to settle for the shallow parts of life. You have a love for thrills and diversity and are passionate and excitable. Half of you is spent getting yourself into trouble while the other half is attempting to get out of it. You can easily slide into the trap thinking that the world provides no comfort or promise because you are inclined to see life from a removed perspective. You may seek out transcendental experiences through spirituality and the occult arts rather than placing your faith in the here and now. No matter how much you attempt to conform and adjust to the world you reside in, you will never stop sensing that you actually belong in another time and place. Your fundamental buoyancy and positive reception of life's biting wit should see you through, no matter how gloomy or estranged you may feel. You have superb diplomatic abilities in addition to purely rational or artistic abilities. You will always hurry to arbitrate any problem in your environs if strain or conflict disrupts things. Law, government, or social service are places this skill in mediation can be applied. You are a pagan and a radical at heart. Disillusionment with the world can bring about an assortment of harmful answers. You are an excellent actor and you may choose to play roles that fit the moment, or you could depart completely. Just being yourself is a challenge. Try to recognize your being and your individuality. Only by discovering from others can you start to believe who you actually are, so be socially engaged. Your sense of humor is one thing you have going for you, and you are able to express amusement with yourself and the human predicament.

SUN IN LIBRA/MOON IN CANCER
Ambassador

You are astute and highly insightful. People are jealous of your peace of mind and air of serenity. They react to your quiet attraction, lightheartedness, and optimism. Your crafty and subtle wit can bring delight to those around you. Because you have surely endured your portion of blows and disenchantments, experience has taught you a lot about how to deal with people and the world. Libra's warmth and aesthetic admiration is added to the emotional astuteness, resourcefulness, and understanding of a Cancer Moon. Your two greatest assets are allure and flexibility. You have certainly learned that compassion, negotiation, and diplomacy can work where hostility and toughness fail. As a result you are a mild, peaceable soul. You know how to get used to the stress and grimness of life and your ability to understand people allows you to go far. Both of your signs are cardinal ones, which indicates you are a lively, determined, and a socially concerned person. Your specialty is people. You can play any role conceivable, knowing instinctively what people desire and expect, but playing roles can be dangerous at times. You are, you will discover, a whole lot tougher and more resilient than you thought you were. Stop fretting so much about what others think and just be yourself. Learn to appreciate and love yourself for who you are. There is almost nothing you are unable to achieve once you have overcome insecurity. You have a wonderful aesthetic sense and a powerful imagination so art, design, and music are all areas in which you can be successful. Your social insight can be used in a creative manner in humanitarian work and diplomacy because you have a keen understanding of people. Former first lady Eleanor Roosevelt was a Libra-Cancer. You are a master negotiator and diplomat. Amazingly you awoke one day unsure of who you actually are. Overaccommodating is something that all Libra-Cancers need to beware of. You are only happy when others seem happy as well, but you must not sacrifice your sense of being for their sake. You believe it is imperative to protect your feelings like all sensitive and psychologically vulnerable people. There is a risk that in protecting yourself you will lose your individuality completely. Do not erect such high walls that your personality loses.

SUN IN LIBRA/MOON IN LEO
Individually Magnetic

You have strong leadership abilities that your Leo Moon gives you. You make sure you are in the focus of things no matter what you are involved with. Maybe you believe you have a mission in life, and you have a powerful sense of purpose. A good example of a very developed Libra-Leo is Mahatma Gandhi. Libra's skills in peacekeeping are improved by Leo's inner self-assurance and high ideals. Your biggest asset is your personality, and it is one reason why people are attracted to you. You have an even temperament in addition to your charisma and charm. Your cheerful nature and positive outlook can improve the blackest mood. You treat others with esteem, compassion, and trust because you believe in their natural decency and dignity. Most people can see your honesty and respond with the same friendliness. A social life is very significant to you, partly resulting from your desire for esteem and attention. The flaw of vanity can easily be an issue for Libra-Leos, because there is constantly the risk that they will become worried about the image they present to people. Seeking popularity can become a major focus for some Libra-Leos. What needs to be remembered is that your social schedule and what it entails may simply be your own way of avoiding reality. Self-fulfillment can be improved by actually doing some of the things you say, but beware of lowering your energies trying to get approval and admiration. Those around you do not always have your view of things. When you learn that some do not have the integrity you do, annoyance often results. You have a lot of luck and it is a strong part of your life. You never feel happy resting on your laurels, and you are active almost all the time. One of the things that you need to learn, however, is to center your passion. You enjoy being involved in a lot of activities at the same time like most Librans, and you may spread out your energies, making it hard for you to choose a profession. A sturdy and righteous sense of mission is something you have, but it may be ill defined. Experience teaches most Libra-Leos, however. You might stick tenaciously to your lofty visions when young, being involved in one cause after another, but with the passage of time your Libra ability to cooperate saves you from complete disillusionment and leads the way to real wisdom. Reason is less important than intuition for you. You tend to behave impetuously because your hunches often prove correct. Rewards actually sometimes come from your recklessness.

SUN IN LIBRA/MOON IN VIRGO
Civil Councilor

You have a strong need to express yourself and express your views. Bashfulness and timidity often stop you from meeting the right people even though you want very much to be well liked. Instead of trying so much to win social recognition by being what you believe people want you to be, you have to learn to be yourself. In your combination, there is a bonding of the logical ability and critical faculties of Virgo along with the aesthetic understanding and social consciousness of Libra, making you a very insightful and rational individual. Until you are asked a question or your views are requested, you are calm, reserved, and a little standoffish. After that you will answer with a long lecture. You like to examine and reason things out, and you are essentially excellent at that. Your interpretations are almost always correct. Two Libra-Virgos are William Faulkner and Miguel Cervantes, and their work shows the extraordinary insight of this combination. You may find yourself compromising some of your very high ideals just to be part of the group. Being with the right people can increase your influence, so you should attempt to broaden the intellectual and creative talents you can give to the world. Areas such as the legal field, social services, writing, and the medical profession can use your extraordinary insight and logical ability. You can easily get perplexed and agitated if your surroundings are tension-filled, and, like all Libras, you need calm, accord, and equilibrium. Look inside yourself to find peace of mind. Quiet contemplation and meditation are excellent for the high-strung Libra-Virgo. Equilibrium, form, and design are your special talents. You find it difficult to think if the colors in your office do not match, or the furniture is somehow not arranged right. Both at work and home, it is absolutely necessary that your environment is synchronized with your preferences. You are fulfilled through work, as are all members of the Moon in Virgo. You are trusted and esteemed by all who know you for your dedication, conscientiousness, and sincerity. Do not let work become the be-all and end-all for you. You will be less apt to fall into a "been there done that" outlook of acquiescence if you develop external interests and try to enjoy as many of life's offerings as possible. Libra-Virgo people often suffer from nervousness and anxiety.

SUN IN LIBRA/MOON IN LIBRA
Party Host

Your insightful inspection crushes the most impenetrable defense mechanism. You hate serenity because you are excitable and drawn to pleasure, no matter how blameless and saintly you may appear. You really love stirring things up. You will commence the most outrageous and contentious argument just to liven things up. You especially enjoy this when the chat slows down to an ordinary pace. You are endlessly fascinated with people: how they behave, what their clothes are, and why they do certain things. You do not have much time left to look within yourself. You can become overly interested in the lives and lifestyles of others. You will not give in until you have learned someone's innermost secrets and not many get away from your observations once they have gotten your attention. Often you get into trouble with that desire for rumor and conspiracy, but if someone points a finger at you accusing you of interfering, you turn on that angelic charm. Venus luck comes immediately to your aid. Some of your actions are tricky enough to bring about violent action, but your charm prevents it. You somehow always manage to stay people's sweetheart in spite the difficulty you find yourself in or the individuals you disaffect. You have variable mood levels, and you need a lot of distractions. For long periods you may be all energy and enthusiasm and then suddenly drop into a dark hole of weariness and indecisiveness that can take can take weeks to get rid of. Be a little more moderate. You have strong parasitic inclinations, and it is important for Libra-Libras to get a lot of professional preparation as young as possible so they can learn to practice their talents fruitfully. In the areas of human relations (particularly labor relations), writing, law, and social work, your perceptivity into human actions can be priceless. Furthermore, you have a sophisticated aesthetic capacity and can shine in art, jewelry design, music, and fashion. Your love life is vital to your general health, and you are quite romantic. It is important that you attempt as much as possible to maintain your emotional scales in balance. You can do this and have fun too. Think things through and scrutinize your own inner workings and try allowing yourself some silent, relaxing moments. You have been blessed with a very good mind, astonishing diplomatic abilities, and a strong imagination. How you employ these things is another matter. Like all Librans, you favor comfort and ease to effort and accountability.

SUN IN LIBRA/MOON IN SCORPIO
Masquerader

You place a high value on being rational and diplomatic, and you try always to stay objective and just in your assessments. Scorpio fervor, aggressiveness, and passion, however, smolder under that cool and calm exterior you present. You have an inner nature that is motivated and obstinate, and although your style might be that of peace, inside lies the motivation and intention of a warrior. Your combination joins peaceable and tactful Libra with forceful, enigmatic, and aggressive Scorpio. All this means that you are a very multifaceted person. You probably show many of the qualities of the Libra outwardly and strive for peace, accord, and inner tranquillity. With your friends and colleagues you are peaceful and thoughtful. At home in your environment you are relaxed with yourself. Regardless of how delightful, naive, and youthful you seem on the exterior, when the time comes to take charge and exploit a personal gain, you can quickly come out as a critical, up-front, and astute individual. Less observant people are caught totally unaware, and you usually end up shocking even your closest friends. Having conceived a goal or idea, you almost never rest until you have followed it through to the end. There is nothing idle or careless about you, but like all Libras, you really enjoy distraction and recreation. Being involved with others is something for which you have a strong need and desire. You often reject the sound advice that others give you. It is a good idea to keep your mind open even though it is important to value your own personal views, especially in times of pressure. Your combination has the potential of academic and spiritual awakening on a big scale and great promise if it is pursued faithfully. With your good leadership you can assist in paving the way to self-realization, as long as the approach is balanced. Presidents Dwight Eisenhower and Jimmy Carter are two examples of this combination. You most likely feel you have a purpose in life and are motivated to assist people and to change outmoded attitudes. You have strong political and diplomatic abilities because of your instinctive knowledge of what makes others tick. Your philosophy is generally realistic and careful, although you are a positive person by nature. You can be fairly closed to a differing perspective and at times people think you are intolerant, even though you may think of yourself as open-minded.

SUN IN LIBRA/MOON IN SAGITTARIUS
Freedom Fighter

You must have the room to believe and do as you want. You most admire honesty, both in yourself and in others. You are never fearful to do what you think is moral or to say precisely what you feel. Your outlook is idealistic and your perspective broad and extensive, but you may have some bewilderment when you find that others do not always match your standards of integrity or subscribe to your strange beliefs. You draw people to you with your free-spirited, courageous, and cheerful nature. Because your character is very self-governing, excitable, and restive, freedom is what you need most. You become incensed when someone tries to limit your expressive style or infringe on your way of life, even though you are even-tempered in most cases. Seeing the world through rose-colored glasses is a Libra-Sagittarian preference, so even if you believe you are always being truthful and uncomplicated in your dealings, there are times when brutal idealism stops you from perceiving the whole truth. Do not allow philosophy to rule every move or blind you to the more pragmatic parts of life just because your convictions are admirable. You like to play with abstract notions and ideas as an intellectual, and details always slow you down. You prefer thinking about the infinity of surveying the universe to balancing your checkbook. Many of your lofty ideas can be put to good use in a more practical realm. Nothing is better for the Libra-Sagittarian than to go off on an African safari or an Alaskan expedition, so go ahead and book your ticket. Any sort of physical exercise is also good for you. You are an idealist with love, as with all things. Fantasizing about your perfect lover is usually the start. You are a great lover and are giving, affectionate, and open. Unfortunately, most of them stay stuck in your mind, just because you lack discipline. Mix it with some good old-fashioned common sense and think of what you could do with all that inspiration. The barriers have been broken before. Imagination is a very powerful aspect of your combination. Do not let your overactive mind take you off into fantasyland in the middle of a chat or a day at work. Fantasy is not a substitute for experience, but you admittedly do need both to be healthy. It is likely that you feel a need to travel to faraway lands because your combination has a lot of restless energy and inquisitiveness.

SUN IN LIBRA/MOON IN CAPRICORN
Name-Dropper

You reach out to understand other people, hoping to find out how to untie and release your own being. Most of all, you search out approval. You more than likely had a tough or unhappy childhood, because the two signs of your combination are in discord and that generally signifies conflict. You may feel you need to gain attention now to make up for the confirmation that may have not been there when you were young. Deep down inside you might feel a lot of doubt, but like other Libras you are delightful, friendly, and sociable. This makes you well liked, but you are a very sensitive and serious individual as well. You may never lose that inner feeling of regret and sadness, but you have a strong sense of self-esteem too. Value and love yourself for what you are instead of what you think you ought to be. Do not judge yourself so harshly. You most likely have strong creative aims like all serious and self-examining people. You can put some of those perceptions into action after you have conquered or resolved your inner battles. Political activism, law, and high-level management are professionally what are best suited for you. While your need for instant acknowledgment and approval can hold back creative development, you may also have musical and artistic abilities. Libras are captured by figure and splendor first and generally have very specific criteria when selecting a partner. Always evaluating and comparing to determine which qualities to admire and copy and which to throw away, you watch others from a distance. You are a great diplomat because of the insight you gain from your constant observations. Politics is your strong point because you are astute but somewhat Machiavellian. Supposedly your motives are to bring about harmony and justice, but your innermost desire is to boost your ego, even if this means dishonesty and exploitation. Your final aim can be merely to improve your own place and increase power, but you are forever blameless in your advance. You may just end up being another firebomb if you use your social talents just to boost your pride. If your aspirations and diplomatic skills are used in a positive manner, however, you could be a hero. How can you do things in a positive way? Gaining more respect and approval for yourself is what comes first. Stop fretting so much about what others think of you and focus on establishing your character.

SUN IN LIBRA/MOON IN AQUARIUS
Altruist

You are particularly attracted to the mysterious and the uncharted. You add tremendous insights into the psychology of people through observation and social contact and are a full-time scholar of human nature. You have no doubt felt strong impulses to assist others many times in your life. When mixed with an Aquarian Moon, the artistic dispositions, sensibility, and social consciousness of Libra are enhanced. You discover yourself and lose yourself via others because you are extremely social, but in most respects you are autonomous and self-sufficient. *Friend* is the word you use the most and you consider everyone a friend of yours until proved to the contrary. You have almost a phobia of loneliness and isolation, but it is essentially ungrounded because it is very rare to find a Libra-Aquarius who is not popular with nearly everyone. Practically no one can resist your cheerful, sociable, and humble spirit. The Aquarian Moon, replacing that with scientific inquisitiveness and compassionate instincts, removes some of the Libran vanity and superficiality. The key to your nature is fascination, and everyone and everything fascinates you. Your powerful imagination and compassion cause you to project far beyond your own self and to identify with the happiness and pain of those near you, as if the feelings were your own. This can be dangerous because that almost Christ-like conscience may carry a heavy burden with too many social duties, as though the sufferings of mankind were completely on you. Your imagination works continuously. You frequently get lost in the deceptions of your mind. You are an idealist and a romantic. There are occasions when you abruptly understand that life does not match your idyllic prospects. If you do not make yourself alter your Pollyanna viewpoint, disenchantment and misfortune may ensue. In mind and spirit you are a maverick. You rebuff the old-fashioned and always look for new ways of expression and purpose. George Gershwin, the jazz composer, personified the creative sensitivity and innovation of Libra-Aquarius. Your cheerful and even-tempered nature hides a very deep, solemn, and often gloomy soul. For Libra-Aquarians depression is common. A more sensible and balanced perspective is the challenge for you to develop. Try not to allow your sense of social concern to turn you from self-analysis, even though your disquiet for others is real. Think more in terms of your own contentment and completion. Then, by example, you will aid others.

SUN IN LIBRA/MOON IN PISCES
Scapegoat

The pain of another person deeply hurts you as well, because you are gentle and sophisticated. Hatred or dishonesty are almost unknown to you, and you are always thoughtful in your dealings with others. Your path to self-realization may be barricaded by tepidness and uneasiness, as with all very sensitive and creative people. You are a very creative, sensitive, highly instinctive, and artistically inclined Libra. Practical expression can be found for many of your abilities. Your seeming tranquillity and serenity amazes people. Working to your advantage in life are your diplomacy, charm, and subtle expressiveness. When young, you were naive and innocent. It was, perhaps, difficult to adapt to some of the tougher realities of life. Luckily, you are flexible and realize when to compromise. Therefore, through experience, you slowly comprehended how to survive in a world you saw as hostile. You run the risk of being repetitive and overly polite in your adult life. You are only happy if those near you are happy, and you too often sacrifice your own happiness for the sake of others. Take control of your surroundings, instead of letting your environment be in charge of you. One of your biggest gifts is intuition. Your noteworthy intuition makes most of your decisions. With money this is particularly true, and you somehow know instinctively the right moment for a venture or investment. You work best in partnerships, as do all Libras, preferably with a person who can balance your tact with aggression. You have a great artistic sense, and your vision is intense. You endure so that others may smile. Moreover, you do not put yourself forward, so others frequently get credit for your ideas. You need to take more chances and be more aggressive. It would be a pity, with so much ability, to let it go to waste. You may succumb to self-disgust or masochism if you someday feel unrealized. Respecting yourself is important for you. Your environment has a lot of influence on your emotional health. You have to be measured when choosing associates and friends because you tend to adapt the moods and positions of those near you. Your relationships should be reexamined from time to time, ascertaining whether they are emotionally confirming or possibly damaging and harmful.

SUN IN SCORPIO/MOON IN ARIES
Dude

You never lose faith in yourself, it does not matter how many times you are set back. People respect you regardless of this, because you have self-respect.

You are sensual and almost decadent. Your purposefulness, strength, and confidence are admired. Furthermore, your combination provides you with incredible powers of insight and intelligence. Of course, how you decide to use these abilities is up to you. You always have an objective or goal in view and are sober and focused. The planet of war, Mars, is the ruler of both signs of your combination, and that gives you a very autonomous and aggressive viewpoint. The word that best fits you is *egocentric*, because no matter how kind and sympathetic you may seem on the outside, you always look out for yourself first and foremost. Regardless of the number of friends you may have, you stay basically a loner, following your own carefully chosen path. There is no need to justify your existence. Your incredible resourceful, spiritual, and leadership abilities can only be used when you recognize that others also deserve to have opinions. You should learn to detach yourself a bit more from your activities, because material success is so important to you. Rather than losing your temper or anxiously sulking, the next time you face defeat or aggravation, try to just relax and see the problem from afar. Even when it comes to yourself, attempt to have a more open-minded, tolerant attitude. Professionally, your combination is perfect for commerce, administration, and leadership positions in general. There are basically two types of Scorpio-Aries; one is kindhearted, spiritual, and compassionate and the other, the more usual kind, is self-embellishing, caring only about enriching their own life with material acquisition and the realization of power. Either type possesses the tenacity, willpower, and courage to be successful, provided that the person is not victimized by their own tragic flaws—extreme pride, bigotry, impatience, and conceit. These are the character traits that warp your perceptions and cause you to undergo defeat and frustration. Compromise with you is extremely difficult. Obstinately you believe you are your own boss, and when you run in to disapproval or disagreement in your work or love life, you are very offended. You need to learn to be flexible sometimes and to work in conjunction with those around you.

SUN IN SCORPIO/MOON IN TAURUS
Commander

You are a person of few words. People see your self-assured bearing and it speaks volumes to them. However, it is astonishing how superstitious you can be at times; reaching out for your favorite good luck charm when in doubt about something. Privacy is your hallmark. You are a complete pragmatist with good sense and a deep apprehension of the way the world works.

You are a very sober person who is astute, pragmatic, and determined. You project a glow of power and self-command and are a natural leader. You think and act on a large scale because your imagination is wide and inclusive. As with all individuals who have self-assurance and believe in themselves, you likely feel as though you have a special purpose in life. After you decide just what that unique goal is, you will go after it with steadfast purpose. You have the energy, vision, and breadth of imagination to accomplish great things, but you always believe you are correct, and this self-satisfied attitude often distorts your judgment and causes you to misplace proper perspective. In order to not bring personal prejudice into every assessment, learn to be more objective in your approach to living. You have acute and elusive abilities of thought. That can make you an awesome sales representative. You would be good in the field of finance because you are good with money. The government or the military could use your very imaginative leadership abilities. Your ambitions and visions can be fulfilled because of your talents. You are a realist, and even a little cynical, but you have depth and understanding for others. You do not let anyone know what you may be thinking. You are nearly always serene and controlled on the outside. You may stew for a bit when you encounter defeat or frustration, but then you come back refreshed and determined. The inclination to protect your thoughts, however, and bottle up your feelings instead of dealing with them honestly and openly, can lead to many mental problems. You must learn to share freely and without reserve. Your combination has signs that are fixed, and that gives you a lot of resolve and purpose but also makes you somewhat stiff and one-sided in your convictions and feelings. You need to make sure that your obstinacy and rigidity do not hold back your progress.

SUN IN SCORPIO/MOON IN GEMINI
Peddler

You are not nearly as deep as some others might believe, even though you appear businesslike and inscrutable. *Cagey* would be a safer word. You present a worldly image because you are so cunning, discerning, and adroit. Humor is one of your best assets. Your strong feel for satire and your discriminating remarks almost always find an objective. Others may charge you with being untactful, but they usually return to be your audience again. You have an uneasy spirit from your Gemini Moon. You are a lot more communicative than other Scorpios, and you can talk to almost anyone. This can make you a great salesperson. There is charm and exuberance to you, and personal magnetism. Others find it difficult to reject your subtle and sophisticated manner. Your self-governing and defiant nature will probably carry you off in search of novelty and adventure. You may use your myriad charms just in pursuit of pleasure, and you are a well-known sex addict and sensualist. Your main problem, strangely enough, is your own cleverness because you may be enticed to live off your quick responses instead of developing something deeper. A sort of self-satisfied sloth may come about, so push yourself to the best of your abilities and do not be so casual about your possibilities. You would be a great reporter or successful in other fact-finding work. Teaching, business, or any other area that involves verbal adroitness are places you can excel. You are inconsistent in love as in many things. Variety is what you need from life. You are, however, just as serious and intent as other Scorpios. Actually you are very detached even if you seem quite emotional. Your flare-ups of passion and poignancy are mostly just for appearance. Frequently, you are not totally sure yourself whether your feelings are real or somehow calculated. Acting is one of your best-loved games, but be sure you do not forget yourself in taking on all those roles. A number of emotional issues can result from going against your real nature. You are somewhat cerebral and you have a love of knowledge, but you never dig too far into things. There is something of the scholar in you because you seem to know something about nearly everything. Focus on one goal or target and learn to narrow the range of your interests and activities. Chasing pleasure can become very strong for many Scorpio-Gemini.

SUN IN SCORPIO/MOON IN CANCER
Attractive Radiance

You always know exactly what you are doing and incisively who you are. You innately prize your own worth, and self-assurance has never been an issue in your life. There is an air of mystery around you, and it can be hard for friends to understand you. They are perfectly happy to follow you anywhere, however. They want to grab some of whatever it is you have, almost as though they feel your inner strength. You are maybe the most charismatic and compelling of all the Sun-Moon combinations and are surefooted, dependable, and flexible. You are esteemed wherever you go. You always seem to be successful, because luck closely follows the Scorpio-Cancer, whether at play or at work. Moreover, appeal, strength, and smarts work to your advantage. You are temperate, calm, and you do not lose your balance. You can play just about any role conceivable, and you are a wonderful actor. This makes you comfortable in almost any conditions. You are seldom interested in taking over despite all those inborn leadership abilities. You are somewhat of a loner because of your self reliance and independence. You require only yourself for comfort and will do your best to maintain a discerning distance from other people, no matter how many want your friendship. You have two water signs, so you might feel strong selfless urges, and your mixture is often seen in charts of clergymen, doctors, and scientists. Your curative powers are likely very apparent, and you should use them in some fashion. You possess a restoring quality, which helps you to bounce back from setbacks with relative ease, and you do not have too many psychological problems. Your only trouble is your inclination to muffle beliefs instead of addressing them candidly and openly. Revealing yourself for examination is just not easy for you. Sadness, heartsickness, and ill humor can result from inhibited feelings in the Scorpio-Cancer. Discuss things more openly and try to put your guard down from time to time. You like to dig beneath appearances to learn the real meaning and significance of things, and are never happy with superficial impressions. You succeed at just about everything you decide to try because of your depth, imagination, and clever realism. Once interested in some undertaking, your absorption and commitment are unmatchable.

SUN IN SCORPIO/MOON IN LEO
Grand Compulsive

You are not part of the crowd. Instead you are a rugged individualist and have great self-assurance and energy. Consequently you do not rely on others for encouragement. Your presence alone draws others, and they believe you are a leader. Your imagination is always at work and your approach is wide ranging, but there are occasions when your emotions can just sweep you away and cause you to lose perspective and accept all kinds of illusions. This combination can result in a person of superior depth, exalted vision, and great leadership, or one can become a constant pleasure-seeker and indulgent sensualist. Your heart is a romantic one, and others can lift you up to great heights of spiritual and cerebral wisdom, or you can be taken away by the absolute power of your emotions. You pay little attention to advice from others because you are so lost in the quest of your own special road to success. You are not one to compromise or be patient. You do not have time for those who are in your way because you are determined to follow your dreams. You can fall in to states of sluggishness and extreme self-indulgence if you run in to disappointment in life, or your goals do not appear to be happening. It is critical for you to learn to remain affirmative and think positively. Your reputation is one of love them and leave them. Lustfulness is something you will not ever overcome, and your Leo Moon gives you a strong desire for variety. You are frequently the first to be disloyal even though allegiance and substance are your ideals. You boast and brag about your latest doings at times, and you have a lot of pride in your activities. You believe that the entire world should be aware of them. Sometimes your bragging can get boring to those around you. Learning to listen as well as talk is very important for you, and acceptance of others is a virtue you must work at. Scorpio-Leo can be extreme at times. Your actions and demeanor are usually designed to attract attention, and you have a strong sense of the dramatic. You seldom do things part way. Try to tone things down occasionally, and give others an opportunity to share the limelight. You have all of the qualifications needed to realize your goals on a big scale with your leadership ability, brains, and astuteness. Stop focusing all your thoughts on yourself. Many Scorpio-Leos may settle for simply wanting earthly pleasures because they are frustrated and bored with the world.

SUN IN SCORPIO/MOON IN VIRGO
Bloodhound

You have some very strong views and beliefs, and you certainly know your own mind. You actually desire to express your beliefs and opinions even though you are reserved and apparently detached. Maybe you are even a bit too conscious of the world around you at times. You try for perfection in yourself and others as all Moons in Virgo individuals do. You run the risk of being a super critical person. You might be happy to be a faultfinder and doing basically nothing to help if things are not what you think they should be. You have the pragmatism and logical abilities of a Virgo with the astuteness, perceptiveness, and insight of a Scorpio. Very little gets past your sharp perception and you are intense, quiet, and soft-spoken. Your sensibility helps you to recognize things that others cannot be aware of. The conclusions you draw about life can be amazingly accurate. In addition, you are logical, inquisitive, and discerning; you are a natural detective. Faultfinding might be turned against you, subjecting you to relentless self-examination and disapproval. If you hope to use your noteworthy talents, you must learn self-acceptance. As long as you do not lock yourself in an ivory tower, intellectual interests are perfect for the Scorpio-Virgo. Detective work, investigative reporting, and scientific pursuits are good choices. You desire an active sex life like all Scorpios. While you were young, however, you may have picked up more than a few inhibitions. Virgo's modesty and Puritanism can tone down the full aspect of your extremely sensual nature. You are able to balance the give-and-take portion of a relationship, and in love you are a consistent, loyal, and devoted partner if you find the right match. Begin to appreciate yourself and then you can appreciate others too. Relax at times and enjoy life for what it is, because the world will not always live up to your visions or your high principles. Just go with the flow more often. Preaching and moralizing are things you should watch out for because your Virgo Moon gives you a very moral and sometimes holier-than-thou attitude. You are quite charismatic, and people somehow realize that you are fundamentally intelligent. This is true of your fellow Scorpios. You are also ambitious and determined. You probably have a strong sense of duty and obligation, and you are fulfilled by work. Leaving enough free time for enjoyment is important.

SUN IN SCORPIO/MOON IN LIBRA
Go-Between

Deep inside you likely feel a lot of doubt, no matter how convincing and self-assured you may seem to people. It is next to impossible for you to set goals and define your purpose in life. You have too much trust in those around you, and this can be a weakness if you always want to hear everyone's views. The people close to you, regardless of whether they are friends or family, powerfully influence you. The way others see you is how you tend to evaluate yourself, instead of by the way you really are. Acting according to your own true wants is important for you to learn. Do not worry too much about what other people might think of your behavior. Others are drawn to your leisurely and elegant personality and attracted to your charming nature. Your combination balances a peaceable and graceful Libra with a hard-driving and forceful Scorpio. You know naturally when to use tact and diplomacy and when it is smart to be assertive. Your power to manage others works to your reward in life, even though you are not as assertive as your other Scorpios. Maintain your freedom and concentrate on doing what you believe is best for you. You are a dreamer and a romantic. You like to delve deeply into things, and you are never happy with surface impressions. You have a strong belief in people and the knowledge that they have. You are too frequently only concerned with instant gratification even though you have the intelligence, charm, and magnetism to achieve a great deal in life. Guard against taking less than you are able of accomplishing, or becoming complacent. Your abilities are well suited to politics, law, and social work. The creativity of the Scorpio enhances Libra Moon and gives you good taste and strong creative interests. You can be disconcerted if a color scheme does not match because you are very sensitive to visual stimulation. For some Scorpio-Libras zealotry is the result of the quest for truth. Your imagination is very strong, and you need to guard against being fooled by charlatans who offer the secrets to the universe. You will hurry to help whenever you sense injustice or when ethical conduct is compromised, because you believe in fair play. You need to be careful about your tendency to preach and moralize because of your code of ethics. Delight and leisure loving are found in the signs of your combination. Basically you are a libertine no matter how high-minded and idealistic you try to be. The barriers to your fulfillment are laziness and self-indulgence.

SUN IN SCORPIO/MOON IN SCORPIO
Fanatic

You can be carried off by the absolute force of your emotions or let them elate you to unearthly and aesthetic heights that few can even conceive of. You have a distinguished presence and enormous powers of concentration. When you enter a room full of people you get attention. Magnetic, forceful, and purposeful, others think you are out to get them. Often they fear you, and somehow and sometimes they are right, because your inordinate jealousy can lead to vengefulness. You accept virtually nothing at face value, and you are continually looking for meaning and significance. To the acute and inventive double Scorpio, even the most commonplace issue can seem promising or suspicious. Depression and preoccupation afflict the double Scorpio. You can be haunted with your own mortality and have a somewhat ghoulish outlook. Not many know what all that silent contemplation is about, because you keep these notions and concerns to yourself. Instead of swallowing it at the expense of your emotional health, learn to express what you are feeling. You subconsciously absorb the impressions, feelings, moods, and even the dreams of those around you. You would be a superb scholar, scientist, or psychologist because you enjoy probing deeply into things. Resource management is another possibility, so long as it is management and not manipulation. It is not easy for you to give to another romantically because you are essentially in love with yourself, but you do have strong sex urges, and this makes you have a lot of sex appeal to many. You might become violent in a super tense or emotionally charged situation because of your very low stress threshold. Many double Scorpios are lawbreakers because they do not believe they have to answer to anyone for their actions. It is vital for you to practice temperance with your indulgent and sensual nature. Your endowments can easily be dispersed through extravagant pleasure seeking, self-love, and in some cases sorrow, but you have the willpower and discipline to master just about anything if you can redirect some of those powerful motivations to loftier enterprises. Possibly you could be a great artist, but if you continually concentrate on the next rung on the ladder, that is not likely. You can stand out in any career involving detective work and analysis in addition to creative avenues of expression.

SUN IN SCORPIO/MOON IN SAGITTARIUS
Prognostic

Many Scorpio-Sagittarians experience a consuming humanitarian and spiritual impulse and know they have a purpose in life. People respect your aim and determination. Most are absorbed into your magnetic and spiritual presence. Kindness rules in your relationships, and you are always open and affectionate. However, you do have an air of distance some construe as haughtiness. This is a result of being such a free spirit and being determined to do your own thing for truth, nirvana, and wisdom. Kindness, profundity, unity, idealism, and all of the better qualities of Scorpio are disclosed when blended with a Sagittarius Moon. You are a beacon of light to others with your grand vision and elevated goals. Your willpower, perseverance, and remarkable perceptiveness help you bring some of those ends into the world. Maybe you are right that you have all the answers, even though you are impertinent and unorthodox. You need a great deal of freedom, and you are a rebel in everything. Any control or imposition on your autonomy is experienced as a menace. You need to do as you please and have room to express yourself, because you have an adventurous and heroic spirit. You would never contravene on the rights of people, because honesty and loyalty are your creeds. Your one large defect is that at times you may be a little too candid as tact is very rare in Scorpio-Sagittarius people. Your frankness can be vicious. You are an idealist in romance and everything else. After you have conferred your tenderness, you are fun loving and unreserved. You are a loyal, trustworthy, and true person. You are concerned with discovering spiritual truth. Self-contemplation is one way of detecting it, because many of the solutions lie inside. Your mental imagery is so potent that sometimes it can take you away and be a root of phobias or delusions. You frequently look at things from a transcendental perspective, which sometimes warps your otherwise good judgment. You are practical though, like your fellow Scorpios. You are essentially a romantic at heart, believing in things that others find hard to penetrate, maybe because you are so far in front of everyone else. But you do sometimes seem astute and sophisticated. Your strength is the courage to explore uncharted new worlds of thinking and feeling. Like all forerunners, you show the way that others will follow tomorrow.

SUN IN SCORPIO/MOON IN CAPRICORN
Energy Collector

You instinctively look out for yourself, no matter how kind you appear to be toward other people. For the headstrong and determined Scorpio-Capricorn ambition can be everything. You possess strong leadership drives, and you are never satisfied unless you are your own boss. Charismatic, obstinate, and autonomous, your astuteness and purpose help you follow through on your ambitions. Calculating, shrewd, vivid, and somewhat manipulative, you take yourself and your activities very seriously. You have a bit of the devil in your nature. You essentially have only one goal in life, and that is to win esteem, deference, and prestige no matter how captivating and warmhearted you seem on the surface. You have your own attraction—if you would only recognize it—so do not always enter a room and feel immediately endangered by the presence of some other striking person. How you use your gifts is strictly up to you, but you have a lot of power and leadership potential. Indira Gandhi is an example of a powerful Scorpio-Capricorn. You need to be careful about becoming too serious a judge of others. You have very high criteria and may acquire a somewhat holier-than-thou and intolerant position toward those who do not live up to your views. Others should be given as much esteem as you expect to be shown. You have a very strong sex drive as do nearly all Scorpios. You know how to use others to get your way because you are severe, worldly, and very subtle. You dislike any show of helplessness in others and are not one for self-pity, perhaps because you worry about your own weaknesses so much. You probably have a great deal of anxiety and confusion deep inside even though you seem confident on the surface. You urgently want to succeed, and this may be one reason. Maybe success is just your manner of assuring yourself that you are all those things individuals say you are. Deep down, you do not believe a word of the kudos bestowed on you. Your goal in life is an endless search for status, whatever the reason. You will lead a really cold existence if you do not expand your spiritual, cerebral, and emotional views. Self-acceptance is something you need to learn. Rather than begrudging those who seem to have more, love and treasure yourself for who you are. No matter how hard or gifted someone may be, everyone has limitations.

SUN IN SCORPIO/MOON IN AQUARIUS
Guiding Light

You know how to adjust to almost any situation, and you are smooth and urbane. Your Aquarius Moon gives you an unusual and unexplored perspective and a strong fascination for science and society. You have an obliging presence and a very strong will, like the typical Scorpio. Your imagination and insights are strange and a bit far-out for most individuals, because you are generally about ten or twelve years in advance of your time. You have a nonrational comprehension and cognizance of people, which assists you in your materialistic philosophy. You know how to coax, bond, and pull strings because you are basically astute, charming, and congenial. People are drawn to your casual, eccentric, and impertinent manner. You love your discoveries and are so proud that you want to announce them to the world. You have a strong need for the companionship of others and are much more extroverted and friendly than most Scorpios. You think an active and wide-ranging social life is necessary to your health, because it is an outlet for your sometimes crazy opinions. Nevertheless, you have a strong autonomous part, and no matter how many friends and people pass through your life, the air of the loner is around you. You are so set in your ways that you have little forbearance for those who do not agree with you. It probably took years of willfulness to make you this way. Instead of people who might offer you challenges or variety, you may surround yourself with boosters and passive disciples. Learn to accept and abide other points of view and keep your mind open to intellectual stimulation. You are essentially very down-to-earth despite that otherworldliness. Your social adroitness works to your advantage, particularly in business. Very few people are more clever or quicker on their feet than a Scorpio-Aquarius. You have a hard time making strong emotional attachments with people and are somewhat detached. This detachment is often your Waterloo. You are dedicated to having your own way and are proud and stubborn. If anyone questions your ideas or opinions, you will take it personally. You must learn how to be more cooperative and more modest. You can be everything from a mystic to innovative scientist or humanitarian, but first you must know that you can only produce at your best when you work in harmony with those near you. Intolerance and self-righteousness are especially a characteristic of Scorpio-Aquarius.

SUN IN SCORPIO/MOON IN PISCES
Hanger-On

Many Scorpio-Pisces have strong idealistic and altruistic urges. At one time or another, you might have felt the call of a religious life. You have a charismatic presence and a lot of willpower, but there are periods when you simply want to get out of the world. You may experience depression and mood swings. Tension in your immediate surrounding is generally the cause of this. Maybe because you fear your own power, forceful people appall you. Your signs are both water signs, and this gives you an uncanny power to adapt promptly to almost any circumstance. You are able to take on the feel of your surroundings. You comprehend things others are unable to. You are tuned in, aware, and have an ability to sense things. You know innately the difference between right or wrong, and no one ever has to tell you. You are very scrupulous. It does not matter how successful you are in life, kindness guides your actions. You are always heedful not to impinge on anyone else's territory. You are very aware of the evil and maliciousness that exists in the world. You are an excellent actor and playing roles is common for the Scorpio-Pisces. However, it is crucial that you be yourself at times. The roles you play do help with advancement, but on the other hand, you could lose your being altogether in the march to try to be everything to everyone. You have a lot to ascertain about yourself like all deep individuals do, and many of the answers you look for can be found within. Just be certain you do not overdo the soul-searching. You may become too withdrawn for your own best interest if you do not stay socially active. Your special ability to assimilate knowledge lets you quickly learn just about anything you want to. You would be excellent in creative and artistic pursuits. Impractical phobias or superstitions should be guarded against because of your limitless imagination. Use it in your profession instead. Scorpio-Pisces are very lucky people. You will not run in to many issues or turmoil in life, because this combination is quite balanced. However, there is a risk of permitting yourself to accept less, rather than taking on the challenges and opportunities that are frequently there for you. Make yourself be more assertive, because you have a lot to give to the world. Self-contemplation is very significant for you.

SUN IN SAGITTARIUS/MOON IN ARIES
Gossiper

Even though you are smart and perceptive, your emotional growth lags behind your understanding. It is almost impossible for you to sit still for very long because you are more like a round-eyed child than a dignified academic. You always want to discover adventure and excitement. There is a duality between the way you show yourself and the way you actually are. The surface is knowledgeable and profound, but the inside is reckless. A Sagittarius-Aries is fearless about speaking his or her mind and has been so since a young age. No other mixture personifies such blunt outspokenness. You have no inhibitions and have the courage to say precisely what you feel. You are active, capricious, and very independent. Everything is as you see it. It does not matter what others think; you are forthright and fearless. You have a philosophical and serious part to your nature too, and there are not many subjects you cannot talk about intelligently. You really like to shock people with your unusual behavior. You do not need to wear a costume at a Halloween party. Wit rates among your greatest pluses. You always manage to annoy some people by pointing out everything they are attempting to ignore. You are satirical and playful. Luckily, people who deserve your attacks are the ones who get them. Using simple nonchalance and purity, you attempt to bring out the hypocrisy you see everywhere. There is a bit of arrogance in your manner even though people may love you. Your penchant is for drama. You really enjoy showing off your humor and courage, and you flourish on competition. From time to time try a little thoughtful contemplation before you speak and be more respectful of the emotions and beliefs of others. It is highly probable you will have several occupations in your life, because this combination connotes diversity. You are both a calculating philosopher and a perennial optimist. In spite of your lack of inhibitions and proper behavior, you always have friends. Others admire your bravery and fresh, alluring charm. You are demonstrative and bighearted. You hunger for an audience and an audience is what you generally find. The comedian, critic, dramatist, and satirist are good for your combination. Mark Twain and James Thurber are both fine examples of Sagittarius-Aries. You need to be careful of that rather big ego of yours, but you are essentially good-hearted and kind.

SUN IN SAGITTARIUS/MOON IN TAURUS
Regretful Inner Voice

You are quite able to realize some of your inspired conceptions, and you are attracted to the aesthetic and artistic. However, too frequently those dreams stay dreams, because, as is the case with all Moon in Taurus people, you need security before you start any campaigns. This means a significant bank balance and a comfortable house. Even if it may prove more profitable in the long run, the pragmatic side of your character holds you back from following a dubious or unconventional career. Security is crucial to everybody, but do not let it be your exclusive pursuit in life. You may always feel an internal discontent if you do not on occasion act on your whims, no matter how materially prosperous you become. You are a person of excellent perceptivity, and you think in wide conceptual terms. Your combination includes the mature wisdom and utility of Taurus with the transcendental and visionary aspect of Sagittarius. Your compassion for people is boundless, which may be another grounds for having difficulty following through on your aspirations. Your judgment is often blocked by sentimentality and sympathy. In the end you are actually a nice person and very softhearted. Saying no is hard for you, and there is nothing you detest more than the thought of rejecting someone. You have a style for business in addition to solely creative or aesthetic pursuits. You know just when to undertake a venture or take a financial chance because you are a good gambler. Charisma and charm work to your advantage, and people feel your inherent dignity. Individuals with this mixture can excel as entrepreneurs and business people. You are always affirmative and positive in your dealings, and setbacks very rarely rattle you even though you are a very serious person. You might feel some guilt feelings deep inside about stepping to the fore and expressing your point of view. Most of your worries are in your mind, because you do have quite a vivid imagination. You are by nature such an affectionate and sharing person you will forever be loved and esteemed no matter what road you choose to take in life. Your nature is very sensual and down-to-earth. You enjoy pursuing pleasure, but comfort is not everything, and you can very easily backslide into self-satisfaction or adopt a smug mind-set. Cultivating a broad range of interests and being active socially is a must for the Sagittarius-Taurus.

SUN IN SAGITTARIUS/MOON IN GEMINI
Cheerful Being

You are anxious and edgy. You do essentially what you want to in life because independence is the one thing you long for most of all, and you are always the maverick. You are extremely autonomous, and you become frightened if anyone tries to regulate you. You have a perky, playful spirit people find irresistible, and you are an eternal optimist. However, you never lose that aura of disengagement no matter how outgoing and friendly you appear. Even though you can get somewhat emotional on the outside, inside you are always very cool. Concentration is difficult for you. Ingenuity and fortune follow you wherever you go, screening you from dangers that anyone else would no doubt suffer. For some reason you always seem to get by no matter how uneasy, whimsical, adventurous, and excessive you may be. You are very much an explorer. You feel a ceaseless impulse to be on the move, and you are likely to search many lands and look into many ideas. A great scholar and trailblazer is the nature of your combination, if you could only acquire the patience called for to master something. You just cannot be calm. Some people may charge you with lying, and some may think you are not consistent. Because you repeatedly change your mind, you often befuddle others by saying one thing and doing something else. You are not actually mean or dishonest, you are honorable to the core; it is just that if you were more careful before speaking, you might not have this problem. Whatever it is you are going to say, be certain you believe it. With romance, as with everything, you are as inconsistent. A person who is able to put up with those mood shifts, or who can walk as quickly and travel as frequently, can be difficult to find. You have spent, from your early years, too much of your time in planning for your next big move. You may feel, as time passes, some tension and maybe even guilt as your failure to employ your gifts leaves you without any purpose or achievement. Eventually, you may discover that you have little to show, even though your life has been eventful. Cultivate the discipline it takes to satisfy yourself. Do not be satisfied depending only on cleverness and luck. You love to interlace stories and tales and have a dramatic imagination. Professions include author, artist, or movie maker. Exaggeration is something you are prone to. The line between fantasy and reality gets fuzzy, and it is sometimes hard for you to keep your great imagination within limits.

SUN IN SAGITTARIUS/MOON IN CANCER
Mastermind

You are a quick learner because your emotional character is receptive, and you are very flexible. Anything that involves the exotic and undiscovered as well as language and society probably intrigues you. You are a very emotional person even though you may have the aura of a scholar. You are controlled, tranquil, and good-hearted and have great depth and perception. The daring, hopeful, and freedom-loving Sagittarius Sun in your combination is connected with the careful, astute, and inventive Cancer Moon. Caution always holds influence over whim in you, and unlike your other Sagittarians you favor looking before you leap. Your manner is self-assured, and you always appear so capable and well versed that many think you are profound. You make friends and judge others according to the way you feel about them because you are extremely intuitive. You are usually correct when you sense a person is not trustworthy or is dishonest. However, there are moments when your feelings and your avant-garde imagination carry you away. Sometimes it is hard for you to distinguish fantasy from reality because you are a dreamer. You could have a smug or self-satisfied viewpoint as time goes by, as with all those who have their Moon in Cancer. You may not carry out those lofty ideals or employ your many endowments because you are too easily contented. You should be able to get past this complacency if your home life is a content one, because from a sound base you can achieve many fantastic things. Joseph Conrad, the writer, is an example of the very insightful and artistic Sagittarius-Cancer. Your appeal and ability will gain you a lot of esteem and admiration. People feel your earnestness and are grateful for your kindness, but you should be careful about too much self-contemplation. You can become very dazed by the things you come across about your own character, and you are very sensitive. You have substantial religious longings and are a spiritual individual. Great adventures can come from the vibrant Cancer imagination, but it can also cause phobias and illusions. Keeping it limited is something you need to learn. If you let your emotions carry you away, your judgment and insight can be affected. You can adapt to nearly any condition or surroundings with your great confidence. Because you recognize that true security is found only inside ourselves, you can make your home almost anywhere.

SUN IN SAGITTARIUS/MOON IN LEO
Know-It-All

You are very energetic and have courage and an innocent interest in people and places. This can take you far and wide in search of reality and self-realization. But there is a good possibility you have it a little too good. With your balanced combination you are so free of inner battles that you may be tempted to just get by and depend only on your fortune, humor, and communication skills. A Leo Moon steadies Sagittarian whimsy and inconsistency. You quest for position and leadership, and you have very high and far-reaching goals. You knew at a young age that your mind's eye, creative drives, and broad capability set you apart from others. You most likely believe you are meant to be a leader. Other people instantly respond to your upbeat and affirmative manner. They also value your sincerity and inborn dignity. You just do not have the issues and inhibitions that hold back so many other people. You are open and outgoing. You direct your aggression into good, productive activities. The Sagittarius-Leo combination can be a happy-go-lucky pleasure seeker or a solemn, goal-oriented philosophical person. Your forte is not introspection, because you are so wrapped up in life that you allow yourself little room for contemplation. If you could just be a bit more meditative, you will discover the way to expand your many gifts. Gustave Flaubert and Benjamin Disraeli are famous members of your combination. Two roadblocks on your way to success are arrogance and bad judgment. Either or both of these could stop your progress. You long for an audience and are demonstrative and playful. At time it is hard to know whether your behavior is real or just designed to produce an effect because you have such a flair for the dramatic. That entire craving for attention is your way of boosting your sense of self, and vanity is emphasized in your signs. It is important for you to note that flattery can easily lead you astray. You need to be reminded of just how great you are. You are naive in romance as in other parts of life even though you are enthusiastic, fervent, and tender. You prefer to go by your own intuition because you do not like to take the suggestions of others. In addition, you do not like to admit your mistakes. You are inclined to take things at face value rather than stopping to look carefully, and this often impairs your judgment. You are unaware that the way things seem can be very deceptive. You need to examine your experience, and you will become less trusting and a bit more alert to the ways of the world.

SUN IN SAGITTARIUS/MOON IN VIRGO
Insightful

You are extremely perceptive. One of your greatest gifts is intuition. You are aware of when it is prudent to take a risk or grab an advantage, as well as when it is smart to remain cool. Your success is assured because of your wisdom, vigilance, and good judgment. Another gift is persuasiveness, and you are charming and soft-spoken. You know precisely how to get to the spirit. You are an outstanding salesman and a convincing leader because of your way with words. An example of a very developed Sagittarius-Virgo is Winston Churchill. You are a lot more reserved and earthy than your fellow Sagittarians. You favor looking before you leap. There is nothing casual or lighthearted about you. Your Virgo inner self provides you with a fixed sense of obligation. Very early in life you most likely had to take on a lot of responsibility, which brought out your clever, pragmatic outlook. You have a very understated, almost wily way about you. You can always spot dishonesty, and your aptitude to sense other people's weaknesses is awesome. You have a restive, autonomous, and unruly spirit even though you prefer to work and live in a conventional lifestyle. Your emotional character is a bit reserved and uncertain even though you are just as fervent and daring as your fellow Sagittarians. You may build up vague feelings of inadequacy or despair whenever you feel you cannot handle the burden of your consummate and aggressive personality. Don't put yourself down. You have many magnificent qualities, which more than compensate for any boldness or courage you may think you lack. You have astonishing powers of scrutiny and an excellent intelligence. Sagittarius provides you the skill to handle the abstract and philosophical, while Virgo gives you ability to set those ideas on a more realistic plateau. A good example of the versatile and intellectual Sagittarius-Virgo is Spinoza, the philosopher. You set exceptionally high, nearly perfectionist goals for yourself, and you are never happy with being second best. When you find you cannot meet the demands you set for yourself, bad temper and nervous tension often come about. Your frustrations might be released on the people closest to you. This includes your sarcasm, which can border on malice at times. More time for enjoying life needs to be set aside. Even though your sense of duty is commendable, do not let your loyalty to work become a compulsion.

SUN IN SAGITTARIUS/MOON IN LIBRA
Bookworm

You have an endless belief in yourself and your future, and you have a strong independent aspect. You have far-reaching aspirations like all confident people. Your aptitude to learn quickly and your attractive charm and good spirits work to your benefit. Since you followed your own unique path to success there is no doubt you will attain recognition. Open-minded, rational Sagittarius, in your combination, is coupled with socially oriented, tender, and inventive Libra. A cheerful, hopeful, delightful, and naive idealist is whom most people know. However there is also a very solemn part to your nature too. It is that of the philosopher who has great subtlety and perceptivity. You have a very vivid imagination and sometimes it is too vivid, because far-fetched fantasies can carry you away. No matter how far you drift, luck is always by your side, and everything seems to be just right. In all likelihood you have a great desire for knowledge, especially theoretical knowledge. You get mixed up by details and prefer to deal with larger concepts. You are much more interested in the meaning of life than by how to balance your budget. Your personality is lively and dynamic. There is always something that is innocent in you no matter how deep and serious you may be. People find it difficult to resist your humor and fresh appeal because you are fun loving and bold. You are apt to gain a lot of respect and power and enjoy a busy social life. You are truthful, devoted, and undemanding professionally. You never compromise your values but know how to work through life's demands. The opposite sex is attracted to you. You spend a lot of time looking for the right partner because you are romantic and idealistic. Your desire for variety, combined with restlessness, often ruins your quest for love. You have a lazy streak, like all those with the Moon in Libra, and your dreams may simply stay dreams unless you gain the strength of mind to follow them through. Recognition may blind your basically sound judgment because you are a bit enthralled by charm and sweet talk. Your specialty is social insight. You have an instinctive understanding of others, and you are a natural diplomat. Any field having to do with human relations or social activism is perfect for the Sagittarius-Libra, including teaching, counseling, law, politics, and sociology.

SUN IN SAGITTARIUS/MOON IN SCORPIO
Campaigner

You populate your life with variety and thrills, and remain free-spirited and adventurous. In the hope of finding salvation for yourself or for others, you have plenty of rebelliousness in you, and many Sagittarius-Scorpios have joined causes and missions. While you are gracious and idealistic, conceit often mars your good intentions. You have some powerful creative and management urges, but you are also very self-determining and prefer to clear your own special path in life. Your combination consists of the idealism, elevated vision, and transcendentalism of Sagittarius, which is fortified by an acute, driven, and ambitious Scorpio Moon. You may be busy building up your own unique perspective on life or book of law that enables you to close your mind to the concepts and beliefs of others. You are a very expressive individual with many prejudices and immovable beliefs and may appear somewhat distant and removed. At times, the utter concentration of your emotions deforms your perspective and good judgment. Those who see you as egotistical are probably correct. You actually do separate yourself from others. Billy the Kid, the American outlaw, is an excellent example of the maverick and rebellious Sagittarius-Scorpio. Renewing yourself is one of your wonderful abilities. You love to dig deeply into unusual subjects, and the exotic and the uncharted fascinate you. You are tempted by the delight of distant places, and you love to travel. You seek to experience as much as possible in life, and you are sensual and pleasure loving. No one can fetter your independent soul, and you have a strong sense of free will. You always get up from falls, no matter how many times you are set back or personal misfortunes you encounter. Your mind is inquisitive and perceptive. You could be a member of the clergy, doctor, scientist, psychologist, or scholar with your wonderful intellectual and spiritual gifts. The necessities for your success in the world are controlling that desire to travel and learning to collaborate with others. Keeping your feelings balanced and guarding against extremes of thought and activity are important for you too. Sensationalizing and exaggerating are things you have a tendency to do. Attempt to detach yourself a bit from your behavior and acquire a more objective viewpoint.

SUN IN SAGITTARIUS/MOON IN SAGITTARIUS
Preoccupied Intellectual

You have the ability to go to great creative and spiritual heights; you nonetheless have real difficulty when it comes to being on Earth. The luck of Jupiter, fortunately, always helps you out at the last minute no matter how out of touch you are. You are capable of stimulating and absorbing an audience with your burning enthusiasm and extent of understanding, and you are a natural teacher. However, you are never really certain exactly where you are on important subjects. For this combination, every side of existence takes on large, abstract dimensions because you are the recurrent philosopher. Nothing in life is simple for the double Sagittarius. You are lifted into the realm of the philosopher-king by lucidity of thought and lofty insights, far above those below. Paying the rent or balancing your budget and other details bog you down. Yours is just not the most sensible of combinations because you are extremely absentminded. The inflow of concepts and visions you have can be overpowering, and you are never exactly sure which set of rules you must follow. However, you are extremely open-minded. You are inclined to change your mind often, although serious and attracted to the abstract. You consider both sides carefully prior to arriving at a decision. You are so careful that it sometimes takes forever for you to take a position. Your worst problem is confusion because the skill to understand mathematics and metaphysics does not help you to know yourself. Once you have mastered a little tolerance and learned to control that restiveness, you may be able to see some of those goals completed. Then you will be all set. You can achieve great success with your wonderful imagination, if you are given the right situation. The Divine is somehow connected to you as well. You also tend to ignore the long-term consequences of your behavior to live almost wholly for the moment. Repeated silliness is common to the double Sagittarius, and caprice rules your decisions. Others may crave gold or fame, but your biggest desire is for total personal freedom. The world is your space for your feelings and thoughts, and you need to move about freely and do precisely as you want. Travel, either in your mind or literally, is critical to your health. It is very unusual for a double Sagittarius to not travel far and wide. It is hard for you to settle down and see some of those grand goals and not have your freedom. You should try to restrain some of those crazier ideas even though your expansive and freedom-loving soul should never be locked up.

SUN IN SAGITTARIUS/MOON IN CAPRICORN
Funnyman

You cover sadness under a painted smile like the laughing clown. As you grew older you probably became powerfully goal oriented even though in youth, you may have been impulsive and given to adventure. You are insecure and in all likelihood feel a lot of doubt and even fear. One way you try to exceed and eliminate those feelings is by proving yourself. You may seem untroubled, affirmative, and playful on the outside, but below that devil-may-care persona is a very compulsive, somewhat profound, and ambitious person. You are a very sober and earthy Sagittarian. Although calculating and practical, you tend to think in big, theoretical terms. You have a pessimistic temperament that often shows through no matter how idealistic and affirmative you may seem. In reality you are very aloof and detached, but to others you seem happy and outgoing. To the career-oriented Sagittarius-Capricorn isolation frequently is a threat. Ambition can become all consuming and can even remove you from those near you because you see the world as a place of difficulty and hardship. Do not let ambition become your life even though you have the vision, astuteness, and persistence to accomplish a lot. Try relaxing more and accepting your real nature and do not place incredible demands on yourself. You do not have any difficulty gathering your thoughts because you invariably know your own mind and you are organized and extremely efficient. You can do a great deal for people by using your mental ability to reveal evil and hypocrisy; your perception of things around you is amazing. Very self-examining, you spend perhaps too much time thinking about yourself. Engrossment with your own issue leads to extreme egoism, but remember your combination shows a lot of wisdom and depth. If you desire to be loved and accepted, you must try to give to people; so remember, you only receive what you give. You have plenty of wit and your keen comments always hit home, even though they generally emphasize the darker side of things. You may elect to play the part of clown or jester socially to defend your sensitivity and prevent getting hurt. However, you are very serious. Writer-humorist Woody Allen and satirist-philosopher Voltaire are both Sagittarius-Capricorns. With your reason and exact mind, you win most debates.

SUN IN SAGITTARIUS/MOON IN AQUARIUS
Pathfinder

You can expect the unexpected when a Sagittarius-Aquarian is present. You are very unpredictable and set quite high goals for yourself. You generally follow them through with honesty and devotion. You get unnerved when anyone tries to restrict your freedom, but you are good-hearted, nice, and warm. Freedom is your favorite expression, and no one can order you around. People seek you out because you are unlike anyone else they know, as well as being captivating, charismatic, and friendly. You can at least count on your identity even if you were to have nothing else on Earth. Activities that suggest change and innovation attract you as do being involved with others. Your greatest gift is foresight. You seem to know instantly what tomorrow has in store, and you are always tuned to the future. You often say and do things that are designed to shock people, and you are restless and unconventional because you hate nothing more than arrogant satisfaction. You get mixed up and impatient when others cannot keep up with you, and you are generally a few steps in front of everyone else. Though you are open-minded and forgiving by nature, your impatience can give you an air of conceit. It is difficult for you to be totally open in your partnerships with others because your essential emotional nature is a bit detached and remote. You have some pretty crazy friends, but friendship is very important to you. Your compelling charm generally works to your advantage, as does your positive approach to others, but there are occasions when a shrewder perspective is better. Eagerness and amiability may take you a long way, but they will not bake any bread. You must have choices in whatever you elect to do for a career. Intellectual pursuits draw you, and you have an intellect for the theoretical. Fields that may attract you are politics, urban planning, and social ethics. People look up to you and try to emulate your freedom. You need to stop now in order to allow the rest of the world to catch up, but you do have certain leadership possibilities. Surprisingly, you have somewhat authoritarian, sanctimonious attitudes even though you verbalize open-minded and democratic visions. After you have formed some of those revolutionary notions and beliefs they stick, so you also have a stubborn streak. Always keep your mind open, but particularly later in life. You have more wisdom and pragmatism than other Sagittarians because of your Aquarian inner nature, but you are still a bit naive.

SUN IN SAGITTARIUS/MOON IN PISCES
Lyricist

You are characterized by flights of fancy. Frequently you may take the easy way out rather than making your numerous gifts work for you. You just adjust and accommodate. You tend to take on the characteristics of those nearest to you, and you are emotionally weak with associates, family, and friends. You may let yourself down because of fear or lethargy, even though you have high principles. Sometimes you seem to live on a distant fantasy island, and there is a dreamlike aspect to the Sagittarius-Pisces. Somehow when it comes to knowing who deserves your trust and who does not, you are led almost solely by your intuition. You can mix up dreams with the real world because you also have an extraordinary imagination. It sometimes carries you away. You are universal in nature, and this allows you to survive in almost any surroundings. You are highly impressionable and adaptable. The one main disadvantage to your vivid imagination and high amount of sensitivity is that it can be hard for you to deal with reality. You may be content to copy, or live using others because you set them up as ideals. This is a shame, because the Sagittarius-Pisces who is more daring will discover that only the smallest amount of effort can lead to better things. You feel the present and future must be happy, and you are an optimist. You have two ways of dealing with negativity in your life: you may simply lie to yourself, accepting a fake kind of happiness, or you will tune out troubles rather than handling them directly. You are extremely romantic and giving in love, and life devoid of love is unimaginable for you. It is essential that you have a good appreciation of yourself before beginning long-term relationships because you take the chance of having unhealthy associations, especially in romance. You almost certainly have a great love of learning and travel as well as exploring other places. Your combination would be good as anthropologists or historians. Ultimately those with Moon in Pisces can be artists or poets if they learn to use their magnificent creative abilities. Hopefully you will get the type of guidance that will set you on the correct path and your talents will be recognized at a young age. You can have enormous happiness and have the capability to take pleasure in life to its fullest.

SUN IN CAPRICORN/MOON IN ARIES
Actively Diligent

You are abrupt and somewhat offhand. Despite what people may say, you are actually not selfish, but self-interest is often obvious in this combination. You have little lenience for those who are inactive, but you just believe that God helps those who help themselves. Tremendous power of attention and will are part of the industrious Capricorn-Aries. Trying to keep up with a Capricorn-Aries is difficult. They move so quickly and it can be exhausting to keep up with them. You are a bundle of energy, and you attend to things swiftly and capably. You are always on the move. An air of intolerance and unfriendliness is the result. You take the rest of the world in good spirits while you take care of things. You can get so caught up in your immediate actions that you forget the rest of the world. You never give up anything and are very ambitious and willful. You are fervent, forceful, and rebellious. You simply are not conventional in any way but are a pioneer. You are always first among those working for change. Your personal life can be a high drama. A lot of tempest and trouble are part of your love affairs. A smooth, monogamous romance is not something your Aries inner nature is cut out for, so you may direct most of your vigor into a career, as well as meeting the goals you set for yourself. You become nervous when things are not progressing as easily and proficiently as you would like. The world will generally know when you get angry about something. Before you head out not knowing the destination, attempt to think things through. With those who cannot equal your tempo, try to be more tolerant. You cannot always set such a fast pace. You should slow down occasionally to let others catch up with you. You are a restless spirit, and it is almost unfeasible for you to sit still. It is not simple for you to find the time for intimate relationships or researching the romantic, spiritual, and logical facets of life, even though you desire love and appreciation for the amazing person you know yourself to be. The respect and approval you get from your work is what you are content with. Ambition is good, but you may end up missing out on a life. Try slowing down now and then. Your interests and activities should be expanded. While generally as careful as other Capricorns, there are periods when you can be quite impetuous, particularly when your blistering Aries soul takes over.

SUN IN CAPRICORN/MOON IN TAURUS
Rooted Commoner

You can quietly coax and persuade almost anyone of almost anything, because your presence is so tranquil and reassuring, and persuasiveness one of your great talents. Your aims are always the best, and you are inherently honest. A problem for the Taurus is obstinacy. With firm resolve you hold on to your beliefs and convictions. It is hard for you to accept a changing society and mores because you are somewhat old-fashioned. Your tragic fault is emotional inflexibility. Your best assets are charisma, inner security, and worldly wisdom, while comfort and material things are your major priorities. You have a very understanding side to your nature, although you are just as determined and goal-oriented as your fellow Capricorns. People believe you because you have an aura of inborn steadiness, knowledge, and good sense. You are a charismatic combination and capable of achieving considerable success and position. The Capricorn-Taurus meets the severities of life with patience and resolve and is not one to wallow in self-pity or regret. You have the stubbornness to follow your objectives through and usually push them on to completion. You must keep your opinions supple and your mind open. Do not let fixed attitudes or bias run your life. Rather than dealing with them truthfully and openly, you also have a propensity to repress your emotions. You fight to preserve that calm and self-controlled front as antagonism, anxiety, or frustration build up. Sometimes it is wise to open up and discuss how you really feel inside. You should do this with someone you can trust. You may be subject to turns of despair or explosions of anger otherwise. You will probably be reluctant to follow such a chancy career even though the financial world may attract you. You require a steady income. In love, you search for a partner who desires all the good things you too want from life. Your perfect relationship would be an unwavering, caring partnership that enhanced your worldly standing and social position. It would be wise for you to be a bit more experimental even though you are affectionate and sensual. You take a chance of adopting a self-satisfied or complacent outlook because your life may be fairly free of tension. You may compromise just because you are so effortlessly contented even though Capricorns are motivated by nature. You may have a penchant to let materialism become your only goal because you love pleasure and are sensual. You have gifts for administration, management, and long-term planning because of your combination.

SUN IN CAPRICORN/MOON IN GEMINI
Absorbed Sponge

You are a thinker, and you have a broad range of interests that lead you to forever try new ideas and theories. Putting some of those novel ideas into practice is probably a strong desire for you. You want to advance in the world like all Capricorns, and fortunately for you, you have the aptitude to do that. You know how to plan, because you are bright as well as philosophical, so on the way up the ladder no one will get in your way. In addition, you love to learn new things. In actuality, that calm and traditional persona is a very agitated and self-determining individual, even though you may seem rather predictable. You are lively and versatile. Capricorns are always aware of their own minds, even with the frequent changes. You are likely to wander far and wide because of your longing for variety and innovation. God for you is knowledge. Although tradition and old values are things you have an enduring admiration for, you are always searching for new means of thought. It is a rare Capricorn-Gemini who can sit still for any period, and internal restlessness keeps you moving. You are not particularly good at concentrating. You find it very hard to focus your abilities no matter how smart you are. You should try cultivating a steady point of view and directing your knowledge in one direction. You become perplexed and are never certain what to do when faced with a very emotional situation. Instant explanations can be a way of handling your sudden rush of feelings. Be careful not to over-intellectualize. Occasionally allow yourself to be influenced by passion. You are a hard worker like all Capricorns, and your vocation is too often allowed precedence over everything else in life. Even when thinking about a holiday weekend you can have nothing but work on your mind. In the final analysis, you may have difficulty deciding where you stand because your interests are so diverse and you are so open to any new theory. After you have tapered down your involvements and activities, you are able to achieve success. Doing things too quickly is another issue for the Capricorn-Gemini. Impatience is the problem. You get puzzled when your labors do not reward you immediately. You want applause right now and seek instant satisfaction and acknowledgment. You may end up assigning responsibility to dutiful underlings because you are in such a hurry to get where you are want to go. Detachment is part of your character.

SUN IN CAPRICORN/MOON IN CANCER
Bruiser

A famous Capricorn-Cancer was Janis Joplin, who had a tough, working-class image that was actually just a disguise for her authentic depth and sensitivity. In this combination the Sun and Moon are in opposite signs, so most likely your early environment was quite poor or even heartless. This nurtured in you a strong sense of self-sufficiency and autonomy as well as a cynical outlook. You attempt to maintain a hard, rough, calm, and removed image on the surface, but notwithstanding that casual air, you are actually a very tender and emotionally susceptible person. Your main problem is insecurity. In order to deal with those entrenched feelings of insufficiency and uncertainty, you can either give in to despair and pessimism or build a hard shell to protect yourself from pain and torment. Consequently many of your anxieties are rooted in your youth. Your challenge is to start to identify your understanding as a strong point rather than a flaw and permit your true self to come forth. You are a competent person, and you should appreciate yourself and your gifts. Two significant things for a Capricorn-Cancer to learn are self-acceptance and self-love. Your combination empowers you with outstanding leadership possibilities and a lot of charm, but you rarely take advantage of these assets. You are not part of the crowd in any way and have no desire to lead others or to be led by someone. You are an independent type, essentially, and prefer the comfort of doing things alone. Unfortunately, voluntary exile can expand into deep isolation and loneliness when added to that glum outlook of yours. It is necessary for you to be fairly active socially, regardless of whether you are your own boss. Emotional issues may prevent a flourishing and equal romantic relationship, but you have an overwhelming need to be loved. You are in many ways clever, affectionate and compassionate. Your skill to see underneath external impressions and your flexibility to change enables you to formulate new ways of understanding. Once you conquer self-doubt, there is little you cannot achieve and the only enemy on the path to success will be you. Isaac Newton, the innovative physicist and mystic, was a Capricorn-Cancer. Your memory is remarkable as is your sharp wit. You are direct and outspoken in pointing out details, including ones that escape even the keenest observer.

SUN IN CAPRICORN/MOON IN LEO
Absolute Ruler

While young you were perhaps very idealistic, somewhat inexperienced, and drawn to social and compassionate causes. However, as you grew older and more calculating, you no doubt sacrificed some of your ideals in order to get the standing, comfort, and status you felt you merited. The pursuit of supremacy for some Capricorn-Leos can become a fixation. You always have the feeling that you are naturally better than other people, and you only feel satisfied when you are the boss. You are a lot more demonstrative and friendly than other Capricorns, and you can be very successful. You have a good appreciation of yourself and your skills and are a determined individual. Others will react to your charisma, magnetism, and resolve, and they admire you because you have self-respect. You have pride and dignity, and want the notice and adulation your ego requires. Very splendid and lofty ideals come from your Leo Moon. This combination can easily result in a despot or a possible tyrant. A good example of this side of a Capricorn-Leo is Mao Tse-tung. Your approach toward others is often condescending, and some may even consider you egotistical. Your ideal is loyalty, and after someone has won your confidence you become concerned, affectionate, and kind to him or her. You can be cruel, cold, and calculating to those who are disloyal to that trust. Insults or slight insults to your vanity or self-esteem are often met with out-of-proportion fury. Your primary concern is maintaining self-respect and decorum. Extreme pride can be your Waterloo. You have the aptitude to renew yourself and achieve anything you really desire. But first you must learn to curb your arrogance and vanity. You inspire others simply with your presence. You are an idealist by nature, and your sunny appeal and enjoyable humor can brighten the darkest heart. Everything you do has a special stamp of innovation. The dramatic is your signature. Strong creative drives are part of a Leo Moon. There are occasions when you are mistaken even though you are wise and intuitive. However, you will never acknowledge it. Because you believe you are always correct and know what is best for you and those you know, you almost never find the middle ground. You have to attempt to become more supple. Obstinacy undermines those goals you set for yourself, and inflexibility will only get you into difficulties. If you do not let your ego get in the way, you are capable of magnificent achievements. Your ultimate strength is willpower.

SUN IN CAPRICORN/MOON IN VIRGO
Grinder

You struggle to get as much status and power as possible to compensate for your fears. Your greatest pleasure comes from the admiration and prestige your work provides, so, like all Capricorns, you are very career minded. You are very responsible, and you are not really happy until you have plenty of power. You have the resolve to conquer any barrier and incredible determination and inner strength. Logical, thrifty, and cautious Virgo in your combination links up with determined, resolute, and career-minded Capricorn. Your strength is cold, hard logic, and you are a person with no illusions. You see things precisely as they are because you are a total pragmatist. Fantasies are a waste of time in your book. Instead of dreaming, you plan and are practical and efficient. Deep inside you most likely feel vague fears or indecision, even though you appear rough, detached, and even a little cold. You also have fantastic powers of attentiveness and quite a mind. You are astute and calculating and know how to convince people of things, but for a lot of Capricorn-Virgos, winning becomes an end in itself. Participate in all the wonders of life, including the romantic and the religious. Do not allow your job and status to be an obsession. All Moons in Virgo people are picky, but your criticisms are frequently directed at yourself. Simply trying to accept yourself is the challenge for you. Your combination is perfectly fitted for managerial and leadership roles. Your rational and shrewd mind is ideal for academic activities. After you put your mind to something, you will not be content until you have mastered it completely. A stable and equal relationship is important to your psychological well-being, but you are not exceptionally romantic. You are actually quite a sensitive person no matter how removed and cool you try to be. Do not try to deny or hide that sensitivity by taking on a role that is at odds with your true nature. Neurosis or self-destructive behavior can result from the fear of actual or imagined failings in life. You despise the idea of having any weaknesses. Capricorn-Virgos are never content. Regardless of how successful you are in life, something in you always tells you that you have not gone far enough. Try to have a little more sympathy for yourself, because we all have limitations. Refrain from dwelling on those tiny imperfections you always think you have.

SUN IN CAPRICORN/MOON IN LIBRA
Blueblood

You continually search for serenity, and somehow you feel those around you can work out the complicated puzzle of your being. You are persistently active, romantically as well as socially, and always seeking some club, philosophy, or individual that will give the inner balance you crave so much. You may constantly have your heart broken in your mission, becoming disenchanted and maybe even bitter as you learn that others cannot always live up to your expectations. You may seem hard, detached, and determined, but deep inside lies a kind, understanding, and very benevolent person. You are a very responsive and optimistic Capricorn, but not as astute as most Capricorns, and your faith in people is so great that it might be a problem. It is only within yourself that true harmony and peace of mind can come. Rather than looking for it elsewhere, try putting some confidence in yourself. Learn to appreciate who you are, and build up a more independent outlook. Your combination has a conflict resulting from strong personal aspirations and Libra's desire to be loved and valued. Even if it is at the expense of your own happiness, you want to see everyone be happy. You are also a little shy about putting yourself forward or giving expression to your ideas and aspirations. You have strong creative needs and a sophisticated aesthetic sense, but for the Capricorn-Libra wisdom rests in self-contemplation and courage: the courage to let your excellent Capricorn strength realize your ideas. You are inclined to idealize your partner and you are very romantic. Make your relationship one that is sensible and healthy, because it is extremely important to you. In addition to material qualities in a partner, look for spiritual qualities as well when choosing a person who intends to remain with you. Always have self-confidence. You act as though someone was watching you, ready to strike and punish you for such assumptions. Eventually you may be very let down in yourself, because your fears may cause you to suppress your ambitions. Oddly enough, you are afraid you will infringe on people if you press on too far. Affirmation instead of self-renunciation is your challenge in life. A self-defeatist attitude can smother your artistic urges if you are not careful.

SUN IN CAPRICORN/MOON IN SCORPIO
Gladiator

You are in fact an exceedingly emotional person even though you may appear distant and cold. There are periods when the strength of your emotions carries you away, but you always have the ability for difficult work and imaginative activity. Your opinions about the world are very fixed and seldom change. You are the type of individual who seems to know what is right for you. You most likely put forward your freedom by dominating all your playmates when you were young. As the nonconformist of the zodiac, few can match you for pure determination, audacity, and aggression. Ultimately you grow wiser and a lot less hotheaded, and fortunately you are fast to learn from your mistakes. Capricorn-Scorpios have two sides that are rather different in nature: the out-of-control sensualist and the painstaking reformer. Capricorn's boredom or inhibition is not at all a part of you. You are never hesitant to say just what you think with frankness and sometimes brutal honesty, because you take the world and yourself with complete seriousness. While very perceptive, you have a strong sanctimonious streak in you, and your prejudices and dug-in attitudes generally have the last word. Your own interests are usually first, and you have a somewhat heartless disregard for others. Often your tastes are founded on whether something is to your benefit. Be careful about being so manipulative. You can probe and search the depths of existence or fly to amazing heights of spiritual wisdom, as can all those who have the Moon in Scorpio. You have most likely done both because you are so curious you want to experience everything. Your future and whatever you do in life is largely up to you, with all that resolve. You are creative and sensual in love, but not very faithful. You are really into adventure like all Capricorns. Anyone who can keep you for a lifetime, considering all of this, is a very rare person. Your approach to reality is to look for gimmicks or places where people might slip up. You could make a brilliant detective, psychologist, or scientist with your fantastic insight and keen perception. As long as you have a clear objective in sight, you will be happy, even though you tend to be somewhat pessimistic in your dealings in life. You are very spirited, and there is nothing you love more than a quarrel, especially an academic one. Having a forum for conveying your views is important for you. It can be chancy trying to keep your beliefs and persuasions locked up inside because you are so emotional. An excellent release for some of those hidden desires is writing.

SUN IN CAPRICORN/MOON IN SAGITTARIUS
Carefree

Although you are subject to intermittent periods of depression and sadness, you never lose your basic sense of humor. Your witty, casual comments always hit the target. You are probably the most balanced of any of the Sun-Moon combinations. You have a wide range of activities and projects. Your profession has to be inside an organized and conventional structure like most Capricorns, but your Sagittarian inner aspect desires adventure and excitement. The Sagittarius part of you is liberal, creative, and freedom loving, while your Capricorn is resolute, determined, and somewhat distant. You have both the resolve and the intelligence to achieve a great deal, and you set long-term goals for yourself. Your allure and casual manner enthrall people. You are much less reserved, and much more sociable, than other Capricorns. You also enjoy having a good time but are a serious and goal-oriented individual. You appear removed, but it does not require much to bring out your ironic smile. It is critical that your job be fulfilling as well as enhances your prestige, because you are very aware of social standing. You must have the liberty to do what you want to because you value your personal freedom. Never happy unless you are the boss, your willpower and intelligence typically take you right to the pinnacle. Your mind is rational, well organized, and sensible, but insight is one of your utmost gifts. You go though impulsive and across-the-board moods as do all Moon in Sagittarius people. You can quickly become an impetuous and adventurous drifter right after being serious and determined for a while. There are times when your moods and visions carry you away and induce you to forget your plans. To direct some of that impatience and inquisitiveness, you need a lot of distraction and external activity. Your need to travel is virtually a requirement for your emotional stability. You respect tradition while you try to see tomorrow's needs, and thus you are the perfect long-term planner. You have a learned and philosophical aura. Perhaps while young you were troubled and had it difficult, but you still acquired a strong intellectual curiosity. You love to experiment with theoretical concepts and analysis. Thus, philosophy attracts you because you want to find truth and a perfect structure with which to manage your life. You would never partake of callous behavior in your search for status and esteem because you are very ethical.

SUN IN CAPRICORN/MOON IN CAPRICORN
Mentor

You are quite a solemn person. You give off a wise image, and you are somewhat introverted and pensive. Indeed, common sense is one of your greatest assets. You seem to have an awareness that goes beyond space and time. You are mostly respected and admired because others see great maturity in you. You most likely recall a lot of rules and regulations and not much love and affection when you reflect on your childhood. Very early in life too, you doubtless had to accept a lot of responsibility, which stopped you from having as much fun as other kids. This is possibly one cause of why you have a somewhat discontented attitude. For you, life is a permanent struggle and, as a result, you can be cold and very cunning. The lack of the support and acceptance you required as a child, and the burden of your early responsibilities, almost certainly drove you to prove yourself to the rest of the world. You are resolute to triumph over whatever reverses you encounter in life, and you are very ambitious as well. Your combination implies tremendous inner strength, determination, and resolve. Your material success is rarely accompanied by emotional satisfaction, but your rise in the world is methodic. You are never happy with your achievements, and you always want more standing, more reputation, and more riches. Your challenge is to have greater concern and human compassion. Do not let a career substitute for love or be an option to everything else in life. Expand and try to appreciate others instead of applying power or position to guard yourself from others. Furthermore, you should attempt to be more understanding and unbiased in your dealings with others. Your stubbornness is mesmerizing and when you meet opposition you do so head on, overcoming your adversaries with level-headedness and sometimes callousness. You are always well prepared, and your mind is reasonable and accurate. Your credo is effectiveness, and centered, creative endeavors are an intrinsic strength. You have a magnificent sense of humor, although very imaginative and generally serious. Consequently, you have a dry liking for the darker and satirical sides of life. Most double Capricorns are attracted to well-planned, ordered professions. You are at ease when risk taking is at a minimum and when you have rules to follow, which makes you well suited for corporate or bureaucratic positions.

SUN IN CAPRICORN/MOON IN AQUARIUS
Whiz Kid

You have a combination of good intelligence, extraordinary intuition, and compelling charm to help you achieve success. You will never be lonely, because your cheerful charm will always draw people to you. You are likely to have many odd and influential friends who are vital to you. You have a very basic conflict in your combination. You have far-ranging and far-out involvements and activities. There is nothing like the ordinary Capricorn about you. You are bothered with the old and worn, so you approach everything with a view to change and innovation, even though you are somber, responsible, and realistic. The uncharted and unknown fascinate you. You also have the bravery to explore new ideas and go down new trails. An Aquarius Moon gives determined Capricorn a solid sense of freedom to go with the Capricorn thirst for status and acclaim. You have an enduring esteem for the past, and you feel you must conform to the influence of culture and parents. All Capricorns feel this. However, your Aquarian inner being gives you an equally firm need to be free and to rebel against conventionality and tradition. You can gain self-assurance and self-esteem by remaining socially active and pursuing an energetic and stimulating professional life. Associating with individuals who can give you emotional support and encourage your plans is important for you. It is just as important that your occupation gives you status and helps boost your satisfaction in yourself. Be careful not to let your vocation take the place of complete emotional satisfaction. Should work turn into everything for you, you may become abrupt and unfeeling even though you actually are very caring. Because your charisma and personality are hard to resist, you have no problem attracting romantic involvement. You may feel a powerful sense of blame, as though somehow you are a deserter whenever you affirm yourself and lead your life according to your own special, independent viewpoint. It would be a waste of your abilities, because you are such a talented and ambitious person, if you decided not to follow your instincts. Your inhibitions are unrealistic, and you have every right to decide on your own unique path to success and self-fulfillment. However, insecurity is often an issue. You probably have vague worries and uncertainties, like all Capricorns, in spite of your informal, self-assured manner. Your Aquarian thoughts can at times multiply this propensity, creating illogical phobias and suspicion.

SUN IN CAPRICORN/MOON IN PISCES
Wizard of Oz

You have many dreams along with the will, practicality, and drive to give form and structure to your goals. You are very career conscious like all Capricorns, and you will work hard to reach some of those ambitions. However, kindness and compassion stop you from resorting to the hostile or immoral behavior, which too often go together with success. On the outside you may be calm, isolated, and unapproachable, but deep within is a very emotional, extremely insightful, and quite perceptive person. You are quite a sensitive Capricorn. That hard facade is just your way of protecting yourself from being hurt. You feel it important to guard your emotions like all sensitive and vulnerable people. Your strength is your imagination. Your ascent in the world will be slow but sure, and you will always take care not to hurt others. Common to the Capricorn-Pisces are unnecessary guilt and confusion. You are very considerate and feel obliged to take care of any minor offense on your part, even if it is imaginary. You have a very active imagination. You have the managerial and practical abilities of Capricorn as well as the metaphysical understanding and lyrical inspiration of Pisces. You are able to move toward things with imagination and suppleness, although you are a practical person. Your compassionate persuasions may draw you to a political or spiritual destination, or your understanding and sensitivity may conduct you to a creative or artistic vocation. Business and economic speculation are possible because of your uncanny instincts. You may feel a bit guilty about your aspirations, but success is important to you. Moreover, you have an inclination to take on the moods and mental issues of those near you, so it is vital that you connect with people who give you emotional balance and support, and avoid individuals who may be harmful to your emotional health. You are devastatingly aware of grief and misfortune in the world and have strong selfless and compassionate feelings. You have a rather gloomy and melancholy viewpoint, which gives you an attraction to the darker side of life. You never have any self-pity, but rather you are inclined to repress your feelings of remorse. You tune in to things at such a profound level that sorrow is often the emotion you feel most powerfully. You have a lot of promise, however.

SUN IN AQUARIUS/MOON IN ARIES
Shoo-In

You desire people to deal with things the way that you do, because you are headstrong and impatient. No matter how bright, flexible, and clever you may be, selfishness and impulsiveness often undermine your efforts. You just have to be your own manager, because teamwork is not your strongest asset. Uneasy, high-strung, and always way ahead of everyone, both mentally and physically, you get mixed up and annoyed when you find that others cannot always maintain your pace. Even though you have imagination, prudence, and innovation, you are not as smart as you think you are. The term that describes you most accurately, in fact, is *individual*. Your manner is sophisticated, and, while you are always nervous about communicating your newest ideas, you have a problem building a relationship with your audience, because your zeal to talk is rarely matched with an eagerness or capacity to listen to others. When you meet what you feel to be ignorance or perplexity, you get worried and annoyed. You believe the best protection is a strong attack. But this tactic usually has the opposite result. To compensate you may adopt a hard offhand manner, and you end up making more foes. While there is a lot that needs to be handled, Aquarius-Aries can be the combination of the visionary dreamer and trailblazer. You have to work on the emotional side of your personality for starters. After that, develop a trust in people. Once you learn to treat others diplomatically and to value what they have to say, there will not be much you cannot accomplish. You are impatient in romance just like you are in everything. Others will judge you a fool as long as you evaluate them so unsympathetically. Be a little more tolerant and understanding if you really want to reach some of those big dreams. An applied scientist, social theorist, or inventor is possible in your future because of your brilliance. Aquarius-Aries are always aimed at the future and can generally be found at the head of their professions, working for progress and change. Being more open to the insights and ideas of others is essential for you to learn. Your intellectual development is ahead of your emotional development. You have a short fuse and are inconsistent, and your anger and indignation can be frightening. You may become unreasonable and unpredictable if you feel threatened. Underlying feelings of uncertainty and insecurity are the cause of this.

SUN IN AQUARIUS/MOON IN TAURUS
Successor

You are a total individualist who sets broad, sweeping goals for yourself. People will follow you anywhere because you are a born leader. You are quite happy to lead them. An Aquarius-Taurus often feels a marked sense of duty to humanity. Some members of this combination include Adlai Stevenson and Ronald Reagan. Your conniving plans are sometimes ostentatious, and some of them are just plain laughable. You can be a hard-nosed and fearsome opponent when challenged, and you are very confident. In your combination, transcendent, idealistic, and caring Aquarius is balanced by sensible, emotionally stable, and secure Taurus. You are somewhat too charming for your own good. Your romanticism and lofty perspective are tempered by astuteness and pragmatism. Your mind is keyed to the theoretical and you enjoy thinking and acting on a grand scale. You are aware of your worth. You are obstinate and will never compromise your ideals, but your beliefs and convictions may change periodically. You are not impulsive like other Aquarians. Before starting on a course of action, you prefer to plan and deliberate, but sometimes you consult the fortune-tellers. Your self-importance and stubbornness can essentially take you over and cause arrogant, self-satisfied, and even obsessive behavior. It is crucial that you learn to be easier going and open to alternative thoughts and opinions. Failing to curb your bias and obstinacy can easily ruin your wonderful plans and dreams. You are friendly and affable socially. Your faithfulness and concern are limitless, and you think of your friends as your brothers and sisters. You are highly superstitious. If it seems rational, because you are determined to put your ambitions into action, you will take a chance. People have a high regard for your self-control and are drawn to your style. No matter how eccentric you can be at times, the confidence that others place in you is justifiable because you are totally trustworthy. If you are not victimized by your own faults, you will be able to achieve a lot in life. You run the risk of becoming too rigid in your positions and demeanor, or foolishly stubborn and biased. When you were young you were experimental, toying with various political theories and lifestyles, but once you decide which are best for you, you stay with them. Having made up your mind about something, you stick to it.

SUN IN AQUARIUS/MOON IN GEMINI
Correspondent

You enjoy toying with theories, ideas, and concepts, even very eccentric ones. You are an intellectual, whether a dabbler or a deep scholar. You also love to examine and explore, and your combination is frequently found in the charts of journalists. Culture and people fascinate you. You are outgoing and amiable. You discover yourself by watching the lives and lifestyles of others. You are attentive, insightful, and particularly mobile. You are a very keen person. Because restlessness and a continuous desire for freshness and excitement keep you on the move, there is not much you have not seen or done. You obtain a worldly wisdom, which is without equal with the experience you gain from your travels, mishaps, and adventures. As a reformer, you frequently become involved in projects and actions that accent modification and innovation. In some way you know just what tomorrow will bring, and intuition is one of your best gifts. However, you live for the future so much that you frequently forget the delights and marvels of the present. You are essentially unemotional but thoughtful to everyone you meet. Because you are wrapped up in your own individuality, it is hard for you to have close emotional ties with anyone. Therefore, regardless of how many friends you have, you will always be a loner. You become bewildered and rattled if you encounter an emotional situation and are never quite sure how to deal with it. Luckily, your happy disposition makes up somewhat for your lack of emotional depth. You are very idealistic, but your compassion is kept for abstracts and ideologies. You are not in the least romantic. You will probably do well with the opposite sex due to your charisma and air of mystery. It is difficult for you to be truly intimate because of your somewhat strong sense of freedom and overall objectivity. Your beguiling and attractive nature is hard to resist and no matter how calm you may seem, you are really happy only when you think all eyes are on you. Worldliness and wit are yours, and somehow you end up getting the attention you think you deserve. Just be cautious that pride does not become an Achilles' heel. Good health, adaptability, and talent are suggested by your combination because it is very harmonious. You may just be gliding along because your life is pretty much free of trouble and inner divergence. If you push yourself to the maximum of your capacities and reject the urge to just get by, it is probable that you will accomplish a great deal in life.

SUN IN AQUARIUS/MOON IN CANCER
Dauntlessness

You always view others as you would view yourself, and you are very aware of your own restrictions and a bit unsure of yourself. You judge others with sympathy, acceptance, and patience. Others sense your honesty and are drawn to your romantic and slightly offbeat approach, so they invariably feel comfortable with you. Your combination is one of the most creative, attractive, and most of all perceptive. It might look as though you are just a detached and remote Aquarian, but beneath that cool, intellectual surface is a very sensitive, understanding, and highly perceptive individual. You have incredible intensity, insight, and instinct. Two of your strengths are empathy and adaptability. You can intuitively understand all sorts of people. You are at home almost anywhere, and there is nothing fake or arrogant about you. There is no limit to your creative imagination. You are capable of reaching your many dreams and goals because you are tuned in. And you have really big dreams. You tend to hold in pain and frustrations ad infinitum, which may cause psychological problems. A great deal, obviously, rests on your early home situation and whether it was secure and emotionally encouraging and helped to develop a positive self-image. However, there is a self-sufficiency available. All Aquarians can get security and a healthy outlook via social activities, no matter what their past is. Your allure and affability almost assures support from friends and mentors later on in life if security was not present in the childhood home. Your inquisitiveness about the world around you is inexhaustible and you are likely to have many pursuits. Aquarius-Cancer combinations include Norman Mailer, Franklin D. Roosevelt, and Clark Gable. A Cancer Moon increases Aquarian incompatibilities and insecurities. For example, men of this combination might attempt to make up for deep-seated fears and hide their emotional vulnerability by taking on a tough, macho exterior. Aquarius-Cancers can simply become eccentric recluses, or that active Cancer imagination can cause a lot of paranoia. While periodic getaways and withdrawal may be important to your emotional health, be careful that it does not become your only reaction to frustration or defeat. In order to fight the more negative expressions of their imaginations, all Cancer-Aquarians should stay active socially.

SUN IN AQUARIUS/MOON IN LEO
Bewildering

Common to every Aquarius-Leo is confusion about who you are or who you should be. However, most finally resolve their difficulties by striking a balance. Instead of denying yourself the rank and authority you long for, you will pursue an ambitious life. Nevertheless, you will always remain thoughtful and sympathetic in your dealings with others. You are a nice individual, a friend to everyone, and you treat others as equals because of your Aquarian nature. However, your Leo inner self is solid, dignified, and controlling. In actuality, you want to be the leader and exercise that authority. You waver between assertiveness and over-accommodation, authority and compliance, and yet you want to be loved and valued by everyone, which often holds you back. The two signs of your combination are totally different in essence and character, which gives you a multifaceted personality with many inner battles. Your combination indicates great force, dedication, and purposefulness as well as a lot of intelligence. You are always unsure of whether to rely on your heart or your mind, and decision making may be hard for you. As with all Aquarians, you see things from a separate, intellectual perspective. However, because your Leo inner nature is very emotional, your heart nearly always has the last word in your life. Many Aquarius-Leos are attracted to the metaphysical and occult and are frequently members of religious cults offering instant salvation. Your extraordinary imagination and self-governing spirit need a constructive outlet for expression. Both of your signs are fixed signs so you must be careful that obstinacy, arrogance, and bigotry do not stand in the way of your path to success. Like all Leos, you long for admiration and attention and you have a strong sense of the theatrical, but your sporadic ostentation and kookiness are often funny. You are prone to behaving on sudden, random hunches because you are impulsive. Unfortunately this often turns out to be catastrophic. Finally, through trial and error, you do well in anything you try, even though you are forgetful and absentminded. You do learn from experience. *Dedication* is one of your preferred words. Devoted and honest, you are not happy until you have mastered whatever you do. Your youth was probably a disaster or limited in some way. Senseless revolt and inner chaos, especially in your youth, may have been the result.

SUN IN AQUARIUS/MOON IN VIRGO
Examiner

Your Virgo Moon provides a fundamental sense of obligation, responsibility, and competence. You tend to hold your affections back for big causes and for humanity as a whole, because you are drawn to the conceptual. Your combination is perfect for medicine, social work, or anything where you need to remain objective relative to the suffering, providing services with reason and detachment. While you share being tolerant, thoughtful, and friendly with other Aquarians, you are also very distant. Your objectivity is one of your strong points. While you are sensitive, you are essentially a thinker, and your ability to calmly detach yourself from your surroundings allows you to see things dispassionately. Your powers of scrutiny and insight are matchless. Sadly, a lot of Aquarius-Virgos examine themselves and everyone else straight out of existence. Life is mental rather than the heart and soul for you. You favor the rational approach to life far away from emotional issues. You have a very deep sense of duty. All of those with a Moon in Virgo find their greatest fulfillment in working hard. Keeping active with outside projects is essential for you. Psychosomatic issues can result from overwork or overexposure to tense or stressful situations. Form and structure to Aquarian inspiration and idealism come for the Virgo Moon. Wonderful creative expressions are possible from some individuals because of their intellectual prowess. Gertrude Stein and James Joyce are two examples of Aquarius-Virgos. Romance is not your thing in a relationship, because your emotional reserve curbs intimacy.

You are a faithful, generous, devoted partner on the positive side. Your combination has a lot of people who go through life feeling somewhat disaffected from those around them but who are bright and creative. Hazy beliefs of superiority might cause you to have a conceited or superior attitude. Avoid insulating yourself behind a barrier of intellectual aloofness and relate to all kinds of people. Because you are so insightful you may become very critical, uptight, and easily disgruntled when things do not live up to your expectations. Accuracy and precision are your goals, but do not let them dominate you. A more broad-minded and accepting outlook needs developing, or you will undergo a lot of stress.

SUN IN AQUARIUS/MOON IN LIBRA
Utopian

You treat everyone with acceptance, respect, and kindness, and most people respond well. You believe in the fundamental goodness of humanity. Admiration and appreciation are the results of your optimistic approach to life. Even though you are trusting and pleasant, confusion takes over when you learn that not everyone possesses your standards of honesty. You are a bit unruffled and detached. Nevertheless, you have a lot of allure and magnetism in your combination. Your resourcefulness and innovation are focused on dreamy, social, and artistic enterprises. You are comparatively free of psychological issues, because you state everything you perceive with complete openness and frankness. You are a very symmetrical combination, and all your many talents can find constructive expression. Moreover, you are very optimistic. Others more astute and crafty pass you by in life, and you probably find yourself watching this uncomprehendingly. You have high ideals, but not everyone else does. You need to develop a more pragmatic viewpoint. Your nature is a dichotomy because while you love stillness and inner peace, you are also very high-strung and feel a regular desire to be active. Therefore, your requirement for harmony can be elusive. One of your best assets is your imagination. Your mind is very visual and you have a very active fantasy life. Just do not lose yourself completely to fantasy. The source of many unreasonable fears might be your overworked imagination. On the other hand, if given the correct focal point and discipline your imagination can be successfully applied in a lot of artistic and creative activities, chiefly music. Human relations work might also be something you would like. A socially oriented person is the result of your combination. Friends are critically important to you, and your social atmosphere often determines your self-image. You should be able to have a positive self-image if you have strong and supportive relationships. Tension and conflict really upset your emotional well-being because you are a peace-loving individual. Attempt to be in a work and home situation that is as free of stress as can be. You need to get away sometimes for self-contemplation and meditation. In your frenetic social involvements you can nearly completely lose your essence and individuality. Refrain from being involved so much with others, and give yourself some time.

SUN IN AQUARIUS/MOON IN SCORPIO
Free Spirit

You will not be told what to do or how to handle your life. Regardless of the number of mistakes, the responsibility is all yours in the end. Rarely listening to the counsel of others, you follow your distinctive path in life. However, your obstinate pride can be your ruin because there is a fundamental clash in your combination. You always leave an enduring and forceful feeling on those you encounter. You are a bit too charismatic for it to be a plus in your character. The impression you leave will be either great or awful, because there is nothing middle-of-the-road about you. Actually, extremism is the most significant trait of the Aquarius-Scorpio. Stubbornness is your negative, but you have very strong needs, unbelievable determination, and a huge respect for your own freedom. Your Scorpio Moon is sharp and a bit self-centered, but an Aquarius Sun gives you powerful compassion and a need to serve society. Thus you are never certain whether to just work toward fulfilling your own desires or follow the call of your lofty ideals. Most Aquarius-Scorpios decide to fulfill the demands of their egos, and frequently guilt is the consequence. As with all those with a Moon in Scorpio, you are always evolving and have the facility to come back from defeat. There is a marked sense of mission and strong creative brilliance in some very evolved Aquarius-Scorpios. It is entirely possible for a Scorpio Moon to strengthen, inspire, and uplift Aquarians. This can lead to a humanism that produces innovative scientists, thinkers, or reformers. But first, materialism must be conquered. You want comfort and acknowledgment above all, but in chasing your goals and dreams you may lose perspective, becoming selfish and even cruel. While you are willing to experiment and are flexible, your Scorpio Moon gives you innate prejudices and entrenched beliefs. Some of them are a bit wild. You can become puzzled and irate when you note that others do not share them. Your signs are both fixed signs, which says that when things get difficult, rather than be flexible, you are more likely to break and take out your anger on others. Developing a more relaxed and, especially, tolerant viewpoint is important. Emotional inflexibility and a sanctimonious attitude are not productive. The good news is, you have the capability to renew yourself.

SUN IN AQUARIUS/MOON IN SAGITTARIUS
Aesthete

While academically inclined, you think that experience is the best teacher and results the best kind of knowledge. You prefer to learn and create your own worlds and ideals instead of relying on the established or the academic. You have a desire for exploring the globe, especially when you were young and your desire for independence reached its summit. Settling down and utilizing your talents does not come easily. The hardest choice for you is to give actual expression to some of those visions of the future by focusing your talents in a single direction. You are tolerant and fond of the unusual as well as very self-sufficient and imaginative. You enjoy the theoretical and the philosophical, and you are a deep thinker. Your combination can result in the irresponsible drifter, happy to roam from one new experience to another, always trying new things, but never learning anything. Inspiration is the essence of your being, but regrettably yours is not always in the realm of practical reality. You get bored with the old and you always look for innovation and exploration. There are many dilettantes in the unique combination of Aquarius-Sagittarius. You are admirable and meticulous, but any obligation to study or work too frequently feels like a burden. This makes it extremely hard for you to develop the control and commitment necessary to accomplish anything meaningful. You attract people to you because of your positive viewpoint and your informal, irreverent manner. Because you are eccentric some may believe you a bit odd, like all Aquarians. Furthermore, some of your more alternative interests may seem a little bizarre to the majority of people. You are not especially interested in the mainstream or conventional. Because you prefer it that way you will always choose your own way. You are a dreamer and a romantic in matters of the heart. Furthermore your inquisitiveness relative to the opposite sex is endless. Consequently, you will surely have a lot of affairs. Your independent nature is commendable and attests to your courage, but it is important for you to understand how to adapt to life's realities. The rebelliousness may last late into life, and finally all that nonconformity may seem like it was just self-interest. There is little you cannot achieve if you can learn to check that propensity. Members of your combination include Charles Lindbergh, Charles Dickens, and Mozart. The Sagittarius Moon can raise up the original imagination and innovation of Aquarius and bring about a very creative and groundbreaking individual. That is possible in politics, the arts, or the sciences.

SUN IN AQUARIUS/MOON IN CAPRICORN
Latest Style Blazer

You always work to create new forms of expression and application, even though you are formal and conventional and have an enduring respect for custom. Not many can match you for pure wit and persuasiveness, and you are a formidable debater. One of your biggest strengths is cold logic. You are an excellent analyst, philosopher, and administrator because of your ability to coolly separate yourself from your emotions and see things objectively. You are sociable, alluring, and enthusiastic like your fellow Aquarians, but you are essentially removed and extremely autonomous. Individualism is your credo. You are a strong believer in the rights and dignity of the individual. You believe that you reap what you sow. A sensible, determined Capricorn Moon together with the Aquarian imagination and prudence grounds you. You have a look about you that suggests genius or, for some, insanity. You never lose your fundamental stability and practicality no matter how enthused you may be. Thomas Edison, Abraham Lincoln, and Charles Darwin are famous Aquarius-Capricorns. Self-respect is part of your character. In addition, you are inventive and fearless about expressing your beliefs and views. You believe the individual is completely accountable for himself and the flaws of others can consequently make you impatient. Nevertheless, you do have deep humanitarian persuasions. You are not mean or heartless. Because you are so independent and secure it is hard for you to comprehend individuals who have psychological problems. Tolerance is something you must learn. More compassion is needed toward those who do not share your gifts. Ambitiousness and the craving for recognition can become all-powerful in some Aquarius-Capricorns. Prejudice or emotion rarely color your views, and you draw your conclusions exactingly from observation. Unfortunately though, once you have determined your positions, you become stuck to them forever. Fanaticism, in some Aquarius-Capricorns' convictions can sometimes come into play. You are extroverted socially. You never lose that aura of isolation even though you are charismatic and pleasant, and this sets you apart. People know that under that bright, cheerful facade is determination you keep hidden. Friendship, as with all Aquarians, is fundamental to you. You are shrewd in choosing friends, however, and prefer those who can help to improve your status and image.

SUN IN AQUARIUS/MOON IN AQUARIUS
Iconoclast

Your interests range from living among native peoples, decoding ancient secrets, or looking through a microscope. Because in your quests you may really discover something, which wins you recognition, there is a good chance you will succeed. Frequently though, double Aquarians become so mired in their unusual pursuits that they begin to lose touch with reality. Or, on occasions, their discoveries are just so futurist that the rest of the world does not value them until many years later. An Aquarius-Aquarius can often be spotted by that distant sparkle in their eyes, and enthrallment is the key to their character. The unusual, the unnoticed, and the untested are things you are alert to. You are always lost in thought with some new, burning interest and are high-strung and very energetic. Your inquisitiveness and taste for the exotic are voracious. You have a special type of intuition together with considerable intelligence and imagination. You always look toward the future and somehow seem to know what it will bring; this holds true even in the distant future. But you do tend to be somewhat inconsistent and unclear. Your concentration and enthusiasm usually weaken quickly even though you start a project with total dedication. Friends are wary when talking to the thrill-seeking and unpredictable double Aquarius. Your biggest issue is to find something that will focus and hold your interest. There is an impulsive aspect about you that can be totally frightening and can cause people to keep their distance. The fact is that you are an odd person and will not change anytime soon. People who cannot accept this will be sadly disappointed. You are attracted to work that permits a lot of freedom and independence and satisfies your never-ending curiosity. Accepting your own uniqueness can perhaps help people find it easier to be comfortable around you. Professionally, science and reporting are fields that might interest a double Aquarius. You are insecure about yourself in spite of your magnetic and extroverted personality. It is vital that you have many assorted, interesting associations, because friends are important to you. And *associations* is the correct term: it is almost impossible for you to become actually intimate with anyone because you are so detached. By the same token it is nearly impossible for you to hate someone, because you like to be a "friend" to everyone. Others are drawn to you because you are unique and your charm is unusual, but some of your more eccentric characteristics and extreme independence can also rebuff them.

SUN IN AQUARIUS/MOON IN PISCES
True Believer

You are a very kind and helpful person and are able to identify and sympathize with almost everybody. Your innocent soul is humble, generous, and sensitive. You know the difference between right and wrong because you have an innate sense of integrity and wisdom. But your spirituality is not always synchronized with pragmatic common sense. You have no cunning or shrewdness and are completely trusting. Your faith in other is total, and you would be eaten alive if other people were not so kind to you. Fortunately, people never fail to respond in a positive way to your innocence. There is a dreamy look that the Aquarius-Pisces have, and it seems they have just woken up and do not know where they are. This approach is used in everything, as though existence is carried on in several dimensions. If you see the entire world at once you get mixed up because you cannot really separate the parts. It is possible a religious path might be for you because you are quite spiritual. Some Aquarius-Pisces are even drawn to the monastic life. Furthermore, you may be especially tuned in to the occult and the mysterious. More mainstream people find this quite odd about you. Sri Rama Krishna, the founder of the Vedanta Society, represents a very evolved Aquarius-Pisces. Your imagination is strong, and you have a very visual mental framework. Given the right motivation and teaching, you might be an artist or other creative entrepreneur. However, you must acquire some direction and discipline from others to be successful. Without this you are a ship with no rudder to guide you to your destination. You are a sponge for the stress or feelings around your environment. That is a strong influence on you. Meditating, reading, or listening to music from time to time is good for you. However, you must be careful that isolation does not take you away from involvement with others. High technology or heavy competition is not suited for you as a career. Involve yourself in a profession where you can use your compassionate and humanitarian feelings. Or perhaps think in terms of using your powerful clairvoyant skills. Because of your detached character, people might think that you are uncaring. Aquarian detachment may lead others to believe that you are not very sensitive, but the opposite is actually true.

SUN IN PISCES/MOON IN ARIES
Dark Horse

You are nice, charitable, and sympathetic, especially to yourself. You are always looking out for your own interests first, and you have a high regard for yourself. It is not a matter of thinking others are unimportant, rather that you are just more important. Ease and a lot of security are what you want from life, and your extraordinary intuition says you will have it. A surface that is reserved and shy hides your true intensity and ambition. You have the impulsive energy and drive of Aries plus the sensitivity and compassion of Pisces. It surprises people when you drop your modest appearance to become frank and decisive. You are not naive even though you appear to be a babe in the woods. Actually, you are a very autonomous and self-sufficient individual. You know how to get your way with charisma and delicate persuasion because you are sly, shrewd, and subtle. This is particularly true of the female Pisces-Aries. You know automatically whom to trust and whom to pass by, because of your amazing sixth sense. You are very impulsive as are all Moons in Aries people, and you love pleasure. Taking chances just for the fun of it may be what you love, but it might also bring you trouble. Curb your impatience and learn to slow down now and then. Your Pisces character is rather inhibited, so when the time comes for action you may be indecisive, but your Aries Moon gives you big aspirations and a need to assert yourself. In addition, not desiring to exceed those who are weaker than you are, maybe you feel a bit guilty about aggressive behavior. Others do not have to pay the price of self-fulfillment, however. It would be good to learn this. Your Sun-Moon combination is favorable to leadership jobs, especially in charitable and service-oriented groups. A career in medicine or engineering, in addition, is possible because of your keen, perceptive mind. You have an emotionally charged Aries inner character, so you could become a productive artist, and your Pisces vision and creative facility are improved by self-expression. Your quick mind, appeal, and flexibility unite to help assure your success once those inhibitions have been defeated. Your real kindness of spirit and consideration will bloom after you have attended to your own needs. Your sympathy is forever with the underdog, and you have strong protective instincts. Do not become condescending though, because for some Pisces-Aries, helping people can just be an ego enhancement.

SUN IN PISCES/MOON IN TAURUS
Virtuoso

You will not be used by others. Hopefully your sensible Taurus Moon will help your Piscean dreams and lyrical visions. You have a vibrant, visual resourcefulness, which can be put to use in very creative ways, and your combination has seen a lot of writers, artists, and musicians. But you may also keep your banal aspect because of the same Taurus Moon, which gives you such an experienced perspective. You have an inner tranquillity and peace of mind that people find convincing and compelling. While you seem to be the typical Pisces who is responsive, thoughtful, and otherworldly, beneath that humble exterior is the firmness, willpower, and common sense of Taurus. You are understanding and conscientious, always willing to lend a helping hand like other Pisces, but you also value yourself, and consequently you know when to say no. You are very determined, and whatever you start to do in life you go about with total devotion and promise. The true abilities of Pisces-Taurus are often not used in their chosen careers. They need something challenging. An easy life attracts you because you are leisure oriented. You will have good health and stability. Consequently, regardless of how far your imagination takes you, you manage to get back unharmed every time. Others sense your wisdom and frequently turn to you for advice. In addition, you have a magnificent inner confidence, but, like all natives of Moon in Taurus, you have a propensity to hold on stubbornly to viewpoints and first impressions. You may seem to be very far-out, or actually be far-out, but you are essentially a conservative. You must attempt to curb some of your prejudices and dug-in attitudes. Lighten up on some of those emotional beliefs and be more tolerant. And while you are at it, do not forget to express some real feelings. What is needed is a more relaxed and open approach to your life. Your emotions can get out of control at times because you are very sentimental. This can cause you to lose your vision and your usually good judgment. A lot of Pisces-Tauruses are so sentimental that they live in the past. There is a big attraction to relax and enjoy the memory of a job well done. While it is okay to be proud of past achievements, you must also learn to live more in the present.

SUN IN PISCES/MOON IN GEMINI
Crafty Rascal

You are very charming in your sly manner, and a great comedian. You acquire friends very easily and need them because, after all, you may need help getting out of the problems you are always having. Another thing you need is your intuition, which also helps you get by. The fact is that although you are clever, you just lack common sense. Scheming is one of your avocations. You change yourself so often that it is hard for people to know the real you because you are more like three or four people than one. A good intelligence, astonishing intuition, and cleverness come from your combination. You are a great character-player, award-winning actor, and con artist above all else. Your wits will take you far in life. You know just what people want, and you are bright and very flexible. You will play any role just to give others what they desire. You never stop moving, and your Gemini Moon provides that restless and feisty nature. On average you might have a dozen ideas, inventions, or ostentatious projects in the works, but you are so flighty that it is unusual for one of them to be completed. Indecisiveness and indecision curse the Pisces-Gemini. Setting an objective or expressing your convictions is hard for you. You are never certain if your latest idea is yours, or if you have unintentionally gotten it from someone else. This is because you are so impressionable. The question you often ask yourself is where are you going. You need to establish your own identity. Deep introspection is great, but the key is to be more disciplined. Cultivate a little patience and control your edgy spirit. Clarify your objectives and stick to them. You are inconsistent in romance, as in all things, and generally have several affairs in progress at once. You truly fall for whoever is nearest. Your actions can at times be very cold and heartless even though you have a bighearted nature. The path is clear to a successful love relationship after you have become more contented with your own individuality. You need to be in an ordered working and living atmosphere. Most importantly, be sure that those around you are positive for you, because you soak up the texture and mood of your environment. Do not get near con artists or unpredictable people. You are a conceptual individual, and your solution to a problem is frequently the most innovative. A lot of your tactics and thoughts are in fact quite resourceful. You must work with a person who has the levelheadedness to bring some of them to completion. There is no telling what you may achieve together in the event you connect with such an associate.

SUN IN PISCES/MOON IN CANCER
Homesteader

You have almost limitless potential talents. Drive is the only thing that is lacking in you. Your difficulty is not one of inner divergence but the nonexistence of it. You are somewhat complacent. There is almost a perfect flow of the elements in your combination. The momentum to attain and to develop your abilities must be refined. If it is not, you settle for second best. The comfortable and the certain satisfy you too easily. Your sensitivity allows you to adapt effortlessly to almost any circumstance without losing yourself in the procedure, and you intuitively know what is needed and what must be done to gain security and contentment. Your combination indicates serenity, emotional balance, and self-reliance. Many excellent artists, dancers, and musicians come from this combination because it is one of the most creative. In difficult times you may be an outstanding survivor, but you do not have the needed vitality to exploit your opportunities when your life is going well. There is great attraction to give up a hopeful career for home and family for a female Pisces-Cancer. The incentive to accomplish often fades early for the male of this combination. Maintaining a disciplined and dynamic life is the challenge for Pisces-Cancer. Long-lasting and rewarding goals should be what you attempt to attain. You can be a permanent dreamer or attain great success. It is up to you. You should have no difficulty in your love life because you are very romantic. There is one exception though: conquering shyness. Your charisma and elegance captivate and hold members of the opposite sex, once you have overcome this timidness. There is no need to quit, no matter how tempted you may be. Involve yourself with individuals who are strongly motivated and fashion an environment that is powerful and demanding. Through the right associations you can obtain the inner drive to completely realize your creative talents. Be careful you do not fall into a martyr role. Your defense mechanisms may already be in use, and you could be thinking of everything you sacrificed your talent for. Incapable of accepting the responsibility for their situation, the Pisces-Cancer can spend a lifetime in self-pity. Keep in mind, there are grand possibilities within you and the sky is the limit.

SUN IN PISCES/MOON IN LEO
Eccentric

You have powerful creative and leadership abilities, as do all natives of Moon in Leo. You cast an image that is trustworthy and self-assured, and occasionally bullying. People sense that you are capable of great things if you are just given the opportunity. Actually you do have the strength, charisma, and imagination to make a success, but several issues stand in your way. For starters, your basic Piscean doubt and reserve often stop you from rising to a position of power or influence. You want your dress, mannerisms, and modus vivendi to reflect your unique, imaginative personality, and so at a party you are typically the most colorful and flamboyant person there. You are not, however, ostentatious or arrogant. You just have quite a personality. You are different and irreverent and known for your frankness, warmth, and fantastic sense of humor. The Leo Moon provides the usually introverted and timid Pisces a very strong sense of independence and purpose. A dramatic and unusual person is the result. You back off when the opportunity comes to use an advantage or grasp a prospect. Most of that audacity and clout is just a show, no matter how confident and self-assured you may appear. You are a great performer. You may experience nervousness and dissatisfaction with yourself when you discover that you cannot follow up on some of those high-flying plans of yours. Be careful not to develop an attitude of acquiescence. Most of your fearfulness is in your mind, and you just have to learn to get rid of those deep-seated insecurities. While others are teaching you, discovering yourself can happen. Be careful about systematizing and categorizing your thinking, because you can be very inflexible at times and even fanatical. You tend to adhere obstinately to your opinions. You must struggle to keep your mind open. Sadly, Pisces-Leo is a very stubborn individual. The challenge for the Pisces-Leo is to dare and to take chances. Do not evade responsibility and challenges that might give you the status and achievement you want. Instead meet them head on. You are essentially egocentric, but you appear demonstrative and friendly. Some Pisces-Leos reside in their own world and view things through rose-colored glasses. This propensity handicaps your capability to learn and at times colors your judgment. Do not shut yourself down.

SUN IN PISCES/MOON IN VIRGO
Compulsive Purist

Early in life you were most likely somewhat self-conscious and inhibited. As you grew older, you slowly gained more confidence. Your Virgo Moon provided you with an astute, sensible, and careful viewpoint. All working to your advantage in life are intelligence, practicality, and almost psychic intuition. In some way you know with certainty who is trustworthy and who to avoid completely. You have a deep sense of accountability and a strong work ethic, because—in all probability—as a child you shouldered more than your portion of obligations. You are a bit too painstaking for your own good. You have an inner core of flexibility and determination that enables you to handle adversity in life with calm forbearance, and you are much more self-directed and tough than your fellow Pisces. By nature you are very shy and reserved. For the devoted and moral Pisces-Virgo guilt is often the curse. Your conscience is huge, and you believe that any misconduct, real or unreal, must be dealt with. You have an innate sense of justice. A little too easily you take on the burdens of those closest to you. Your ethics are commendable, but taken to an extreme they can bring on neurosis and asceticism. Do not sacrifice yourself for the sake of others. You find comfort and satisfaction in your work, as with all Moon in Virgo natives. Stress and anxiety often plague the Pisces-Virgo. Because you are so sensitive, you too easily soak up the tensions and bad feelings of the people near you, especially those in your work situation. It is critical that you get plenty of relaxation because of your low tolerance for stress. Time away for meditation and introspection is a wise move. Your desire to help people can be applied creatively in a lot of fields, and you have strong humanitarian instincts. Doctors, clergy, and public servants are common in your combination. You generally know which romantic partner is best for you because of your good intuition. You are always devoted and genuine, and your sense of duty is part of a need to feel desired. Your work should not be everything. You are at risk of becoming a workaholic because you are industrious by nature. Outside interests and activities need to be developed. You are enormously hard on yourself. You fall into depression when you discover that you cannot hold up the perfectionist standards you set for yourself.

SUN IN PISCES/MOON IN LIBRA
Equanimity

The arts appeal to you. You are most likely a very creative person because you have an exact comprehension of form, beauty, and aesthetics. Your romantic soul extends to all things. Nat King Cole, Frederic Chopin, and Rudolf Nureyev are natives of your combination. Your spiritual nature enables you to experience great joy. For example, you can experience awe over hearing a bird sing. On the other hand, your refined emotions can also be a problem. People respond well to your soft-spoken kindness, and you have an aura of peace. In your combination the gentle, peace-loving, romantic Libra enhances the emotional strength, appeal, and sensitivity of Pisces. The secret to your combination is devotion. Once you have set your goals in life, few can match you for commitment and determination. You are also agonizingly aware of the rougher realities of life just as you are connected to the finer things. For a lot of Pisces-Libras reality can be quite hard to deal with. Your unusual imagination might be put to use facing life's problems. That way you choose to escape reality. Possibly you just pick the path of least resistance and select a profession that offers little challenge or reward. A woman will be tempted by an expedient marriage; one that gives shelter from the world. We all need comfort and security, but we should not settle for less to get it. Do not waste the many natural endowments and gifts you have. Your main demand in your life and work is tranquillity. Your emotional balance can be upset by tension, and this will cause you to go back in your shell. It is vital that your life and work environment be equally peaceful even though your combination is conducive to inner harmony. In many ways you are the ideal partner because you are extremely romantic and capable of getting lost in love. In a relationship you know how to balance the give-and-take. Do not let your partner make all your decisions and become overbearing or controlling. You need a relationship based on equality. You are a nice and sharing individual, but be careful of being used by others. You are not happy unless those around you are. It is very possible that you are sacrificing your own happiness for others. There is nothing wrong with being a bit more selfish and self-assertive. Needless guilt is frequently an issue for the Pisces-Libra. It is absurd for you to feel guilty just because you are standing up for yourself.

SUN IN PISCES/MOON IN SCORPIO
Cyclone

You enjoy deep exploration into whatever you find. Even the most ordinary matter can take on cosmic and meaningful implications for some Pisces-Scorpios. You have a far-reaching and powerful imagination. Your mind is always active, taking things in and forming impressions of everything no matter how still or modest you may seem. You have to deal with many difficulties like all serious, emotional people. Pisces can be lifted up and given focus by the emotional strength, passion, and regenerating qualities of a Scorpio Moon. You are high powered, sober, and introspective. You are a very philosophical individual who is never content with external impressions. The dazzling heights of consciousness you reach based on that same emotional power can also pull you to the depths of misery and regret. This combination can create very neurotic, criminally inclined individuals, or it can result in spiritual and creative individuals. Charismatic, strong-minded, and apparently your own boss, you are, however, heavily influenced by your environment. You cling stubbornly to old ways of behaving, and your initial responses are too frequently your only ones. This combination has vast possibilities; however, if you do not utilize your creative possibilities constructively, you might turn all that fervor and energy in on yourself. Unleashing it on others is possible, and this can open the way to cruel or malicious behavior. Be careful of excesses of any sort, especially in romance, as in all things, because there is also the hidden possibility of addiction in your combination. The character of the Pisces-Scorpio is often prejudiced and stubborn. Furthermore, you have an extremely sensual, indulgent nature, and enjoyment seeking can effortlessly become the opponent of the Pisces-Scorpio. To help you direct some of your abilities and to keep your emotions within bounds, you need lots of organization, discipline, and educational training. There is no end to what you can do if your powerful sensual drives can be channeled into creative or spiritual pursuits. Direction is the key here. You take the slightest criticism as an affront. You are very touchy. Try to be a little less single-minded and become more tolerant. Do not focus so much on yourself, but turn your energies outward. It is not unusual to find yourself by losing yourself first.

SUN IN PISCES/MOON IN SAGITTARIUS
Sophist

You will probably travel the world because of your craving for adventure and novelty. You are under the power of your luck because you are a bit fearless. You believe completely in your good fortune and rightfully so, because it always comes through for you. Your greatest resource is faith. The farsighted Sagittarian Moon enhances the inspired intuitive and poetic imagination of Pisces. You are always fresh and appealing, and your optimism and enthusiasm are boundless. Extremely bright, your mind likes the theoretical, the spiritual, and the philosophical. You set high goals for yourself, and you have versatile, creative, and artistic talents. Both in spirit and in thought, liberty is the thing you crave most, and this makes you a very inventive and tolerant individual. Victor Hugo, Albert Einstein, and Maxim Gorky are some outstanding natives of your combination. Your charm is very innocent and brings out the protective feelings of others. You are an idealist and lover of life, like most Pisces-Sagittarius. You think this is the best of all possible worlds, even if others do not agree. You are, for some reason, in a constant state of confusion. Kierkegaard or Nietzsche are not a problem for you, but your checkbook is because you cannot balance it. There is not a pragmatic bone in your body—you reside in a world of ideas and impressions, and the ordinary details of life just annoy you. However, you do have a keen intuition that manages to move you away from dangers. You have a huge faculty for happiness and are always an optimist. You see nothing but a sunny future for yourself. It is possible that you can fool yourself into thinking that things are better than they really are. Rather than handle them head on, the Pisces-Sagittarius often tunes out issues and difficulties, and certainly this can cause more problems. As might be expected, you are not the business type. Organization and structure are critical for your work and home life because you have a tendency to drift about. If you hope to apply yourself, your intellectual talent and imagination need a foundation and structure. Without this, your dreams could remain only dreams. Associate with individuals who are strong willed and have a positive effect on you, because you are very suggestible and gullible. There is little you are unable to achieve after you have gotten the proper training and focus. There is nothing traditional about you, and thus everything you do is, in a sense, original and aimed at change.

SUN IN PISCES/MOON IN CAPRICORN
Nonbeliever

You are very conscious of your limitations like all Moon in Capricorn natives, but perhaps too much so. You brood instead of valuing your abilities, and you think about your imperfections, even if they are imaginary, which they frequently are. You think of things you are unable to do rather than envisioning the wonderful things at which you can succeed. Pisces-Capricorns have a fixed pessimism and cynicism, which is their curse. You have the very sophisticated depth to be successful in highly creative ventures, but your gloomy approach to life might restrain you. While you are a very sensitive person, you are more tuned in to the depressing and miserable parts of life. The result is a melancholy and negative philosophy of life. Your unlimited Piscean imagination is imprisoned by a Capricorn inner nature that is careful and old-fashioned. While you show an image that is worldly and self-confident, you are actually not as confident as you appear. Beginning in your youth, you probably had to deal with a lot of fear and uncertainty. As you grew older, in order to balance your insecurity, you devoted much of your energy to your career. You will eventually become your own boss, or at the least go very far, through your resolve and determination. You will never be the dictator type, regardless of how far your drives take you. In fact, kindness and sympathy are traits that Pisces-Capricorns are well known for. Your approach to love is unconventional. Capricorn coolness stops you from giving everything in a relationship, but you also want to be romantic and have that faraway look. Until you have found a person who makes you feel secure, it will be hard to have true intimacy. Your unusual situation will continue until that happens. You have to first understand how to love and appreciate yourself, of course, before true love is possible. In the end, it will happen for you and perhaps that hidden romantic can surface. An organized, conventional framework is where you work best. You still need to have structure in your life and work in spite of your independence and self-sufficiency. Especially in business matters you have an excellent intuitive awareness of people, which is a big advantage. Being freer about your feelings is one thing you should learn. It is okay to open up and share them once in a while. When you keep in your resentments, frustrations, or tensions, depression often enters the picture.

SUN IN PISCES/MOON IN AQUARIUS
Sparkplug

Your nature is sober and reserved, and you cannot stand showiness. You are compulsively truthful and thorough, and you value and respect loyalty and sincerity in others. There is a wisdom and deep understanding of human nature revealed in your eyes. You project your sympathy and concern for people to the entire world. The social reformer, the fervent missionary, and the revolutionary are members of this combination. Moreover, your interest in science and the mysterious urges you to press the borders of human knowledge. The result of this mixture of signs can be confusing. In your combination the intellectual inquisitiveness, peculiarity, and social concern of Aquarius is paired with the deep kindness and compassion of Pisces. You have a bearing that suggests you are from the distant past. You have totally changeable moods. You might gaze off into space at a party, or look like you just arrived from the twilight zone. But if your musings are interrupted, you do not miss a beat. Your password is experimentation. You glide easily through a wide range of concepts and pursuits, until you find the one that suits you best. Once you have discovered your specialty, whether in science or the occult, you fixate on it with resolve and an extraordinary sense of mission. Your moods need to be gotten under control for any kind of happiness. It is a mystery to you why anyone would desire all the attention that love involves. Your mate in life is treated equally, but like a friend or coworker. It is consequently critical that your partner understand your intellectual and eccentric activities. Because you are known for your patience and ability to forgive and forget, you are an easy person to get along with. The issue of finding the right person is very critical here. You can be charming and funny one moment, then suddenly go totally silent the next. Maybe the most important part of your life, even though you do not acknowledge it, is people. You do not like the idea of frightening them off with your erratic and at times illogical behavior. You want a feeling of camaraderie with a lot of people of both genders. The opposite sex is probably captivated by your otherworldly allure, innocence, and transcendental presence. People in general are more meaningful to you than are individuals, so you do not have much time for a romance with any single person.

SUN IN PISCES/MOON IN PISCES
Visionary

Things that others cannot understand, natives of your combination have an intuitive understanding of; they experience their environment on a level that is very delicate, almost awe-inspiring. With their marked spiritual gifts and empathy, they cannot handle seeing suffering. You are mysterious and carry this with you. You are not totally from this planet and are a tremendously sensitive and vulnerable soul. You are almost free of cunning, malice, or deceit. You are innocent, unquestioning, and conscientious, and all of this makes you very vulnerable. You are saved by intuition, and it is almost your only defense. Without it, your innocence would leave you open to too much adversity. Practically as though guided by a guardian angel, you always seem to know just when to charge and when to withdraw, who to trust and who to avoid. Other worlds concern you more than this one. Because your imagination is intense, Pisces-Pisces finds it hard to differentiate between fantasy and reality at times. You are a very self-examining person with a lot of sympathy. If people thought you were self-centered and worldly when you were young, it was because you were so fearful of not having the comfort and security that you grabbed all the material possessions you could gather. In fact, you will always have everything you need to get along in life, because your allure and refinement assure that. You find it difficult to concentrate. Your mind tends to drift off in daydreams and fantasies because you are so sensitive and emotionally open to your environment that you need to remove yourself at times. All of a sudden, while working on a meaningful project, or in the middle of a serious discussion, your eyes will fade out of focus and you will be right in the middle of some captivating trance and out of contact. You must have some technical training and find some discipline if your artistic potential is ever to be realized. The male may be drawn to a job that offers permanence while the female Pisces-Pisces is frequently interested in the security and shelter of an early marriage. They must both fight the urge to withdraw from society and this is important for both the male and female double Pisces. You may find it hard to adjust to the business of the contemporary world because you are shy and vulnerable. But you always have your intuition to guide you. Creative and artistic talents are usually obvious even though strong ambition and drive are not visible in the double Pisces. Your mind is highly visual and powerful. Michelangelo, an artist known to the world, was a double Pisces.

MOON CHARTS 1940–2030

1940

Jan.	Feb.	Mar.	Apr.	May	June	July	Aug.	Sep.	Oct.	Nov.	Dec.
1 Lib	2 Sag	2 Cap	1 Aqr	1 Pis	2 Tau	2 Gem	3 Leo	1 Vir	2 Sco	1 Sag	3 Aqr
3 Sco	4 Cap	7 Pis	3 Pis	3 Ars	4 Gem	4 Can	5 Vir	3 Lib	4 Sag	3 Cap	5 Pis
6 Sag	5 Aqr	10 Ars	6 Ars	6 Tau	7 Can	6 Leo	7 Lib	5 Sco	6 Cap	5 Aqr	7 Ars
8 Cap	9 Pis	12 Tau	8 Tau	8 Gem	9 Leo	8 Vir	9 Sco	7 Sag	9 Aqr	7 Pis	10 Tau
10 Aqr	11 Ars	15 Gem	11 Gem	10 Can	11 Vir	10 Lib	11 Sag	10 Cap	11 Pis	10 Ars	13 Gem
13 Pis	14 Tau	17 Can	13 Can	13 Leo	13 Lib	13 Sco	13 Cap	12 Aqr	14 Ars	13 Tau	15 Can
15 Ars	16 Gem	19 Leo	15 Leo	15 Vir	15 Sco	15 Sag	15 Aqr	14 Pis	16 Tau	15 Gem	17 Leo
18 Tau	19 Can	21 Vir	18 Vir	17 Lib	17 Sag	17 Cap	18 Pis	17 Ars	18 Gem	18 Can	19 Vir
20 Gem	21 Leo	23 Lib	20 Lib	19 Sco	20 Cap	19 Aqr	20 Ars	19 Tau	21 Can	20 Leo	21 Lib
22 Can	23 Vir	25 Sco	22 Sco	21 Sag	22 Aqr	22 Pis	23 Tau	22 Gem	24 Leo	22 Vir	24 Sco
24 Leo	25 Lib	27 Sag	24 Sag	23 Cap	24 Pis	24 Ars	25 Gem	24 Can	26 Vir	24 Lib	26 Sag
26 Vir	27 Sco	29 Cap	26 Cap	25 Aqr	27 Ars	27 Tau	28 Can	26 Leo	28 Lib	26 Sco	28 Cap
28 Lib	29 Sag		28 Aqr	28 Pis	29 Tau	29 Gem	30 Leo	28 Vir	30 Sco	28 Sag	30 Aqr
30 Sco				30 Ars		31 Can		30 Lib		30 Cap	

1941

Jan.	Feb.	Mar.	Apr.	May	June	July	Aug.	Sep.	Oct.	Nov.	Dec.
1 Pis	3 Tau	2 Tau	1 Gem	1 Can	2 Vir	1 Lib	1 Sag	2 Aqr	2 Pis	3 Tau	2 Gem
4 Ars	5 Gem	5 Gem	3 Can	3 Leo	4 Lib	3 Sco	4 Cap	4 Pis	4 Ars	5 Gem	5 Can
6 Tau	8 Can	7 Can	5 Leo	5 Vir	6 Sco	5 Sag	6 Aqr	7 Ars	6 Tau	8 Can	7 Leo
9 Gem	10 Leo	9 Leo	8 Vir	7 Lib	8 Sag	7 Cap	8 Pis	9 Tau	9 Gem	10 Leo	10 Vir
11 Can	12 Vir	11 Vir	10 Lib	9 Sco	10 Cap	9 Aqr	10 Ars	11 Gem	11 Can	13 Vir	12 Lib
13 Leo	14 Lib	13 Lib	12 Sco	11 Sag	12 Aqr	12 Pis	12 Tau	14 Can	14 Leo	15 Lib	14 Sco
16 Vir	16 Sco	16 Sco	15 Sag	13 Cap	14 Pis	14 Ars	15 Gem	16 Leo	16 Vir	17 Sco	16 Sag
18 Lib	18 Sag	18 Sag	17 Cap	16 Aqr	17 Ars	16 Tau	17 Can	18 Vir	18 Lib	19 Sag	18 Cap
20 Sco	20 Cap	20 Cap	19 Aqr	18 Pis	19 Tau	19 Gem	19 Leo	21 Lib	20 Sco	21 Cap	20 Aqr
22 Sag	23 Aqr	23 Aqr	21 Pis	20 Ars	22 Gem	21 Can	21 Vir	23 Sco	23 Sag	23 Aqr	22 Pis
24 Cap	25 Pis	25 Pis	23 Ars	23 Tau	24 Can	24 Leo	24 Lib	25 Sag	25 Cap	25 Pis	25 Ars
26 Aqr	27 Ars	27 Ars	26 Tau	25 Gem	26 Leo	26 Vir	26 Sco	27 Cap	27 Aqr	27 Ars	27 Tau
29 Pis		29 Tau	28 Gem	28 Can	29 Vir	28 Lib	29 Sag	29 Aqr	29 Pis	30 Tau	30 Gem
31 Ars				30 Leo		30 Sco	31 Cap		31 Ars		

1942

Jan.	Feb.	Mar.	Apr.	May	June	July	Aug.	Sep.	Oct.	Nov.	Dec.
1 Can	2 Vir	2 Vir	2 Sco	2 Sag	2 Aqr	2 Pis	3 Tau	1 Gem	1 Can	3 Vir	2 Lib
4 Leo	5 Lib	4 Lib	4 Sag	4 Cap	4 Pis	4 Ars	5 Gem	4 Can	4 Leo	5 Lib	4 Sco
6 Vir	7 Sco	6 Sco	6 Cap	6 Aqr	7 Ars	6 Tau	8 Can	6 Leo	6 Vir	7 Sco	7 Sag
8 Lib	9 Sag	8 Sag	9 Aqr	8 Pis	9 Tau	9 Gem	11 Leo	9 Vir	8 Lib	9 Sag	9 Cap
11 Sco	11 Cap	10 Cap	11 Pis	10 Ars	12 Gem	11 Can	13 Vir	11 Lib	11 Sco	11 Cap	11 Aqr
13 Sag	13 Aqr	12 Aqr	13 Ars	13 Tau	14 Can	14 Leo	15 Lib	13 Sco	13 Sag	13 Aqr	13 Pis
15 Cap	15 Pis	15 Pis	16 Tau	15 Gem	17 Leo	16 Vir	17 Sco	15 Sag	15 Cap	15 Pis	15 Ars
17 Aqr	17 Ars	17 Ars	18 Gem	18 Can	19 Vir	19 Lib	19 Sag	18 Cap	17 Aqr	18 Ars	17 Tau
19 Pis	20 Tau	19 Tau	21 Can	20 Leo	21 Lib	21 Sco	21 Cap	20 Aqr	19 Pis	20 Tau	20 Gem
21 Ars	22 Gem	22 Gem	23 Leo	23 Vir	24 Sco	23 Sag	23 Aqr	22 Pis	21 Ars	22 Gem	22 Can
23 Tau	25 Can	24 Can	25 Vir	25 Lib	26 Sag	25 Cap	25 Pis	24 Ars	24 Tau	25 Can	25 Leo
26 Gem	27 Leo	27 Leo	28 Lib	27 Sco	28 Cap	27 Aqr	28 Ars	26 Tau	26 Gem	27 Leo	27 Vir
29 Can		29 Vir	30 Sco	29 Sag	30 Aqr	29 Pis	30 Tau	29 Gem	29 Can	30 Vir	30 Lib
31 Leo		31 Lib		31 Cap		31 Ars			31 Leo		

1943

Jan.	Feb.	Mar.	Apr.	May	June	July	Aug.	Sep.	Oct.	Nov.	Dec.
1 Sco	1 Cap	1 Cap	1 Pis	1 Ars	2 Gem	1 Can	3 Vir	1 Lib	1 Sco	2 Cap	1 Aqr
3 Sag	3 Aqr	3 Aqr	3 Ars	3 Tau	4 Can	4 Leo	5 Lib	4 Sco	3 Sag	4 Aqr	3 Pis
5 Cap	5 Pis	5 Pis	6 Tau	5 Gem	6 Leo	6 Vir	7 Sco	6 Sag	5 Cap	6 Pis	5 Ars
7 Aqr	8 Ars	7 Ars	8 Gem	8 Can	9 Vir	9 Lib	10 Sag	8 Cap	8 Aqr	8 Ars	7 Tau
9 Pis	10 Tau	9 Tau	10 Can	10 Leo	11 Lib	11 Sco	12 Cap	10 Aqr	10 Pis	10 Tau	10 Gem
11 Ars	12 Gem	11 Gem	13 Leo	13 Vir	14 Sco	13 Sag	14 Aqr	12 Pis	12 Ars	12 Gem	12 Can
13 Tau	15 Can	14 Can	15 Vir	15 Lib	16 Sag	15 Cap	16 Pis	14 Ars	14 Tau	15 Can	15 Leo
16 Gem	17 Leo	16 Leo	18 Lib	17 Sco	18 Cap	17 Aqr	18 Ars	16 Tau	16 Gem	17 Leo	17 Vir
18 Can	20 Vir	19 Vir	20 Sco	20 Sag	20 Aqr	19 Pis	20 Tau	18 Gem	18 Can	20 Vir	20 Lib
21 Leo	22 Lib	21 Lib	22 Sag	22 Cap	22 Pis	21 Ars	22 Gem	21 Can	21 Leo	22 Lib	22 Sco
23 Vir	24 Sco	24 Sco	24 Cap	24 Aqr	24 Ars	24 Tau	25 Can	24 Leo	23 Vir	25 Sco	24 Sag
26 Lib	27 Sag	26 Sag	26 Aqr	26 Pis	26 Tau	26 Gem	27 Leo	26 Vir	26 Lib	27 Sag	26 Cap
28 Sco		28 Cap	29 Pis	28 Ars	29 Gem	28 Can	30 Vir	29 Lib	28 Sco	29 Cap	28 Aqr
30 Sag		30 Aqr		30 Tau		31 Leo			30 Sag		30 Pis

1944

Jan.	Feb.	Mar.	Apr.	May	June	July	Aug.	Sep.	Oct.	Nov.	Dec.
2 Ars	2 Gem	1 Gem	2 Leo	1 Vir	3 Sco	2 Sag	1 Cap	2 Pis	1 Ars	2 Gem	1 Can
4 Tau	4 Can	3 Can	4 Vir	3 Lib	5 Sag	5 Cap	3 Aqr	4 Ars	3 Tau	4 Can	3 Leo
6 Gem	7 Leo	5 Leo	7 Lib	6 Sco	7 Cap	7 Aqr	5 Pis	6 Tau	5 Gem	6 Leo	6 Vir
8 Can	10 Vir	7 Vir	9 Sco	9 Sag	9 Aqr	9 Pis	7 Ars	8 Gem	7 Can	9 Vir	8 Lib
11 Leo	12 Lib	10 Lib	11 Sag	11 Cap	12 Pis	11 Ars	9 Tau	10 Can	10 Leo	11 Lib	11 Sco
13 Vir	15 Sco	13 Sco	14 Cap	13 Aqr	14 Ars	13 Tau	11 Gem	12 Leo	12 Vir	14 Sco	13 Sag
16 Lib	17 Sag	15 Sag	16 Aqr	15 Pis	16 Tau	15 Gem	14 Can	15 Vir	15 Lib	16 Sag	16 Cap
18 Sco	19 Cap	18 Cap	18 Pis	17 Ars	18 Gem	18 Can	16 Leo	17 Lib	17 Sco	18 Cap	18 Aqr
20 Sag	21 Aqr	20 Aqr	20 Ars	20 Tau	20 Can	20 Leo	19 Vir	20 Sco	20 Sag	21 Aqr	20 Pis
23 Cap	23 Pis	22 Pis	22 Tau	22 Gem	23 Leo	22 Vir	21 Lib	22 Sag	22 Cap	23 Pis	22 Ars
25 Aqr	25 Ars	24 Ars	24 Gem	24 Can	25 Vir	25 Lib	24 Sco	25 Cap	24 Aqr	25 Ars	24 Tau
27 Pis	27 Tau	26 Tau	27 Can	26 Leo	28 Lib	27 Sco	26 Sag	27 Aqr	26 Pis	27 Tau	26 Gem
29 Ars		28 Gem	29 Leo	29 Vir	30 Sco	30 Sag	29 Cap	29 Pis	29 Ars	29 Gem	29 Can
31 Tau		30 Can		31 Lib			31 Aqr		31 Tau		31 Leo

1945

Jan.	Feb.	Mar.	Apr.	May	June	July	Aug.	Sep.	Oct.	Nov.	Dec.
2 Vir	1 Lib	3 Sco	2 Sag	1 Cap	2 Pis	2 Ars	2 Gem	3 Leo	2 Vir	1 Lib	1 Sco
5 Lib	3 Sco	5 Sag	4 Cap	4 Aqr	4 Ars	4 Tau	4 Can	5 Vir	5 Lib	3 Sco	3 Sag
7 Sco	5 Sag	8 Cap	6 Aqr	6 Pis	6 Tau	6 Gem	6 Leo	7 Lib	7 Sco	6 Sag	6 Cap
10 Sag	8 Cap	10 Aqr	9 Pis	8 Ars	8 Gem	8 Can	9 Vir	10 Sco	10 Sag	8 Cap	8 Aqr
12 Cap	11 Aqr	12 Pis	11 Ars	10 Tau	10 Can	10 Leo	11 Lib	12 Sag	12 Cap	11 Aqr	10 Pis
15 Aqr	13 Pis	14 Ars	13 Tau	12 Gem	13 Leo	12 Vir	14 Sco	15 Cap	15 Aqr	13 Pis	13 Ars
17 Pis	15 Ars	16 Tau	15 Gem	14 Can	15 Vir	15 Lib	16 Sag	17 Aqr	17 Pis	15 Ars	15 Tau
19 Ars	17 Tau	18 Gem	17 Can	16 Leo	17 Lib	17 Sco	19 Cap	19 Pis	19 Ars	17 Tau	17 Gem
21 Tau	19 Gem	21 Can	19 Leo	19 Vir	20 Sco	19 Sag	21 Aqr	21 Ars	21 Tau	19 Gem	19 Can
23 Gem	21 Can	23 Leo	21 Vir	21 Lib	22 Sag	22 Cap	23 Pis	23 Tau	23 Gem	21 Can	21 Leo
25 Can	23 Leo	25 Vir	24 Lib	24 Sco	25 Cap	24 Aqr	25 Ars	25 Gem	25 Can	23 Leo	23 Vir
27 Leo	26 Vir	28 Lib	26 Sco	26 Sag	27 Aqr	27 Pis	27 Tau	28 Can	27 Leo	26 Vir	25 Lib
30 Vir	28 Lib	30 Sco	29 Sag	29 Cap	29 Pis	29 Ars	29 Gem	30 Leo	29 Vir	28 Lib	28 Sco
				31 Aqr		31 Tau	31 Can				31 Sag

1946

Jan.	Feb.	Mar.	Apr.	May	June	July	Aug.	Sep.	Oct.	Nov.	Dec.
2 Cap	1 Aqr	2 Pis	1 Ars	2 Gem	1 Can	2 Vir	1 Lib	2 Sag	2 Cap	1 Aqr	1 Pis
4 Aqr	3 Pis	4 Ars	3 Tau	4 Can	3 Leo	5 Lib	3 Sco	5 Cap	5 Aqr	3 Pis	3 Ars
7 Pis	5 Ars	7 Tau	5 Gem	6 Leo	5 Vir	7 Sco	6 Sag	7 Aqr	7 Pis	6 Ars	5 Tau
9 Ars	7 Tau	9 Gem	7 Can	9 Vir	7 Lib	10 Sag	8 Cap	10 Pis	9 Ars	8 Tau	7 Gem
11 Tau	10 Gem	11 Can	9 Leo	11 Lib	10 Sco	12 Cap	11 Aqr	12 Ars	11 Tau	10 Gem	9 Can
13 Gem	12 Can	13 Leo	11 Vir	14 Sco	12 Sag	15 Aqr	13 Pis	14 Tau	13 Gem	12 Can	11 Leo
15 Can	14 Leo	15 Vir	14 Lib	16 Sag	14 Cap	17 Pis	15 Ars	16 Gem	15 Can	14 Leo	13 Vir
17 Leo	16 Vir	18 Lib	16 Sco	19 Cap	16 Aqr	19 Ars	18 Tau	18 Can	17 Leo	16 Vir	16 Lib
20 Vir	18 Lib	20 Sco	19 Sag	21 Aqr	19 Pis	21 Tau	20 Gem	20 Leo	20 Vir	18 Lib	18 Sco
22 Lib	21 Sco	23 Sag	21 Cap	23 Pis	22 Ars	24 Gem	22 Can	23 Vir	22 Lib	21 Sco	20 Sag
24 Sco	23 Sag	25 Cap	24 Aqr	26 Ars	24 Tau	26 Can	24 Leo	25 Lib	24 Sco	23 Sag	23 Cap
27 Sag	26 Cap	27 Aqr	26 Pis	28 Tau	26 Gem	28 Leo	26 Vir	27 Sco	27 Sag	26 Cap	25 Aqr
29 Cap	28 Aqr	30 Pis	28 Ars	30 Gem	28 Can	30 Vir	28 Lib	30 Sag	29 Cap	28 Aqr	28 Pis
			30 Tau		30 Leo		31 Sco				30 Ars

1947

Jan.	Feb.	Mar.	Apr.	May	June	July	Aug.	Sep.	Oct.	Nov.	Dec.
2 Tau	2 Can	1 Can	2 Vir	1 Lib	2 Sag	2 Cap	1 Aqr	2 Ars	2 Tau	2 Can	2 Leo
4 Gem	4 Leo	3 Leo	4 Lib	4 Sco	5 Cap	5 Aqr	3 Pis	4 Tau	4 Gem	4 Leo	4 Vir
6 Can	6 Vir	6 Vir	6 Sco	6 Sag	7 Aqr	7 Pis	5 Ars	7 Gem	6 Can	6 Vir	6 Lib
8 Leo	8 Lib	8 Lib	9 Sag	8 Cap	10 Pis	10 Ars	7 Tau	9 Can	8 Leo	9 Lib	8 Sco
10 Vir	11 Sco	10 Sco	11 Cap	11 Aqr	12 Ars	12 Tau	9 Gem	11 Leo	10 Vir	11 Sco	10 Sag
12 Lib	13 Sag	12 Sag	14 Aqr	14 Pis	14 Tau	14 Gem	12 Can	13 Vir	12 Lib	13 Sag	13 Cap
14 Sco	15 Cap	15 Cap	16 Pis	16 Ars	17 Gem	16 Can	14 Leo	15 Lib	14 Sco	16 Cap	15 Aqr
17 Sag	18 Aqr	17 Aqr	18 Ars	18 Tau	19 Can	18 Leo	16 Vir	17 Sco	17 Sag	18 Aqr	18 Pis
19 Cap	20 Pis	20 Pis	21 Tau	20 Gem	21 Leo	20 Vir	19 Lib	19 Sag	19 Cap	21 Pis	20 Ars
22 Aqr	23 Ars	22 Ars	23 Gem	22 Can	23 Vir	22 Lib	21 Sco	22 Cap	22 Aqr	23 Ars	23 Tau
24 Pis	25 Tau	24 Tau	25 Can	24 Leo	25 Lib	24 Sco	23 Sag	24 Aqr	24 Pis	25 Tau	25 Gem
27 Ars	27 Gem	26 Gem	27 Leo	26 Vir	27 Sco	27 Sag	26 Cap	27 Pis	27 Ars	27 Gem	27 Can
29 Tau		29 Can	29 Vir	29 Lib	30 Sag	29 Cap	28 Aqr	29 Ars	29 Tau	30 Can	29 Leo
31 Gem		31 Leo		31 Sco			31 Pis		31 Gem		31 Vir

1948

Jan.	Feb.	Mar.	Apr.	May	June	July	Aug.	Sep.	Oct.	Nov.	Dec.
2 Lib	1 Sco	1 Sag	2 Aqr	2 Pis	1 Ars	1 Tau	2 Can	2 Vir	2 Lib	2 Sag	2 Cap
4 Sco	3 Sag	4 Cap	5 Pis	5 Ars	4 Tau	3 Gem	4 Leo	4 Lib	4 Sco	4 Cap	4 Aqr
7 Sag	5 Cap	6 Aqr	7 Ars	7 Tau	6 Gem	5 Can	6 Vir	6 Sco	6 Sag	7 Aqr	7 Pis
9 Cap	8 Aqr	9 Pis	10 Tau	9 Gem	8 Can	7 Leo	8 Lib	8 Sag	8 Cap	9 Pis	9 Ars
12 Aqr	10 Pis	11 Ars	12 Gem	12 Can	10 Leo	9 Vir	10 Sco	11 Cap	11 Aqr	12 Ars	12 Tau
14 Pis	13 Ars	14 Tau	14 Can	14 Leo	12 Vir	11 Lib	12 Sag	13 Aqr	13 Pis	14 Tau	14 Gem
17 Ars	15 Tau	16 Gem	17 Leo	18 Vir	14 Lib	14 Sco	15 Cap	16 Pis	16 Ars	17 Gem	16 Can
19 Tau	18 Gem	18 Can	19 Vir	18 Lib	16 Sco	16 Sag	17 Aqr	18 Ars	18 Tau	19 Can	18 Leo
21 Gem	20 Can	20 Leo	21 Lib	20 Sco	19 Sag	18 Cap	20 Pis	21 Tau	20 Gem	21 Leo	21 Vir
23 Can	22 Leo	22 Vir	23 Sco	22 Sag	21 Cap	21 Aqr	22 Ars	23 Gem	23 Can	23 Vir	23 Lib
25 Leo	24 Vir	28 Lib	22 Vir	24 Lib	28 Sco	23 Sco	25 Sag	27 Cap	22 Sag	25 Cap	25 Aqr
27 Vir	26 Lib	26 Sco	27 Cap	27 Aqr	26 Pis	26 Ars	27 Gem	28 Leo	27 Vir	28 Sco	27 Sag
29 Lib	28 Sco	29 Sag	30 Aqr	30 Pis	28 Ars	28 Tau	29 Can	30 Vir	29 Lib	30 Sag	29 Cap
		31 Cap				31 Gem	31 Leo		31 Sco		

1949

Jan.	Feb.	Mar.	Apr.	May	June	July	Aug.	Sep.	Oct.	Nov.	Dec.
1 Aqr	2 Ars	1 Ars	2 Gem	2 Can	1 Leo	2 Lib	3 Sag	1 Cap	1 Aqr	2 Ars	2 Tau
3 Pis	4 Tau	4 Tau	4 Can	4 Leo	3 Vir	4 Sco	6 Cap	3 Aqr	4 Tau	4 Gem	4 Gem
5 Ars	6 Gem	6 Gem	7 Leo	6 Vir	5 Lib	6 Sag	7 Aqr	6 Pis	5 Ars	7 Gem	6 Can
7 Tau	9 Can	9 Can	9 Vir	9 Lib	7 Sco	9 Cap	9 Pis	8 Ars	8 Tau	9 Can	9 Leo
10 Gem	11 Leo	11 Leo	11 Lib	11 Sco	9 Sag	11 Aqr	12 Ars	11 Tau	11 Gem	12 Leo	11 Vir
12 Can	13 Vir	13 Vir	13 Sco	13 Sag	11 Cap	13 Pis	14 Tau	13 Gem	13 Can	14 Vir	13 Lib
15 Leo	15 Lib	15 Lib	15 Sag	15 Cap	13 Aqr	16 Ars	17 Gem	16 Can	15 Leo	16 Lib	15 Sco
17 Vir	17 Sco	17 Sco	17 Cap	17 Aqr	16 Pis	18 Tau	19 Can	18 Leo	17 Vir	18 Sco	17 Sag
19 Lib	19 Sag	19 Sag	20 Aqr	19 Pis	18 Ars	21 Gem	22 Leo	20 Vir	20 Lib	20 Sag	19 Cap
21 Sco	22 Cap	21 Cap	22 Pis	22 Ars	21 Tau	23 Can	24 Vir	22 Lib	22 Sco	22 Cap	22 Aqr
23 Sag	24 Aqr	23 Aqr	25 Ars	24 Tau	23 Gem	25 Leo	26 Lib	28 Sco	24 Sag	24 Aqr	24 Pis
26 Cap	27 Pis	26 Pis	27 Tau	27 Gem	26 Can	27 Vir	28 Sco	28 Sag	26 Cap	27 Pis	26 Ars
28 Aqr		28 Ars	30 Gem	29 Can	28 Leo	29 Lib	30 Sag	28 Cap	28 Aqr	29 Ars	29 Tau
30 Pis		31 Tau			30 Vir	31 Sco			30 Pis		31 Gem

1950

Jan.	Feb.	Mar.	Apr.	May	June	July	Aug.	Sep.	Oct.	Nov.	Dec.
3 Can	1 Leo	1 Leo	2 Lib	1 Sco	1 Cap	1 Aqr	2 Ars	1 Tau	3 Can	2 Leo	1 Vir
5 Leo	4 Vir	3 Vir	4 Sco	3 Sag	3 Aqr	3 Pis	4 Tau	3 Gem	5 Leo	4 Vir	4 Lib
7 Vir	6 Lib	5 Lib	6 Sag	5 Cap	6 Pis	5 Ars	7 Gem	6 Can	8 Vir	6 Lib	6 Sco
9 Lib	8 Sco	7 Sco	8 Cap	7 Aqr	9 Pis	8 Tau	9 Can	8 Leo	10 Lib	8 Sco	8 Sag
12 Sco	10 Sag	9 Sag	10 Aqr	9 Pis	11 Tau	10 Gem	12 Leo	10 Vir	12 Sco	10 Sag	10 Cap
14 Sag	12 Cap	11 Cap	12 Pis	12 Ars	13 Gem	13 Can	14 Vir	12 Lib	14 Sag	12 Cap	12 Aqr
16 Cap	14 Aqr	14 Aqr	14 Ars	14 Tau	16 Can	15 Leo	16 Lib	15 Sco	16 Cap	14 Aqr	14 Pis
18 Aqr	17 Pis	16 Pis	17 Tau	17 Gem	18 Leo	18 Vir	18 Sco	17 Sag	28 Aqr	16 Pis	16 Ars
20 Pis	19 Ars	18 Ars	20 Gem	19 Can	20 Vir	20 Lib	20 Sag	19 Cap	20 Pis	19 Ars	19 Tau
23 Ars	22 Tau	21 Tau	22 Can	21 Leo	22 Lib	22 Sco	22 Cap	21 Aqr	23 Ars	21 Tau	21 Gem
25 Tau	24 Gem	23 Gem	25 Leo	23 Vir	25 Sco	24 Sag	25 Aqr	23 Pis	25 Tau	24 Gem	24 Can
28 Gem	27 Can	26 Can	27 Vir	26 Lib	27 Sag	26 Cap	27 Pis	25 Ars	28 Gem	27 Can	26 Leo
30 Can		28 Leo	29 Lib	28 Sco	29 Cap	28 Aqr	29 Ars	28 Tau	30 Can	29 Leo	29 Vir
		30 Vir		30 Sag		30 Pis		30 Gem			31 Lib

1951

Jan.	Feb.	Mar.	Apr.	May	June	July	Aug.	Sep.	Oct.	Nov.	Dec.
2 Sco	1 Sag	2 Cap	2 Pis	2 Ars	1 Tau	3 Can	2 Leo	3 Lib	2 Sco	1 Sag	2 Aqr
4 Sag	3 Cap	4 Aqr	5 Ars	4 Tau	3 Gem	5 Leo	4 Vir	5 Sco	4 Sag	3 Cap	4 Pis
6 Cap	6 Aqr	6 Pis	7 Tau	7 Gem	6 Can	8 Vir	6 Lib	7 Sag	7 Cap	5 Aqr	6 Ars
8 Aqr	7 Pis	8 Ars	10 Gem	9 Can	8 Leo	10 Lib	9 Sco	9 Cap	9 Aqr	7 Pis	8 Tau
10 Pis	9 Ars	11 Tau	12 Can	12 Leo	11 Vir	13 Sco	11 Sag	11 Aqr	11 Pis	9 Ars	11 Gem
13 Ars	11 Tau	13 Gem	15 Leo	14 Vir	13 Lib	15 Sag	13 Cap	13 Pis	13 Ars	12 Tau	14 Can
15 Tau	14 Gem	16 Can	17 Vir	17 Lib	15 Sco	17 Cap	15 Aqr	16 Ars	15 Tau	14 Gem	16 Leo
18 Gem	16 Can	18 Leo	19 Lib	19 Sco	17 Sag	19 Aqr	17 Pis	18 Tau	18 Gem	16 Can	19 Vir
20 Can	19 Leo	21 Vir	21 Sco	21 Sag	19 Cap	21 Pis	19 Ars	20 Gem	20 Can	19 Leo	21 Lib
23 Leo	21 Vir	23 Lib	23 Sag	23 Cap	21 Aqr	23 Ars	21 Tau	23 Can	23 Leo	21 Vir	23 Sco
25 Vir	23 Lib	25 Sco	25 Cap	25 Aqr	23 Pis	25 Tau	24 Gem	25 Leo	25 Vir	24 Lib	26 Sag
27 Lib	25 Sco	27 Sag	27 Aqr	27 Pis	25 Ars	2b Gem	26 Can	28 Vir	27 Lib	26 Sco	28 Cap
29 Sco	28 Sag	29 Cap	30 Pis	29 Ars	28 Tau	30 Can	29 Leo	30 Lib	30 Sco	28 Sag	30 Aqr
		31 Aqr			30 Gem		31 Vir			30 Cap	

1952

Jan.	Feb.	Mar.	Apr.	May	June	July	Aug.	Sep.	Oct.	Nov.	Dec.
1 Pis	1 Tau	2 Gem	1 Can	1 Leo	2 Lib	2 Sco	2 Cap	1 Aqr	2 Ars	1 Tau	3 Can
3 Ars	4 Gem	5 Can	3 Leo	3 Vir	4 Sco	4 Sag	4 Aqr	3 Pis	4 Tau	3 Gem	5 Leo
5 Tau	6 Can	7 Leo	6 Vir	6 Lib	7 Sag	6 Cap	6 Pis	5 Ars	7 Gem	5 Can	8 Vir
7 Gem	9 Leo	10 Vir	8 Lib	8 Sco	9 Cap	8 Aqr	8 Ars	7 Tau	9 Can	8 Leo	10 Lib
10 Can	11 Vir	12 Lib	11 Sco	10 Sag	11 Aqr	10 Pis	11 Tau	10 Gem	11 Leo	10 Vir	13 Sco
12 Leo	14 Lib	14 Sco	13 Sag	12 Cap	13 Pis	12 Ars	13 Gem	12 Can	14 Vir	13 Lib	15 Sag
15 Vir	16 Sco	17 Sag	15 Cap	14 Aqr	15 Ars	14 Tau	15 Can	15 Leo	16 Lib	15 Sco	17 Cap
17 Lib	18 Sag	19 Cap	17 Aqr	16 Pis	17 Tau	17 Gem	18 Leo	17 Vir	19 Sco	17 Sag	19 Aqr
20 Sco	20 Cap	21 Aqr	19 Pis	19 Ars	19 Gem	19 Can	20 Vir	19 Lib	21 Sag	20 Cap	21 Pis
22 Sag	22 Aqr	23 Pis	21 Ars	21 Tau	22 Can	22 Leo	23 Lib	22 Sco	23 Cap	22 Aqr	23 Ars
24 Cap	24 Pis	25 Ars	23 Tau	23 Gem	24 Leo	24 Vir	25 Sco	24 Sag	26 Aqr	24 Pis	25 Tau
26 Aqr	27 Ars	27 Tau	26 Gem	26 Can	27 Vir	27 Lib	28 Sag	26 Cap	28 Pis	26 Ars	27 Gem
28 Pis	29 Tau	29 Gem	28 Can	28 Leo	29 Lib	29 Sco	30 Cap	28 Aqr	30 Ars	28 Tau	30 Can
30 Ars				31 Vir		31 Sag		30 Pis		30 Gem	

1953

Jan.	Feb.	Mar.	Apr.	May	June	July	Aug.	Sep.	Oct.	Nov.	Dec.
1 Leo	3 Lib	2 Lib	1 Sco	3 Cap	1 Aqr	1 Pis	1 Tau	2 Can	1 Leo	3 Lib	2 Sco
3 Vir	5 Sco	4 Sco	3 Sag	5 Aqr	3 Pis	3 Ars	3 Gem	4 Leo	4 Vir	5 Sco	5 Sag
6 Lib	8 Sag	6 Sag	5 Cap	7 Pis	5 Ars	5 Tau	5 Can	7 Vir	6 Lib	8 Sag	7 Cap
8 Sco	10 Cap	9 Cap	8 Aqr	9 Ars	7 Tau	7 Gem	8 Leo	9 Lib	9 Sco	10 Cap	10 Aqr
11 Sag	12 Aqr	11 Aqr	10 Pis	11 Tau	10 Gem	10 Can	10 Vir	12 Sco	11 Sag	12 Aqr	12 Pis
13 Cap	14 Pis	13 Pis	12 Ars	13 Gem	12 Can	12 Leo	13 Lib	14 Sag	14 Cap	14 Pis	14 Ars
15 Aqr	16 Ars	15 Ars	14 Tau	15 Can	14 Leo	14 Vir	15 Sco	16 Cap	16 Aqr	17 Ars	16 Tau
17 Pis	18 Tau	17 Tau	16 Gem	18 Leo	17 Vir	16 Lib	18 Sag	19 Aqr	18 Pis	19 Tau	18 Gem
19 Ars	20 Gem	19 Gem	18 Can	20 Vir	19 Lib	19 Sco	20 Cap	21 Pis	20 Ars	21 Gem	20 Can
22 Tau	22 Can	22 Can	20 Leo	23 Lib	22 Sco	21 Sag	22 Aqr	23 Ars	22 Tau	23 Can	22 Leo
24 Gem	25 Leo	24 Leo	23 Vir	25 Sco	24 Cap	24 Cap	24 Pis	25 Tau	24 Gem	25 Leo	25 Vir
26 Can	27 Vir	27 Vir	26 Lib	28 Sag	26 Aqr	26 Aqr	26 Ars	27 Gem	26 Can	27 Vir	27 Lib
29 Leo		29 Lib	28 Sco	30 Cap	28 Pis	28 Pis	28 Tau	29 Can	29 Leo	30 Lib	30 Sco
31 Vir			30 Sag			30 Ars	30 Gem		31 Vir		

1954

Jan.	Feb.	Mar.	Apr.	May	June	July	Aug.	Sep.	Oct.	Nov.	Dec.
1 Sag	2 Aqr	2 Aqr	2 Ars	2 Tau	2 Can	2 Leo	2 Lib	1 Sco	1 Sag	2 Aqr	2 Pis
4 Cap	4 Pis	4 Pis	4 Tau	4 Gem	4 Leo	4 Vir	5 Sco	4 Sag	4 Cap	5 Pis	4 Ars
6 Aqr	6 Ars	6 Ars	6 Gem	6 Can	6 Vir	6 Lib	8 Sag	6 Cap	7 Aqr	7 Ars	6 Tau
8 Pis	8 Tau	8 Tau	8 Can	8 Leo	9 Lib	9 Sco	10 Cap	9 Aqr	8 Pis	9 Tau	8 Gem
10 Ars	10 Gem	10 Gem	11 Leo	10 Vir	12 Sco	11 Sag	12 Aqr	11 Pis	11 Ars	11 Gem	10 Can
12 Tau	13 Can	12 Can	13 Vir	13 Lib	14 Sag	14 Cap	15 Pis	13 Ars	13 Tau	13 Can	12 Leo
14 Gem	15 Leo	14 Leo	15 Lib	15 Sco	16 Cap	16 Aqr	17 Ars	15 Tau	15 Gem	15 Leo	15 Vir
16 Can	17 Vir	17 Vir	18 Sco	18 Sag	19 Aqr	18 Pis	19 Tau	17 Gem	17 Can	17 Vir	17 Lib
19 Leo	20 Lib	19 Lib	20 Sag	20 Cap	21 Pis	21 Ars	21 Gem	19 Can	19 Leo	20 Lib	20 Sco
21 Vir	22 Sco	22 Sco	23 Cap	23 Aqr	23 Ars	23 Tau	23 Can	22 Leo	21 Vir	22 Sco	23 Sag
24 Lib	25 Sag	24 Sag	25 Aqr	25 Pis	25 Tau	25 Gem	25 Leo	24 Vir	24 Lib	24 Sag	25 Cap
26 Sco	27 Cap	27 Cap	28 Pis	27 Ars	27 Gem	27 Can	28 Vir	26 Lib	26 Sco	27 Cap	27 Aqr
29 Sag		29 Aqr	30 Ars	29 Tau	29 Can	29 Leo	30 Lib	29 Sco	29 Sag	30 Aqr	29 Pis
31 Cap		31 Pis		31 Gem		31 Vir			31 Cap		

1955

Jan.	Feb.	Mar.	Apr.	May	June	July	Aug.	Sep.	Oct.	Nov.	Dec.
1 Ars	1 Gem	2 Can	1 Leo	3 Lib	1 Sco	1 Sag	2 Aqr	1 Pis	1 Ars	1 Gem	1 Can
3 Tau	3 Can	5 Leo	3 Vir	5 Sco	4 Sag	4 Cap	5 Pis	3 Ars	3 Tau	3 Can	3 Leo
5 Gem	5 Leo	7 Vir	5 Lib	8 Sag	6 Cap	6 Aqr	7 Ars	6 Tau	5 Gem	5 Leo	5 Vir
7 Can	7 Vir	9 Lib	8 Sco	10 Cap	9 Aqr	9 Pis	9 Tau	8 Gem	7 Can	8 Vir	7 Lib
9 Leo	10 Lib	12 Sco	10 Sag	13 Aqr	11 Pis	11 Ars	11 Gem	10 Can	9 Leo	10 Lib	10 Sco
11 Vir	12 Sco	14 Sag	13 Cap	15 Pis	14 Ars	13 Tau	13 Can	12 Leo	11 Vir	12 Sco	12 Sag
13 Lib	15 Sag	17 Cap	15 Aqr	17 Ars	16 Tau	15 Gem	16 Leo	14 Vir	14 Lib	15 Sag	15 Cap
15 Sco	17 Cap	19 Aqr	18 Pis	19 Tau	18 Gem	17 Can	18 Vir	16 Lib	16 Sco	17 Cap	17 Aqr
18 Sag	20 Aqr	21 Pis	20 Ars	21 Gem	20 Can	19 Leo	20 Lib	19 Sco	19 Sag	20 Aqr	19 Pis
21 Cap	22 Pis	23 Ars	22 Tau	23 Can	22 Leo	21 Vir	22 Sco	21 Sag	21 Cap	22 Pis	21 Ars
23 Aqr	24 Ars	26 Tau	24 Gem	25 Leo	24 Vir	24 Lib	25 Sag	24 Cap	23 Aqr	25 Ars	23 Tau
26 Pis	26 Tau	28 Gem	26 Can	28 Vir	26 Lib	26 Sco	27 Cap	26 Aqr	26 Pis	27 Tau	26 Gem
28 Ars	28 Gem	30 Can	28 Leo	30 Lib	29 Sco	28 Sag	30 Aqr	29 Pis	28 Ars	29 Gem	28 Can
30 Tau			30 Vir			31 Cap			30 Tau		30 Leo

1956

Jan.	Feb.	Mar.	Apr.	May	June	July	Aug.	Sep.	Oct.	Nov.	Dec.
1 Vir	2 Sco	3 Sag	2 Cap	2 Aqr	3 Ars	2 Tau	1 Gem	1 Leo	1 Vir	1 Sco	1 Sag
3 Lib	5 Sag	5 Cap	4 Aqr	4 Pis	5 Tau	5 Gem	3 Can	3 Vir	3 Lib	4 Sag	3 Cap
6 Sco	7 Cap	8 Aqr	6 Pis	6 Ars	7 Gem	7 Can	5 Leo	5 Lib	5 Sco	6 Cap	6 Aqr
8 Sag	10 Aqr	10 Pis	9 Ars	9 Tau	9 Can	9 Leo	7 Vir	8 Sco	7 Sag	9 Aqr	8 Pis
11 Cap	12 Pis	13 Ars	11 Tau	11 Gem	11 Leo	11 Vir	9 Lib	10 Sag	10 Cap	11 Pis	11 Ars
13 Aqr	14 Ars	15 Tau	13 Gem	13 Can	13 Vir	13 Lib	11 Sco	12 Cap	12 Aqr	14 Ars	13 Tau
16 Pis	17 Tau	17 Gem	16 Can	15 Leo	15 Lib	15 Sco	14 Sag	15 Aqr	15 Pis	16 Tau	16 Gem
18 Ars	19 Gem	19 Can	18 Leo	17 Vir	18 Sco	17 Sag	16 Cap	17 Pis	17 Ars	18 Gem	18 Can
20 Tau	21 Can	21 Leo	20 Vir	19 Lib	20 Sag	20 Cap	18 Aqr	20 Ars	20 Tau	20 Can	20 Leo
23 Gem	23 Leo	23 Vir	22 Lib	21 Sco	22 Cap	22 Aqr	21 Pis	22 Tau	22 Gem	22 Leo	22 Vir
25 Can	25 Vir	26 Lib	24 Sco	23 Sag	24 Aqr	25 Pis	24 Ars	24 Gem	24 Can	24 Vir	24 Lib
27 Leo	27 Lib	28 Sco	27 Sag	26 Cap	27 Pis	27 Ars	26 Tau	27 Can	26 Leo	27 Lib	26 Sco
29 Vir	29 Sco	30 Sag	29 Cap	29 Aqr	30 Ars	30 Tau	28 Gem	29 Leo	28 Vir	29 Sco	28 Sag
31 Lib				31 Pis			30 Can		30 Lib		31 Cap

1957

Jan.	Feb.	Mar.	Apr.	May	June	July	Aug.	Sep.	Oct.	Nov.	Dec.
2 Aqr	1 Pis	3 Ars	1 Tau	1 Gem	2 Leo	1 Vir	2 Sco	2 Cap	2 Aqr	1 Pis	1 Ars
5 Pis	4 Ars	5 Tau	3 Gem	3 Can	4 Vir	3 Lib	4 Sag	5 Aqr	5 Pis	3 Ars	3 Tau
7 Ars	6 Tau	8 Gem	6 Can	5 Leo	6 Lib	5 Sco	6 Cap	7 Pis	7 Ars	6 Tau	6 Gem
10 Tau	8 Gem	10 Can	8 Leo	8 Vir	8 Sco	8 Sag	9 Aqr	10 Ars	10 Tau	8 Gem	8 Can
12 Gem	10 Can	12 Leo	10 Vir	10 Lib	10 Sag	10 Cap	11 Pis	12 Tau	12 Gem	11 Can	10 Leo
14 Can	12 Leo	14 Vir	12 Lib	12 Sco	13 Cap	12 Aqr	14 Ars	15 Gem	14 Can	13 Leo	12 Vir
16 Leo	14 Vir	16 Lib	14 Sco	14 Sag	15 Aqr	15 Pis	16 Tau	17 Can	17 Leo	15 Vir	14 Lib
18 Vir	16 Lib	18 Sco	17 Sag	16 Cap	18 Pis	17 Ars	19 Gem	19 Leo	19 Vir	17 Lib	16 Sco
20 Lib	19 Sco	20 Sag	19 Cap	19 Aqr	20 Ars	20 Tau	21 Can	21 Vir	21 Lib	19 Sco	19 Sag
22 Sco	21 Sag	22 Cap	21 Aqr	21 Pis	22 Tau	22 Gem	23 Leo	23 Lib	23 Sco	21 Sag	21 Cap
25 Sag	23 Cap	25 Aqr	24 Pis	24 Ars	25 Gem	24 Can	25 Vir	25 Sco	25 Sag	23 Cap	23 Aqr
27 Cap	26 Aqr	28 Pis	26 Ars	26 Tau	27 Can	26 Leo	27 Lib	27 Sag	27 Cap	26 Aqr	26 Pis
29 Aqr	28 Pis	30 Ars	29 Tau	28 Gem	29 Leo	28 Vir	29 Sco	30 Cap	29 Aqr	28 Pis	28 Ars
				31 Can		30 Lib	31 Sag				31 Tau

1958

Jan.	Feb.	Mar.	Apr.	May	June	July	Aug.	Sep.	Oct.	Nov.	Dec.
2 Gem	1 Can	2 Leo	1 Vir	2 Sco	1 Sag	2 Aqr	1 Pis	2 Tau	2 Gem	1 Can	3 Vir
4 Can	3 Leo	4 Vir	3 Lib	4 Sag	3 Cap	4 Pis	3 Ars	5 Gem	5 Can	3 Leo	5 Lib
6 Leo	5 Vir	6 Lib	5 Sco	6 Cap	5 Aqr	7 Ars	5 Tau	7 Can	7 Leo	5 Vir	7 Sco
8 Vir	7 Lib	8 Sco	7 Sag	9 Aqr	7 Pis	10 Tau	9 Gem	9 Leo	9 Vir	8 Lib	9 Sag
11 Lib	9 Sco	10 Sag	9 Cap	11 Pis	10 Ars	12 Gem	11 Can	12 Vir	11 Lib	10 Sco	11 Cap
13 Sco	11 Sag	13 Cap	11 Aqr	14 Ars	12 Tau	14 Can	13 Leo	14 Lib	13 Sco	12 Sag	13 Aqr
15 Sag	13 Cap	15 Aqr	14 Pis	16 Tau	15 Gem	17 Leo	15 Vir	16 Sco	15 Sag	14 Cap	15 Pis
17 Cap	16 Aqr	17 Pis	16 Ars	18 Gem	17 Can	19 Vir	17 Lib	18 Sag	17 Cap	16 Aqr	18 Ars
19 Aqr	18 Pis	19 Ars	19 Tau	21 Can	19 Leo	21 Lib	19 Sco	20 Cap	19 Aqr	18 Pis	20 Tau
22 Pis	21 Ars	22 Tau	21 Gem	23 Leo	21 Vir	23 Sco	21 Sag	22 Aqr	22 Pis	21 Ars	23 Gem
24 Ars	23 Tau	25 Gem	24 Can	25 Vir	24 Lib	25 Sag	24 Cap	25 Pis	24 Ars	23 Tau	25 Can
27 Tau	26 Gem	27 Can	26 Leo	28 Lib	26 Sco	27 Cap	26 Aqr	27 Ars	27 Tau	26 Gem	27 Leo
29 Gem	28 Can	30 Leo	28 Vir	30 Sco	28 Sag	30 Aqr	28 Pis	30 Tau	29 Gem	28 Can	30 Vir
			30 Lib		30 Cap		31 Ars			30 Leo	

1959

Jan.	Feb.	Mar.	Apr.	May	June	July	Aug.	Sep.	Oct.	Nov.	Dec.
1 Lib	2 Sag	1 Sag	1 Aqr	1 Pis	2 Tau	2 Gem	1 Can	2 Vir	1 Lib	2 Sag	1 Cap
3 Sco	4 Cap	3 Cap	4 Pis	3 Ars	5 Gem	5 Can	3 Leo	4 Lib	3 Sco	4 Cap	3 Aqr
5 Sag	6 Aqr	5 Aqr	6 Ars	6 Tau	7 Can	7 Leo	6 Vir	6 Sco	5 Sag	6 Aqr	6 Pis
7 Cap	8 Pis	7 Pis	9 Tau	8 Gem	10 Leo	9 Vir	8 Lib	8 Sag	8 Cap	8 Pis	8 Ars
10 Aqr	11 Ars	10 Ars	11 Gem	11 Can	12 Vir	12 Lib	10 Sco	10 Cap	10 Aqr	11 Ars	11 Tau
12 Pis	13 Tau	12 Tau	13 Can	13 Leo	14 Lib	14 Sco	12 Sag	12 Aqr	12 Pis	13 Tau	13 Gem
14 Ars	16 Gem	15 Gem	16 Leo	16 Vir	16 Sco	16 Sag	14 Cap	15 Pis	14 Ars	16 Gem	16 Can
17 Tau	18 Can	17 Can	18 Vir	18 Lib	18 Sag	18 Cap	16 Aqr	17 Ars	17 Tau	18 Can	18 Leo
19 Gem	20 Leo	20 Leo	21 Lib	20 Sco	20 Cap	20 Aqr	18 Pis	19 Tau	19 Gem	21 Leo	20 Vir
22 Can	23 Vir	22 Vir	23 Sco	22 Sag	22 Aqr	22 Pis	21 Ars	22 Gem	22 Can	23 Vir	23 Lib
24 Leo	25 Lib	24 Lib	25 Sag	24 Cap	25 Pis	24 Ars	23 Tau	24 Can	24 Leo	25 Lib	25 Sco
26 Vir	27 Sco	26 Sco	27 Cap	26 Aqr	27 Ars	27 Tau	26 Gem	27 Leo	27 Vir	27 Sco	27 Sag
28 Lib		28 Sag	29 Aqr	28 Pis	29 Tau	29 Gem	28 Can	29 Vir	29 Lib	29 Sag	29 Cap
31 Sco		30 Cap		31 Ars			31 Leo		31 Sco		31 Aqr

1960

Jan.	Feb.	Mar.	Apr.	May	June	July	Aug.	Sep.	Oct.	Nov.	Dec.
2 Pis	1 Ars	1 Tau	3 Can	2 Leo	1 Vir	1 Lib	2 Sag	2 Aqr	1 Pis	2 Tau	2 Gem
4 Ars	3 Tau	4 Gem	5 Leo	5 Vir	4 Lib	3 Sco	4 Cap	4 Pis	4 Ars	4 Gem	4 Can
7 Tau	5 Gem	6 Can	8 Vir	7 Lib	6 Sco	5 Sag	6 Aqr	6 Ars	6 Tau	7 Can	7 Leo
9 Gem	8 Can	9 Leo	10 Lib	9 Sco	8 Sag	7 Cap	8 Pis	8 Tau	8 Gem	9 Leo	9 Vir
12 Can	10 Leo	11 Vir	12 Sco	11 Sag	10 Cap	9 Aqr	10 Ars	11 Gem	11 Can	12 Vir	12 Lib
14 Leo	13 Vir	13 Lib	14 Sag	13 Cap	12 Aqr	11 Pis	12 Tau	13 Can	13 Leo	14 Lib	14 Sco
17 Vir	15 Lib	18 Sco	16 Cap	15 Aqr	14 Pis	13 Ars	14 Gem	16 Leo	16 Vir	17 Sco	16 Sag
19 Lib	17 Sco	18 Sag	18 Aqr	18 Pis	16 Ars	15 Tau	17 Can	18 Vir	18 Lib	19 Sag	18 Cap
21 Sco	19 Sag	20 Cap	20 Pis	20 Ars	18 Tau	18 Gem	19 Leo	21 Lib	20 Sco	21 Cap	20 Aqr
23 Sag	22 Cap	22 Aqr	23 Ars	22 Tau	21 Gem	21 Can	22 Vir	23 Sco	22 Sag	23 Aqr	22 Pis
25 Cap	24 Aqr	24 Pis	25 Tau	25 Gem	25 Can	23 Leo	24 Lib	25 Sag	24 Cap	25 Pis	24 Ars
27 Aqr	28 Pis	26 Ars	27 Gem	27 Can	26 Leo	26 Vir	27 Sco	27 Cap	27 Aqr	27 Ars	27 Tau
29 Pis	28 Ars	29 Tau	29 Can	30 Leo	28 Vir	28 Lib	29 Sag	29 Aqr	29 Pis	29 Tau	29 Gem
		31 Gem				30 Sco	31 Cap		31 Ars		

1961

Jan.	Feb.	Mar.	Apr.	May	June	July	Aug.	Sep.	Oct.	Nov.	Dec.
1 Can	2 Vir	1 Vir	2 Sco	2 Sag	2 Aqr	2 Pis	3 Tau	1 Gem	3 Leo	2 Vir	2 Lib
3 Leo	4 Lib	4 Lib	4 Sag	4 Cap	4 Pis	4 Ars	4 Gem	3 Can	5 Vir	4 Lib	4 Sco
6 Vir	7 Sco	6 Sco	7 Cap	6 Aqr	6 Ars	6 Tau	7 Can	6 Leo	7 Lib	7 Sco	6 Sag
8 Lib	9 Sag	8 Sag	9 Aqr	8 Pis	9 Tau	8 Gem	9 Leo	8 Vir	10 Sco	9 Sag	9 Cap
10 Sco	11 Cap	10 Cap	11 Pis	10 Ars	11 Gem	11 Can	12 Vir	11 Lib	12 Sag	11 Cap	11 Aqr
13 Sag	13 Aqr	12 Aqr	13 Ars	12 Tau	13 Can	13 Leo	14 Lib	13 Sco	15 Cap	13 Aqr	13 Pis
15 Cap	15 Pis	15 Pis	15 Tau	15 Gem	16 Leo	16 Vir	17 Sco	15 Sag	17 Aqr	16 Pis	15 Ars
17 Ars	17 Ars	17 Ars	17 Gem	17 Can	18 Vir	18 Lib	19 Sag	17 Cap	19 Pis	18 Ars	17 Tau
19 Pis	19 Tau	19 Tau	19 Can	20 Leo	21 Lib	21 Sco	21 Cap	20 Aqr	21 Ars	20 Tau	19 Gem
21 Ars	22 Gem	21 Gem	21 Leo	22 Vir	23 Sco	23 Sag	23 Aqr	22 Pis	23 Tau	22 Gem	22 Can
23 Tau	24 Can	24 Can	24 Vir	25 Lib	26 Sag	25 Cap	25 Pis	24 Ars	26 Gem	24 Can	24 Leo
25 Gem	27 Leo	26 Leo	27 Lib	27 Sco	28 Cap	27 Aqr	27 Ars	26 Tau	28 Can	27 Leo	26 Vir
28 Can		28 Vir	29 Sco	29 Sag	30 Aqr	29 Pis	30 Tau	28 Gem	30 Leo	29 Vir	29 Lib
30 Leo		31 Lib	31 Cap			31 Ars		30 Can			31 Sco

1962

Jan.	Feb.	Mar.	Apr.	May.	June.	July	Aug.	Sep.	Oct.	Nov.	Dec.
3 Sag	1 Cap	1 Cap	1 Pis	1 Ars	1 Gem	1 Can	2 Vir	1 Lib	3 Sag	2 Cap	1 Aqr
5 Cap	3 Aqr	3 Ars	3 Ars	3 Tau	3 Can	3 Leo	4 Lib	3 Sco	5 Cap	4 Aqr	3 Pis
7 Aqr	5 Pis	5 Pis	5 Tau	6 Gem	6 Leo	6 Vir	7 Sco	6 Sag	8 Aqr	6 Pis	6 Ars
9 Pis	7 Ars	7 Ars	7 Gem	7 Can	8 Vir	8 Lib	9 Sag	8 Cap	10 Pis	8 Ars	8 Tau
11 Ars	10 Tau	9 Tau	9 Can	9 Leo	11 Lib	10 Sco	12 Cap	10 Aqu	12 Ars	10 Tau	10 Gem
13 Tau	12 Gem	11 Gem	12 Leo	12 Vir	13 Sco	13 Sag	14 Aqr	12 Pis	14 Tau	12 Gem	12 Can
16 Gem	15 Can	13 Can	15 Vir	14 Lib	16 Sag	15 Cap	16 Pis	14 Ars	16 Gem	14 Can	14 Leo
18 Can	17 Leo	16 Leo	17 Lib	17 Sco	18 Cap	17 Aqr	19 Ars	16 Tau	18 Gem	17 Leo	16 Vir
20 Leo	19 Vir	18 Vir	20 Sco	19 Sag	20 Aqr	19 Pis	21 Tau	18 Gem	20 Leo	19 Vir	19 Lib
23 Vir	22 Lib	21 Lib	22 Sag	22 Cap	22 Pis	22 Ars	23 Gem	21 Can	23 Vir	21 Lib	21 Sco
25 Lib	24 Sco	23 Sco	24 Cap	24 Aqr	24 Ars	24 Tau	25 Can	23 Leo	25 Lib	24 Sco	24 Sag
28 Sco	26 Sag	26 Sag	27 Aqr	26 Pis	26 Tau	26 Gem	27 Leo	25 Vir	28 Sco	26 Sag	26 Cap
30 Sag		28 Cap	29 Pis	28 Ars	29 Gem	28 Can	28 Vir	28 Lib	30 Sag	29 Cap	28 Aqr
		30 Aqr		30 Tau		30 Leo		30 Sco			31 Pis

1963

Jan.	Feb.	Mar.	Apr.	May	June	July	Aug.	Sep.	Oct.	Nov.	Dec.
2 Ars	2 Gem	1 Gem	2 Leo	2 Vir	1 Lib	3 Sag	2 Cap	3 Pis	2 Ars	1 Tau	2 Can
4 Tau	4 Can	4 Can	5 Vir	4 Lib	3 Sco	6 Cap	4 Aqr	5 Ars	4 Tau	3 Gem	4 Leo
6 Gem	7 Leo	6 Leo	7 Lib	7 Sco	5 Sag	8 Aqr	6 Pis	7 Tau	6 Gem	5 Can	6 Vir
8 Can	9 Vir	8 Vir	10 Sco	9 Sag	8 Cap	10 Pis	8 Ars	9 Gem	8 Can	7 Leo	9 Lib
10 Leo	11 Lib	11 Lib	12 Sag	12 Cap	10 Aqr	12 Ars	10 Tau	11 Can	10 Leo	9 Vir	11 Sco
13 Vir	14 Sco	13 Sco	15 Cap	14 Aqr	12 Pis	14 Tau	13 Gem	13 Leo	13 Vir	11 Lib	14 Sag
15 Lib	16 Sag	16 Sag	17 Aqr	16 Pis	15 Ars	16 Gem	15 Can	15 Vir	15 Lib	14 Sco	16 Cap
18 Sco	19 Cap	18 Cap	19 Pis	18 Ars	17 Tau	18 Can	18 Leo	18 Lib	18 Sco	16 Sag	19 Aqr
20 Sag	21 Aqr	21 Aqr	21 Ars	21 Tau	19 Gem	21 Leo	20 Vir	20 Sco	20 Sag	19 Cap	21 Pis
22 Cap	23 Pis	23 Pis	23 Tau	23 Gem	21 Can	23 Vir	23 Lib	23 Sag	23 Cap	21 Aqr	23 Ars
23 Aqr	25 Ars	25 Ars	25 Gem	25 Can	23 Leo	25 Lib	24 Sco	25 Cap	25 Aqr	24 Pis	25 Tau
27 Ars	27 Tau	27 Tau	27 Can	27 Leo	25 Vir	28 Sco	27 Sag	28 Aqr	27 Pis	26 Ars	27 Gem
29 Ars		29 Gem	29 Leo	29 Vir	28 Lib	30 Sag	29 Cap	30 Pis	30 Ars	28 Tau	29 Can
31 Tau		31 Can			30 Sco		31 Aqr			30 Gem	31 Leo

1964

Jan.	Feb.	Mar.	Apr.	May	June	July	Aug.	Sep.	Oct.	Nov.	Dec.
3 Vir	1 Lib	S Sco	1 Sag	1 Cap	2 Pis	2 Ars	2 Gem	1 Can	2 Vir	1 Lib	3 Sag
5 Lib	4 Sco	5 Sag	3 Cap	3 Aqr	4 Ars	4 Tau	4 Can	3 Leo	4 Lib	3 Sco	5 Cap
7 Sco	6 Sag	7 Cap	6 Aqr	6 Pis	6 Tau	8 Gem	6 Leo	5 Vir	7 Sco	5 Sag	8 Aqr
10 Sag	9 Cap	10 Aqr	8 Pis	8 Ars	8 Gem	8 Can	8 Vir	7 Lib	9 Sag	8 Cap	10 Pis
12 Cap	11 Aqr	12 Pis	10 Ars	10 Tau	10 Can	10 Leo	10 Lib	9 Sco	11 Cap	10 Aqr	13 Ars
14 Aqr	13 Pis	14 Ars	13 Tau	12 Gem	12 Leo	12 Vir	13 Sco	12 Sag	14 Aqr	13 Pis	15 Tau
17 Pis	16 Ars	16 Tau	15 Gem	14 Can	15 Vir	14 Lib	15 Sag	14 Cap	16 Pis	15 Ars	17 Gem
19 Ars	18 Tau	18 Gem	17 Can	18 Leo	17 Lib	16 Sco	18 Cap	17 Aqr	19 Ars	17 Tau	19 Can
21 Tau	20 Gem	20 Can	19 Leo	20 Lib	19 Sco	18 Cap	20 Aqr	19 Pis	21 Tau	19 Gem	21 Leo
24 Gem	22 Can	23 Leo	21 Vir	23 Sco	21 Sag	22 Cap	23 Pis	21 Ars	23 Gem	21 Can	23 Vir
26 Can	24 Leo	25 Vir	23 Lib	25 Sag	24 Cap	24 Aqr	25 Ars	23 Tau	25 Can	23 Leo	25 Lib
28 Leo	26 Vir	27 Lib	26 Sco	28 Cap	27 Aqr	28 Pis	27 Tau	28 Can	27 Leo	26 Vir	27 Sco
30 Vir	29 Lib	29 Sco	28 Sag	30 Aqr	29 Pis	31 Tau	29 Gem	30 Leo	29 Vir	28 Lib	30 Sag
										30 Sco	

1965

Jan.	Feb.	Mar.	Apr.	May	June	July	Aug.	Sep.	Oct.	Nov.	Dec.
1 Cap	3 Pis	2 Pis	1 Ars	2 Gem	1 Cap	2 Ars	1 Lib	2 Sag	1 Cap	3 Pis	2 Ars
4 Aqr	5 Ars	4 Ars	3 Tau	4 Can	3 Leo	4 Lib	3 Sco	4 Cap	3 Aqr	5 Ars	5 Tau
6 Pis	7 Tau	6 Tau	5 Gem	7 Leo	5 Vir	7 Sco	5 Sag	6 Aqr	6 Pis	7 Tau	7 Gem
9 Ars	10 Gem	9 Gem	7 Can	9 Vir	7 Lib	9 Sag	8 Cap	8 Pis	9 Ars	10 Gem	9 Can
11 Tau	12 Can	11 Can	9 Leo	11 Lib	9 Sco	11 Cap	10 Aqr	11 Ars	11 Tau	13 Can	11 Leo
13 Gem	14 Leo	13 Leo	11 Vir	13 Sco	12 Sag	14 Aqr	13 Pis	14 Tau	13 Gem	15 Leo	14 Vir
15 Can	16 Vir	15 Vir	14 Lib	15 Sag	14 Cap	18 Pis	15 Ars	16 Gem	16 Can	17 Vir	15 Lib
17 Leo	18 Lib	17 Lib	16 Sco	18 Cap	17 Aqr	19 Ars	18 Tau	18 Can	18 Leo	19 Lib	18 Sco
19 Vir	20 Sco	19 Sco	18 Sag	20 Aqr	19 Pis	21 Tar	20 Gem	20 Leo	20 Vir	21 Sco	20 Sag
21 Lib	22 Sag	22 Sag	21 Cap	23 Pis	21 Ars	24 Gem	22 Can	22 Vir	22 Lib	23 Sag	22 Cap
24 Sco	25 Cap	24 Cap	23 Aqr	25 Ars	24 Tau	28 Can	24 Leo	25 Lib	24 Sco	25 Cap	25 Aqr
26 Sag	27 Aqr	26 Aqr	26 Pis	28 Tau	28 Gem	28 Leo	26 Vib	27 Sco	26 Sag	27 Aqr	27 Pis
29 Cap		29 Pis	28 Ars	30 Gem	28 Can	30 Sco	28 Lib	29 Sag	29 Cap	30 Pis	30 Ars
31 Aqr			30 Tau		30 Leo		30 Sco		31 Aqr		

1966

Jan.	Feb.	Mar.	Apr.	May	June	July	Aug.	Sep.	Oct.	Nov.	Dec.
1 Tau	2 Can	1 Can	2 Vir	1 Lib	2 Sag	1 Cap	3 Pis	1 Ars	1 Tau	2 Can	2 Leo
4 Gem	4 Leo	4 Leo	4 Lib	3 Sco	4 Cap	4 Aqr	5 Ars	4 Tau	4 Gem	4 Leo	4 Vir
6 Can	6 Vir	6 Vir	6 Sco	6 Sag	6 Aqr	6 Pis	8 Tau	6 Gem	6 Can	7 Vir	6 Lib
8 Leo	8 Lib	7 Lib	8 Sag	8 Cap	9 Pis	9 Ars	10 Gem	9 Can	8 Leo	9 Lib	8 Sco
10 Vir	10 Sco	10 Sco	10 Cap	10 Aqr	11 Ars	11 Tau	12 Can	11 Leo	10 Vir	11 Sco	10 Sag
12 Lib	12 Sag	12 Sag	13 Aqr	13 Pis	14 Tau	14 Gem	14 Leo	13 Vir	12 Lib	13 Sag	12 Cap
14 Sco	15 Cap	14 Cap	15 Pis	15 Ars	16 Gem	16 Can	16 Vir	15 Lib	14 Sco	15 Cap	15 Aqr
16 Sag	17 Aqr	17 Aqr	18 Ars	18 Tau	19 Can	18 Leo	18 Lib	17 Sco	16 Sag	17 Aqr	17 Pis
19 Cap	20 Pis	19 Pis	20 Tau	20 Gem	21 Leo	20 Vir	20 Sco	19 Sag	19 Cap	20 Pis	20 Ars
21 Aqr	22 Ars	22 Ars	23 Gem	22 Can	23 Vir	22 Lib	23 Sag	21 Cap	21 Aqr	22 Ars	22 Tau
24 Pis	25 Tau	24 Tau	25 Can	24 Leo	25 Lib	24 Sco	25 Cap	24 Aqr	23 Pis	25 Tau	25 Gem
26 Ars	27 Gem	26 Gem	27 Leo	26 Vir	27 Sco	26 Sag	27 Aqr	26 Pis	26 Ars	27 Gem	27 Can
29 Tau		29 Can	29 Vir	29 Lib	29 Sag	29 Cap	30 Pis	29 Ars	28 Tau	29 Can	29 Leo
31 Gem		31 Leo		31 Sco		31 Aqr			31 Gem		31 Vir

1967

Jan	Feb	Mar.	Apr.	May	June	July	Aug.	Sep.	Oct.	Nov.	Dec.
2 Lib	1 Sco	2 Sag	1 Cap	3 Pis	1 Ars	1 Tau	2 Can	1 Leo	1 Vir	1 Sco	1 Sag
4 Sco	3 Sag	4 Cap	3 Aqr	5 Ars	4 Tau	4 Gem	5 Leo	3 Vir	3 Lib	3 Sag	3 Cap
7 Sag	5 Cap	7 Aqr	5 Pis	8 Tau	6 Gem	6 Can	7 Vir	5 Lib	5 Sco	5 Cap	5 Aqr
9 Cap	7 Aqr	9 Pis	8 Ars	10 Gem	9 Can	8 Leo	9 Lib	7 Sco	7 Sag	7 Aqr	7 Pis
11 Aqr	10 Pis	12 Ars	10 Tau	12 Can	11 Leo	11 Vir	11 Sco	9 Sag	9 Cap	10 Pis	9 Ars
13 Pis	12 Ars	14 Tau	13 Gem	15 Leo	13 Vir	13 Lib	13 Sag	12 Cap	11 Aqr	12 Ars	12 Tau
16 Ars	15 Tau	17 Gem	15 Can	17 Vir	15 Lib	15 Sco	15 Cap	14 Aqr	13 Pis	15 Tau	14 Gem
18 Tau	17 Gem	19 Can	18 Leo	19 Lib	17 Sco	17 Sag	18 Aqr	16 Pis	16 Ars	17 Gem	17 Can
21 Gem	20 Can	21 Leo	20 Vir	21 Sco	20 Sag	19 Cap	20 Pis	19 Ars	18 Tau	20 Can	19 Leo
23 Can	22 Leo	23 Vir	22 Lib	23 Sag	22 Cap	21 Aqr	22 Ars	21 Tau	21 Gem	22 Leo	22 Vir
25 Leo	24 Vir	25 Lib	24 Sco	25 Cap	24 Aqr	24 Pis	25 Tau	24 Gem	23 Can	24 Vir	24 Lib
27 Vir	26 Lib	27 Sco	26 Sag	27 Aqr	26 Pis	26 Ars	27 Gem	26 Can	26 Leo	27 Lib	26 Sco
30 Lib	28 Sco	29 Sag	28 Cap	30 Pis	29 Ars	29 Tau	30 Can	28 Leo	28 Vir	29 Sco	28 Sag
			30 Aqr			31 Gem			30 Lib		30 Cap

1968

Jan.	Feb.	Mar.	Apr.	May	June	July	Aug.	Sep.	Oct.	Nov.	Dec.
1 Aqr	2 Ars	3 Tau	2 Gem	2 Can	3 Vir	2 Lib	1 Sco	1 Cap	3 Pis	1 Ars	1 Tau
3 Pis	6 Tau	5 Gem	4 Can	4 Leo	5 Lib	4 Sco	3 Sag	3 Aqr	5 Ars	4 Tau	3 Gem
6 Ars	7 Gem	8 Can	7 Leo	6 Vir	6 Sco	6 Sag	5 Cap	5 Pis	7 Tau	6 Gem	6 Can
8 Tau	10 Can	10 Leo	9 Vir	9 Lib	9 Sag	8 Cap	7 Aqr	8 Ars	10 Gem	9 Can	8 Leo
11 Gem	12 Leo	13 Vir	11 Lib	11 Sco	11 Cap	10 Aqr	9 Pis	10 Tau	12 Can	11 Leo	11 Vir
13 Can	14 Vir	15 Lib	13 Sco	13 Sag	13 Aqr	13 Pis	11 Ars	12 Gem	15 Leo	14 Vir	13 Lib
16 Leo	16 Lib	17 Sco	15 Sag	15 Cap	15 Pis	15 Ars	14 Tau	15 Can	17 Vir	16 Lib	15 Sco
18 Vir	18 Sco	19 Sag	17 Cap	17 Aqr	18 Ars	17 Tau	18 Gem	17 Leo	19 Lib	18 Sco	17 Sag
20 Lib	21 Sag	21 Cap	19 Aqr	19 Pis	20 Tau	20 Gem	19 Can	20 Vir	22 Sco	20 Sag	19 Cap
22 Sco	23 Cap	23 Aqr	22 Pis	21 Ars	23 Gem	22 Can	21 Leo	22 Lib	24 Sag	22 Cap	21 Aqr
24 Sag	25 Aqr	25 Pis	24 Ars	24 Tau	25 Can	25 Leo	24 Vir	24 Sco	25 Cap	24 Aqr	23 Pis
26 Cap	27 Pis	28 Ars	27 Tau	26 Gem	28 Leo	27 Vir	26 Lib	26 Sag	28 Aqr	26 Pis	26 Ars
29 Aqr	29 Ars	30 Tau	29 Gem	29 Can	30 Vir	29 Lib	28 Sco	28 Cap	30 Pis	28 Ars	28 Tau
31 Pis				31 Leo			30 Sag	30 Aqr			31 Gem

1969

Jan.	Feb.	Mar.	Apr.	May	June	July	Aug.	Sep.	Oct.	Nov.	Dec.
2 Can	1 Leo	3 Vir	1 Lib	1 Sco	1 Cap	1 Aqr	1 Ars	2 Gem	2 Can	1 Leo	1 Vir
5 Leo	3 Vir	5 Lib	4 Sco	3 Sag	3 Aqr	3 Pis	4 Tau	5 Can	5 Leo	4 Vir	3 Lib
7 Vir	6 Lib	7 Sco	6 Sag	6 Cap	6 Pis	5 Ars	6 Gem	7 Leo	7 Vir	6 Lib	6 Sco
9 Lib	8 Sco	9 Sag	8 Cap	7 Aqr	8 Ars	7 Tau	9 Can	10 Vir	10 Lib	8 Sco	8 Sag
12 Sco	10 Sag	11 Cap	10 Aqr	9 Pis	10 Tau	10 Gem	11 Leo	12 Sco	12 Sco	10 Sag	10 Cap
14 Sag	12 Cap	14 Aqr	12 Pis	11 Ars	12 Gem	12 Can	14 Vir	15 Sco	14 Sag	12 Cap	12 Aqr
16 Cap	14 Aqr	16 Pis	14 Ars	14 Tau	15 Can	15 Leo	16 Lib	17 Sag	16 Cap	14 Aqr	14 Pis
18 Aqr	18 Pis	18 Ars	17 Tau	18 Gem	18 Leo	17 Vir	18 Sco	19 Cap	18 Aqr	17 Pis	16 Ars
20 Pis	18 Ars	20 Tau	19 Gem	19 Can	20 Vir	20 Lib	20 Sag	21 Aqr	20 Pis	19 Ars	18 Tau
22 Ars	21 Tau	23 Gem	21 Can	21 Leo	22 Lib	22 Sco	23 Cap	23 Pis	22 Ars	21 Tau	20 Gem
24 Tau	23 Gem	25 Can	24 Leo	24 Vir	25 Sco	24 Sag	25 Aqr	25 Ars	25 Tau	23 Gem	23 Can
27 Gem	26 Can	28 Leo	26 Vir	26 Lib	27 Sag	26 Cap	27 Pis	27 Tau	27 Gem	26 Can	26 Leo
29 Can	28 Leo	30 Vir	29 Lib	28 Sco	29 Cap	28 Aqr	29 Ars	30 Gem	30 Can	28 Leo	28 Vir
				30 Sag		30 Pis	31 Tau				30 Lib

1970

Jan.	Feb.	Mar.	Apr.	May	June	July	Aug.	Sep.	Oct.	Nov.	Dec.
2 Sco	1 Sag	2 Cap	3 Pis	2 Ars	3 Gem	2 Can	1 Leo	2 Lib	2 Sco	1 Sag	2 Aqr
4 Sag	3 Cap	4 Aqr	5 Ars	4 Tau	5 Can	5 Leo	3 Vir	5 Sco	4 Sag	3 Cap	4 Pis
6 Cap	5 Aqr	6 Pis	7 Tau	6 Gem	7 Leo	7 Vir	6 Lib	7 Sag	7 Cap	5 Aqr	7 Ars
8 Aqr	7 Pis	8 Ars	9 Gem	9 Can	10 Vir	10 Lib	8 Sco	9 Cap	9 Aqr	7 Pis	9 Tau
10 Pis	9 Ars	10 Tau	11 Can	11 Leo	12 Lib	12 Sco	11 Sag	12 Aqr	11 Pis	9 Ars	11 Gem
12 Ars	11 Tau	12 Gem	14 Leo	14 Vir	15 Sco	14 Sag	13 Cap	14 Pis	13 Ars	11 Tau	13 Can
15 Tau	13 Gem	15 Can	16 Vir	16 Lib	17 Sag	17 Cap	15 Aqr	16 Ars	15 Tau	14 Gem	15 Leo
17 Gem	16 Can	17 Leo	19 Lib	18 Sco	19 Cap	19 Aqr	17 Pis	18 Tau	17 Gem	16 Can	18 Vir
19 Can	18 Leo	20 Vir	21 Sco	21 Sag	21 Aqr	21 Pis	19 Ars	20 Gem	19 Can	18 Leo	20 Lib
22 Leo	21 Vir	22 Lib	23 Sag	23 Cap	23 Pis	23 Ars	21 Tau	22 Can	22 Leo	21 Vir	23 Sco
24 Vir	23 Lib	25 Sco	26 Cap	25 Aqr	25 Ars	25 Tau	23 Gem	24 Leo	24 Vir	23 Lib	25 Sag
27 Lib	26 Sco	27 Sag	28 Aqr	27 Pis	28 Tau	27 Gem	26 Can	27 Vir	27 Lib	26 Sco	28 Cap
29 Sco	28 Sag	29 Cap	30 Pis	29 Ars	30 Gem	29 Can	28 Leo	30 Lib	29 Sco	28 Sag	30 Aqr
		31 Aqr		31 Tau			31 Vir			30 Cap	

1971

Jan.	Feb.	Mar.	Apr.	May	June	July	Aug.	Sep.	Oct.	Nov.	Dec.
1 Pis	1 Tau	1 Tau	2 Can	1 Leo	3 Lib	2 Sco	1 Sag	2 Aqr	1 Pis	2 Tau	1 Gem
3 Ars	3 Gem	3 Gem	4 Leo	3 Vir	5 Sco	5 Sag	3 Cap	4 Pis	3 Ars	4 Gem	3 Can
5 Tau	6 Can	5 Can	6 Vir	6 Lib	7 Sag	7 Cap	5 Aqr	6 Ars	5 Tau	6 Can	5 Leo
7 Gem	8 Leo	7 Leo	9 Lib	8 Sco	9 Cap	9 Aqr	7 Pis	8 Tau	7 Gem	8 Leo	8 Vir
9 Can	11 Vir	10 Vir	11 Sco	11 Sag	12 Aqr	11 Pis	9 Ars	10 Gem	9 Can	10 Vir	10 Lib
12 Leo	13 Lib	12 Lib	14 Sag	13 Cap	14 Pis	13 Ars	12 Tau	12 Can	12 Leo	13 Lib	13 Sco
14 Vir	16 Sco	15 Sco	16 Cap	15 Aqr	16 Ars	15 Tau	14 Gem	15 Leo	14 Vir	15 Sco	15 Sag
17 Lib	18 Sag	17 Sag	18 Aqr	18 Pis	18 Tau	17 Gem	16 Can	17 Vir	17 Lib	18 Sag	18 Cap
19 Sco	20 Cap	20 Cap	20 Pis	20 Ars	20 Gem	20 Can	18 Leo	19 Lib	19 Sco	20 Cap	20 Aqr
22 Sag	22 Aqr	22 Aqr	22 Ars	22 Tau	22 Can	22 Leo	21 Vir	22 Sco	22 Sag	23 Aqr	22 Pis
24 Cap	24 Pis	24 Pis	24 Tau	24 Gem	25 Leo	24 Vir	23 Lib	24 Sag	24 Cap	25 Pis	24 Ars
26 Aqr	26 Ars	26 Ars	26 Gem	26 Can	27 Vir	27 Lib	26 Sco	27 Cap	27 Aqr	27 Ars	25 Tau
28 Pis		28 Tau	29 Can	28 Leo	30 Lib	29 Sco	28 Sag	29 Aqr	29 Pis	29 Tau	28 Gem
30 Ars		30 Gem		31 Vir			31 Cap		31 Ars		31 Can

1972

Jan.	Feb.	Mar.	Apr.	May	June	July	Aug.	Sep.	Oct.	Nov.	Dec.
2 Leo	1 Vir	1 Lib	3 Sag	2 Can	1 Aqr	1 Pis	1 Tau	2 Can	1 Leo	2 Lib	2 Sco
4 Vir	2 Lib	4 Sco	5 Cap	5 Aqr	3 Pis	3 Ars	3 Gem	4 Leo	3 Vir	4 Sco	4 Sag
7 Lib	5 Sco	6 Sag	7 Aqr	7 Pis	6 Ars	5 Tau	5 Can	6 Vir	6 Lib	7 Sag	7 Cap
9 Sco	8 Sag	9 Cap	10 Pis	9 Ars	8 Tau	7 Gem	8 Leo	8 Lib	8 Sco	9 Cap	9 Aqr
12 Sag	10 Cap	11 Aqr	12 Ars	11 Tau	10 Gem	9 Can	10 Vir	11 Sco	11 Sag	12 Aqr	12 Pis
14 Cap	13 Aqr	13 Pis	14 Tau	13 Gem	12 Can	11 Leo	12 Lib	13 Sag	13 Cap	14 Pis	14 Ars
16 Aqr	15 Pis	15 Ars	16 Gem	15 Can	14 Leo	13 Vir	15 Sco	16 Cap	16 Aqr	17 Ars	15 Tau
18 Pis	17 Ars	17 Tau	18 Can	17 Leo	16 Vir	16 Lib	18 Sag	18 Aqr	18 Pis	19 Tau	18 Gem
21 Ars	19 Tau	19 Gem	20 Leo	20 Vir	18 Lib	18 Sco	20 Cap	21 Pis	20 Ars	21 Gem	20 Can
23 Tau	21 Gem	21 Can	22 Vir	22 Lib	21 Sco	21 Sag	22 Aqr	23 Ars	22 Tau	23 Can	22 Leo
25 Gem	23 Can	24 Leo	25 Lib	25 Sco	23 Sag	23 Cap	24 Pis	25 Tau	24 Gem	25 Leo	24 Vir
27 Can	26 Leo	26 Vir	27 Sco	27 Sag	26 Cap	26 Aqr	26 Ars	27 Gem	25 Can	27 Vir	26 Lib
29 Leo	28 Vir	29 Lib	30 Sag	30 Cap	28 Aqr	28 Pis	28 Tau	29 Can	28 Leo	30 Lib	29 Sco
		31 Sco				30 Ars	30 Gem		31 Vir		31 Sag

1973

Jan.	Feb.	Mar.	Apr.	May	June	July	Aug.	Sep.	Oct.	Nov.	Dec.
3 Cap	2 Aqr	1 Aqr	2 Ars	2 Tau	2 Can	1 Leo	2 Lib	1 Sco	3 Cap	2 Aqr	2 Pis
5 Aqr	4 Pis	3 Pis	4 Tau	4 Gem	4 Leo	3 Vir	4 Sco	3 Sag	6 Aqr	4 Pis	4 Ars
8 Pis	6 Ars	5 Ars	6 Gem	6 Can	6 Vir	6 Lib	7 Sag	6 Cap	8 Pis	7 Ars	6 Tau
10 Ars	9 Tau	8 Tau	8 Can	8 Leo	8 Lib	8 Sco	9 Cap	8 Aqr	10 Ars	9 Tau	8 Gem
12 Tau	11 Gem	10 Gem	10 Leo	10 Vir	11 Sco	11 Sag	12 Aqr	11 Pis	12 Tau	11 Gem	10 Can
14 Gem	13 Can	12 Can	13 Vir	12 Lib	13 Sag	13 Cap	14 Pis	13 Ars	15 Gem	13 Can	12 Leo
16 Can	15 Leo	14 Leo	15 Lib	15 Sco	16 Cap	16 Aqr	17 Ars	15 Tau	17 Can	15 Leo	14 Vir
18 Leo	17 Vir	16 Vir	17 Sco	17 Sag	18 Aqr	18 Pis	19 Tau	17 Gem	19 Leo	17 Vir	17 Lib
21 Vir	19 Lib	19 Lib	20 Sag	20 Cap	21 Pis	20 Ars	21 Gem	19 Can	21 Vir	19 Lib	19 Sco
23 Lib	22 Sco	21 Sco	22 Cap	22 Aqr	23 Ars	23 Tau	23 Can	22 Leo	23 Lib	22 Sco	21 Sag
25 Sco	24 Sag	23 Sag	25 Aqr	25 Pis	25 Tau	25 Gem	25 Leo	24 Vir	25 Sco	24 Sag	24 Cap
28 Sag	27 Cap	26 Cap	27 Pis	27 Ars	27 Gem	27 Can	27 Vir	26 Lib	28 Sag	27 Cap	26 Aqr
30 Cap		28 Aqr	29 Ars	29 Tau	29 Can	29 Leo	29 Lib	28 Sco	30 Cap	29 Aqr	29 Pis
		31 Pis		31 Gem		31 Vir		30 Sag			31 Ars

1974

Jan.	Feb.	Mar.	Apr.	May	June	July	Aug.	Sep.	Oct.	Nov.	Dec.
3 Tau	1 Gem	3 Can	1 Leo	2 Lib	1 Sco	1 Sag	2 Aqr	1 Pis	3 Tau	1 Gem	1 Can
5 Gem	3 Can	5 Leo	3 Vir	5 Sco	3 Sag	3 Cap	4 Pis	3 Ars	5 Gem	3 Can	3 Leo
7 Can	5 Leo	7 Vir	5 Lib	7 Sag	6 Cap	6 Aqr	7 Ars	5 Tau	7 Can	6 Leo	5 Vir
9 Leo	7 Vir	9 Lib	7 Sco	9 Cap	8 Aqr	8 Pis	9 Tau	8 Gem	9 Leo	8 Vir	7 Lib
11 Vir	9 Lib	11 Sco	10 Sag	12 Aqr	11 Pis	11 Ars	12 Gem	10 Can	11 Vir	10 Lib	9 Sco
13 Lib	12 Sco	13 Sag	12 Cap	14 Pis	13 Ars	13 Tau	14 Can	12 Leo	14 Lib	12 Sco	12 Sag
15 Sco	14 Sag	16 Cap	15 Aqr	17 Ars	16 Tau	15 Gem	16 Leo	14 Vir	16 Sco	14 Sag	14 Cap
18 Sag	16 Cap	18 Aqr	17 Pis	19 Tau	18 Gem	17 Can	18 Vir	16 Lib	18 Sag	17 Cap	16 Aqr
20 Cap	19 Aqr	21 Pis	19 Ars	21 Gem	20 Can	19 Leo	20 Lib	18 Sco	20 Cap	19 Aqr	19 Pis
23 Aqr	21 Pis	23 Ars	22 Tau	23 Can	22 Leo	21 Vir	22 Sco	20 Sag	23 Aqr	22 Pis	21 Ars
25 Pis	24 Ars	25 Tau	24 Gem	25 Leo	24 Vir	23 Lib	24 Sag	23 Cap	25 Pis	24 Ars	24 Tau
28 Ars	26 Tau	28 Gem	26 Can	28 Vir	26 Lib	25 Sco	27 Cap	25 Aqr	28 Ars	26 Tau	26 Gem
30 Tau	28 Gem	30 Can	28 Leo	30 Lib	28 Sco	28 Sag	29 Aqr	28 Pis	30 Tau	29 Gem	28 Can
			30 Vir			30 Cap		30 Ars			30 Leo

1975

Jan.	Feb.	Mar.	Apr.	May	June	July	Aug.	Sep.	Oct.	Nov.	Dec.
1 Vir	2 Sco	1 Sco	2 Cap	2 Aqr	1 Pis	3 Tau	2 Gem	2 Leo	2 Vir	2 Sco	2 Sag
3 Lib	4 Sag	3 Sag	4 Aqr	4 Pis	3 Ars	5 Gem	4 Can	4 Vir	4 Lib	4 Sag	4 Cap
6 Sco	6 Cap	6 Cap	7 Pis	7 Ars	6 Tau	8 Can	6 Leo	6 Lib	6 Sco	7 Cap	6 Aqr
8 Sag	9 Aqr	8 Aqr	9 Ars	9 Tau	8 Gem	10 Leo	8 Vir	8 Sco	8 Sag	9 Aqr	9 Pis
10 Cap	11 Pis	11 Pis	12 Tau	12 Gem	10 Can	12 Vir	10 Lib	11 Sag	10 Cap	11 Pis	11 Ars
13 Aqr	14 Ars	14 Ars	14 Gem	14 Can	12 Leo	14 Lib	12 Sco	13 Cap	13 Aqr	14 Ars	14 Tau
15 Pis	16 Tau	18 Tau	17 Can	16 Leo	14 Vir	16 Sco	14 Sag	15 Aqr	15 Pis	16 Tau	16 Gem
16 Ars	19 Gem	20 Gem	19 Leo	18 Vir	17 Lib	18 Sag	17 Cap	18 Pis	18 Ars	19 Gem	18 Can
20 Tau	21 Can	23 Can	21 Vir	20 Lib	19 Sco	20 Cap	19 Aqr	20 Ars	20 Tau	21 Can	21 Leo
22 Gem	23 Leo	25 Leo	23 Lib	22 Sco	21 Sag	23 Aqr	21 Pis	23 Tau	22 Gem	23 Leo	23 Vir
25 Can	25 Vir	27 Vir	25 Sco	25 Sag	23 Cap	25 Pis	24 Ars	25 Gem	25 Can	26 Vir	25 Lib
27 Leo	27 Lib	29 Lib	27 Sag	27 Cap	25 Aqr	28 Ars	27 Tau	28 Can	27 Leo	28 Lib	27 Sco
29 Vir		31 Sco	29 Cap	29 Aqr	28 Pis	30 Tau	29 Gem	30 Leo	29 Vir	30 Sco	29 Sag
31 Lib					30 Ars		31 Can		31 Lib		31 Cap

1976

Jan.	Feb.	Mar.	Apr.	May	June	July	Aug.	Sep.	Oct.	Nov..	Dec.
3 Aqr	1 Pis	2 Ars	1 Tau	1 Gem	2 Leo	1 Vir	2 Sco	2 Cap	2 Aqr	3 Ars	2 Tau
5 Pis	4 Ars	5 Tau	3 Gem	3 Can	4 Vir	3 Lib	4 Sag	4 Aqr	4 Pis	5 Tau	5 Gem
7 Ars	6 Tau	7 Gem	6 Can	5 Leo	6 Lib	5 Sco	6 Cap	7 Pis	6 Ars	8 Gem	8 Can
10 Tau	9 Gem	10 Can	8 Leo	8 Vir	8 Sco	8 Sag	8 Aqr	9 Ars	9 Tau	10 Can	10 Leo
12 Gem	11 Can	12 Leo	10 Vir	10 Lib	10 Sag	10 Cap	10 Pis	12 Tau	11 Gem	13 Leo	12 Vir
15 Can	13 Leo	14 Vir	12 Lib	12 Sco	12 Cap	12 Aqr	13 Ars	14 Gem	14 Can	15 Vir	14 Lib
17 Leo	15 Vir	16 Lib	14 Sco	14 Sag	14 Aqr	14 Pis	15 Tau	17 Can	16 Leo	17 Lib	17 Sco
19 Vir	17 Lib	18 Sco	16 Sag	16 Cap	17 Pis	17 Ars	18 Gem	19 Leo	19 Vir	19 Sco	19 Sag
21 Lib	20 Sco	20 Sag	18 Cap	18 Aqr	19 Ars	19 Tau	20 Can	21 Vir	21 Lib	21 Sag	21 Cap
23 Sco	22 Sag	22 Cap	21 Aqr	20 Pis	22 Tau	22 Gem	23 Leo	23 Lib	23 Sco	23 Cap	23 Aqr
25 Sag	24 Cap	24 Aqr	23 Pis	23 Ars	24 Gem	24 Can	25 Vir	25 Sco	25 Sag	25 Aqr	25 Pis
28 Cap	26 Aqr	27 Pis	26 Ars	25 Tau	26 Can	26 Leo	27 Lib	27 Sag	27 Cap	28 Pis	27 Ars
30 Aqr	29 Pis	29 Ars	28 Tau	28 Gem	29 Leo	28 Vir	29 Sco	29 Cap	29 Aqr	30 Ars	30 Tau
				30 Can		31 Lib	31 Sag		31 Pis		

1977

Jan.	Feb.	Mar.	Apr.	May	June	July	Aug.	Sep.	Oct.	Nov.	Dec.
1 Gem	3 Leo	2 Leo	1 Vir	2 Sco	1 Sag	2 Aqr	1 Pis	2 Tau	1 Gem	3 Leo	2 Vir
4 Can	5 Vir	4 Vir	3 Lib	4 Sag	3 Cap	4 Pis	3 Ars	4 Gem	4 Can	5 Vir	5 Lib
6 Leo	7 Lib	6 Lib	5 Sco	6 Cap	5 Aqr	6 Ars	5 Tau	7 Can	6 Leo	7 Lib	7 Sco
8 Vir	9 Sco	8 Sco	7 Sag	8 Aqr	7 Pis	9 Tau	8 Gem	9 Vir	9 Vir	10 Sco	9 Sag
11 Lib	11 Sag	10 Sag	9 Cap	10 Pis	9 Ars	11 Gem	10 Can	11 Vir	11 Lib	12 Sag	11 Cap
13 Sco	13 Cap	13 Cap	11 Aqr	13 Ars	12 Tau	14 Can	13 Leo	14 Lib	13 Sco	14 Cap	13 Aqr
15 Sag	15 Aqr	15 Aqr	13 Pis	15 Tau	14 Gem	16 Leo	15 Vir	16 Sco	15 Sag	16 Aqr	15 Pis
17 Cap	18 Pis	17 Pis	16 Ars	18 Gem	17 Can	19 Vir	17 Lib	18 Sag	17 Cap	18 Pis	17 Ars
19 Aqr	20 Ars	19 Ars	18 Tau	20 Can	19 Leo	21 Lib	19 Sco	20 Cap	19 Aqr	20 Ars	20 Tau
21 Pis	22 Tau	22 Tau	21 Gem	23 Leo	22 Vir	23 Sco	22 Sag	22 Aqr	22 Pis	22 Tau	22 Gem
24 Ars	25 Gem	24 Gem	23 Can	25 Vir	24 Lib	25 Sag	24 Cap	24 Pis	24 Ars	25 Gem	25 Can
26 Tau	27 Can	27 Can	26 Leo	28 Lib	26 Sco	27 Cap	26 Aqr	27 Ars	26 Tau	27 Can	27 Leo
29 Gem		29 Leo	28 Vir	30 Sco	28 Sag	29 Aqr	28 Pis	29 Tau	29 Gem	30 Leo	30 Vir
31 Can			30 Lib		30 Cap		30 Ars		31 Can		

1978

Jan.	Feb.	Mar.	Apr.	May	June	July	Aug.	Sep.	Oct.	Nov.	Dec.
1 Lib	2 Sag	1 Sag	2 Aqr	1 Pis	2 Tau	1 Gem	3 Leo	1 Vir	1 Lib	2 Sag	1 Cap
3 Sco	4 Cap	3 Cap	4 Pis	3 Ars	4 Gem	4 Can	5 Vir	4 Lib	3 Sco	4 Cap	3 Aqr
5 Sag	6 Aqr	5 Aqr	6 Ars	5 Tau	7 Can	6 Leo	8 Lib	6 Sco	6 Sag	6 Aqr	5 Pis
7 Cap	8 Pis	7 Pis	8 Tau	8 Gem	9 Leo	9 Vir	10 Sco	8 Sag	8 Cap	8 Pis	8 Ars
9 Aqr	10 Ars	9 Ars	10 Gem	10 Can	12 Vir	11 Lib	12 Sag	11 Cap	10 Aqr	10 Ars	10 Tau
11 Pis	12 Tau	12 Tau	13 Can	13 Leo	14 Lib	14 Sco	14 Cap	13 Aqr	12 Pis	13 Tau	12 Gem
14 Ars	15 Gem	14 Gem	15 Leo	15 Vir	16 Sco	16 Sag	16 Aqr	15 Pis	14 Ars	15 Gem	15 Can
16 Tau	17 Can	17 Can	18 Vir	18 Lib	18 Sag	18 Cap	18 Pis	17 Ars	16 Tau	17 Can	17 Leo
18 Gem	20 Leo	19 Leo	20 Lib	20 Sco	20 Cap	20 Aqr	20 Ars	19 Tau	19 Gem	20 Leo	20 Vir
21 Can	22 Vir	22 Vir	22 Sco	22 Sag	22 Aqr	22 Pis	23 Tau	21 Gem	21 Can	22 Vir	22 Lib
24 Leo	25 Lib	24 Lib	25 Sag	24 Cap	24 Pis	24 Ars	25 Gem	24 Can	24 Leo	25 Lib	25 Sco
26 Vir	27 Sco	26 Sco	27 Cap	26 Aqr	27 Ars	26 Tau	27 Can	26 Leo	26 Vir	27 Sco	27 Sag
28 Lib		28 Sag	28 Aqr	28 Pis	29 Tau	29 Gem	30 Leo	29 Vir	28 Lib	29 Sag	29 Cap
31 Sco		30 Cap		30 Ars		31 Can			31 Sco		31 Aqr

1979

Jan.	Feb.	Mar.	Apr.	May	June	July	Aug.	Sep.	Oct.	Nov.	Dec.
2 Pis	2 Tau	2 Tau	3 Can	3 Leo	1 Vir	1 Lib	2 Sag	1 Cap	3 Pis	1 Ars	2 Gem
4 Ars	5 Gem	4 Gem	5 Leo	5 Vir	4 Lib	4 Sco	5 Cap	3 Aqr	5 Ars	3 Tau	5 Can
6 Tau	7 Can	6 Can	8 Vir	8 Lib	6 Sco	6 Sag	7 Aqr	5 Pis	7 Tau	5 Gem	7 Leo
8 Gem	10 Leo	9 Leo	10 Lib	10 Sco	9 Sag	8 Cap	9 Pis	7 Ars	9 Gem	7 Can	9 Vir
11 Can	12 Vir	11 Vir	13 Sco	12 Sag	11 Cap	10 Aqr	11 Ars	9 Tau	11 Can	10 Leo	12 Lib
13 Leo	15 Lib	14 Lib	15 Sag	14 Cap	13 Aqr	12 Pis	13 Tau	11 Gem	13 Leo	12 Vir	15 Sco
16 Vir	17 Sco	16 Sco	17 Cap	17 Aqr	15 Pis	14 Ars	15 Gem	14 Can	16 Vir	15 Lib	17 Sag
18 Lib	19 Sag	19 Sag	19 Aqr	19 Pis	17 Ars	16 Tau	17 Can	16 Leo	18 Lib	17 Sco	19 Cap
21 Sco	22 Cap	21 Cap	21 Pis	21 Ars	19 Tau	19 Gem	20 Leo	19 Vir	21 Sco	19 Sag	21 Aqr
23 Sag	24 Aqr	23 Aqr	24 Ars	23 Tau	21 Gem	21 Can	22 Vir	21 Lib	23 Sag	22 Cap	23 Pis
25 Cap	26 Pis	25 Pis	26 Tau	25 Gem	24 Can	24 Leo	24 Lib	23 Sco	25 Cap	24 Aqr	25 Ars
27 Aqr	28 Ars	27 Ars	28 Gem	27 Can	26 Leo	26 Vir	27 Sco	26 Sag	28 Aqr	26 Pis	28 Tau
29 Pis		29 Tau	30 Can	29 Vir		29 Lib	30 Sag	28 Cap	30 Pis	28 Ars	30 Gem
31 Ars		31 Gem				31 Sco		30 Aqr		30 Tau	

1980

Jan.	Feb.	Mar.	Apr.	May	June	July	Aug.	Sep.	Oct.	Nov.	Dec.
1 Can	2 Vir	3 Lib	2 Sco	1 Sag	2 Aqr	2 Pis	2 Tau	1 Gem	2 Leo	1 Vir	1 Lib
3 Leo	5 Lib	5 Sco	4 Sag	4 Cap	5 Pis	4 Ars	4 Gem	3 Can	5 Vir	4 Lib	3 Sco
6 Vir	7 Sco	8 Sag	7 Cap	6 Aqr	7 Ars	6 Tau	7 Can	5 Leo	7 Lib	6 Sco	6 Sag
8 Lib	10 Sag	10 Cap	9 Aqr	8 Pis	9 Tau	8 Gem	9 Leo	8 Vir	10 Sco	9 Sag	8 Cap
11 Sco	12 Cap	12 Aqr	11 Pis	10 Ars	11 Gem	10 Can	11 Vir	10 Lib	12 Sag	11 Cap	11 Aqr
13 Sag	14 Aqr	15 Pis	13 Ars	12 Tau	13 Can	13 Leo	14 Lib	13 Sco	15 Cap	13 Aqr	13 Pis
15 Cap	16 Pis	17 Ars	15 Tau	14 Gem	15 Leo	15 Vir	16 Sco	15 Sag	17 Aqr	16 Pis	15 Ars
18 Aqr	18 Ars	19 Tau	17 Gem	17 Can	18 Vir	17 Lib	19 Sag	17 Cap	19 Pis	18 Ars	17 Tau
20 Pis	20 Tau	21 Gem	19 Can	19 Leo	20 Lib	20 Sco	21 Cap	20 Aqr	21 Ars	20 Tau	19 Gem
22 Ars	22 Gem	23 Can	21 Leo	21 Vir	23 Sco	22 Sag	23 Aqr	22 Pis	23 Tau	22 Gem	21 Can
24 Tau	25 Can	25 Leo	24 Virg	24 Lib	25 Sag	25 Cap	25 Pis	24 Ars	25 Gem	24 Can	23 Leo
26 Gem	27 Leo	28 Vir	26 Lib	26 Sco	27 Cap	27 Aqr	27 Ars	26 Tau	27 Can	26 Leo	26 Vir
28 Can	29 Vir	30 Lib	29 Sco	29 Sag	30 Aqr	29 Pis	29 Tau	28 Gem	30 Leo	28 Vir	28 Lib
31 Leo				31 Cap		31 Ars		30 Can			31 Sco

1981

Jan.	Feb.	Mar.	Apr.	May	June	July	Aug.	Sep.	Oct.	Nov.	Dec.
2 Sag	1 Cap	3 Aqr	1 Pis	1 Ars	1 Gem	1 Can	1 Vir	2 Sco	2 Sag	1 Cap	1 Aqr
5 Cap	3 Aqr	5 Pis	3 Ars	3 Tau	3 Can	3 Leo	4 Lib	5 Sag	5 Cap	4 Aqr	3 Pis
7 Aqr	5 Pis	7 Ars	5 Tau	5 Gem	5 Leo	5 Vir	6 Sco	7 Cap	7 Aqr	6 Pis	5 Ars
9 Pis	8 Ars	9 Tau	7 Gem	7 Can	8 Vir	7 Lib	9 Sag	10 Aqr	10 Pis	8 Ars	8 Tau
11 Ars	10 Tau	11 Gem	9 Can	9 Leo	10 Lib	10 Sco	11 Cap	12 Pis	12 Ars	10 Tau	10 Gem
13 Tau	12 Gem	13 Can	12 Leo	11 Vir	12 Sco	12 Sag	13 Aqr	14 Ars	14 Tau	12 Gem	12 Can
16 Gem	14 Can	15 Leo	14 Vir	14 Lib	15 Sag	15 Cap	16 Pis	16 Tau	16 Gem	14 Can	14 Leo
18 Can	16 Leo	18 Vir	16 Lib	16 Sco	17 Cap	17 Aqr	18 Ars	18 Gem	18 Can	16 Leo	16 Vir
20 Leo	18 Vir	20 Lib	19 Sco	19 Sag	20 Aqr	19 Pis	20 Tau	20 Can	20 Leo	18 Vir	18 Lib
22 Vir	21 Lib	23 Sco	21 Sag	21 Cap	22 Pis	22 Ars	22 Gem	23 Leo	22 Vir	21 Lib	20 Sco
24 Lib	23 Sco	25 Sag	24 Cap	24 Aqr	24 Ars	24 Tau	24 Can	25 Vir	25 Lib	23 Sco	23 Sag
27 Sco	26 Sag	28 Cap	26 Aqr	26 Pis	27 Tau	26 Gem	26 Leo	27 Lib	27 Sco	26 Sag	26 Cap
30 Sag	28 Cap	30 Aqr	29 Pis	28 Ars	29 Gem	28 Can	29 Vir	30 Sco	29 Sag	28 Cap	28 Aqr
				30 Tau		30 Leo	31 Lib				30 Pis

1982

Jan.	Feb.	Mar.	Apr.	May	June	July	Aug.	Sep.	Oct.	Nov.	Dec.
2 Ars	2 Gem	2 Gem	2 Leo	1 Vir	2 Sco	2 Sag	1 Cap	2 Pis	2 Ars	3 Gem	2 Can
4 Tau	4 Can	4 Can	4 Vir	4 Lib	5 Sag	5 Cap	3 Aqr	5 Ars	4 Tau	5 Can	4 Leo
6 Gem	6 Leo	6 Leo	7 Lib	6 Sco	7 Cap	7 Aqr	6 Pis	7 Tau	6 Gem	7 Leo	6 Vir
8 Can	9 Vir	8 Vir	9 Sco	9 Sag	10 Aqr	10 Pis	8 Ars	9 Gem	8 Can	9 Virg	8 Lib
10 Leo	11 Lib	10 Lib	11 Sag	11 Cap	12 Pis	12 Ars	11 Tau	11 Can	10 Leo	11 Lib	11 Sco
12 Vir	13 Sco	13 Sco	14 Cap	14 Aqr	15 Ars	14 Tau	13 Gem	13 Leo	13 Vir	13 Sco	13 Sag
14 Lib	16 Sag	15 Sag	16 Aqr	16 Pis	17 Tau	16 Gem	15 Can	15 Vir	15 Lib	16 Sag	15 Cap
17 Sco	18 Cap	17 Cap	19 Pis	18 Ars	19 Gem	18 Can	17 Leo	17 Lib	17 Sco	18 Cap	18 Aqr
19 Sag	21 Aqr	20 Aqr	21 Ars	21 Tau	21 Can	20 Leo	19 Vir	20 Sco	19 Sag	21 Aqr	21 Pis
22 Cap	23 Pis	22 Pis	23 Tau	23 Gem	23 Leo	22 Vir	21 Lib	22 Sag	22 Cap	23 Pis	23 Ars
24 Aqr	25 Ars	25 Ars	25 Gem	25 Can	25 Vir	25 Lib	23 Sco	25 Cap	24 Aqr	26 Ars	25 Tau
27 Pis	27 Tau	27 Tau	27 Can	27 Leo	27 Lib	27 Sco	26 Sag	27 Aqr	27 Pis	28 Tau	27 Gem
29 Ars		29 Gem	29 Leo	29 Vir	30 Sco	29 Sag	28 Cap	30 Pis	29 Ars	30 Gem	29 Can
31 Tau		31 Can		31 Lib			31 Aqr		31 Tau		31 Leo

1983

Jan.	Feb.	Mar.	Apr.	May	June	July	Aug.	Sep.	Oct.	Nov.	Dec.
2 Vir	1 Lib	2 Sco	1 Sag	1 Cap	2 Pis	2 Ars	1 Tau	2 Can	1 Leo	1 Lib	1 Sco
5 Lib	3 Sco	5 Sag	4 Cap	3 Aqr	5 Ars	5 Tau	3 Gem	4 Leo	3 Vir	4 Sco	3 Sag
7 Sco	5 Sag	7 Cap	6 Aqr	6 Pis	7 Tau	7 Gem	5 Can	6 Vir	5 Lib	6 Sag	5 Cap
9 Sag	8 Cap	10 Aqr	9 Pis	8 Ars	9 Gem	9 Can	7 Leo	8 Lib	7 Sco	8 Cap	8 Aqr
12 Cap	11 Aqr	12 Pis	11 Ars	11 Tau	11 Can	11 Leo	9 Vir	10 Sco	9 Sag	11 Aqr	10 Pis
14 Aqr	13 Pis	15 Ars	13 Tau	13 Gem	13 Leo	13 Vir	11 Lib	12 Sag	12 Cap	13 Pis	13 Ars
17 Pis	15 Ars	17 Tau	16 Gem	15 Can	15 Vir	15 Lib	13 Sco	14 Cap	14 Aqr	16 Ars	15 Tau
19 Ars	18 Tau	19 Gem	18 Can	18 Leo	18 Lib	17 Sco	16 Sag	17 Aqr	17 Pis	18 Tau	18 Gem
22 Tau	20 Gem	22 Can	20 Leo	19 Vir	20 Sco	19 Sag	18 Cap	19 Pis	19 Ars	20 Gem	20 Can
24 Gem	22 Can	24 Leo	22 Vir	21 Lib	22 Sag	22 Cap	21 Aqr	22 Ars	22 Tau	22 Can	22 Leo
26 Can	24 Leo	26 Vir	24 Lib	24 Sco	25 Cap	24 Aqr	23 Pis	24 Tau	24 Gem	25 Leo	24 Vir
28 Leo	26 Vir	28 Lib	26 Sco	26 Sag	27 Aqr	27 Pis	26 Ars	27 Gem	26 Can	27 Vir	26 Lib
30 Vir	28 Lib	30 Sco	29 Sag	28 Cap	30 Pis	29 Ars	28 Tau	29 Can	28 Leo	29 Lib	28 Sco
				31 Aqr			30 Gem		30 Vir		30 Sag

1984

Jan.	Feb.	Mar.	Apr.	May	June	July	Aug.	Sep.	Oct.	Nov.	Dec.
2 Cap	3 Pis	1 Pis	2 Tau	2 Gem	1 Can	2 Vir	1 Lib	1 Sag	1 Cap	2 Pis	2 Ars
4 Aqr	6 Ars	4 Ars	5 Gem	4 Can	3 Leo	4 Lib	3 Sco	3 Cap	3 Aqr	4 Ars	4 Tau
7 Pis	8 Tau	6 Tau	7 Can	7 Leo	5 Vir	7 Sco	5 Sag	6 Aqr	6 Pis	7 Tau	7 Gem
9 Ars	10 Gem	9 Gem	9 Leo	9 Vir	7 Lib	9 Sag	7 Cap	8 Pis	8 Ars	9 Gem	9 Can
12 Tau	13 Can	11 Can	12 Vir	11 Lib	9 Sco	11 Cap	10 Aqr	11 Ars	11 Tau	12 Can	11 Leo
14 Gem	15 Leo	13 Leo	14 Lib	13 Sco	11 Sag	13 Aqr	12 Pis	13 Tau	13 Gem	14 Leo	13 Vir
16 Can	17 Vir	15 Vir	16 Sco	15 Sag	14 Cap	16 Pis	15 Ars	16 Gem	16 Can	16 Vir	16 Lib
18 Leo	19 Lib	17 Lib	18 Sag	17 Cap	16 Aqr	18 Ars	17 Tau	18 Can	18 Leo	18 Lib	18 Sco
20 Vir	21 Sco	19 Sco	20 Cap	20 Aqr	18 Pis	21 Tau	20 Gem	20 Leo	20 Vir	20 Sco	20 Sag
22 Lib	23 Sag	21 Sag	22 Aqr	22 Pis	21 Ars	23 Gem	22 Can	23 Vir	22 Lib	22 Sag	22 Cap
24 Sco	25 Cap	24 Cap	25 Pis	25 Ars	23 Tau	25 Can	24 Leo	25 Lib	24 Sco	25 Cap	24 Aqr
27 Sag	28 Aqr	26 Aqr	27 Ars	27 Tau	26 Gem	28 Leo	26 Vir	27 Sco	26 Sag	27 Aqr	27 Pis
29 Cap		28 Pis	30 Tau	29 Gem	28 Can	30 Vir	28 Lib	29 Sag	28 Cap	29 Pis	29 Ars
31 Aqr		31 Ars			30 Leo		30 Sco		30 Aqr		

1985

Jan.	Feb.	Mar.	Apr.	May	June	July	Aug.	Sep.	Oct.	Nov.	Dec.
1 Tau	2 Can	1 Can	2 Vir	1 Lib	2 Sag	1 Cap	2 Pis	1 Ars	1 Tau	2 Can	2 Leo
3 Gem	4 Leo	3 Leo	4 Lib	3 Sco	4 Cap	3 Aqr	4 Ars	3 Tau	3 Gem	4 Leo	4 Vir
5 Can	6 Vir	5 Vir	6 Sco	5 Sag	6 Aqr	5 Pis	7 Tau	6 Gem	6 Can	7 Vir	6 Lib
8 Leo	8 Lib	7 Lib	8 Sag	7 Cap	8 Pis	8 Ars	9 Gem	8 Can	8 Leo	9 Lib	8 Sco
10 Vir	10 Sco	9 Sco	10 Cap	10 Aqr	11 Ars	11 Tau	12 Can	11 Leo	10 Vir	11 Sco	10 Sag
12 Lib	12 Sag	12 Sag	12 Aqr	12 Pis	13 Tau	13 Gem	14 Leo	13 Vir	12 Lib	13 Sag	12 Cap
14 Sco	15 Cap	14 Cap	15 Pis	14 Ars	16 Gem	16 Can	16 Vir	15 Lib	14 Sco	15 Cap	14 Aqr
16 Sag	17 Aqr	16 Aqr	17 Ars	17 Tau	18 Can	18 Leo	18 Lib	17 Sco	16 Sag	17 Aqr	16 Pis
18 Cap	19 Pis	18 Pis	20 Tau	20 Gem	21 Leo	20 Vir	21 Sco	19 Sag	18 Cap	19 Pis	19 Ars
21 Aqr	22 Ars	21 Ars	22 Gem	22 Can	23 Vir	22 Lib	23 Sag	21 Cap	21 Aqr	22 Ars	21 Tau
23 Pis	24 Tau	23 Tau	25 Can	24 Leo	25 Lib	24 Sco	25 Cap	23 Aqr	23 Pis	24 Tau	24 Gem
25 Ars	27 Gem	26 Gem	27 Leo	27 Vir	27 Sco	26 Sag	27 Aqr	26 Pis	25 Ars	27 Gem	26 Can
28 Tau		28 Can	29 Vir	29 Lib	29 Sag	29 Cap	29 Pis	28 Ars	28 Tau	29 Can	29 Leo
30 Gem		31 Leo		31 Sco		31 Aqr			30 Gem		31 Vir

1986

Jan.	Feb.	Mar.	Apr.	May	June	July	Aug.	Sep.	Oct.	Nov.	Dec.
2 Lib	1 Sco	2 Sag	3 Aqr	2 Pis	1 Ars	3 Gem	2 Can	1 Leo	3 Lib	1 Sco	1 Sag
5 Sco	3 Sag	4 Cap	5 Pis	4 Ars	3 Tau	5 Can	4 Leo	3 Vir	5 Sco	3 Sag	3 Cap
7 Sag	5 Cap	6 Aqr	7 Ars	7 Tau	6 Gem	8 Leo	7 Vir	5 Lib	7 Sag	5 Cap	5 Aqr
9 Cap	7 Aqr	9 Pis	10 Tau	9 Gem	8 Can	10 Vir	9 Lib	7 Sco	9 Cap	7 Aqr	7 Pis
11 Aqr	9 Pis	11 Ars	12 Gem	12 Can	11 Leo	13 Lib	11 Sco	9 Sag	11 Aqr	9 Pis	9 Ars
13 Pis	12 Ars	13 Tau	15 Can	14 Leo	13 Vir	15 Sco	13 Sag	11 Cap	13 Pis	12 Ars	11 Tau
15 Ars	14 Tau	16 Gem	17 Leo	17 Vir	15 Lib	17 Sag	15 Cap	14 Aqr	15 Ars	14 Tau	14 Gem
18 Tau	17 Gem	18 Can	20 Vir	19 Lib	18 Sco	19 Cap	17 Aqr	16 Pis	18 Tau	17 Gem	16 Can
20 Gem	19 Can	21 Leo	22 Lib	21 Sco	20 Sag	21 Aqr	20 Pis	18 Ars	20 Gem	19 Can	19 Leo
23 Can	21 Leo	23 Vir	24 Sco	23 Sag	22 Cap	23 Pis	22 Ars	20 Tau	23 Can	22 Leo	21 Vir
25 Leo	24 Vir	25 Lib	26 Sag	25 Cap	24 Aqr	25 Ars	24 Tau	23 Gem	25 Leo	24 Vir	24 Lib
27 Vir	26 Lib	27 Sco	28 Cap	27 Aqr	26 Pis	28 Tau	27 Gem	25 Can	28 Vir	26 Lib	26 Sco
30 Lib	28 Sco	29 Sag	30 Aqr	29 Pis	28 Ars	30 Gem	29 Can	28 Leo	30 Lib	29 Sco	28 Sag
		31 Cap			30 Tau			30 Vir			30 Cap

1987

Jan.	Feb.	Mar.	Apr.	May	June	July	Aug.	Sep.	Oct.	Nov.	Dec.
1 Aqr	2 Ars	1 Ars	2 Gem	2 Can	1 Leo	3 Lib	2 Sco	2 Cap	2 Aqr	2 Ars	2 Tau
3 Pis	4 Tau	3 Tau	4 Can	4 Leo	3 Vir	5 Sco	4 Sag	4 Aqr	4 Pis	4 Tau	4 Gem
5 Ars	6 Gem	6 Gem	7 Leo	6 Vir	6 Lib	7 Sag	6 Cap	6 Pis	6 Ars	7 Gem	6 Can
8 Tau	9 Can	8 Can	9 Vir	9 Lib	8 Sco	9 Cap	8 Aqr	8 Ars	8 Tau	9 Can	9 Leo
10 Gem	11 Leo	11 Leo	12 Lib	11 Sco	10 Sag	11 Aqr	10 Pis	10 Tau	10 Gem	11 Leo	11 Vir
13 Can	14 Vir	13 Vir	14 Sco	14 Sag	12 Cap	13 Pis	12 Ars	13 Gem	13 Can	14 Vir	14 Lib
15 Leo	16 Lib	15 Lib	16 Sag	16 Cap	14 Aqr	16 Ars	15 Tau	15 Can	15 Leo	16 Lib	16 Sco
18 Vir	19 Sco	18 Sco	18 Cap	18 Aqr	16 Pis	18 Tau	17 Gem	18 Leo	18 Vir	19 Sco	18 Sag
20 Lib	21 Sag	20 Sag	20 Aqr	20 Pis	18 Ars	20 Gem	19 Can	20 Vir	20 Lib	21 Sag	20 Cap
22 Sco	23 Cap	22 Cap	23 Pis	22 Ars	21 Tau	23 Can	21 Leo	23 Lib	22 Sco	23 Cap	22 Aqr
24 Sag	25 Aqr	24 Aqr	25 Ars	24 Tau	23 Gem	25 Leo	23 Vir	25 Sco	25 Sag	25 Aqr	24 Pis
26 Cap	27 Pis	26 Pis	27 Tau	27 Gem	25 Can	28 Vir	26 Lib	27 Sag	27 Cap	27 Pis	27 Ars
28 Aqr		28 Ars	29 Gem	29 Can	28 Leo	30 Lib	28 Sco	29 Cap	29 Aqr	29 Ars	29 Tau
30 Pis		31 Tau			30 Vir		31 Sag		31 Pis		31 Gem

1988

Jan.	Feb.	Mar.	Apr.	May	June	July	Aug.	Sep.	Oct.	Nov.	Dec.
3 Can	1 Leo	2 Vir	1 Lib	1 Sco	1 Cap	1 Aqr	1 Ars	2 Gem	1 Can	3 Vir	3 Lib
5 Leo	4 Vlr	5 Llb	3 Sco	3 Sag	3 Aqr	3 Pls	3 Tau	4 Can	4 Leo	5 Lib	5 Sco
8 Vir	6 Lib	7 Sco	6 Sag	5 Cap	6 Pis	5 Ars	6 Gem	7 Leo	6 Vir	8 Sco	7 Sag
10 Lib	9 Sco	9 Sag	8 Cap	7 Aqr	8 Ars	7 Tau	8 Can	9 Vir	9 Lib	10 Sag	10 Cap
12 Sco	11 Sag	12 Cap	10 Aqr	9 Pis	10 Tau	9 Gem	10 Leo	12 Lib	11 Sco	12 Cap	12 Aqr
15 Sag	13 Cap	14 Aqr	12 Pis	11 Ars	12 Gem	12 Can	13 Vir	14 Sco	14 Sag	15 Aqr	14 Pis
17 Cap	15 Aqr	16 Pis	14 Ars	14 Tau	14 Can	14 Leo	15 Lib	17 Sag	16 Cap	17 Pis	16 Ars
19 Aqr	17 Pis	18 Ars	16 Tau	16 Gem	17 Leo	17 Vir	17 Sag	19 Cap	18 Aqr	19 Ars	18 Tau
21 Pis	19 Ars	20 Tau	18 Gem	18 Can	19 Vir	19 Lib	20 Sag	21 Aqr	20 Pis	21 Tau	20 Gem
23 Ars	21 Tau	22 Gem	21 Can	20 Leo	22 Lib	22 Sco	23 Cap	23 Pis	23 Ars	23 Gem	23 Can
25 Tau	24 Gem	24 Can	23 Leo	23 Vir	24 Sco	24 Sag	25 Aqr	25 Ars	25 Tau	25 Can	26 Leo
27 Gem	26 Can	27 Leo	26 Vir	25 Lib	27 Sag	26 Cap	27 Pis	27 Tau	27 Gem	28 Leo	27 Vir
30 Can	29 Leo	29 Vir	28 Lib	28 Sco	29 Cap	27 Aqr	29 Ars	29 Gem	29 Can	30 Vir	30 Lib
				30 Sag		29 Ars	31 Tau		31 Leo		
						30 Pis					

1989

Jan.	Feb.	Mar.	Apr.	May	June	July	Aug.	Sep.	Oct.	Nov.	Dec.
1 Sco	2 Cap	2 Cap	3 Pis	1 Ars	2 Gem	2 Can	3 Vir	2 Lib	1 Soc	3 Cap	2 Aqr
4 Sag	5 Aqr	4 Aqr	5 Ars	4 Tau	5 Can	4 Leo	5 Vib	4 Sco	4 Sag	5 Aqr	5 Pis
6 Cap	7 Pis	6 Pis	7 Tau	6 Gem	7 Leo	6 Vir	8 Sco	7 Sag	6 Cap	7 Pis	7 Ars
8 Aqr	9 Ars	8 Ars	9 Gem	8 Can	9 Vir	9 Lib	10 Sag	9 Cap	9 Aqr	9 Ars	9 Tau
10 Pis	11 Tau	10 Tau	11 Can	10 Leo	12 Lib	11 Sco	13 Cap	11 Aqr	11 Pis	11 Tau	11 Can
12 Ars	13 Gem	12 Gem	13 Leo	13 Vir	14 Sco	14 Sag	15 Aqr	13 Pis	13 Ars	13 Gem	13 Can
14 Tau	15 Can	14 Can	15 Vir	15 Lib	17 Sag	16 Cap	17 Pis	15 Ars	15 Tau	15 Can	15 Leo
17 Gem	18 Leo	17 Leo	17 Lib	18 Sco	19 Cap	19 Aqr	19 Ars	17 Tau	17 Gem	18 Leo	17 Vir
19 Can	20 Vir	19 Vir	21 Sco	20 Sag	21 Aqr	21 Pis	21 Tau	20 Gem	19 Can	20 Vir	20 Lib
21 Leo	23 Lib	22 Lib	23 Sag	23 Cap	23 Pis	23 Ars	23 Gem	22 Can	21 Leo	22 Lib	22 Soc
24 Vir	25 Sco	24 Sco	25 Cap	25 Aqr	26 Ars	25 Tau	25 Can	24 Leo	24 Vir	25 Sco	25 Sag
26 Lib	28 Sag	27 Sag	28 Aqr	27 Pis	28 Tau	27 Gem	28 Leo	26 Vir	26 Lib	27 Sag	27 Cap
29 Sco		29 Cap	30 Pis	19 Ars	30 Gem	29 Can	30 Vir	29 Lib	29 Sco	30 Cap	29 Aqr
31 Sag		31 Aqr		31 Tau		31 Leo			31 Sag		

1990

Jan.	Feb.	Mar.	Apr.	May	June	July	Aug.	Sep.	Oct.	Nov.	Dec.
1 Pis	1 Tau	1 Tau	1 Can	1 Leo	1 Lib	1 Sco	3 Cap	1 Aqr	1 Pis	2 Tau	1 Gem
3 Ars	3 Gem	3 Gem	3 Leo	3 Vir	4 Sco	4 Sag	5 Aqr	4 Pis	3 Ars	4 Gem	3 Can
5 Tau	6 Can	5 Can	6 Vir	5 Lib	6 Sag	6 Cap	7 Pis	6 Ars	5 Tau	6 Can	5 Leo
7 Gem	8 Leo	7 Leo	8 Lib	8 Sco	9 Cap	9 Aqr	10 Ars	8 Tau	7 Gem	8 Leo	7 Vir
9 Can	10 Vir	9 Vir	10 Sco	10 Sag	11 Aqr	11 Pis	12 Tau	10 Gem	9 Can	10 Vir	10 Lib
11 Leo	12 Lib	12 Lib	13 Sag	13 Cap	14 Pis	13 Ars	14 Gem	12 Can	12 Leo	12 Lib	12 Sco
14 Vir	15 Sco	14 Sco	16 Cap	15 Aqr	16 Ars	15 Tau	16 Can	14 Leo	14 Vir	15 Sco	15 Sag
16 Lib	17 Sag	17 Sag	18 Aqr	18 Pis	18 Tau	16 Can	18 Leo	17 Vir	16 Lib	17 Sag	17 Cap
19 Sco	20 Cap	19 Cap	20 Pis	20 Ars	20 Gem	18 Gem	20 Vir	19 Lib	19 Sco	20 Cap	20 Aqr
21 Sag	22 Aqr	22 Aqr	22 Ars	22 Tau	22 Can	20 Can	23 Lib	21 Sco	21 Sag	22 Aqr	22 Pis
23 Cap	24 Pis	24 Pis	24 Tau	24 Gem	24 Leo	22 Leo	25 Sco	24 Sag	24 Cap	25 Pis	24 Ars
26 Aqr	27 Ars	26 Ars	26 Gem	26 Can	26 Vir	24 Leo	27 Sag	26 Cap	26 Aqr	27 Ars	27 Tau
28 Pis		28 Tau	28 Can	28 Leo	29 Lib	26 Lib	30 Cap	29 Aqr	28 Pis	29 Tau	29 Gem
30 Ars		30 Gem		30 Vir		29 Sco			31 Ars		31 Can
						31 Sag					

1991

Jan.	Feb.	Mar.	Apr.	May	June	July	Aug.	Sep.	Oct.	Nov.	Dec.
2 Leo	2 Lib	2 Lib	3 Sag	3 Cap	1 Aqr	1 Pis	2 Tau	1 Gem	2 Leo	1 Vir	2 Sco
4 Vir	5 Sco	4 Sco	5 Cap	5 Aqr	4 Pis	4 Ars	4 Gem	3 Can	4 Vir	3 Lib	5 Sag
6 Lib	7 Sag	6 Sag	8 Aqr	8 Pis	6 Ars	6 Tau	6 Can	5 Leo	6 Lib	5 Sco	7 Cap
8 Sco	10 Cap	9 Cap	10 Pis	10 Ars	9 Tau	8 Gem	8 Leo	7 Vir	9 Sco	7 Sag	10 Aqr
11 Cap	12 Aqr	12 Aqr	13 Ars	12 Tau	11 Gem	10 Can	10 Vir	9 Lib	11 Sag	10 Cap	10 Aqr
13 Cap	15 Pis	14 Pis	15 Tau	14 Gem	13 Can	12 Leo	13 Lib	11 Sco	13 Cap	12 Aqr	12 Pis
16 Aqr	17 Ars	16 Ars	17 Gem	16 Can	15 Leo	14 Vir	15 Sco	14 Sag	16 Aqr	15 Pis	15 Ars
18 Pis	19 Tau	18 Tau	19 Can	18 Leo	17 Vir	16 Lib	17 Sag	16 Cap	18 Pis	17 Ars	17 Tau
21 Ars	21 Gem	20 Gem	21 Leo	20 Vir	19 Lib	18 Sco	20 Cap	19 Aqr	21 Ars	19 Tau	19 Gem
23 Tau	23 Can	23 Can	23 Virg	23 Lib	21 Sco	21 Sag	22 Aqr	21 Pis	23 Tau	22 Gem	21 Can
25 Gem	25 Leo	25 Leo	25 Libr	25 Sco	24 Sag	23 Cap	25 Pis	23 Ars	25 Gem	24 Can	23 Leo
27 Can	28 Vir	27 Vir	28 Sco	27 Sag	26 Cap	26 Aqr	27 Ars	26 Tau	27 Can	26 Leo	25 Vir
29 Leo		29 Lib	30 Sag	30 Cap	29 Aqr	28 Pis	29 Tau	28 Gem	29 Leo	28 Vir	27 Lib
31 Vir		31 Sco				31 Ars		30 Can		30 Lib	29 Sco

1992

Jan.	Feb.	Mar.	Apr.	May	June	July	Aug.	Sep.	Oct.	Nov.	Dec.
1 Sag	2 Aqr	3 Pis	2 Ars	1 Tau	2 Can	1 Leo	2 Lib	3 Sag	2 Cap	1 Aqr	1 Pis
3 Cap	5 Pis	5 Ars	4 Tau	4 Gem	4 Leo	3 Vir	4 Sco	5 Cap	5 Aqr	4 Pis	3 Ars
6 Aqr	7 Ars	8 Tau	6 Gem	6 Can	6 Vir	6 Lib	6 Sag	7 Aqr	7 Pis	6 Ars	6 Tau
8 Pis	9 Tau	10 Gem	8 Can	8 Leo	8 Lib	8 Sco	9 Cap	10 Pis	10 Ars	8 Tau	8 Gem
11 Ars	12 Gem	12 Can	11 Leo	10 Vir	10 Sco	10 Sag	11 Aqr	12 Ars	12 Tau	11 Gem	10 Can
13 Tau	14 Can	14 Leo	13 Vir	12 Lib	13 Sag	12 Cap	14 Pis	15 Tau	15 Gem	13 Can	12 Leo
15 Gem	16 Leo	16 Vir	15 Lib	14 Sco	15 Cap	15 Aqr	16 Ars	17 Gem	17 Can	15 Leo	15 Vir
17 Can	18 Vir	18 Lib	17 Sco	16 Sag	18 Aqr	17 Pis	19 Tau	20 Can	19 Leo	17 Vir	17 Lib
19 Leo	20 Lib	20 Sco	19 Sag	19 Cap	20 Pis	20 Ars	21 Gem	22 Leo	21 Vir	19 Lib	19 Sco
21 Vir	22 Sco	23 Sag	21 Cap	21 Aqr	23 Ars	22 Tau	23 Can	24 Vir	23 Lib	22 Sco	21 Cap
23 Lib	24 Sag	25 Cap	24 Aqr	24 Pis	25 Tau	25 Gem	25 Leo	26 Lib	25 Sco	24 Sag	23 Cap
26 Sco	27 Cap	28 Aqr	27 Pis	26 Ars	27 Gem	27 Can	27 Vir	28 Sco	27 Sag	26 Cap	26 Aqr
28 Sag	29 Aqr	30 Pis	29 Ars	29 Tau	29 Can	29 Leo	29 Lib	30 Sag	30 Cap	28 Aqr	28 Pis
31 Cap				31 Gem		31 Vir	31 Sco				31 Ars

1993

Jan.	Feb.	Mar.	Apr.	May	June	July	Aug.	Sep.	Oct.	Nov.	Dec.
2 Tau	1 Gem	3 Can	1 Leo	3 Lib	1 Sco	3 Cap	1 Aqr	2 Ars	2 Tau	1 Gem	1 Can
5 Gem	3 Can	5 Leo	3 Vir	5 Sco	3 Sag	5 Aqr	4 Pis	5 Tau	5 Gem	3 Can	3 Leo
7 Can	5 Leo	7 Vir	5 Lib	7 Sag	5 Cap	7 Pis	6 Ars	7 Gem	7 Can	6 Leo	5 Vir
9 Leo	7 Vir	9 Lib	7 Sco	9 Cap	8 Aqr	10 Ars	9 Tau	10 Can	9 Leo	8 Vir	7 Lib
11 Vir	9 Lib	11 Sco	9 Sag	11 Aqr	10 Pis	12 Tau	11 Gem	12 Leo	12 Vir	10 Lib	9 Sco
13 Lib	11 Sco	13 Sag	11 Cap	14 Pis	12 Ars	15 Gem	13 Can	14 Vir	14 Lib	12 Sco	11 Sag
15 Sco	14 Sag	15 Cap	14 Aqr	16 Ars	15 Tau	17 Can	16 Leo	16 Lib	16 Sco	14 Sag	14 Cap
17 Sag	16 Cap	18 Aqr	16 Pis	19 Tau	17 Gem	19 Leo	18 Vir	18 Sco	18 Sag	16 Cap	16 Aqr
20 Cap	18 Aqr	20 Pis	19 Ars	21 Gem	20 Can	21 Vir	20 Lib	20 Sag	20 Cap	18 Aqr	18 Pis
22 Aqr	21 Pis	23 Ars	21 Tau	23 Can	22 Leo	23 Lib	22 Sco	22 Cap	22 Aqr	21 Pis	21 Ars
25 Pis	23 Ari	25 Tau	24 Gem	26 Leo	24 Vir	25 Sco	24 Sag	25 Aqr	24 Pis	23 Ars	23 Tau
27 Ars	26 Tau	28 Gem	26 Can	28 Vir	26 Lib	28 Sag	26 Cap	27 Pis	27 Ars	26 Tau	26 Gem
30 Tau	28 Gem	30 Can	28 Leo	30 Lib	28 Sco	30 Cap	28 Aqr	30 Ars	29 Tau	28 Gem	28 Can
			30 Vir		30 Sag		31 Pis				30 Leo

1994

Jan.	Feb.	Mar.	Apr.	May	June	July	Aug.	Sep.	Oct.	Nov.	Dec.
1 Vir	2 Sco	1 Sco	2 Cap	1 Aqr	2 Ars	2 Tau	1 Gem	4 Vir	2 Vir	2 Sco	2 Sag
3 Lib	4 Sag	3 Sag	4 Aqr	4 Pis	5 Tau	5 Gem	3 Can	6 Lib	4 Lib	4 Sag	4 Cap
6 Sco	6 Cap	5 Cap	6 Pis	6 Ars	7 Gem	7 Can	6 Leo	9 Sco	6 Sco	6 Cap	6 Aqr
8 Sag	8 Aqr	8 Aqr	9 Ars	9 Tau	10 Can	9 Leo	8 Vir	11 Sag	8 Sag	8 Aqr	8 Pis
10 Cap	11 Pis	10 Pis	11 Tau	11 Gem	12 Leo	12 Vir	10 Lib	13 Cap	10 Cap	11 Pis	10 Ars
12 Aqr	13 Ars	12 Ars	14 Gem	14 Can	14 Vir	14 Lib	12 Sco	15 Aqr	12 Aqr	13 Ars	13 Tau
14 Pis	16 Tau	15 Tau	16 Can	16 Leo	17 Lib	16 Sco	14 Sag	17 Pis	14 Pis	16 Tau	15 Gem
17 Ars	18 Can	18 Gem	19 Leo	18 Vir	19 Sco	18 Sag	17 Cap	20 Ars	17 Ars	18 Gem	18 Can
19 Tau	21 Can	20 Can	21 Vir	20 Lib	21 Sag	20 Cap	19 Aqr	22 Tau	19 Tau	21 Can	20 Leo
22 Gem	23 Leo	22 Leo	23 Lib	22 Sco	23 Cap	22 Aqr	21 Pis	25 Gem	22 Gem	23 Leo	23 Vir
24 Can	25 Vir	25 Vir	25 Sco	24 Sag	25 Aqr	25 Pis	23 Ars	27 Can	24 Can	26 Vir	25 Lib
27 Leo	27 Lib	27 Lib	27 Sag	26 Cap	27 Pis	27 Ars	26 Tau	30 Leo	27 Leo	28 Lib	27 Sco
29 Vir	29 Sco	29 Sco	29 Cap	29 Aqu	30 Ars	29 Tau	28 Gem		29 Vir	30 Soc	29 Sag
		31 Sag		31 Pis			31 Can		31 Lib		31 Cap

1995

Jan.	Feb.	Mar.	Apr.	May	June	July	Aug.	Sep.	Oct.	Nov.	Dec.
2 Aqr	1 Pis	2 Ars	1 Tau	1 Gem	2 Leo	2 Vir	1 Lib	1 Sag	1 Cap	1 Pis	1 Ars
4 Pis	3 Ari	5 Tau	4 Gem	4 Can	5 Vir	4 Lib	3 Sco	3 Cap	3 Cap	3 Ars	3 Tau
7 Ars	6 Tau	7 Gem	6 Can	6 Leo	7 Lib	7 Sco	5 Sag	5 Aqr	5 Pis	6 Tau	5 Gem
9 Tau	8 Gem	10 Can	9 Leo	8 Vir	9 Sco	9 Sag	7 Cap	8 Pis	7 Ars	8 Gem	8 Can
12 Gem	11 Can	12 Leo	11 Vir	11 Lib	11 Sag	11 Cap	9 Aqr	10 Ars	9 Tau	11 Can	10 Leo
14 Can	13 Leo	15 Vir	13 Lib	13 Sco	13 Cap	13 Aqr	11 Pis	12 Tau	12 Gem	13 Leo	13 Vir
17 Leo	15 Vir	17 Lib	15 Sco	15 Sag	15 Aqr	15 Pis	13 Ars	14 Gem	14 Can	16 Vir	15 Lib
19 Vir	18 Lib	19 Sco	17 Sag	17 Cap	17 Pis	17 Ars	16 Tau	17 Can	17 Leo	18 Lib	18 Sco
21 Lib	20 Sco	21 Sag	19 Cap	19 Aqr	20 Ars	19 Tau	18 Gem	19 Leo	19 Vir	20 Sco	20 Sag
23 Sco	22 Sag	23 Cap	22 Aqr	21 Pis	22 Tau	22 Gem	21 Can	22 Vir	22 Lib	22 Sag	22 Cap
26 Sag	24 Cap	25 Aqr	24 Pis	23 Ars	25 Gem	24 Can	23 Leo	24 Lib	24 Sco	24 Cap	24 Aqr
28 Cap	26 Aqr	28 Pis	26 Ars	26 Tau	27 Can	27 Leo	25 Vir	26 Sco	26 Sag	26 Aqr	26 Pis
30 Aqr	28 Pis	30 Ars	28 Tau	28 Gem	30 Leo	29 Vir	28 Lib	28 Sag	28 Cap	28 Pis	30 Tau
				31 Can			30 Sco		30 Aqr		

1996

Jan.	Feb.	Mar.	Apr.	May	June	July	Aug.	Sep.	Oct.	Nov.	Dec.
2 Gem	3 Leo	1 Leo	2 Lib	2 Sco	1 Sag	2 Aqr	2 Ars	1 Tau	1 Gem	2 Leo	2 Vir
4 Can	5 Vir	4 Vir	5 Sco	4 Sag	3 Cap	4 Pis	5 Tau	3 Gem	3 Can	4 Vir	4 Lib
7 Leo	8 Lib	6 Lib	7 Sag	6 Cap	5 Aqr	6 Ars	7 Gem	6 Can	6 Leo	7 Lib	7 Sco
9 Vir	10 Sco	8 Sco	9 Cap	8 Aqr	7 Pis	8 Tau	9 Can	8 Leo	8 Vir	9 Sco	9 Sag
12 Lib	12 Sag	11 Sag	11 Aqr	10 Pis	9 Ars	11 Gem	12 Leo	11 Vir	11 Lib	11 Sag	11 Cap
14 Sco	14 Cap	13 Cap	13 Pis	13 Ars	11 Tau	13 Can	15 Vir	13 Lib	13 Sco	14 Cap	13 Aqr
16 Sag	16 Aqr	15 Aqr	15 Ars	15 Tau	14 Gem	16 Leo	17 Lib	16 Sco	15 Sag	16 Aqr	15 Pis
18 Cap	19 Pis	17 Pis	18 Tau	17 Gem	16 Can	18 Vir	19 Sco	18 Sag	17Cap	18 Pis	17 Ars
20 Aqr	21 Ars	19 Ars	20 Gem	20 Can	18 Leo	21 Lib	22 Sag	20 Cap	18 Pis	20 Ars	19 Tau
22 Pis	23 Tau	21 Tau	22 Can	22 Leo	21 Vir	23 Sco	24 Cap	22 Aqr	20 Aqr	22 Tau	22 Gem
24 Ars	25 Gem	24 Gem	25 Leo	25 Vir	23 Lib	25 Sag	26 Aqr	24 Pis	22 Pis	24 Gem	24 Can
26 Taur	28 Can	26 Can	27 Vir	27 Lib	26 Sco	27 Cap	28 Pis	26 Ars	24 Ars	27 Can	27 Leo
29 Gem		29 Leo	30 Lib	29 Sco	28 Sag	29 Aqr	30 Ars	28 Tau	26 Tau	29 Leo	29 Vir
31 Can		31 Vir			30 Cap	31 Pis			28 Gem		
									30 Can		

1997

Jan.	Feb.	Mar.	Apr.	May	June	July	Aug.	Sep.	Oct.	Nov.	Dec.
1 Lib	2 Sag	1 Sag	2 Aqr	1 Pis	2 Tau	1 Gem	2 Leo	1 Vir	3 Sco	2 Sag	1 Cap
3 Sco	4 Cap	3 Cap	4 Pis	3 Ars	4 Gem	3 Can	4 Vir	3 Lib	5 Sag	4 Cap	3 Aqr
5 Sag	6 Aqr	5 Aqr	6 Ars	5 Tau	6 Can	6 Leo	7 Lib	6 Sco	8 Cap	6 Aqr	6 Pis
7 Cap	8 Pis	7 Pis	8 Tau	7 Gem	8 Leo	9 Vir	9 Sco	8 Sag	10 Aqr	8 Pis	8 Ars
9 Aqr	10 Ars	9 Ars	10 Gem	10 Can	11 Vir	11 Lib	12 Sag	11 Cap	12 Pis	11 Ars	10 Tau
11 Pis	12 Tau	11 Tau	12 Can	12 Leo	13 Lib	13 Sco	14 Cap	13 Aqr	14 Ars	13 Tau	12 Gem
13 Ars	14 Gem	14 Gem	15 Leo	14 Vir	16 Sco	16 Sag	16 Aqr	15 Pis	16 Tau	15 Gem	14 Can
16 Tau	17 Can	16 Can	17 Vir	17 Lib	18 Sag	18 Cap	18 Pis	17 Ars	18 Gem	17 Can	16 Leo
18 Gem	19 Leo	18 Leo	20 Lib	19 Sco	20 Cap	20 Aqr	20 Ars	19 Tau	20 Can	19 Leo	19 Vir
20 Can	22 Vir	21 Vir	22 Sco	22 Sag	22 Aqr	22 Pis	22 Tau	21 Gem	23 Leo	22 Vir	21 Lib
23 Leo	24 Lib	23 Lib	24 Sag	24 Cap	25 Pis	24 Ars	24 Gem	23 Can	25 Vir	24 Lib	24 Sco
25 Vir	27 Sco	26 Sco	27 Cap	26 Aqr	27 Ars	26 Tau	27 Can	25 Leo	28 Lib	27 Sco	26 Sag
28 Lib		28 Sag	29 Aqr	28 Pis	29 Tau	28 Gem	29 Leo	28 Vir	30 Sco	29 Sag	29 Cap
30 Sco		31 Cap		30 Ars		31 Can		30 Lib			31 Aqr

1998

Jan.	Feb.	Mar.	Apr.	May	June	July	Aug.	Sep.	Oct.	Nov.	Dec.
2 Pis	2 Tau	2 Tau	2 Can	2 Leo	1 Vir	3 Sco	2 Sag	1 Cap	2 Pis	1 Ars	2 Gem
4 Ars	5 Gem	4 Gem	5 Leo	4 Vir	3 Lib	5 Sag	4 Cap	3 Aqr	5 Ars	3 Tau	4 Can
6 Tau	7 Can	6 Can	7 Vir	7 Lib	6 Sco	8 Cap	6 Aqr	5 Pis	6 Tau	5 Gem	6 Leo
8 Gem	9 Leo	8 Leo	10 Lib	9 Sco	8 Sag	10 Aqr	9 Pis	7 Ars	8 Gem	7 Can	9 Vir
11 Can	12 Vir	11 Vir	12 Sco	12 Sag	11 Cap	12 Pis	11 Ars	9 Tau	11 Can	9 Leo	11 Lib
13 Leo	14 Lib	13 Lib	15 Sag	14 Cap	13 Aqr	14 Ars	13 Tau	11 Gem	13 Leo	11 Vir	14 Sco
15 Vir	17 Sco	16 Sco	17Cap	17 Aqr	15 Pis	17 Tau	15 Gem	13 Can	15 Vir	14 Lib	16 Sag
18 Lib	19 Sag	18 Sag	19 Aqr	19 Pis	17 Ars	19 Gem	17 Can	16 Leo	18 Lib	16 Sco	19 Cap
20 Sco	21 Cap	21 Cap	22 Pis	21 Ars	19 Tau	21 Can	19 Leo	18 Vir	20 Sco	19 Sag	21 Aqr
23 Sag	24 Aqr	23 Aqr	24 Ars	23 Tau	21 Gem	23 Leo	22 Vir	20 Lib	23 Sag	21 Cap	23 Pis
25 Cap	26 Pis	25 Pis	26 Tau	25 Gem	23 Can	25 Vir	24 Lib	23 Sco	25 Cap	24 Aqr	26 Ars
27 Aqr	28 Ars	27 Ars	28 Gem	27 Can	26 Leo	28 Lib	27 Sco	25 Sag	28 Aqr	26 Pis	28 Tau
29 Pis		29 Tau	30 Can	29 Leo	28 Vir	30 Sco	29 Sag	28 Cap	30 Pis	28 Ars	30 Gem
		30 Aqr			30 Lib			30 Aqr		30 Tau	

1999

Jan.	Feb.	Mar.	Apr.	May	June	July	Aug.	Sep.	Oct.	Nov.	Dec.
1 Can	2 Vir	1 Vir	2 Sco	2 Sag	1 Cap	3 Pis	1 Ars	2 Gem	1 Can	2 Vir	1 Lib
3 Leo	4 Lib	3 Lib	5 Sag	4 Cap	3 Aqr	5 Ars	3 Tau	4 Can	3 Leo	4 Lib	4 Sco
5 Vir	6 Sco	6 Sco	7 Cap	7 Aqr	5 Pis	7 Tau	5 Gem	6 Leo	5 Vir	6 Sco	6 Sag
8 Lib	9 Sag	8 Sag	10 Aqr	9 Pis	8 Ars	9 Gem	8 Can	8 Vir	8 Lib	9 Sag	9 Cap
10 Sco	11 Cap	11Cap	12 Pis	11 Ars	10 Tau	11 Can	10 Leo	10 Lib	10 Sco	11 Cap	11 Aqr
13 Sag	14 Aqr	13 Aqr	14 Ars	13 Tau	12 Gem	13 Leo	12 Vir	13 Sco	13 Sag	14 Aqr	14 Pis
15 Cap	16 Pis	15 Pis	16 Tau	15 Gem	14 Can	15 Vir	14 Lib	15 Sag	15 Cap	16 Pis	16 Ars
17 Aqr	18 Ars	18 Ars	18 Gem	17 Can	16 Leo	18 Lib	16 Sco	18 Cap	18 Aqr	19 Ars	18 Tau
20 Pis	20 Tau	20 Tau	20 Can	19 Leo	18 Vir	20 Sco	19 Sag	20 Aqr	20 Pis	21 Tau	20 Gem
22 Ars	22 Gem	22 Gem	22 Leo	22 Vir	20 Lib	23 Sag	21 Cap	23 Pis	22 Ars	23 Gem	22 Can
24 Tau	24 Can	24 Can	24 Vir	24 Lib	23 Sco	25 Cap	24 Aqr	25 Ars	24 Tau	25 Can	24 Leo
26 Gem	27 Leo	26 Leo	27 Lib	27 Sco	25 Sag	28 Aqr	26 Pis	27 Tau	26 Gem	27 Leo	26 Vir
28 Can		28 Vir	29 Sco	29 Sag	28 Cap	30 Pis	28 Ars	29 Gem	28 Can	29 Vir	29 Lib
30 Leo		31 Lib			30 Aqr		31 Tau		30 Leo		31 Sco

2000

Jan.	Feb.	Mar.	Apr.	May	June	July	Aug.	Sep.	Oct.	Nov.	Dec.
2 Sag	1 Car	2 Aqr	1 Pis	1 Ars	1 Gem	1 Can	1 Vir	2 Sco	1 Sag	3 Aqr	3 Pis
5 Cap	4 Aqr	4 Pis	3 Ars	3 Tau	3 Can	3 Leo	3 Lib	4 Sag	4 Cap	5 Pis	5 Ars
7 Aqr	6 Pis	7 Ars	5 Tau	5 Gem	5 Leo	5 Vir	5 Sco	7 Cap	6 Aqr	8 Ars	7 Tau
10 Pis	9 Ars	9 Tau	7 Gem	7 Can	7 Vir	7 Lib	8 Sag	9 Aqr	9 Pis	10 Tau	10 Gem
12 Ars	11 Tau	11 Gem	10 Can	9 Leo	9 Lib	9 Sco	10 Cap	12 Pis	11 Ars	12 Gem	12 Can
15 Tau	13 Gem	13 Can	12 Leo	11 Vir	12 Sco	12 Sag	13 Aqr	14 Ars	14 Tau	14 Can	14 Leo
17 Gem	15 Can	15 Leo	14 Vir	13 Lib	14 Sag	14 Cap	15 Pis	16 Tau	16 Gem	16 Leo	16 Vir
19 Can	17 Leo	18 Vir	16 Lib	16 Sco	17 Cap	17 Aqr	18 Ars	19 Gem	18 Can	18 Vir	18 Lib
21 Leo	19 Vir	20 Lib	18 Sco	18 Sag	19 Aqr	19 Pis	20 Tau	21 Can	20 Leo	21 Lib	20 Sco
23 Vir	21 Lib	22 Sco	21 Sag	21 Cap	22 Pis	22 Ars	22 Gem	23 Leo	22 Vir	23 Sco	22 Sag
25 Lib	24 Sco	24 Sag	23 Cap	23 Aqr	24 Ars	24 Tau	24 Can	25 Vir	24 Lib	25 Sag	25 Cap
27 Sco	26 Sag	27 Cap	26 Aqr	26 Pis	27 Tau	26 Gem	26 Leo	27 Lib	27 Sco	28 Cap	27 Aqr
30 Sag	29 Cap	29 Aqr	28 Pis	28 Ars	29 Gem	28 Can	28 Vir	29 Sco	29 Sag	30 Aqr	30 Pis
				30 Tau		30 Leo	31 Lib		31 Cap		

2001

Jan.	Feb.	Mar.	Apr.	May	June	July	Aug.	Sep.	Oct.	Nov.	Dec.
1 Ars	2 Gem	2 Gem	2 Leo	2 Vir	2 Sco	2 Sag	3 Aqr	2 Pis	1 Ars	2 Gem	2 Can
4 Tau	5 Can	4 Can	4 Vir	4 Lib	4 Sag	4 Cap	5 Pis	4 Ars	4 Tau	5 Can	4 Leo
6 Gem	7 Leo	6 Leo	6 Lib	6 Sco	7 Cap	6 Aqr	8 Ars	7 Tau	6 Gem	7 Leo	6 Vir
8 Can	8 Vir	8 Vir	8 Sco	8 Sag	9 Aqr	9 Pis	10 Tau	9 Gem	8 Can	9 Vir	8 Lib
10 Leo	10 Lib	10 Lib	11 Sag	10 Cap	12 Pis	12 Ars	13 Gem	11 Can	11 Leo	11 Lib	10 Sco
12 Vir	13 Sco	12 Sco	13 Cap	13 Aqr	14 Ars	14 Tau	15 Can	13 Leo	13 Vir	13 Sco	13 Sag
14 Lib	15 Sag	14 Sag	16 Aqr	15 Pis	17 Tau	16 Gem	17 Leo	15 Vir	15 Lib	15 Sag	15 Cap
16 Sco	17 Cap	17 Cap	18 Pis	17 Ars	19 Gem	18 Can	19 Vir	17 Lib	17 Sco	18 Cap	17 Aqr
19 Sag	20 Aqr	19 Aqr	21 Ars	20 Tau	21 Can	20 Leo	21 Lib	19 Sco	19 Sag	20 Aqr	20 Pis
21 Cap	22 Pis	22 Pis	23 Tau	22 Gem	23 Leo	22 Vir	23 Sco	21 Sag	21 Cap	22 Pis	22 Ars
24 Aqr	25 Ars	24 Ars	25 Gem	25 Can	25 Vir	24 Lib	25 Sag	24 Cap	24 Aqr	25 Ars	25 Tau
26 Pis	27 Tau	27 Tau	27 Can	27 Leo	27 Lib	27 Sco	28 Cap	26 Aqr	26 Pis	27 Tau	27 Gem
29 Ars		29 Gem	29 Leo	29 Vir	29 Sco	29 Sag	30 Aqr	29 Pis	29 Ars	30 Gem	29 Can
31 Tau		31 Can		31 Lib		31 Cap			31 Tau		31 Leo

2002

Jan.	Feb.	Mar.	Apr.	May	June	July	Aug.	Sep.	Oct.	Nov.	Dec.
2 Vir	1 Lib	2 Sco	1 Sag	3 Aqr	1 Pis	1 Ars	3 Gem	1 Can	1 Leo	2 Lib	1 Sco
5 Lib	3 Sco	4 Sag	3 Cap	5 Pis	4 Ars	4 Tau	5 Can	4 Leo	3 Vir	4 Sco	3 Sag
7 Sco	5 Sag	7 Cap	5 Aqr	8 Ars	7 Tau	6 Gem	7 Leo	6 Vir	5 Lib	6 Sag	5 Cap
9 Sag	7 Cap	9 Aqr	8 Pis	10 Tau	9 Gem	9 Can	9 Vir	8 Lib	7 Sco	8 Cap	7 Aqr
11 Cap	10 Aqr	12 Pis	10 Ars	13 Gem	11 Can	11 Leo	11 Lib	10 Sco	9 Sag	10 Aqr	10 Pis
14 Aqr	12 Pis	14 Ars	13 Tau	15 Can	13 Leo	13 Vir	13 Sco	12 Sag	11 Cap	12 Pis	12 Ars
16 Pis	15 Ars	17 Tau	15 Gem	17 Leo	16 Vir	15 Lib	15 Sag	14 Cap	14 Aqr	15 Ars	15 Tau
19 Ars	17 Tau	19 Gem	18 Can	20 Vir	18 Lib	17 Sco	18 Cap	16 Aqr	16 Pis	17 Tau	17 Gem
21 Tau	20 Gem	22 Can	20 Leo	22 Lib	20 Sco	19 Sag	20 Aqr	19 Pis	18 Ars	20 Gem	19 Can
24 Gem	22 Can	24 Leo	22 Vir	24 Sco	22 Sag	21 Cap	22 Pis	21 Ars	21 Tau	22 Can	22 Leo
26 Can	24 Leo	26 Vir	24 Lib	26 Sag	24 Cap	24 Aqr	25 Ars	24 Tau	24 Gem	25 Leo	24 Vir
28 Leo	26 Vir	28 Lib	26 Sco	28 Cap	26 Aqr	26 Pis	27 Tau	26 Gem	26 Can	27 Vir	26 Lib
30 Vir	28 Lib	30 Sco	28 Sag	30 Cap	29 Pis	29 Ars	30 Gem	29 Can	28 Leo	29 Lib	28 Sco
			30 Cap			31 Tau			30 Vir		30 Sag

2003

Jan.	Feb.	Mar.	Apr.	May	June	July	Aug.	Sep.	Oct.	Nov.	Dec.
1 Cap	2 Pis	2 Pis	3 Tau	3 Gem	1 Can	1 Leo	2 Lib	2 Sag	2 Cap	2 Pis	2 Ars
4 Aqr	5 Ars	4 Ars	5 Gem	5 Can	4 Leo	3 Vir	4 Sco	4 Cap	4 Aqr	5 Ars	4 Tau
6 Pis	7 Tau	7 Tau	8 Can	8 Leo	6 Vir	6 Lib	6 Sag	7 Aqr	6 Pis	7 Tau	7 Gem
8 Ars	10 Gem	9 Gem	10 Leo	10 Vir	8 Lib	8 Sco	8 Cap	9 Pis	8 Ars	10 Gem	10 Can
11 Tau	12 Can	12 Can	13 Vir	12 Lib	10 Sco	10 Sag	10 Aqr	11 Ars	11 Tau	12 Can	12 Vir
13 Gem	15 Leo	14 Leo	15 Lib	14 Sco	12 Sag	12 Cap	13 Pis	14 Tau	13 Gem	15 Leo	14 Vir
16 Can	17 Vir	16 Vir	17 Sco	16 Sag	14 Cap	14 Aqr	15 Ars	16 Gem	16 Can	17 Vir	17 Lib
18 Leo	19 Lib	18 Lib	19 Sag	18 Cap	17 Aqr	16 Pis	17 Tau	19 Can	18 Leo	19 Lib	19 Sco
20 Vir	21 Sco	20 Sco	21 Cap	20 Aqr	19 Pis	18 Ars	20 Gem	21 Leo	21 Vir	21 Sco	21 Sag
22 Lib	23 Sag	22 Sag	23 Aqr	22 Pis	21 Ars	21 Tau	22 Can	23 Vir	23 Lib	23 Sag	23 Cap
25 Sco	25 Cap	24 Cap	25 Pis	25 Ars	24 Tau	23 Gem	25 Leo	25 Lib	25 Sco	25 Cap	25 Aqr
27 Sag	27 Aqr	27 Aqr	28 Ars	27 Tau	26 Gem	26 Can	27 Vir	27 Sco	27 Sag	27 Aqr	27 Pis
29 Cap		29 Pis	30 Tau	30 Gem	29 Can	28 Leo	29 Lib	29 Sag	29 Cap	30 Pis	29 Ars
		31 Vir					31 Sco		31 Aqr		

2004

Jan.	Feb.	Mar.	Apr.	May	June	July	Aug.	Sep.	Oct.	Nov.	Dec.
1 Tau	2 Can	3 Leo	2 Vir	1 Lib	2 Sag	1 Cap	2 Pis	3 Tau	2 Gem	1 Can	1 Leo
3 Gem	5 Leo	5 Vir	4 Lib	3 Sco	4 Cap	3 Aqr	4 Ars	5 Gem	5 Can	4 Leo	3 Vir
6 Can	7 Vir	7 Lib	6 Sco	5 Sag	6 Aqr	5 Pis	6 Tau	7 Can	7 Leo	6 Vir	6 Lib
8 Leo	9 Lib	10 Sco	8 Sag	7 Cap	8 Pis	7 Ars	9 Gem	10 Leo	10 Vir	8 Lib	8 Sco
11 Vir	11 Sco	12 Sag	10 Cap	9 Aqr	10 Ars	10 Tau	11 Can	12 Vir	12 Lib	11 Sco	10 Sag
13 Lib	13 Sag	14 Cap	12 Aqr	12 Pis	13 Tau	12 Gem	14 Leo	15 Lib	14 Sco	13 Sag	12 Cap
15 Sco	16 Cap	16 Aqr	14 Pis	14 Ars	15 Gem	15 Can	16 Vir	17 Sco	16 Sag	15 Cap	14 Aqr
17 Sag	18 Aqr	18 Pis	17 Ars	16 Tau	17 Can	17 Leo	18 Lib	19 Sag	18 Cap	17 Aqr	16 Pis
19 Cap	20 Pis	20 Ars	19 Tau	19 Gem	20 Leo	20 Vir	21 Sco	21 Cap	21 Aqr	19 Pis	18 Ars
21 Aqr	22 Ars	23 Tau	22 Gem	21 Can	23 Vir	22 Lib	23 Sag	23 Aqr	23 Pis	21 Ars	21 Tau
23 Pis	24 Tau	25 Gem	24 Can	23 Leo	25 Lib	24 Sco	25 Cap	25 Pis	25 Ars	24 Tau	23 Gem
26 Ars	27 Gem	28 Can	27 Leo	26 Vir	27 Sco	27 Sag	27 Aqr	28 Ars	27 Tau	26 Gem	26 Can
28 Tau	29 Can	30 Leo	29 Vir	29 Lib	29 Sag	29 Cap	29 Pis	30 Tau	30 Gem	28 Can	28 Leo
31 Gem				31 Sco		31 Aqr	31 Ars				31 Vir

2005

Jan.	Feb.	Mar.	Apr.	May	June	July	Aug.	Sep.	Oct.	Nov.	Dec.
2 Lib	1 Sco	2 Sag	1 Cap	2 Pis	1 Ars	2 Gem	1 Can	2 Vir	2 Lib	1 Sco	3 Cap
4 Sco	3 Sag	4 Cap	3 Aqr	4 Ars	3 Tau	5 Can	4 Leo	5 Lib	5 Sco	3 Sag	5 Aqr
7 Sag	5 Cap	6 Aqr	5 Pis	7 Tau	5 Gem	7 Leo	6 Vir	7 Sco	7 Sag	5 Cap	7 Pis
9 Cap	7 Aqr	9 Pis	7 Ars	9 Gem	8 Can	10 Vir	9 Lib	10 Sag	9 Cap	7 Aqr	9 Ars
11 Aqr	9 Pis	11 Ars	9 Tau	11 Can	10 Leo	12 Lib	11 Sco	12 Cap	11 Aqr	10 Pis	11 Tau
13 Pis	11 Ars	13 Tau	11 Gem	14 Leo	13 Vir	15 Sco	13 Sag	14 Aqr	13 Pis	12 Ars	13 Gem
15 Ars	13 Tau	15 Gem	14 Can	16 Vir	15 Lib	17 Sag	15 Cap	16 Pis	15 Ars	14 Tau	16 Can
17 Tau	16 Gem	18 Can	16 Leo	19 Lib	17 Sco	19 Cap	17 Aqr	18 Ars	17 Tau	16 Gem	18 Leo
19 Gem	18 Can	20 Leo	19 Vir	21 Sco	20 Sag	21 Aqr	19 Pis	20 Tau	20 Gem	18 Can	21 Vir
22 Can	21 Leo	23 Vir	21 Lib	23 Sag	22 Cap	23 Pis	21 Ars	22 Gem	22 Can	21 Leo	23 Lib
24 Leo	23 Vir	25 Lib	24 Sco	25 Cap	24 Aqr	25 Ars	24 Tau	25 Can	24 Leo	23 Vir	26 Sco
27 Vir	26 Lib	27 Sco	26 Sag	27 Aqr	26 Pis	27 Tau	26 Gem	27 Leo	27 Vir	26 Lib	28 Sag
29 Lib	28 Sco	29 Sag	28 Cap	29 Pis	28 Ars	30 Gem	28 Can	30 Vir	29 Lib	28 Sco	30 Cap
			30 Aqr		30 Tau		31 Leo			30 Sag	

2006

Jan.	Feb.	Mar.	Apr.	May	June	July	Aug.	Sep.	Oct.	Nov.	Dec.
1 Aqr	1 Ars	1 Ars	1 Gem	1 Can	2 Vir	2 Lib	1 Sco	2 Cap	2 Aqr	2 Ars	2 Tau
3 Pis	4 Tau	3 Tau	4 Can	4 Leo	5 Lib	5 Sco	3 Sag	4 Aqr	4 Pis	4 Tau	4 Gem
5 Ars	6 Gem	5 Gem	6 Leo	6 Vir	7 Sco	7 Sag	6 Cap	6 Pis	6 Ars	6 Gem	6 Can
7 Tau	8 Can	7 Can	9 Vir	9 Lib	10 Sag	9 Cap	8 Aqr	8 Ars	8 Tau	8 Can	8 Leo
10 Gem	11 Leo	10 Leo	11 Lib	11 Sco	12 Cap	11 Aqr	10 Pis	10 Tau	10 Gem	11 Leo	10 Vir
12 Can	13 Vir	12 Vir	14 Sco	13 Sag	14 Aqr	13 Pis	12 Ars	12 Gem	12 Can	13 Vir	13 Lib
14 Leo	16 Lib	15 Lib	16 Sag	16 Cap	16 Pis	16 Ars	14 Tau	15 Can	14 Leo	16 Lib	15 Sco
17 Vir	18 Sco	17 Sco	18 Cap	18 Aqr	18 Ars	18 Tau	16 Gem	17 Leo	17 Vir	18 Sco	18 Sag
19 Lib	21 Sag	20 Sag	21 Aqr	20 Pis	20 Tau	20 Gem	18 Can	20 Vir	19 Lib	21 Sag	20 Cap
22 Sco	23 Cap	22 Cap	23 Pis	22 Ars	23 Gem	22 Can	21 Leo	22 Lib	22 Sco	23 Cap	22 Aqr
24 Sag	25 Aqr	24 Aqr	25 Ars	24 Tau	25 Can	25 Leo	23 Vir	25 Sco	24 Sag	25 Aqr	25 Pis
26 Cap	27 Pis	26 Pis	27 Tau	26 Gem	27 Leo	27 Vir	26 Lib	27 Sag	27 Cap	27 Pis	27 Ars
28 Aqr		28 Ars	29 Gem	29 Can	30 Vir	30 Lib	28 Sco	29 Cap	29 Aqr	29 Ars	29 Tau
30 Pis							31 Sag		31 Pis		31 Gem

2007

Jan.	Feb.	Mar.	Apr.	May	June	July	Aug.	Sep.	Oct.	Nov.	Dec.
2 Can	1 Leo	2 Vir	1 Lib	1 Sco	2 Cap	2 Aqr	2 Ars	1 Tau	2 Can	1 Leo	3 Lib
4 Leo	3 Vir	5 Lib	4 Sco	3 Sag	4 Aqr	4 Pis	4 Tau	3 Gem	4 Leo	3 Vir	5 Sco
7 Vir	6 Lib	7 Sco	6 Sag	6 Cap	7 Pis	6 Ars	7 Gem	5 Can	7 Vir	5 Lib	8 Sag
9 Lib	8 Sco	10 Sag	9 Cap	8 Aqr	9 Ars	8 Tau	9 Can	7 Leo	9 Lib	8 Sco	10 Cap
12 Sco	11 Sag	12 Cap	11 Aqr	10 Pis	11 Tau	10 Gem	11 Leo	10 Vir	12 Sco	11 Sag	13 Aqr
14 Sag	13 Cap	15 Aqr	13 Pis	13 Ars	13 Gem	12 Can	13 Vir	12 Lib	14 Sag	13 Cap	15 Pis
17 Cap	15 Aqr	17 Pis	15 Ars	15 Tau	15 Can	15 Leo	16 Lib	14 Sco	17 Cap	15 Aqr	17 Ars
19 Aqr	17 Pis	19 Ars	17 Tau	17 Gem	17 Leo	17 Vir	18 Sco	17 Sag	19 Aqr	18 Pis	19 Tau
21 Pis	19 Ars	21 Tau	19 Gem	19 Can	20 Vir	19 Lib	21 Sag	19 Cap	21 Pis	20 Ars	21 Gem
23 Ars	21 Tau	23 Gem	21 Can	21 Leo	22 Lib	22 Sco	23 Cap	22 Aqr	24 Ars	22 Tau	23 Can
25 Tau	23 Gem	25 Can	23 Leo	23 Vir	25 Sco	24 Sag	25 Aqr	24 Pis	26 Tau	24 Gem	25 Leo
27 Gem	26 Can	27 Leo	26 Vir	26 Lib	27 Sag	27 Cap	28 Pis	26 Ars	28 Gem	26 Can	28 Vir
29 Can	28 Leo	30 Vir	28 Lib	28 Sco	29 Aqr	30 Ars	30 Ars	28 Tau	30 Can	28 Leo	30 Lib
				31 Sag	31 Pis			30 Gem		30 Vir	

2008

Jan.	Feb.	Mar.	Apr.	May	June	July	Aug.	Sep.	Oct.	Nov.	Dec.
2 Sco	3 Cap	1 Cap	2 Pis	2 Ars	2 Gem	2 Can	2 Vir	1 Lib	1 Sco	2 Cap	2 Aqr
4 Sag	5 Aqr	4 Aqr	5 Ars	4 Tau	4 Can	4 Leo	5 Lib	3 Sco	3 Sag	5 Aqr	4 Pis
7 Cap	8 Pis	6 Pis	7 Tau	6 Gem	6 Leo	6 Vir	7 Sco	6 Sag	6 Cap	7 Pis	7 Ars
9 Aqr	10 Ars	8 Ars	9 Gem	8 Can	9 Vir	8 Lib	9 Sag	8 Cap	8 Aqr	9 Ars	9 Tau
11 Pis	12 Tau	10 Tau	11 Can	10 Leo	11 Lib	11 Sco	12 Cap	11 Aqr	11 Pis	11 Tau	11 Gem
14 Ars	14 Gem	12 Gem	13 Leo	12 Vir	13 Sco	13 Sag	14 Aqr	13 Pis	13 Ars	13 Gem	13 Can
16 Tau	16 Can	14 Can	15 Vir	15 Lib	16 Sag	16 Cap	17 Pis	15 Ars	15 Tau	15 Can	15 Leo
18 Gem	18 Leo	17 Leo	17 Lib	17 Sco	18 Cap	18 Aqr	19 Ars	18 Tau	17 Gem	17 Leo	17 Vir
20 Can	21 Vir	19 Vir	20 Sco	20 Sag	21 Aqr	21 Pis	21 Tau	20 Gem	19 Can	20 Vir	19 Lib
22 Leo	23 Lib	21 Lib	22 Sag	22 Cap	23 Pis	23 Ars	23 Gem	22 Can	21 Leo	22 Lib	21 Sco
24 Vir	25 Sco	24 Sco	25 Cap	25 Aqr	26 Ars	25 Tau	26 Can	24 Leo	23 Vir	24 Sco	24 Sag
26 Lib	28 Sag	26 Sag	27 Aqr	27 Pis	28 Tau	27 Gem	28 Leo	26 Vir	26 Lib	27 Sag	26 Cap
29 Sco		29 Cap	30 Pis	29 Ars	30 Gem	29 Can	30 Vir	28 Lib	28 Sco	29 Cap	29 Aqr
31 Sag		31 Aqr		31 Tau					30 Sag		

2009

Jan.	Feb.	Mar.	Apr.	May	June	July	Aug.	Sep.	Oct.	Nov.	Dec.
1 Pis	1 Tau	1 Tau	1 Can	1 Leo	1 Lib	1 Sco	2 Cap	1 Aqr	3 Ars	2 Tau	1 Gem
3 Ars	4 Gem	3 Gem	3 Leo	3 Vir	3 Sco	3 Sag	4 Aqr	3 Pis	5 Tau	4 Gem	3 Can
5 Tau	6 Can	5 Can	5 Vir	5 Lib	6 Sag	6 Cap	7 Pis	6 Ars	7 Gem	6 Can	5 Leo
7 Gem	8 Leo	7 Leo	8 Lib	7 Sco	8 Cap	8 Aqr	9 Ars	8 Tau	10 Can	8 Leo	7 Vir
9 Can	10 Vir	9 Vir	10 Sco	9 Sag	11 Aqr	11 Pis	12 Tau	10 Gem	12 Leo	10 Vir	9 Lib
11 Leo	12 Lib	11 Lib	12 Sag	12 Cap	13 Pis	13 Ars	14 Gem	12 Can	14 Vir	12 Lib	12 Sco
13 Vir	14 Sco	14 Sco	15 Cap	15 Aqr	16 Ars	15 Tau	16 Can	14 Leo	16 Lib	14 Sco	14 Sag
15 Lib	17 Sag	16 Sag	17 Aqr	17 Pis	20 Gem	18 Gem	18 Leo	16 Vir	18 Sco	17 Sag	16 Cap
18 Sco	19 Cap	18 Cap	20 Pis	19 Ars	22 Can	20 Can	20 Vir	19 Lib	20 Sag	19 Cap	19 Aqr
20 Sag	22 Aqr	21 Aqr	22 Ars	22 Tau	24 Vir	22 Leo	22 Lib	21 Sco	23 Cap	22 Aqr	21 Pis
23 Cap	24 Pis	23 Pis	24 Tau	24 Gem	26 Vir	24 Vir	24 Sco	23 Sag	25 Aqr	24 Pis	24 Ars
25 Aqr	26 Ars	26 Ars	26 Gem	26 Can	28 Lib	26 Lib	27 Sag	25 Cap	28 Pis	27 Ars	26 Tau
28 Pis		28 Tau	28 Can	28 Leo		28 Sco	29 Cap	28 Aqr	30 Ars	29 Tau	29 Gem
30 Ars		30 Gem		30 Vir		30 Sag		30 Pis			31 Can

2010

Jan.	Feb.	Mar.	Apr.	May	June	July	Aug.	Sep.	Oct.	Nov.	Dec.
2 Leo	2 Lib	2 Lib	2 Sag	2 Cap	1 Aqr	1 Pis	2 Tau	1 Gem	2 Leo	1 Vir	2 Sco
4 Vir	4 Sco	4 Sco	5 Cap	4 Aqr	3 Pis	3 Ars	4 Gem	3 Can	4 Vir	3 Lib	4 Sag
6 Lib	7 Sag	6 Sag	7 Aqr	7 Pis	6 Ars	6 Tau	6 Can	5 Leo	6 Lib	5 Sco	6 Cap
8 Sco	9 Cap	8 Cap	10 Pis	9 Ars	8 Tau	8 Gem	8 Leo	7 Vir	8 Sco	7 Sag	9 Aqr
10 Sag	11 Aqr	11 Aqr	12 Ars	12 Tau	10 Gem	10 Can	10 Vir	9 Lib	10 Sag	9 Cap	11 Pis
13 Cap	14 Pis	13 Pis	14 Tau	14 Gem	13 Can	12 Leo	12 Lib	11 Sco	13 Cap	11 Aqr	14 Ars
15 Aqr	17 Ars	16 Ars	17 Gem	16 Can	15 Leo	14 Vir	15 Sco	13 Sag	15 Aqr	14 Pis	16 Tau
18 Pis	19 Tau	18 Tau	19 Can	18 Leo	17 Vir	16 Lib	17 Sag	15 Cap	18 Pis	16 Ars	19 Gem
20 Ars	21 Gem	21 Gem	21 Leo	20 Vir	19 Lib	18 Sco	19 Cap	18 Aqr	20 Ars	19 Tau	21 Can
23 Tau	23 Can	23 Can	23 Vir	23 Lib	21 Sco	20 Sag	22 Aqr	20 Pis	23 Tau	21 Gem	23 Leo
25 Gem	26 Leo	25 Leo	25 Lib	25 Sco	23 Sag	23 Cap	24 Pis	23 Ars	25 Gem	24 Can	25 Vir
27 Can	28 Vir	27 Vir	27 Sco	27 Sag	25 Cap	25 Aqr	27 Ars	25 Tau	27 Can	26 Leo	27 Lib
29 Leo		29 Lib	30 Sag	29 Cap	28 Aqr	28 Pis	29 Tau	28 Gem	30 Leo	28 Vir	29 Sco
31 Vir		31 Sco				30 Ars		30 Can		30 Lib	

2011

Jan.	Feb.	Mar.	Apr.	May	June	July	Aug.	Sep.	Oct.	Nov.	Dec.
1 Sag	1 Aqr	1 Aqr	2 Ars	2 Tau	3 Can	2 Leo	1 Vir	1 Sco	1 Sag	1 Aqr	1 Pis
3 Cap	4 Pis	3 Pis	4 Tau	4 Gem	5 Leo	5 Vir	3 Lib	3 Sag	3 Cap	4 Pis	4 Ars
5 Aqr	6 Ars	6 Ars	7 Gem	7 Can	7 Vir	7 Lib	5 Sco	6 Cap	5 Aqr	6 Ars	6 Tau
8 Pis	9 Tau	8 Tau	9 Can	9 Leo	9 Lib	9 Sco	7 Sag	8 Aqr	8 Pis	9 Tau	9 Gem
10 Ars	11 Gem	11 Gem	12 Leo	11 Vir	12 Sco	11 Sag	9 Cap	10 Pis	10 Ars	11 Gem	11 Can
13 Tau	14 Can	13 Can	14 Vir	13 Lib	14 Sag	13 Cap	12 Aqr	13 Ars	13 Tau	14 Can	13 Leo
15 Gem	16 Leo	15 Leo	16 Lib	15 Sco	16 Cap	15 Aqr	14 Pis	15 Tau	15 Gem	16 Leo	16 Vir
17 Can	18 Vir	17 Vir	18 Sco	17 Sag	18 Aqr	18 Pis	17 Ars	18 Gem	18 Can	18 Vir	18 Lib
19 Leo	20 Lib	19 Lib	20 Sag	19 Cap	20 Pis	20 Ars	19 Tau	20 Can	20 Leo	21 Lib	20 Sco
21 Vir	22 Sco	21 Sco	22 Cap	22 Aqr	23 Ars	23 Tau	22 Gem	23 Leo	22 Vir	23 Sco	22 Sag
23 Lib	24 Sag	23 Sag	24 Aqr	24 Pis	25 Tau	25 Gem	24 Can	25 Vir	24 Lib	25 Sag	24 Cap
26 Sco	26 Cap	26 Cap	27 Pis	27 Ars	28 Gem	28 Can	26 Leo	27 Lib	26 Sco	27 Cap	26 Aqr
28 Sag		28 Aqr	29 Ars	29 Tau	30 Can	30 Leo	28 Vir	29 Sco	28 Sag	29 Aqr	28 Pis
30 Cap		30 Pis		31 Gem			30 Lib		30 Cap		31 Ars

2012

Jan.	Feb.	Mar.	Apr.	May	June	July	Aug.	Sep.	Oct.	Nov.	Dec.
2 Tau	1 Gem	2 Can	1 Leo	3 Lib	1 Sco	2 Cap	1 Aqr	2 Ars	1 Tau	3 Can	3 Leo
5 Gem	4 Can	4 Leo	3 Vir	5 Sco	3 Sag	5 Aqr	3 Pis	4 Tau	4 Gem	5 Leo	5 Vir
7 Can	6 Leo	7 Vir	5 Lib	7 Sag	5 Cap	7 Pis	5 Ars	7 Gem	7 Can	8 Vir	7 Lib
10 Leo	8 Vir	9 Lib	7 Sco	9 Cap	7 Aqr	9 Ars	8 Tau	9 Can	9 Leo	10 Lib	9 Sco
12 Vir	10 Lib	11 Sco	9 Sag	11 Aqr	9 Pis	11 Tau	10 Gem	12 Leo	11 Vir	12 Sco	11 Sag
14 Lib	12 Sco	13 Sag	11 Cap	13 Pis	12 Ars	14 Gem	13 Can	14 Vir	13 Lib	14 Sag	13 Cap
16 Sco	15 Sag	15 Cap	13 Aqr	15 Ars	14 Tau	17 Can	15 Leo	16 Lib	16 Sco	16 Cap	15 Aqr
18 Sag	17 Cap	17 Aqr	15 Pis	18 Tau	17 Gem	19 Leo	18 Vir	18 Sco	18 Sag	18 Aqr	18 Pis
20 Cap	19 Aqr	20 Pis	18 Ars	20 Gem	19 Can	21 Vir	20 Lib	20 Sag	20 Cap	20 Pis	20 Ars
23 Aqr	21 Pis	22 Ars	21 Tau	23 Can	22 Leo	23 Lib	22 Sco	22 Cap	22 Aqr	23 Ars	22 Tau
25 Pis	24 Ars	24 Tau	23 Gem	25 Leo	24 Vir	26 Sco	24 Sag	24 Aqr	24 Pis	25 Tau	25 Gem
27 Ars	26 Tau	27 Gem	26 Can	28 Vir	26 Lib	28 Sag	26 Cap	27 Pis	26 Ars	28 Gem	27 Can
30 Tau	29 Gem	29 Can	28 Leo	30 Lib	28 Sco	30 Cap	28 Aqr	29 Ars	29 Tau	30 Can	30 Leo
			30 Vir		30 Sag		30 Pis		31 Gem		

2013

Jan.	Feb.	Mar.	Apr.	May	June	July	Aug.	Sep.	Oct.	Nov.	Dec.
1 Vir	2 Sco	1 Sco	2 Cap	1 Aqr	2 Ars	1 Tau	3 Can	2 Leo	1 Vir	2 Sco	2 Sag
4 Lib	4 Sag	3 Sag	4 Aqr	3 Pis	4 Tau	4 Gem	5 Leo	4 Vir	4 Lib	4 Sag	4 Cap
6 Sco	6 Cap	6 Cap	6 Pis	6 Ars	7 Gem	6 Can	8 Vir	6 Lib	6 Sco	6 Cap	6 Aqr
8 Sag	8 Aqr	8 Aqr	8 Ars	8 Tau	9 Can	9 Leo	10 Lib	9 Sco	8 Sag	8 Aqr	8 Pis
10 Cap	10 Pis	10 Pis	11 Tau	10 Gem	12 Leo	11 Vir	12 Sco	11 Sag	10 Cap	11 Pis	10 Ars
12 Aqr	13 Ars	12 Ars	13 Gem	13 Can	14 Vir	14 Lib	15 Sag	13 Cap	12 Aqr	13 Ars	12 Tau
14 Pis	15 Tau	14 Tau	16 Can	15 Leo	17 Lib	16 Sco	17 Cap	15 Aqr	14 Pis	15 Tau	15 Gem
16 Ars	17 Gem	17 Gem	18 Leo	18 Vir	19 Sco	18 Sag	19 Aqr	17 Pis	17 Ars	18 Gem	17 Can
19 Tau	20 Can	19 Can	21 Vir	20 Lib	21 Sag	20 Cap	21 Pis	19 Ars	19 Tau	20 Can	20 Leo
21 Gem	22 Leo	22 Leo	23 Lib	22 Sco	23 Cap	22 Aqr	23 Ars	21 Tau	21 Gem	22 Leo	22 Vir
24 Can	25 Vir	24 Vir	25 Sco	24 Sag	25 Aqr	24 Pis	25 Tau	24 Gem	24 Can	25 Vir	25 Lib
26 Leo	27 Lib	26 Lib	27 Sag	26 Cap	27 Pis	26 Ars	27 Gem	26 Can	26 Leo	27 Lib	27 Sco
28 Vir		29 Sco	29 Cap	28 Aqr	29 Ars	29 Tau	30 Can	29 Leo	29 Vir	30 Sco	29 Sag
31 Lib		31 Sag		31 Pis		31 Gem			31 Lib		31 Cap

2014

Jan.	Feb.	Mar.	Apr.	May	June	July	Aug.	Sep.	Oct.	Nov.	Dec.
2 Aqr	1 Pis	2 Ars	1 Tau	3 Can	2 Leo	1 Vir	3 Sco	1 Sag	1 Cap	1 Pis	1 Ars
4 Pis	3 Ars	4 Tau	3 Gem	5 Leo	4 Vir	4 Lib	5 Sag	3 Cap	3 Aqr	3 Ars	3 Tau
6 Ars	5 Tau	7 Gem	5 Can	8 Vir	7 Lib	6 Sco	7 Cap	5 Aqr	5 Pis	5 Tau	5 Gem
9 Tau	7 Gem	9 Can	8 Leo	10 Lib	9 Sco	9 Sag	9 Aqr	7 Pis	7 Ars	8 Gem	7 Can
11 Gem	10 Can	12 Leo	10 Vir	13 Sco	11 Sag	11 Cap	11 Pis	9 Ars	9 Tau	10 Can	10 Leo
14 Can	12 Leo	14 Vir	13 Lib	15 Sag	13 Cap	13 Aqr	13 Ars	12 Tau	11 Gem	12 Leo	12 Vir
16 Leo	15 Vir	17 Lib	15 Sco	17 Cap	15 Aqr	15 Pis	15 Tau	14 Gem	13 Can	15 Vir	15 Lib
19 Vir	17 Lib	19 Sco	17 Sag	19 Aqr	17 Pis	17 Ars	17 Gem	16 Can	16 Leo	17 Lib	17 Sco
21 Lib	20 Sco	21 Sag	20 Cap	21 Pis	19 Ars	19 Tau	20 Can	19 Leo	18 Vir	20 Sco	19 Sag
23 Sco	22 Sag	23 Cap	22 Aqr	23 Ars	22 Tau	21 Gem	22 Leo	21 Vir	21 Lib	22 Sag	22 Cap
26 Sag	24 Cap	25 Aqr	24 Pis	25 Tau	24 Gem	24 Can	25 Vir	24 Lib	23 Sco	24 Cap	24 Aqr
28 Cap	26 Aqr	28 Pis	26 Ars	28 Gem	26 Can	26 Leo	27 Lib	26 Sco	25 Sag	26 Aqr	26 Pis
30 Aqr	28 Pis	30 Ars	28 Tau	30 Can	29 Leo	29 Vir	30 Sco	28 Sag	28 Cap	28 Pis	28 Ars
		31 Lib	30 Gem						30 Aqr		30 Tau

2015

Jan.	Feb.	Mar.	Apr.	May	June	July	Aug.	Sep.	Oct.	Nov.	Dec.
1 Gem	2 Leo	1 Leo	3 Lib	3 Sco	1 Sag	1 Cap	1 Pis	2 Tau	1 Gem	2 Leo	2 Vir
4 Can	5 Vir	4 Vir	5 Sco	5 Sag	4 Cap	3 Aqr	3 Ars	4 Gem	4 Can	5 Vir	4 Lib
6 Leo	7 Lib	7 Lib	8 Sag	7 Cap	6 Aqr	5 Pis	6 Tau	6 Can	6 Leo	7 Lib	7 Sco
8 Vir	10 Sco	9 Sco	10 Cap	9 Aqr	8 Pis	7 Ars	8 Gem	9 Leo	8 Vir	10 Sco	9 Sag
11 Lib	12 Sag	11 Sag	12 Aqr	12 Pis	10 Ars	9 Tau	10 Can	11 Vir	11 Lib	12 Sag	12 Cap
13 Sco	14 Cap	14 Cap	14 Pis	14 Ars	12 Tau	12 Gem	12 Leo	14 Lib	13 Sco	15 Cap	14 Aqr
16 Sag	17 Aqr	16 Aqr	16 Ars	16 Tau	14 Gem	14 Can	15 Vir	16 Sco	16 Sag	17 Aqr	16 Pis
18 Cap	18 Pis	18 Pis	18 Tau	18 Gem	16 Can	16 Leo	17 Lib	19 Sag	18 Cap	19 Pis	18 Ars
20 Aqr	20 Ars	20 Ars	20 Gem	20 Can	19 Leo	19 Vir	20 Sco	21 Cap	21 Aqr	21 Ars	21 Tau
22 Pis	23 Tau	22 Tau	23 Can	22 Leo	21 Vir	21 Lib	22 Sag	23 Aqr	23 Pis	23 Tau	23 Gem
24 Ars	25 Gem	24 Gem	25 Leo	25 Vir	24 Lib	24 Sco	25 Cap	25 Pis	25 Ars	25 Gem	25 Leo
26 Tau	27 Can	26 Can	28 Vir	27 Lib	26 Sco	26 Sag	27 Aqr	27 Ars	27 Tau	27 Can	27 Leo
28 Gem		29 Leo	30 Lib	30 Sco	29 Sag	28 Cap	29 Pis	29 Tau	29 Gem	30 Leo	29 Vir
		31 Vir				30 Aqr	31 Ars		31 Can		

2016

Jan.	Feb.	Mar.	Apr.	May	June	July	Aug.	Sep.	Oct.	Nov.	Dec.
1 Lib	2 Sag	3 Cap	2 Aqr	1 Pis	2 Tau	1 Gem	2 Leo	3 Lib	2 Scor	1 Sag	1 Cap
3 Sco	5 Cap	5 Aqr	4 Pis	3 Ars	4 Gem	3 Can	4 Vir	5 Sco	5 Sag	4 Cap	3 Aqr
6 Sag	7 Aqr	7 Pis	6 Ars	5 Tau	6 Can	5 Leo	6 Lib	8 Sag	7 Cap	6 Aqr	6 Pis
8 Cap	9 Pis	9 Ars	8 Tau	7 Gem	8 Leo	7 Vir	9 Sco	10 Cap	10 Aqr	8 Pis	8 Ars
10 Aqr	11 Ars	11 Tau	10 Gem	9 Can	10 Vir	10 Lib	11 Sag	12 Aqr	12 Pis	11 Ars	10 Tau
12 Pis	13 Tau	13 Gem	12 Can	11 Leo	13 Lib	12 Sco	14 Cap	15 Pis	14 Ars	13 Tau	12 Gem
15 Ars	15 Gem	16 Can	14 Leo	14 Vir	15 Sco	15 Sag	16 Aqr	17 Ars	16 Tau	15 Gem	14 Can
17 Tau	17 Can	18 Leo	16 Vir	16 Lib	18 Sag	17 Cap	18 Pis	19 Tau	18 Gem	17 Can	16 Leo
19 Gem	20 Leo	20 Vir	19 Lib	19 Sco	20 Cap	20 Aqr	20 Ars	21 Gem	20 Can	19 Leo	18 Vir
21 Can	22 Vir	23 Lib	22 Sco	21 Sag	22 Aqr	22 Pis	22 Tau	23 Can	22 Leo	21 Vir	21 Lib
23 Leo	24 Lib	25 Sco	24 Sag	24 Cap	25 Pis	24 Ars	24 Gem	25 Leo	25 Vir	23 Lib	23 Sco
26 Vir	27 Sco	28 Sag	26 Cap	26 Aqr	27 Ars	26 Tau	27 Can	27 Vir	27 Lib	26 Sco	26 Sag
28 Lib	29 Sag	30 Cap	29 Aqr	28 Pis	29 Tau	28 Gem	29 Leo	30 Lib	30 Sco	28 Sag	28 Cap
31 Sco				31 Ars		30 Can	31 Vir				31 Aqr

2017

Jan.	Feb.	Mar.	Apr.	May	June	July	Aug.	Sep.	Oct.	Nov.	Dec.
2 Pis	3 Tau	2Tau	2 Can	2 Leo	3 Lib	2 Sco	1 Sag	2 Aqr	2 Pis	1 Ars	2 Gem
4 Ars	5 Gem	4 Gem	4 Leo	4 Vir	5 Sco	5 Sag	4 Cap	5 Pis	4 Ars	3 Tau	4 Can
6 Tau	7 Can	6 Can	7 Vir	6 Lib	7 Sag	7 Cap	6 Aqr	7 Ars	6 Tau	5 Gem	6 Leo
8 Gem	9 Leo	8 Leo	9 Lib	9 Sco	10 Cap	10 Aqr	8 Pis	9 Tau	8 Gem	7 Can	8 Vir
10 Can	11 Vir	10 Vir	11 Sco	11 Sag	12 Aqr	12 Pis	11 Ars	11 Gem	11 Can	9 Leo	11 Lib
13 Leo	13 Lib	13 Lib	14 Sag	14 Cap	15 Pis	14 Ars	13 Tau	13 Can	13 Leo	11 Vir	13 Sco
15 Vir	16 Sco	15 Sco	16 Cap	16 Aqr	17 Ars	17 Tau	15 Gem	16 Leo	15 Vir	13 Lib	16 Sag
17 Lib	18 Sag	18 Sag	19 Aqr	19 Pis	19 Tau	19 Gem	17 Can	18 Vir	17 Lib	16 Sco	18 Cap
19 Sco	21Cap	20 Cap	21 Pis	21 Ars	21 Gem	21 Can	19 Leo	20 Lib	20 Sco	18 Sag	21 Aqr
22 Sag	23 Aqr	23 Aqr	24 Ars	23 Tau	23 Can	23 Leo	21 Vir	22 Sco	22 Sag	21 Cap	23 Pis
24 Cap	26 Pis	25 Pis	26 Tau	25 Gem	25 Leo	25 Vir	24 Lib	25 Sag	25 Cap	23 Aqr	26 Ars
27 Aqr	28 Ars	27 Ars	28 Gem	27 Can	28 Vir	27 Lib	26 Sco	27 Cap	27 Aqr	26 Pis	28 Tau
29 Pis		29 Tau	30 Can	29 Leo	30 Lib	30 Sco	28 Sag	29 Pis	29 Pis	28 Ars	30 Gem
31 Ars		31 Gem		31 Vir			31 Cap			30 Tau	

2018

Jan.	Feb.	Mar.	Apr.	May	June	July	Aug.	Sep.	Oct.	Nov.	Dec.
1 Can	1 Vir	1 Vir	1 Sco	1 Sag	2 Aqr	2 Pis	1 Ars	2 Gem	1 Can	2 Vir	1 Lib
3 Leo	3 Lib	3 Lib	4 Sag	4 Cap	5 Pis	5 Ars	3 Tau	4 Can	3 Leo	4 Lib	3 Sco
5 Vir	6 Sco	5 Sco	6 Cap	6 Aqr	7 Ars	7 Tau	6 Gem	6 Leo	5 Vir	6 Sco	6 Sag
7 Lib	8 Sag	7 Sag	9 Aqr	9 Pis	10 Tau	10 Gem	8 Can	8 Vir	8 Lib	8 Sag	8 Cap
9 Sco	11 Cap	10 Cap	11 Pis	11 Ars	12 Gem	13 Leo	10 Leo	10 Lib	10 Sco	11 Cap	10 Aqr
12 Sag	13 Aqr	12 Aqr	14 Ars	13 Tau	14 Can	15 Vir	12 Vir	12 Sco	12 Sag	13 Aqr	13 Pis
14 Cap	16 Pis	15 Pis	16 Tau	15 Gem	16 Leo	17 Lib	14 Lib	15 Sag	14 Cap	16 Pis	16 Ars
17 Aqr	18 Ars	17 Ars	18 Gem	17 Can	18 Vir	20 Sco	16 Sco	17 Cap	17 Aqr	18 Ars	18 Tau
19 Pis	20 Tau	20 Tau	20 Can	19 Leo	20 Lib	22 Sag	18 Sag	19 Aqr	19 Pis	20 Tau	20 Gem
22 Ars	23 Gem	22 Gem	22 Leo	22 Vir	22 Sco	24Cap	21 Cap	22 Ars	22 Ars	23 Gem	22 Can
24 Tau	25 Can	24 Can	24 Vir	24 Lib	24 Sag	27 Aqr	23 Aqr	24 Ars	24 Tau	25 Can	24 Leo
26 Gem	27 Leo	26 Leo	27 Lib	26 Sco	27 Cap	29 Pis	26 Pis	27 Tau	26 Gem	27 Leo	26 Vir
28 Can		28 Vir	29 Sco	28 Sag	30 Aqr		28 Ars	29 Gem	28 Can	29 Vir	28 Lib
30 Leo		30 Lib		31 Cap			31 Tau		31 Leo		31 Sco

2019

Jan.	Feb.	Mar.	Apr.	May	June	July	Aug.	Sep.	Oct.	Nov.	Dec.
2 Sag	1 Cap	2 Aqr	1 Pis	1 Ars	2 Gem	2 Can	2 Vir	2 Sco	2 Sag	1 Cap	3 Pis
4 Cap	3 Aqr	5 Pis	4 Ars	3 Tau	4 Can	4 Leo	4 Lib	5 Sag	4 Cap	3 Aqr	5 Ars
7 Aqr	6 Pis	7 Ars	6 Tau	6 Gem	6 Leo	6 Vir	7 Sco	7 Cap	7 Aqr	5 Pis	8 Tau
9 Pis	8 Ars	10 Tau	8 Gem	8 Can	8 Vir	8 Lib	9 Sag	9 Aqr	9 Pis	8 Ars	10 Gem
12 Ars	11 Tau	12 Gem	11 Can	10 Leo	11 Lib	10 Sco	11 Cap	12 Pis	12 Ars	10 Tau	12 Can
14 Tau	13 Gem	14 Can	13 Leo	12 Vir	13 Sco	12 Sag	14 Aqr	14 Ars	14 Tau	13 Gem	15 Leo
17 Gem	15 Can	17 Leo	15 Vir	14 Lib	15 Sag	14 Cap	16 Pis	17 Tau	17 Gem	15 Can	17 Vir
19 Can	17 Leo	19 Vir	17 Lib	16 Sco	17 Cap	17 Aqr	18 Ars	19 Gem	19 Can	17 Leo	19 Lib
21 Leo	19 Vir	21 Lib	19 Sco	19 Sag	20 Aqr	19 Pis	21 Tau	22 Can	21 Leo	20 Vir	21 Sco
23 Vir	21 Lib	23 Sco	21 Sag	21 Cap	22 Pis	22 Ars	23 Gem	24 Leo	23 Vir	22 Lib	23 Sag
25 Lib	23 Sco	25 Sag	23 Cap	23 Aqr	25 Ars	24 Tau	25 Can	26 Vir	25 Lib	24 Sco	25 Cap
27 Sco	25 Sag	27 Cap	26 Aqr	26 Pis	27 Tau	27 Gem	27 Leo	28 Lib	27 Sco	26 Sag	28 Aqr
29 Sag	28 Cap	30 Aqr	28 Pis	28 Ars	29 Gem	29 Can	29 Vir	30 Sco	29 Sag	28 Cap	30 Pis
				31 Tau		31 Leo				30 Aqr	

2020

Jan.	Feb.	Mar.	Apr.	May	June	July	Aug.	Sep.	Oct.	Nov.	Dec.
2 Ars	1 Tau	1 Gem	2 Leo	2 Vir	2 Sco	2 Sag	2 Aqr	1 Pis	1 Ars	2 Gem	2 Can
4 Tau	3 Gem	4 Can	4 Vir	4 Lib	4 Sag	4 Cap	5 Pis	3 Ars	3 Tau	4 Can	4 Leo
7 Gem	5 Can	6 Leo	6 Lib	6 Sco	6 Cap	6 Aqr	7 Ars	6 Tau	6 Gem	7 Leo	6 Vir
9 Can	7 Leo	8 Vir	8 Sco	8 Sag	9 Aqr	8 Pis	10Tau	8 Gem	8 Can	9 Vir	9 Lib
11 Leo	9 Vir	10 Lib	10 Sag	10 Cap	11 Pis	11 Ars	12 Gem	11 Can	11 Leo	11 Lib	11 Sco
13 Vir	11 Lib	12 Sco	13 Cap	12 Aqr	13 Ars	13 Tau	14 Can	13 Leo	13 Vir	13 Sco	13 Sag
15 Lib	14 Sco	14 Sag	15 Aqr	15 Pis	16 Tau	16 Gem	17 Leo	15 Vir	15 Lib	15 Sag	15 Cap
17 Sco	16 Sag	16 Cap	17 Pis	17 Ars	18 Gem	18 Can	19 Vir	17 Lib	17 Sco	17 Cap	17 Aqr
19 Sag	18 Cap	19 Aqr	20 Ars	20 Tau	21 Can	20 Leo	21 Lib	19 Sco	19 Sag	19 Aqr	19 Pis
22 Cap	20 Aqr	21 Pis	22 Tau	22 Gem	23 Leo	22 Vir	23 Sco	21 Sag	21 Cap	22 Pis	21 Ars
24 Aqr	23 Pis	24 Ars	25 Gem	24 Can	25 Vir	25 Lib	25 Sag	23 Cap	23 Aqr	24 Ars	24 Tau
26 Pis	25 Ars	26 Tau	27 Can	27 Leo	27 Lib	27 Sco	27 Cap	26 Aqr	25 Pis	27 Tau	26 Gem
29 Ars	28 Tau	29 Gem	30 Leo	29 Vir	29 Sco	29 Sag	30 Aqr	28 Pis	28 Ars	29 Gem	29 Can
		31 Can		31 Lib		31 Cap			30 Tau		31 Leo

2021

Jan.	Feb.	Mar.	Apr.	May	June	July	Aug.	Sep.	Oct.	Nov.	Dec.
3 Vir	1 Lib	2 Sco	1 Sag	2 Aqr	1 Pis	1 Ars	2 Gem	1 Can	1 Leo	1 Lib	1 Sco
5 Lib	3 Sco	4 Sag	3 Cap	5 Pis	3 Ars	3 Tau	4 Can	3 Leo	3 Vir	4 Sco	3 Sag
7 Sco	5 Sag	7 Cap	5 Aqr	7 Ars	6 Tau	6 Gem	7 Leo	5 Vir	5 Lib	6 Sag	5 Cap
9 Sag	7 Cap	9 Aqr	7 Pis	9 Tau	8 Gem	8 Can	9 Vir	8 Lib	7 Sco	8 Cap	7 Aqr
11 Cap	10 Aqr	11 Pis	10 Ars	12 Gem	11 Can	11 Leo	11 Lib	10 Sco	9 Sag	10 Aqr	9 Pis
13 Aqr	12 Pis	13 Ars	12 Tau	15 Can	13 Leo	13 Vir	14 Sco	12 Sag	11 Cap	12 Pis	11 Ars
15 Pis	14 Ars	16 Tau	15 Gem	17 Leo	16 Vir	15 Lib	16 Sag	14 Cap	13 Aqr	14 Ars	14 Tau
18 Ars	17 Tau	18 Gem	17 Can	19 Vir	18 Lib	17 Sco	18 Cap	16 Aqr	16 Pis	17 Tau	16 Gem
20 Tau	19 Gem	21 Can	20 Leo	22 Lib	20 Sco	19 Sag	20 Aqr	18 Pis	18 Ars	19 Gem	19 Can
23 Gem	22 Can	23 Leo	22 Vir	24 Sco	22 Sag	21 Cap	22 Pis	21 Ars	20 Tau	22 Can	21 Leo
25 Can	24 Leo	26 Vir	24 Lib	26 Sag	24 Cap	24 Aqr	24 Ars	23 Tau	23 Gem	24 Leo	24 Vir
28 Leo	26 Vir	28 Lib	26 Sco	28 Cap	26 Aqr	26 Pis	27 Tau	26 Gem	25 Can	27 Vir	26 Lib
30 Vir	28 Lib	30 Sco	28 Sag	30 Aqr	28 Pis	26 Ars	29 Gem	28 Can	28 Leo	29 Lib	28 Sco
			30 Cap			30 Tau			30 Vir		30 Sag

2022

Jan.	Feb.	Mar.	Apr.	May	June	July	Aug.	Sep.	Oct.	Nov.	Dec.
1 Cap	2 Pis	1 Pis	2 Tau	2 Gem	1 Can	1 Leo	2 Lib	2 Sag	2 Cap	2 Pis	2 Ars
3 Aqr	4 Ars	4 Ars	5 Gem	4 Can	3 Leo	3 Vir	4 Sco	5 Cap	4 Aqr	4 Ars	4 Tau
6 Pis	6 Tau	6 Tau	7 Can	7 Leo	6 Vir	5 Lib	6 Sag	7 Aqr	6 Pis	7 Tau	6 Gem
8 Ars	9 Gem	8 Gem	10 Leo	9 Vir	8 Lib	8 Sco	8 Cap	9 Pis	8 Ars	9 Gem	9 Can
10 Tau	11 Can	11 Can	12 Vir	12 Lib	10 Sco	10 Sag	10 Aqr	11 Ars	10 Tau	12 Can	11 Leo
13 Gem	14 Leo	13 Leo	14 Lib	14Sco	12 Sag	12 Cap	12 Pis	13 Tau	13 Gem	14 Leo	14 Vir
15 Can	16 Vir	16 Vir	17 Sco	16 Sag	14 Cap	14 Aqr	14 Ars	15 Gem	15 Can	17 Vir	16 Lib
18 Leo	19 Lib	18 Lib	19 Sag	18 Cap	16 Aqr	16 Pis	17 Tau	18 Can	18 Leo	19 Lib	19 Sco
20 Vir	21 Sco	20 Sco	21 Cap	20 Aqr	18 Pis	18 Ars	19 Gem	20 Leo	20 Vir	21 Sco	21 Sag
22 Lib	23 Sag	22 Sag	23 Aqr	22 Pis	21 Ars	20 Tau	22 Can	23 Vir	23 Lib	23 Sag	23 Cap
25 Sco	25 Cap	24 Cap	25 Pis	24 Ars	23 Tau	23 Gem	24 Leo	25 Lib	25 Sco	25 Cap	25 Aqr
27 Sag	27 Aqr	27 Aqr	27 Ars	27 Tau	25 Gem	25 Can	27 Vir	27 Sco	27 Sag	27 Aqr	27 Pis
29 Cap		29 Pis	30 Tau	29 Gem	28 Can	28 Leo	29 Lib	30 Sag	29 Cap	30 Pis	29 Ars
31 Aqr						30 Vir	31 Sco		31 Aqr		31 Tau

2023

Jan.	Feb.	Mar.	Apr.	May	June	July	Aug.	Sep.	Oct.	Nov.	Dec.
3 Gem	1Can	1 Can	2 Vir	2 Lib	3 Sag	2 Cap	1 Aqr	1 Ars	1 Tau	1 Can	1 Leo
5 Can	4 Leo	3 Leo	4 Lib	4 Sco	5 Cap	4 Aqr	3 Pis	3 Tau	3 Gem	4 Leo	4 Vir
8 Leo	6 Vir	6 Vir	7 Sco	6 Sag	7 Aqr	6 Pis	5 Ars	5 Gem	5 Can	6 Vir	6 Lib
10 Vir	9 Lib	8 Lib	9 Sag	8 Cap	9 Pis	8 Ars	7 Tau	8 Can	7 Leo	9 Lib	9 Sco
13 Lib	11 Sco	11 Sco	11 Cap	11 Aqr	11 Ars	10 Tau	9 Gem	10 Leo	10 Vir	11 Sco	11 Sag
15 Sco	14 Sag	13 Sag	13 Aqr	13 Pis	13 Tau	13 Gem	11 Can	13 Vir	13 Lib	14 Sag	13 Cap
17 Sag	16 Cap	15 Cap	15 Pis	15 Ars	16 Gem	15 Can	14 Leo	15 Lib	15 Sco	16 Cap	15 Aqr
19 Cap	18 Aqr	17 Aqr	18 Ars	17 Tau	18 Can	18 Leo	16 Vir	18 Sco	17 Sag	18 Aqr	17 Pis
21 Aqr	20 Pis	19 Pis	20 Tau	19 Gem	20 Leo	20 Vir	19 Lib	20 Sag	20 Cap	20 Pis	19 Ars
23 Pis	22 Ars	21 Ars	22 Gem	22 Can	23 Vir	23 Lib	21 Sco	22 Cap	22 Aqr	22 Ars	22 Tau
25 Ars	24 Tau	23 Tau	24 Can	24 Leo	25 Lib	25 Sco	24 Sag	24 Aqr	24 Pis	24 Tau	24 Can
27 Tau	26 Gem	26 Gem	27 Leo	27 Vir	28 Sco	28 Sag	26 Cap	26 Pis	26 Ars	27 Gem	26 Can
30 Gem		28 Can	29 Vir	29 Lib	30 Sag	30 Cap	28 Aqr	29 Ars	28 Tau	29 Can	29 Leo
							30 Pis		30 Gem		31 Vir

2024

Jan.	Feb.	Mar.	Apr.	May	June	July	Aug.	Sep.	Oct.	Nov.	Dec.
3 Lib 5 Sco 7 Sag 10 Cap 12 Aqr 14 Pis 16 Ars 18 Tau 20 Gem 22 Can 25 Leo 27 Vir 30 Lib	1 Sco 4 Sag 6 Cap 8 Aqr 10 Pis 12 Ars 14 Tau 16 Gem 19 Can 21 Leo 24 Vir 26 Lib 29 Sco	2 Sag 4 Cap 7 Aqr 9 Pis 11 Ars 13 Tau 15 Gem 17 Can 19 Leo 22 Vir 24 Lib 27 Sco 29 Sag	1 Cap 3 Aqr 5 Pis 7 Ars 9 Tau 11 Gem 13 Can 16 Leo 18 Vir 21 Lib 23 Sco 26 Sag 28 Cap 30 Aqr	2 Pis 4 Ars 6 Tau 8 Gem 11 Can 13 Leo 15 Vir 18 Lib 20 Sco 23 Sag 25 Cap 27 Aqr 30 Pis	1 Ars 3 Tau 5 Gem 7 Can 9 Vir 12 Vir 14 Lib 17 Sco 19 Sag 21 Cap 24 Aqr 26 Pis 28 Ars 30 Tau	2 Gem 4 Can 7 Leo 9 Vir 12 Lib 14 Sco 17 Sag 19 Cap 21 Aqr 23 Pis 25 Ars 27 Tau 29 Gem	1 Can 3 Leo 5 Vir 8 Lib 10 Sco 13 Sag 15 Cap 17 Aqr 19 Pis 21 Ars 24 Tau 26 Can 28 Can 30 Leo	2 Vir 4 Lib 7 Sco 9 Sag 12 Cap 14 Aqr 16 Pis 18 Ars 20 Tau 22 Gem 24 Can 26 Leo 29 Vir	1 Lib 4 Sco 6 Sag 9 Cap 11 Aqr 13 Pis 15 Ars 17 Tau 19 Gem 21 Can 24 Leo 26 Vir 29 Lib 31 Sco	3 Sag 5 Cap 7 Aqr 10 Pis 12 Ars 14 Tau 16 Gem 18 Can 20 Leo 22 Vir 25 Lib 28 Sco 30 Sag	2 Cap 5 Aqr 7 Pis 9 Ars 11 Tau 13 Gem 15 Can 17 Leo 20 Vir 22 Lib 25 Sco 27 Sag 30 Cap

2025

Jan.	Feb.	Mar.	Apr.	May	June	July	Aug.	Sep.	Oct.	Nov.	Dec.
1 Aqr 3 Pis 5 Ari 7 Tau 10 Gem 12 Can 14 Leo 16 Vir 19 Lib 21 Sco 24 Sag 26 Cap 28 Aqr 30 Pis	2 Ars 4 Tau 6 Gem 8 Can 10 Leo 13 Vir 15 Lib 18 Sco 20 Sag 22 Cap 25 Aqr 27 Pis	1 Ars 3 Tau 5 Gem 7 Can 9 Leo 12 Vir 14 Lib 17 Sco 19 Sag 22 Cap 24 Aqr 26 Pis 28 Ars 30 Tau	1 Gem 3 Can 6 Leo 8 Vir 11 Lib 13 Sco 16 Sag 18 Cap 20 Aqr 23 Pis 25 Ars 27 Tau 29 Gem	1Can 3 Leo 5 Vir 8 Lib 10 Sco 13 Sag 15 Cap 18 Aqr 20 Pis 22 Ars 24 Tau 26 Gem 28 Can 30 Leo	2 Vir 4 Lib 7 Sco 9 Sag 12 Cap 14 Aqr 16 Pis 18 Ars 21 Tau 23 Gem 25 Can 27 Leo 29 Vir	1 Lib 4 Sco 6 Sag 9 Cap 11 Aqr 13 Pis 16 Ars 18 Tau 20 Gem 22 Can 24 Leo 26 Vir 29 Lib 31 Sco	3 Sag 5 Cap 8 Aqr 10 Pis 12 Ars 14 Tau 16 Gem 18 Can 20 Leo 23 Vir 25 Lib 28 Sco 30 Sag	2 Cap 4 Aqr 6 Pis 8 Ars 10 Tau 12 Gem 15 Can 17 Leo 19 Vir 21 Lib 24 Sco 26 Sag 29 Cap	1 Aqr 4 Pis 6 Ars 8 Tau 10 Gem 12 Can 14 Leo 16 Vir 19 Lib 21 Sco 24 Sag 26 Cap 29 Aqr 31 Pis	2 Ars 4 Tau 6 Gem 8 Can 10 Leo 12 Vir 15 Lib 17 Sco 20 Sag 22 Cap 25 Aqr 27 Pis 30 Ars	2 Tau 4 Gem 6 Can 8 Leo 10 Vir 12 Lib 15 Sco 17 Sag 20 Cap 22 Aqr 25 Pis 27 Ars 29 Tau 31 Gem

2026

Jan.	Feb.	Mar.	Apr.	May	June	July	Aug.	Sep.	Oct.	Nov.	Dec.
2 Can 4 Leo 6 Vir 9 Lib 11 Sco 13 Sag 16 Cap 18 Aqr 21 Pis 23 Ars 25 Tau 27 Gem 29 Can	1 Leo 3 Vir 5 Lib 7 Sco 10 Sag 12 Cap 15 Aqr 17 Pis 19 Ars 21 Tau 24 Gem 26 Can 28 Leo	2 Vir 4 Lib 7 Sco 9 Sag 12 Cap 14 Aqr 16 Pis 19 Ars 21 Tau 23 Gem .25 Can 27 Leo 29 Vir	1 Lib 3 Sco 5 Sag 8 Cap 10 Aqr 13 Pis 15 Ars 17 Tau 19 Gem 21 Can 23 Leo 26 Vir 28 Lib 30 Sco	3 Sag 5 Cap 8 Aqr 10 Pis 13 Ars 15 Tau 17 Gem 19 Can 21 Leo 23 Vir 25 Lib 28 Sco 30 Sag	2 Cap 4 Aqr 7 Pis 9 Ars 11 Tau 13 Gem 15 Can 17 Leo 19 Vir 21 Lib 24 Sco 26 Sag 29 Cap	1 Aqr 4 Pis 6 Ars 8 Tau 10 Gem 12 Can 14 Leo 17 Vir 19 Lib 21 Sco 24 Sag 26 Cap 29 Aqr 31 Pis	2 Ars 5 Tau 7 Gem 9 Can 11 Leo 13 Vir 15 Libr 17 Sco 20 Sag 22 Cap 25 Aqr 27 Pis 30 Ars	1 Tau 3 Gem 5 Can 7 Leo 9 Vir 11 Lib 14 Sco 16 Sag 19 Cap 21 Aqr 24 Pis 26 Ars 28 Tau 30 Gem	2 Can 4 Leo 7 Vir 9 Lib 11 Sco 14 Sag 16 Cap 19 Aqr 21 Pis 23 Ars 25 Tau 28 Gem 30 Can	1 Leo 3 Vir 5 Lib 7 Sco 10 Sag 12 Cap 15 Aqr 17 Pis 20 Ars 22 Tau 24 Gem 26 Can 28 Leo	2 Lib 5 Sco 7 Sag 10 Cap 12 Aqr 15 Pis 17 Ars 19 Tau 21 Gem 23 Can 25 Leo 27 Vir 30 Vir

2027

Jan.	Feb.	Mar.	Apr.	May	June	July	Aug.	Sep.	Oct.	Nov.	Dec.
1 Sco 3 Sag 6 Cap 8 Aqr 11 Pis 13 Ars 16 Tau 18 Gem 20 Can 22 Leo 24 Vir 26 Lib 28 Sco 31 Sag	2 Cap 5 Aqr 7 Pis 10 Ars 12 Tau 14 Gem 16 Can 18 Leo 20 Vir 22 Lib 25 Sco 27 Sag	1 Cap 4 Aqr 6 Pis 9 Ars 11 Lau 13 Gem 16 Can 18 Leo 20 Vir 22 Lib 24 Sco 26 Sag 29 Cap 31 Aqr	3 Pis 5 Ars 7 Tau 10 Gem 12 Can 14 Leo 16 Vir 18 Lib 20 Sco 23 Sag 25 Cap 28 Aqr 30 Pis	3 Ars 5 Tau 7 Gem 9 Can 11 Leo 13 Vir 15 Lib 18 Sco 20 Sag 22 Cap 25 Aqr 27 Pis 30 Ars	3 Gem 5 Can 7 Leo 10 Vir 12 Lib 14 Sco 16 Sag 19 Cap 21 Aqr 24 Pis 26 Ars 29 Tau	1 Gem 3 Can 5 Leo 7 Vir 9 Lib 11 Sco 14 Sag 16 Cap 19 Aqr 21 Pis 24 Ars 26 Tau 28 Gem 30 Can	1 Leo 3 Vir 5 Lib 7 Sco 10 Sag 12 Cap 15 Aqr 17 Pis 20 Ars 22 Tau 24 Gem 27 Can 29 Leo 31 Vir	2 Lib 4 Sco 6 Sag 9 Cap 11 Aqr 14 Pis 16 Ars 18 Tau 21 Gem 23 Can 25 Leo 27 Vir 29 Lib	1 Sco 3 Sag 6 Cap 8 Aqr 11 Pis 13 Ars 16 Tau 18 Gem 20 Can 22 Leo 24 Vir 27 Lib 29 Sco 31 Sag	2 Cap 5 Aqr 7 Pis 10 Ars 12 Tau 14 Gem 16 Can 19 Leo 21 Vir 23 Lib 25 Sco 27 Sag 30 Cap	2 Aqr 5 Pis 7 Ars 9 Tau 12 Gem 14 Can 16 Leo 18 Vir 20 Lib 22 Sco 24 Sag 27Cap 29 Aqr

2028

Jan.	Feb.	Mar.	Apr.	May	June	July	Aug.	Sep.	Oct.	Nov.	Dec.
1 Pis	2 Tau	3 Gem	1 Can	1 Leo	1 Lib	1 Sco	1 Cap	2 Pis	2 Ars	1 Tau	1 Gem
3 Ars	4 Gem	5 Can	3 Leo	3 Vir	3 Sco	3 Sag	4 Aqr	5 Ars	5 Tau	3 Gem	3 Can
6 Tau	7 Can	7 Leo	6 Vir	5 Lib	5 Sag	5 Cap	6 Pis	8 Tau	7 Gem	6 Can	5 Leo
8 Gem	9 Leo	9 Vir	8 Lib	7 Sco	8 Cap	7 Aqr	9 Ars	10 Gem	10 Can	8 Leo	7 Vir
10 Can	11 Vir	11 Lib	10 Sco	9 Sag	10 Aqr	10 Pis	11 Tau	12 Can	12 Leo	10 Vir	10 Lib
12 Leo	13 Lib	13 Sco	12 Sag	11 Cap	13 Pis	12 Ars	14 Gem	14 Leo	14 Vir	12 Lib	12 Sco
14 Vir	15 Sco	15 Sag	14 Cap	14 Aqr	15 Ars	15 Tau	16 Can	17 Vir	16 Lib	14 Sco	14 Sag
16 Lib	17 Sag	18 Cap	16 Aqr	16 Pis	18 Tau	17 Gem	18 Leo	19 Lib	18 Sco	16 Sag	16 Cap
18 Sco	19 Cap	20 Aqr	19 Pis	19 Ars	20 Gem	20 Can	20 Vir	20 Sco	20 Sag	19 Cap	18 Aqr
21 Sag	22 Aqr	23 Pis	21 Ars	21 Tau	22 Can	22 Leo	22 Lib	23 Sag	22 Cap	21 Aqr	21 Pis
23 Cap	24 Pis	25 Ars	24 Tau	24 Gem	24 Leo	24 Vir	24 Sco	25 Cap	25 Aqr	23 Pis	23 Ars
26 Aqr	27 Ars	28 Tau	26 Gem	26 Can	26 Vir	26 Lib	26 Sag	27 Aqr	27 Pis	26 Ars	26 Tau
28 Pis	29 Tau	30 Gem	29 Can	28 Leo	28 Lib	28 Sco	29 Cap	30 Pis	30 Ars	28 Tau	28 Gem
31 Ars				30 Vir		30 Sag	31 Aqr				30 Can

2029

Jan.	Feb.	Mar.	Apr.	May	June	July	Aug.	Sep.	Oct.	Nov.	Dec.
2 Leo	2 Lib	2 Lib	2 Sag	1 Cap	2 Pis	2 Ars	1 Tau	2 Can	2 Leo	1 Vir	2 Sco
4 Vir	4 Sco	4 Sco	4 Cap	4 Aqr	5 Ars	5 Tau	4 Gem	5 Leo	4 Vir	3 Lib	4 Sag
6 Lib	6 Sag	6 Sag	6 Aqr	6 Pis	7 Tau	7 Gem	6 Can	7 Vir	6 Lib	5 Sco	6 Cap
8 Sco	9 Cap	8 Cap	9 Pis	9 Ars	10 Gem	10 Can	8 Leo	9 Lib	8 Sco	7 Sag	8 Aqr
10 Sag	11 Aqr	10 Aqr	11 Ars	11 Tau	12 Can	12 Leo	10 Vir	11 Sco	10 Sag	9 Cap	11 Pis
12 Cap	13 Pis	13 Pis	14 Tau	14 Gem	15 Leo	14 Vir	13 Lib	13 Sag	12 Cap	11 Aqr	13 Ars
15 Aqr	16 Ars	15 Ars	16 Gem	16 Can	17 Vir	16 Lib	15 Sco	15 Cap	15 Aqr	13 Pis	15 Tau
17 Pis	18 Tau	18 Tau	19 Can	18 Leo	19 Lib	18 Sco	17 Sag	17 Aqr	17 Pis	16 Ars	18 Gem
20 Ars	21 Gem	20 Gem	21 Leo	21 Vir	21 Sco	20 Sag	19 Cap	20 Pis	19 Ars	18 Tau	20 Can
22 Tau	23 Can	23 Can	23 Vir	23 Lib	23 Sag	23 Cap	21 Aqr	22 Ars	22 Tau	21 Gem	23 Leo
25 Gem	25 Leo	25 Leo	25 Lib	25 Sco	25 Cap	25 Aqr	23 Pis	25 Tau	24 Gem	23 Can	25 Vir
27 Can	28 Vir	27 Vir	27 Sco	27 Sag	27 Aqr	27 Pis	26 Ars	27 Gem	27 Can	26 Leo	27 Lib
29 Leo		29 Lib	29 Sag	29 Cap	30 Pis	30 Ars	28 Tau	30 Can	29 Leo	28 Vir	30 Sco
31 Vir		31 Sco					31 Gem			30 Lib	

2030

Jan.	Feb.	Mar.	Apr.	May	June	July	Aug.	Sep.	Oct.	Nov.	Dec.
1 Sag	1 Aqr	3 Pis	1 Ars	1 Tau	2 Can	2 Leo	1 Vir	1 Sco	1 Sag	1 Aqr	1 Pis
3 Cap	3 Pis	5 Ars	4 Tau	4 Gem	5 Leo	4 Vir	3 Lib	4 Sag	3 Cap	3 Pis	3 Ars
5 Aqr	6 Ars	7 Tau	6 Gem	6 Can	7 Vir	7 Lib	5 Sco	6 Cap	5 Aqr	6 Ars	5 Tau
7 Pis	8 Tau	10 Gem	9 Can	9 Leo	10 Lib	9 Sco	7 Sag	8 Aqr	7 Pis	8 Tau	8 Gem
9 Ars	11 Gem	13 Can	11 Leo	11 Vir	12 Sco	11 Sag	9 Cap	10 Pis	10 Ars	11 Gem	10 Can
12 Tau	13 Can	15 Leo	14 Vir	13 Lib	14 Sag	13 Cap	11 Aqr	12 Ars	12 Tau	13 Can	13 Leo
14 Gem	16 Leo	17 Vir	16 Lib	15 Sco	16 Cap	15 Aqr	14 Pis	15 Tau	14 Gem	16 Leo	15 Vir
17 Can	18 Vir	19 Lib	18 Sco	17 Sag	18 Aqr	17 Pis	16 Ars	17 Gem	17 Can	18 Vir	18 Lib
19 Leo	20 Lib	21 Sco	20 Sag	19 Cap	20 Pis	19 Ars	18 Tau	20 Can	19 Leo	20 Lib	20 Sco
21 Vir	22 Sco	23 Sag	22 Cap	21 Aqr	22 Ars	22 Tau	21 Gem	22 Leo	22 Vir	23 Sco	22 Sag
24 Lib	24 Sag	25 Cap	24 Aqr	23 Pis	25 Tau	24 Gem	23 Can	24 Vir	24 Lib	25 Sag	24 Cap
26 Sco	26 Cap	28 Aqr	26 Pis	26 Ars	27 Gem	27 Can	26 Leo	27 Lib	26 Sco	27 Cap	26 Aqr
28 Sag	28 Aqr	30 Pis	29 Ars	28 Tau	30 Can	29 Leo	28 Vir	29 Sco	28 Sag	29 Aqr	28 Pis
30 Cap							30 Lib		30 Cap		30 Ars

To find any Moon Sign not on the these charts go to
www.moonsigncalendar.net/moonphase.asp.

Chinese and Western Combinations

In a Western astrological year there are twelve signs. Each sign lasts for about one month. They have corresponding Chinese animal signs with corresponding year, month, day, time, triad, and allies. We'll explain more after the table on page 214.

Your Chinese animal sign is based on the *year* of your birth. It is easy to follow. If you were born in the year of the Horse you are a Horse, and once you know your animal sign you can find the corresponding Western sign, month, day, time, triad, and secret allies. There is, however, an exception to this simple rule. The Chinese New Year does not start until mid-January or February, so check the animal year charts at the end of this chapter to see when the new year begins and ends (see pages 453–58). If you are a Capricorn born in January or an Aquarius born in either January or February, you may have been born at the end of the current Chinese year and, of course, wear the animal sign of that year.

The strongest animal influence comes from the *year*—followed by the *month*, *day*, and *time*—for your compatibility with your triad and allies. For each Chinese animal year there are Earth elements that move in the *creative cycle* of the Taoist Five Element Theory in the animal year sequence, as seen in the chart on the next page starting with the Rat year. According to Five Element Astrology tradition you are also under the influence of one element every 12 years of your life as follows: *Wood Energy (Spring) 1–12 years old; Fire Energy (Summer) 13–24 years old; Earth Energy (Indian*

CHINESE ANIMALS, WESTERN SIGNS, AND THEIR ATTRIBUTES

Year	Western Signs	Month	Earthly Branch	Time of Day	Chinese Triad	Secret Allies
Rat	Sagittarius	11/23–12/22	Yang Water	11pm–1am	Dragon, Monkey	Snake & Monkey
Buffalo	Capricorn	12/22–01/20	Yin Earth	1am–3am	Snake, Rooster	Horse & Ram
Tiger	Aquarius	01/21–02/19	Yang Wood	3am–5am	Horse, Dog	Dragon & Boar
Rabbit	Pisces	02/20–03/20	Yin Wood	5am–7am	Ram, Boar	Rooster & Dog
Dragon	Aries	03/21–04/20	Yang Earth	7am–9am	Monkey, Rat	Tiger & Boar
Snake	Taurus	04/21–05/21	Yin Fire	9am–11am	Rooster, Buffalo	Rat & Monkey
Horse	Gemini	05/22–06/21	Yang Fire	11am–1pm	Dog, Tiger	Ram & Buffalo
Ram	Cancer	06/22–07/23	Yin Earth	1pm–3pm	Boar, Rabbit	Buffalo & Horse
Monkey	Leo	07/24–08/23	Yang Metal	3pm–5pm	Rat, Dragon	Snake & Rat
Rooster	Virgo	08/24–09/23	Yin Metal	5pm–7pm	Buffalo, Snake	Dog & Ram
Dog	Libra	09/24–10/23	Yang Earth	7pm–9pm	Tiger, Horse	Ram & Rooster
Boar	Scorpio	10/24–11/22	Yin Water	9pm–11pm	Rabbit, Ram	Dragon & Tiger

Summer) 24–36 years old; Metal Energy (Fall) 36–48 years old; Water Energy (Winter) 48–60 years old; and then it repeats itself for a second cycle, then third, or fourth time. You also have other secondary element influences in your energy pattern but your birth-year element is your primary influence having the most impact on your persona. You can determine your element by the descriptions that follow on pages 219–451.

Each element has a different phase and texture of the animal as the elements of nature. Additionally, each day has an element. Sunday is associated with the Sun, Monday with the Moon, Tuesday with Fire, Wednesday with Water, Thursday with Wood, Friday with Metal, and Saturday with Earth. Each day also has a corresponding animal sign based on the Earthly Branch in Four Pillar Chinese astrology (see Vincent Koh's *Hsia Calendar 1924–2024* to determine the Earthly Branch).

Triads are made up of animals that are born four years apart. Each animal has two other animal signs in the triad that are extremely compatible in their personalities, thinking, and likability. Each triad has the same understandings and communicates extremely well together in business, relationships, personal life, and communities. It is important for you to know your triad and animal counterparts. Along with the animal triad, each animal sign has *secret allies*, or friends who support and collaborate with them on all phases of life, so it is important to know animal allies too.

There are twelve animals with five elements each, so to complete one full cycle of the animals and their elements takes *sixty years*. As an example, 1948 is the year of the Earth Rat and it would take sixty years, until 2008, before another Earth Rat would be born in the progression.

CHINESE AND WESTERN COMBINATIONS IN THEORY AND PRACTICE

The third phase to develop your persona is to compare your Western sign (month) to your Chinese sign (year), which comes up with a new angle and dimension of your persona. If you are a Scorpio (Boar) and were born in 1948, then you are a Scorpio-Rat. Simply take your regular, familiar astrological sign and match it with the animal sign of the year you were born. Everybody has a dual nature. Some people are naturally greedy and grasping about money, but the same people can be generous to a fault in emotional ways. The combination of the different aspects of an individual's persona, including sentiment, affection, and phase, could explain this seemingly contradictory behavior. It is true as well in relationships: there are some people you can get along with and care for easily, others who just rub you the wrong way or get on your nerves, and still others who attract and fascinate you. In order to understand your attraction or dislike for a person—by yourself, without the aid of a psychiatrist—you can now use this book to determine his or her persona and apply these discoveries about how to communicate effectively with each individual's internal energy pattern.

This approach attempts to help us understand human behavior within the universe through the marriage of Western and Chinese astrologies.

The Chinese have divided time differently from Westerners. Western time is divided into 100-year-long centuries, while the Chinese have repeating cycles of sixty years. In the West we divide our centuries into ten decades. The Chinese divide their sixty-year spans into "dozen-cades," or twelve-year periods. In the West we divide our year up twelve times by its moons. Each month is between twenty-eight and thirty-one days long and overlaps with one or two of twelve Western astrological signs. Every year the Western cycle begins anew. In the East each year within the dozen-cade has its own astrological name. At the end of each twelve-year period, the Chinese cycle begins anew.

To review, the twelve Western months have celestial sign names: Aries, Taurus, Gemini, Cancer, Leo, Virgo, Libra, Scorpio, Sagittarius, Capricorn, Aquarius, and Pisces. The twelve Chinese years have animal sign names: Rat, Buffalo, Tiger, Rabbit, Dragon, Snake, Horse, Ram, Monkey, Rooster, Dog, and Boar. In both cases the astrological sign name refers to the character of people named under its influence. Everyone has a Western "month" sign and a Chinese "year" sign. One sign is complementary to the other, and each Western sign also interacts with its corresponding Chinese sign. The Western month signs and Chinese year signs correspond as follows:

Western Month Sign	Chinese Year Sign
Aries	Dragon
Taurus	Snake
Gemini	Horse
Cancer	Ram
Leo	Monkey
Virgo	Rooster
Libra	Dog
Scorpio	Boar
Sagittarius	Rat
Capricorn	Buffalo
Aquarius	Tiger
Pisces	Rabbit

Taken together, these correspondences show us more about the individual than either one can on its own. If someone is born in Pisces and is also born in a Snake year, they were born the month of the Rabbit (Pisces) and the year of the Snake or a Rabbit/Snake, which are a lot different from a Rabbit/Horse or Rabbit/Tiger. There are 144 different Western and Chinese combinations. This will help you to refine your understanding of your persona. Through this process we can learn to get along better with our friends, family, and loved ones. We can find out why we tend not to harmonize with certain people, which can further improve our knowledge of those individuals, and of ourselves.

Each Chinese year is ruled by one the Five Elements.

Metal: Monkey and Rooster. Movement = Chopping. Decision Maker, Orderly, Inflexible, Organized, and Systematic.

Water: Rat and Boar. Movement = Flowing. Stable, Shy, Predictable, Polite, Pleasant, Non-Confrontational.

Wood: Tiger and Rabbit. Movement = Sprouting. Kindness, Sensitive, Gentle, Criers, Worriers, Caring.

Fire: Snake and Horse. Movement = Blazing. Impatient, Narcissism, Impulsive, Quick, Passionate.

Earth: Buffalo, Dragon, Ram, and Dog. Movement = Grounding. Balance Keepers, Peacemakers, Communicators, Supporters.

Western astrology uses four ruling elements: Fire, Air, Earth, and Water. Each sign is ruled by only one of the elements.

Fire: Aries, Leo, and Sagittarius characterized by Movement, Obsession, and Energy.

Air: Gemini, Libra, and Aquarius characterized by Receptiveness, Intellect, and Aspiration.

Earth: Taurus, Virgo, and Capricorn characterized by Function, Practicality, and Solidity.

Water: Cancer, Scorpio, and Pisces characterized by Emotion, Compassion, and Perception.

One or more of ten planets or heavenly bodies rule each sign in Western astrology. The planets influence a sign's character. Their position in the heavens helps to predict the future.

Aries is ruled by Mars representing: Impulse, Action, and Bravery.

Taurus is ruled by Venus representing: Acceptance, Vanity, and Love.

Gemini is ruled by Mercury representing: Intelligence, Change, and Adaptability.

Cancer is ruled by the Moon representing: Receptivity, Emotion, and Viscera.

Leo is ruled by the Sun representing: Assertiveness, Will, and Majesty.

Virgo is ruled by Mercury representing: Analysis, Absorption, and Logic.

Libra is ruled by Venus representing: Sociability, Persuasion, and Luxury.

Scorpio is ruled by Mars/Pluto representing: Courage and Obligation.

Sagittarius is ruled by Jupiter representing: Expansion, Vision, and Justice.

Capricorn is ruled by Saturn representing: Solitude, Rigidity, and Ambition.

Aquarius is ruled by Saturn/Uranus representing: Individuality and Cosmic Consciousness.

Pisces is ruled by Neptune/Jupiter representing: Enigma, Inspiration, and Compassion.

Western astrology also uses three different qualities: Cardinal, Fixed, and Mutable.

Cardinal: Aries, Cancer, Libra, and Capricorn—Dynamic, Authoritative, Active, and Energetic.

Fixed: Taurus, Scorpio, Leo, and Aquarius—Concrete, Limited, Purposeful, and Conscientious.

Mutable: Gemini, Virgo, Sagittarius, and Pisces—Moving, Adaptable, Harmonizing, and Versatile.

All these aspects are taken into consideration with the analysis of each of the 144 month and year personas. This combination will give you the third phase of your persona, based on the combination of the month and year you were born.

In each of the Western sign (Month) and Chinese Animal (Year) combinations that follow, the first bold term classifies the energy pattern of that particular Western sign (e.g., Being, Possess, Reflect, etc.). This is followed by its Planet, Western Element (Air, Water, Earth, Fire), and Quality. The second bold term describes the energy pattern of the Chinese Animal sign (e.g., Observer, Regulator, Take Charge, etc.), followed by its Yin/Yang Charge and Chinese Element (Metal, Water, Wood, Fire, Earth).

Aries (Dragon) Month Combined with Rat Year

"Being" Mars, Fire, Cardinal   **"Regulator"** Yin-Positive Water

Characteristics: Charisma, Intellectual, Enterprise, Courage, Skill, Domination, Naïveté, Acquisitiveness, Influence, Nervousness, Power, Willfulness, Thirst, Excess, Sanctimony, Talent, Affability, Drive, Heartiness, Ostentation

Aries-Rats will help people they love in all sorts of situations, but they are not inclined to waste time helping those who refuse to help themselves. They are fearless about exploring new places and will happily go alone. This is no ordinary Aries: it is an Aries-Rat. With the talkativeness of the Aries, it is the craftiest of the combinations. There is the friendliness of the Rat combined with the jovial side of the Aries. Mixing the two results in a very good personality with charisma from the Rat and self-confidence from Aries. Extraordinary energy is the result. All of this is done with painstaking detail and beautiful script. In the Aries-Rat's bedroom there is a notebook full of her own poems, and in the kitchen refrigerator there are meals that have been planned, home cooked, and wrapped. The result is a person who cannot tolerate lazy people. There are plans and projects scattered everywhere in the life of an Aries-Rat. There might be plans for new additions to the house on your desk at work. Or in the den at home you might find plans for a new library that will be presented to the city council at its monthly meeting.

Romance: Impatience is a part of the Aries-Rat. With a quick and tense mind, help will always be provided in spite of the numerous plans and projects—but it might be of the prickly variety. They have no right to a coffee break. Besides, there is no time. The schedule is booked with projects, chores, trips, meetings, ceremonies, and errands. What we have in the Aries-Rat is a person akin to an innocent ruler but who nevertheless is concerned with ruling. Following the rulebook, being stern, and playing cop are all part of being a boss. Generally, people do not like those who are their bosses. Aries-Rats are not able to tolerate being hated and the loneliness of a king or queen is deadly to Aries-Rats. They find it very hard to talk to anyone because of their impatience.

Relationships: The gentle, patient, and funny youth is taken by a deep seriousness about everything, including love. The powerful fixation on doing the right things is the cause of losing a lot of the fun of being in love. Stiffness, tightness, and near panic take over in this combination with age.

There is a moderating effect with children, social status, and the necessary material accoutrements of life. With the passage of time, the Aries-Rat is less mellow.

Family Life: Aries-Rats are fantastic parents who are even lovingly strict. The story with siblings is another matter; they are overly critical and superior. An Aries-Rat parent is the ultimate hands-on type, participating to the max and joining in everything. All of this starts before birth and actually never stops. Aries-Rat dads carry their kids on nature treks beginning at age two, later they go bird-watching and join scouts. Aries-Rat moms make costumes for Halloween and school plays. She is chairperson of the school bazaar, bakes cookies, and helps with rehearsals.

Livelihood: Regardless of their profession they are gifted. In fact, they find it joyful not just to work things out but to plan and organize and even fill in forms. With essentially no apparent effort, they are successful. They rise above, and that is where they want to be, whether in lifestyle or career. Quite obviously, this type of person is hardcore in the ambition department. If there is a task, they work: it does not matter what it is.

Famous Aries-Rats: Marlon Brando, Sarah Vaughan, Raymond Barre, John Cheever, Gloria Steinem.

Aries (Dragon) Month Combined with Buffalo Year

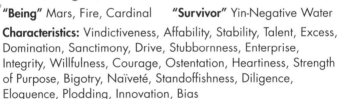

"Being" Mars, Fire, Cardinal   **"Survivor"** Yin-Negative Water

Characteristics: Vindictiveness, Affability, Stability, Talent, Excess, Domination, Sanctimony, Drive, Stubbornness, Enterprise, Integrity, Willfulness, Courage, Ostentation, Heartiness, Strength of Purpose, Bigotry, Naïveté, Standoffishness, Diligence, Eloquence, Plodding, Innovation, Bias

The Aries character of this combination strolls out into the world at a young age, strong and hopeful. The powerful but slow walk of the Buffalo diligently carries the proud Aries, prepared for any eventuality, toward serious, demanding destinations. This sign is so powerful it is seemingly carrying Earth on its little finger. Sheer might sends this combination directly toward accomplishment. Pragmatism, for Aries-Buffalos, depends instead on a concrete effect. This is not about games, rather the Aries-Buffalo must be permitted to work and get things accomplished and solve actual problems. This is their element and the way they sparkle. But in the modern technological-urban world, shows of physical strength generally do not count. Aries-Buffalos are achievers, and there is no doubt about it because of their in-your-face lack of subtlety. There is not much friendship here, but neither is there hate. Communication does not come easy for this loving colossus. Aries-Buffalo shyness runs to the ominous. The oddness here is that the Aries-Buffalo can be a well-expressed narrator but be incapable of chatting with the mail carrier. Aries-Buffalos are ungainly.

Romance: There is not a lot of original seduction in the Aries-Buffalo nature. Sex simply is not the highest priority here. The emphasis is on accomplishment or at times displeasure. But sentimentality is shunned entirely. The Aries-Buffalo offers the actual ideal love and astounding faithfulness. Aries-Buffalos love with quiet succinct ardor. They are a mountain of love and dependable security. Creativity is another matter.

Relationships: Virgo-Tigers annoy this combination because they are arrogant. They are not crazy about Libra-Rabbits and ghostly Pisces-Rams. Their romantic partners include Leo-Roosters, -Rats, and -Monkeys. But that is not all. Virgo-Pigs like their strength, and they will be drawn to Sagittarius-Dragons and -Monkeys. Their hearts skip a beat with Gemini-Snakes.

Family Life: A family comfortable at home is where the Aries-Buffalo rests and sleeps best. The safety of home is the Aries-Buffalo's choice. Everything about this combo functions better and smoother at home. Perfection is what is desired, and anything less will not be tolerated. Moreover, the Aries-Buffalo is the CEO at home and that is that. Offspring of Aries-Buffalos will tend to be gifted but obstinate. A highly discontent Aries-Buffalo results if there is even a hint of competition for that role. The throne, in the end, belongs to them. Adapt or leave. In a breakup they can be difficult and end saying rather unflattering things about their loved one. The alternative, if one does not want to lose all those comforts in the dream home, is to just placate the Aries-Buffalo for a week or so. This combo will lighten right up.

Livelihood: A large dose of reflection and vigilance are part of the character by as young as thirty. Gullibility dissipates from the joyful Aries by that time, and generally not many enjoy having commerce with them. Nobody wants to buy anything from a grump. The aptitude to accumulate a lot of money is in the hands of the Aries-Buffalo. A lot of this depends on working hard while young. Doing that guarantees security. It would be much harder later in life, if youth is wasted. There is, however, no laziness here ever.

Famous Aries-Buffalos: Lionel Hampton, Karl Malden, Melvyn Douglas, Merle Haggard.

Aries (Dragon) Month Combined with Tiger Year

"Being" Mars, Fire, Cardinal   **"Observer"** Yang-Positive Wood

Characteristics: Authority, Intemperance, Itinerancy, Courage, Drive, Naïveté, Heartiness, Willfulness, Ostentation, Affability, Talent, Sanctimony, Excess, Enterprise, Magnetism, Disobedience, Good Luck, Benevolence, Fervor, Domination, Swagger, Impetuosity, Hotheadedness, Bravery

The question for Aries-Tigers is one of ability to face inactivity or boredom. Tigers cannot handle it. Aries is more effective in this regard and, of course, that is one of the qualities of Aries. They can deal with the tiresome effectively. It is not that Tigers only want to have fun, but they do enjoy it, and Aries are a bit more realistic in that regard. There is, therefore, a tugging on the Aries-Tiger soul, but this still does not rein in their ability to accomplish things. The picture created when we think of an Aries-Tiger can be one of a cartoon, or, more seriously perhaps, a tattoo. Tigers take risks while dragons are the stuff of children's songs. Buddies striding down the road together, full of plans and ideas, represent the essence of an Aries-Tiger. Tigers, of course, are known for attacking, and that is what this combination does. They have lots of methods for this. Consequently, the issue in question pertains to successful people. Everyone knows that Aries people are serious folks. They do not undertake projects lightly. Like the large cat it is, Tigers play with their prey and sometimes forget it. They attack and carry through. Aries might not have Tiger-eyes, but they are serious, much more serious than tigers.

Romance: There is not much interest in a one-person relationship here. There could be a lot of changing of partners, flirtations, or even extracurricular activities. It is not meanness or cruelty. It is a matter of moving on. This is a beautiful, fun, innocent, and youthful combination. It is a sort of mixture of the ridiculous and the sublime, or perhaps the tragic comedy. They are two aspects that should not go together but do. The result is a very popular and sought-after person. In romance the new and the exciting and challenging are needed.

Relationships: There are many choices for this combination in terms of romance. Probably first on the list are Leo-Dogs or Sagittarius-Dragons or -Horses. A very close second are Aquarius-Dogs, -Boars, and -Dragons. Some combinations wise to avoid are Libra-Buffalos, Capricorn-Monkeys, or Capricorn-Snakes. Cancer-Snakes are not a good idea either.

Family Life: This combination is also loyal and dedicated to the family. The children of this combination are not any more moved by such rational explanations than any other children, yet they do turn out to be quite lovely in their own right. Everyone, including other parents and teachers, like the children of this combination. It is not exactly the perfect middle-class family, but it tends in that direction, along with sprinklings of liberalism. The result is a person who not only remembers all holidays, birthdays, and anniversaries but who also is reasonable. And reasonable includes the child-rearing philosophy that you can reason children into good behavior or achievement. This combination is the mother at the supermarket explaining to her screaming two-year-old why candy is bad for her health.

Livelihood: Their attitude about money actually helps in this regard; it helps, at least, in terms of happiness. They, as a matter of fact, do have abilities to see to it that they are taken care of. They execute their plans and build their castles, right here on Earth. Aries-Tigers are a really interesting combination, because, for starters, they are not money signs. They can get by without money, and it is not all that important in their value system. However, they are go-getters and want to accomplish things, make their lives better, and bring their dreams into reality.

Famous Aries-Tigers: Alec Guinness, John Fowles, Jerry Brown.

Aries (Dragon) Month Combined with Rabbit Year

"Being" Mars, Fire, Cardinal   **"Withdraw"** Yin-Negative Wood

Characteristics: Heartiness, Complexity, Prudence, Pedantry, Longevity, Dilettantism, Ambition, Domination, Hypochondria, Tact, Secretiveness, Finesse, Squeamishness, Virtue, Willfulness, Naïveté, Affability, Enterprise, Excess Talent, Courage, Sanctimony, Drive, Ostentation

We have a kind of classicist in Aries-Rabbits, and their interest is not an avocation. It is their purpose and goal in life. There is not a trace of a con artist here, and indeed they have, or wish they had, old money. They will not give up their journey in the realm of Plato's Forms. There is not a single sign of quit in them. The Aries-Rabbit has fine qualities that boggle the mind. It might be easier to say what they are not rather than say what they are. For starters, they are akin to the Platonic Ideal of Rabbithood. The old, the new, the sacred, and the culturally valuable are just some of the concerns of this combination. Not only do they downright care, but they are nice, polite, and, on the less obvious side, philosophers in the real meaning of the term: lovers of wisdom. This combination could actually end up being the philosopher king, steadfast in the face of adversity but never forgetting the quest for quality in the aesthetic sense, for this combination has the soul of a professor of aesthetics coupled with energy of the hero hidden underneath. Headed off into the world, they search for the beautiful. They search for true peace. Aries-Rabbits do not work at a discount retailer. They have probably never even been in one. What they are probably doing is either rereading Aristotle's *Poetics*, or at least having a mental dialogue with Aristotle himself.

Romance: They like their freedom and doing things their own way. It is not that they are the radical philosophical types so much as the fact that while a spouse and two children in the suburbs seems theoretically pleasant, it is too confining in actual practice. This combination is not the walk-hand-in-hand-through-the-mall sort. In addition, the suburban angst is too much for the Aries side. Given the sort of Jimmy Stewart nature of this combination, it is surprising to find out that they are not exactly the most faithful partners on Earth. They are, like a rabbit, very inclined to jump from love to love.

Relationships: Cancer-Dragons and -Roosters, as well as Capricorn-Tigers, are near the bottom of the possibilities. They should pretty much stay away from Capricorn-Tigers and Libra-Dragons and -Tigers. The relationship pyramid is something like this: at the top are Leo-Dogs or -Boars. One tier down are Sagittarius-Rams and Gemini-Boars or -Rams. Also in the mix are Aquarius-Boars and -Snakes.

Family Life: Being the eccentric that they are, at least in some sense, they want their own space. In addition, they are not particularly good about expressing themselves. They are, to be sure, good people, but breaking through that veil of idealism and search for beauty is almost impossible. Generally, the internal battle results in individualism prevailing, even if it means erecting a wall and establishing boundaries. There are issues pertaining to the family facing the Aries-Rabbit. There is a question whether they are actually suited to be the family type. The core of the issue is their individualism and that they plan and put into practice a life that is about them. This is not exactly selfish, but they follow their personal preferences.

Livelihood: This combination is made up of avid readers, and when something catches their interest they are off and running. Like the rabbit, they will jump—in this case from one area to another. If a member of this combination goes missing, check the library or museum first. The ambition in the Aries-Rabbit is not typical of others. They do not want to be rich or famous. They will settle for happiness, if that means they can continue learning and growing. They are sociable for the same reason: to talk and listen and learn.

Famous Aries-Rabbits: Ali MacGraw, David Frost, Muddy Waters, Arturo Toscanini.

Aries (Dragon) Month Combined with Dragon Year

"Being" Mars, Fire, Cardinal   **"Take Charge"** Yang-Positive Wood

Characteristics: Volubility, Sentimentality, Rigidity, Heartiness, Dissatisfaction, Mistrust, Braggadocio, Infatuation, Good Health, Domination, Strength, Willfulness, Enthusiasm, Pluck, Success, Excess Talent, Affability, Courage, Naïveté, Sanctimony, Enterprise, Ostentation, Drive

Aries-Dragons know they are winners, so there is no need for pretense in that regard. They are capable of staggering feats of deception and actions that shock not just neighborhoods but entire countries. Their manners, however, incline people to believe that they are dealing with a naive parochial school student. This combination does have an Achilles' heel though: actually, it is more like an Achilles' foot. They are bleeding hearts of sympathy. They never saw a movie that did not make them cry, and they never heard a tale of tragedy they did not believe. Tell them you lost all your money to an Internet scam and they will cover your mortgage for a year. The Aries-Dragon is a mind-boggling combination of energy, refinement, and street smarts. You might think of them as Donald Trump with a Ph.D. in etiquette. This combination is slick, and that is unusual for an Aries. It is just that there is such a deep drive for success that their native intelligence can morph into cunning. All this is nicely hidden behind a perfectly polite and engaging persona that is supremely self-assured.

Romance: There are two ways for a person in love with an Aries-Dragon to handle this. First, relish those times together, because they are such great lovers you may forget about transgressions. The second approach is to use the above-mentioned sob story technique. Whine and cry and act heartbroken. This is sure to work, at least for a while. This combination is the romantic, the seducer, and the seduced. Love, if you want to call it that, or sex, if you are the cynical type, is this combination's middle name. That means that loyalty to a partner is not part of this combination's makeup.

Relationships: Unpleasant matches are Cancer-Dogs and -Buffalos, Capricorn-Buffalos and Libra-Dogs. Problems of compatibility are likely in those combinations. Good matches for the Aries-Dragon are Gemini-Rats and -Monkeys, Aquarius-Monkeys, Sagittarius-Rats, and Leo-Rats and -Monkeys.

Family Life: They might be perfectly good spouses or parents, but that is not enough for this combination, who need challenges in life to feel fulfilled and complete. This combination shuns the routine in favor of the limelight. Aries-Dragons are after some kind of fame and adulation. Fortune is fine as a challenge, but it is other people whom they want as their currency, and that means something beyond the family.

Livelihood: What about starting a youth symphony, establishing a language school, or saving endangered parrots in the Amazon? All of this is done in the Aries-Dragon's spare time from her profession as a lawyer in Washington, D.C., where she law clerks for the Supreme Court. Plainly put, this sign is driven. Aries-Dragons live for challenges for their entire life. They are A students who get into the finest schools while lettering in track and play saxophone in a blues band on the weekend. They are first violinist in the city orchestra. If such opportunities do not present themselves, the Aries-Dragon will create challenges from whole cloth.

Famous Aries-Dragons: Verlaine, Irving Wallace, Anita Bryant.

Aries (Dragon) Month Combined with Snake Year

"Being" Mars, Fire, Cardinal   "Feel" Yang-Negative Fire

Characteristics: Clairvoyance, Sagacity, Domination, Compassion, Attractiveness, Intuition, Heartiness, Discretion, Willfulness, Talent, Affability, Excess, Presumption, Sanctimony, Exclusiveness, Drive, Courage, Ostentation, Naïveté, Dissimulation, Laziness, Cupidity, Enterprise, Extravagance

The Aries in Snakeskin is not necessarily a bad thing, because the wisdom, experience, and reality-based Snake can bring the ambitious and headstrong Aries back to Earth. What is very possible is that all the ambition and daring of the Aries is mixed with Snake wisdom such that the result can yield a rather profound individual. The gaudy teenager fashion tastes of the Aries are mitigated by the subtle style of the Snake. Some of the self-righteousness goes too and is replaced by self-reflection. The combination of Aries and the Snake is fire, because both signs are fire. That does not mean, however, that there is balance and internal peace in this combination. Aries and the Snake have fundamentally different characters, so the result is a battle between the impatient Aries who is always ready to do something and the Snake who sits back and waits and thinks. Who wins these internal wars is a consequence of who has the strength at any given point in time. We do not know if it is the intuitive planner in the form of the Snake or the go-getter Aries who wants to test everything.

Romance: The term *intuitive* was probably invented to describe Snakes. Their powers of intuition coupled with observation are mind-boggling. They see and sense things, particularly in people, that others cannot see. This gives them uncanny instincts and is another gift to the Aries. This fortunate asset carries over into love and relationships, and it is a good thing that it does because Snakes cannot live without love. It is the fuel of their soul. That instinct helps them find a partner and helps prevent heartbreak. It also helps round out Aries people emotionally, because they are generally not loving and caring to any significant degree.

Relationships: In the ballpark are Leo-Dragons or -Boars and Aquarius-Buffalos or -Roosters. To be avoided are Cancer-Tigers and Libra-Boars and -Snakes. Top tier romantic possibilities are Gemini-Roosters or -Buffalos. Very near the top are Sagittarius-Dragons.

Family Life: Raising children, decorating, cooking, and family entertaining are their calling. This combination is a model of family life. They do not just dream of the perfect family, they create it. In fact, there is, in their innermost being, the family itself. What happens with this internal essence is that it is externalized in the form of projects and of making things. To visit their home is to visit a virtual museum of their character. Home is where the heart is, and it is, after all, love that Snakes crave. The result here, with the intuitive Snake and the ambitious Aries, is someone who loves the home and everything about it.

Livelihood: Action is an important part of this combination so they like to be busy. Business lunches and trips to conventions are often little more than junkets or the desire to have a meal at a high-class establishment. It would not, however, be wise for someone to say anything. Considering what has been discussed, it should not come as a surprise that Snakes externalize results into the finer things of life, and the money to acquire them. They are friendly and nice and like to be involved with business.

Famous Aries-Snakes: Julie Christie, Aretha Franklin.

Aries (Dragon) Month Combined with Horse Year

"Being" Mars, Fire, Cardinal   **"Command"** Yang-Positive Fire

Characteristics: Pragmatism, Accomplishment, Naïveté, Courage, Rebellion, Style, Unscrupulousness, Autonomy, Haste, Popularity, Sanctimony, Persuasiveness, Enterprise, Selfishness, Domination, Drive, Heartiness, Ostentation, Affability, Excess, Willfulness, Talent, Anxiety, Dexterity

This combination is stubborn but filled with energy. None of this is to say that the Aries-Horse lacks good points. There are many. In spite of their pushiness, they are nice people. They are positive, and this rubs off on others at times because of the full tank of energy they always seem to have. There is a lot of ego in the Aries-Horse, and it motivates as well as drives them. The result is that they are pushy. They are sharp and slick but not always as responsible as one would like, and that creates problems. The problem is exacerbated because this trait is found in both the Aries and the Horse. Their half-full-glass attitude is both innocent and catching. They will not be deterred from a vision of a better world. They are geniuses at it and basically well beyond your ordinary fix-it types. Logic is what they use; Aries-Horses are incorrigibly practical. They can fix almost anything and make almost anything, from wooden toys to houses. They are able to remodel homes and decorate like professionals. Their main weapon for trying to establish such an environment is the truth, which they tell without shame and with frequency. They care about goodness and virtue and really can buckle down and work toward noble and lofty goals.

Romance: Sadly, unlike other collections, it is hard to be satisfied over time when collecting romance because it can never be deep enough. The Aries-Horse is doomed to disappointment in this department. Aries-Horses are collectors, and they are very enthusiastic about what they collect. But love is not baseball cards, coins, or antiques. They fall in love at the drop of a hat. The curves or tone of voice grab them, or it might be the hair or the way the object of their attraction moves.

Relationships: Libra-Rats and -Monkeys and Capricorn-Rats and -Boars are not good choices. The best matches for the Aries-Horse are Sagittarius-Rams, Gemini-Tigers, or Gemini-Dogs. Aquarius-Rams are a possibility.

Family Life: This combination is efficient and the no-nonsense type. They do not like people who drag their feet or who slowly muddle through things. There will be no procrastinating and there will be no halfhearted efforts. They like to get it done quickly and get it done right. It is clear whether a particular home is that of an Aries-Horse by the way it is decorated. It is conservative but tasteful. More than likely, things have a natural appearance, because this combination shuns the gaudy or any sort of frills. However, the home is not boring or banal because the Aries-Horse has a great imagination. This combination in their home is clearly the one in charge.

Livelihood: Since this combination is the enthusiastic type, it is easy to shift gears. There are usually two stages in the careers of the Aries-Horse. In youth this combination is generally attracted to the arts. It might be music or acting or even the visual arts. As time goes by the practical nature of their being usually takes over. Their intelligence also plays a role in them changing to a more practical career, one that is more mainstream. As a general rule, they switch from the artistic to the secure but bring with them their creativity, intelligence, and enthusiasm. Still, the choice is one that reflects their fundamental being, just as their home does.

Famous Aries-Horses: Nikita Khrushchev, Pearl Bailey, Sandra Day O'Connor, Michael York.

Aries (Dragon) Month Combined with Ram Year

"Being" Mars, Fire, Cardinal   **"Reliance"** Yang-Negative Fire

Characteristics: Heartiness, Impracticality, Worry, Perseverance, Whimsy, Tardiness, Pessimism, Domination, Invention, Parasitism, Good Manners, Lack of Foresight, Affability, Sensitivity, Willfulness, Excess, Sanctimony, Talent, Courage, Enterprise, Taste, Naïveté, Drive, Ostentation

This combination is made up of sharply dressed men and women who are staggeringly creative. This makes them almost compulsive about their appearance. Their glass is 90 percent full at minimum most of the time. That is the good news. The bad news is that there is always the possibility of it being 90 percent (or more) empty. That can destroy them. It is true that they are freethinkers who stand out from the crowd. It is true that they are rebels. What is hidden in all of this is that they need to reveal their unique character on their own terms and in their own way. That means security. Ram the rebel and Aries the entrepreneur coexist in this walking contradiction. The Ram, who likes to smell the flowers, generally loses to Aries, who wants to get up and get going. The Aries-Ram, even more than most people, needs security. While all human beings feel a tug and pull of the dialectic of security-freedom, this is truer of this combination than others. They need to feel safe.

Romance: Aries-Rams should be quite careful in the choice of a mate. They need someone who is truly faithful and monogamous. This is a "togetherness" combination. The best match for them is one where there are mutual interests and things like vacations dovetail, as do hobbies or other interests. This combination does not match well with certain types, so caution is in order. The dialectic of the Aries-Ram is further exemplified in the concept of love. Those who want security want love; however, there is always risk in love: the risk of losing the other person. The need for love comes from the Ram and is its highest priority, which all results in a person who is deeply possessive. They are jealous and cling to the other person day and night. The only exception might be allowing their partner to leave for a while for financial reasons.

Relationships: This combination should rule out Capricorns, particularly -Tiger and -Dog. Cancer- and Scorpio-Buffalos are virtual no-goes. Aquarius-Boars and -Rabbits and Sagittarius-Rabbits and -Horses are the top matches. Gemini-Rabbits and Leo-Horses and -Rabbits are good.

Family Life: This combination entertains at home, employing their gourmet cooking skills and decorating their own birthday cakes. They vacation in the same place every year and hold firmly onto their routine, one which is set by others. This combination is essentially the Florida suburbanite with 2.5 children, living in a comfortable upscale house with a swimming pool and flower garden. They are comfortable and secure among their friends and family. They are happy taking care of the home or commuting to their job, and baking pies and cakes; mowing the lawn and barbequing suit them wonderfully. Warmth, peace, and security are theirs.

Livelihood: What these individuals do have is a loyalty so deep that they strive mightily for the success of the person they love. Those who want support, loyalty, and a solid home could not do any better than choosing this combination. Neither greed nor wealth are the prime movers of this combination. They are not particularly materialistic, although they do like comfort.

Famous Aries-Rams: Arthur Murray, McGeorge Bundy, Hugh Carey.

Aries (Dragon) Month Combined with Monkey Year

"Being" Mars, Fire, Cardinal   **"Arrange"** Yin-Positive Metal

Characteristics: Zeal, Sanctimony, Enterprise, Self-involvement, Stability, Wit, Silliness, Leadership, Domination, Opportunism, Deceit, Improvisation, Ruse, Loquacity, Willfulness, Cunning, Affability, Excess, Courage, Talent, Naïveté, Ostentation, Drive, Heartiness

This combination is highly loquacious but never boring. In addition, this combination is exceedingly empathetic. They have strong and sincere feelings for others. To say that Aries-Monkeys are frank and straight talking is not to do them justice. If you want the truth, the whole truth, and nothing but the truth, you should talk to someone in this combination. Not only will it be blunt and honest, it will be thorough and interesting. Aries-Monkeys are born to succeed, and they can do this in virtually any area they choose. The reason for their success is as straightforward as their speech. They want to get ahead, so they do. No combination is more motivated in this regard. For them doing well has intrinsic value. They want it for its own sake, not for the sake of other things, like material gains. They have an appeal based on this real compassion for others combined with motivation and intelligence. All this adds up to a very worthwhile personality and character. To be a friend of theirs is to have a nonstop talker with you everywhere you go. They can sometimes be heavy and difficult to follow. You feel like a student again, listening to a professor. But this professor is never boring.

Romance: Aries-Monkeys are highly social and require others to verify their being. They like to hold forth in conversation with an audience, although they are not terrible at listening either. They can be unfaithful, but it would not be fair to say they are prone to it. They do, however, have a deep-seated passion in their soul and make fantastic lovers. Aries-Monkeys are not the Rock of Gibraltar in the love and marriage category. They can, however, appear to others like a good and solid spouse. They most certainly are not the stay-at-home types who watch family videos or go to the mall on weekends.

Relationships: Capricorn- and Cancer-Tigers and -Boars are not good for this combination. Do not be deceived by the Libra-Snake. The best relationship for this combination is the Leo-Dragon or -Rat. Also good are Gemini-, Aquarius-, and Sagittarius-Rats.

Family Life: This combination is, after all, a Monkey, and that means lots of monkey business, especially with the children. The practical joking, silly, and active mom or dad is built in to the character of this combination. The playful Aries-Monkey wants attention and wants to play. They are also extremely talkative. A good outlet for this combination is children. Especially fun for them is teaching their kids. It could be sports or the arts, but as long as they can talk and participate they are fine.

Livelihood: If there is a project or family gathering, Aries-Monkeys are in their element. This aptitude can translate into a job or profession. Of course, all this talent is topped off with a super personality that attracts people and sells things, be they products or ideas. There might be only one drawback in this picture of the Aries-Monkey: jealousy. They are so talented and so popular that this can cause resentments in others. Aries-Monkeys are very adaptable and flexible people. This shows itself in abilities to accomplish a variety of things. They can build, make, and fix things. They can cook nearly anything, and they can organize parties and gatherings.

Famous Aries-Monkeys: Howard Cosell, Bette Davis, Joan Crawford, Jack Webb, Omar Sharif.

Aries (Dragon) Month Combined with Rooster Year

"Being" Mars, Fire, Cardinal   **"Conqueror"** Yang-Negative Metal

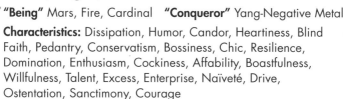

Characteristics: Dissipation, Humor, Candor, Heartiness, Blind Faith, Pedantry, Conservatism, Bossiness, Chic, Resilience, Domination, Enthusiasm, Cockiness, Affability, Boastfulness, Willfulness, Talent, Excess, Enterprise, Naïveté, Drive, Ostentation, Sanctimony, Courage

The Aries brings to the table a pleasant and open personality, and a character that is generous as well as extroverted. Lazy is a total antonym for them, for they are go-getters. If it is unusual, foreign, or from another part of the world, this combination is interested in it. The Aries-Rooster is a combination that is an endless source of enthusiasm coupled with relentless curiosity. The former stems primarily from the Rooster and the latter primarily from the Aries, but both signs embody these characteristics. They long for excitement and experience. They want to try doing and experiencing *every-thing*, and that is not an overstatement. They are on-call twenty-four hours a day for adventure and excitement. The Aries-Rooster might be found living in Mongolia as a nomad in a yurt. If they do not have one, they will find a person who does. Living among the pygmies in the Congo would be a dream come true for this combination. If this sounds as though Aries-Roosters are antisocial, they are not. They are, to some extent, clotheshorses, but have style in this regard too. Because of their nature, however, they are apt to try the far-out and cutting edge at times, but their style of choice cannot be pinpointed, because it varies from person to person. Suffice it to say that how they look is of importance to them. They can socialize with anyone, including those pygmies. Their good personality assures an ample number of friends who they enjoy hanging out with and celebrating many festivities, including exotic ones. This could very well take place, if not in a yurt, in their own home that has been decorated with exotic style and grace.

Romance: While they are sociable and well liked, they are frank and direct with their speech. This can cause them problems at times, but they are generally more affectionate in nature. Aries-Roosters depend on other people both to verify their being and to enhance their self-worth. Consequently, they are not loners. Indeed, they need others to more or less reflect their existence. This gives them an ability to read other people's reactions to them.

Relationships: Cancer-Rabbits and Libra-Snakes, as well as Leo-Dogs, are not good. Capricorns, especially Capricorn-Dogs, are not good for this combination. There is a mutual attraction between Sagittarius and Aries-Roosters. The best choices in the romance department are the Gemini-Snake and -Buffalo. Really good are Leo-Buffalo or Leo-Snake, or Aquarius-Dragon or -Snake.

Family Life: Aries-Roosters will fulfill their obligations to their family. They will go to all-important occasions, especially visiting their parents. In spite of the fact that some of these events and celebrations might be boring, they do them. Their character dictates this. Publicly, this is what you see when you look at the life of this combination. The Aries-Rooster has a strong sense of duty, especially to his family and close friends. They tend to always do the right thing.

Livelihood: The difficulty in terms of career for this combination might be the fact that there are so many choices, it is hard to narrow them down to just one. But regardless of their choice, there is a high likelihood of success. It is essentially impossible to say what is the best vocation for an Aries-Rooster. They can be essentially anything they like, and their interests are diverse. They are talented in creative endeavors, humanitarian activities, and practical careers.

Famous Aries-Roosters: Peter Ustinov, Simone Signoret, General Patton.

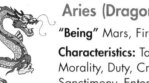

Aries (Dragon) Month Combined with Dog Year

"Being" Mars, Fire, Cardinal   **"Concerned"** Yin-Positive Metal

Characteristics: Tactlessness, Excess, Talent, Uneasiness, Morality, Duty, Criticism, Courage, Naïveté, Domination, Sanctimony, Enterprise, Unsociability, Constancy, Respectability, Intelligence, Self-righteousness, Cynicism, Ostentation, Heroism, Drive, Heartiness, Willfulness, Affability

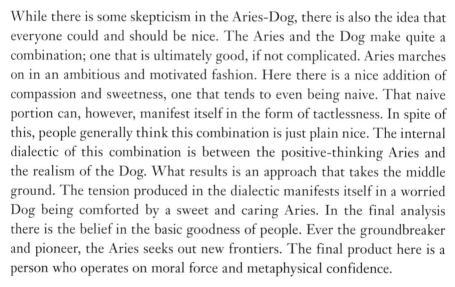

While there is some skepticism in the Aries-Dog, there is also the idea that everyone could and should be nice. The Aries and the Dog make quite a combination; one that is ultimately good, if not complicated. Aries marches on in an ambitious and motivated fashion. Here there is a nice addition of compassion and sweetness, one that tends to even being naive. That naive portion can, however, manifest itself in the form of tactlessness. In spite of this, people generally think this combination is just plain nice. The internal dialectic of this combination is between the positive-thinking Aries and the realism of the Dog. What results is an approach that takes the middle ground. The tension produced in the dialectic manifests itself in a worried Dog being comforted by a sweet and caring Aries. In the final analysis there is the belief in the basic goodness of people. Ever the groundbreaker and pioneer, the Aries seeks out new frontiers. The final product here is a person who operates on moral force and metaphysical confidence.

Romance: Human nature being what it is, truth in relationships is hard to find, and being totally honest with another takes a lot of faith. However, Aries-Dogs insist on it, and the slightest sign of dishonesty in a partner results in breakups. Generally speaking, age brings a more realistic attitude, and they become more accepting of others' foibles. The happy medium approach is employed in the personal life of the Aries-Dog. They shun problems and take the middle ground. As with most individuals, this combination does marry and have a family, but that often is done later than most people. In their youth, Aries-Dogs are busy sorting out epistemological issues. They are relentless seekers of the truth.

Relationships: The Aquarius-Tigers are not the best choice, even though there might be an attraction for this combination. Do not consider Cancer-Rooster, -Dragon, and -Ram. Libra-Rams and Capricorn-Dragons are not good picks. The best romantic choices for this combination are the Gemini-Rabbit or –Tiger, as well as the Leo-Horse or -Tiger. Also good selections are the Sagittarius-Rabbits and -Tigers.

Family Life: Essentially this combination is content and accepting. Perhaps their only flaw is their tendency to hurt people's feelings. They do not do this deliberately, and it is just a trait that seems to haunt all Dogs. The Aries-Dog has a deep and abiding sense of place. They know where they are in a profound way. They can establish their territory and make it their own. Materialism is not in their character, but they do need space. They want space for themselves, and they want space for those they love.

Livelihood: Among this combination, there are other talents involving creativity, including the arts. They have huge hearts and love humanitarian causes. Slips of the tongue are to be guarded against, however, because they often take a form that hurts people's feelings. Generally speaking though, their kind, open-minded, and flexible nature lets their good hearts shine through. The Aries-Dog is highly flexible and adaptable. Their interests and aptitudes are many. Because of their ability to organize they can be a boss or manager, but their nature is also suited to being an employee.

Famous Aries-Dogs: Henry Luce, Paul Robeson, Eileen Ford, Carmen McRae, Ved Mehta.

Aries (Dragon) Month Combined with Boar Year
"Being" Mars, Fire, Cardinal   **"Cultivator"** Yin-Negative Water
Characteristics: Boar-headedness, Honesty, Drive, Talent, Hesitation, Materialism, Voluptuousness, Culture, Domination, Scrupulousness, Credulity, Gourmandize, Gallantry, Willfulness, Wrath, Sincerity, Excess, Sanctimony, Affability, Enterprise, Naïveté, Courage, Ostentation, Heartiness

Aries-Boars are virtually selfless, and to be their friend is an honor as well as a joy. The Aries-Boar is probably the kindest person on the planet. If something needs doing, they are there to do it or to help others do it. They volunteer for everything and assist their friends in every possible way: from babysitting to moving house. They are the ones who stay after Thanksgiving dinner and help with the dishes and who take the kids to the county fair.

Obviously, this makes them extremely popular individuals. Their gifts run across the spectrum to include artistic and musical ability. Their lives are not always blessed with good fortune, and they give far more than they receive. If you have an Aries-Boar among your family or friends, you are truly blessed. If you need a volunteer or someone to head a committee, seek out someone from this combination, and they will surely agree. They are totally trustworthy. Combine this with the fact that they have superior organizational skills and you have someone capable of easily being elected to the school board, or even state senate. And they will probably set a record for the youngest person ever elected to the position. They have pleasant personalities and enjoy entertaining others and doing things with their family.

Romance: Aries-Boars cling to a belief that they can fix anything, including broken relationships or serious issues pertaining to communication or other important parts of a relationship. Without caution, the end result can be not only frustration but also failure in the area of romance. Romance is not always smooth sailing for this combination. For starters, the Aries-Boar makes friends with everyone, beginning as just a young child. The distinct possibility here is that there will be an early marriage, which is not always the best of all possible worlds.

Relationships: In this combination the Cancer-Monkeys, -Dogs, or -Horses are not a good choice. Avoid Libra-Roosters or Capricorn-Tigers or -Roosters. Do not be fooled by Libra-Tigers. Good choices in the realm of romance are Gemini- or Leo-Dragons and -Rabbits. Sagittarius-Rabbits and Aquarius-Rabbits and -Dragons are also good. On the other hand, Snakes of any sign are not good for Boars.

Family Life: Aries-Boars create dependent people in their own home and can create dependent people in the extended family such that they are unable to function on their own. Furthermore, it is possible that any effort to establish independence, including children as they grow up, will be seen as betrayal. Because for the Aries-Boar the family is such an important part of their being, any attempts to disrupt patterns will not be appreciated. The be-all and end-all of life for the Aries-Boar is the family, and that means the entire extended family. The primary concern and care of this combination is, of course, the spouse and children, but it goes beyond that to parents, uncles, cousins, nephews, and nieces. This love, care, and concern is not all positive, because it creates neediness on the part of both parties.

Livelihood: This combination is so ready to take on projects that there can be, at times, issues about following through to completion, but generally this is not a big problem. The aptitude of this combination combined with the go-getter spirit translates into fine career opportunities. They are the first choice on any boss's team because of their abilities and flexibility. Another significant aspect of Aries-Boars is their affinity for projects. They project themselves into the future when planning and implementing these ideas. As a result there is very little they do not like in terms of business, creativity, or management.

Famous Aries-Boars: Tennessee Williams, Bismarck, Dudley Moore.

Taurus (Snake) Month Combined with Rat Year

"Possess" Venus, Earth, Fixed   **"Regulator"** Yin-Positive Water

Characteristics: Meddling, Languor, Thirst for Power, Acquisitiveness, Intellectual, Guile, Charisma, Complacency, Logic, Skill, Sensuality, Nervousness, Jealousy, Determination, Influence, Intractability, Prejudice, Patience, Gluttony, Industry, Appeal, Sociability, Verbosity, Thrift, Ardor

Taurus-Rats do not want to be kings or queens who rule over people. What they want is dignity and respect. They enjoy being highly regarded. Perhaps it is the aura and presentation of power and control that they like, for there is no appearance of sentimentality about this combination. Taurus-Rats are tightly strung but powerful. The string on their bow is not likely to break. Implant a hyperactive Rat into the deliberate and strong Taurus and you have a marriage of energy and strength. As a result, there is a character that loves power. One cannot read the minds of this combination because they maintain their poker face at all times. However, they are great at bluffing their way to winning hands because they have their strong will and mental focus. Added to this is another layer of shrewdness: the ability to seem to be unaffected by things around them. There is a definite stoicism in their character. Taurus-Rats do not cry over sad movies nor get misty-eyed over days gone by. Rats are tricky but are extremely appealing. Their power is mental, combined with shrewdness and an impenetrable mask they always wear.

Romance: In this combination betrayal of any sort will not be tolerated. Caution is in order too, because Taurus-Rats are the highly jealous type. To have a relationship with them means a long-term and deep commitment to them and the family. They can put up with all sorts of foibles and missteps, but betrayal is not one of them. This combination is the Rock of Gibraltar type; at least, that is what they aspire to be. A routine and secure life appeals to them, yet they are somewhat the sultry and erotic type. They do not mind the occasional flirtation; however, loyalty is at the top of their list of values. A bit of fantasy is acceptable, and this combination might engage in some of that too. But it is paramount to be reality bound in the long run.

Relationships: For this combination Horses are not good in general, but that is especially true of the Leo-, Scorpio-, and Aquarius-Horses. Rabbits, especially Aquarius-Rabbits, are a poor choice. A very good romantic choice is the Pisces-Buffalo or -Tiger. Also good are Cancer-, Virgo-, or Capricorn-Monkeys and Capricorn-Boars.

Family Life: Most likely the Taurus-Rat is the family type and the center of the family and home. That is not to say that this combination is a homebody. They love their home, but they also love their work, and it often takes them away. As might be expected, this combination is highly traditional in their views and in their environment. This is reflected in their decor at home and at work, as well as what they read and their hobbies.

Livelihood: Taurus-Rats are dedicated and responsible. They like money, but they are willing to work for it. They have a mind like a mousetrap and remember everything down to the smallest details. They consequently make excellent employees or bosses. This combination is the ultimate multitasker. Their clock is polychromic, and they can do a dozen things at once and do them well. There is no perfect job for them because they are good at most things and great at the rest.

Famous Taurus-Rats: William Shakespeare, Charlotte Bronte, Ayatollah Khomeini, Studs Terkel, Zubin Mehta, Charles Aznavour.

Taurus (Snake) Month Combined with Buffalo Year

"Possess" Venus, Earth, Fixed   **"Survivor"** Yin-Negative Water

Characteristics: Vindictiveness, Eloquence, Stability, Bias, Integrity, Standoffishness, Plodding, Diligence, Bigotry, Innovation, Jealousy, Strength of Purpose, Stubbornness, Patience, Intractability, Gluttony, Logic, Determination, Complacency, Ardor, Prejudice, Languor, Industry, Sensuality

The Taurus is the quiet one while at the same time being well-spoken. The Buffalo is slow but powerful. Supremely patient, the Buffalo moves slowly but surely. They are calm. They can wait. There is nothing impulsive about

them. The Taurus-Buffalo is a combination of heavyweights. While it might appear that they would be left in the dust of others, the fact is that they have superb endurance. If ever there was a strong silent type, this is it. The patience quotient is significant here too, because that means this combination can wait for gratification of all sorts, including the sensual, which it clearly enjoys. This sign is not, therefore, stodgy in any way. Quite the contrary is the case. They think about things and take their time doing them. They cogitate. Like most cogitators, they often make wise decisions, certainly wiser than would have been made had they rushed. In their deliberations they are serious, as with most things. It is not that they do not enjoy a night at the cinema or even cheering for their favorite team. No, the case is that they have these things in perspective. Perhaps their philosophy can be summarized as "first things first."

Romance: In this combination they will do what it takes to win, and it will be done harshly. Overall, however, if you are kind and loyal to this combination, they make great friends or tender lovers. Just do not cross them. It would be a mistake to consider the Taurus-Buffalo a smiling, big, stuffed animal. A part of them can actually be cruel and cutting. Caution is necessary. If you make them feel threatened, there will be a fight and it will be vicious. There are neither Queensbury rules nor the Geneva Convention in a battle with them.

Relationships: In this combination there are possibilities of a relationship of Pisces- or Capricorn-Monkeys, but probably not for long-term relationships. Avoid Leo-, Aquarius-, and Scorpio-Tigers and Scorpio-Rams. Pisces- or Cancer-Rats or Cancer-Snakes are a good selection on the romantic front, as are Roosters from these signs. Capricorn- and Virgo-Rats and Virgo-Snakes and -Roosters are possibilities.

Family Life: In the case of this combination, work furthers the goals of the Taurus-Buffalo. For this combination, achievement is important, and so the home must assist in that capacity. That generally means a boost of some kind to this combination's social image. The home of the Taurus-Buffalo will not be featured in *Home and Garden Magazine*. Decorating is not among their talents or interests. They like a degree of tidiness and certainly demand some comfort. Aside from that, the home is seen as something that is fairly utilitarian. If it works, then it is fine.

Livelihood: This combination values working hard, being responsible, never quitting, and being industrious. Applying those values in life guarantees not only success but also long-lasting success. As might be expected, this combination does not place a great deal of value on beauty or youth or other passing assets. The only assets that matter are those that are timeless.

Famous Taurus-Buffalos: Adolf Hitler, Gary Cooper, Jack Nicholson, Billy Joel.

Taurus (Snake) Month Combined with Tiger Year

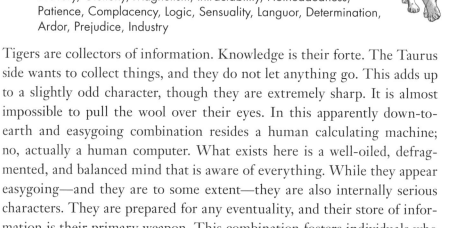

"Possess" Venus, Earth, Fixed　　**"Observer"** Yang-Positive Wood

Characteristics: Itinerancy, Authority, Good Luck, Disobedience, Benevolence, Swagger, Intemperance, Fervor, Impetuosity, Jealousy, Bravery, Gluttony, Magnetism, Intractability, Hotheadedness, Patience, Complacency, Logic, Sensuality, Languor, Determination, Ardor, Prejudice, Industry

Tigers are collectors of information. Knowledge is their forte. The Taurus side wants to collect things, and they do not let anything go. This adds up to a slightly odd character, though they are extremely sharp. It is almost impossible to pull the wool over their eyes. In this apparently down-to-earth and easygoing combination resides a human calculating machine; no, actually a human computer. What exists here is a well-oiled, defragmented, and balanced mind that is aware of everything. While they appear easygoing—and they are to some extent—they are also internally serious characters. They are prepared for any eventuality, and their store of information is their primary weapon. This combination fosters individuals who are born leaders and who prefer leading to following. At one and the same time they are royal but also self-effacing. They are secure within themselves and know who they are, and that gives them a sense of distinction. Taurus-Tigers are not arrogant by any stretch of the imagination, but they do love being the leader. They also do well in groups. They love to be around others, not necessarily to show off, but to people watch and perhaps store more information.

Romance: Taurus-Tigers probably invented unconditional love, and they are the paradigm example of this. Their love and devotion are beautiful to behold with the one obvious exception: should they lose their beloved, they can fall into a bottomless pit of heartbreak from which they might never escape. No one loves deeper, longer, and stronger than the Taurus-Tiger. They open their entire heart and soul and turn it over to the beloved. They are profoundly loyal and completely selfless with the one they love.

Relationships: In this combination Scorpio-Monkeys or -Snakes should be ruled out. Leo-Snakes and Aquarius-Snakes, -Buffalos, and -Monkeys are not good selections either. The choice is ultimately personal, of course, but because of the devotion and strong love of this combination, extra caution should be used. The best romantic selections for this combination are Cancer, Virgo, and Capricorns who are Dragons, Dogs, or Horses. Another choice might be the Pisces-Dragon or -Dog. Another option is the Scorpio-Dog.

Family Life: This combination has the temper of a tiger and inflexibility of the Taurus, so it is little wonder that there would be issues. This combination does not have a character that lends itself to compromise, and problems are inevitable. Domestic tranquillity is hard to find in the home life of a Taurus-Tiger, despite their mighty love and devotion. For some reason they have a home life of quakes, aftershocks, and frequent tremors.

Livelihood: As an employee, this combination can create serious problems. However, they do ultimately make good workers as well as managers once they have checked things out for themselves. It is just a matter of getting them used to the rule book and seeing the point of things. Those willing to tolerate the approach of this combination will end up with a responsible and faithful employee who is levelheaded and task oriented. The Taurus-Tiger is a unique individual, with the emphasis on *individual*. Their theme song is probably "I Did It My Way." They have to examine and check everything for their personal brand of truth.

Famous Taurus-Tigers: Robespierre, Karl Marx, Ho Chi Minh, Remain Gary, Elizabeth II.

Taurus (Snake) Month Combined with Rabbit Year

"Possess" Venus, Earth, Fixed   **"Withdraw"** Yin-Negative Wood

Characteristics: Complexity, Prudence, Pedantry, Dilettantism, Longevity, Ambition, Hypochondria, Jealousy, Secretiveness, Tact, Finesse, Intractability, Patience, Squeamishness, Virtue, Gluttony, Logic, Complacency, Languor, Sensuality, Ardor, Determination, Prejudice, Industry

This combination's primary asset is imagination and vision. They are creative and innovative in every aspect of life. Whether it is science or the arts, they are revolutionary. However, this combination is also a homebody. After finding a partner and a home, it nearly requires explosives to dislodge them. This, of course, is related to their need for security. The primary value of the Taurus-Rabbit is security, and nothing is more important than that. They need insurance, assurance, contracts, pledges, and guarantees to be happy. Everything must be lined up carefully and completed properly and in a responsible fashion. Failing to have an ordered life, this combination is nearly helpless and, at minimum, vulnerable. The ideal situation for Taurus-Rabbits is to find a mate, settle down, mow the lawn in the summer, sit by the fire in the winter, and snuggle with their partner at night. They may live in their hometown for their entire lives and not stray beyond a hundred miles. They are the ultimate keepers of the nest. Because of their fantastic innovative minds they often achieve their goals. What bothers them is the freedom that is taken away from them in exchange for the success. They have built their castle, found their love and comfort, and they do not want it invaded. Neither do they want to hang out with all kinds of people they know nothing of and care nothing about. Unfortunately that is where the difficulties begin. Every rose has its thorns: success often brings with it people and attention, and that is something this combination does not particularly care for. Yes, they do enjoy the comforts and the financial security, but they far prefer to have commerce with those they choose.

Romance: The Taurus-Rabbit is detail minded but in their own unique way. Nagging this combination is definitely not recommended. Leave them alone and things will be taken care of properly. A kind and charitable heart resides in the Taurus-Rabbit. The dialectic of this combination is refinement butting heads with obstinacy. There is a heavy portion of desire in the sensual sense in the mix as well. This combination insists on things being simple and abhors difficulties and problems. Whining drives them up the wall: they shun complaining or listening to those who wallow in their sorrows. Their notion of love entails a mixture of knights on white horses combined with comfort and security.

Relationships: In this combination a good choice is the Virgo-Rabbit. Also possibilities are Pisces-Boars and -Rams. Leos are not a good idea. Good romantic matches for the Taurus-Rabbit are Capricorn- or Cancer-Rams and Cancer-Dogs or -Boars.

Family Life: For Taurus-Rabbits, the style and the price tag are top of the line, but they are not in-your-face showy. Rather, they are graceful. If you want a lesson in good taste, visit the home of a Taurus-Rabbit. The home is the castle and nest of this combination. It is a place of retreat but not surrender. Loving the nest as they do, Taurus-Rabbits tend to go for the comfy and warm approach to a home. To walk into their home is to feel welcomed and, of course, secure.

Livelihood: Generally there is a middle-age slump when reality slaps these individuals in the face and they realize they have pretty much what they are going to get out of life. Still, in the end, most can be moderately successful and content. The peak time in the professed life of a Taurus-Rabbit is roughly between twenty-five and forty-five. They have the potential to soar to the great heights during this portion of their life span. Of course, this period in most people's lives is one of a certain amount of naïveté coupled with blind ambition.

Famous Taurus-Rabbits: Orson Welles, Dr. Benjamin Spock, Judy Collins.

Taurus (Snake) Month Combined with Dragon Year

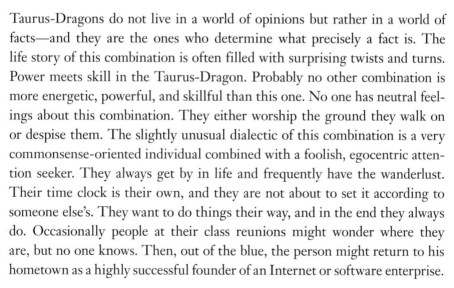

"Possess" Venus, Earth, Fixed **"Take Charge"** Yang-Positive Wood

Characteristics: Dissatisfaction, Volubility, Infatuation, Pluck, Mistrust, Braggadocio, Jealousy, Success, Rigidity, Strength, Good Health, Intractability, Enthusiasm, Gluttony, Logic, Patience, Complacency, Sensuality, Languor, Sentimentality, Ardor, Prejudice, Determination, Industry

Taurus-Dragons do not live in a world of opinions but rather in a world of facts—and they are the ones who determine what precisely a fact is. The life story of this combination is often filled with surprising twists and turns. Power meets skill in the Taurus-Dragon. Probably no other combination is more energetic, powerful, and skillful than this one. No one has neutral feelings about this combination. They either worship the ground they walk on or despise them. The slightly unusual dialectic of this combination is a very commonsense-oriented individual combined with a foolish, egocentric attention seeker. They always get by in life and frequently have the wanderlust. Their time clock is their own, and they are not about to set it according to someone else's. They want to do things their way, and in the end they always do. Occasionally people at their class reunions might wonder where they are, but no one knows. Then, out of the blue, the person might return to his hometown as a highly successful founder of an Internet or software enterprise.

Romance: This combination remembers anniversaries and Valentine's Day. They are the type who love to be with their partners. This is a wonderful combination for love and romance. For starters, the Dragon is highly romantic.

On top of this, in the Taurus, there is a deep loyalty and faithfulness. The result is that the Taurus-Dragon deeply loves and cares for his or her partner.

Relationships: It is not only possible but, indeed, certain that the Taurus-Dragon is extraordinarily jealous and craves attention. If you do not give them the attention they need, or if you give the slightest hint that there is some interest other than them, there will be a price to be paid. In general, however, this combination is a true-blue partner. This combination is, for the most part, faithful and loyal to their partners. They are, however, human, and can be led into temptation like anyone else. They are not likely to have a flashy, headline-making adulterous affair. But, straying is a possibility under the right circumstances.

Family Life: In this combination perhaps a bit of caution needs to be in place with Leo- and Scorpio-Buffalos and Scorpio-Dogs, but they are not actually dangerous. Furthermore, while Aquarius-Buffalos and -Dogs might be good friends, romance is probably not advisable. Dragons can get along with almost anyone and that includes the powerful and skillful Taurus-Dragon. Romantically speaking, nearly every combination is possible.

Livelihood: The love in this combination is most certainly of the give-and-take variety because Dragons are, deep in their hearts, very affectionate by nature. While they do not appear to be the overly affectionate huggy, kissy types with their children, they are deeply moved and interested in everything they do. Even though this combination has the wanderlust, a Taurus-Dragon is a good spouse and excellent with the children. Taurus-Dragons take excellent care of those they love, and in return there is love and respect aplenty.

Famous Taurus-Dragons: Salvador Dali, Sigmund Freud, Jean Cabin, Shirley Temple, Yehudi Menuhin.

 ## Taurus (Snake) Month Combined with Snake Year

"Possess" Venus, Earth, Fixed   **"Feel"** Yang-Negative Fire

Characteristics: Compassion, Industry, Exclusiveness, Discretion, Sagacity, Laziness, Cupidity, Presumption, Clairvoyance, Jealousy, Intractability, Intuition, Attractiveness, Dissimulation, Extravagance, Patience, Gluttony, Complacency, Logic, Sensuality, Languor, Ardor, Determination, Prejudice

The Snake portion of this combination is the economic advisor and is extraordinarily good at it. Considering this combination is highly materialistic, this is probably a good thing. The Taurus-Snake is a fascinating mixture of the ostentatious but tasteful person combined with financial wizard. And that is only the tip of the iceberg. Fortunately, the Taurus side holds some sway in the combination and takes the Snake down a couple of notches to something more manageable. The Taurus, too, is acquisitive. Considering this, and the fact that Snakes generally have fine taste, more than likely this combination has a strong attachment to fine art and comfort. They are extremely aesthetic and materialistically driven. The end result is probably akin to a marriage of an award-winning chef with the curator of the Museum of Modern Art. Unfortunately, this affliction attacks them from both sides of their combination, and coupled with this is an obstinacy that renders them inflexible at times. In spite of the show they put on, there is a lack of self-assurance. Because of the Snake element and the plodding Taurus, however, financial success is usually assured. They know their stuff. Taurus-Snakes' most serious problem is that they tend to be lazy, very lazy. They lean toward being lackadaisical procrastinators and daydreamers who frequently eat too much.

Romance: What this combination needs more than anything is a regime that makes it clear life has responsibilities, and sometimes unpleasant chores. If they are actually going to accomplish anything, they need some discipline. Notwithstanding the above, the Taurus-Snake is one of the beautiful people of the world and they know it. They expect things to be handed to them on silver platters and to be fed with silver spoons. This is not a wise thing to do.

Relationships: Leo-Tigers and -Boars are not recommended in this combination. Avoid Scorpio- or Aquarius-Tigers. The tendency for fantasy in romance needs to be avoided. Good relationship choices are Cancer-, Virgo-, Capricorn-, and Pisces-Buffalos and Pisces-Dragons and -Roosters.

Family Life: Keeping in mind their lackadaisical nature and penchant for laziness, it should not be a surprise that comfort is very significant to them. However, given the highly aesthetic mind-set of their being, this comfort must be of top quality and supremely stylish. You will find any number of places to lounge around in their homes and the most comfortable beds on the planet. The environment of Taurus-Snakes is of supreme importance to them. This does not mean that they are tree-huggers; it means that their home's accoutrements play a vital role in their happiness.

Livelihood: Individuals of this combination want to be professionals because the money and security are there. Thus they gravitate toward things like accounting or academia. In management positions they tend to let the Taurus' plodding and slow style dominate too much. They are excellent with money but are not gamblers. They shun risk taking.

Famous Taurus-Snakes: Johannes Brahms, Henry Fonda, I. M. Pei, Audrey Hepburn, Daniele Darrieux.

Taurus (Snake) Month Combined with Horse Year

"Possess" Venus, Earth, Fixed   **"Command"** Yang-Positive Fire

Characteristics: Accomplishment, Autonomy, Pragmatism, Style, Popularity, Rebellion, Dexterity, Ardor, Anxiety, Haste, Jealousy, Unscrupulousness, Persuasiveness, Logic, Intractability, Selfishness, Patience, Complacency, Gluttony, Languor, Sensuality, Prejudice, Determination, Industry

In this combination there are no major issues until the age of puberty, when socialization sets in, bringing the influence of those from outside the home. It means peer pressure. People with gifts often tend not to fit in, of course, but that does not stop the Taurus-Horse from trying. The evolution of a Taurus-Horse is dominated by the intelligence and talent of the Horse, grounded by the strength of the Taurus. Unfortunately the result is not always as happy as it might seem. For starters, the early life of this combination is generally highly successful in some fashion. This near genius could be in the form of anything from music to sports. Whatever it is, they have the limelight and that gives them a taste for power. Unfortunately, people with special gifts and talents frequently do not conform, try as they may. The eventual result is often an individual who craves power over other people. Resentment and animosity can set in because they feel being the conductor of the State Orchestra is beneath them. They deserve the New York Philharmonic. The challenge for them is to recognize the limits of their greatness; even though they might be excellent at something, not everyone can play at Carnegie Hall.

Romance: Fortunately, individuals in this combination are ever concerned about the views other people have of them, and that lends itself to a certain degree of prudence. This carries across to the approach this individual takes toward love. Surprisingly, what some may take to be an egocentric, narcissistic, attention-seeker turns out to be a loving romantic partner, perhaps too much so. Love is the only area of this combination's life where they are egalitarians. Ironically, their sort of populist approach to love inclines them to frequent love affairs where they dedicate their affections without reservation.

Relationships: Essentially off the list are Leo-, Scorpio-, and Aquarius-Rats in this combination. Avoid Leo-Monkeys, Aquarius-Buffalos and -Boars, and Scorpio-Boars. Good romantic selections are Virgo- and Capricorn-Tigers and Capricorn-Roosters and -Goats. Pisces-Tigers make the list too. This combination would match well with a Pisces-Ram, but that might not be easy to achieve.

Family Life: This combination does not quite understand children. It is not that they are bad parents. They are not. Rather, it is the innocence and the love that they give so freely and willingly. In the end though, a family is the best medicine for Taurus-Horses to escape their own egos. Taurus-Horses love the home. It is not only their castle, it is their fortress against a world that does not give just rewards and a refuge from those who lack an understanding of real talent. In their home, Taurus-Horses can be comfortable among their things, their trophies from days gone by, and perhaps with a select few whom they trust.

Livelihood: In this combination it is entirely possible that individuals can direct their talent to being a superior boss or excellent and much appreciated employee. As with a lot of things in life, attitude is the key. Sometimes there can be an entirely different story in the evolution of the Taurus-Horse. There is the possibility that they channel their gifts, whatever they may be, in such a way that an actual career comes about; perhaps a career as an art teacher or manager of some sort.

Famous Taurus-Horses: Ulysses S. Grant, Mike Wallace, Barbara Streisand.

Taurus (Snake) Month Combined with Ram Year

"Possess" Venus, Earth, Fixed   **"Reliance"** Yang-Negative Fire

Characteristics: Worry, Impracticality, Tardiness, Perseverance, Whimsy, Invention, Pessimism, Complacency, Parasitism, Taste, Lack of Foresight, Manners, Determination, Jealousy, Ardor, Industry, Patience, Prejudice, Logic, Sensuality, Languor, Intractability, Gluttony, Sensitivity

In this combination the Taurus element is always grounded, slow but steady, and sensuous. The Ram element is more like waves on the ocean. This portion of the combination pushes then rests, and makes progress in this fashion. The Taurus is not a quitter and keeps marching and plodding onward. The Ram charges ahead, butts its head, backs up, charges again, repeatedly. All gifts are also curses, and this can certainly be true of the Taurus-Ram, although it need not be. The gift is genius. The curse is also genius, because if it is not properly cultivated it goes totally to waste in a sea of frustration and disappointment. There is an unusual kind of mutuality in the dynamics of this combination, one with a lot of potential. It can be a deliberate, hard-charging, well-balanced combination if conditions permit. Steadfastness and sure footing harmonize well. This combination has patience with perseverance that totally calms any human being. This happens because the two signs individually are compatible and work well together on all levels. This makes their logic and inventiveness work together, giving them wisdom and understanding, especially in difficult situations in life and love.

Romance: In this combination, individuals crave security but are essentially inept at providing it. None of this, in their view, is any fault of their own. A relationship with a Taurus-Ram is not terrifically rewarding for most people. It might be harsh to say that love and romance for the Taurus-Ram is a one-way street, but sometimes the truth is harsh. For starters, they are not very good at loving other people in most cases. Unfortunately, they are very needy in the love department.

Relationships: Perhaps the cream of the crop in this combination is Capricorn-Monkey, but there is not a lot of chance of catching one. Bad choices are Leo-Buffalos or -Dogs and Scorpio-Tigers and -Buffalos. Perhaps the worst picks are Aquarius-Dogs or -Tigers. Making the A list are Pisces-Boars and -Horses. Also good choices are Virgo-Rabbits and Virgo-Boars. In the running too are Capricorns and Cancers, both -Monkeys and -Horses.

Family Life: Taurus-Rams are, of course, gifted, and these gifts can take the form of doing all kinds of things children like, from puppetry to baking. Consequently, all is not lost. Quite the contrary; in the proper environment the Taurus-Ram can flourish and help those near them flourish too. All homes need a dependable person. This generally is not the Taurus-Ram, so the question is a matter of who it is. Should there be a person filling this role, this combination can be good parent. They could also add other positive features like humor. Of course one reason they make good parents is that they enjoy their playtime. Kids are wonderful playmates.

Livelihood: As for family life, the outlook is not optimistic. That does not mean it is hopeless. What it means is that a strong effort of willpower combined with a serious attitude adjustment is in order. This combination is very difficult to say much about, because some traits are so deeply ingrained in a person's nature that it is unlikely they will be changed.

Famous Taurus-Rams: Laurence Olivier, Honore de Balzac, Rudolph Valentino.

Taurus (Snake) Month Combined with Monkey Year

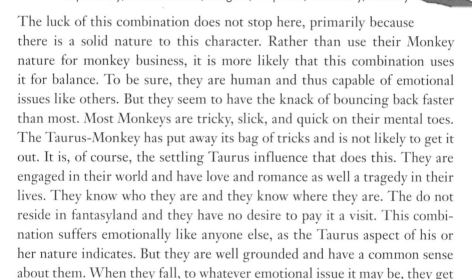

"Possess" Venus, Earth, Fixed   *"Arrange"* Yin-Positive Metal

Characteristics: Leadership, Self-involvement, Silliness, Wit, Opportunism, Jealousy, Zeal, Improvisation, Cunning, Deceit, Ruse, Stability, Ardor, Gluttony, Intractability, Patience, Logic, Loquacity, Complacency, Determination, Languor, Prejudice, Sensuality, Industry

The luck of this combination does not stop here, primarily because there is a solid nature to this character. Rather than use their Monkey nature for monkey business, it is more likely that this combination uses it for balance. To be sure, they are human and thus capable of emotional issues like others. But they seem to have the knack of bouncing back faster than most. Most Monkeys are tricky, slick, and quick on their mental toes. The Taurus-Monkey has put away its bag of tricks and is not likely to get it out. It is, of course, the settling Taurus influence that does this. They are engaged in their world and have love and romance as well a tragedy in their lives. They know who they are and they know where they are. The do not reside in fantasyland and they have no desire to pay it a visit. This combination suffers emotionally like anyone else, as the Taurus aspect of his or her nature indicates. But they are well grounded and have a common sense about them. When they fall, to whatever emotional issue it may be, they get back up, dust themselves off, and carry on. The grounding also provides a strong sense of reality.

Romance: This combination has a high regard for other people and respect for others is part of the Taurus-Monkey nature. In return they expect to be respected equally. How all of this plays out in terms of being faithful varies. What is not in question is that the Taurus-Monkey will be fair. The Taurus-Monkey is loyal and loving. They make excellent friends. They can and do love, but their love comes with a condition. They are not willing to threaten their own personal liberty, and they will not be involved in relationships that do. Their perspective is not one way, and they are certainly willing to allow their partner the same freedom.

Relationships: A very good choice for this combination might be a Pisces-Rat. Scorpio-Tigers are in the mix too, but that probably would not last long. Bad choices are the Leo-Buffalo, -Tiger, and -Horse. Other combinations that value respect, and are consequently good matches, are Capricorn- and Pisces-Dragons, as well as Dragons and Monkeys. Additionally, Cancer-, Virgo-, and Capricorn-Rats are good.

Family Life: There is a possibility they will not be parents, but if they are, they are dedicated and very caring. They are also good providers. Being dedicated, furthermore, this combination would do nearly anything for a family member such as a child, nephew, niece, or anyone else. This combination can be excellent at parenthood. Being monkeys, they are, of course, playful. Taurus-Monkeys make excellent relatives and are great fun for kids, playing with them, taking them places, giving them gifts, and being happy to be one of them.

Livelihood: Regardless of what they do, they will probably do it well, and they will probably be financially successful too. They are not afraid to work hard, and they enjoy helping others. The financial success they will probably enjoy is good, because they also happen to be good at spending money. It is not that they are wasteful; it is just a corollary of the other things mentioned in relationship to the character of this combination. This combination is very well rounded in nearly every part of life. They are excellent at making money, making friends, doing things, and learning things. Because of this they might be very good at jobs in public relations or sales.

Famous Taurus-Monkeys: J. M. Barrie, Leonardo da Vinci, Harry Truman, Sugar Ray Leonard, Jill Clayburgh, Pope John Paul II.

Taurus (Snake) Month Combination with Rooster Year

"Possess" Venus, Earth, Fixed   *"Conqueror"* Yang-Negative Metal

Characteristics: Humor, Jealousy, Sensuality, Resilience, Enthusiasm, Conservatism, Candor, Industry, Patience, Intractability, Gluttony, Logic, Bossiness, Complacency, Ardor, Chic, Dissipation, Languor, Determination, Cockiness, Prejudice, Blind Faith, Boastfulness, Pedantry

Taurus-Roosters have their eyes on their goal and will not be shaken on their way to it. Fortunately, among their gifts is enthusiasm, giving them the strength to keep on going. In addition, almost from birth, they are the sort of person who seems to rise above a situation and is able to dominate it. None of this is to say that they are necessarily popular, although they might be. Neither is it the case that they are joiners, overly friendly, great athletes, or any of the things that often are associated with success. The Taurus-Rooster is a person who often rises to the top of their chosen field because of their wisdom and motivation. Combined with this is a self-assurance bordering on, but not crossing the line in to, arrogance. Most of the qualities necessary for success in life are found in this combination. Life, perhaps like the home or office, has a place for everything and everything needs to be in its place. The place of the Taurus-Rooster is not at the bottom of the ladder. To look at them is to know this. One indication that there is no falsehood about this combination is their compassion. They know that some people do not have the same wherewithal as they do, and they are happy to help them. This part of their being comes to them naturally, and it comes to them sincerely. Furthermore, they are not the pushy and overly aggressive types. They are people who stand out from the crowd. They ride this aura, and the concomitant ability, to a very high rank in society.

Romance: Because they are hard charging, highly serious, hardworking individuals, Taurus-Roosters enjoy a break from time to time, and that break often comes in the form of a lightweight but very entertaining partner. The match may simply be for variety. The situation is as simple as this. They are with them to fill in the gaps in their own life. It is not uncommon to see this high-flying, wise, and astute individual with a partner who is a bit on the flaky side. And that is putting it kindly.

Relationships: For this combination the not particularly good picks are Leo-Rabbits or -Roosters. Additional bad choices are Aquarius- and Scorpio-Dogs and Scorpio-Rabbits. The best romantic choices for this combination are Cancer-, Virgo-, and Capricorn-Buffalos and Capricorn-Dragons or -Snakes. Also good are Pisces-Buffalos or -Snakes.

Family Life: This combination will be the first one to RSVP a yes for attendance. Furthermore, they will be a great addition to any party or function because they love parties or events of all kinds. In family matters this combination will be a shining star and the type that everyone is happy to see. The Taurus-Rooster is ideal for parenthood and all family matters. They are extraordinarily fond of children and having a large family is certainly within the realm of possibility. Unlike some other combinations, they enjoy family gatherings of all types and sizes and for all ages.

Livelihood: This combination needs more autonomy in the work environment. Given that, they will be content because they do enjoy work. This, of course, indicates that they will be financially secure, and while that is true, it does not imply that money has intrinsic value for them. It does not. They enjoy a reasonable amount of comfort and security as do most of us, but that is sufficient for them. The Taurus-Rooster's ability extends across the entire spectrum. There is very little that they are not capable of. All of the professions, from medicine through academia, are a possibility. Management and business ownership are also very real possibilities. This combination is just plain talented. There is, however, in this rosy picture, one thing that a Taurus-Rooster finds difficult to do and does not do well: they plainly are not cut out to be in lower positions that demand strict adherence to authority.

Famous Taurus-Roosters: Rod McKuen, Peter Townshend, Annie Dillard.

Taurus (Snake) Month Combined with Dog Year

"Possess" Venus, Earth, Fixed   **"Concerned"** Yin-Positive Metal

Characteristics: Tactlessness, Morality, Heroism, Respectability, Cynicism, Self-righteousness, Duty, Intelligence, Logic, Ardor, Sensuality, Complacency, Jealousy, Languor, Constancy, Unsociability, Intractability, Determination, Prejudice, Industry, Patience, Gluttony, Uneasiness, Criticism

For starters, the Taurus-Dog has an almost profound lack of self-confidence. That alone could doom them to be far less than they are actually capable of being. The Taurus-Dog has a lot of positive traits. They are responsible, likable, and generally others enjoy their company. Furthermore, this combination has a wide variety of interests and a lot of capability, and all in all this looks like a very promising picture for the Taurus-Dog. Unfortunately, as we all know, looks can be deceiving. There is something wrong with this situation. The empirical manifestation of this lack of self-confidence results in what, for lack of a better word, translates as being a chronic whiner. There is a hero hidden deep within them, but they do not seem to have the luck to let that side show itself either. The one thing that is lacking, self-confidence, is not likely to mend itself. If it does, all the wonderful and positive things that the Taurus-Dog is can be released. It is not merely that they complain, they do it with gusto and they do it relentlessly. Life does not give what they think they deserve, it does not offer what it should offer, and what is available is rigged. They believe that they are the unluckiest person ever born. Others get all the breaks. None of this should lead one to believe that the Taurus-Dog is a wimp, far from it.

Romance: This combination's love is so awesome that it is nearly impossible for anyone to match it, but it is precisely that which the Taurus-Dog expects. Ethically speaking, it is reasonable to ask people to be fair and to be just and to be kind. It is not reasonable to ask people to be superhuman, but that is almost what it would take to be in a relationship with this combination. So, perhaps, they are doomed to disappointment here too. The Taurus-Dog is very loving and dedicated. They make exceptionally loyal and devoted lovers and there is almost nothing they will not do for their partner. Both sides of the combination contribute to this character. They are also very romantically inclined. Once again, we have a positive picture, but the picture does not tell the entire story. The problem is precisely the degree and strength of their love. It is well beyond the call of duty and perhaps is the hero element mentioned above.

Relationships: In this combination very poor choices of compatibility are Leo-, Scorpio-, or Aquarius-Tigers and Aquarius-Dragons or -Rams. Excellent possibilities for this combination are Cancer-, Virgo-, Capricorn-, and Pisces-Rabbits and Pisces-Horses and -Tigers.

Family Life: Individuals in this combination enjoy doing things with their own special mark on them, but that can be something as ordinary as the color of tablecloth or which kind of coasters to get. The Taurus-Dog lives up to what you might expect in terms of the home and its surroundings. Easygoing and personal are the keys. Style or the latest designs are not significant. There is no concern for antiques either, and used furniture is fine, as long as it is not plastic. The fake in general is not well liked by this combination.

Livelihood: Taurus-Dogs have a talent for details and a flair for the personal touch. Furthermore, Dogs, when treated properly, are extremely loyal, and that is very true of the Taurus variety. They are also responsible, if not a bit awkward at times. They have a lovable and friendly nature that makes them popular with coworkers and clients alike. Whether young or old, you can teach the Taurus-Dog new tricks, and, in this case, that means new ways of doing things or new and challenging tasks. There are lots of positive things to say in the area of family life with regard to the Taurus-Dog. As might be expected from the Taurus side of things, this is a very hard worker who plods on until the job gets done. That job might be done slowly on occasions, but it is done with diligence and is nearly always appreciated.

Famous Taurus-Dogs: Lenin, Golda Meir, Shirley MacLaine.

Taurus (Snake) Month Combined with Boar Year

"Possess" Venus, Earth, Fixed   **"Cultivator"** Yin-Negative Water

Characteristics: Honesty, Ardor, Boar-headedness, Logic, Industry, Culture, Hesitation, Voluptuousness, Credulity, Materialism, Gourmandism, Scrupulousness, Gallantry, Wrath, Jealousy, Sincerity, Patience, Intractability, Sensuality, Gluttony, Complacency, Languor, Determination, Prejudice

Taurus-Boars will accept nothing less than what they are entitled to. However, what they feel they are entitled to is to be in charge and to get precisely what they want. The Taurus-Boar is not just the upper crust. It is the aged, high society, royal upper crust. There is a certain amount of mahogany here, so it is not necessarily all gold and gems. As with all old money, the situation is not just one of economic advantages. There is, of course, position, and along with position there are privileges. But mahogany is dear too. While these things might not necessarily have been earned, they are expected. Given the privilege, there is little that they cannot do with the proper training and education they have received. From art to athletics or board games, and, of course, to academics, they do well. These are not the only things the Taurus-Boar does well. They have a big, kind, and giving heart. This combination has as much substance and as much weight as that mahogany. As much as some might like to put such people down as having been born with everything and never having to raise a finger in their lives, that will not hold water. They know how to love others and work hard. They are very capable of doing well on their own and usually do. They are capable of finding and sharing love on their own. There is no need for them to be arrogant, and they are not. They are not prideful about their standing or their looks or their finances.

Romance: This combination also knows how to keep and decorate a home. The last comment they would want to hear applied to their home is "tacky." They are comfortable, not showy. Old-school style and grace is what it is. Picture mahogany and you have an image of their home. Little else need be said. In terms of love and romance, the accolades continue. This sign is romantic and loving. They know how to care and how to treat a person. Further, they know about loyalty and kindness, giving and sharing. They know how to respect a partner.

Relationships: In this combination out of the running are Leo-Snakes or -Monkeys, as are Scorpio-Tigers, -Roosters, and -Dogs. They should strictly avoid Aquarius-Snakes, -Roosters, or -Monkeys, but at the top of the list for romance are Capricorn-Rabbit or Cancer-Rabbit, -Dragon, or -Ram. Additional good choices are Rabbits and Dragons who are Virgo or Pisces. Good, but probably not marriage material, are the Virgo- or Pisces-Ram.

Family Life: This combination accepts responsibilities that include not just the spouse and children but the parents and siblings and even friends as well. This combination is kindness on top of responsibility. Of course, as with all things, the Taurus-Boar is the model of a good family person. They love their families, and they show it at every possible opportunity. They show it not just with the fun things like parties or holidays, but also with things that are not always so much fun, like chores.

Livelihood: This combination has other qualities they work with. In addition to the bossy element, there is obstinacy about this combination, but that too is small in the overall picture of things. This Taurus-Boar combination is not a person who likes to work alone. They are not very good at being an individualist. What they are good at is working with others, in spite of their bossy nature.

Famous Taurus-Boars: Fred Astaire, Vladimir Nabokov, Oliver Cromwell, William Randolph Hearst.

Gemini (Horse) Month Combined with Rat Year

"Reflect" Mercury, Air, Mutable   **"Regulator"** Yin-Positive Water

Characteristics: Intellectual Skill, Power, Charisma, Guile, Meddling, Influence, Nervousness, Thirst for Performance, Acquisitiveness, Self-deception, Dexterity, Inconstancy, Wittedness, Superficiality, Glibness, Impatience, Perspicacity, Versatility, Flexibility, Appeal, Thrift, Verbosity, Quick-witted, Indecisiveness, Sociability

Gemini-Rats are at once lovely to behold and tiring to watch because of their boundless renewable energy. Think of a personality trait, almost any personality trait, and that is probably something that can be said of the

Gemini-Rat. The Gemini-Rat is the social party animal meets genius. This is one of the smoothest and most ego-bound combinations there is. This combination is filled with tales and experiences, and some of them are actually true. To see them at a social gathering is to see a brightly colored butterfly who captures everybody's eye and whom everyone wants to land on them. They are generous, yes, almost to a fault. This combination walks the walk and they talk the talk; actually, they run and give award-winning speeches. Their huge ego does not get in the way of loyalty, so long as that ego is stroked often, and they can also be extraordinarily responsible. Add heavy doses of humor and a three-dimensional personality to the mix and you have a winner. They have probably given away trunk-loads of shirts off their backs. They are talented, of course, but they are nice enough to stay away from talent shows because they know they would win them all.

Romance: This combination's propensity to play is connected to great skills at seduction. They are extraordinarily enticing. In the end there is probably a great desire for dominion as much as anything. They are not the dictatorial type, however. Rather, they just relish being looked up to. The Gemini-Rat is not without fault. One fault is, perhaps, related to the issue of ego mentioned above. That fault is carried by the Gemini side and relates to infidelity. This combination is not the Rock of Gibraltar in many ways.

Relationships: Poor choices for this combination are Virgo-, Scorpio-, Sagittarius-, or Pisces-Rabbits. It would be wise also to keep away from Horses but the Aries-Buffalo or Libra-Tiger are okay. Good choices for the Gemini-Rat are Aries, Leo, Libra, or Aquarius. Those who are Dragons or Monkeys are the best.

Family Life: Gemini-Rats like to lead a comfortable life and are willing to work, but they are not happy about home handyperson projects on the weekend. They do not have a home workshop or sewing machine. They are not the primary caregivers of the children, but they are happy to play with them and tell them bedtime stories. None of this is particularly negative, but it is particularly Gemini-Rat and that is the only way this combination will function. The Gemini-Rat is a reasonably good family member, but it would be misleading to say they are self-sacrificing. While they are excellent knights in shining armor, protecting their spouse and children from assorted evils, they are not the type who will dedicate their life working two jobs so their child can attend college.

Livelihood: This combination is very perceptive and always has a quick and frequently humorous comeback. In spite of their egos, they are very reality based and able to call a spade a spade. Gemini are communicators and that holds particularly true of the Rat variety. They tend to be too easy on themselves, frequently finding excuses for their transgressions, but they are also too easy on others.

Famous Gemini-Rats: Thomas Hardy, John Cheever, Mary McCarthy.

Gemini (Horse) Month Combined with Buffalo Year

"Reflect" Mercury, Air, Mutable   **"Survivor"** Yin-Negative Water

Characteristics: Performance, Versatility, Dexterity, Self-deception, Inconstancy, Glibness, Plodding, Quick-wittedness, Impatience, Innovation, Diligence, Bias, Perspicacity, Standoffishness, Flexibility, Superficiality, Stubbornness, Indecisiveness, Integrity, Strength of Purpose, Bigotry, Vindictiveness, Eloquence, Stability

About the time a person thinks they are talking to a bore, they will be introduced to the other twin: the one who is anything but boring. Yes, they once actually did scale Mount Everest. In the long run then, the communicator, who in this case is the other twin, is revealed. But, like anyone who scales Mount Everest, they need to know each step of the way and keep their feet firmly planted on the ground. The philosophically minded Gemini is not lost, but there is not likely to be a Ph.D. dissertation on the Metaphysical Implications of the Fibonacci Spirals either. All of this is to say that with the Gemini-Buffalo, what you see is not what you get. This Gemini is one who is different from others; different from what we expect because of a mixing of the shooting star with the solid earth. While this combination is not exactly the 1960s TV show *Father Knows Best*, the Gemini-Buffalo is a family oriented Gemini, as unusual as that may sound.

Romance: Forget any other concepts of love. That there are two, or twin, parts to any Gemini is a function of the basic character of this sign. Gemini-Buffalos love home and family life, but there is a completely hidden side to their nature. They are also sexually driven, and that drive extends well beyond their own backyards. It should not come as surprising that there is a bifurcation of love for the Gemini-Buffalo. Even though, in part, these two sides seem wildly contradictory, they do exist side by side in this combination. For this combination there is sexual love and there is family love.

Relationships: This combination is not compatible with Virgo-, Capricorn-,

Sagittarius-, or Pisces-Tiger or Pisces-Ram. Pisces-Monkeys are a poor choice as well. Aries-Rats, -Snakes, and -Roosters would be fine selections in terms of romance. The Leo-Snake or Leo-Rat are fine too, as is the Libra-Rat or -Rooster. Additionally Aquarius-Rats, -Snakes, and -Roosters are appealing.

Family Life: Gemini-Buffalos are not particularly industrious, but their home is their nonsentient love. It might even be their first love, and there is some possibility it is their only long-term love. Gemini-Buffalos love their home environment and everything about it. So, perhaps in that sense, there is a third kind of love for this combination. Love in this case means comfort and quality. From accoutrements to rooms, to furniture, to electronics, this home has everything and it is dusted, polished, and ready to use.

Livelihood: If you like sarcasm, then you will love the vicious tongue of this combination. Few, however, enjoy that. Some of these apparent negatives do have a plus side. This combination accomplishes things. In addition, they are intelligent and deep. There are positive aspects about the Gemini-Buffalo, like steadfast responsibility, and there are qualities that are less than desirable. They are not just hardnosed; they can be way overboard in terms of demands. Given their awkward stance on love, it should not be shocking to note that they are not mushy and lovey-dovey.

Famous Gemini-Buffalos: William Butler Yeats, William Styron, Colleen McCullough, Waylon Jennings.

Gemini (Horse) Month Combined with Tiger Year

"Reflect" Mercury, Air, Mutable   **"Observe"** Yang-Positive Wood

Characteristics: Hotheadedness, Disobedience, Swagger, Itinerancy, Benevolence, Magnetism, Intemperance, Perspicacity, Superficiality, Indecisiveness, Authority, Fervor, Bravery, Impetuosity, Flexibility, Performance, Versatility, Dexterity, Self-deception, Quick-wittedness, Impatience, Glibness, Good Luck, Inconstancy

Gemini-Tigers are not just hotheaded, they are hot about everything. If they were a car, it would be one designed for drag racing. And those qualities just describe the Gemini portion of this combination. Spontaneity is not this combination's middle name; spontaneity is its first name. Blink your eyes and the Gemini-Tiger is in a new place with a new project involving new people. A supreme self-image comes from the Tiger part. They are number one and they know it. The extraordinary thing about all this is that it is essentially correct. Individuals in this combination tend to be leaders and they are frequently successful. However, there is a catch to this latter point. They need others, perhaps more than most. Who will they lead, who will they be popular with, and, for that matter, who will they get in trouble with if not with other human beings? It is precisely for this reason that they need to back off occasionally and stick to one thing, or, in a lot of cases, one person. This combination is an awesome creature who is loaded with charm and has the popularity to prove it. Yes, they find themselves in trouble from time to time, but they are sharp enough to get themselves out of it as often as not.

Romance: Gemini-Tigers are not cruel, and they do not like this idea. They do not try to hurt the other person. But, the long and short of it is that they do and they frequently do it big time. As a corollary of this, they like to be the center of attention in groups or special places. Wine them and dine them, especially among the rich and famous, and you might actually hook them. But, with the elusive Gemini-Tiger, it is hard to say for sure. It is not that the Gemini-Tiger collects romantic partners. It is not even that they are stuck on themselves or that they are egomaniacs. It is that they enjoy, that is to say relish, being the center of someone's affections, the center of their life. Somewhere in their hearts they realize that the other person is going to suffer horribly from a disappointment or breakup.

Relationships: Virgo- and Scorpio-Snakes and Scorpio-Tigers and -Monkeys are not suggested for this combination, and they should avoid Sagittarius-Horses, -Rabbits, and -Rams as well as Pisces-Snakes. Good combinations for relationships are Aries-Dogs and -Horses, Leo-Dogs or –Horses, and Libra-Dogs or -Horses. Additionally, Aquarius-Dragons are fine as are Aquarius-Dogs.

Family Life: Individuals in this combination can be great parents and dearly love and care for their children. This is particularly true in the area of learning, because this combination inherently knows the value of a good education. As might be expected, this combination is not exactly a homebody. Mowing lawns and making new drapes are not for the Gemini-Tiger. That is not mobile enough, and they do need to be on the move. Sure, the home can be awesome—the stuff that magazine articles are made of—but that is because this combination loves a show and loves to be noticed.

Livelihood: If you want the real McCoy and the whole enchilada, this combination is for you. They are, to put it plainly, different. They do not hear the same music other people do and consequently do not march the same. In fact, they probably do not march at all. They dance and people love it. That is why, in the end, so many of this combination are successful. There is no one like the Gemini-Tiger. There are people as fast, but not many. There are people as flexible, but not many. If you want a good manager or supervisor, do not employ this combination. If you want a good worker, they are not for you.

Famous Gemini-Tigers: Yuri Andropov, Barbara McClintock, Marilyn Monroe.

Gemini (Horse) Month Combined with Rabbit Year

"Reflect" Mercury, Air, Mutable **"Withdraw"** Yin-Negative Wood

Characteristics: Ambition, Longevity, Complexity, Hypochondria, Finesse, Prudence, Squeamishness, Pedantry, Virtue, Dilettantism, Self-deception, Tact, Superficiality, Secretiveness, Indecisiveness, Flexibility, Dexterity, Versatility, Performance, Inconstancy, Glibness, Quick-wittedness, Perspicacity, Impatience

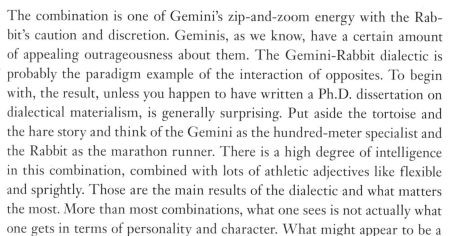

The combination is one of Gemini's zip-and-zoom energy with the Rabbit's caution and discretion. Geminis, as we know, have a certain amount of appealing outrageousness about them. The Gemini-Rabbit dialectic is probably the paradigm example of the interaction of opposites. To begin with, the result, unless you happen to have written a Ph.D. dissertation on dialectical materialism, is generally surprising. Put aside the tortoise and the hare story and think of the Gemini as the hundred-meter specialist and the Rabbit as the marathon runner. There is a high degree of intelligence in this combination, combined with lots of athletic adjectives like flexible and sprightly. Those are the main results of the dialectic and what matters the most. More than most combinations, what one sees is not actually what one gets in terms of personality and character. What might appear to be a Rabbit running from one flower to the next and chomping them all away is actually a Swiss watch that is perfectly timed.

Romance: In a way this combination needs to have a live-in loving and caring boss, a person who does the dirty work. This part of the Gemini-Rabbit is easily broken but nevertheless amiable, sophisticated, and traditional. All in all, this combination makes a good match for most people. The Gemini-Rabbit is, for lack of a better description, needy in the love department. That is not to say that they make bad mates, because they do not. What it means is that to them love is important, very important. They need it for security and for personal growth.

Relationships: Out of the running for this combination are Virgo-Rats and -Roosters. Sagittarius-Tigers and Pisces-Dragons or -Roosters are not recommended. Autonomy is important to this combination, but so is being at ease. Excellent choices for this combination in the realm of romance are Aries- and Libra-Ram and Libra-Dog or -Boar. There will probably be an attraction to Leo-Dogs and -Boars and Aquarius-Rams and -Boars.

Family Life: This combination makes a good spouse for those who want to have a homebody as their partner. But please take note that part of the Gemini-Rabbit's character is more interested in relaxing at home rather than chopping wood or folding clothes. In a world full of sound and fury, what the Gemini-Rabbit needs is peace and quiet. What their home signifies to them is a refuge. It is comfy but graceful with a touch of sophistication. Yes, this combination can be a great parent and family member, but these individuals do not want seventeen hyperactive children running around. Give them one or two well-behaved kids and they function very well.

Livelihood: The liability here is that Gemini-Rabbits cannot develop their own business plans and are therefore challenged in the area of business management and development. They are, however, perfectly able to manage issues and strategies developed by others. In the long run, this combination might not have the hard edge needed for business. In terms of business, the Gemini-Rabbit is a bit difficult to grasp. This combination plays a great violin but generally more in the category of second fiddle. That may sound like a reduced role, but those who know orchestras know that the second violin is both a key and a talent in producing successful music.

Famous Gemini-Rabbits: Bob Hope, Marguerite Yourcenar, Margaret Drabble, Queen Victoria.

Gemini (Horse) Month Combined with Dragon Year

"Reflect" Mercury, Air, Mutable **"Take Charge"** Yang-Positive Wood

Characteristics: Self-infatuation, Strength, Braggadocio, Glibness, Sentimentality, Impatience, Volubility, Quick-wittedness, Success, Enthusiasm, Pluck, Good Health, Perspicacity, Mistrust, Deception, Indecisiveness, Superficiality, Dissatisfaction, Flexibility, Rigidity, Dexterity, Versatility, Performance, Inconstancy

The Gemini-Dragon has an excess of confidence coupled with flamboyance. These individuals are attention getters. A large portion of this attention getting is used to attract people to do their bidding for them. This is another highly energized and captivating Gemini combination. To meet one is to forever remember them. They are powered by excitement and a mind that can grasp almost anything. But their engines stall at times because they have the attention span of a two-year-old. If they cannot get someone to install the new ceiling fan for free, which is entirely possible, they will find the perfect person to hire to do it. Hidden in the background of all this is the specter of boredom. This combination can be bored easily. They can plan, they can lead, they can dream up all kinds of activities and events, but they cannot be bored. It drives them right up the wall. They are so good at this it is probable they headed a human resource department in a previous life. If the job is unpleasant, say for example filling out income tax forms, they will not do it. Someone else will do it for them.

Romance: There will be no hint of monkey business in this combination. Nothing short of blind and total love and loyalty are acceptable. Gemini-Dragons are among the most loyal, faithful, and loving partners one can find. They are not shallow and do not get bored in this department. They will love a person like they have never been loved, and that means loving their entire being: every single metaphysical sinew and epistemological nerve ending. That love and that loyalty are not free. In fact, the price is too much for some. What they want in exchange for what they gladly give is the same in return.

Relationships: Virgo-Buffalo as well as Scorpio-, Sagittarius-, or Pisces-Dogs or Pisces-Buffalos are poor choices for this combination. Aries-Rats, -Monkeys, and -Boars are all excellent choices. Leo-Rats, -Tigers, and -Monkeys all capture their attention, but there is reason for caution. Libra- or Aquarius-Rats are great. If anyone is perfect, and of course that is impossible, it is the Libra-Monkey.

Family Life: This combination is kind and charitable to all people. Plainly put, this is a person who cares and acts on it. Yes they talk, but they also act. There is, in this as with all things in life, something to be careful about. It is not wise to make Gemini-Dragons feel like they are stagehands rather than stars. They need to shine at all times. Gemini-Dragons are wonderful family people in nearly every way. They are happy to have lots of children around, all the relatives are welcome, and people can drop in to their homes at any time.

Livelihood: The fundamental issue here is whether they have the stick-to-itiveness to continue in a position. The creeping boredom of this combination comes to the forefront again: Can they stay or will they go? Gemini-Dragons have talent, charm, and ability. They have vast quantities of energy and a mind capable of taking on almost anything and doing a great job. They not only dress for success, they have that special activeness that radiates ability.

Famous Gemini-Dragons: Ralph Bellamy, James Brown.

Gemini (Horse) Month Combined with Snake Year

"Reflect" Mercury, Air, Mutable   **"Feel"** Yang-Negative Fire

Characteristics: Extravagance, Self-attractiveness, Discretion, Laziness, Quick-wittedness, Exclusiveness, Impatience, Glibness, Cupidity, Sagacity, Clairvoyance, Compassion, Presumption, Superficiality, Inconstancy, Deception, Indecisiveness, Dissimulation, Perspicacity, Intuition, Flexibility, Performance, Versatility, Dexterity

In this combination there is a deep and almost profound nature that can be tapped. At the same time they have an extra sense—they can see what others cannot see. These qualities have the potential to be astonishing gifts, but gifts of character are always just that—potential. They must be actualized to mean anything. This combination is an odd one and perhaps the most perplexing of them all. There is a very unique aspect to the Gemini-Snake, and there is no doubt they can lead a life that is highly successful. The contradictory personality of this combination, however, is that the Gemini-Snake has seemingly dozens of hurdles to jump and traps to avoid in order to make it. One of the biggest issues that this combination has to deal with is that they are otiose. Plainly put, they are lazy. They also think they are God's gift—not only to the world, but to the entire cosmos itself. They are adored and they have fans, followers, and groupies. They probably have lovers galore. This is twofold because they do attain their awesome potential and, most importantly, they are happy. There are no easy answers for this, and generalizations are risky. But there are hints about those questions. Those qualities almost guarantee that problems will develop on the road to success. In fact, the road might be so filled with potholes and collapsed bridges that it will be impossible to reach the end. To overcome the challenges is practically impossible, even for the intellectual and intuitive Gemini-Snake.

Romance: Individuals in this combination have to relentlessly fight their lethargy and never cease smiling through their gloom. But this, for a highly intelligent individual, is possible, so they tend to do it. Most Gemini-Snakes do attain some level of success as, for example, college professors. Most go through life experiencing a certain degree of angst born of the intellect and the fact that they have a pretty good idea of what tomorrow might bring. Again, a level of contentment is possible for some.

Relationships: Virgos, in particular Tigers and Boars, are not suggested for this combination. Additional combinations to avoid are Sagittarius-Tigers or -Boars or Pisces-Tigers or -Monkeys. Scorpios, particularly the Tigers, should be strictly avoided. Recommendations for this combination are Aries and Aquarius, particularly -Roosters and -Buffalos. Also, Leo-Dragons and -Buffalos as well as Libra-Dogs and -Buffalos are good choices.

Family Life: The Gemini-Snake makes a good enough aunt or uncle who pays a visit from time to time, but being mommy or daddy is just not the best thing for a person who lives in a state of existential tension and ontological suspension. The nature of this combination is not especially suited for parenthood, especially for small children. They do not feel comfortable with hand puppets, dolls, or making silly noises. Even watching cartoons is out of the question.

Livelihood: Generally they are highly educated individuals and tend to do the things that one would expect of the educated, both in their vocation and avocations. There is little doubt that the Gemini-Snake will reach some level of accomplishment. They are very astute and anything regarding mental work is generally easy for them. They can be educators, lawyers, or writers, or one of myriad other professions.

Famous Gemini-Snakes: Bob Dylan, John Fitzgerald Kennedy, Beverly Sills, Jean Paul Sartre.

Gemini (Horse) Month Combined with Horse Year

"Reflect" Mercury, Air, Mutable   **"Command"** Yang-Positive Fire

Characteristics: Selfishness, Autonomy, Pragmatism, Haste, Rebellion, Unscrupulousness, Dexterity, Accomplishment, Anxiety, Perspicacity, Superficiality, Deception, Indecisiveness, Performance, Persuasiveness, Flexibility, Dexterity, Style, Versatility, Inconstancy, Quick-wittedness, Glibness, Impatience, Popularity

This combination is loaded with ability of all sorts. Given all this, one would think that the Gemini-Horse is away and running and the winner of the Triple Crown. The problem is that they are at war with themselves, and

that gets in the way. The Gemini-Horse wants liberty, popularity, and soul. Particularly the latter relates to this combination, and it does so in every sense of the word. They will not be pushed, and they want to be themselves. Their artistic selves cry out for expression, and they are absolutely able to express themselves, usually in music or the visual arts. Their refusal to conform to other people's wishes—including, for example, the boss—and their insistence on being themselves thwarts their drive and significant success. It is entirely possible that they will find a career in a field they love. Maybe they are members of a band or maybe they are successful in the visual arts. Maintaining that success, and most certainly moving higher on the ladder, can be very difficult for a combination that is a rebel with a cause and that cause is usually themselves. This combination is not lazy. They work and they generally do so responsibly. But they want to work sexy and they want to work cool and they want to work popular. Often that is not possible.

Romance: This combination needs someone who is kind, compassionate, giving, talented, good looking, understanding, tolerant, sexy, and perfect. Of course they are not likely to find such a person, and this results in problems with relationships and romance. The result might be a series of shallow love affairs full of bells and whistles but residing in an abandoned factory. This combination is looking for the knight in shining armor, and he must be tall, dark, and handsome. They are looking for their princess: the most beautiful one in the world. What they want is an ideal.

Relationships: Best left off the list for this combination are Virgo- or Scorpio-Buffalos and the Sagittarius-Buffalo for compatibility. Do not consider Virgo-, Pisces-, and Sagittarius-Rats or a Pisces-Boar. Probably at the top of the list of romantic candidates are Leo- and Aquarius-Dogs and Aquarius-Tigers. Aries-Rams, however, as well as -Tigers and Libra-Rams also make the list.

Family Life: This combination loves the home, but that is not necessarily to say that these individuals are homebodies. They are not. Yes, they do take very good care of their abode and it works for them. It is a place to rest and recover from the assorted explosions that are generally a part of this combination's life: some of which take place in that very home. The house might be made of stone or bricks and it is very hard to crumble, but it might be tested by the Gemini-Horse themselves. There might be more than the average number of hot colors in the decor as well, perhaps reflecting a highly charged person.

Livelihood: Their home base is ego centered, however. Their reflections are of themselves and, in particular, the problems they have in life. At that point they often return to their stable, being led rather than being pushed. Gemini-Horses are at one and the same time directed inwardly and outwardly. Needless to say, this is problematic. The outward direction is often a push against others, flying in the face of their own distaste for being pushed.

Famous Gemini-Horses: Igor Stravinsky, Josephine Baker, Margaret Bourke-White, Paul McCartney.

Gemini (Horse) Month Combination with Ram Year
"Reflect" Mercury, Air, Mutable   *"Reliance"* Yang-Negative Fire
Characteristics: Whimsy, Tardiness, Good Manners, Pessimism, Lack of Foresight, Impracticality, Sensitivity, Taste, Perseverance, Self-deception, Inconstancy, Superficiality, Invention, Indecisiveness, Flexibility, Perspicacity, Versatility, Worry, Performance, Dexterity, Quick-wittedness, Glibness, Impatience, Parasitism

This combination can be absolutely needy when it comes to others. Ramming (no pun intended) headfirst into this neediness is the Gemini in a reversal of characters, because they tend to be shooting stars. Dialectical combinations make for some interesting characters, and the Gemini-Ram is certainly one. They can be busy as bees, but most certainly not all the time—they get tired. One trait that tends to rise to the surface is akin to cynicism and results in frequent sharp and critical comments to others. But it should be clear that they do need people to make these very comments to. These individuals are not exactly psychic, but they are very insightful, probably because of their skills at communication. This is also reflected in their aptitude in the arts. Finally, in the communications department, the Gemini-Ram is a shameless gossip. However, what they need more than anything else is security. The Gemini is also a communicator, so the result here can be razor-sharp comments sprinkled with intelligence and humor. Their bite and their humor can just as easily be focused on themselves.

Romance: This combination loves and needs the company of other people. They also love and need a certain amount of flexibility in the loyalty realm, especially when they are younger. This combination is not known for its fidelity, but this is in fact quite the contrary. Living up to the image of many Gemini, they enjoy playing and they enjoy it a lot. This does not mean they want to live alone. They do not.

Relationships: Because of Gemini-Rams' tendency toward utilizing their freedom, they need someone who is more like a rock. That means staying away from Virgo- or Scorpio-Buffalos, as well as Virgo-, Sagittarius-, and Pisces-Dogs and Pisces-Tigers. Some good romantic picks are the Aries-Rabbit or Libra-Horse or -Boar. Aquarius-Rabbits and -Boars and Leo-Horses also capture this combination's attention.

Family Life: This combination is the general and tactician and the person to whom everyone looks for guidance. The Gemini-Ram makes a good parent and, with someone who is open-minded and somewhat tolerant, a good spouse. The Gemini-Ram is a natural parent and loving family member. While they do go on journeys, both literal and metaphorical, they enjoy time at home with those they love. The home is the headquarters of their heart, and that headquarters is the location of all the significant activities of their life. In addition, it is comfortable and there is a place for everything and everything is in its place, including the children.

Livelihood: This combination makes excellent followers but not particularly good leaders. They prefer not to be in management positions. This combination is a good worker and, even though negative and complaining at times, is responsible. These individuals have an aptitude for the artistic and perhaps the performing arts where it is possible they can be successful.

Famous Gemini-Rams: Arthur Conan Doyle, John Wayne, Herve Alphand, Pauline Kael, Brooke Shields.

Gemini (Horse) Month Combined with Monkey Year

"Reflect" Mercury, Air, Mutable   **"Arrange"** Yin-Positive Metal

Characteristics: Leadership, Silliness, Wit, Ruse, Opportunism, Zeal, Deceit, Improvisation, Cunning, Loquacity, Stability, Self-involvement, Self-deception, Dexterity, Superficiality, Inconstancy, Perspicacity, Indecisiveness, Flexibility, Performance, Versatility, Quick-wittedness, Glibness, Impatience

Both the Gemini and the Monkey have an abundance of energy and are very spontaneous. Of course the Gemini is a talker, and the Monkey exacerbates this in this combination. Part of that comes from the performing Monkey element in the combination; they are shameless show-offs of the most blatant type. The Gemini-Monkey combination is a bundle of energy mixed with a bundle of loquaciousness and large doses of party animal thrown in for good measure. They are a human perpetual motion machine that shuns sleep in favor of action. This penchant for the big show carries over to the home and throughout their lives. All this is perhaps the origin of the saying "more fun than a barrel full of monkeys." That many, however, might be a bit much for those of us who are mere mortals in this area. If you want a party, an extravaganza, or even a presidential inauguration, this is the combination for you. It will all go off without a hitch, and it will go down in the annals of people's lives as the most successful and the most fun ever. They love it and they can plan it.

Romance: Flying to Paris for the weekend is not out of the question for this combination. If, in the unlikely event that they are not that affluent, they will serenade their lover under their bedroom window and throw chocolates at them. This combination can sweep people off their feet, and they do it with passion and creativity. This combination is the ultimate romantic and perhaps the most highly charged one you have ever met. In love and in the bedroom, they tend to get their way. That is true not so much because they are obnoxiously demanding, it is true because they are so skilled at seduction and so creative in their methods. If there is money involved, the Gemini-Monkey will spend it on romance.

Relationships: Poor choices for this combination include the Virgo-Tiger or -Snake, or a Sagittarius-Buffalo, -Snake, or -Dog. Perhaps the worst of all is the Capricorn-Snake. A couple of good romantic choices for compatibility are the Libra-Rat or -Dragon. Additionally there are Aries-Dragons and -Monkeys as well as Leo-Rats and Aquarius-Dragons among the possibilities.

Family Life: Comfort, as it is with many Geminis, is the key for them, although they do not object to stylishness as long as it is not flashy. Classic refinement is more to their liking. This combination makes good parents but tends to be on the serious side and insists on good manners. Gemini-Monkeys enjoy the home. In their case, however, home needs to be plural because they frequently like more than one. Several, in radically different environments, would be best. That desire is not necessarily a part of their inclination for showmanship, at least not relative to showing off class or status or finances.

Livelihood: This combination likes change and flexibility. In fact, they might like it more than any other combination. Being entrenched in a position that does not allow variety and diversity is not for the Gemini-Monkey. They do not generally make good accountants. The seriousness these people possess actually is ingrained deeply in their being. It is, in many ways, a gift for them. The gift is one that gives them an aptitude for doing intellectual jobs that require detail and exactitude. But this should not be taken to imply that they want to remain in one position for their entire life. They may do well as a scientist or automobile designer.

Famous Gemini-Monkeys: Paul Gauguin, Marquis de Sade, Ian Fleming, Duchess of Windsor.

Gemini (Horse) Month Combined with Rooster Year

"Reflect" Mercury, Air, Mutable *"Conqueror"* Yang-Negative Metal
Characteristics: Impatience, Quick-wittedness, Candor, Blind Faith, Dissipation, Conservatism, Pedantry, Bossiness, Humor, Perspicacity, Flexibility, Cockiness, Chic, Versatility, Performance, Glibness, Dexterity, Resilience, Superficiality, Boastfulness, Enthusiasm, Inconstancy, Self-deception, Indecisiveness

This is the great communicator in the form of the Gemini and the wonderfully attired Rooster parading around with total self-assurance. Anything requiring standing in front of crowds and the entertainment field in any capacity is designed for this combination. There is no better actor, performer, and entertainer than the Gemini-Rooster. There probably are none better on the planet, at least when it comes to confidence, presentation, and flexibility. That includes the act put on by doctors with good bedside manners. Knock them down or put them down and they will arise every time. They will not push you or punish you. It is fine to carry on doing things your own way, but there is a strong likelihood you will lose the benefit of their wisdom. They will entertain you regardless of what you elect to do. They do not quit. Reject them or neglect them and they are unfazed. There is a deep and profound sense of confidence in this sign. If you want to do something correctly, ask them politely and they will tell you—and yes, they do know how to do things correctly.

Romance: There is probably a bit of a flirt still residing in this combination because of the Gemini element, but these individuals are faithful to the core and there is no question about that. For nearly any combination, but particularly a Gemini, there is exceptional loyalty. They do not forget their lovers, no matter what they have been through in life. They stick with their friends, and there is a good chance that they still know their first love; in fact, they might have married them.

Relationships: Virgo-, Sagittarius-, Capricorn-, and Pisces-Rabbits are not good choices for this combination. Additionally, Sagittarius- and Pisces-Roosters, and Sagittarius-Boars and Pisces-Dogs are not good choices either. There are some excellent romantic picks for this combination including Aries- or Libra-Snakes as well as Leo-Dragons and Aquarius-Buffalos.

Family Life: To some they might appear to be homebody family people, and to some degree that is true. But this combination wants to travel and to experience life. One of the anchors for their home is their children, whom they dearly love. They are, as a result, good parents. The Gemini-Rooster likes to be mobile. That is not to say that they do not enjoy their family, children, and home, but they have itchy feet and a touch of the wanderlust.

Livelihood: Of course anything involving performing is right up Gemini-Roosters' alley, and they would be brilliant at it. As employees they can be good as long as they are given some responsibility, a chance for creativity, and a few people to be subordinates. There are a wide variety of professions at which the Gemini-Rooster can succeed. This combination can lead departments, take care of minute details, or be in positions of leadership.

Famous Gemini-Roosters: Errol Flynn, Anne Murray, Joan Collins, Jane Russell.

Gemini (Horse) Month Combined with Dog Year

"Reflect" Mercury, Air, Mutable   *"Concerned"* Yin-Positive Metal
Characteristics: Self-righteousness, Heroism, Intelligence, Morality, Uneasiness, Criticism, Tastelessness, Duty, Indecisiveness, Quick-wittedness, Cynicism, Constancy, Self-deception, Respectability, Inconstancy, Unsociability, Performance, Dexterity, Impatience, Superficiality, Glibness, Flexibility, Perspicacity, Versatility

This combination has an excellent sense of humor and perhaps more than anything is exceedingly generous and caring. Added to this fine mixture is a lot of talent. The Gemini-Dog lives up to both sides of this combination and in so doing puts a new twist to both. The Gemini in this combination remains friendly and talkative. People can count on them to be responsible and do things right. The kindhearted aspect of the Gemini-Dog has the potential to go too far and weigh down the lighthearted portion. They need to keep the problems of the world, the neighborhood, and themselves in perspective in order to be happy. This combination tends toward the intellectual and the active. Any success they achieve will be done by hard work and following the book strictly. Not only are they moral individuals, they are selfless when it comes to helping others. They can frequently be found heavily involved in charity work. As would be expected from the Gemini element, they are fine communicators and can be quite entertaining.

Romance: They may not sell their soul for the person they love, but they sell everything else. Their lover is perfect in every way. Given this perspective, it is clear that these individuals need someone who is loyal and dedicated to them. If they do not have such a person, they are inclined to flights of fancy where they actually do get in their cars and go to the airport. They need an anchor at home. Operas and romantic Broadway musicals have probably been written about the Gemini-Dog. They are the lead character in every romance ever written, and they wrote the music too.

Relationships: Leo- and Libra-Rabbits are also good picks for this combination, as are Libra- or Aquarius-Tiger, or Virgo-, Sagittarius-, Capricorn- and Pisces-Rams and Pisces-Dragons. Loyalty is paramount to them. Excellent romantic picks for the Gemini-Dog are Aries-, Leo-, and Aquarius-Horses.

Family Life: Their creative character takes the form of a taste for good art and classic design. They love their home, if it is in the right location, and they love their family. While responsible family members, they also see them as a built-in audience for their shows; those tend to be comedic but can be dramatic as well. Gemini-Dogs are drawn to nature and aesthetics. They prefer a home where there are ample forests and streams as part of the surroundings. A connection with Mother Nature is very important to them and their well-being. The big city, with its pollution and crowds and nothing green to be found, disquiets them.

Livelihood: There is a huge element of drama surrounding Gemini-Dogs, and people actually listen to their existential tales and feel the pain. The Gemini-Dog is a traveling circus coupled with a drive-in theater. The tendency toward the aesthetic follows the Gemini-Dog into a profession. The performing arts are fine for them, either as a director or performer. They were born to act and perhaps the dramatic comedy is best suited to them. Professions in the visual arts, including decorating or antiques, are also possibilities.

Famous Gemini-Dogs: Judy Garland, Rainer Werner Fassbinder, Gilda Radner.

Gemini (Horse) Month Combined with Boar Year

"Reflect" Mercury, Air, Mutable   **"Cultivator"** Yin-Negative Water

Characteristics: Honesty, Voluptuousness, Wrath, Materialism, Scrupulousness, Boar-headedness, Credulity, Gallantry, Culture, Sincerity, Superficiality, Inconstancy, Self-deception, Indecisiveness, Versatility, Perspicacity, Flexibility, Performance, Dexterity, Impatience, Hesitation, Quick-wittedness, Glibness

The energetic Gemini tilts some of the sluggish Boar nature in a more positive direction. As with other Gemini combinations, it is hard to thwart them to the point where they will not try again. The Gemini-Boar is an excellent combination with many positive characteristics. Some of the negative aspects of each sign are mitigated by the balanced influence of the complementary sign. This combination is careful but highly flexible. The Boar adds bulk to that nature so that they can blast their way through problems they cannot circumvent. There is, however, the emotional element that is found in most Boars. The stodginess of the Boar is relieved by the gift of humor from the Gemini too. The Gemini-Boar has a quick mind, especially when it comes to problem solving. They have an analytical mind in spite of the occasional weekend in fantasyland.

Romance: Sometimes in love this combination falls for the package instead of what is in it. Sometimes it is because there is nothing in the package, even though it is wrapped well. Fortunately for the Gemini-Boar, there is a strong streak of individualism and they can handle being alone. There is a good person here who unfortunately has a serious problem in the realm of love. Not only do they fall in love easily, but they fall in love with the wrong person in many cases.

Relationships: Poor choices for this combination are a Virgo- and Sagittarius-Monkey. Caution is in order with a Pisces-Rooster. Avoid the Virgo-, Scorpio-, or Pisces-Snake. Fine selections for the Gemini-Boar are the Aries-, Libra-, and Aquarius-Rabbit. Difficulties might arise financially with the Leo- and Aquarius-Ram. However, a Libra-Buffalo is a real possibility.

Family Life: This combination makes excellent parents and becomes involved in the children's lives in a positive way. Because of their ability to problem solve, they tend to have fewer serious problems and a more stable environment. The entire extended family is frequently involved in many aspects of life, including holidays and celebrations. The family life of a Gemini-Boar, after finally finding an appropriate partner, is generally happy. This combination is excellent in terms of taking care of the home front and the family at large.

Livelihood: This combination is, for the most part, fortunate in many aspects of life. Success is written all over the Gemini-Boar, particularly that of the financial variety. You name it and they have the ability. Furthermore, they have the ability not just to do things well, but also to do them happily and to make those they associate with happy. They can manage, organize, sell, bargain, negotiate, and be responsible.

Famous Gemini-Boars: Jacques Cousteau, Henry Kissinger, the Dalai Lama, Christo Francoise.

Cancer (Ram) Month Combined with Rat Year

"Sense" Moon, Water, Cardinal   **"Regulator"** Yin-Positive Water
Characteristics: Sociability, Thirst for Power, Meddling, Guile, Intellectual, Charisma, Skill, Thrift, Appeal, Verbosity, Moodiness, Hypersensitivity, Influence, Nervousness, Affection, Acquisitiveness, Caring, Despondency, Caution, Imagination, Avarice, Irritability, Insight, Tenacity, Possessiveness

There is a reclusive homebody in this combination who shuns the limelight and keeps his personal choices under lock and key. That, however, is not the only side of the Cancer-Rat. The dialectic of the Cancer-Rat combines shrewdness with heavy emotional elements. The moon plays a significant role here. There is a teetering back and forth between external motivational forces and internal ones. By the same token there is unpredictability about them. This combination can, on occasion, be extremely social and extroverted. They are not interested in being ordinary. They want to be unique without being absurd, and they are generally successful at it. It is unlikely that anything vaguely resembling the banal will be found in, on, or around them. That includes everything pertaining to their being and the accoutrements that they showcase. In addition to this, while not flamboyant, they can be a bit showy in terms of their finances, and this usually mean things, expensive things. Their choices in that department vary. It can be art or automobiles. It might be stamps or books. Baseball cards or expensive dolls are even possibilities. In addition to the likelihood of a fine automobile, which is somewhat portable, they appreciate style when it comes to clothing.

Romance: This combination wants to keep the flame of passion and infatuation alive with love itself and is able to because of their intuition and intelligence. Many Cancer-Rats are highly desirable, but all are difficult to tie down and hold on to. They can run and they can hide; they frequently do precisely that. As might be expected, the predicable is of little interest in the area of romance for this combination. They are swift, secure, and secretive in romance as with life.

Relationships: This combination is probably not compatible with Horses, particularly those that are Aries-, Libra-, and Capricorn-. Best ignored are Libra- or Capricorn-Rabbits. This combination cares about love and romance, and thus good picks are Taurus, Virgo, Scorpio, and Pisces. The best choices in those signs are Buffalos and Monkeys.

Family Life: This combination is not necessarily wasteful or compulsive shoppers, though. They are highly protective of not only their home but also especially their family. They are also rather possessive and demanding parents. The Cancer-Rat is materialistic with heavy elements of good taste and style. They like to show their possessions and usually they are well worth showing because of their unique and well-appointed nature. In addition to this, the Cancer-Rat tends to be a collector, not just of the fine things in life, but of food, clothing, or gifts for future use.

Livelihood: There is an extremely strong tendency for Cancer-Rats to be writers. This can perhaps be thought of as a need for self-expression, and that is generally something not well suited for run-of-the-mill jobs. Perhaps some form of art or other creative endeavor can fulfill this need.

Famous Cancer-Rats: Louis Armstrong, Lord Louis Mountbatten, Art Linkletter, Sidney Lumet, Bess Meyerson.

Cancer (Ram) Month Combined with Buffalo Year

"Sense" Moon, Water, Cardinal   "Survivor" Yin-Negative Water

Characteristics: Vindictiveness, Innovation, Bias, Purpose, Stability, Standoffishness, Bigotry, Diligence, Eloquence, Caution, Plodding, Integrity, Hypersensitivity, Strength of Despondency, Stubbornness, Possessiveness, Affection, Caring, Avarice, Moodiness, Imagination, Irritability, Insight, Tenacity

This combination has an almost staggering power and force of creativity, one that is not found in any other combination. The combination of Cancer and the Buffalo is often destined to be an artist of some kind. While this might be surprising to some, an examination of the history of art reveals it to be a fact. The reason for this is because the combination is one of feeling emanating from the Cancer side, along with strength of mind on the part of the Buffalo. There are also qualities of motivation, emotion, and originality. People born under the sign of Cancer-Buffalo invariably are compulsive about not just completing things but about completing them thoroughly and well. Failure is not an option for them. The family and friends of this combination are blessed with a person in their life who returns fidelity and love tenfold. While they are to an extent perfectly capable of being alone, to betray them is to risk serious and sometimes even dangerous wrath. They can have feelings of superiority, and it often shows. They are also insistent on doing things their own way. This carries over into other portions of their life where they tend to resist being told what to do. Because of their insistence on doing things as they see fit, they can be overbearing and occasionally rude to those who do not accept their terms.

Romance: Contrary to other aspects of their life, this combination loves deeply enough to practice give-and-take in their relationship. They can be extremely romantic and loving. As with other parts of their life, however, it is unwise to betray a Cancer-Buffalo. The Cancer-Buffalo is a dedicated and loving partner in romance and in life itself. They tend to be monogamous and loyal to the one they love. In addition, they often have lifelong relationships with the one they marry or partner with.

Relationships: In this combination an Aries- or Libra-Ram would probably not be a wise selection. Additional poor choices are Libra-Tigers and Capricorn-Tigers and -Dragons. Good relationship choices are the Virgo-, Pisces-, or Taurus-Rooster. Other good selections would be a Virgo-, Scorpio-, or Pisces-Rat. Scorpio- and Pisces-Snakes are also possibilities in the love department.

Family Life: The importance that the combination places on their family shows clearly in their home; it is lovely, loving, and shines with loyalty. There is a strong tendency toward home in this combination, and that translates into a base that is both welcoming and beautiful.

Livelihood: At the core, this combination is probably not an accountant, stockbroker, or physicist. What there is, and very much so, is more than likely an artist. This combination is the sort of person who has probably known what they wanted to be and planned for it since youth. There is water, water everywhere because both signs are water signs. Water is powerful but also soft.

Famous Cancer-Buffalos: Peter Paul Rubens, Henry David Thoreau, Jean Cocteau, Barbara Cartland, Tom Stoppard, David Hockney, Merv Griffin, Meryl Streep, Princess Diana.

Cancer (Ram) Month Combined with Tiger Year

"Sense" Moon, Water, Cardinal   **"Observe"** Yang-Positive Wood

Characteristics: Authority, Intemperance, Hotheadedness, Itinerancy, Swagger, Magnetism, Impetuosity, Disobedience, Good Luck, Caution, Hypersensitivity, Bravery, Benevolence, Moodiness, Fervor, Despondency, Caring, Affection, Possessiveness, Avarice, Irritability, Imagination, Tenacity, Insight

Restlessness mingles with moderation in the Cancer-Tiger, and the more sensitive Cancer probably cannot contain the Tiger side. It is not that Cancers do not have good common sense; they do. Rather, it is that they are so sensitive that they will probably be unable to advise restraint. There is a strong likelihood of some kind of dialectical clash here with diametrically opposed traits residing in the same psyche. Consider the existential pessimism of the Cancer mixed with the person who longs to be a Thai boxer; this is the result. The sensitivity of the Cancer is blended with a person who is easily bored and likes to go on the prowl. All of this can potentially lead to either a train wreck or an Academy Award for the best dramatic comedy. Heavy doses of learned advice phrased to get the Tiger's attention are necessary but likely not forthcoming from the Cancer who is too busy buried in a restraining mood of one sort or another. This combination can be a difficult one. It is entirely possible that bad faith can result from this, and the fantasyland of delusion can be the result.

Romance: There is no need for flash or glitter with this combination, but there is a need for substance and there is a need for respect. Like most of us, flattery can get you everywhere with a Cancer-Tiger. After the slow start lessons are learned, and it is likely this combination will have a meaningful love life when more mature. The Cancer-Tiger is a slow bloomer in the area of love and romance. At first it might appear that they have no luck whatsoever. A lot of time is wasted on what turns out to be infatuations and shallow relationships. While they might be full of sexual attraction and other fun and games, they lead nowhere.

Relationships: For this combination, Aries-, Libra-, or Capricorn-Monkeys are no-gos, as are Aries- and Libra-Snakes. Also to be avoided are Aries-

and Libra-Buffalos. Finally, the Libra-Ram is certainly a poor choice. Taurus-, Virgo-, and Scorpio-Dogs are fine choices in the romance department. Additionally, Scorpio- and Pisces-Dragons and Pisces-Horses, are very real and good possibilities. Among the better selections, too, is the Pisces-Boar.

Family Life: The temperamental Cancer confronts the highly charged and positive Tiger and a canyon of difference results. However, in the area of parenthood, this combination is excellent because of the home-loving Cancer and the adventure-seeking Tiger. Children are drawn to this and a special bonding takes place. Quite clearly in the area of the home there are issues with the Cancer-Tiger combination. Cancers are homebodies who are family oriented, and, to put it mildly, Tigers are not. There are opposites involved here, and the life and home of this combination reflects that.

Livelihood: In this combination, while there is the ability, there is sometimes not the full toolbox to complete the task in the innovation department. The plans are drawn or the novel is written, and it remains in a drawer, never to be acted on. With the right partner, spouse, or mentor this unfortunate waste can be avoided. This combination is not especially materialistic. While it is true that planning, purpose, home, and family are among the elements in this mixture, the Tiger makes for an individual who is touchy and fidgety, perhaps even distracted. In the long run this will result in the creativity of the Cancer dissipating and being lost.

Famous Cancer-Tigers: Richard Rodgers, Elisabeth Kübler-Ross, Diana Rigg.

Cancer (Ram) Month Combined with Rabbit Year

"Sense" Moon, Water, Cardinal   **"Withdraw"** Yin-Negative Wood

Characteristics: Hypochondria, Dilettantism, Longevity, Complexity, Squeamishness, Ambition, Pedantry, Secretiveness, Moodiness, Caring, Tact, Hypersensitivity, Finesse, Prudence, Virtue, Affection, Imagination, Caution, Possessiveness, Tenacity, Avarice, Insight, Despondency, Irritability

The home of this combination is neither a castle nor a fortress, but it is where they like to be. That does not mean, however, that all of their time is spent there. They are quite social creatures and love to visit and party with friends. This combination has essentially no clash at all in terms of its fundamental nature. The Cancer-Rabbit is a home-home combination. That is where their heart and everything they value resides. The value they place on their home shows care, style, comfort, and detail. It is lived in, but it is attractive. They can talk of days gone by without a trace of nostalgia but with a strong sense of place and history. This perhaps stems from their very deep love of their home and a curiosity about how others feel about theirs. So while they may not always be found at home, their interest, and of course their heart, will always be there. They enjoy good conversation and comfort. While there is not a melancholy characteristic about them, there is an interest in history and a longing to visit the past.

Romance: This combination cares for family as well and all the ornaments that go on the family tree. For those who want love, there is no better choice to consult than this combination. Perhaps more than any other combination, the Cancer-Rabbit knows what love is. They care about it so much that they love love itself. They are not interested in passing flings or short-lived infatuations. They do not care about one-night stands or even one-year stands. They need, want, and know love. They also know how to give it. A home for their family that is comfortable physically and emotionally is in the cards for them.

Relationships: In this combination Aries-, Libra-, or Capricorn-Tigers and Capricorn-Dragons or -Roosters are not recommended. Concentrate on those signs and combinations interested in the home and the family: Taurus, Virgo, and Scorpio. Among those signs the best are Rams, Dogs, and Boars. Pisces-Rabbits are also fine choices for this combination.

Family Life: This combination enjoys their home, and when seen there, their joy is obvious in their smile. Finally, the Cancer-Rabbit is a fantastic parent. They are loving, caring, and sharing. They tend to push their children a bit, but it is done with a loving touch. Yes, it is the home that is the main focus once again. If a person is looking for a Cancer-Rabbit, the first place to look is there. Their home is not something from the army five minutes prior to inspection, but it is totally and completely organized. The motto of this combination is obviously a place for everything and everything in its place.

Livelihood: This combination can be nearly anything they choose. Education is a good choice, but so are things pertaining to the written word such as printing or writing itself. Finally, they are excellent and responsible employees. They are as loyal at work as they are at home, and they are always interested in new developments in their chosen field. This is the ultimate homebody. That means that they are happy and busy there. They have endless projects they love. The word *boredom* is not in their vocabulary. None of this is to say that their talents are only domestically oriented.

Famous Cancer-Rabbit: Neil Simon.

Cancer (Ram) Month Combined with Dragon Year

"Sense" Moon, Water, Cardinal *"Take Charge"* Yang-Positive Wood

Characteristics: Sentimentality, Braggadocio, Enthusiasm, Volubility, Hypersensitivity, Pluck, Dissatisfaction, Mistrust, Infatuation, Caution, Success, Despondency, Rigidity, Strength, Affection, Good Health, Avarice, Caring, Moodiness, Possessiveness, Imagination, Irritability, Insight, Tenacity

In this combination the Dragon mollifies the angst of the Cancer, and the boastfulness of the Dragon is lightened by the poise of the Cancer. A charming and sensual individual enters the picture. The strength of this combination resides in psychological resilience. They have an ability to feel but also have vim and vigor. There is, of course, the Cancer's deep sensitivity in this personality, but at the same time there is the courage and force of the Dragon. Mix in some passion and an extraordinary ability to sense the nature of life, and a forceful figure arises. There is, however, an element of internal conflict in the dialectic of the Cancer-Dragon. Dragons tend to be above the schmaltzy, but not the Cancer-Dragon. Emotions are always right below the surface with this individual, and that is often the direction that they tilt when it comes to decision making. While they do have a persona of power and ability, they are often deeply sensitive underneath that facade. Home is a magnet for the Cancer element, but the Dragon wants to sail the seas and visit every port. As with all dialectical issues, something generally comes into the picture to decide issues, and in the case of the Cancer-Dragon it is the sentimental character of its nature.

Romance: Supreme self-confidence conjoins in this combination with abject insecurity. This part of the life of a Cancer-Dragon is difficult at best, and it is exacerbated by sentimentality and thin skin. Clearly for any sort of happiness in this area to ever happen, risks must be taken, but they should be taken with caution. Of course the same emotional mix found in the overall character of the Cancer-Dragon is present in the area of love and romance, and it is a very stormy mix. Ambivalence rules a lot of time, and love versus hatred can almost be a way of life.

Relationships: This combination should avoid Aries-, Libra-, or Capricorn-Dogs, Capricorn- or Libra-Buffalos, and Aries-Rabbits. Worth looking at are Taurus-, Scorpio-, and Pisces-Monkeys. Also good possibilities are Scorpio- or Pisces-Rats. On the list too are Taurus- or Pisces-Snakes, as well as Taurus-Boars and -Roosters.

Family Life: This combination has a large and deluxe presence, and the home probably needs a gardener to maintain the spacious grounds. The point is to be impressive and the result is exactly that. The Cancer-Dragon is a fine parent who dearly loves the children. In exchange for love and, of course, security, this combination wants a well-behaved offspring who can be shown off to others. It should come as no surprise that the home is important, because that is true for all Cancers. The issues are the elements added by the Dragon. The influence here results in something less than gaudy but more than the stylish.

Livelihood: This combination possesses an aura of leadership, so management positions are a real possibility. This is true in general, but others sometimes have difficulty being as demanding as necessary for others to respect them. Fortunately they have enough intuition to sort things out in most cases. Education is important in the life of this combination because their natural leadership abilities can be brought forward by acquiring the right credentials. Fortunately the Cancer-Dragon loves learning and is a responsible and active student.

Famous Cancer-Dragons: Haile Selassie, Pablo Neruda, Jean-Baptiste Camille Corot, Pearl Buck, Olivia de Havilland, Ringo Starr.

Cancer (Ram) Month Combined with Snake Year

"Sense" Moon, Water, Cardinal　　　*"Feel"* Yang-Negative Fire

Characteristics: Exclusiveness, Presumption, Compassion, Caring, Laziness, Discretion, Sagacity, Clairvoyance, Cupidity, Caution, Dissimulation, Hypersensitivity, Affection, Intuition, Attractiveness, Possessiveness, Despondency, Moodiness, Avarice, Imagination, Irritability, Insight, Tenacity, Extravagance

This combination has the influence of the Snake, which is fortunate. The positive influence of the Cancer creates a Snake that is less likely to bite, has less venom, and is less cold-blooded. The Cancer-Snake has a more realistic view of themselves than most other Cancers. There is a keen awareness of the flaws in their own personality and character coupled with a deep sense of family and, of course, home. The emotional lows of this combination are not as low as those of other Cancers, and the lows are not as long lasting. Cancers might play the blues, but that can charm the Snake. This combination cannot only be charmed, they can also be charming—but not to the degree that they think. Seeking an Oscar, they generally settle for a bit part, but their cleverness is able to manipulate this into bigger and better things. This combination, thanks to the Snake, is slick and sneaky. They are not above bending the truth. They are, however, quite intelligent about it and are seldom caught because of their slippery personalities. They are, quite clearly, able to find openings of all sorts: openings for escape and openings for opportunity.

Romance: Because of the relentless temptations the combination faces, they are not especially loyal, particularly in love. However, they most certainly are enticing and beguiling. In addition they are very kind and caring people with huge hearts. That is true with nearly all who are close to them. The Cancer-Snake is highly desirable and sought after for their looks and their sex appeal. Some actually have something akin to groupies. Hidden from view are some qualities that are not necessarily flattering, including a desire to control, requiring more than should be expected, and being almost unmanageable.

Relationships: Aries-Tigers or -Monkeys probably don't even make the short list for this combination. Capricorn-Tigers and -Boars and Libra-Boars are left off completely. Almost all Roosters make the list of possible lovers. Perhaps the best choices are Taurus, Virgo, Scorpio, and Pisces. Additionally, Buffalos of these types are fine picks.

Family Life: Given the financing, they would have homes scattered all over the world and in every type of environment imaginable: the mountains, the beach, the city, Paris, the Alps, and maybe one in Kathmandu as well. The impressive thing is there are children everywhere, as well as friends, relatives, household staff, and more. This is a high-powered home combination. Of course, home is profoundly important to this combination and nearly doubly so. That might even be tripled, because the Cancer-Snake likes not just home but the plural, *homes*.

Livelihood: With maturity this combination changes, and that change comes from the realization that work and money are connected. Paying the piper means hearing the song. That does not mean that vacations and weekends are not used for rest and relaxation, but it does mean that the bugle call is answered when money is involved. In almost typical youthful fashion, the Cancer-Snake avoids work, study, and responsibility as much as possible. Sleeping in instead of mowing the lawn and being late with the book report are to be expected.

Famous Cancer-Snakes: Andrew Wyeth, Peter Maas, Ashley Montagu.

Cancer (Ram) Month Combined with Horse Year

"Sense" Moon, Water, Cardinal **"Command"** Yang-Positive Fire

Characteristics: Anxiety, Insight, Pragmatism, Accomplishment, Autonomy, Unscrupulousness, Rebellion, Popularity, Style, Haste, Persuasiveness, Caution, Dexterity, Hypersensitivity, Selfishness, Caring, Despondency, Affection, Avarice, Moodiness, Imagination, Possessiveness, Tenacity, Irritability

This combination loves so deeply and is so giving that they will even do so with no reciprocation whatsoever on the part of their partner. The Cancer-Horse is probably the most dedicated and loving partner of all the combinations. Many people claim that they would do anything for the person they love. In the case of the Cancer-Horse, this is literally true. This is all the result of the extraordinary romantic streak in the Horse coupled with the love of home and family of the Cancer. The Cancer-Horse will work two jobs to take care of their partner and the children and essentially do it alone because of their dedication and forbearance, but mostly from pure, unselfish, and unconditional love. This combination is careful in their decision-making process. They have a firm list of priorities, and that list is populated with those they love and the home they share. Of course, involved here is a stoicism and patience well beyond that of most mere mortals. Stoicism, as a philosophy, is a guiding principle and this combination is bound by principles. They also have intelligence, which helps them navigate stormy waters and live a rich and meaningful internal life.

Romance: The romantic fervor in this combination is unlikely to fade with the passage of time. The trickiest part of all for this combination is not necessarily to find someone deserving of them but to find someone who understands them and reciprocates their love—at least to some degree. The Cancer-Horse has love to share and love to spare. All they need is a person to share it with. This necessitates finding a deserving person, and whoever it is should probably consider themselves lucky. This combination is tender and affectionate, and that is more than likely something that will continue throughout a relationship.

Relationships: Very bad choices for this combination are Aries-, Libra-, and Capricorn-Rats. Also to be avoided are Aries- or Libra-Buffalos, as well as Aries- or Capricorn-Boars. Some top-of-the-line romantic picks for the Cancer-Horse are Taurus, Virgo, Scorpio, and Pisces, especially those in the Tiger, Ram, and Dog categories. For Dogs, the best choices are Taurus and Scorpio.

Family Life: In this combination their refrigerator is open to their friends, and there is no need to worry about turning on their TV. They chat in a homespun style and gossip with the best of them. They make people happy. And, once this is accomplished, they themselves are happy. The Cancer-Horse is friendly and welcoming. Of course their home must be friendly too, and that means comfortable. This combination's home is not a museum or a showcase; this home is a place to live. It is clean and well kept, but it is not a place that causes fear about relaxing.

Livelihood: Workers from this combination are diligent, creative, and well liked. Not many can work harder than the Cancer-Horse, with the exception of the Buffalo. As a result, they tend to do just fine financially. Both those who hire them and those who work for them are fortunate. They are excellent at hosting parties and always willing to spend some of their hard-earned cash. This combination is multitalented and multifaceted. They are capable of doing nearly anything from crafts to poetry. As a result their family is well taken care of, and their children have good foundations.

Famous Cancer-Horses: Rembrandt, Duke of Windsor, Ingmar Bergman, Karen Black.

Cancer (Ram) Month Combined with Ram Year

"Sense" Moon, Water, Cardinal   **"Reliance"** Yang-Negative Fire

Characteristics: Taste, Impracticality, Perseverance, Manners, Worry, Good Affection, Tardiness, Pessimism, Whimsy, Caution, Caring, Lack of Foresight, Invention, Hypersensitivity, Parasitism, Avarice, Imagination, Insight, Tenacity, Despondency, Irritability, Moodiness, Possessiveness, Sensitivity

This combination does not just make the children laugh, they make everyone laugh, and they make everyone happy. Along with all this is a deep sensitivity. Friends and lovers alike hurt them, but they are, nevertheless, loyal to the end. Whether they fall or they are pushed, they invariably get up. The Cancer-Ram combination is cute but strong. They have a terrific sense of humor. Like most Cancers, they know what love is, and when they love it is completely and for the long-term. In addition to this, there is kind of an endearing craziness about them. This combination, like some others in their group, is of the "place for everything and everything in its place" approach to life. They take good citizenship seriously and are probably active in a civic group or charity. They are at minimum survivors and can stage comebacks so great they might even be heroes. A lot of this is probably the result of the child in them, and that child is not just an inner one. It is there for all to see. They fall off their bikes, bruised and scraped, and get right back on. This combination is friendly and generous with everyone. They strive for fairness in all things, perhaps because they have been treated unfairly at some time in their life. That, among other difficulties, is something the Cancer-Ram has risen above and recovered from.

Romance: Once again, this is a Cancer who gives unconditional love to his or her partner and to their children. They love activities with the family no matter what they may be. In exchange for this loving gift, the Cancer-Ram wants attention. That does not mean they want to be the boss or even have the leading role. What it means is they want to be at the center of things. For this combination it is about love. No doubt they have a Ph.D. in that field. They know how to love, how to show it, and how to feel it. Devotion is this combination's middle name. In addition to this endearing quality, they can laugh not just with others but at themselves as well.

Relationships: The Dog sign does not make the best sexual partner for this combination. Aries- and Capricorn-Buffalos are not good choices either. Not making the list at all are Libra- and Capricorn-Tigers. Top-of-the-line romantic choices for this combination are Taurus-, Virgo-, and Scorpio-Horses. Other fine choices are Taurus-, Scorpio-, or Pisces-Rabbits. Also in the mix are Taurus-, Virgo-, Scorpio-, and Pisces-Boars, as well as Aries-, Libra-, and Capricorn-Dogs.

Family Life: This combination is about Earth. They are a child of the Earth, and they welcome all who come from the Earth. They are not necessarily the most diligent in terms of memory, but they are probably the most loving person you have ever met. It is not surprising that this combination loves their family, and that includes the extended family. All are welcome, not only aunts and uncles but cousins and of course the children and the children's third cousins twice removed and great-aunts and -uncles. Bring them all, including the in-laws, their neighbors, and the family dog.

Livelihood: This combination will happily spend money on their family and close friends. They like to throw a good party and give presents to far-flung relatives on their birthdays. Creative jobs are possible for the Cancer-Ram. This includes assorted types of designers and the fashion industry too. The Cancer-Ram does not have the mind of an accountant or the interests of a stockbroker. They are, plainly put, terrible about planning financial matters. The bill will be paid late, but probably before there is a penalty due. They probably have not been as good as they should about saving for retirement.

Famous Cancer-Rams: Franz Kafka, Buckminster Fuller, Iris Murdoch.

Cancer (Ram) Month Combined with Monkey Year

"Sense" Moon, Water, Cardinal   **"Arrange"** Yin-Positive Metal

Characteristics: Zeal, Opportunism, Stability, Silliness, Loquacity, Hypersensitivity, Self-involvement, Caution, Wit, Leadership, Ruse, Improvisation, Despondency, Deceit, Cunning, Affection, Caring, Possessiveness, Moodiness, Insight, Avarice, Irritability, Tenacity, Imagination

This combination likes to turn things on their heads to examine them from another perspective. They check out the unpopular to discover what is wrong. They have a streak of nonconformity in them and also an ability to discern its potential. The Cancer-Monkey is active, alert, and always thinking. They cannot only organize like most Cancers, they can figure things out. Sure they have the will to find the way, but most important they have the intelligence to figure out solutions. New ideas from others do not put this combination off, and they are perfectly able to develop their own too. Collecting things, both literally and intellectually, is a trait from the Monkey side of the combination. Sure, like most people, they love some sort of stature or recognition, but they are tasteful if not delicate about it. In the end this combination will probably get what they want and do it without stepping on toes. They know the steps to getting there and the slippery slopes to avoid. They like bits of information and unusual objects, perhaps bracelets from Cambodia or pieces of marble from Indiana. None of this makes the Cancer-Monkey an effete intellectual snob. They actually are down-to-earth individuals with a tendency to march to the beat of their own conga drum.

Romance: People in this combination are always worried that their partner is off doing exactly what they are doing. It is not that they are bad people or disloyal in other areas. It is just that their call of duty is different from most people, and they generally heed the call. Phrasing the approach to sex that this combination takes requires a bit of delicacy. However, it is necessary to be frank and honest as well. The Cancer-Monkey likes sex and they like it a lot. This can, and usually does, lead to unfaithfulness to varying degrees. It is just that they have an irrepressible libido. As if this were not enough of a problem, they are very jealous and constantly worried about what their spouse is up to.

Relationships: For this combination it is best to avoid the Libra-Buffalo. Also to be avoided are Aries-, Libra-, and Capricorn-Dogs, as well as Aries- and Capricorn-Horses. Completely out of the picture are Aries-Boars. Excellent selections for this combination are Taurus, Virgo, Scorpio, and Pisces who are Dragons or Rats.

Family Life: As with most Cancers, the Monkey types are very family oriented. They will help and assist all members of their family at any time. There is one possible exception to this, however. Some members of this combination believe that they are better than others in their family, particularly brothers and sisters. This can lead to cool relationships with some members of the family.

Livelihood: While this combination probably will not end up being the president of a company or a world-famous artist, they can attain high-level management positions or make an excellent living as a professional artist. Of course the choice as to area of interest is up to them. Cancers are known to be more sensitive than most, and this is true of the Cancer-Monkey. This has the potential to be a stumbling block in the professional realm. In terms of a profession the sky is not the limit, but there is a good possibility that the Cancer-Monkey can sail above the clouds. This combination has numerous aptitudes in areas aplenty. Consequently it is difficult to select one to emphasize. They are highly motivated and do not, to say the least, avoid positions of power. Quite the contrary, they seek out such positions.

Famous Cancer-Monkeys: Julius Caesar, Lord Byron, Amedeo Modigliani, Nelson Rockefeller, Yul Brynner, Amy Vanderbilt.

Cancer (Ram) Month Combined with Rooster Year

"Sense" Moon, Water, Cardinal **"Conqueror"** Yang-Negative Metal

Characteristics: Bossiness, Humor, Boastfulness, Dissipation, Pedantry, Candor, Conservatism, Chic, Blind Faith, Caution, Resilience, Hypersensitivity, Enthusiasm, Cockiness, Despondency, Moodiness, Possessiveness, Caring, Imagination, Insight, Tenacity, Affection, Irritability, Avarice

The Rooster element in this combination throws a curveball into what might be expected from a Cancer. It's true that they follow the pattern of being sensitive and tender and, to a degree, loving. But there is a sharp, sometimes hurtful tongue in the character of this individual. The Cancer-Rooster combination has an excellent sense of humor. They love to make others laugh and usually succeed. Frequently, and befitting the Cancer, the stories they tell are of home, family, and kids: humorous anecdotes beloved by grandmothers and maiden aunts. However, by all appearances that would not seem to be true. Frequently there is a look of Santa Claus or Mrs. Claus about them. They have succumbed, perhaps more than most Cancers, to the desire for stature. They just do not usually show it. Additionally, they can hold grudges and be extraordinarily vengeful. The Cancer-Rooster works, and they work hard. They help other workers. In short, they make good employees, as long as they are not crossed or caught at a bad moment. They are happy to help others, groups, causes, and neighbors. But they are moody and can come off as without feelings. That smiling, nice, helpful person can turn into a hypercritical, short-tempered complainer.

Romance: This combination was designed to be domestically focused, whether it is with the kitchen or the lawn. The Cancer-Rooster probably invented the saying "home sweet home." The Cancer-Rooster is a faithful and loyal spouse or partner. They can be depended on. They are fundamentally homebodies who like a quiet and peaceful life. Activities around the home are enjoyed, as are other aspects of a more traditional family life. A peaceful and quiet home life is critical to this individual's being.

Relationships: This combination should avoid Aries-, Libra-, and Capricorn-Rabbits. Poor choices are Aries- or Capricorn-Dogs. Out of the question are Libra-Roosters. A Taurus-Horse is not a bad choice, but far better are the Virgo, Scorpio, and Pisces signs that are Buffalos, Dragons, or Snakes. Taurus-Snakes are an especially good choice in the area of romance.

Family Life: In this dialectical struggle, the Cancer influence dominates.

Cancer-Roosters then, in general, are home centered and take a lot of pride in a quality home as well as a quality home life. All Cancers center their being around their homes. On the other hand, the Rooster side of this combination is not particularly concerned about home life. The same can be said about the Rooster's interest in children. It is not that they are bad parents; they just do not define their essence by their offspring.

Likelihood: The Cancer-Rooster is a hardnosed boss who is sometimes difficult to get along with and extremely demanding. They like being the boss because deep inside they like power. However, they are willing to accept a lower post provided that it gives some status or position. The essential nature of this person is serious. They work hard and work well. They pay attention to details and get things done. They are the no-nonsense type and have no interest whatsoever in wasting time or energy.

Famous Cancer-Roosters: John Glenn, Carly Simon, Stavros Niarchos.

Cancer (Ram) Month Combined with Dog Year

"Sense" Moon, Water, Cardinal   **"Concerned"** Yin-Positive Metal

Characteristics: Constancy, Heroism, Morality, Tastelessness, Moodiness, Unsociability, Self-righteousness, Respectability, Insight, Tenacity, Caution, Cynicism, Hypersensitivity, Intelligence, Irritability, Possessiveness, Despondency, Uneasiness, Affection, Caring, Imagination, Criticism, Duty, Avarice

When there is something wrong, a cruel remark or a rude clerk, they are mortified. Everyone and everything has the potential to be the Big Bad Wolf. If someone is a friend of this combination, they will frequently be called on to protect him or her or to reassure him or her that everything is fine. Cancer-Dogs are sensitive, emotional, touchy, easily hurt, thin-skinned, and just about any other adjective one can think of in this department. They have very deep feelings about everything. No matter what it might be in their environment, they are affected by it. They are the sort who frequently asks others what is the matter when there is absolutely no reason to worry about anything. As with all human beings, of course, they have real lives and lead them, and they are not necessarily lives of quiet desperation. They can be happy and fulfilling lives with a family and all the trappings that the rest of humanity has. Cancer-Dogs work hard, and their avocations are generally something creative such as music or art. Of course, as Cancers, home decorating, gardening, and other domestic pursuits are likely. Finally, there are hints of a compulsive character here: a person driven to finish things on time and to never forget anything. Appointment books and calendars were made with them in mind. It is entirely possible that art will be part of their lives, because they have a strong inclination in that area. Regardless of, or perhaps because of, their sensitivity, they are fine problem solvers. They are thoughtful and supremely patient.

Romance: Generally, some sincere and meaningful reassurance and love will put an end to that hypersensitivity. What they need on a steady and reliable basis is attention, affection, and tenderness. If they have that, they can let their love shine through. As with some others of the Cancer group, this individual is very loving. There are a couple of twists in that mix, however. The hypersensitivity of this combination means that they can lash out at people when they feel unloved.

Relationships: This combination should probably not consider the Aries, Libra, and Capricorn signs such as Dragons and Rams. Not making the list at all is the Aries-Boar. At the top of the romance list are Virgo- and Pisces-Rabbits. Additional good choices are Taurus-, Scorpio-, and Virgo-Tigers, and also worth looking at are Taurus-Rats.

Family Life: This combination does not have nests as much as they have beautifully designed and well-kept birdhouses. The reason that things must be beautiful is because of love, and this combination loves their family perhaps more deeply and more truly than any other. The ties here are bound together for eternity. Of course the home is critical, but the essence of this combination is aesthetics. Things that matter are things that are beautiful, and things that are beautiful are loved. That is the internal sensibility that makes a Cancer-Dog tick, and it is what is reflected externally.

Livelihood: Because of this combination's fundamental character they are capable of success in many areas, but it is in the kind of vague realm of caring and empathizing that they do best. They simply are not meant to be robots in a bureaucracy or cogs in a corporate machine. The circle is not broken in the life of a Cancer-Dog. It begins with sensitivity, and it ends there. That means that a profession that is in need of sensitive and creative people is the best for this individual.

Famous Cancer-Dogs: Claude Debussy, Marcel Proust, Jean Anouilh, Alexander Calder, Donald Sutherland, Sylvester Stallone.

Cancer (Ram) Month Combined with Boar Year

"Sense" Moon, Water, Cardinal **"Cultivator"** Yin-Negative Water

Characteristics: Gourmandism, Boar-headedness, Honesty, Tenacity, Culture, Sincerity, Voluptuousness, Hesitation, Materialism, Caution, Gallantry, Hypersensitivity, Credulity, Scrupulousness, Wrath, Affection, Despondency, Moodiness, Possessiveness, Caring, Imagination, Insight, Avarice, Irritability

This combination does not need adulation, commendations, or undying love aimed in their direction. None of this is to say that they do not care about others or desire to be totally left alone. It just means that they are capable of performing on their own. They are kind, generous, and friendly. It is probably safe to say that John Donne, famous for saying "No man is an island entire of itself," never knew a Cancer-Boar, because that is precisely what this combination is. The Platonic Ideal representing self-sufficiency was created by this combination and probably the advertising slogan "Just Do It" was as well. As would be expected, they love their homes and their families. Because Boars like luxury and Cancers like home, it is pretty clear what the result will be: a luxurious home. The Cancer-Boar combination is not one to waste money. They just happen to be very good at managing it. There is, probably because of the Cancer influence, a special knack when it comes to art: especially new talent. They are on the cutting edge in this department. Finances are often invested in real estate and art and this leads to more luxury, and so the ripples in the pond multiply.

Romance: In romance the traditional character of the Cancer-Boar remains in place but is supplemented with an unduly harsh asceticism. This combination needs a vacation from time to time but probably will not take one. It is all about love with this combination, and that means huge, vast, and deep love. Oddly enough, however, the Cancer-Boar's nature often has an equally deep-seated peculiarity in the area of associations. This can and frequently does lead to serious problems in both relationships and psyches alike. Rebounds in negativity are possible. This sometimes results in cynicism in a combination that is extremely sensitive.

Relationships: What is not recommended for this combination are Aries- or Libra-Monkeys or Libra-Snakes. Capricorn-Snakes and -Roosters are not on the list at all. A good romantic selection, and one that this combination is drawn to, is the Taurus-Tiger. Also good choices are Virgo-, Scorpio-, or Pisces-Rabbits or Pisces-Rams. Taurus-Rats are also a real possibility.

Family Life: This combination is loving and generous when it comes to the young in general and have a special knowledge that they, indeed, are the future. Cancer-Boars are lovers of the family. That means the entire family tree, no matter who or where they are. They love the Girl Scouts who sell cookies, the boy who shovels the snow, their grandnephew, and children in need everywhere. Of course they are totally and deeply loving and tender to their own children.

Livelihood: This combination can do it themselves, and they can do it with royal bugles being blown to announce their arrival. They are, at the very least, to be considered for greatness, and there is a chance that they will make it. Besides, there is nothing wrong with being second in line for the throne. This combination is one that monarchs are made of. Yes there is the self-sufficiency, but there is also the persona that they put forward. Walking down the sidewalk on Main Street, they would be recognized as the king or queen regardless of their attire and lack of attendants. They do not need or want attendants.

Famous Cancer-Boars: Henry VIII, Ernest Hemingway, Federico Garcia Lorca, Georges Pompidou, Marc Chagall, John D. Rockefeller.

Leo (Monkey) Month Combined with Rat Year

"Willpower" Sun, Fire, Fixed   **"Regulator"** Yin-Positive Water

Characteristics: Intellectual, Meddling, Skill, Loyalty, Charisma, Sociability, Appeal, Verbosity, Immodesty, Thrift, Nervousness, Thirst for Power, Influence, Philanthropy, Acquisitiveness, Vanity, Tyranny, Warmth, Protection, Promiscuity, Guile, Arrogance, Nobility, Power, Self-satisfaction

If a party planner is needed, even at the very last minute, the Leo-Rat is there. Leo-Rats can also be natural-born motivational speakers or very effective counselors. The Leo-Rat is extremely positive and very talented. They love to have a good time and are capable of turning a negative situation into a party at the drop of a hat. If a person needs cheering up, this is the combination that person should contact. They make fine sports coaches because of their ability to motivate and inspire. This combination is extremely energetic and easily capable of multitasking. Most people would get tired just following them around for the day, even without doing the work they do at each stop. This combination shares and cares but knows how to manage money. They give a helping hand but do not martyr themselves in the process. It is very possible that they will be quite financially successful because of all their abilities and talents. They are joiners and leaders. They can solve problems as well as chitchat with the elite. Creativity is another one of their aptitudes. If you want something designed, they can do it. Other and, in fact all, forms of creativity are in their sights because music and the dramatic arts call them as well.

Romance: This combination works hard. They do not dawdle and they do not care for those who do. They have a deep and long-lasting passion for the things and people they care about, and they have no interest in fiddling around with far-flung places, far-out ideas, or far-fetched love affairs. Leo-Rat is a combination that loves deeply and usually loves forever. They spread their love far and wide. In general, they fall for a "people person" and enjoy being around crowds and ceremonial gatherings.

Relationships: Poor selections for this combination are Taurus-, Scorpio-, or Aquarius-Horses. Really bad picks are Scorpio- or Aquarius-Rabbits. At the top of the list for romance is the Buffalo who is a Gemini, Libra, Capricorn, or Sagittarius. Other good choices are Dragons who are Gemini, Libra, Sagittarius, or Capricorn. Further good choices are Aries-, Gemini-, Libra-, and Capricorn-Monkeys.

Family Life: This combination is terrific at taking care of the home and the family. That is true not just in the food and shelter categories but in the shelter from the storm category too. The family feels safe in their environment. They do that faithfully and they do that well. Fairly obviously stemming from the Rat's influence, this combination likes to have goods safely stored in the house.

Livelihood: In the event that this combination comes into money, they will use it wisely and develop a plan to maximize their assets. If they are not born with a silver spoon in their mouth, they will soon be able to afford their own. A tireless worker, this combination will almost certainly be successful in some area. The most likely areas for success are business, either in the field of management or as a business owner.

Famous Leo-Rats: James Baldwin, Yves St. Laurent, Leon Uris, Gene Kelly, Mata Hari.

Leo (Monkey) Month Combined with Buffalo Year

"Willpower" Sun, Fire, Fixed   **"Survivor"** Yin-Negative Water

Characteristics: Eloquence, Vindictiveness, Plodding, Stability, Immodesty, Standoffishness, Innovation, Diligence, Bias, Bigotry, Integrity, Stubbornness, Strength of Purpose, Arrogance, Vanity, Philanthropy, Warmth, Tyranny, Promiscuity, Protection, Nobility, Loyalty, Power, Self-satisfaction

There is sort of a General George Patton quality to this combination, including the hard outer shell that implies they are both heartless and relentless. They are severe, they are strict, and they are sober. The Leo-Buffalo sets goals, and those goals are attained. The Leo-Buffalo radiates power in everything they do, and that power is real. There is a terrific force in this combination. They are quite capable of lording it over others, and thus they are born leaders. They might not win popularity contests, but people realize and respect their strength. In addition to this they are shrewd and able to find opportunities to exploit. This combination needs to be the focus of everyone's attention at work or committees or clubs. They give speeches but tend to ignore others. Fortunately the Leo-Buffalo has good verbal skills when they choose to employ them. They are intelligent and analytic as well. But do not try to tell them anything; they know it already. They have nerves of steel and relish a good battle, usually winning. Their personalities are distant, reserved at best and off-putting at times. For a good chat, this combination is not the best choice. They are silent and removed, unless it involves a group.

Romance: This combination needs a partner who is both patient and fun loving. They require someone who can humor them out of their seriousness and release someone who can relax and enjoy themselves with love, romance, and the things associated with it, particularly sex. In the love and romance department there is a slightly misaligned dialectic. Buffalos want sex and often that is the extent of it for them. Leos, however, can be reasonably good in the bedroom even though they are not the best. Having fun is the difficulty, because this combination is serious when it comes to nearly everything.

Relationships: Poor choices are Scorpio- and Taurus-Dragons. Also poor selections are Scorpio- and Aquarius-Tigers and Aquarius-Rams. The Taurus-Monkey should be avoided too. Excellent choices for love partnership are Rats, Snakes, and Roosters who are Aries, Gemini, Libra, Sagittarius, and Capricorn signs.

Family Life: You can practically bet this combination will have a home office or special work area and use it because they are hard workers. They are also excellent at planning and preparing nearly anything. They are clean, neat, and tidy. Order prevails in the home of a Leo-Buffalo. The books on their shelves are in alphabetical order and so are the spices in the kitchen. Those spices are used, because this combination is often a terrific chef.

Livelihood: This combination neither looks nor acts like someone who is ready to laugh and joke. To visit friends when a Leo-Buffalo is present is probably to witness them disappear into their study, without comment, in order to get some work accomplished. This combination is not easy for almost any partner. Their dedication to work and their stoic nature do not incline them toward being fun. While it is true that they can be funny in their own way, that humor tends to be caustic for the most part.

Famous Leo-Buffalos: Napoleon, Oscar Peterson, Russell Baker, Robert Redford, Dustin Hoffman.

Leo (Monkey) Month Combination with Tiger Year

"Willpower" Sun, Fire, Fixed   *"Observe"* Yang-Positive Wood

Characteristics: Authority, Good Luck, Disobedience, Itinerancy, Fervor, Swagger, Intemperance, Benevolence, Immodesty, Magnetism, Vanity, Impetuosity, Hotheadedness, Bravery, Protection, Philanthropy, Warmth, Promiscuity, Tyranny, Arrogance, Nobility, Self-satisfaction, Power, Loyalty

When taken singularly, each aspect of this combination is not a problem. However, when Leo is mixed with the Tiger personality, the result is someone who not only thinks they are royalty but also knows they are royalty. As a result they are extraordinarily snobbish. It is difficult to be tactful about some of the issues facing the Leo-Tiger. They are, of course, royalty. Plainly put, they feel superior to everyone and it shows in the way they talk and in the way they carry themselves. What does not show is that being so much better than everyone else is lonely. Leo-Tigers refuse to see themselves for what they are and become cute despite their royalty. Everyone, other than himself or herself, recognizes this for what it is and knows the fundamental insincerity. There is some chance they can come to their own rescue from these difficulties because they possess a great deal of courage, and that is precisely what it takes for a Leo-Tiger to view themselves for what they are. This combination occasionally makes friends, but it is hard for them to keep them. Royalty does not want to have equals around; they want to have yes-men and yes-women around. As if this alone was not difficulty enough, the Leo-Tiger tries to sugarcoat their essence using bad faith.

Romance: Sexual adventures are allowed though, because it is it possible to perhaps find someone who is willing to acknowledge the royal essence of this combination. This mixture makes domestic life essentially impossible, because there are not many who are willing to polish Leo-Tiger's throne on a regular basis. Arrogance is not attractive to most individuals. Romance and emotional attachments are not in the Leo-Tiger's field of vision. What they demand in a partner is almost impossible to find, because, in their eyes, there is essentially no one who is worthy of marrying them.

Relationships: To be avoided in this combination are Taurus-, Scorpio-, or Aquarius-Monkeys as well as Taurus- and Aquarius-Buffalos. Taurus- and Scorpio-Snakes are a certain no-go. A Taurus-Rabbit is also out of the question. There are some possible combinations for the Leo-Tiger to investigate in terms of romance. They are the Aries, Gemini, Sagittarius, and Capricorn signs in the years of the Dragon, Horse, and Dog. Unfortunately the list is short because of the nature of the combination.

Family Life: There is a misconception in the self-image of this combination; they believe that they are a vagabond or a gypsy. Somewhere they view themselves as revolutionary heroes—perfect ones, of course. Leo-Tigers are not so much frugal as they are practical, and that is most certainly obvious in their home. The home, more than anything, is real as well as comfortable. It will most certainly not be filled with fine art or ancient artifacts. It is not cheap, because this combination wants quality for its staying power.

Livelihood: Furthermore, this combination is individualistic. That is the area where they might be best off. Or, perhaps they are right: they are a revolutionary in search of a cause. If they find their cause, that might be right up their alley as a vocation. Charity work or political work, even as a leader, is possible. If that is where they end up, they can put on a real white hat and let go of the pretense. There might be a manager inside the Leo-Tiger, but this is not the best world for them. Their drive toward being human might interfere with telling people what to do.

Famous Leo-Tigers: Emily Bronte, Eric Hoffer, Natalie Wood.

Leo (Monkey) Month Combined with Rabbit Year

"Willpower" Sun, Fire, Fixed   **"Withdraw"** Yin-Negative Wood

Characteristics: Pedantry, Dilettantism, Complexity, Prudence, Immodesty, Longevity, Ambition, Hypochondria, Secretiveness, Tact, Philanthropy, Finesse, Vanity, Squeamishness, Virtue, Tyranny, Loyalty, Warmth, Protection, Promiscuity, Arrogance, Nobility, Power, Self-satisfaction

This combination loves their freedom but maintains the regal and dignified element as well. Greatness is written all over them. The stumbling block here is that this combination does not want to be in the spotlight or to be the leader of the pack. The dialectic that constitutes the Leo-Rabbit is, frankly speaking, awesome. As is often the case in life, however, that does not mean that the result is awesome. Potential is not actuality. This combination is flexible and fast. They move about so quickly that a person might actually not spot them. The Leo-Rabbit has, of course, the royal persona. The combination is intelligent along with being generous, and perhaps that plays a role in them eschewing power. The main cause, however, is that they have delicate characters. They avoid fights of any sort. This combination tends to be, in a manner similar to many Cancers, homebodies. They make excellent friends and avoid trouble deftly. The Leo-Rabbit knows that they are stupendous and does not need others to verify this. Still, there is no sign of egoism, and they make excellent friends. This combination likes to be busy and generally this means they are financially secure. Of course as a Leo, they have a certain amount of vanity in them and love admiration. This is kept somewhat in check, but is, nevertheless, present. Furthermore, as royalty, they do not appreciate being wrong. There is no blatant arrogance about this combination however. They have enough self-confidence to be sure that they are stupendous, so they do not need verification from others.

Romance: This combination can inadvertently come off as being too aggressive in the area of sex. The quick mind of the Leo-Rabbit is more interested in fitting a partner into the metaphysical framework of their life, however, and not so much mere sexuality. They go about things like love and even giving their heart in a rather slow and well-thought-out fashion. This combination is polite and always a lady or a gentleman. Their home and their peace come before most things in their life, and this most certainly includes sex. The Leo-Rabbit is among the most popular signs of all relative to interest by the opposite sex. When they are young they will have admirers aplenty. When they mature it will be difficult to decide which to select.

Relationships: This combination likes people who are involved with their world. That rules out Taurus-, Scorpio-, or Aquarius-Rats and Aquarius-Tigers and -Roosters. Scorpio-Dragons or Taurus-Rabbits are probably best avoided. Fine selections in the area of romance are Aries-, Libra-, and Capricorn-Rams and Capricorn-Boars. Sagittarius-Boars are also possibilities. Members of the Dog family are excellent picks, especially Libra or Sagittarius.

Family Life: This combination makes an excellent home, and the individuals also make fine parents. They tend to push their children a bit, but in the right direction and with loving tenderness. They are also on the strict side and there will be no computer games in the house, and even if there are, the time on them will be limited. When children, Leo-Rabbits are the stay-at-home type and love to study. Expect lots of awards. The Leo-Rabbit needs to inform others that they are a royal person, and this is done with grace and style in the home. Antiques are a must for the Leo-Rabbit. This combination can, on rare occasions, give in to the ostentatious, but that is not done on a large scale and is usually avoided.

Livelihood: In addition to having a wide range of abilities, the Leo-Rabbit is proficient at nearly everything and great at a lot. All of this gives this combination something they love: respect and admiration. While they can get it because of their royal bearing, they prefer to earn it and they do. Regardless of their station in life, this combination accepts it. The fact is though, they are very likely to rise to the top of their profession. The Leo-Rabbit is one of those types who can do anything. Their abilities carry across the brawn category all the way over to brains. For them, work has intrinsic value and is its own reward.

Famous Leo-Rabbits: Fidel Castro, Ring Lardner, Peter Bogdanovich.

Leo (Monkey) Month Combined with Dragon Year

"Willpower" Sun, Fire, Fixed   **"Take Charge"** Yang-Positive Wood

Characteristics: Mistrust, Volubility, Pluck, Infatuation, Braggadocio, Vanity, Dissatisfaction, Rigidity, Strength, Success, Philanthropy, Sentimentality, Good Health, Enthusiasm, Warmth, Immodesty, Promiscuity, Tyranny, Arrogance, Protection, Power, Self-satisfaction, Nobility, Loyalty

This combination is loaded with kindness, courage, and personality. It is true that they carry themselves with a somewhat portentous bearing, but people recognize that they, in fact, deserve to. This combination reigns supreme. There is probably not another as royal as the Leo-Dragon. It is difficult to be this combination and to not realize it, and so the idea that they have big heads is probably academic. Of course in the world of combinations, there is no such thing as one being superior. The fact is, though, that the Leo-Dragon has a unique and supreme nobility about them. Others watch them pass and marvel at their magnificence. The adjectives that can be applied to this combination are virtually endless. The Dragon influence in this combination is terrifically important, because it lets the sun shine and dissipates the clouds. It erases some of the negative elements in other Leo combinations. For shelter from the storm, warmth in the cold, and protection in the face of danger, this sign is there for their friends and family. This sign is the monarch of monarchs. Among them are the good-hearted, and a person would be hard-pressed to find a kinder member of royalty. They are steadfast and can be counted on in any number of situations. They talk the magnificent talk, but they also walk the dynamic walk.

Romance: Among the other difficulties mixed in with a romantic scenario is the fact that this combination is profoundly difficult for a partner to handle. Plainly put, living with a person who is convinced that they are superior is not an easy task. Only those willing to trail behind hoisting the Leo-Tiger's robes will be happy. Such individuals do exist and will be rewarded with kindness and protection. However, sometimes being patronized is not enjoyable. Being a member of royalty does, at times, have drawbacks, and this reveals itself, unfortunately, in the area of the Leo-Dragon's love life. The difficulty here is what might be called ego-interference. This combination knows full well what they want, and they are used to getting it.

Relationships: Poor choices for this combination are Taurus-, Scorpio-, and Aquarius-Buffalos and Aquarius-Dogs. Possibilities for a romantic relationship include Aries, Gemini, Libra, Sagittarius, and Capricorn. The best picks among those are Gemini-, Aries-, and Capricorn-Snakes; Aries-, Libra-, and Sagittarius-Monkeys; Gemini-, Aries-, and Sagittarius-Rats; and sometimes the Sagittarius-Rooster.

Family Life: Leo-Dragons love to be parents. Because there is a chance of divorce there is a possibility that children from other marriages will be involved. This is of no consequence to the Leo-Dragon because they love children and play no favorites. A Leo-Dragon rules from his home, which is both castle and headquarters. As might be expected, the castle and the throne room are generally populated with people. In a more literal sense, this combination enjoys having friends and relatives around them. They welcome everyone. As might be expected, they like their surroundings to be fit for royalty. That means art objects, antiques, and precious metals and gems.

Livelihood: Failure is not part of their vocabulary, and in those rare cases when they do not make the grade it is devastating. Royalty does not handle removal from office well. Leo-Dragons are multitalented and can succeed at nearly anything they try. In their case "anything" should be interpreted literally. The other operative word is *trying*. Given effort they will do it and do it well: from the academic to the mechanical to the technical to the physical.

Famous Leo-Dragons: George Bernard Shaw, Karlheinz Stockhausen, Stanley Kubrick.

Leo (Monkey) Month Combined with Snake Year

"Willpower" Sun, Fire, Fixed **"Feel"** Yang-Negative Fire

Characteristics: Laziness, Protection, Exclusiveness, Clairvoyance, Compassion, Sagacity, Cupidity, Immodesty, Intuition, Attractiveness, Dissimulation, Vanity, Philanthropy, Nobility, Attractiveness, Tyranny, Warmth, Arrogance, Power, Loyalty, Presumption, Self-satisfaction, Promiscuity, Discretion

The twist here is that in a lot of cases this combination is exactly right on the money, especially on personal matters. It should not be inferred from this that the Leo-Snake is an obnoxious know-it-all. They are not. The Leo-Snake is intelligent, and they enjoy a certain amount of psychic ability as well. The Snake element brings calmness to the combination. The Leo tends to sit on a throne, however, directing people to do what they deem right and true. The mixture results in a person who believes they are right about nearly everything. Furthermore, this combination can be very parsimonious. All of this is exacerbated when, in their self-pride, they refuse to allow anyone to come to the rescue, or even give basic help in times of need. In the event that intelligence can win in an internal battle with pride, there is a lot of hope for this combination. Sadly, pride generally takes the day. The Snake is a sunshine character and has a warm and caring personality, but yes, it is true, there is a strong portion of conceit as well. Obviously having a big head with a Snake body can create problems, so this combination is not without its issues. There is an element of determination mixed with an element of lethargy. Then too, there is the question of Leo's strong will.

Romance: The Platonic form for love in its human form is probably the Leo-Snake. They hold on to lovers tightly and then set them free, leaving the former partners with wonderful memories and broken hearts, under the window crying, Wherefore art thou? The Leo-Snake is a love magnet. While it is true that they will likely have partners, friends, lovers, significant others, spouses, and groupies, the simple fact is that people love to love them. They seem to never be without a lover and can attract them from Timbuktu to Kathmandu. They make Romeo look like the street sweeper and Juliet the cleaning lady.

Relationships: While most people are drawn to this combination, Leo-Snakes should avoid Libra-Roosters; Taurus-, Scorpio-, and Aquarius-Tigers; and Aquarius-Boars. Top choices in the romance area are Gemini-, Libra-, Sagittarius-, and Capricorn-Buffalos. Also excellent are Aries-, Libra-, and Capricorn-Dragons, as well as Capricorn-Roosters.

Family Life: The butler draws their bath and they put on their robes or lacey finery or other luxuries so they can sit and sip expensive wine while making an engagement with their stockbroker. They entertain and travel and are always perfectly coifed. Love might be a many-splendored thing, but so is the home of a Leo-Snake. Maids, gardeners, butlers, and cooks are probably needed in their homes. They mosey around their estate in riding gear, leading their horses and returning them to the stableboy when finished.

Livelihood: If there is a profession suited to them it would most certainly be one that is academic or mentally creative in some fashion. It would certainly not be a manual job or skilled labor. They shine best in the area of intelligence. They also shine best when left to their own devices because they are, at heart, individuals. Leo-Snakes are thinkers and oftentimes not doers. They move mountains in their minds but cannot be bothered to weed the garden at home.

Famous Leo-Snakes: Cecil B. De Mille, Dorothy Parker, Mae West, Gracie Allen, Jackie Kennedy Onassis, Robert Mitchum.

Leo (Monkey) Month Combined with Horse Year

"Willpower" Sun, Fire, Fixed   **"Command"** Yang-Positive Fire

Characteristics: Pragmatism, Accomplishment, Power, Haste, Loyalty, Autonomy, Rebellion, Popularity, Style, Dexterity, Anxiety, Unscrupulousness, Immodesty, Selfishness, Persuasiveness, Vanity, Protection, Philanthropy, Warmth, Promiscuity, Tyranny, Arrogance, Self-satisfaction, Nobility

Leo-Horses are competitors, but usually just with themselves, wanting to exceed their previous attempts and move to higher levels. A focus like this means they can triumph, because barriers do not faze them and challenges are undertaken with vigor. The Leo-Horse is a doer and a cheerful one at that. In addition, they are generally champions. While human and to an extent possessing the skittishness of a Horse, they are also not easily deterred. They are the type that people speak of as a role model. Regardless of what it is—mundane tasks that someone must do, or great events—the Leo-Horse gets them accomplished. They can scrub floors or run the marathon in the Olympics. They are well aware that their winning smile can only get them so far in life. Leo-Horses can be taken for a ride, and this can do damage to their souls even though they are essentially strong. While they are not pouters or sulkers, they do have feelings and, most of all, they are the type who relentlessly asks why things are the way they are. All they hear for an answer is an echo. A lot of success comes from struggling alone in the night doing thankless tasks. There is a strong trusting character in this combination and while that is generally good, it can be harmful. Not everyone is sincere with his or her handshake, and most contracts have the fine print.

Romance: This combination is both extra hot-blooded and super beguiling. There is, unfortunately, an amoral approach to passion on the part of this combination. For them, it is a one-way street rife with lack of responsibility and failure in communication. Disappearing acts are a strong likelihood, leaving their partner to worry and wonder. The Leo-Horse is a combination that is made up of two movers and shakers in the passion department. They are enthusiastically red hot and smashingly seductive. Generally this combination is a passionate creature, full of dash and vigor. Leo is no slouch in the ardor department either.

Relationships: This combination should avoid Taurus-, Scorpio-, or Aquarius-Rats and Aquarius-Monkeys. They are strictly bad luck. Terrific choices for romance are Aries-, Gemini-, Libra-, Sagittarius-, and Capricorn-Tigers.

Dogs with these sign are good too. Additional good choices are Aries- and Capricorn-Rams.

Family Life: Fine points matter to this combination. They make excellent parents and their children are generally well behaved. This is due to a moderately strict style of parenting that is not overbearing. Comfort is the key in the home of the Leo-Horse. They do not lean in the direction of the flashy or magnificent. They are pragmatists, and that means their house must work properly. The decor is on the traditional side but it does call attention to itself.

Livelihood: Business is probably a good place for this combination because they are independent and abhor authority. In addition, they are extremely good at turning nothing into something. The Leo-Horse is capable of a vast variety of jobs and professions. There is essentially nothing they cannot do. Much of this is based on their staggering willpower. If they want something, including success, there is a good likelihood that they will get it.

Famous Leo-Horses: Percy Bysshe Shelley, Aldous Huxley, Ted Hughes, John Huston.

Leo (Monkey) Month Combined with Ram Year

"Willpower" Sun, Fire, Fixed   **"Reliance"** Yang-Negative Fire

Characteristics: Perseverance, Impracticality, Tardiness, Worry, Immodesty, Whimsy, Good Manners, Pessimism, Taste, Invention, Vanity, Parasitism, Sensitivity, Lack of Foresight, Philanthropy, Arrogance, Warmth, Promiscuity, Tyranny, Protection, Nobility, Power, Self-satisfaction, Loyalty

There is a wide and awe-inspiring spirit in this combination. To be sure, there is a touch of madness too, brought, of course, by the Ram. But the Leo influence adds some serious sense to the combination. Consequently, there is very likely to be a person who is destined for something incredible. This combination is nearly in the "What more could you ask for?" category. There is serious drive and motivation here. However, there is a catch. Remaining as part of the character is the Ram's lack of coherence. They simply do not have a lot of foresight. There is an immediate vision of the world. The Leo-Ram has thin skin and has horrible difficulty accepting criticism. That is not a good trait in the arts. Furthermore, they are needy and depend on others and can even be accused of exploiting them to varying degrees. Yes, they are perceptive and original, but this is often not enough to overcome some of the liabilities. This combination lives for now. Teleological thinking goes right out the window. There is a mine of creative resources in their character, and there is essentially nothing in the field of art they cannot do. Again, however, their thin skin is a roadblock.

Romance: The Leo-Ram wants to be taken care of. Clearly, they need the right person to do this because a lot of potential mates find it annoying. If they find someone who is willing to do this, all will go well. All of this is accomplished by the Leo-Ram in a fairly benign and lovely fashion. The Leo-Ram is highly attractive. But, as is becoming clear, there are issues and stumbling blocks at every turn. In the case of love it is the dependency that shows up. They fall in love rather quickly, of course, because there is only the present, and after winning their partner over get needy and dependent.

Relationships: Out of the running for this combination are Taurus-, Scorpio-, and Aquarius-Buffalos and Aquarius-Dogs. For real love, the best choices for this combination are Aries-, Gemini-, Sagittarius-, and Capricorn-Boars. They can usually put up with the neediness of the Leo-Ram. Other candidates are Libra-, Sagittarius-, and Capricorn-Horses. Capricorn- and Libra-Rabbits are possibilities too.

Family Life: This combination is not conservative but rather desires physical well-being and sophistication. Lots of room makes them feel at ease. Because they are often good at making things and are individualistic, they frequently create things for the home with their own hands. They tend to be loving and wonderful parents. This combination needs security at home but that does not necessarily mean they live in the place they were born. They are impulsive and it is possible they live in a far-off place or even another land. When it comes to their home their theme song is "I Did It My Way."

Livelihood: This combination is probably not cut out to be the CEO of the company, but they can rise to a fairly high position. Superiors should watch them closely though, because of their tendency to be spontaneous. They tend to be good employees because they enjoy money and what it can do. Leo-Rams are a highly creative combination. They excel at the arts, no matter what form they might take. That can be visual or the written word. They are excellent at determining what others like and can, as a result, be trendsetters. There is a lot of vigor in this combination. There is also a fairly open mind.

Famous Leo-Rams: Benito Mussolini, Andy Warhol, Geraldine Chaplin, Robert De Niro, Jean-Claude Killy.

Leo (Monkey) Month Combined with Monkey Year

"Willpower" Sun, Fire, Fixed   **"Arrange"** Yin-Positive Metal

Characteristics: Leadership, Self-involvement, Ruse, Silliness, Wit, Self-satisfaction, Zeal, Opportunism, Nobility, Arrogance, Power, Deceit, Protection, Improvisation, Immodesty, Promiscuity, Cunning, Vanity, Loyalty, Tyranny, Warmth, Philanthropy, Stability, Loquacity

This combination has a genius for verbal communication and can readily bring about a laugh or a tear in the most stoic of personalities. Being a mixture of the Lion and the Monkey, there is a royal but agile bearing that this combination carries everywhere. That translates as clout in a small package. The Leo-Monkey is a fabulous combination that blends numerous appealing characteristics into one fine individual. They are enchantment personified. Among the things that draw people to this combination are compassion and intelligence. While the Leo-Monkey does display their royalty, they do it in a way that is modest thanks to the Monkey influence. They bring a certain tact that wards off feelings of superiority. This combination does appreciate a bit of adoration, particularly in terms of their appearance, which they are careful to maintain. In addition to the compassion and other fine traits in the person of a Leo-Monkey, they have a great deal of insight into their own being. They know themselves well. There is also a surprise in store in that this combination can handle criticism: something that is rare for a Leo indeed. They do not automatically assume they are the boss, but it would be misleading to say that they do not have a slight edge of superiority. Their egos do not need to be endlessly stroked, and they do not need hordes of people around nodding their heads in agreement.

Romance: The Leo-Monkey is inclined to be somewhat controlling and has the green eyes of jealousy. To be the partner of a Leo-Monkey means to experience questioning who, what, when, where, and why on frequent occasions. The area of romance is the spot that the Leo-Monkey has decided to be a donkey. It is a shame, because they are really great people. Like most ointments one must be careful of flies, and to be sure there is an issue with this combination, and unfortunately it comes with matters of the heart. It seems that it is here that the Leo ego has decided to be most forceful, and this causes some errors of judgment and false steps.

Relationships: Poor choices for this combination are Scorpio- or Aquarius-Snakes. Taurus- and Aquarius-Horses are not particularly good either.

Topping the choices are the Gemini-, Libra-, Sagittarius-, or Capricorn-Rat. Aries-, Gemini-, Sagittarius-, and Capricorn-Dragons are also excellent.

Family Life: This combination is terrific with children, because they are enthralling and somewhat childish themselves. Neatness in the home is not their highest priority, but things get done even though this combination is not strict. It is hard to see them as authority figures instead of wizards. They live in comfortable homes with a unique but not strange feel to them. They enjoy making their lives and their family's life less of a burden. A relationship with the Leo-Monkey is a true partnership in every sense of the word. They are loving and involved members of the family who are responsible, caring, helpful, and do their share. Regardless of gender, they help with the kids from birth. They use their humor and enthusiasm to a great benefit.

Livelihood: While this is an odd combination to find in one being, it works for the Leo-Monkey. It also permits a wide range of professions and interests. It would be remiss to not point out something rather obvious: the Monkey loves sports. Possible professions are physical education, the travel industry, or any of the helping professions. The Leo-Monkey might not have a double major in Philosophy and Religion, they might not meditate or read Immanuel Kant, but they are metaphysicians and spiritually minded nonetheless. They are poets who swing from trees and ride magic carpets. In all of this, however, they are folks: real, down-to-earth people who make good neighbors and friends.

Famous Leo-Monkeys: Alexandre Dumas fils, Henri Cartier-Bresson, Salvador Allende, Ray Bradbury, Mick Jagger, Bella Abzug.

Leo (Monkey) Month Combined with Rooster Year

"Willpower" Sun, Fire, Fixed **"Conqueror"** Yang-Negative Metal

Characteristics: Dissipation, Chic, Pedantry, Cockiness, Bossiness, Immodesty, Conservatism, Humor, Enthusiasm, Resilience, Promiscuity, Philanthropy, Boastfulness, Tyranny, Vanity, Warmth, Protection, Nobility, Arrogance, Power, Self-satisfaction, Loyalty, Candor, Blind Faith

There is a nice balance in this combination, and gaps in needed areas tend to be filled. Finance is an area that requires care, caution, and even serious warnings and alerts. On the Leo side of this there is a strong influence of self-pride. The Rooster amplifies this trait. That might be trouble enough, but in the case of this combination there is a very strong craving for money.

The dialectic of the Leo-Rooster provides many opportunities for this combination if they elect to put them to proper use. One positive consequence is a royal compassion brought, of course, by the Leo side. This exaggerated desire affects nearly everything in the life of the Leo-Rooster, and, alas, without it the effect can be extremely negative and even life threatening. The lack of money can cause depression with this combination, and as if that was not bad enough, it can cause dangerous efforts to ease the depression. These efforts can include alcohol or drug abuse. Consequently there is a real possibility of extreme mood swings. Fortunately they tend to be the survivor type. They fall but they get up. Someone knocks them down and bloodies them but they endure. As often as not, however, when they do get up, away they go on a pride trip again, risking more of the same. They can bring about any number of other addictions including—but not restricted to—gambling, hoarding, sex, and overeating. It is worth recalling that this is initiated by excessive pride. There is also an element of "mirror, mirror on the wall" syndrome involved here, as would be expected.

Romance: This combination is very much a homebody who loves his children and has projects around the house. That portion of the mixture is wonderful, but anyone interested in a long-term relationship with this individual needs to prepare themselves for a yo-yo at best and roller coaster at worst in terms of temperament. This combination is an excellent lover and a loyal partner. The Leo-Rooster mates for life. Fortitude is a prerequisite for anyone who partners with this individual.

Relationships: At the bottom of the list are Aquarius-Dogs. Top choices are the Buffalo, the Snake, and the Dragon. The best signs among this group are the Aries, Libra, Sagittarius, and Capricorn. Taurus, Scorpio, and Aquarius individuals are not demonstrative enough for the Leo-Rooster, so they do not make the short list. That is especially true of Rabbits and Roosters in those signs.

Family Life: At times this combination is distant in literal terms too, because they love to travel. While it is true that they are often middle-class people masquerading as vagabonds, they believe themselves to be the real article, especially when they are young. They are somewhat flexible in terms of where their actual home is, but they do love it and get homesick fairly easily. Unfortunately for their lovers, there is nothing that can be done about Leo-Rooster's distance other than wait.

Livelihood: This combination must always remember Nietzsche's concept that whatever does not kill me makes me stronger. If they can get through these early rough spots, the likelihood of great success increases dramatically. The Leo-Rooster needs to be resilient. They will be knocked down repeatedly when younger. They have extraordinarily bad luck and some of it is painful. It appears at times that the only luck they have is unfortunate, because they get sick, have accidents, and fall on their face again and again.

Famous Leo-Roosters: Alex Haley, Jacqueline Susann, Jerry Falwell, Roman Polanski.

Leo (Monkey) Month Combined with Dog Year
"Willpower" Sun, Fire, Fixed   **"Concerned"** Yin-Positive Metal

Characteristics: Morality, Tastelessness, Righteousness, Protection, Respectability, Self-promiscuity, Power, Cynicism, Immodesty, Intelligence, Constancy, Loyalty, Warmth, Vanity, Criticism, Uneasiness, Duty, Philanthropy, Self-satisfaction, Tyranny, Heroism, Arrogance, Nobility, Unsociability

The traits in this combination, including loving-kindness and compassion, generate a giving and charitable person. When they sign a letter "Sincerely yours," they mean it. They are probably the most sincere people on the planet. The Leo-Dog is one of those combinations that leaves a person in awe. The imagination could not dream up a person with such exceptional courage and blind allegiance, the former coming from the Dog and the latter from the Leo. They also care about their friends, family, and, yes, all sentient beings. They probably care about nonsentient life as well. They personify devotion. Regardless of what a person has done or is thought to have done, if they are a friend, the Leo-Dog is on their side. Even their pessimism, which they do in fact possess, does not make them cynical. They believe their friends and relatives even if they must resort to a fantastical approach to the matter; it is perfectly acceptable to believe something that is absurd. That is ultimate loyalty. All of this implies that the Leo-Dog does things; and yes, they are doers with those they love. They happily get the newspaper for their master even though they cannot read it. Life does not disappoint them, and they do not whine and complain. This combination, in spite of the Dog influence, has faith, and that is why they do what they do and are what they are.

Romance: There is no suspension of belief here. There is deep and lasting belief and faith. They may stray, they may remarry, and they may lust in their heart, but they will never stop caring. Those who love this combination need to be aware of not only that but also the fact that they are touchy when it comes to issues of maintaining face. A Leo-Dog cares for a lifetime. Nothing can break the ties that bind this individual to those they love now or those they loved in the past or those they love in the future. That does not necessarily imply strict adherence to the principles of monogamy. It means an uninterrupted connection for a lifetime.

Relationships: Taurus-, Scorpio-, or Aquarius-Dragons or Aquarius-Rams do not make the elite list for this combination. There is too much negativity surrounding them. What is needed is an agreeable, jolly person who lifts their spirits and gives enough praise. Some suggestions in the area of romance are Aries, Gemini, Libra, Sagittarius, and Capricorns who are Rabbits or Tigers. Another serious possibility is the Gemini-Horse.

Family Life: The Leo-Dog is not interested in impressing people or having fine art and antiques. Those things do nothing in the comfort department. They are not dirty individuals but perhaps a bit untidy. This combination is a great member of the family. They are responsible and loving with the children and more than happy to help out. They like social gatherings and will help with the arrangements as well as the grunt work. This combination's house has one and only one thing as its purpose. A house is somewhere to be cool in the summer, warm in the winter, and sheltered from the elements. It is a place to eat and sleep. It is certainly comfortable and obviously used.

Livelihood: This combination is individualistic in their work, meaning they like to work by themselves. They can be trusted to do this, as they are loyal employees. Should they end up in a higher position, they are quite fair and just. They are also fully capable of permitting a bit of slack when it comes to joking or fooling around on the job. The Leo-Dog is a multi-talented combination. Their forte is patience and care with details. They have extremely logical minds and are capable of solving difficult problems through careful and painstaking analysis.

Famous Leo-Dogs: Norman Lear and Alain Robbe-Grillet.

Leo (Monkey) Month Combined with Boar Year

"Willpower" Sun, Fire, Fixed   **"Cultivator"** Yin-Negative Water

Characteristics: Honesty, Hesitation, Boar-headedness, Materialism, Gourmandism, Voluptuousness, Culture, Credulity, Immodesty, Philanthropy, Gallantry, Sincerity, Vanity, Scrupulousness, Warmth, Promiscuity, Arrogance, Self-satisfaction, Wrath, Tyranny, Protection, Power, Loyalty, Nobility

The desire for fun and a good time for this combination accompanies their humor. In fact, this combination is prone to overdo everything. Name something that most people enjoy, say food, and the Leo-Boar excels at it. That runs the gamut from sex to philanthropy. All combinations have a least one thing that stands out among their characteristics. With the Leo-Boar it is humor. They are just plain funny, and they can always bring about at least a smile with those they encounter. There is a strong-willed and responsible person here too, but it is the humor that people notice the most. It is a natural sort of comedic being that is simply part of their personality. It is not planned; it just happens spontaneously in the best of times and the worst of times. It is quite easy to determine that this is true of the Leo-Boar simply by asking them. They are also exceedingly honest. Luxury is not something that is an extra in the life of this combination. Luxury is a need. It must shine, glitter, be famous, and most of all, expensive. In the food department too, only the gourmet will do. There is absolutely nothing over the top with this combination, and they are just not ostentatious. They have class and a lot of it. In spite of what some might assume, this combination loves the home. They need a firm and secure home base. They want to be with those they love, and they want them to be well. Everything about this combination is gift-wrapped in humor and fun. Clothing is only acceptable if it comes from the finest designers and is up to date. It should not be inferred that this combination only worries about themselves. They are quite generous and willing to share with everyone. This too they tend to overdo and many friends wonder why they give away so much to so many. The reason is, like the other traits, they simply cannot help themselves.

Romance: There will be neither wild headlines nor even local gossip about the happenings in the relationship of a Leo-Boar. Having said this, there is a bit of a double standard operating here, in that this individual demands blind faith and allegiance. The Leo side of this combination loves to get attention, and sometimes that comes in the form of running around a bit in the sexual sense. The Boar side, however, does balance out this tendency a bit, if not completely. Boars are inward looking and strongly emphasize good judgment.

Relationships: Snakes, particularly Aries-, Taurus-, Scorpio-, and Aquarius-Snakes, should be avoided. Maybe the very best choice of all is a Gemini-Dog. Humor comes to the forefront here in love and romance too, and thus recommended are Aries-, Gemini-, Libra-, Sagittarius-, or Capricorn-Buffalos and Capricorn-Rabbits and -Rams.

Family Life: The home of this combination might make the cover of *Home and Garden* magazine. It could be on the list of sights to see in town. They are fussy about all of this, and it will be done their way. Yes, they do maintain their sense of humor, but they shall not be moved, not one inch. No posters taped to the wall in the kid's room will be permitted. The man of the house cannot collect beer cans. Handwoven carpets are fine, but throw rugs are not. Style and class are the essence of this combination at home. They want and will accept nothing but the very best: from the bedroom to the patio to the garden, it must be perfect. Silk sheets are standard issue in the home of a Leo-Boar.

Livelihood: Consequently this combination pushes on, striving for perfection, but never finding anything but fault with themselves. Fortunately, they can laugh it off. A Leo-Boar overdoes in the area of achieving things just as they do everything else. At the same time, they are not satisfied that they have accomplished enough.

Famous Leo-Boars: Carl Jung, Henry Ford, Lucille Ball, Alfred Hitchcock.

Virgo (Rooster) Month Combined with Rat Year

"Study" Mercury, Earth, Mutable **"Regulator"** Yin-Positive Water

Characteristics: Charisma, Intellect, Skill, Acquisitiveness, Lucidity, Nervousness, Thirst for Power, Decorum, Service, Influence, Practicality, Reserve, Meticulousness, Crankiness, Nit-picking, Appeal, Discrimination, Courtesy, Negativism, Verbosity, Snobbery, Thrift, Guile, Sociability, Meddling

This combination is quite good and successful with most things in life, but of course not all. They take their time thinking things through, and they are exceedingly calm. Stress does not get to them because they will not be pressured. This is a very productive combination that is organized as well. Both the Virgo and the Rat add power so we have power in both hands. It might not be heavyweight power, but it is power nonetheless. The double power shows up as energy and logic. Being Rats, there is a cunning side to this combination. They are not the greatest listener on the planet either, especially when it comes to suggestions or advice from others. What they are though, are data and information sponges. It goes in one ear and stays there as though no exit was available. However, this tends to bring about personal and subjective interpretations of the data at times. The Rat's tendency to do battle is balanced by the Virgo. The sharpness and logic carry across most sides of this character but, unfortunately, not the romantic side of things. Maybe it is their desire for freedom and the great ability to be so self-sufficient that causes the issues in the area of love. It might be the fact that they need to think things over so carefully.

Romance: This combination believes every lie and deceit that is handed over to them and has no ability to think things through. A train wreck is sure to happen in the emotions, and it does because this combination believes others are as principled as they are. The place where subjectivity runs head first into the Virgo-Rat is love. They suddenly become blind, illogical, and dizzy individuals; this is the opposite of what they are in the rest of their being. They invented crazy love and have a patent on it. They worship the ground that their lovers walk on.

Relationships: This combination should best pass on the Gemini, Libra, Sagittarius, and Pisces who are Horses or Rabbits. Very fine romantic picks are a Buffalo, a Monkey, or a Dragon who is Taurus, Cancer, Scorpio, or Capricorn. A bit of caution might be necessary with the Dragon.

Family Life: The catch with this combination is that there are regulations, and the main one is obedience. They are not armed and dangerous, but respect is paramount to them. This does not mean that they will not have, to put it tactfully, unruly children. To be fair though, there is an emphasis on the principle of treating others as an individual wants to be treated. The Virgo-Rat is a model of the nurturing and caring family person. They are practically excessive in some ways, particularly in what they give and what they permit.

Livelihood: Science is an area where this combination's work might help people, and in that they are truly excellent. For that matter, any job or profession that entails interaction with others would be wonderful. Their calm and patient demeanor is made to order for positions such as retail and customer service. The analytical mind of this combination might come into play in the choice of a profession. Science or professions that require research are possibilities.

Famous Virgo-Rats: Leo Tolstoy, Joseph Kennedy Sr., Maurice Chevalier, Lauren Bacall.

Virgo (Rooster) Month Combined with Buffalo Year

"Study" Mercury, Earth, Mutable **"Survivor"** Yin-Negative Water

Characteristics: Stability, Vindictiveness, Bias, Strength of Purpose, Crankiness, Bigotry, Plodding, Reserve, Eloquence, Decorum, Standoffishness, Stubbornness, Innovation, Courtesy, Integrity, Diligence, Meticulousness, Discrimination, Snobbery, Practicality, Service, Lucidity, Nit-picking, Negativism

This combination is very cautious in what they do. The most obvious description of this combination, the king of their characteristics, is righteousness. There are probably pictures of them in dictionaries under that entry. The Virgo-Buffalo can be counted on, but in all they do they are individualistic. The Virgo-Buffalo is a walking, talking study in the old school, and that means they are conventional and stuffy. There are some good qualities to this combination, but they are hard to find and reserved for a select few. Of course, reserved is an operative word with this combination, in more ways than one. Trudging along through life with their austere lifestyle the Virgo-Buffalo can, to be kind, be thought of as traditional and genuine. Things must be done their way, and generally they are done alone. This combination is very well mannered. In addition there is a creative streak in them, albeit one that is not necessarily interestingly innovative. If there is any other fun stuff about them, it is well hidden under a relentlessly solemn demeanor. Perhaps it can be added, though, that this combination is a good communicator and often a fine orator. They do not like help or to ask for it. They rule themselves. Occasional exceptions occur when absolutely necessary, and in those cases this combination depends on those that are close to them. To be close requires sharing a kinship in values, if not blood. Extraordinary care is taken when choosing who is close. In the fluffy department of personal qualities there is not much that can be said. There may be a glimpses of these qualities, however, for the ones closest to this combination.

Romance: This combination has extraordinary caution in choosing whom they associate with, which is a great help in the selection of a mate. What they want is someone who is industrious to the core, someone who grew up that way and has remained that way. The Virgo-Buffalo is a pragmatist and seeks love in all the right places. This combination is careful and knows what they want. What is desired is someone who is functional. There is a bit of slack in how they define functional, but not much. They consider sex appeal or intelligence as frosting on the cake; they like it, but do not require it.

Relationships: Probably this combination should best avoid Gemini-Dragons, -Horses, and -Rams. A distance should be maintained with Sagittarius-Rams and -Tigers. To be avoided at all costs are Pisces-Rams and -Tigers. Excellent choices for the Virgo-Buffalo are the Taurus, Cancer, Scorpio, or Capricorn signs, especially those who are Snakes or Dragons. If a Cancer is involved, the odds are they will be Horses or Dogs.

Family Life: The Virgo-Buffalo feels no need for the luxurious. To know this combination is to be totally aware of what their home will be like, even though it has not been seen yet. There are absolutely no surprises upon the first visit. In fact, the Virgo-Buffalo lot does not like surprises. Conservative and long lasting, as well as tough, are probably some adjectives for this combination's home. There is no hint of the showy or the flashy here. Being a pragmatist, this person's home and the things in it must work. They probably subscribe to the "if it is not broken, don't fix it" school of thought. This is not based on penny-pinching but on practicality.

Livelihood: The work this combination does is precise and complete. This combination is intelligent and quite responsible. The projects they undertake are completed correctly. They are capable of being fine in supervisory positions and have no problem enforcing rules. This combination is not fond of the city with its noise, hustle, and bustle. They are country people, but most certainly not hayseeds. While they are not plantation owners, they might be the stoic rancher type.

Famous Virgo-Buffalos: Lafayette, Peter Sellers, Robert Bresson.

Virgo (Rooster) Month Combined with Tiger Year

"Study" Mercury, Earth, Mutable **"Observe"** Yang-Positive Wood

Characteristics: Intemperance, Benevolence, Itinerancy, Authority, Magnetism, Lucidity, Disobedience, Hotheadedness, Good Luck, Reserve, Impetuosity, Decorum, Swagger, Crankiness, Fervor, Bravery, Practicality, Courtesy, Meticulousness, Snobbery, Discrimination, Service, Nit-picking, Negativism

This combination knows what they are doing, and it is probably not a good idea to try to pull the wool over their eyes. Those foolhardy enough to do this will surely pay a price, because the Virgo-Tiger can figure things out and zap a person who tries to scam or befuddle them. While it is true that they can be a bit on the touchy or even on the irritable side, they have so many positives it hardly matters. Sometimes dialectical interactions work, and that is the case with the Virgo-Tiger. For starters, this combination has a really good heart. Balancing this out is a worldly-wise person who does not fall for things. They even have enough to cover the fact that they think they know more than they actually do. Nearly all of the negatives that can be associated with the Tiger are smoothed over. The Virgo element helps them keep their sharp tongue in check. Furthermore, this combination borders on being a workaholic. They are so dedicated and work so hard, it is tiring just to watch them. They are practically serfs, or even slaves. Virgo-Tigers will clean the house, take care of the children, pick up the dry cleaning, and have the car serviced, and all that is before lunch, which they prepare for everyone. None of this is done from a perspective of subservience or feelings of inadequacy. Rather, the motive for this is pure and straight-ahead duty. So maybe they are more like soldiers than slaves or serfs.

Romance: This combination is as good in lovemaking as most people are. They enjoy it and release themselves to it. There is, though, way in the back of their heads maybe, a feeling that they should be mowing the lawn, baking bread, or rearranging the garage. Other than this small warning, most combinations can do no better in the romance category than the Virgo-Tiger. It is difficult to imagine a partner that can surpass the Virgo-Tiger. In fact, there are not any. There is a slight cautionary note attached to that, however. While this combination is respectable, reliable, hardworking, and dedicated, that sense of duty can, at times, be annoying.

Relationships: The Aries-Buffalo is not a good pick for this combination nor is the Gemini-Ram. Additional poor choices are Gemini-, Sagittarius-, and Pisces-Snakes and Pisces-Monkeys. Capricorns are possibilities for romance because they share some of their natural qualities. This is especially true of Capricorn-Horses and -Dogs. Additional good choices are Taurus-, Cancer-, and Scorpio-Horses and Scorpio-Dogs.

Family Life: There is in this combination—at least in some sense—a flower person, if not a flower child, in the home, because there will almost surely be freshly cut flowers in the home at all times. In a related category, there will be teas, and that is plural: a wide range of aromatic and herbal teas. Do not forget exotic jams, jellies, cheese, home-baked bread, and maybe even some new age music. One leaves the home of this combination exclaiming, "Oh my, what a pretty home you have!" However, speaking of children, this combination is not exactly a kid lover. They might have one very well-behaved child who eats the jam on toast in the kitchen, not in the living room. That will likely be the extent of it. The home of the Virgo-Tiger is conservative in style. There are probably some antiques tastefully placed. Other aspects of the home show a very small trace of perhaps a former hippie. The colors can be a bit loud.

Livelihood: Somewhere inside this combination is a revolutionary spirit, one that is unlikely to show itself, and they easily adapt to working in the system. They can do things at the spur of the moment, and they do have a temper. Like most folks, they like their creature comforts and they are good at providing them both for themselves and for those they love. They have a good heart, at least to the point of giving to causes they believe in. A child of Mother Earth, this combination gets their big store of energy from natural and renewable sources.

Famous Virgo-Tigers: Kitty Carlisle, Karl Lagerfeld, Elliott Gould.

Virgo (Rooster) Month Combined with Rabbit Year

"Study" Mercury, Earth, Mutable **"Withdraw"** Yin-Negative Wood

Characteristics: Secretiveness, Hypochondria, Pedantry, Complexity, Nit-picking, Meticulousness, Squeamishness, Tact, Lucidity, Dilettantism, Discrimination, Service, Decorum, Crankiness, Reserve, Picking, Negativism, Snobbery, Courtesy, Finesse, Practicality, Virtue, Longevity, Prudence, Ambition

This combination likes to stay home and contemplate, read, and stare out the window. They are ever on their guard. There is a better than average probability that they will spend their lives alone. This too will be done without complaint and probably with some degree of satisfaction. The Virgo-Rabbit tends to be a loner who strictly avoids conflict of any kind. They are exceedingly careful. There is no whining or grumbling from this combination. It is entirely possible that they will go through life completely unnoticed. Communicating is not their forte either. Some things, gossip for example, make them very uncomfortable. It is not that Virgo-Rabbits are prudes or do-gooders. The way they are and the way they act is the essence of their being. They do not necessarily judge people so much as wonder why they partake of some activities. There are things to do that are more rewarding than wasting time chatting about neighbors, coworkers, or mutual friends. They like to undertake projects, perhaps around the home, but they would rather do this on their own. Hobnobbing with others is stupendously boring to them, and they abhor it. It is a total waste of time.

Romance: Because the Virgo-Rabbit is neither crazy nor foolish deep down in their being, they come to their senses at about the age of thirty. What their senses tell them is to remove themselves from the carnival and go home: wherever that might be. This period might become the missing years of their life. People at reunions may ask what happened to them, and no one knows. They do eventually turn up, and where they have been can be a surprise. They might, for example, have worked their way up in the State Department and been the Deputy Ambassador to Monaco. What they surely have become is a caring and giving person, a person who pulls for the underdog and helps the less fortunate. There will probably be an odd history in the story of the Virgo-Rabbit's romantic life. In their early years they might be quite crazy, participating in any number of escapades and romantic adventures. They will find partners who support their craziness and more than likely make a huge number of errors.

Relationships: Not on this combination's list are Gemini-, Sagittarius-, or Pisces-Roosters. Totally out of bounds are Gemini- and Sagittarius-Rats, as are Pisces-Dragons. Taurus-, Cancer-, Scorpio-, and Capricorn-Boars are premium choices in the love category. They will make this combination quite happy. Also good are Taurus-, Scorpio-, and Capricorn-Rams and Capricorn-Dogs. Also a fine pick is Taurus-Rabbit.

Family Life: For some reason, subtle colors appeal to the Virgo-Rabbit with gold being the exception. There is a traditional feeling to their home. As parents, they are responsible. They place a priority on the intellectual, so time with the children could mean classical music concerts and plays rather than heavy metal or hip-hop venues. Given this combination's need for security, that aspect will be important in their home. That means assorted alarms and locks. Besides this, the furniture is nicely chosen and has some class. There will probably be art and antiques of some sort.

Livelihood: This combination does work and work very hard. There is a high probability of achieving at least a secure retirement. Virgo-Rabbits are fine financial planners, and this probably stems from their need for security. The work they tend to do is designed to accumulate a totally safe and secure financial setup that lasts for generations. That goal is sometimes missed, however. The reason for this is their complete unwillingness to take a chance.

Famous Virgo-Rabbits: Ingrid Bergman, Jack Lange, Memphis Slim.

Virgo (Rooster) Month Combined with Dragon Year

"Study" Mercury, Earth, Mutable **"Take Charge"** Yang-Positive Wood

Characteristics: Braggadocio, Good Health, Volubility, Sentimentality, Crankiness, Enthusiasm, Dissatisfaction, Pluck, Infatuation, Courtesy, Decorum, Rigidity, Reserve, Mistrust, Success, Nit-picking, Strength, Practicality, Snobbery, Meticulousness, Lucidity, Service, Negativism, Discrimination

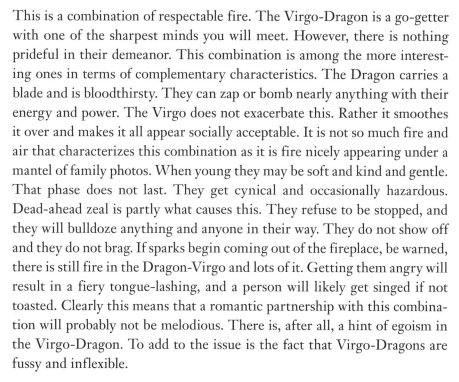

This is a combination of respectable fire. The Virgo-Dragon is a go-getter with one of the sharpest minds you will meet. However, there is nothing prideful in their demeanor. This combination is among the more interesting ones in terms of complementary characteristics. The Dragon carries a blade and is bloodthirsty. They can zap or bomb nearly anything with their energy and power. The Virgo does not exacerbate this. Rather it smoothes it over and makes it all appear socially acceptable. It is not so much fire and air that characterizes this combination as it is fire nicely appearing under a mantel of family photos. When young they may be soft and kind and gentle. That phase does not last. They get cynical and occasionally hazardous. Dead-ahead zeal is partly what causes this. They refuse to be stopped, and they will bulldoze anything and anyone in their way. They do not show off and they do not brag. If sparks begin coming out of the fireplace, be warned, there is still fire in the Dragon-Virgo and lots of it. Getting them angry will result in a fiery tongue-lashing, and a person will likely get singed if not toasted. Clearly this means that a romantic partnership with this combination will probably not be melodious. There is, after all, a hint of egoism in the Virgo-Dragon. To add to the issue is the fact that Virgo-Dragons are fussy and inflexible.

Romance: The Virgo-Dragon must circle the globe, because their street is one way and U-turns are not allowed. Watch, cheer, and tune in, but you probably will end up just another fan. The Virgo-Dragon is not the best romantic match for most people. They are very attractive and have enormous sex appeal. That is not the problem. The problem is that zeal for success and demand for career. The suitors and groupies are put on hold. The phone calls are not returned.

Relationships: Gemini-, Sagittarius-, and Pisces-Dogs irritate and are probably not good choices for this combination. Sagittarius- and Pisces-Buffalos do not make the list at all. Topping the list of romantic picks for the Virgo-Dragon are Rats. Among those, Taurus- and Capricorn-Rats are the best choices. Additional good choices are Taurus- and Cancer-Roosters as well as Taurus-, Cancer-, and Capricorn-Monkeys. The Scorpio-Snake is someone to keep an eye on.

Family Life: This combination makes very responsible parents, but they are strict and demanding. Their middle years bring a kind of sappiness to their nature. Or perhaps it would be better to say they get more easy-going. Finally, as senior citizens they spoil their grandchildren horribly. The Virgo-Dragon has good taste and this will show in the furniture, even though it is not the most comfortable you have used. It gets your attention for its harsh nature. Everything is straight-edged, sharp. They enjoy visitors, but please call ahead and do not overstay your welcome. This combination blooms late in the parenthood department.

Livelihood: This combination is focused, and they are a well-directed person. They breathe and eat fire at the appropriate moments; they are also generally fair about things. Do not obstruct their path or make them angry. The Virgo-Dragon is multitalented and consequently able to succeed at most anything. That means they can be happy anywhere, because they are the type that love their work.

Famous Virgo-Dragons: Paul Williams, Raquel Welch, Jimmy Connors.

Virgo (Rooster) Month Combined with Snake Year

"Study" Mercury, Earth, Mutable   **"Feel"** Yang-Negative Fire

Characteristics: Presumption, Clairvoyance, Service, Compassion, Extravagance, Exclusiveness, Discretion, Attractiveness, Laziness, Crankiness, Sagacity, Dissimulation, Reserve, Decorum, Intuition, Meticulousness, Cupidity, Snobbery, Courtesy, Lucidity, Practicality, Discrimination, Negativism, Nit-picking

This combination speaks well, and many of their points are made indirectly. To some they seem too serious, but there is a smile there if one looks at the right time and in the right place. They have the unusual ability to solve serious technical problems while at the same time being tuned in to the cosmos. The Virgo-Snake is deep, exceedingly and mysteriously deep. It is true that they are intellectual and can out-analyze almost anyone. That is not really the point. Something different begins to become obvious when someone notices the intuition of this combination. The understanding that is part of their being is a wisdom that seems to stretch to eternity, and this is coupled with the beautiful side of them. People are drawn to the Virgo-Snake almost as though they were human magnets. Not only is there the beautiful, there is an aura of sensuality about them. Make no mistake though: among the things they can instantly analyze are people, and they use this to their advantage. They want to be loved and respected. This makes them very good friends. None of this is to imply that they do not get angry, because they do. Bickering or downright verbal disputes are not uncommon with this combination. They do not like games, and they do not like people to play with them. They are serious planners and know every curve, hill, and pothole on the road they are driving. Their quiet interest in human nature results in fundamental honesty in the sense of sincerity. If they say something, they mean it. Their hobby is collecting friends, acquaintances, and lovers, and then admiring them.

Romance: This combination finds it rather easy to flip a switch and become friends with a former lover or even an ex-spouse. Management of a partner from this combination is strictly a laissez-faire approach; leave them alone and things will be fine. Push, bug, harass, and manipulate them at one's own risk. The Virgo-Snake's love dialectic is difficult to get in focus. On the one hand, the Snake enjoys going this way and that way and is not typically a paragon of faithfulness. However, Virgos tend to be steadier while, nonetheless, being erotically inclined as well. The result can have some novel but worthwhile consequences.

Relationships: Not particularly good choices for this combination are Gemini-, Sagittarius-, or Pisces-Tigers. The same is true of the Gemini-Monkey. Strictly and totally to be avoided are Boars. Buffalos and Roosters who are Taurus, Scorpio, and Capricorns are top-of-the-line picks for this combination.

Family Life: As parents they tend to spoil their children. They give in to just about everything because their personalities are not inclined to be dictators. Besides, they enjoy having fun with the children and have an excellent sense of humor. Virgo-Snakes have a bit of the wanderlust and they most certainly are not homebodies. This is reflected in their homes, where they are not the least bit materialistic or interested in making a show. They want to be able to move about and perhaps to move on. While, like nearly everyone, they like to be comfortable, the story ends there in the decor department. While not gourmets, they do enjoy decent food, and their cupboards will not be bare.

Livelihood: This combination is made up of smart individuals who have a particular ability in the realm of science and mathematics. Perhaps the part of the mind that makes this combination calculating, literally, distracts them from being especially charitable. In general, the Virgo-Snake is okay with work, but they can lean toward laziness at times. They have a knack for fixing and making things and are technically inclined. This aptitude will be evident from an early age.

Famous Virgo-Snakes: Goethe, Greta Garbo, Jessica Mitford.

Virgo (Rooster) Month Combined with Horse Year

"Study" Mercury, Earth, Mutable   **"Command"** Yang-Positive Fire

Characteristics: Pragmatism, Anxiety, Service, Accomplishment, Autonomy, Unscrupulousness, Rebellion, Popularity, Haste, Persuasiveness, Crankiness, Reserve, Decorum, Selfishness, Meticulousness, Courtesy, Snobbery, Practicality, Dexterity, Style, Nit-picking, Negativism, Discrimination, Lucidity

This combination has a nice balance to it. There is a leveling off of pride but an increase in self-confidence for the Virgo side. The combination is not so prone to go prancing off foolishly thinking it can win every steeplechase. Instead of shyly staying inside, fearful of meeting others, or going out and finding fault, the Virgo-Horse carries itself well and proceeds to work toward success. The Virgo-Horse is a smooth combination, because the two aspects not only complement one another but also help to smooth out rough edges or negative characteristics. The Virgo-Horse has an air of dignity about them. Of course the Horse element makes for hard workers who are vibrant. Horses parade and strut, can be silly and too ardent. The Virgo element adds a portion of inhibition. They hold back and take few chances in life. They are discerning but frequently fussy. The smoothing influence mentioned above helps minimize the drawbacks in both the Horse and

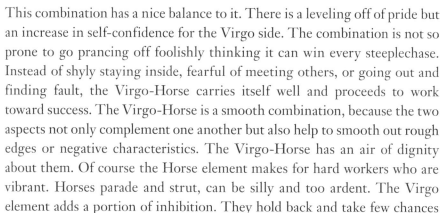

the Virgo. Finally, there is ability and talent that comes by the bushel for this combination. The wonderful imagination remains largely intact, but creativity does not run amok. The rebel without a cause undertakes reasonable and acceptable causes. Duty steps to the forefront. The final result is an extremely appealing individual: a modest but self-confident character. All of this lets the natural physical attraction shine through. Rather than the ostentatious attire that some Horses might choose, style wins the day. Charm is allowed to bloom.

Romance: In lovemaking this combination lives up to what the admirers thought they were: remarkable. They are supremely passionate and skilled in the art of love, and others seem to know this instinctively. To say that this combination has what it takes in the love and sex appeal category is a gross understatement. People practically worship them. The Virgo-Horse has a romantic air, but they exude this monumental seductive personality. Furthermore, that is not merely appearance; it is reality, too.

Relationships: Poor partners for compatibility in this combination are Gemini-, Sagittarius-, or Pisces-Rats. Also ruled out are Pisces-Monkeys. Excellent romantic fits are the Taurus, Cancer, Scorpio, and Capricorn. The cream of the crop among those are Dogs or Tigers. Also good choices are Scorpio- and Cancer-Rams.

Family Life: This combination makes a good mother or father. Family events and kids' activities are frequent. As parents, however, this combination is strict, and their children behave themselves. Manners and schoolwork are particularly emphasized. Finally, the Virgo-Horse loves to throw a shindig, and they are good at it. This combination tends toward middle-class values, and that will be evident in the home. Furniture is supposed to be right in the just-right home. Finances permitting, there will be domestic help.

Livelihood: It is a strong possibility that this combination will be in politics or other realms in public life. This combination has charisma and is able to use their magic before audiences, including large ones. This obviously makes them suitable to be in the spotlight, wherever that may be. Related to this is the fact that they are creative, but in this case that means the artistic. Overall, they are gifted in many areas, including business. They tend to exceed most others, regardless of the endeavor of their choice.

Famous Virgo-Horses: Leonard Bernstein, Vera Miles, Sean Connery, Alan Jay Lerner.

Virgo (Rooster) Month Combined with Ram Year

"Study" Mercury, Earth, Mutable **"Reliance"** Yang-Negative Fire

Characteristics: Crankiness, Taste, Worry, Impracticality, Decorum, Lack of Good Foresight, Reserve, Parasitism, Invention, Sensitivity, Whimsy, Perseverance, Pessimism, Tardiness, Courtesy, Snobbery, Nit-picking, Meticulousness, Practicality, Service, Lucidity, Manners, Negativism, Discrimination

There is a direct channel from a Virgo-Ram's perceptions to their mouths. In spite of the deep inner need for security, this combination tends to be a snob. Friends know the truth: that the stylish clothes and transportation are a mask made of wool covering their eyes. Some combinations lead to individuals who find themselves in precarious positions. That is the case with the Virgo-Ram. The end result is a person who is uncertain of their being. That is the case, because the zip of the Virgo is influenced by the neediness of the Ram. In addition, Rams are a highly materialistic type and love opulence. Virgos tend to be good workers, and that is certainly what this individual wants to be, or at least how they want to appear. The Ram influence disturbs the developmental process in that regard, however. The end result is someone who is, to put it gently, opinionated but easily manipulated by the slick and sly. The final result, especially as the years go by, is a peculiar person. They do not censor, and they rarely think before they opine. Sometimes their chatter can be pleasant, however. Security is one of their top priorities, and if they have it they tend to have fewer issues. Family, friends, and those whose function in life is to help others need to surround this individual. None of that means that this combination is shy and reserved. They are not.

Romance: The real lesson for this combination needs to incorporate a dose of reality in their sense of self, that is, realize who they really are. After learning these lessons there is a possibility of real love, romance, and marriage. There is, to be bold about it, a chance of true happiness. Those who find themselves interested in a Virgo-Ram should proceed with caution. Love and romance for a Virgo-Ram is a tough call. There is the snobbery to deal with and the tongue with no bridle. This combination is unpredictable, because it acts on impulse. A self-improvement class for this combination needs to begin with a lesson in humility.

Relationships: Probably unwise picks for this combination are Gemini, Sagittarius, and Pisces who are Buffalos or Dogs. Pisces-Tigers will not run the distance, and besides, they will just make this combination insecure. High-ranking romantic choices are Taurus, Cancer, Scorpio, and Capricorn. The best in those ranks are the Rabbit and Boar. Also good choices are Cancer- and Scorpio-Horses.

Family Life: The Virgo-Ram is one of those combinations for which style is a statement. They want people to notice their status so they feel secure. There is no plastic or polyester in this home. Everything is natural and reeks of elegance.

Livelihood: This combination also likes to throw a party, and they do it well. Parenthood is a mixture and switching between being a boss and being Santa Claus. They love playing with children and would probably like to sit on Santa's lap and ask for a few things themselves. "Steady as she goes" is what the Virgo-Ram wants in a profession. At work this combination can communicate well, and they have an ability for public speaking. Not surprising is the fact that this combination, being so opinionated, is biased and in some cases downright prejudiced. Vocations that appreciate a unique perspective work for this combination. As for being in charge, there is no possibility here whatsoever.

Famous Virgo-Rams: William Carlos Williams, George Wallace.

Virgo (Rooster) Month Combined with Monkey Year

"Study" Mercury, Earth, Mutable   **"Arrange"** Yin-Positive Metal

Characteristics: Cunning, Opportunism, Stability, Zeal, Self-reserve, Reserve, Involvement, Wit, Leadership, Decorum, Practicality, Crankiness, Courtesy, Improvisation, Ruse, Deceit, Snobbery, Meticulousness, Nit-picking, Service, Lucidity, Silliness, Negativism, Discrimination, Loquacity

Virgos want to ride on the crest of the wave; they want to associate with the high and mighty. They need that security. Monkeys are much more pragmatic and fly economy class. It is this gap difference in approaches to life that can lead to a lot of issues. There is a wide gap resulting from the dialectical interaction of Virgo and the Monkey. The Virgo side of things is, of course, superior; at least they tend to think this is the case. The Monkey side is not the least bit worried about lording it over others or even pretending to be better than they are. This results in a life that is a shade difficult at times. There is no issue of huge suffering here, but there is the issue of having to work very hard to get anywhere. There is not much in common between the high and mighty, say the CEO of the electric company, and the Monkey. They want so desperately to be in charge of their own being and, for that matter, the beings of lots of other people too. In the end, this is almost never possible, and the wave crashes into the rocks and the Virgo-Monkey is forced to try once again to figure out who they are. They are frequently, especially to Monkeys, boring and superficial and, most of all, selfish. So, besides having some personal and internal struggles that are no fun whatsoever, the result is a Nervous Nelly sort, trembling about the choices they make.

Romance: This combination wants to own those they love. If a person gives them the title to their soul, all will go well. The Virgo-Monkey will take care of, work for, sacrifice for, and die for that person. Total and complete love for a total and complete price is the bargain that must be agreed to. The Virgo-Monkey is totally, completely, and overwhelmingly serious about love. They may not have invented it, but they know how to do it; almost, that is. If this combination gets attracted to a person and then decides they love them, it is full steam ahead. Let the courting and the subsequent seduction begin. No is not an option. The drawback, and it is a huge drawback, is that it can feel smothering.

Relationships: Not good choices for this combination are Gemini-, Sagittarius-, or Pisces-Tigers. Also in the poor choice category are Gemini- and Sagittarius-Boars. Pisces-Snakes and Sagittarius-Buffalos do not make the cut either. The best choices are Taurus-, Cancer-, and Scorpio-Rats and Scorpio-Dragons. Capricorns who are Rats or Dragons are good too.

Family Life: This combination is not lazy. A lot of the work in fixing, decorating, renovating, landscaping, and other things will be done by the Virgo-Monkey themselves. In parenthood the controller returns and rules over their estate and all who live there with a firm—albeit loving—hand. As with the spouse, the children best not leave the grounds without being accompanied. The Virgo-Monkey wants the house on the hill: the expensive one with the antique gates and the guesthouse bigger than most people's homes. This desire stems from security and their fundamental need for it.

Livelihood: This combination wants to move ahead, and that means way ahead. They tend to want to replace their own bosses and take over for themselves. The Virgo-Monkey is a detail-minded person and is quite good in that regard. They are compulsive about things, including work, and almost never miss a day and are seldom late. Things must be lined up and strictly in order. Yes, there is a pragmatic motivation for this, but there is also just the fact that they are that way in their character.

Famous Virgo-Monkeys: Maxwell Perkins, William Saroyan, Lyndon Johnson, Craig Claiborne, Jacqueline Bisset.

Virgo (Rooster) Month Combined with Rooster Year
"Study" Mercury, Earth, Mutable **"Conqueror"** Yang-Negative Metal
Characteristics: Service, Conservatism, Humor, Chic, Crankiness, Negativism, Decorum, Resilience, Reserve, Enthusiasm, Courtesy, Practicality, Snobbery, Candor, Bossiness, Meticulousness, Nit-picking, Dissipation, Boastfulness, Discrimination, Lucidity, Cockiness, Blind Faith, Pedantry

This combination is acutely aware of their position in society, and their resolve will push them to attain class: very high class. They compulsively strive for the finer things in life, so they can be displayed as a show of membership in the upper crust. The Virgo-Rooster is one of the most determined combinations on the planet. Virtually nothing can stop them on their march to triumph. Resolve is this combination's middle name, and money is at the top of their priorities. This is especially true if they grew up in a needy family. That motivation carries over to them craving social standing. They have a knack for minutiae and are excellent in discovering what the actual facts in a given case are. This is not only helpful for them but is useful in a broader context. The source of this area of their character is their intelligence. They are sly, and coupled with this is discretion. They, along with members of their group, have the ability and wherewithal to pull off major deceptions. They are the type of person who knows useless and unusual facts. They are able to solve obscure mathematical puzzles. Finally, lurking in the background of the Virgo-Rooster is a native craftiness.

Romance: Love is defined on their terms, and that means that their partners must have a high regard for them. While they do not enjoy inflicting pain on the person they love, they will push harder than most to get their way, and that, at the very least, can be uncomfortable. Love and romance are not easy for Virgo-Roosters. While it is true that they desire to be seen as having status, their intelligence keeps them from being overbearing in ordinary daily situations. They do want to be liked, after all. Romance, however, is another matter. For starters, they are controllers and want things done their way.

Relationships: Out of bounds for this combination are Gemini-, Sagittarius-, or Pisces-Rabbits as well as Sagittarius-Roosters. To be totally avoided is the Pisces-Dog. The best choices are the Taurus-, Cancer-, Scorpio-, or even Capricorn-Snakes. Among these, Snakes are the best. Also great picks in the area of romance are the Taurus- or Capricorn-Buffalo as well as the Capricorn-Dragon.

Family Life: The decor represents a repository of artifacts or a peculiar secondhand shop. Clearly it is difficult to have children roaming around among huge antique vases and exotic Thai musical instruments. This is a home of a single person. An old cat or a medium-size well-behaved dog might be around, but there will be few if any jungle animals masquerading as children. The home of the Virgo-Rooster's is what might be expected from an absentminded professor of classics. It is messy but not dirty. Books are the first thing that will be noticed, and they are all over the house. Many of them are open or facedown, marking a page.

Livelihood: This combination is probably suited best for closet archaeologists or curators of museums. Professions like that provide both money and great personal satisfaction, and, of course, status. When speaking of the opera, the Virgo-Rooster immediately comes to mind. They do not want drama in their lives, but they love drama on the stage. Run-of-the-mill jobs will not pay for the home on or in the canyon where nature is visible and a lovely curvy road leads to the big city in fifteen minutes.

Famous Virgo-Roosters: Cardinal Richelieu, D. H. Lawrence, Elia Kazan, Ben Bradlee.

Virgo (Rooster) Month Combined with Dog Year

"Study" Mercury, Earth, Mutable   **"Concerned"** Yin-Positive Metal

Characteristics: Righteousness, Tastelessness, Intelligence, Morality, Self-meticulousness, Heroism, Respectability, Unsociability, Service, Discrimination, Crankiness, Decorum, Duty, Reserve, Cynicism, Uneasiness, Negativism, Practicality, Courtesy, Snobbery, Criticism, Nit-picking, Lucidity, Constancy

The Virgo-Dog may seem moody and grouchy frequently, but that is not the nature of this combination. The soul and perhaps the inspiration, too, of this person can be seen on their countenance. Look at the face carefully and there is a deep kindness and concern. One can forget what appears to be class and erudition. What one sees in a casual glance is a mask and not the real person. The Virgo-Dog is two people, but not in the way the Gemini is. This combination has the external and visible side of their being and the internal side. The latter is the real one and the one that matters. When help is needed this combination is there, especially for those they care about, but for society at large too. If a person needs a shoulder to cry on or an ear to hear one's troubles, the Virgo-Dog is the choice. They are not the bubbliest people on Earth, and they may not have a reputation as a do-gooder. This combination is also very family-oriented, and they take good care of those they love. They also enjoy sharing time with them. Inside this combination, though, is a person who really cares. While the Virgo-Dog may not be a human calculating machine, they will need a big calculator to add up the sums of money they will likely make. The likelihood of this comes from one place: hard work. Few can outwork this combination. While generous, they do watch their finances, and silly money-making schemes are not for them.

Romance: This combination does have that external moodiness that shows itself from time to time, but they are honorable. To keep things smooth on the domestic front, a partner of this combination would be advised to inject loads of humor into things. Virgo-Dogs are not desperate for love. They probably do not frequent dating websites, and if they do their profile is modest. They are not seekers of attention. They do want to marry, but if they do, a life without drama with lots of quiet and humor is what works for them.

Relationships: For this combination poor choices are Scorpio- and Capricorn-Horses. Additional combinations to avoid are Gemini-, Sagittarius-, and Pisces-Rams. To be strictly avoided are Sagittarius or Pisces-Dragons. Top romantic choices for the Virgo-Dog are Taurus, Cancer, Scorpio, and Capricorn people. Among these, the best are Taurus-, Scorpio-, and Capricorn-Tigers. Also good are Cancer-, Capricorn-, and Scorpio-Rabbits.

Family Life: In terms of style, the home is somewhat plain but attractive. It works well. Just like with the Virgo-Dog himself, one needs to look below the surface. Underneath the starkness there is a light of kindness that loved ones cannot miss. The pride of home ownership for the Virgo-Dog stems from a deep connection to the home. That connection is related to the fact that they built it themselves, at least in some sense of that phrase. They worked hard, and they endured to make it a reality.

Livelihood: The only problem they seem to encounter at work is sometimes not following things through to completion. The astute boss will notice that this is because the Virgo-Dog is helping his coworkers who are either inept at something or just downright lazy. Caution in the area of overworking is recommended for this combination. Virgo-Dogs are responsible workers. In fact they are exceptionally and beyond the call of duty responsible. Their aptitudes run in the direction of projects requiring meticulous work and problem solving. This might make them good in mechanically oriented professions.

Famous Virgo-Dogs: Rene Levesque, Kate Millet, Sophia Loren, Barry Gibb, Michael Jackson, Jean-Louis Barrault.

Virgo (Rooster) Month Combined with Boar Year

"Study" Mercury, Earth, Mutable **"Cultivator"** Yin-Negative Water
Characteristics: Boar-headedness, Gourmandism, Sincerity, Honesty, Culture, Hesitation, Materialism, Voluptuousness, Crankiness, Gallantry, Decorum, Scrupulousness, Reserve, Credulity, Courtesy, Nit-picking, Snobbery, Meticulousness, Practicality, Service, Lucidity, Negativism, Discrimination, Wrath

There are loads of excellent qualities in the character of the Virgo-Boar. They are hardworking and have a lot of common sense. They are disciplined and thorough. If you believe in rose-colored glasses then you have an understanding for the Virgo-Boar. Each and every thing in the universe, the animate as well as the inanimate, is good. Evil does not exist. The philosophical ramification of this view is too complicated to discuss here and so it can be left as just mentioning that this combination is naive and pure-hearted. All of this is topped off with a pleasant portion of sensuality. Some of these characteristics, particularly common sense, tell this combination that evil does exist in the world, but it is dismissed as the fault of society, not of individuals. Finally, in terms of the sort of person this combination is, it would be remiss to not mention that they are very good with their hands relative to craftsmanship. In fact, a quick summary of the nature of this combination could simply be that they are good people. Those that appear to be bad are actually victims in need of help. Perhaps it would be all right to leave things at that and, if one disagrees, just maintain that they are a fool with a bleeding heart. The problem is, however, that this combination is wide open to deception, scams, and actual danger because of their lily-white being and their purity of spirit.

Romance: Jewels, flowers, expensive dates—nothing is too great an expense or effort to capture the heart of someone they cannot resist. One cautionary note needs to be made. While this combination does not get angry often, when they do get angry, it is the rage of the gods. Fidelity and loyalty are the essence of the Virgo-Boar in love. Without hesitation, but with total commitment, this combination will be dedicated to those they love: partners, friends, spouses. Nothing is too great a sacrifice. The prelude to this kind of devotion is a staggering effort in an attempt to win over those they desire.

Relationships: This combination must avoid Gemini-, Sagittarius-, and Pisces-Snakes. Other bad selections are Gemini- or Pisces-Monkeys. Pisces-Dragons are totally out of the question. The Aries-Buffalo might just be the right sort of romantic connection for the Virgo-Boar. The other possibilities are Taurus-, Scorpio-, and Capricorn-Rabbits and Capricorn-Rams. Other picks are the Taurus-Tiger or -Boar.

Family Life: Parenthood is a snap for this combination because it comes naturally. They want good children but are willing to give a lot of effort too. Handmade Halloween costumes done with love and care come from this kind of parent. They drive their kids weekly to violin lessons and then to contests hundreds of miles away. Homework gets done and flu shots are not forgotten. The Virgo-Boar wants to be comfortable in a nice home with all the trappings. The trappings in this case might include antiques, art, and fine fabrics. Of course, because of the influence of the Boar, assorted fineries in the food realm are desired, so there will be gourmet tastes aplenty in this home. Unlike some Boars, however, there is a certain restraint in the area of materialism and food stores. There will be nothing ostentatious or reaching to the absurd here. This Boar is not a glutton.

Livelihood: This combination does not mind spending money, but they are extremely capable of earning it too. As people in charge they are respected, partly because they are willing to get their hands dirty and help out or even do the job themselves. As workers they are dependable. Virgo-Boars are industrious as well as being artistic. They are good at nearly anything with the exception of professions that involve science. Plainly put, they do not like that subject and cannot be bothered to study it.

Famous Virgo-Boars: Jorge Luis Borges, Robert Benchley, Stephen King, Ken Kesey.

Libra (Dog) Month Combined with Rat Year

"Steady" Venus, Air, Cardinal **"Regulator"** Yin-Positive Water

Characteristics: Thirst for Power, Charisma, Intellectual, Influence, Meddling, Talkativeness, Self-indulgence, Nervousness, Acquisitiveness, Idealism, Gentility, Procrastination, Aesthetics, Equilibrium, Justice, Indecision, Quarrelsomeness, Sociability, Manipulation, Appeal, Charm, Verbosity, Thrift, Guile

This combination believes the cosmos itself is the limit. The Libra-Rat is the most positive person on the planet. The power they have and the power they believe they will attain is not a power over other human beings. The Libra-Rat has delusions of power combined with loquaciousness. To phrase it more gently, they are eternally optimistic. The thing is that their optimism has no bounds and they fully expect to be major leaguers who play in a famous rock band in the off-season. They will have their own cooking show and be well-known brain surgeons. They are not self-centered, but rather have an interest in other people too. They care for them and tend to speak up for them. Libra-Rats are affable and open. Those who are friends with the Libra-Rat will never be bored with them because they are endlessly both interesting and interested. It is just a full-fledged belief that they will climb the highest mountain and sail the widest sea. They will do this and write poetry about it. They are, at their cores, poets. They are also excellent talkers. They are walking and talking filibusters. They will tell you everything about anything and leave no detail unexamined or unexplained. They are extremely friendly about all of this, of course.

Romance: This combination is extraordinarily sensitive. They need to be handled like fine handblown glass. They do, of course, take great pleasure in talking with those they love, so one should be prepared to communicate. Libra-Rats know love and never play games with it. They recognize how fragile it is and use their emotions with care. A person's feelings are sacred, both their own and those of others. Love and romance put new and complicated twists on this feeling. While they are cautious in the love department, they are not necessarily faithful partners. What this means is they understand love, but they do not always live up to the monogamist ideal.

Relationships: Not particularly good choices for this combination are Leo-Dragons or Aries-, Cancer-, or Capricorn-Horses. Horses in general are not good picks. Best avoided are Cancer- and Capricorn-Rabbits. There is a serious romantic attraction to Gemini, Leos, Sagittarians, and Aquarians, but the Monkeys are the best pick. Additional good picks are Dragons and Buffalos of the Monkey group.

Family Life: This combination makes fine parents who are responsible and loving. They are excellent about being with and communicating with their families. With the children they are a bit on the strict side. Libra-Rats love to be comfy and require a pleasant environment. The problem is that they are not particularly creative in this department. Neither are they particularly handy around the house. This combination is more oriented toward things intellectual. Regardless of whether a decorator is used or not, the Libra-Rat's home is organized around pragmatic principles. It must work.

Livelihood: This combination is excellent at convincing others, and they are quite social. They do tend to involve themselves in the affairs of others without being invited. They care about attaining some status in their careers and have the ability to do well. There is a balance in the combination that allows them to be fair judges. Libra-Rats have virtually no censoring mechanism between their brains and their mouths. They say what they think and they think a lot. Their aptitude in life centers on dealing with people because they communicate so well.

Famous Libra-Rats: T. S. Eliot, Eugene O'Neill, Truman Capote, Jimmy Carter, Jim Henson.

Libra (Dog) Month Combined with Buffalo Year

"Steady" Venus, Air, Cardinal **"Survivor"** Yin-Negative Water

Characteristics: Vindictiveness, Integrity, Bias, Innovation, Stability, Plodding, Strength of Purpose, Justice, Bigotry, Eloquence, Talkativeness, Standoffishness, Indecision, Equilibrium, Idealism, Gentility, Stubbornness, Diligence, Charm, Procrastination, Quarrelsomeness, Self-indulgence, Manipulation, Aesthetics

The Libra-Buffalo, like all human beings, has faults. The problems here center on the fundamental humanity of this combination and the fact that they have emotions. It is the emotions that rattle this seemingly unflappable person. The Libra-Buffalo is the paradigm of dialectics resulting in mind-boggling contradictions and conflicts. One side of this combination is a relentless perfectionist. They appear to be one of the most meticulous people in any circle. They strive for purity of perception and reality both. They will have the lovely house and the kids and pets and maybe even some horses. The house, however, and all the trappings, is fragile and perhaps made of straw. The wind that blows it down might come from the Libra-Buffalo themselves. It might be a wind born of emotions that have run amok. While they are gentle and tend to be kind, they sometimes appear to desire a life on the edge of psychosis and emotional turmoil. They want high drama even though they appear to want a happy family in the suburbs. And yes, the fact is that they are, in one very real sense, the beautiful and gentle person that one sees. They will more than likely attain what they seek.

Romance: For those who dare risk love and romance with this combination, the home will always be there and be a place of security. Romance in the case of this combination is either a can of worms or a kettle of fish. In any case, it is complicated. The Libra-Buffalo hides a number of emotional issues and difficulties that need to be dealt with. These include, but are not limited to, an argumentative nature coupled with a demanding and manipulative personality.

Relationships: For this combination some poor picks are Aries-, Cancer-, and Capricorn-Tigers as well as Cancer-Dragons, -Horses, and -Monkeys. Capricorn-Rams are way out of bounds. The very best romantic choices are Gemini, Leo, Sagittarius, and Aquarius. Snakes are the best among these signs. Leo-, Sagittarius-, and Aquarius-Rats are also fine selections. Further good choices are Gemini- and Sagittarius-Buffalo. Leo- and Aquarius-Roosters are also good.

Family Life: This combination desires to be the head of the family, and that might be best in order to keep their emotions in check. Springing from the need to have a place for everything and everything in its place, the Libra-Buffalo thinks they are kind, good-hearted and generous. Everyone in the household should nominate them for the leader of the pack. Libra-Buffalos are family people through and through. They are devoted and will maintain the family unit at all costs.

Livelihood: This combination can be counted on to do the job well and on time. In general they get along with others, but because of their extreme fussiness, they can be a chore to have as a boss. Surprisingly, they tend to be fairly tactful. Libra-Buffalos tend to be successful to varying degrees and usually do quite well. The main reason for their success is that they are excellent workers. They tend to be extremely reliable and responsible.

Famous Libra-Buffalos: Chester Alan Arthur, Art Buchwald, Gore Vidal.

Libra (Dog) Month Combined with Tiger Year

"Steady" Venus, Air, Cardinal   **"Observe"** Yang-Positive Wood

Characteristics: Intemperance, Benevolence, Itinerancy, Authority, Good Luck, Hotheadedness, Disobedience, Magnetism, Swagger, Bravery, Indecision, Talkativeness, Fervor, Idealism, Impetuosity, Justice, Self-indulgence, Charm, Aesthetics, Gentility, Equilibrium, Manipulation, Quarrelsomeness, Procrastination

This combination has a high level of appeal to everyone. It could, for example, begin with their awesome sense of humor. Something about the Libra-Tiger will grab people's attention though, regardless of what it is. The frosting on the cake, however, and what everyone notices, is their fundamental cuteness. The Libra-Tiger is a unique, one of a kind combination. From the moment you meet this combination you will be won over completely. It seems at times as though their mission in life is to make others happy. While some may perceive them as disingenuous, the fact is they win others over. They are delightful and charming. This group has many friends and admirers and is esteemed by all. As a rule though, they do walk the walk and are happy about helping others, being kind and doing the right thing. This is not to be understood as having reverence for the establishment or a conservative worldview. Quite the contrary. They are hugely impertinent and break social mores at every opportunity. They are successful though because of their charm and their work ethic. There is sort of a magic about them, but alas, magic usually involves tricks. They are not hypocrites or fakes though. They work hard in the world and pay their dues. It is just that concrete solid self-confidence can feel a bit over the top to some.

Romance: This combination is sensitive, but oddly enough they can seem a bit hostile and aggressive at times. Overall, however, they are among the coolest of the combinations in terms of dress, composure, and flair. This combination is excellent for many other combinations because of its overall balance. Libra-Tigers are excellent partners and have a sweet disposition. They tend toward placing a value on being romantic. The sexual aspect of romance is ample, but it is certainly not at the top of their list of priorities.

Relationships: Poor choices for this combination are Aries-, Cancer-, or Capricorn-Rabbits. Additional unwise selections are Aries-Snakes. Capricorn- and Cancer-Buffalos as well as Cancer-Rams are totally off the list of possibilities. Some superb choices for a partner are the Gemini, Leo,

Sagittarius, or Aquarius who are Dogs. Sagittarius- and Aquarius-Dragons are also fine.

Family Life: This combination makes for good parents who are caring and thoughtful. They set a good example and are fun for the children at the same time. The Libra-Tiger loves their home totally and completely. In fact, they may love it just a tad too much if one judges things on a financial basis. Plainly put, they spend a lot of money on their home. They want nothing but the best, and nothing short of a sumptuous environment will satisfy them. They adorn not just the big picture at home but the details as well. Everything from the knobs on the faucets to the hinges on the doors has to be first class.

Livelihood: On top of everything, the Libra-Tiger is a charmer. They are capable of using this quality in conjunction with their hard work to better themselves and to help their family. They are ready, willing, and able to take leadership roles. Libra-Tigers are excellent workers and are happy to do more than their share. They pitch in and help when needed and do it with a sense of caring. They have a lot of energy.

Famous Libra-Tigers: Rimbaud, Oscar Wilde, Dwight D. Eisenhower, Thor Heyerdahl, Michel Foucault, Valery Giscard d'Estaing, Mary McFadden.

Libra (Dog) Month Combined with Rabbit Year

"Steady" Venus, Air, Cardinal   **"Withdraw"** Yin-Negative Wood

Characteristics: Longevity, Hypochondria, Ambition, Squeamishness, Pedantry, Virtue, Complexity, Dilettantism, Prudence, Secretiveness, Indecision, Talkativeness, Idealism, Tact, Finesse, Equilibrium, Self-indulgence, Aesthetics, Justice, Charm, Gentility, Quarrelsomeness, Procrastination, Manipulation

The Libra-Rabbit tends to be a homebody. Earning the trust of this combination takes times because they refrain from taking any sort of leap of faith. At times they reflect on a decision so long that by the time they make up their minds their opportunity is long gone. Careful and sophisticated are the first two adjectives that are associated with the Libra-Rabbit. It is not surprising that they have superior skills in the area of aesthetics because both the Libra and the Rabbit possess this quality. They personify indecision, and this comes from both the Libra, who hates to judge, and the Rabbit, who is edgy. They appear to be quite levelheaded as well as calm and cool. The reality is quite different. They are often so indecisive that it occasionally reaches the point of confusion. This can result in the inability to make a decision. They avoid any hint of conflict and virtually refuse to be the attacker. Furthermore, this aspect of the Libra-Rabbit's being can lead to missed opportunities and regret. Of course, like most people, there is an inner self and an outer self. In the case of this combination, there is an appearance of self-assurance and reliability.

Romance: Any individual who falls in love with the Libra-Rabbit needs to be extraordinarily patient in trying to catch them permanently. In addition, techniques that lead them to believe they are doing the catching need to be employed from time to time. Playing hard to get, up to a point, works in snagging the fickle heart of the Libra-Rabbit. This combination loves romance and the occasional intrigue that comes with it. They can be prone to falling in love in a serial fashion. The Libra-Rabbit, plainly put, is a nice person to be around. They make excellent companions. They also, stemming from their Libra side, enjoy talking a bit. As a result, they not only like to be in love, they like to talk about love. They also happen to be quite good at it. They are loving, bighearted, and ardent. The problem is that they are reluctant to choose a single individual to be with.

Relationships: Poor choices for this combination are Cancer- or Capricorn-Roosters or Capricorn-Rats. Of course, go slowly in any serious romance with a Libra-Rabbit. Excellent choices in love and romance are Gemini, Leo, Sagittarius, and Aquarius individuals. Of those, the Ram, Dog, or Boar are the top of the line. Not such a good choice is Aries-Buffalo.

Family Life: This combination might not be the model spouse or particularly high-quality parent, because this sometimes involves conflict and that is something they do not do well. In fact, they avoid it. Being a disciplinarian is not something this combination was cut out to be, in spite of the best intentions in the realm of parenthood. The home of the Libra-Rabbit is plush but old-fashioned to the extent that it is sophisticated. There will probably be leather with thick carpeting. There could be marble and wallpaper with a heavy mantle over the fireplace. There is no attempt to be showy or gaudy with this combination. Rather there is an attempt to reflect their own being. In terms of the family, particularly being a parent, the Libra-Rabbit will fulfill their responsibilities.

Livelihood: One thing this combination does not do is make a good boss. Should they end up in a situation where one is needed, they would have to employ an enforcer. The Libra-Rabbit is good at professions requiring some independence, but that most certainly does not include being a self-starting entrepreneur. That requires too much hard-nosed competition and conflict. This does not mean that they lack character, however, because the opposite is the case. They leave a good impression with others always.

Famous Libra-Rabbits: George C. Scott, Arthur Miller, Gunter Grass.

Libra (Dog) Month Combined with Dragon Year

"Steady" Venus, Air, Cardinal   **"Take Charge"** Yang-Positive Wood

Characteristics: Enthusiasm, Sentimentality, Braggadocio, Volubility, Infatuation, Idealism, Mistrust, Pluck, Dissatisfaction, Indecision, Good Charm, Talkativeness, Strength, Rigidity, Success, Equilibrium, Procrastination, Self-indulgence, Gentility, Justice, Quarrelsomeness, Manipulation, Aesthetics, Health

This combination is most certainly not the shy type, largely because there are some mismatches in character here. There is a potential storm brewing, but the Libra-Dragon often averts it and leads a charmed and lucky life. This is a moderate to strong clash of signs dialectically speaking. The Libra element can figure out a method for getting its way but always wants things balanced. The Dragon adds mistrust as well as a demand to be noticed. The natural tact of the Libra often allows them to calm the storm. Much of the time, however, the Dragon will hear nothing of this. The Dragon, of course, has a particularly loud voice and is not afraid to use it to inform others it is right. Energy is expended, but there might be some debate as to whether it is wasted. The reason for this is that the Libra-Dragon clash, as often as not, passes the test of success. They are highly creative, and this quality helps in every manner of accomplishment. As if all this was not enough, they also happen to be a high-energy combination that works hard for what they have and what they want. In the end, therefore, and in spite of dialectical considerations, this is a combination that does what it needs to do and gets what it wants in life. While they can be almost shameless in that pursuit, results are achieved.

Romance: This combination demands total focus, appreciation, compliments, and a person to bounce ideas off. Anyone not ready, willing, and able to provide these attentions is simply not suitable for them. Consequently, being the partner of a Libra-Dragon can be exhausting and difficult work. Nevertheless, most seem to find a more than suitable partner and tend to live somewhat happily ever after. The romantic life of a Libra-Dragon is a bit of a roller coaster ride. They certainly do not like to be tied down too early in life and love to play the field. After some time doing that, there is a good likelihood that they will find an excellent match. Extending the period prior to tying the knot is the fact that this combination is not easily satisfied. The primary attribute they demand is attention. Actually, that is a bit of an understatement.

Relationships: For this combination poor selections are Aries-, Cancer-, or Capricorn-Rabbits or Capricorn-Dogs. Totally out of the running are Cancer-Buffalos. Excellent love and romance choices are Gemini-, Leo-, Sagittarius-, or Aquarius-Rats. Additional picks are Gemini-, Leo-, and Aquarius-Monkey individuals. The good choices continue with Leo- and Sagittarius-Roosters as well as Leo-Snakes.

Family Life: Libra-Dragons make fine parents. Part of this relates to the fact the Libra-Dragons like to be looked up to by anyone, but especially by their children. Of course teens are not well known for looking up to their parents, so there will probably be some of the usual difficulties there. Libra-Dragons know what they want in terms of clothing and decor in their homes. They tend to do both well, even though their physical appearance is not necessarily what everyone wants. They are the sort of people who can project themselves onto their world because of their fine taste and awareness of aesthetics. They do this so well that it is actually an advantage in their lives.

Livelihood: This combination is destined for success. Perhaps one area where they are lacking a bit is the area of patience, but that is not a major obstacle. They make good managers and coworkers who are popular among those they work with. The Libra-Dragon is generally a totally terrific employee. They can work and run circles around most, and they have a vim and vigor that is awesome to behold. This is true regardless of what profession they undertake: from the classroom to the boardroom, from outer space to the factory. They are so good at so much that they will probably not remain a lower tier employee for long.

Famous Libra-Dragons: Nietzsche, Sarah Bernhardt, Graham Greene, John Lennon, Rex Reed, Angie Dickinson, Christopher Reeve.

Libra (Dog) Month Combined with Snake Year

"Steady" Venus, Air, Cardinal   **"Feel"** Yang-Negative Fire

Characteristics: Presumption, Compassion, Laziness, Clairvoyance, Exclusiveness, Extravagance, Discretion, Style, Attractiveness, Intuition, Dissimulation, Idealism, Charm, Talkativeness, Self-indulgence, Sagacity, Procrastination, Cupidity, Gentility, Equilibrium, Aesthetics, Indecision, Quarrelsomeness, Manipulation, Justice

Dealing with this combination generally means dancing around a headstrong individual. Often the only way to do the deal is their way. Because they frequently have admirers around them, getting others to accomplish tasks for them is not as difficult as it is for some. The Libra-Snake is a social magnet who attracts people in unparalleled numbers. Of course, no life is all roses and cherries, and that is true of these individuals as well, because they do have a broad stubborn streak. They can unite people in a family of emotions that is both brotherly and motherly. While they can appear somewhat flaccid, that passivity carries a strength that creates fervent followers. This combination tends, in spite of the stubbornness, to provide others with feelings of purpose and security. They give people direction. The Libra-Snake has keen senses bordering on the psychic. They have a special kind of intuition, and they have a knack for knowing what others want from them, particularly in the emotional realm. At times they are capable of bringing out the sentimental in the hardest heart. In fact, they can do that with groups as well as individuals.

Romance: Besides everything else, they have a bit of an independent side and enjoy doing things on their own. This requires patience and self-sufficiency in any partner. Whether they are worth the effort is not really an issue, because for those who adore them the answer is most certainly a resounding yes. Libra-Snakes are beautiful and sensual people who know feelings and that means romance. They make excellent partners in most ways, but, alas, they tend not to be in relationships for the long haul. They are too desirable for that. They also happen to be a lot of fun in a wacky kind of way.

Relationships: Not the best of choices for compatibility in this combination are Aries- and Capricorn-Monkeys. Cancer- and Capricorn-Boars are also poor choices as are Cancer-Tigers. An excellent start in the search for romance is Roosters. The best picks among them are Gemini, Leo, Sagittarius, and Aquarius. Leo-, Sagittarius-, and Aquarius-Buffalos are also good selections.

Family Life: This combination is the grand protector of all creatures great and small. They also enjoy their kids so much that they join in with fun and use a special magic to entertain them. The Libra-Snake is not, however, beyond giving a good lecture to a wayward yearling. Comfort and luxury are the hallmarks of the Libra-Snake home. The finest fabrics and plenty of artwork need to be employed. All of this luxury must, however, be exceedingly comfortable. Libra-Snakes like others to view their environment, so people can drop in for a visit without notice and feel quite welcome. The fact that these individuals love parenting is demonstrated by the large families they tend to have. Essentially the Libra-Snake likes having people around, including the family.

Livelihood: In the end, they are usually in charge because of their abilities with people. All of this works fine unless the Libra-Snake abuses his power. Then it gets ugly. Fortunately, this is unlikely to happen for this combination. They do not want to step on the necks of others, but neither do they want to be stepped on. The Libra-Snake attracts followers without trying and, in some cases, without particularly wanting them. For certain what they do not want is hostility or even competition. What they have to offer is their beauty and their transcendent good feelings.

Famous Libra-Snakes: Mahatma Gandhi, Thelonious Monk, Jesse Jackson.

Libra (Dog) Month Combined with Horse Year

"Steady" Venus, Air, Cardinal   **"Command"** Yang-Positive Fire

Characteristics: Dexterity, Anxiety, Accomplishment, Pragmatism, Unscrupulousness, Autonomy, Popularity, Rebellion, Haste, Selfishness, Indecision, Talkativeness, Idealism, Persuasiveness, Self-indulgence, Charm, Gentility, Procrastination, Equilibrium, Quarrelsomeness, Aesthetics, Justice, Manipulation

Tugging at its reins, the Libra makes an effort to calm the Horse. Generally, this takes time and a lot of effort. The eventual goal is a respectable member of society or, barring that, a bit of taming. It is not a matter of the Libra side being bothered by the unpredictability of the Horse. The Libra-Horse combinations are kind of a push and pull dialectic. Libras are noble and seek equilibrium. Libras want harmony. Countering this is a Horse personality that is defiant and stubborn. To the contrary, Libras rather approve of that. What is desired is a willingness to be a part of the establishment when necessary so that material possessions, sought after by the Libra, are not lost. Horses, when properly controlled and educated, have a wonderful stately and almost majestic presence. This is very much desired by the Libra aspect. They are agile and have an ability to advance toward success with an ease not granted to most. Of course, the fact that the Libra-Horse is not the least bit lazy and is willing to work hard for that success does not hurt either. In addition, they have an air of confidence and charm made all the better by doing well before audiences. This combination has a ticket to ride and the ticket is in first class. They have a destiny that includes not only fame but also fortune if the jumps are made well. Luck is on the side of these fortunate individuals in many cases, because they seem to appear, just in time, at the precise place that they were supposed to be.

Romance: Libra-Horses do like to be noticed when they go places. Many have refined the fine art of flirting, and this comes easy because there is something highly appealing about most members of this combination. They tend to be a bit of work to have as a partner for these reasons, and because they are lacking somewhat in the giving department. This latter point, in particular, can be an issue. The Libra-Horse tends to march to the beat of his own drummer; in some cases it is the beat of his own brass band. In terms of a partner, this means that they choose someone who has something that they like or appreciate. It is not a matter of appearance. Looks are not a particularly important factor. Principles, ideals, or material possessions are more important than appearance.

Relationships: Aries-, Cancer-, or Capricorn-Rats are not recommended for this combination. Capricorn-Rams are a no-go as well. The Gemini-, Leo-, Sagittarius-, or Aquarius-Tiger are fine selections in the area of romance. Additional good picks are a Gemini- or Leo-Ram. The positive choices continue with Sagittarius- and Aquarius-Dogs.

Family Life: This combination is the type who has automatic this and computerized that in the home and on the grounds. The sprinklers go on automatically as do the lights. The house has flowers arranged to perfection in exactly the right places. Friends are welcome but they must behave and dress appropriately. The Libra-Horse absolutely must have luxury at home as well as every gadget known to humankind. The house is a showplace for friends to come and be impressed. The sofa is so luxurious that people might be afraid to sit on it. The curtains and all the other trappings are nothing but the finest.

Livelihood: Libra-Horses' primary motivation at work is to get ahead, and they are not particularly good at compromising unless it is self-serving. They are the paradigm of a "dress for success" person. If they play their cards right, they do, in most cases, succeed at a high level. The Libra-Horse is excellent at logic and communication. The result is that they can convince people of almost anything. That is fortunate because they tend to be fond of arguing. Obvious jobs that are suitable for them are those that utilize verbal abilities and clear thinking.

Famous Libra-Horses: Dmitri Shostakovitch, Rita Hayworth, Penny Marshall.

Libra (Dog) Month Combined with Ram Year

"Steady" Venus, Air, Cardinal   **"Reliance"** Yang-Negative Fire

Characteristics: Parasitism, Sensitivity, Tardiness, Pessimism, Taste, Worry, Quarrelsomeness, Justice, Aesthetics, Charm, Gentility, Manipulation, Procrastination, Self-indulgence, Equilibrium, Indecision, Idealism, Talkativeness, Invention, Lack of Foresight, Perseverance, Whimsy, Good Manners, Impracticality

Libra-Rams are quite serious much of the time, and they want people to recognize that about them. While they do not want to be placed on a pedestal, they do want to be well liked by their associates. Balance is important to most Libras. However, Libra-Rams are the exception to the rule because they are not concerned about balance and peace. Plainly put, they are difficult and hard to get along with a lot of the time. They enjoy a good argument that gets the blood pressure up a bit. They are experimental and like to try new things. They can be lazy at times but have a taste for flair and sophistication. In terms of style, they lean toward the conservative or timeless. Libra-Rams are somewhat air headed, but they are absolutely genuine. There is nothing fake about them. They have a sense of security and self-awareness. There is a large dose of creativity in this combination. They probably will not be famous artists, but they are skilled at many crafts and have basic artistic talents. This combination is not interested in the latest fad or current trend. They climb the ladder of success by being cultured, not by drinking martinis. Rule them out as party animals and associate them with art galleries.

Romance: Libra-Rams would be lost on their own. They are huggers and kissers and terms of endearment people. For those courting a Libra-Ram, this means performing the necessary romantic rituals and being exceptionally tender and sentimental. Libra-Rams are romantics and know what they are doing in that area. They have the necessary emotional makeup to use candles at the dinner table and have surprise birthday parties. They love walks on the beach and moonlit nights. They are good in the sexual portion of love too. They are not exactly needy, but they are made to be part of a couple.

Relationships: Ruled out for compatibility in this combination are Aries-, Cancer-, and Capricorn-Dogs as are Cancer- and Capricorn-Buffalos. Capricorn-Tigers do not make the list either. Rabbits are a great romantic choice and of those the top of the line are Gemini, Leo, Sagittarius, and Aquarius. Horses are also good and among that group the best are Gemini, Sagittarius, or Aquarius. Continuing the rather large number of good picks are Leo- and Aquarius-Boars.

Family Life: This combination is the messy type. They make good parents and strive to have educated and cultured children. Their natures allow them to be overwhelmed by their children from time to time because they are most certainly not disciplinarians. The Libra-Ram has more of the absentminded professor approach to home decorating. Essentially, they are not particularly worried about their environment as long as it works. Neither are they out to impress others. They are the intellectual type and thus not meant to be home decorators. Comfort is the first priority.

Livelihood: This combination is particularly good in areas involving imagination and innovation. Others do need to encourage them because they can be very sensitive if not supported. They are most certainly not multitaskers, so their assignment sheet needs to be kept to a minimum. Libra-Rams were not meant to be on their own. They do not work well that way and they do not do well at home that way. They need others to help them stay organized. They are gifted and original in many areas. The Libra-Ram presents themselves well and is well spoken.

Famous Libra-Rams: Pierre Trudeau, Doris Lessing, Chevy Chase, Barbara Walters, Catherine Deneuve.

Libra (Dog) Month Combined with Monkey Year

"Steady" Venus, Air, Cardinal   **"Arrange"** Yin-Positive Metal

Characteristics: Opportunism, Silliness, Justice, Loquacity, Self-involvement, Cunning, Stability, Zeal, Leadership, Indecision, Talkativeness, Idealism, Manipulation, Improvisation, Deceit, Charm, Equilibrium, Procrastination, Wit, Gentility, Self-indulgence, Ruse, Quarrelsomeness, Aesthetics

This combination is not the most peaceful internally. Libra loves balance and a stable home life, while the Monkey is talkative and enjoys a good fight from time to time. The Libra-Monkey is an artist who paints with words. They can do virtually anything with their verbal skills, both negative and positive. They are able to use words for wonderful and creative things or they can manipulate them for less-desirable motives. Clearly they are fantastic conversationalists, and there is never a boring moment when in their company. The Libra-Monkey is highly capable of rationalizing anything that is borderline in the manipulation department. This combination is perfectly capable of using its intelligence and way with words to exploit people. They know they always want what is best for others and it is just a coincidence that it happens to be in their best interest as well. This is a bright and amusing combination. They are very easygoing in many ways, thanks to the Monkey influence. There is a fidgety element in the nature of the Libra-Monkey, and they sometimes suffer from a kind of wanderlust on a small scale. They want to move from spot to spot.

Romance: In the end, the Libra-Monkey wants a two-way street of mutuality in all things. Consequently they make for a good choice for many individuals. The overall picture in terms of romance for the Libra-Monkey is one where the relationship is important and devotion is present. That is not to say that everything is perfect. This combination can, for example, be selfish. Sometimes this can overcome the natural tendency to be fair.

Relationships: Cancer-Boars and Capricorn-Buffalos are ruled out entirely for this combination. Dragons are a good choice in the area of love and romance. The best bets are Gemini, Leo, Sagittarius, or Aquarius individuals. Other good picks include Leo-, Sagittarius-, and Aquarius-Rats. Lower on the list are Aries- or Cancer-Horses as are Cancer- or Capricorn-Tigers.

Family Life: This combination's security is not based in their real estate. The Libra-Monkey makes good parents. They are loving and caring. In addition, many of them are still kids at heart. This combination has a home to live in and to go to after work. They are not particularly interested in making a big production out of things. Like most people, they do enjoy comfort and luxury, but they do not need a villa. In addition, while they are not the type to pack up and move to Fiji on the spur of the moment, they simply do not need that much.

Livelihood: This combination makes wonderful friends and coworkers and is able to be in positions that utilize their verbal ability and human relations aptitude. As bosses they are able to gain respect because of their intelligence and communication skills. Libra-Monkeys carry themselves well and have an appearance of stature. There is a dignity about them. They have a wonderful ability to use words. Additionally they are able to convert words into more concrete notions. This make them especially good at jobs such as public relations that require those abilities.

Famous Libra-Monkeys: Glenn Gould, Buster Keaton, F. Scott Fitzgerald, Jacques Tati, John Kenneth Galbraith, Timothy Leary.

Libra (Dog) Month Combined with Rooster Year

"Steady" Venus, Air, Cardinal   **"Conqueror"** Yang-Negative Metal

Characteristics: Dissipation, Bossiness, Humor, Quarrelsomeness, Blind Faith, Enthusiasm, Candor, Boastfulness, Conservatism, Cockiness, Indecision, Talkativeness, Idealism, Resilience, Pedantry, Aesthetics, Indulgence, Justice, Gentility, Charm, Equilibrium, Chic, Manipulation, Procrastination

This combination is balanced to some extent by the character of the Libra, but that seems primarily to focus on the Rooster's somewhat arrogant and bossy streak. The Libra also lightens up the sometimes stodgy nature of the Rooster. Finally, the Libra side gives a more balanced frame of reference in terms of reactions, whereas the Rooster tends to go a bit over the top. Libras are far more thoughtful in the way they react to the world and are almost reluctant to make judgments about anything. The Libra-Rooster is another one of those hills and valleys combinations. Emotionally they climb high, only to fall into depression. In fact, the Libra-Rooster might be the most easygoing Rooster of all. The Rooster element can motivate the Libra side to be more active because of its down-to-earth but fervent nature. The best medicine, in many cases, is activity, which the Rooster promotes. In the long run, in spite of some issues, this combination is a fortunate one indeed. While the Libra is not passive, they do tend to relax a little too much and need to be prodded on occasion. The Rooster is very handy in this regard. They can remind the Libra of the wide world around them that needs exploring. Still, because of this kind of tilting and rotating character, this combination does suffer from rather extreme mood swings.

Romance: This combination has deep and sincere feelings for those they love and are committed to. For those who have a Libra-Rooster as a mate, there is generally respect as well. However, this combination is extremely sensitive and requires a rather high degree of affection. While they may be slow to commit to love, once they have, they stick with it. Probably no combination is more loyal than this one. The Libra-Rooster tends to stick to one mate for their entire life. There is one important element there, however. It is absolutely critical that they have respect for their partner. This combination has a lot to offer and can make a wonderful spouse. Fortunately, they do take their time in deciding who their partner will be.

Relationships: Poor picks for this combination include Aries-Boars, Cancer-Roosters, and Capricorn-Rabbits. The Libra-Rooster needs a levelheaded and calm partner in order to attain happiness. That quality is paramount in any romantic match that might come along. Gemini-, Leo-, Sagittarius-, or Aquarius-Buffalos and Aquarius-Snakes are superb choices in the love and romance department.

Family Life: This combination is more the mental sort. In the areas of parenting this combination is not a model of the hands-on approach. Libra-Roosters are not the type who change diapers nor do they have an interest in being a Scout leader. As half of a couple, they do quite well, however. Libra-Roosters are more outdoor- and intellectual-type characters and consequently do not have a taste for interior decorating. They are not the type who enjoys making homemade quilts or needlepoint pillowcases. They are not slobs and do prefer to keep their homes looking presentable, but they do not use them as a showpiece. Practical, do-it-yourself home chores have little appeal to this individual.

Livelihood: Artistry comes to the forefront in particular when this combination is younger. If developed, there is no stopping them. While they may need, on occasion, to fit into some sort of establishment framework, it is possible that they can design this on their own. Regardless, however, they will more than likely achieve at a very high level. There is talent and a highly special quality about the Libra-Rooster that tends to make fame and fortune more likely. It starts with the creative nature of the combination. Furthermore, while Libras are not inclined to put themselves forward, the Rooster steps in here to promote a more active and confident approach to life.

Famous Libra-Roosters: Giuseppe Verdi, Louis Aragon, William Faulkner, Al Capp, Yves Montand.

Libra (Dog) Month Combined with Dog Year

"Steady" Venus, Air, Cardinal   **"Concerned"** Yin-Positive Metal

Characteristics: Morality, Intelligence, Tastelessness, Heroism, Justice, Self-righteousness, Unsociability, Respectability, Boastfulness, Indulgence, Indecision, Equilibrium, Idealism, Procrastination, Aesthetics, Gentility, Charm, Manipulation, Cynicism, Criticism, Duty, Uneasiness, Quarrelsomeness, Constancy

The Libra-Dog is a caring individual who does not mind people crying on his or her shoulder. They have the ability to make others feel better about themselves and consequently are terrific friends. The Libra-Dog has many roles and is a seriously complicated person. To begin with, this combination is an idealist, and this is probably reflected best in the fact that they are so generous. Their idealism, however, does not preclude them from worrying and complaining. An additional characteristic includes a highly artistic nature. There is a lot more to this combination, and the list is practically endless. They also make wonderful and creative coworkers. The balance that Libra brings allows this combination to deal with things fairly and empathetically. However, they can be reluctant to stick their necks out for causes or for individuals. That is because of their ability to comprehend both sides of the coin. The complaints that this combination registers are about the unfairness of life and how the needy should be helped. The mixture of the Libra and the Dog is a very compassionate one who endlessly cares about the poor and needy of the world. The end result does not make for the happiest of lives for this combination, but it does make for a generally good person who is admired and appreciated. The Dog side of the combination adds reluctance for conflict to the balancing act of the Libra. This results in a person who absolutely does not want to hurt anyone or anything. Only self-defense would cause them to do that.

Romance: The Libra-Dog is in no hurry to move in with someone. Being their partner also requires a bit of a thick skin, because they can be very critical people. That is often a one-way street, because they do not particularly like people criticizing them. The best approach in dealing with this combination is to agree with them a lot about their ideas and give them space of their own from time to time. Libra-Dogs are social animals and hang out with all sorts of people. In the area of love and commitment, however, they are very careful and methodical. They take their own sweet time. They are wonderful lovers, but sometimes have a fear of being intimate. To catch this sign for marriage requires a lot of patience.

Relationships: For this combination Dragons can be ruled out, and this is doubly true if they are Aries, Cancer, or Capricorn. Also not making the list are Cancer- or Capricorn-Rams. Totally out of the question are Cancer-Monkeys. Tigers make an excellent romantic partner for the Libra-Dog, especially if they are Gemini, Sagittarius, or Aquarius. Additional good selections are Gemini-, Leo-, or Aquarius-Rabbits. Really good choices can be found among Leo- and Sagittarius-Horses as well as Gemini-Snakes.

Family Life: This combination thinks so long about a commitment that they are often late to marry and thus do not tend to have children. They do like children, though, and get along with them famously. There is a sardonic side to their nature that some find unappealing. They are good providers for their family and make good family members. This is a country person, and it is there that they are happy. The Libra-Dog finds the city hard and unkind. They are too tender to handle that. Their home has somewhat the appearance of a neatnik. They like things kept organized. Even though a country person, they are inclined toward more modern design at home. However, they do like colors that reflect the Earth and the seasons.

Livelihood: This combination is supremely tender and considerate. That can be both a blessing and a curse for them, because they can be taken advantage of. As bosses they are fair and just. Their subordinates tend to like them and work hard for them. While not exactly nerds, this sign is drawn to technical professions and they do quite well in that area. This probably stems from their inclination to be organized and orderly, which is a mirror of logic. They are also interested in current events and, oddly enough, poetry as well.

Famous Libra-Dogs: Charles Ives, George Gershwin, Brigitte Bardot.

Libra (Dog) Month Combined with Boar Year

"Steady" Venus, Air, Cardinal **"Cultivator"** Yin-Negative Water

Characteristics: Honesty, Culture, Boar-headedness, Gourmandism, Materialism, Wrath, Sincerity, Hesitation, Voluptuousness, Indecision, Scrupulousness, Idealism, Talkativeness, Credulity, Gentility, Charm, Self-indulgence, Manipulation, Procrastination, Equilibrium, Justice, Quarrelsomeness, Aesthetics, Gallantry

Everything the Libra-Boar does is centered on their love relationship. Another issue that crops up here is the concept of a one-dimensional person. Nothing comes close to the love of their life. The Libra-Boar has one focus and that is love; essentially everything else does not make it into their heart and soul. They are, as a result of this, excellent lovers. They are faithful to the one they love and there is no one else on the planet—forever. This, of course, gets highly intense and is way over the top for many, especially when the green monster of jealousy is added to the mixture. They may have interests, but they are a distant second. Libra seeks the lovely and the beautiful. It seems that without it, they will surely die. Boars want material possessions and quiet. The result is an individual who wants an easygoing life of love and luxury. This combination is cultured, and they love all the finer things in life. They need a spouse who reflects their ideals and their dreams. Sorrow and depression can result if there is even a hint of betrayal. Everything in their lives is directed by and toward their spouse or partner. They work and they wait for their fantasy ship to reach their shore, and when it does they can lead a life of overindulgence—to have the love of their life caress and hold them as harps play and flowers bloom. Riches and gourmet food will be at hand, and their lover will be theirs and theirs alone.

Romance: This combination needs almost nothing else to be happy. They might spend their entire lives trying to figure out who they are and what they like. Love, however, is never called into question. It is the summum bonum—the highest good. Perhaps, way in the inner resources of their being, there is an artist. It seldom sees the light of day, however. The Libra-Boar, with its single-minded approach to life, must find love in order to attain happiness. In the love department they will give entirely of themselves to their partner and do anything to help them succeed. Their world is a world of secondhand happiness as their lover climbs the ladder of fame or accomplishment.

Relationships: Poor choices for this combination come from Snakes, and the poorest of all are Aries-, Cancer-, or Capricorn-Snakes. Capricorn-Monkeys are not a good idea either. The best place to start looking for love and romance is with Rabbits and Rams. Of those, the Gemini, Sagittarius, Leo, or Aquarius are the best picks.

Family Life: As parents they love their children and do a fine job. They are tender and caring. Nonetheless, they do tend to put their spouse ahead of their children. The picture of a happy and comfortable home requires happy children, however, and that is generally what the family of this combination is like. Libra-Boars like to show off their homes and generally they are beautiful indeed. The love of beauty is what this combination brings to the table. It will not be a house that sacrifices comfort in favor of lavishness.

Livelihood: There is talent in this combination, but it is generally not revealed, at least not without serious motives pertaining to the person they love. They need a huge amount of togetherness in order to make use of their abilities. The same statement can be made about professions. As bosses they are not especially strong. The Libra-Boar is, to a degree, a social climber, but there needs to be a qualification to that statement. They want to climb the social ladder for the benefit of their partner in life, not for themselves.

Famous Libra-Boars: Le Corbusier, Julie Andrews, Cheryl Tiegs.

Scorpio (Boar) Month Combined with Rat Year

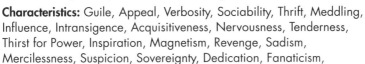

"Form" Mars, Water, Fixed   **"Regulator"** Yin-Positive Water

Characteristics: Guile, Appeal, Verbosity, Sociability, Thrift, Meddling, Influence, Intransigence, Acquisitiveness, Nervousness, Tenderness, Thirst for Power, Inspiration, Magnetism, Revenge, Sadism, Mercilessness, Suspicion, Sovereignty, Dedication, Fanaticism, Discipline, Skill, Intellectual, Charisma

This combination is very likeable and sociable. They have a friendly and personable appearance, and this tends to relax others. There is, however, a secret hiding behind the appearance. The Scorpio-Rat is a straight talker and always speaks their mind. They are loquacious and sometimes their words bite. This combination is flexible and very spirited. That includes both the mental and physical aspects of their being. There is a good likelihood that the Scorpio-Rat will be into sports and do well at them. This combination is generous and outgoing in a self-interested manner. This is mostly hidden, except with those they love, with whom they are frank. There is a good awareness of both the political and the aesthetic. They are as crafty as they are clever. The Scorpio-Rat loves power and is motivated to acquire it. That does not mean that they want to be king, queen, president, or prime minister. It means they want to control their environment. The Scorpio-Rat has internal fortitude, and there is nothing soft about them. They have goals in life and they set out directly to attain them. They might be a bit more surreptitious than some Rats when it comes to their ambitions. They are able to temper themselves enough that people do not notice their drive so much.

Romance: This is a sensual combination. They are extraordinarily passionate, particularly in the early adult years. An inner voice seems to tell them that they need someone to keep an eye on them and help stop them from straying. This combination often ends up with a desirable but fairly straitlaced spouse, which is precisely what they need to achieve their goals. Romance and intrigue are the name of the Scorpio-Rat's game. This combination does not do one-night stands when it comes to love. They want the best, and the best has to be supremely special.

Relationships: Some caution for compatibility is needed with the Taurus-, Leo-, or Aquarius-Horse. Out of the question are Taurus- and Aquarius-Rabbits. Terrific choices in romance are Cancer-, Virgo-, and Pisces-Buffalo individuals. Also making the list of possibilities are Cancer-, Capricorn-, or Pisces-Dragons, along with Cancer-, Virgo-, and Capricorn-Monkeys.

Family Life: This combination tends to be artistic, and it is usually on display in their homes. As parents, this combination is responsible and watches out for their children. They are prepared for nearly any eventuality from physical health to schoolwork. This combination is loaded with willpower. Their environment needs to make a statement about who they are and what they have done. It needs to be unique to them. The home of the Scorpio-Rat is generally super modern in its decor, and they like to feel like they are on the cutting edge of art and design.

Livelihood: The law, medicine, business, and entertainment are ideally suited for the aptitudes of this combination. Additionally, their happy and friendly nature makes their perspectives easier to accept. A Scorpio-Rat can view things and find problems fairly easily. They have a keen eye for details and are very analytical. This makes for a good critic. Also, their willingness to tell it like it is can be helpful for those who want real and honest feedback.

Famous Scorpio-Rats: Claude Monet, Aaron Copland, Dick Cavett, Prince Charles.

Scorpio (Boar) Month Combined with Buffalo Year

"Form" Mars, Water, Fixed   **"Survivor"** Yin-Negative Water

Characteristics: Vindictiveness, Intransigence, Revenge, Diligence, Innovation, Tenderness, Suspicion, Bigotry, Discipline, Stability, Standoffishness, Eloquence, Plodding, Bias, Sadism, Fanaticism, Inspiration, Sovereignty, Strength of Purpose, Magnetism, Dedication, Stubbornness, Mercilessness, Integrity

The Scorpio side of things in this combination brings a rather different dynamic. They will surprise people and attract people to them. They are a bit on the thorny side, however. They are probably the most agile bulldozer known to man. The Scorpio-Buffalo is sharp: very sharp. They are a bit on the wacky side as well. To all external appearances this combination is plain and ordinary. While it is true that they tend to do things somewhat slowly, they are very careful and detail oriented in what they do. They have an ability to sense the moves of others as well as a fine intuitive mind. These qualities help them get what they want, and what they want is to have a very high degree of success with the salary to match. They do not mind being merciless in attaining this goal. If one looks carefully at the Scorpio-Buffalo, the superiority that they feel will be evident. But it requires a very close look to spot. The combination of the slow but straight-ahead Buffalo with the unpredictable Scorpio results in a person who is the second cousin to a bulldozer at the Indy 500. The determination that the Scorpio-Buffalo has is aided by the fact that they are slick.

Romance: Here is some of the drama invented by this combination: crying, breaking up, arguing, every other conceivable show of emotion. Clearly being the spouse of someone like this is, to put it mildly, challenging. Maybe the passion and the attractiveness are worth it for some. This combination is also a bit of a vagabond in the romance department too. The nutty side of the Scorpio-Buffalo shows up in personal relationships. Actually nutty is putting it kindly. This combination is quite crazy in that regard. For starters, they want an attractive piece of clay for a partner: someone they can mold and show off. They have no interest in a mate with brains. Besides being attractive, they want someone they can have frequent personal problems with: big personal problems.

Relationships: Poor choices for this combination include Gemini-, Taurus-, Leo-, and Aquarius-Rams. Also not worth checking are Taurus- and Gemini-Dragons. Not in the ballpark are Taurus-Monkeys, Gemini-Horses, or

Aquarius-Tigers. Good places to look for romance are with Cancer-, Virgo-, Capricorn-, and Pisces-Rats. Roosters are also fine choices, especially if they are Cancer, Capricorn, or Pisces. Cancer-, Virgo-, or Capricorn-Snakes are additional choices.

Family Life: There must, if possible, be servants who take care of the grounds and the children. A stableboy and butler are essential. This crew is needed because the Scorpio-Buffalo is jet-setting around being impressive and making money. The far-out meets the homebody is the character of this combination. Of course there is Mother Earth, and this means living in the country. There is nature and the sun and moon. There is home. Somewhere there must be the outrageous and it might come with the home itself, perhaps it's a mansion on a hill or a huge old farmhouse. It is luxurious.

Livelihood: This combination can lead people and move people emotionally or politically. So, appearing before an audience is what it was destined to do. Acting on stage or the movies is possible, but then teachers and comedians move people too. They are good at moving others from behind the scenes as well, so directors, writers, or mass communication are all open possibilities. The issue for this combination is which of the high-powered professions it is capable of will it choose. They are performers and movers, not to mention shakers. It is here that their genius shows the most.

Famous Scorpio-Buffalos: Andre Malaraux, Robert Kennedy, Vivien Leigh, Richard Burton, Jonathan Winters, Johnny Carson.

Scorpio (Boar) Month Combined with Tiger Year

"Form" Mars, Water, Fixed   **"Observe"** Yang-Positive Wood

Characteristics: Itinerancy, Intemperance, Hotheadedness, Authority, Disobedience, Magnetism, Swagger, Good Luck, Discipline, Magnetism, Fervor, Intransigence, Impetuosity, Benevolence, Bravery, Suspicion, Revenge, Tenderness, Inspiration, Sadism, Dedication, Sovereignty, Mercilessness, Fanaticism

This combination does nearly everything to the maximum. There is no middle path or moderation in the Scorpio-Tiger. They wake up in the morning and rush out of the house trying to change things and live dangerously. The idea of doing things slowly and carefully does not occur to this combination. This dialectic results in a person related to a bungee jumper who is trying to show up a person they had an argument with. They may have gone to the grocery store without a shopping list and decided on the spur of the moment to jump. Maybe the only thing they do deliberately is place themselves in precarious situations. If you know someone who likes to paint a living room prior to going out for some games of beach volleyball and then entertaining friends for a gourmet meal, they are Scorpio-Tigers. The Tiger may not have nine lives, but this combination intends to squeeze nine lives into one. They attract people and others find them extremely interesting to be around. The Scorpio-Tiger has a quick temper, which ignites without warning. There is some fairness to the claim that they are totally crazy. They want to experience everything on the planet and after that is accomplished move on to outer space.

Romance: In the partner category they are true blue if they find someone who appreciates their color scheme. First the partner must defer to them in matters of craziness. This combination needs to be the big cheese in the crazy department. In order to do that, they need to be balanced with a person who appears respectable. If all this is accomplished, then marital bliss is possible. This combination chooses a partner carefully and takes their sweet time doing it. Among the reasons are the varied and active lives they lead. They are fond of movement and movement means changes. That does not mean they change partners, they just like to rearrange items in their lives from time to time: perhaps move to Timbuktu or, barring that, redo the garden. Movement helps keep their unsavory appetites in check, for without change they might be overcome with a vice or two.

Relationships: For this combination poor choices include Aries-, Taurus-, or Aquarius-Rams. Taurus-Snake, -Monkey, and -Boar are not on the list of choices either. Ruled out completely are Gemini-Tigers and Aquarius-Buffalos. Top tier selections in the area of love and romance are Cancer-, Virgo-, Capricorn-, or Pisces-Horses. Also very fine picks are Dogs who are Cancer, Virgo, Capricorn, or Pisces. Pisces-Dragons are superb selections too.

Family Life: With children this combination is a loving and caring parent. They tend to bring up children who are independent but who have been raised relatively strictly so as to cultivate obedience and purpose. This combination does not care in the least about impressing people. The Scorpio-Tiger decorates, if that is what it is, by impulse, intuition, and instinct. Their home reflects them and no one else. This is a nutty home that might have black lights and candelabra and furniture from the Jimmy Carter era. If they like it or those they love like it, then it becomes part of the decor.

Livelihood: This combination has their own version of tough love; they are loving but pushy. They make for polite bosses who tend to suggest rather than order. They can hold audiences and communicate well with others. They are good at dealing with people as well as persuading people. This combination might be considered a natural law anarchist—a person who makes up his or her own rules. They do not like to follow those of the others. That does not translate to chaos, because they are organized people and highly capable. They also, in spite of their independent tendencies, are reasonably obedient.

Famous Scorpio-Tigers: Mohammed, Dylan Thomas, Charles de Gaulle, Pete Townshend, Jean Seberg, Ted Turner, Jane Pauley, Jeane Kirkpatrick.

Scorpio (Boar) Month Combined with Rabbit Year

"Form" Mars, Water, Fixed   **"Withdraw"** Yin-Negative Wood

Characteristics: Complexity, Hypochondria, Pedantry, Ambition, Dilettantism, Prudence, Tact, Longevity, Suspicion, Magnetism, Intransigence, Secretiveness, Fanaticism, Mercilessness, Revenge, Inspiration, Discipline, Finesse, Sadism, Tenderness, Dedication, Squeamishness, Sovereignty, Virtue

This combination earns both respect and money, and they know how to hold on to both. Part of the persona that the world sees is peaceful and sophisticated. Of course most people do not show all of themselves to the external world, and inside the Scorpio-Rabbit is someone who knows human nature well. The Scorpio-Rabbit in a sense is a severe person. That does not mean they are unfriendly or standoffish. It means they have a rather awesome presence. They impress people just with their persona. They are, consequently, able to overcome fear and meet difficulty straight on. The Rabbit brings kindness into the mixture and is a brave, humanitarian defender of the needy. The timid Rabbit does occasionally bring in some fear, but the Scorpio generally overrides this in action. For starters, they talk straight and need to be taken seriously. They can dance around difficult situations and put out fires before they get going. While there is nothing foreboding about them, they know the concept of dread and its causes. The balance they have and the straight walk they walk is largely the influence of the Rabbit, who gives them self-confidence. The Scorpio gives some balance to the combination by adding daring.

Romance: The primary need for a mate for the Scorpio-Rabbit is as a kind of manager and executive security officer. They need management so they are able to get the important things done. Love for this combination is often born of respect. Being the spouse of this combination will probably involve an evolution of sorts: one that is hinted at, requested, and indirectly pushed for by their partner. Scorpio-Rabbits need and care about love. They tend to go after the real McCoy fairly quickly and do not care to fool around playing the field. They have places to go and things to accomplish and consequently have no time for passing affairs or infatuations. This combination tends to be relatively faithful but can, on occasion, stray off the path. Generally this is not the cause of serious breakups or restarts.

Relationships: Totally out of the running for compatibility are Taurus-, Leo-, and Aquarius-Roosters. The Leo-Rat would also be a mistake as a romantic partner. The best choice in the department of love and romance are Cancer-, Virgo-, Capricorn-, or Pisces-Rams. Dogs and Boars in those signs are good too.

Family Life: As parents, this combination is responsible and caring. Here too, however, deference must be shown to the way things are designed by the Scorpio-Rabbit. Above all is respect. This combination has a lot of social status and has probably earned it themselves with diligence and a good work ethic. The Scorpio-Rabbit, while not a Rooster, does rule the roost at home. It is strictly their domain and things will be done their way. This rule is true in spades when it comes to the living room of the house. It totally belongs to them. As for the remainder of the home, it is distinguished and has the imprint of the Scorpio-Rabbit. While some individual choice will be allowed in rooms other than the main room, everything must match and fit and be refined. The goal is a home that is more or less synchronized.

Livelihood: As employers they can, to put it kindly, be testy. They can also have a very sharp tongue. Positions they might be good at run the gamut from music to science and religion. This combination was meant for a responsible position. They desire to help others, and the concern that they have for their peers and all members of the group is very admirable. They are a no-frills and get-the-job-done-right individual.

Famous Scorpio-Rabbits: Martin Luther, Evelyn Waugh, Marie Curie, Roland Barthes, Grace Slick.

Scorpio (Boar) Month Combined with Dragon Year

"Form" Mars, Water, Fixed   **"Take Charge"** Yang-Positive Wood

Characteristics: Enthusiasm, Intransigence, Discipline, Sentimental, Tenderness, Suspicion, Fanaticism, Success, Inspiration, Dedication, Revenge, Magnetism, Good Health, Braggadocio, Rigidity, Pluck, Mistrust, Mercilessness, Strength, Sovereignty, Infatuation, Dissatisfaction, Sadism

This combination's reputation of being extravagant is, most certainly, overstated. The presentation too is one of being piquant and, to put it more roughly, hot. The reason for this is that the combination brings out the ultimate in the portions it was mixed with. The Scorpio-Dragon is a high-flying combination and a fragrant mixture. This combination has an air of inscrutability from the Scorpio and, of course, mercilessness too. There is a kind of larger-than-life persona here, but not in the ordinary sense. There is no Dragon like this Dragon and no Scorpio like this Scorpio. The Scorpio-Dragon meets perhaps more than their fair share. While they are ambitious they are mildly prone to giving up: to throwing in the towel, to abandoning the ship. Most, however, keep both the towel and the ship and keep on moving on toward their destiny: one that is filled with riches, status, and, with some luck, happiness too. They are ambitious and head straight for what they desire. Their huge charisma will help get them there. They are so ambitious that they can have nearly anything they desire, at least that is what they think. There is a rather large obstacle in all this optimism and wealth. Life for everyone has difficulties and challenges.

Romance: The way to keep the Scorpio-Dragon in line is to first recognize how beautiful and wonderful they are and show it. Next, just be extremely relaxed and have a sort of planned attitude of not particularly caring what they do. They have enough jealousy for two individuals anyway, so that too can be used as a preventive. The Scorpio-Dragon is a sexual creature and it is fairly easy for them to carry out that role in their life. They are extremely attractive and sought after by many. If that is not enough, they also are well aware of this fact. It is possible, because they do tend to enjoy being unpredictable, for them to be very faithful and loyal spouses.

Relationships: In general the Dragon is friendly in this combination and appealing to most people. The exceptions for compatibility are the Leo- and Aquarius-Buffalo, the Taurus- and the Leo-Rabbit, and Taurus-, Leo-, and Aquarius-Dog. Fine picks for love and romance are the Virgo-, Capricorn-, or Pisces-Buffalo or Pisces-Monkey. Near the top of the list are Cancer-, Capricorn-, and Pisces-Tigers. On the more erotic side of the matter, the Cancer-Rat and Pisces-Rat are suggested, as are Cancer- and Virgo-Roosters. A superior choice is the Cancer-Snake.

Family Life: This combination enjoys entertaining and has frequent visitors. The Scorpio-Dragon personality speaks for itself, and these individuals do not need to impress with things or by showing off. They are superior parents and love their children. They do what they can to help their children succeed, and that success is very important to the Scorpio-Dragon mom or dad. Comfort is probably the main goal of the Scorpio-Dragon in terms of their home. They are not particularly a handy person, nor do they have an especially green thumb. There is no particular reason, in their book, to spend time designing, decorating, and improving. If it is comfortable, leave it alone. Cleanliness is, however, important to them, as is neatness.

Livelihood: This combination wants what they want and they want it now. That often means premature celebrations and disappointments. That disappointment comes when this combination does not attain the power that they desire. They need a supporting spouse and some frolicking children to help keep them focused. In their professional life is where the Scorpio-Dragon might run in to difficulty. They are intelligent and very educated. The problems are twofold though. They can have a fairly wicked tongue, and, most importantly, they can stop or give up too quickly.

Famous Scorpio-Dragons: Walter Cronkite, Francois Mitterrand.

Scorpio (Boar) Month Combined with Snake Year

"Form" Mars, Water, Fixed   **"Feel"** Yang-Negative Fire

Characteristics: Intransigence, Compassion, Discipline, Clairvoyance, Exclusiveness, Tenderness, Cupidity, Discretion, Suspicion, Laziness, Presumption, Inspiration, Revenge, Sadism, Extravagance, Sagacity, Attractiveness, Sovereignty, Fanaticism, Mercilessness, Intuition, Magnetism, Dedication, Dissimulation

This combination is super sensitive with deep feelings, considering they are a Snake. Of course, Scorpio brings the element of being sensual. There is also a perception of aristocracy. Self-examination and introspection are

part and parcel of the Scorpio-Snake. Scorpio-Snakes love things that stir up the emotions and tactile sensations. They are a combination of beauty and opulence, kindness and excessiveness. Without these things they feel their life is meaningless. The Snake adds a certain kind of wisdom born of the philosophical nature of the combination. This combination is fussy about its appearance, and they take meticulous care to not be part of the crowd. They will be noticed and commented on for their appearance, and that is their point. They are compulsive about their grooming habits as well. While they do not actually wear costumes, they do tend to be showy and dramatic even in the most ordinary of situations. They have an extra sense as well as super-sharp intuitive abilities. They seem to have a keen ability to determine what others want. Deep is probably one way to think of them: deep thinkers. As with many who go under the surface of things, they can experience emotional pain and turmoil.

Romance: One might as well get used to having all the attention focused on their partner when they go out as a couple. The Scorpio-Snake tends to choose mates based on their being subservient. This combination wants to be the boss at home as well as in the overall relationship. Being the partner of a Scorpio-Snake is somewhat akin to being married to a movie star, and that star shines brightly. People love to love this combination. They radiate beauty and coolness, and people turn into fans. One thing that helps to keep them on the straight and narrow in the area of loyalty is the fact that they are very picky about who they get involved with. Nearly everyone is a follower and fan of this combination.

Relationships: Taurus- and Leo-Tigers do not have what it takes to make a good match for this combination. Eliminated from contention are Taurus- and Gemini-Boars. Virgo-, Capricorn-, and Pisces-Dragons are excellent choices for love and romance. Cancer-, Virgo-, Capricorn-, and Pisces-Roosters are also premium selections. Another fine choice is the Cancer-Buffalo. Lower down on the list are Taurus-, Leo-, and Aquarius-Monkeys.

Family Life: This combination makes good parents and believes in spoiling the children. They do, however, get pretty uncomfortable if their children get more attention and adulation than they do. That just is not supposed to happen. Their children are filled with energy and are very good-looking. Like the Scorpio-Dragon parent, they will probably need bodyguards to keep away the hordes of admirers too. The Scorpio-

Snake has a home that is, broadly speaking, in the showcase category. It is luxurious and expensive. Exotic and natural fabrics are emphasized. There is a customized feeling to it as though most of it has been handmade. The statement they are making is somewhat akin to appearance actually is reality.

Livelihood: This combination is fine at being a boss but does not like to work for others. They are power oriented. If they believe someone has been disloyal to them or otherwise offended their sensibilities, they can be down-right cruel in their revenge. The Scorpio-Snake is a creative combination that is flexible and adaptable. They are able to handle most things. They like inventive and pragmatic schemes. They have no problem fitting into an established order as long as people recognize what they perceive as their worth both in terms of reputation and finances.

Famous Scorpio-Snakes: Pablo Picasso, Grace Kelly, Indira Gandhi, Henri Gault.

Scorpio (Boar) Month Combined with Horse Year

"Form" Mars, Water, Fixed   *"Command"* Yang-Positive Fire

Characteristics: Accomplishment, Style, Anxiety, Intransigence, Pragmatism, Dexterity, Tenderness, Suspicion, Discipline, Selfishness, Rebellion, Revenge, Fanaticism, Popularity, Inspiration, Magnetism, Sadism, Unscrupulousness, Sovereignty, Autonomy, Persuasiveness, Dedication, Mercilessness, Haste

This combination is convincing, animated, devoted, and stylish. This is a freedom-loving combination that is capable of acting responsibly on their own. They are sharp and have a great deal of energy. Jobs that others shy away from the Scorpio-Horse excels at doing. There are a lot of positive situations going on with the Scorpio-Horse. That is because this combination possesses most of the positive qualities of each sign. This combination does a great job of self-ruling. They have a view and approach to things that is outside the box. This combination is so good in these areas that they are prone to overconfidence and can allow themselves to take a trip to fantasyland. This is something they need to guard against. Their independent streak tends to set them apart so far that they can be misfits with their peers. There is something almost heroic and magical about them at times. They can look at a task, analyze it, and carry it out with expertise. Their appearance and their touch have a perception of success.

Romance: This combination is magnificent with those they love and give a warm and fuzzy feeling to them. They also happen to be a little odd, but that only adds interest. The Scorpio-Horse is fun to be with and to play with. They appreciate help with the tasks in their lives but are autonomous and need some space at times. There is a serious pragmatic side to the Scorpio-Horse, and that is the guiding principle they have in the area of romance. It must work, and that includes feeling comfortable and being hassle free. They are not beyond straying a tad, but those they stray with are not the people they will marry.

Relationships: Rats, in general, are poor picks for compatibility. Other combinations to stay away from are Taurus-, Gemini-, Leo-, and Aquarius-Horses. Emphatically out of the question are Aquarius-Rabbits. Top-notch selections in the area of love and romance are the Cancer-, Virgo-, Capricorn-, or Pisces-Tiger or Pisces-Ram. More good selections are Virgo- and Pisces-Dogs.

Family Life: When children enter the picture that is whom Scorpio-Horses dedicate their lives to. Their kids pick up on the love and are marvelous themselves. They seem to be born wise. In addition, they are extraordinarily well behaved. They are enjoyable to be around from a very young age. The home of the Scorpio-Horse is marked by aesthetics and comfort. It will be attractive and highly organized. In addition, it will be extremely clean. This combination must have order in their home. Their homes are pleasing to visit. The Scorpio-Horse totally and completely loves their children and would do absolutely anything for them.

Livelihood: This combination likes to do things according to their own procedure, method, and time frame. They make better leaders than followers but it is best if they work alone. If they are left to their own devices, things do get done because they are very responsible. The heart beating in the chest of a Scorpio-Horse is the heart of an artist. They are someone who creates. While they can do most jobs, those that involve creativity are the best. Like most artists, they hear a tune of their own, and that is the way they work. They dislike being constrained inside a rigid structure.

Famous Scorpio-Horses: Teddy Roosevelt, Paul Simon, Daniel Barenboim.

Scorpio (Boar) Month Combined with Ram Year

"Form" Mars, Water, Fixed   **"Reliance"** Yang-Negative Fire

Characteristics: Good Manners, Discipline, Impracticality, Worry, Taste, Sensitivity, Whimsy, Perseverance, Tardiness, Pessimism, Magnetism, Invention, Parasitism, Intransigence, Lack of Foresight, Tenderness, Suspicion, Dedication, Revenge, Inspiration, Sadism, Sovereignty, Mercilessness, Fanaticism

This combination needs some kind of external structure or framework because they are without it themselves. There is a degree of self-knowledge so it is possible for them to come to grips with what they are and move on and attain some success. Where the framework for their lives originates varies. The Scorpio-Ram is a very creative but highly unpredictable and a somewhat goofy individual. To be sure, they have intelligence, and it is in their creativity that most of their intelligence resides. They also work hard, in spite of beliefs to the contrary. Perhaps a spouse or even their own children will help them in that regard. It might come from their job. The fact is, though, it is always external. They simply do not know what is useful. They can be geniuses at times to be sure. They can be talented visual artists. They can be, and truly are, highly idealistic. What they are not, and never can be, are practical. The inner workings of the Scorpio-Ram are another matter. They are the eccentric inventor perhaps, with an endless stream of new and fanciful ideas. They are, whatever it might be, quite wacky. Their problems in this regard are a total lack of pragmatism.

Romance: This combination is selfish as well. They have the willpower to push for things to be done their way, and push they do. What is good about them makes up for a lot of this. They are terrifically interesting individuals. They are loyal as well. There is opportunity in romance and marriage for the Scorpio-Ram. They can, using this mechanism, find someone to give them guidance and rein in their eccentric behavior when necessary. They can even hint at some rules to follow. This situation and potential is often destroyed, however. The reason things can go afoul is that the Scorpio-Ram is, to put it mildly, argumentative. To put it less mildly, they love to argue, and anyone who is partnered with them better get used to the idea that there are going to be issues.

Relationships: Toward the bottom of the ladder for compatibility in this combination are Taurus- or Aquarius-Buffalos. Leo-Dogs and Aquarius-Tigers are not particularly good either. Really good choices in the romance department are Cancer-, Virgo-, Capricorn-, and Pisces-Boars. Additional good matches can be found with Virgo-, Capricorn-, or Pisces-Rabbits. Also fine choices are Virgo- and Pisces-Horses.

Family Life: This combination is not much interested in culinary arts, so their kitchen might be a bit on the sparse side. They are pretty artsy though, and signs of this will be seen. There will be fine art prints or nifty artistic photographs on the walls. In terms of parenting, the Scorpio-Ram is a mixed bag. They clearly love and care for their children. They just happen to be awkward in knowing how to handle them. The home of a Scorpio-Ram is generally quite tasteful and can even be in the well-appointed category. They have a creative streak in the interior-decorating department with a hint of the offbeat.

Livelihood: This combination does not make especially good bosses. They are popular, but it does not go much deeper than this. Financially they are a little devious. They do not like others to know their situation, but odds are it is much better than they let on. There is potential for awesome accomplishment with this combination. Given opportunities they are capable of being professional artists. The medical field is also within their grasp. Unfortunately, the Scorpio-Ram is lacking in stick-to-itiveness. They might give up during their education or after they have barely begun. Their noses do tend to wander away from the grindstone.

Famous Scorpio-Rams: Shah of Iran, Morley Safer, Annie Girardot, Joni Mitchell.

Scorpio (Boar) Month Combined with Monkey Year

"Form" Mars, Water, Fixed   *"Arrange"* Yin-Positive Metal

Characteristics: Zeal, Opportunism, Stability, Cunning, Discipline, Self-involvement, Wit, Silliness, Loquacity, Leadership, Improvisation, Deceit, Revenge, Magnetism, Tenderness, Inspiration, Suspicion, Ruse, Dedication, Sadism, Mercilessness, Fanaticism, Sovereignty

This combination has a bullwhip for a tongue, is cunning and unfathomable. All this might be hard to perceive, because the Scorpio-Monkey can come off as cheerful and even childish. There is always the darkness below the bright surface. Both the Monkey and the Scorpio are slippery and deceitful. The Scorpio-Monkey is a complicated combination. They have both creativity as well as shrewdness. Lightning is going to strike somewhere. This, of course, makes them perfect for leadership. There is a lot of passion in the Monkey, while that space is filled with resentment in the Scorpio. All of this leads to an internal clash, and the result can cause confusion in this combination. Frequently it boils down to what they should do: fool some of the people as often as possible, or try to work their tails off. The Monkey side of this character is playing around while the Scorpio side is quite serious. There are a number of opposing characteristics between Monkeys and Scorpios. For example, Monkeys enjoy making things, while Scorpios like to knock things down.

Romance: Anyone involved with this combination must be prepared for someone who is primarily sexual in their approach to life. Among the corollaries that come with sexual gratification for the Scorpio-Monkey is self-esteem. This is how they get their egos boosted. This combination is high-octane sexual. Start with the super sexy Scorpio and then blend that with the titillating Monkey and you have a person who is focused on sex. There also happens to be a lot of energy powering this person. The eroticism and sexual drive of this combination must be of the highest quality: no half-baked frolicking in the hay here.

Relationships: Aquarius-Buffalos and -Rams are a very poor choice in the realm of love. Cancer-, Virgo-, Capricorn-, or Pisces-Rats are at the top of the list for romance. In addition, Cancer-, Capricorn-, and Pisces-Dragons are good for the Scorpio-Monkey. Taurus- and Leo-Tigers are not the best of choices nor are Leo-Horses and Leo-Boars.

Family Life: This combination likes to display things from their travels. As if this were not enough, their car is, to put it very gently, different—supremely different. Not only is it a wreck, it might actually be a Mercedes turned into a pickup truck. This is the person who never grew up, which makes for a very fun-loving parent. They probably know more knock-knock jokes than their child. The Scorpio-Monkey wants some homegrown individuality in their house. Strange or personal stuff will be hanging on walls and fill up shelves. There will be several distinctively weird things in their home: maybe a suit of armor or collection of hats.

Livelihood: Professionally they need a lot of freedom and flexibility. Their fuse is short when they are uncomfortable at work. They probably do not make good bosses and more than likely eschew power and try to replace it with freedom. Creativity is the hallmark of the Scorpio-Monkey. They have other talents as well. They can figure things out with ease. They can weave stories that please the young and old alike. They have quick minds that categorize things logically. While they are not comfortable before large audiences, they do very well in more personal situations.

Famous Scorpio-Monkeys: James Kilpatrick, Louis Malle, Alistair Cooke.

Scorpio (Boar) Month Combined with Rooster Year

"Form" Mars, Water, Fixed   **"Conqueror"** Yang-Negative Metal

Characteristics: Blind Faith, Bossiness, Dissipation, Humor, Candor, Resilience, Conservatism, Discipline, Pedantry, Chic, Intransigence, Sadism, Enthusiasm, Cockiness, Magnetism, Inspiration, Revenge, Sovereignty, Tenderness, Dedication, Suspicion, Mercilessness, Fanaticism, Boastfulness

There seems to be a wonderful intelligence here, and the Scorpio-Rooster appears to know that he has what it takes. This combination is capable of drawing energy from others and prone to use it for their many gifts. *Strength* might be the right word for the Scorpio-Rooster because they have it to spare. Yes, there is passion here too, and it is a powerful passion for life. There are many other qualities than can be attributed to this character. They are mystifying and enigmatic. They see the world through an idealist's pair of glasses. Scorpio-Roosters are obviously highly sexy people. That should never be mistaken for promiscuity or immorality. Under all that sex appeal and ready to rock-and-roll appearance is a traditional person. Perhaps nowhere is their energy more apparent than when they have been bruised, battered, wounded, and left for dead. It is not that they just get up and carry on. They get up with a smile on their face looking proper enough to go to a State Dinner. Mr. or Ms. Cool is what these individuals represent.

Romance: Fooling around, flirting, and philandering are strictly out. In their quest for the Holy Grail of love, the Scorpio-Rooster meets resistance and encounters failures: lots of them. They are so insistent on this vision of love that they sometimes end up living the single life. They prefer this to anything they consider half-baked, murky, or risky. Scorpio-Roosters seek love and for them that ideal love must be formulated by Plato himself. It must be perfect, and it must be forever. When one loves, that love has to be directed to one person and reflected back by that one person. There are no eyes for anyone else.

Relationships: Leading off the poor matches for this combination is the

Taurus-Boar. Even poorer choices are Leo-Rabbits and -Roosters. Completely out of the question are Aquarius-Rats. Snakes are a good choice for the Scorpio-Rooster, and of those the romance scale is higher with Cancer, Virgo, Capricorn, and Pisces. Additional fine picks are Capricorn and Pisces-Buffalos. The list of positive picks continues with Capricorn- and Pisces-Dragons.

Family Life: As parents the Scorpio-Roosters are very loving and caring. Birthdays for their kids are extravaganzas of three-ring circuses and county fairs. They believe totally in happy childhoods and do everything that they can to make that the case. Scorpio-Rooster homes are staggeringly fantastic. It is hard to know where to begin. There are the antiques, of course; real ones and lots of them. There are the gadgets and appliances. The home is perfectly maintained and has the finest everything, including the stuff that cannot be seen: the wiring for instance. A game room is a must, and there will be a fully stocked bar.

Livelihood: This combination sees a challenge, and they undertake it with joy. They can learn languages, play sports, take awesome photographs, and that is before lunch. This person is a cut above your average Joe in everything. This combination oozes talent, charisma, and responsibility. Plainly put, there is very little they cannot do. Huge projects that take years can be done as well as tiny projects requiring detail and focus. They are disciplined and versatile.

Famous Scorpio-Roosters: Ezra Pound, Katharine Hepburn, Neil Young, Goldie Hawn.

Scorpio (Boar) Month Combined with Dog Year

"Form" Mars, Water, Fixed   **"Concerned"** Yin-Positive Metal

Characteristics: Tastelessness, Intelligence, Morality, Heroism, Tenderness, Respectability, Mercilessness, Self-righteousness, Sovereignty, Intransigence, Cynicism, Suspicion, Discipline, Uneasiness, Fanaticism, Revenge, Magnetism, Inspiration, Sadism, Dedication, Constancy, Criticism, Duty, Unsociability

While there are some very different aspects to the Scorpio and the Dog, they are similar in that they are committed and loyal individuals. The sexual and confident nature of the Scorpio can get the Dog a little mixed up, however, especially when they are young. The dialectic involved with the Scorpio-Dog is perhaps an unusual one. The Dog is a softhearted and giving individual. They are open and speak their minds. However, Scorpio adds a heavy dose of the green monster to the combination. Another shared trait is direct speech on all manner of topics. The Scorpio tends to be somewhat loquacious. Dogs tend to bite, but Scorpios are snipers. The result here is someone who can do some serious damage with his or her use of the language. That frequently comes in the form of sarcasm. That is only half the picture though, because this combination is sincerely nice and sincerely kind. The point is not to provoke this combination to anger. Only regret will result. Scorpio-Dogs do not hold back on their opinions of anything. The Dog portion tends to speak from on high a bit more than the Scorpio. They believe they know almost everything.

Romance: Love for them is a two-way street. They will happily provide their share, but it must be reciprocated. They are sensitive and careful in the event that their heart is broken. If they fail and have serious emotional pain, they will never take a chance again. The Scorpio-Dog is very likable in spite of the vicious tongue. They have big hearts and can be wonderful to everyone. Respect is important for this combination. They must have someone to look up to and admire. They do not want someone who wants to be ordered around, but rather a partner, someone to share their insights with.

Relationships: On the negative side of the list are Gemini- and Aquarius-Dragons. Poor choices for compatibility in this combination include the Taurus-Rooster or -Boar. It is possible that the Aquarius-Ram has an attraction, but that combination should be avoided. Cancer-, Virgo-, Capricorn-, and Pisces-Tigers are great choices in the romance area. Additional good selections are Cancer-, Capricorn-, and Pisces-Rabbits and Pisces-Horses.

Family Life: This combination practically worships their children. Everything possible will be done to ensure that the children have a good and successful future. Education is therefore paramount. The home of the Scorpio-Dog needs to be comfortable and secure. Wanting others to feel welcome and at ease is more important to this combination than making a show. Things need to be designed to create a relaxed ambience. Books lining the walls, easy chairs, quilts, and perhaps a woodstove are in the home. The house does not look expensive, and that is why there is money in the bank.

Livelihood: This combination is responsible, but the environment must be suitable. They work hard and are seldom out of work. Freedom is the key to happiness in the work life of the Scorpio-Dog. They are easy to get along with but do have that tendency to snap at people. They do not mind authority per se, but will not tolerate people who restrain them. Routine also annoys them. There needs to be some variety in their professional life.

Famous Scorpio-Dogs: Voltaire, Magritte, Carl Sagan, Kurt Vonnegut, Sally Field, David Stockman.

Scorpio (Boar) Month Combined with Boar Year

"Form" Mars, Water, Fixed   **"Cultivator"** Yin-Negative Water

Characteristics: Boar-headedness, Gourmandism, Honesty, Culture, Discipline, Hesitation, Voluptuousness, Materialism, Wrath, Scrupulousness, Intransigence, Tenderness, Credulity, Gallantry, Magnetism, Inspiration, Revenge, Sadism, Suspicion, Sovereignty, Fanaticism, Dedication, Mercilessness, Sincerity

As with other Scorpios, this combination has a mysterious quality to it; one that only adds to its stature. They are very ambitious, and they know who to know to get there. They lead a life that is designed to get them ahead. They do suffer a bit from being aggressive in getting their way. The Scorpio-Boar is one of those combinations that is probably born for success. For starters they have the halo effect—they are frequently good looking to the max. There is a regal air to their good looks. One can almost see the hordes of admiring subjects lining the roadside. Far from being innocent and gullible, this combination is so suspicious that it borders on paranoia. They both push as well as shove. Furthermore, they are a bit too heavy on the verbal side of things. When young this combination could almost be a farmer they are so busy sowing wild oats. They tend to tone this down a notch as they get older. All in all, the combination is a good mixture. They have, in addition to everything else, a very sensual nature that is derived from both the Scorpio and the Boar side. They can talk the talk and dress the dress as well, being smooth in both areas.

Romance: This combination has a huge and terrifying temper if they get jealous, and this is not enjoyable for anyone. Another somewhat negative trait is that they like to play games with people's emotions. Loving a Scorpio-Boar is a difficult and challenging business. Nevertheless, people will get in line to do it. Ego can be an issue for the Scorpio-Boar. To be sure, this combination does work and does try, but when it comes right down to it, they are self-serving. They are challenging. One thing that needs to be said is that the Scorpio-Boar is intelligent. Let's also not forget their wonderful sense of humor. Combine this with their looks and you have a creature to behold. When they love they love deeply. They also like to have people behind them to worship the ground they walk on.

Relationships: Not particularly good selections for this combination are Taurus and Leo-Snakes. Taurus-Horses are best avoided as well. Bringing up the rear in the negative category are Aquarius-Monkeys. Top-tier choices in the department of love are Cancer-, Virgo-, Capricorn-, and Pisces-Ram. Additional good choices are Cancer-, Virgo-, and Pisces-Rabbits.

Family Life: There is a traditional and somewhat conservative feeling to the home for this combination. Much of the creative and handyperson work alike will have been done by the Scorpio-Boar himself. There is no point in having such a home if the rich and famous do not see it, so receptions and parties are a must. In the parenthood department this combination is strict and insistent but very loving. Style and grace are the be-all and end-all of the Scorpio-Boar's home. Surely, they believe that life is not worth living without decor suitable to the high rank they have or will attain. Plush, expensive, luxurious, and similar adjectives come to mind. Each room has its own theme, but the home matches and fits into a pattern that takes the breath away.

Livelihood: Riches and comfort and wonderful possessions matter to this combination. The early years might be difficult for them, because they are threatening to the establishment. Time teaches them that they need to tone things down a tad and put people at ease. Having done this, they can reach their goals. This combination can attain fortune in the financial professions. It is therefore important to choose correctly. The Scorpio-Boar will not work for peanuts even if they happen to be large peanuts. There is a goal in their minds, and that goal is the pinnacle of success.

Famous Scorpio-Boars: Marie Antoinette, Alain Delon, Richard Dreyfuss.

Sagittarius (Rat) Month Combined with Rat Year

"Witness" Jupiter, Fire, Mutable   **"Regulator"** Yin-Positive Water

Characteristics: Reason, Meddling, Contradiction, Charisma, Sociability, Carelessness, Appeal, Bad Manners, Acquisitiveness, Honor, Vacillation, Thrift, Skill, Intellectual, Guile, Solicitude, Openhandedness, Influence, Valor, Verbosity, Recklessness, Outspokenness, Nervousness, Cheerfulness, Thirst for Power

The Sagittarius-Rat is not particularly concerned about what others think of him. What the Sagittarius-Rat wants is to keep on the road to success. This results in a person who is rather direct with others. The dialectic of the Sagittarius-Rat results in a bubbly person who is constantly moving. They are generally very healthy and loaded with get-up-and-go. This combination is also totally comfortable and is generally involved in numerous social activities. They are extraordinarily real in their dealings with people. They love being around other people and are excellent hosts. Oddly enough, however, they are somewhat reticent in their interactions. There is an almost dismissive approach to those who do not agree with them. They may host the party, but they are not usually the focus of the party. They let others fill this role. They do not have the charm of many Rats and are a no-nonsense person. If that is not your cup of tea it is perfectly okay with this combination that you do not belong to the same circle that they do. They are too busy taking care of business to be bothered by people who cannot relate to them, and they do not try to make converts of them. They do not have a wall around them, but it is almost impossible to access their true being. They are the glue of gatherings, but they have no need to be encircled by followers or groupies. They like facilitating things, and for them seeing others happy is a reward in itself.

Romance: This combination has the wanderlust and is enamored by out-of-the-ordinary cultures and places. They are adventurers, and this means they are hard-pressed to find a suitable partner. Those who do fall for the Sagittarius-Rat should be prepared for a life of travel and exploration. They definitely need a ticket to ride. The Sagittarius-Rat is an idealist in the love category. If things do not pan out for them in romantic relationships they are supremely disappointed; so much so that they may never marry. There is a hidden rebel in this combination, and they are very leery of society's norms. Huggy, kissy, comfy homebody relationships are not for them.

Relationships: For this combination less than desirable choices are Gemini-, Virgo-, and Pisces-Horses and Pisces-Rabbits. In the area of love and romance, Aries-, Leo-, Libra-, and Aquarius-Dragons are top choices. Additional good selections are Leo-, Libra-, and Aquarius-Monkeys and Aquarius-Buffalos. There is a seriously strong attraction to the Libra-Ram.

Family Life: As for the family, there is safety and security. In the event that this combination has servants, they are treated as part of the family. There is no trace of arrogance in the Sagittarius-Rat. They make fine parents although they are not constantly fretting about their children. The Sagittarius-Rat carries the fact that it is real and genuine into its environment. The home of this combination is both luxurious and comfortable.

But above all, it is honest. Yes, there are paintings and sculptures and the expensive imported furniture. More than anything else, however, is the atmosphere of authenticity.

Livelihood: This combination's spirit of adventure leads to a craving for freedom and flexibility in the workplace. They do not need to lord it over others and are usually coolheaded. They are capable, however, of being firm as bosses and have no problem firing employees who are not earning their keep. In the end, though, they are often not happy campers as employees. The Sagittarius-Rat possesses characteristics that are unusual. While they are not psychic, they can understand things quickly and spot truth with a very limited exposure to a person or experience. This makes them suitable for professions involving decision making. This combination does not give up easily.

Famous Sagittarius-Rats: Toulouse-Lautrec, Eugene Ionesco, Carlo Ponti, Tip O'Neill, Abbie Hoffman, Lou Rawls.

Sagittarius (Rat) Month Combined with Buffalo Year

"Witness" Jupiter, Fire, Mutable   **"Survivor"** Yin-Negative Water

Characteristics: Innovation, Carelessness, Reason, Bias, Standoffishness, Contradiction, Vacillation, Stability, Vindictiveness, Bad Manners, Diligence, Bigotry, Solicitude, Honor, Eloquence, Recklessness, Plodding, Integrity, Valor, Openhandedness, Strength of Purpose, Outspokenness, Cheerfulness, Stubbornness

This combination is a human generator. They are easygoing but sizzling. Their verbal skills are amazing, and they are super orators. They possess a strength that includes a deep concern for the human condition. The dialectic of the Sagittarius-Buffalo results in an extremely talented individual with loads of luck. For example, the Buffalo is able to do wonders at work, but the Sagittarius-Buffalo can do even more. They are straight shooters who seek power and authority. Status is important to them, and they want to hold an influential place in society. While not hungry for money, they are well aware of its importance. A large factor in their success simply comes from them working hard. Per capita, this combination leads the pack of the rich, famous, and brave. The Sagittarius-Buffalo can out distance them all. They burn the midnight oil and place their nose directly on the grindstone. The Sagittarius-Buffalo is rational and, to a degree, this sets them apart from other Buffalos. There is a kind of shamelessness about this combination; this one is effervescent. When they set a goal for themselves, odds are good they will attain it; in fact, it generally comes easy. Failure is not a part of their vocabulary, and they are just completely blind to the concept.

Romance: No matter how large or small the accomplishment, they will inform others about it. There is, of course, a large amount of self-interest in doing this because it is quite self-congratulatory. In addition, they are deeply and profoundly loyal. It is practically unheard of for them to cheat on their partner. This combination is usually married, and others are generally well aware of it. The Sagittarius-Buffalo advertises their partner. For some reason, this individual enjoys bragging about the person in their life and they do it frequently.

Relationships: Poor choices for this combination are Gemini, Leo, Virgo, and Pisces. There is a problem with Virgo-Monkeys as well as Gemini-Horses, Gemini- and Virgo-Rams, and Pisces-Tigers. The cream of the crop in the romance department is the Leo-, Libra-, and Aquarius-Rat and Aquarius-Snake. Another excellent choice is Aquarius-Rooster. This individual should be careful with Dragons.

Family Life: Their hobbies, likes, and significant accomplishments are on display. Their violin might be hanging on the living room wall, for example, and their degrees on display in their study. Regardless of the profession they chose, they are capable and competent. With their children they are loving, but patience is not their virtue. In addition they are stubborn. The Sagittarius-Buffalo does not have a lot of free time, so they need a home that is economical with the clock. Good organization is the key, and this combination has it. Furthermore, their home is a happy and bright place. It makes a statement about what they are, and what they are is cheery and efficient.

Livelihood: This combination needs a life that is secure and that is probably the origin of their fussiness. They take care of themselves, and while they are at it they take care of everyone else they know as well. They are destined to be bosses and will be good ones. Their hard work pays off in the end, and they become the king of the hill. Sagittarius-Buffalos are dedicated to succeeding, and that total dedication means they make it to the top far more often than not. They are not particularly after money but in spite of that usually end up with it, and that means lots of it. They are astute when it comes to details, and almost nothing gets by them. They are the type that checks their credit card statement carefully and, while they are at it, pays it in full every month.

Famous Sagittarius-Buffalos: Walt Disney, William Blake, William Buckley, Willy Brandt, Alexander Godunov, Gary Hart, Sammy Davis Jr., Margaret Meade, Jane Fonda, Jean Marais.

Sagittarius (Rat) Month Combined with Tiger Year

"Witness" Jupiter, Fire, Mutable   **"Observe"** Yang-Positive Wood

Characteristics: Contradiction, Intemperance, Authority, Reason, Benevolence, Swagger, Itinerancy, Good Luck, Honor, Carelessness, Disobedience, Solicitude, Magnetism, Bad Manners, Valor, Vacillation, Hotheadedness, Recklessness, Openhandedness, Bravery, Fervor, Outspokenness, Cheerfulness, Impetuosity

This combination dreams of being great adventurers and explorers who sail the seven seas in search of buried treasure. That dream for this combination is not possible. They will travel but probably only as far as their grown kids' house for a weekend. The Sagittarius-Tiger can probably best be thought of as someone who does not want to grow up. They are not immature, nor are they irresponsible. They just have these dreams and desires that are young. They are very charming people, and some of the things that they want are doable for them. Take, for example, gadgets. They love gadgets and gizmos of every type and variety. That is pretty reasonable and pretty attainable. If their kids live on the other side of the country the Sagittarius-Tiger will pay for tickets for them to fly home. This combination has an excellent sense of humor, but they simply do not want to be away from their home base for long in spite of their fantasies about adventure. Those fantasies are generally realized by watching the Travel Channel. Traveling for business is probably okay with them, and they can ward off homesickness. They are not stick-in-the-muds. They just would rather do things in an easy-does-it manner, and that means the manner that is easiest for them. This is the type of person who prefers staying with friends or relatives rather than getting a hotel. They can climb mountains and swim in the sea as long as it does not interfere with work. Their adventures are generally restricted to the local fishing hole or the closest national park. They might go snorkeling in the nearby river or seashore if there is one. That is where their great discoveries will be made and not 20,000 leagues under the sea.

Romance: Alas, this combination is not exactly in the "what you see is what you get" category. They are super sensitive for starters, and things can go bad quickly. There is often pessimism waiting to spring out. Those attracted to the Sagittarius-Tiger need to know that this combination must be handled with kid gloves. The mistrusting nature of the Sagittarius-Tiger makes love and romance a challenge. They seem determined to find fault with potential partners and the tiniest flaw is often blown into a major problem. They are, however, the type of person that members of the opposite sex are drawn to. They are, after all, kind and considerate. Frequently, at the beginning of a relationship, things go swimmingly.

Relationships: For this combination poor choices include Virgo, Gemini, or Pisces born in Buffalo, Rabbit, or Snake. Moving down the list of negative picks are Virgo- and Pisces-Monkeys. Finally, Gemini-Rams are not recommended at all. In the area of love or romance, good choices are Aries-, Leo-, Libra-, and Aquarius-Horses. More good picks can be found with Leo-, Libra-, and Aquarius-Dogs.

Family Life: The Sagittarius-Tiger is not a huge family person. If they have children, they will have someone to play with though, and they enjoy that part of the picture. The home and family start to matter a little more once they get past middle age, but these things are never a major priority. For this combination the home is a place to live and be comfortable. There is not much more to it than that. Sagittarius-Tigers do not worry about design, fashion, or decorating. Of course, as an eternal child this pretty much makes sense. They need a TV, computer for their games, and stereo for their music. Other than that, they just want to be comfortable while they dream dreams of faraway lands and adventures.

Livelihood: This combination is quite capable of managing extremely large projects. Because of their wide-ranging interests, they can also manage things that entail numerous phases and aspects. A weakness might be that they do not respect hierarchical procedure. Who their boss might be is irrelevant to them, and they are not fond of work that is repetitive. This combination is driven to work hard. They have a great deal of ambition. They are oblivious to what others may think of them when it comes to seeking their goals, and they are willing to attain that goal by any means necessary. This attitude opens up possibilities in their profession. They are, for example, willing to undertake unpopular projects.

Famous Sagittarius-Tigers: Beethoven, Emily Dickinson, Cristina Onassis, Tracy Austin.

Sagittarius (Rat) Month Combined with Rabbit Year

"Witness" Jupiter, Fire, Mutable   **"Withdraw"** Yin-Negative Wood

Characteristics: Complexity, Contradiction, Prudence, Ambition, Solicitude, Honor, Carelessness, Dilettantism, Longevity, Openhandedness, Bad Manners, Virtue, Valor, Pedantry, Vacillation, Hypochondria, Recklessness, Reason, Finesse, Squeamishness, Cheerfulness, Tact, Outspokenness, Secretiveness

This Sagittarian is not as unruly as other Sagittarians. There is an awareness and sensitivity brought to the table by the Rabbit. There is more of an awareness of the surroundings and the need for being tactful with others. The Sagittarius-Rabbit has a cautious side, which comes from the Rabbit. On the other hand, the Sagittarius is more lighthearted. The blending of these two signs results in diminishing the unruliness of the Sagittarius. The motive for much of this is that Rabbits have a serious interest in advancing themselves financially and professionally. There is no retreat and there is no surrender in their beings. Rather, the rough edges have been smoothed over and the energy left in place. They have accepted their blows from the past and resolved to move on with a new and even more powerful frame of mind. They possess a kind of wisdom in things pertaining to their career. While they have a lot of energy and pizzazz, this combination has a side that can seem downhearted. If one looks carefully in the eyes of a Sagittarius-Rabbit, that part of their nature might be visible. Interestingly enough though, the Sagittarius-Rabbit seems to use their melancholy as a source of strength.

Romance: This combination cannot contain all of that sexual energy all of the time, however. The result is often serial monogamy, but they are certainly not beyond straying beyond the bonds that they have created. Neither are they beyond helping the partners of others stray beyond their promises. In the long run they do have an ability to hold on to previous lovers as friends, and at least in this sense they are loyal and faithful. The Sagittarius-Rabbit is a person who frequently has one relationship after another; it's almost as though they are looking for something special. While there is a big sexual drive in this combination, a lot of that is repressed and directed in other ways.

Relationships: Not making the list for compatibility are Gemini-, Virgo-, and Pisces-Roosters. Their Tiger equivalents are not suggested either. Fine selections for love and romance are Aries-, Leo-, and Aquarius-Dogs. Also high on the list of possibilities are Leo-, Libra-, and Aquarius-Boars. There are even more good picks with Aries- and Aquarius-Rams. Aries-Snakes are generally quite attractive to the Sagittarius-Rabbit.

Family Life: Odds are that their primary home will be a country estate that is highly comfortable. In addition, there will probably be some domestic help who are treated with loving-kindness. As a parent the Sagittarius-Rabbit tends to not be extremely involved and leaves much of the actual parenting to his partner. The older the child gets, however, the more interest this combination will have. In the same manner that Sagittarius-Rabbits might partake of serial monogamy, they might also partake of having multiple homes. But in this case they are likely to be happening all at the same time. The members of this combination are wanderers. Something in their being calls them to roam, and they must answer that call. Further, the travel must be first-class travel. Without this there is a lack of completion. None of this is to say that the Sagittarius-Rabbit will not have one primary place that they consider home. They will.

Livelihood: This combination needs to make sure they do not have personal problems that distract them. Having set their goal, they need to focus on it. If this is done, they are capable of many things. Opening a business or managing a company or virtually anything is possible. Finally, this combination is good with groups and is a person looked up to and listened to by others. Sagittarius-Rabbits are talented individuals. They can be artistic and creative or more business oriented. It is possible they even have a technical aptitude. The point is that they will have some ability that stands out, and they will be able to utilize this. Because they can be multitalented, they need to be careful not to spread themselves too thin.

Famous Sagittarius-Rabbits: Edith Piaf, Augusto Pinochet, Frank Sinatra.

Sagittarius (Rat) Month Combined with Dragon Year

"Witness" Jupiter, Fire, Mutable" "**Take Charge**" Yang-Positive Wood

Characteristics: Volubility, Contradiction, Infatuation, Sentimentality, Good Health, Honor, Pluck, Braggadocio, Carelessness, Reason, Enthusiasm, Dissatisfaction, Vacillation, Valor, Openhandedness, Success, Mistrust, Recklessness, Bad Manners, Solicitude, Outspokenness, Strength, Cheerfulness, Rigidity

This combination does forge ahead through enemy lines with a brilliance and dedication exceeded by none. They smile in the face of danger and tap-dance on the edge of cliffs. The Sagittarius-Dragon is good-looking and determined. Sagittarius-Dragons are fearless soldiers dedicated to the proposition that they will prevail. That does not mean that they are rude, harsh, or rough. Quite the contrary; they are well mannered, gentle, and stately. In addition, they are clever and outsmart their foes. They are so gifted that they make former enemies into converts. They are not egotists nor are they selfish. Rather they are utilitarian, wanting the greatest good for the greatest number of people. They have goals and dreams and a vision of how to attain them. This combination is right more often than not. The Sagittarius-Dragon is modest in spite of being triumphant. There is not so much as one iota of arrogance in them. They are friendly with everyone and quite down-to-earth. They do not carry an air of supremacy around with them. They are the friendly type in spite of their ambition and are quite happy to have others join with them in their quest to make dreams come true.

Romance: Big dreams are part of this individual, and that includes everything across the board. They want a huge house with zillions of children. The size of the dreams demands a partner who has real standing and real depth. Being married to a Sagittarius-Dragon is an experience indeed. The Sagittarius-Dragon is shrewd when it comes to marriage and does not rush things. Their overall demeanor of friendliness and confidence is attractive to others. This combination is not interested in merely the external. They want a real partner in life: someone who will help them attain their aspirations.

Relationships: Poor choices for compatibility are Dogs who are Gemini, Virgo, and Pisces. Excellent picks in the realm of romance are Aries, Leo, Libra, and Aquarius. The best of these are Aries-Buffalo, -Tiger, -Monkey, and -Boar, as well as the Leo-Rat, -Monkey, or -Rooster. Additional fine choices are the Libra-Tiger and -Monkey or Aquarius-Rat and -Monkey.

Family Life: This combination must be seen shopping only at the best stores. Discount department stores are not for them. They are original and creative in terms of their home. It will be unique, it will be cool, but most of all it will be impressive. This combination makes excellent parents. They are dependable and caring. They are encouraging. Status is primary for the Sagittarius-Dragon. In the beginning they do not require luxury, but as time passes they want only the finest. They do not care to live on the wrong side of the tracks; rather, it must be a neighborhood with standing. When they have children, they must go to quality schools.

Livelihood: This combination is charming overall, and that too helps them get to the mountaintop. They have a staggering amount of self-confidence without being pompous about it. This is a highly attractive combination. Sagittarius-Dragons mean what they say and say what they mean. If that is not enough, they do what they say they are going to do. That includes succeeding. They will not quit. Of course they do not walk on water, so mistakes are possible, but infrequent.

Famous Sagittarius-Dragons: Louisa May Alcott, Betty Grable, Richard Pryor.

Sagittarius (Rat) Month Combined with Snake Year

"Witness" Jupiter, Fire, Mutable   **"Feel"** Yang-Negative Fire

Characteristics: Compassion, Reason, Exclusiveness, Contradiction, Dissimulation, Sagacity, Carelessness, Cupidity, Honor, Clairvoyance, Laziness, Solicitude, Discretion, Bad Manners, Valor, Presumption, Attractiveness, Openhandedness, Recklessness, Extravagance, Cheerfulness, Intuition, Outspokenness, Vacillation

These individuals carry themselves with poise and bearing. They are extraordinarily well mannered and the pinnacles of virtue. If one were to look up the word *sophisticated* in the dictionary there would be a picture of a Sagittarius-Snake. Perhaps the word *attentive* best summarizes the Sagittarius-Snake. Sagittarius-Snakes care deeply about others in general and those they love in particular. It is not just people that they care for but inanimate objects as well. They are attentive when it comes to their home, their office, or their yard. This combination is a high-class article with a discount price. They are well spoken and delicate with the tone of their voice. There is a very good chance this combination will succeed beyond anything anyone in his or her family ever has or ever imagined. Idealism is a big motivator for them, and it often pushes them upward. They work; they believe and rise up through the ranks. They are the type who speaks softly but carries a big stick. People pay attention to them. They do not announce themselves with bugles and marching bands. The Sagittarius-Snake does not attack head-on. This combination is a reasonable person with emphasis on the word *reason*. They can use logic to figure things out, explain them, and communicate.

Romance: This combination is a supremely dedicated spouse with a great deal of class. This sort of person is wonderful but of course requires reciprocation that is equally wonderful. That means pressure to be virtuous. The Sagittarius-Snake takes her time in making a marriage commitment. It is possible that she will have a long live-together relationship before marriage.

Sagittarius-Snakes are quiet types, and sometimes their partners wonder what is going on with them. The fact is that they are very loyal and faithful partners and would never get involved in betrayal or an extramarital affair because they find it disgusting and unseemly.

Relationships: Probably not especially good suggestions are Virgo, Gemini, and Pisces. This is doubly true of the Gemini-Monkey, Virgo-Tiger and -Boar, and Pisces-Tiger, -Monkey, and -Boar. First-class relationship possibilities are Leo-, Libra-, and Aquarius-Buffalos. Further fine picks are Aries- and Aquarius-Roosters.

Family Life: This combination will have no part of anything that is not authentic. There is no flash and no glitter about this individual. As parents they are superb. They care and are creative. There is a tad of doting in their parenting, but this stems from caring. This combination insists on an aesthetically pleasing home. In addition to that, it must be real and perhaps a bit understated. There is no nouveau about it. The antiques that they are fond of are precisely that—antiques. Everything surrounding them is the real McCoy, including jewelry, art, and kitchenware.

Livelihood: As bosses this combination is good at delegating authority. They are fair and make wonderful employees or bosses. The Sagittarius-Snake does, however, get frustrated if all his ducks are not lined up properly. Professions in the area of caring are right up this combination's alley. They are excellent with people. They also have good organizational abilities. The paperwork often associated with such professions does not bother them because they are meticulous and pay attention to details. Tricky situations between individuals can generally be dealt with in a soft-spoken and tactful manner.

Famous Sagittarius-Snakes: Pope John XXIII, Munro Leaf, Ossie Davis, Howard Hughes.

Sagittarius (Rat) Month Combined with Horse Year

"Witness" Jupiter, Fire, Mutable   *"Command"* Yang-Positive Fire

Characteristics: Pragmatism, Contradiction, Haste, Accomplishment, Unscrupulousness, Vacillation, Carelessness, Valor, Honor, Dexterity, Selfishness, Autonomy, Bad Manners, Solicitude, Popularity, Style, Anxiety, Openhandedness, Recklessness, Cheerfulness, Reason, Persuasiveness, Outspokenness, Rebellion

This combination seemingly has a giant power generator producing power twenty-four hours a day. They never sleep. They never get tired; or so it seems. The old-fashioned character of the Sagittarius-Horse is evident in his manner. The Sagittarius-Horse is like the statue in the park in terms of strength and power. Notable too is the fact that this statue is predominantly Horse. There is a homely wisdom to the character and values of this individual. They are in control not only of themselves but also of their surroundings. These individuals stare straight ahead focused firmly on their goals. They are ever polite and ever considerate. When people say the Sagittarius-Horse is classy, they are not talking about merely their presentation to the world. This combination does not want to be viewed as part of the crowd, and they generally succeed in not being thought of in that manner. They proudly march to the beat of their own drummer. They have grace and demeanor in social settings. They carry themselves with their heads held high and their shoulders back, and people sense their presence. The internal workings of the Sagittarius-Horse reflect an individual who approaches arrogance but does not cross the line.

Romance: This combination wants a spouse strong enough to be responsible and take care of those things necessary for maintaining a secure home and family. The Sagittarius-Horse insists on doing things their way and takes care of business while their partner takes care of the home front. The Sagittarius-Horse is likely to slip up in the area of romance when they are younger, but they will not be major foibles. This is a passionate combination and has a lot of oats that it can sow in its early years. Maturity does come to the Sagittarius-Horse, however, and they grasp the concept of having a partner suitable for their goals.

Relationships: Out of the running for compatibility are Virgo-, Gemini-, and Pisces-Rats. In the area of romance, combined with the desire for success, the best choices are Aries-, Libra-, Leo-, and Aquarius-Tigers. Other superb choices are Aries-, Leo-, and Libra-Ram. Continuing the list of positive partner choices are Libra- and Aquarius-Dogs.

Family Life: This combination must have their workspace at home and there are no exceptions. It does not matter where it is: in the attic, basement, or spare bedroom, they make it what it is. They spare no expense to make it work and to make it attractive. There is the proper lighting, plenty of electrical outlets, all the gadgets they need, and plenty of countertop and workspace. It is all there, and it is all first-class. The Sagittarius-Horse essentially has no interest in the decor of their home. They are happy to make do with hand-me-downs. They like to be comfortable like everyone does, but that is the extent of it. If their home is decorated or attractive, it is certain that it has been done by their spouse.

Livelihood: This combination has excellent managerial skills and is a born organizer. They are also good in front of groups and have superb leadership skills. While they are on the authoritarian side, they do have a degree of tact as well. Professions that need a degree of perceptiveness are best for the Sagittarius-Horse. That includes, of course, work demanding acute skills of observation. They are also good in the area of problem solving, especially when it comes to the issues of others.

Famous Sagittarius-Horses: Leonid Brezhnev, James Thurber, Alexander Solzhenitsyn, Jean-Luc Godard, Jimi Hendrix, Jean-Louis Trintignant.

Sagittarius (Rat) Month Combined with Ram Year

"Witness" Jupiter, Fire, Mutable   *"Reliance"* Yang-Negative Fire

Characteristics: Impracticality, Reason, Worry, Contradiction, Good Manners, Pessimism, Carelessness, Whimsy, Honor, Taste, Perseverance, Sensitivity, Bad Manners, Solicitude, Tardiness, Valor, Lack of Foresight, Openhandedness, Vacillation, Recklessness, Invention, Cheerfulness, Outspokenness, Parasitism

The fact is that if any aspect of this combination's life is out of balance or threatened even to a small degree, they have a very difficult time functioning. The monkey wrench could come in the form of rumors at work, personal problems at home, or bad news in the stock market. This combination is extraordinarily imaginative and innovative. The Sagittarius-Ram is a highly creative individual. There is a sort of vitality to this logical and astute person. Of course, no one is perfect and everyone has some challenges. In the case of the Sagittarius-Ram it is almost a desperate need for security that he seeks. Sagittarius-Rams seem to have an extra sense relative to when help is needed and when help is appropriate. They also happen to be excellent in providing assistance to those in need. This individual is not a wimp or a coward; quite the contrary. They are brave and spirited. The primary challenge that they face is attaining security for themselves and their families. They are very poised and proud individuals who present themselves with charm and elegance. The manners come from the Sagittarius side, as does the kindness that they show others. The mixture in the sign means that they are careful about all things.

Romance: The need for freedom is also there, and even after marriage this combination wants to have a flexible mate. The Sagittarius-Ram expects to be respected and has a rather high level of self-esteem. They also expect to have a relatively high degree of deference shown them. The desire for security coupled with the desire for independence leads this person to be relatively slow in marrying. This is generally true in regard to most major decisions but particularly a life-long commitment. They must feel financially secure and have sorted things out in their lives. The necessary backup mechanisms must be in order and everything needs to be rock solid.

Relationships: Negative picks for compatibility are Gemini-, Virgo-, or Pisces-Dogs. Poor selections are also Gemini-Tigers and Virgo- and Pisces-Buffalos. Romance and love can best be found with Aries-, Libra-, and Aquarius-Rabbits. Further fine choices are Leo-, Libra-, and Aquarius-Boars. Continuing along the list of positive combinations is the Aries-Horse.

Family Life: This combination tends to have no-frill homes that are strong and comfortable. They are generally remote. The Sagittarius-Ram makes a fine parent. They care deeply for their children and find it easy to show interest in everything that they do. Sagittarius-Rams are suitable for the country life because they have a strong dislike for crowds, noise, and pollution. Those things tend to disconcert this combination. They are more of the meditative type and prefer peace and quiet. They love nature, including moonlit nights and powerful streams running through crevices. Nature restores them and provides the motivation for major accomplishments.

Livelihood: This combination gets along well with others, and they work hard, especially if permitted to work independently. They make fine bosses and are well liked as well as respected by those who work for them. This combination looks to the future and to change. They are cautious souls and plan well. Sagittarius-Rams have deep feelings about their families and take good care of them because they are so bound to the concept of security. They are well aware of what is happening in the larger society in spite of the fact that they tend to live rather private and remote lives.

Famous Sagittarius-Rams: Jane Austen, Mark Twain, Andrew Carnegie, Anna Freud, Alberto Moravia, Busby Berkeley, Randy Newman.

Sagittarius (Rat) Month Combined with Monkey Year

"Witness" Jupiter, Fire, Mutable   **"Arrange"** Yin-Positive Metal

Characteristics: Zeal, Contradiction, Leadership, Opportunism, Honor, Loquacity, Carelessness, Silliness, Bad Manners, Stability, Vacillation, Self-involvement, Wit, Reason, Openhandedness, Outspokenness, Recklessness, Valor, Cunning, Ruse, Solicitude, Cheerfulness, Improvisation, Deceit

This combination knows who he is, likes who he is, and is comfortable with who he is. This makes him fairly outgoing. This combination is kind and compassionate and enjoys sharing with and helping other people. Of course no combination is all roses and cherries, and that is true of the Sagittarius-Monkey. The Sagittarius-Monkey is an open-minded explorer of the future. They are smooth and care deeply about their fellow humans. Verbally they shoot straight and believe in participating in good works. They are essentially happy campers. This fundamental description is true of both the Sagittarius and Monkey side of the combination. Perhaps that is why their personalities are basically in harmony. The outwardly directed and people-oriented Sagittarius side is not in complete accord with the crafty and indirect Monkey. A powerful and charismatic leader is born of this dialectic. They have the necessary power and passion to attract and convince followers. They are opportunistic and sly and thus are perfect for anything involving a political approach to matters. The Sagittarius in this combination likes to take chances, but the Monkey is cautious. Monkeys primarily think about themselves. This apparent rift and conflict actually has a happy ending, however. The overall interactions of the two signs push this combination toward leadership. Furthermore, it all comes about as simply as a stroll in the park.

Romance: This combination's emotional makeup is such that they have a difficult time coming to grips with it. To put it plainly, they just do not take responsibility for their emotions. It is difficult for someone to capture the heart of a Sagittarius-Monkey. They are a barrel of laughs and are extremely friendly. Serious commitment is another matter. The Sagittarius-Monkey is reluctant to make a serious commitment in a relationship. Intimacy scares them a bit, and they worry that time will erode deep feelings of love and romance. Marriage is something that they shy away from.

Relationships: Top selections in the field of romance and love are Aries-, Libra-, and Aquarius-Rats. Additional good picks are the Leo-, Libra-, or Aquarius-Dragon. Oddly enough, Pisces-Snakes are quite a wonderful choice, but the chances are very much against ever hooking up with one. For compatibility in this combination poor choices are Virgo-, Gemini-, or Pisces-Boars. Also out of the running are Gemini- and Pisces-Buffalos. Continuing the somewhat lengthy list of negative selections are Virgos who are Rabbits or Tigers.

Family Life: In all likelihood this combination will not marry early. This combination's career usually comes first and marriage and kids a bit later. Their personal appearance is also fairly functional and conventional. This combination is not Mr. or Ms. Flashy or Showy. Getting things accomplished is more important than gaining attention. The Sagittarius-Monkey is fundamentally a pragmatic person. There is no flamboyance in their nature and this fact is reflected in their home. While they might have some interesting items from their globetrotting, their goal is not to impress people. They have a home that is comfortable, and they are fairly neat and orderly. As with most pragmatists, the point of their home is that it works well.

Livelihood: With this kind of personality and approach to life, there is only one slot for them in the world of employment: they are bosses. Fortunately, they do a fairly good job at being in leadership positions and are generally liked by those under them. This combination loves a challenge and does not shy away from problems. Problem solving, in fact, is their forte, and they have the acumen to deal with the toughest and most difficult issues placed before them. There is no such thing, in their mind, as a problem without a solution. They invented the saying, "if life gives you lemons, make lemonade." In those rare occasions where they are not familiar with the issues or the focus, they can make sensible noises anyway.

Famous Sagittarius-Monkeys: John Milton, Claude Levi-Strauss, Ellen Burstyn, Larry Bird.

Sagittarius (Rat) Month Combined with Rooster Year

"Witness" Jupiter, Fire, Mutable   **"Conqueror"** Yang-Negative Metal

Characteristics: Humor, Contradiction, Chic, Dissipation, Bossiness, Conservatism, Cockiness, Pedantry, Blind Faith, Bad Manners, Valor, Reason, Carelessness, Enthusiasm, Openhandedness, Honor, Candor, Recklessness, Solicitude, Boastfulness, Outspokenness, Cheerfulness, Vacillation, Resilience

This combination is impressive just walking down the street or entering a room. People notice them. They are jet-setting wanderers who have been nearly everywhere on Earth, and they are walking and talking Wikipedia entries on geography. All this might lead one to believe that this combination is rash or even irresponsible. Actually, quite the opposite is the case. The Sagittarius-Rooster is a frank, honest and extremely realistic individual. They are vagabonds, albeit nervous ones. Both the Sagittarius and the Rooster side of this combination are loaded with energy but also edginess. They are enthusiastic and flamboyant. The hidden inner workings of this individual show a person who is cautious, careful, sensible, and organized. In addition, they are kind and want to help others. There is a good chance that they will volunteer or travel widely to assist the poor, the sick, and the homeless. Whatever it might be, they put their energy to good use in humanitarian causes. Verbally they are straight shooters who speak their minds. They are the proverbial "what you see is what you get" type of individual. They might lean a bit toward the do-gooder side of the scale and do not mind imagining a world that is just, fair, and kind. There is absolutely nothing fake about the Sagittarius-Rooster, and they abhor anything that is a phony. One of their primary missions in life, and it is a mission, is to assist those in need.

Romance: A bit of caution is in order in the realms of passion and jealousy for this combination. The Sagittarius-Rooster is the type who sometimes falls for people that are projects, someone with problems and in need of help. This too is not always the best course of action. The Sagittarius-Rooster generally has some difficulty in their love life because of the nature of their character. For starters they can be quite pushy with their partners. On the other hand they generally find that approach not particularly useful, so they go to the other extreme and get pushed around. Neither approach is fruitful. In addition, they are so frank that they talk about things in a relationship that are best left unspoken. It is not wise to tell one's partner every single thought and be totally open and honest. Flattery sometimes is in order, even if it is a bit of an untruth. Telling one's significant other that a new workmate is attractive is not wise either.

Relationships: Poor choices for compatibility are Virgo- and Gemini-Roosters. Additional negative selections are Pisces-Dogs and Virgo- and Pisces-Rabbits. Superb romantic and love selections are Aries-, Leo-, Libra-, and Aquarius-Snakes. Additionally Leo-, Libra-, and Aquarius-Buffalos are quite good as well. Romance is nearly ideal with Leo- and Libra-Dragons.

Family Life: The Sagittarius-Rooster is a borderline neat freak. Order and cleanliness are next to Godliness. This overall worldview demands the right address with the right home and the right sort of decorating. This combination, in spite of the emphasis on the home, is on the road a lot. They are generally quite busy individuals, and this can interfere with them becoming parents. While parenthood appeals to them, that does not top their list of priorities. Unlike many combinations, the Sagittarius-Rooster in not primarily focused on comfort in their home. Rather, they have a clean but elegant place with a very respectable address. They believe in things being both eye-catching and highly regarded. There is no arrogance in the Sagittarius-Rooster, but there is a highly conservative approach to life.

Livelihood: This combination has a kind of metaphysical perspective on the universe and can see the interconnectedness of things where others miss them. They are not space cadets, however, but rather have a lot of common sense. Nevertheless, they are very decisive. Vocations that entail travel are very well suited to this combination. They were destined to move about. The Sagittarius-Rooster is loquacious and can talk to most people about most things. Their verbal skills are excellent, and it is possible they are multilingual. They have an excellent awareness of future trends, fads, and styles.

Famous Sagittarius-Roosters: Deanna Durbin, Tim Conway, Flip Wilson.

Sagittarius (Rat) Month Combined with Dog Year

"Witness" Jupiter, Fire, Mutable **"Concerned"** Yin-Positive Metal

Characteristics: Heroism, Carelessness, Reason, Intelligence, Contradiction, Tastelessness, Cynicism, Vacillation, Self-solicitude, Bad Manners, Righteousness, Criticism, Honor, Openhandedness, Respectability, Duty, Valor, Uneasiness, Morality, Unsociability, Recklessness, Outspokenness, Cheerfulness, Constancy

This combination generally speaks straight from the heart with both frankness and passion. They can talk and usually say too much. Their mouths get them in trouble at times, and they possess a knockout punch second to none. In spite of this they are highly regarded. The Sagittarius-Dog has verbal skills and can bite. They love exploration; the more idealistic the trip, the better. There is a hero in hiding here with a keen sense of what is over the next mountain and the brilliance to find their way. It would be difficult to find a person who is more principled and dependable. When they open their mouths and start talking, one should be prepared for them to hold forth. Sagittarius-Dogs do not beat around the bush and are not timid about expressing themselves. They are friends with the movers and the shakers and know the right places to go at the right time. As if this were not enough, they have an uncanny ability to fix things and are often turned to when a problem needs solving. Their credibility is unquestioned. They are almost bulletproof. Antagonists cannot deal with the heat and leave the kitchen. This is one very courageous combination and is not intimidated by confrontation. They are well versed in a wide range of topics and have more honor than Eagle Scouts.

Romance: For this combination private matters belong in private, and there are to be no public hearings or sightings of what belongs behind closed doors. Impolite and offensive behavior is shunned. Anyone involved romantically should know that the Sagittarius-Dog is a wanderer. There is a shy side to this powerful individual, and they can be quite gentle and caring. They have a very good personality and can be faithful to their partner. Furthermore, their passion lasts and they are supremely loving and caring. They have an aversion to having their private life become public. This leads to discretion in terms of how and when they display their love and their romantic side.

Relationships: In the area of compatibility, poor picks are Gemini-, Leo-, Virgo-, and Pisces-Dragons. Further poor choices are Gemini-, Virgo-, and Pisces-Rams. Perhaps the worst possible pick is the Gemini-Monkey. Tigers are excellent choices for love and romance. Of those, the Leo, Libra, and Aquarius are the cream of the crop, and Horses from these same signs are also excellent. Leo-Rabbits are another good selection.

Family Life: This combination cares about work and the world in general. Given the financial resources, this combination will have household staff. The same is true where a nanny and private tutors for the children are employed. This individual is a caring but serious and strict mother or father. The Sagittarius-Dog is firmly rooted in family and tradition. This means, of course, that funerals, weddings, and baptisms are important. There is probably a serious interest in genealogy, and there is an authentic coat of arms. One would think that home was quite important to this combination, but oddly enough, it is not. A place that is reasonably well decorated is, of course, desired, but other things, for example proximity to work, are more significant. This is not a handyperson around the house or someone who spends the weekend redecorating the living room.

Livelihood: As bosses this combination can do a good job even though they have a sharp and biting manner to their speech. They are strictly business and want things done right. While somewhat strict, they actually are kind individuals who care about those they work with. The Sagittarius-Dog is an intelligent worker and does best in positions where his intellect can be utilized. They do not like bossy or bad-tempered individuals in positions of authority over them. Neither are they interested in hanging out by the water cooler and gossiping about Sally or Sam. They want independence. In exchange for that, they work very hard, almost to the workaholic level. However, the Sagittarius knows how to leave their work where it belongs—on their desks—and exercise their freedom.

Famous Sagittarius-Dogs: Jean Genet, Winston Churchill, Abe Burrows.

Sagittarius (Rat) Month Combined with Boar Year

"Witness" Jupiter, Fire, Mutable **"Cultivator"** Yin-Negative Water

Characteristics: Contradiction, Reason, Boar-headedness, Honesty, Solicitude, Materialism, Culture, Gourmandism, Carelessness, Valor, Vacillation, Bad Manners, Sincerity, Credulity, Hesitation, Honor, Gallantry, Openhandedness, Recklessness, Wrath, Cheerfulness, Scrupulousness, Outspokenness, Voluptuousness

Sagittarius-Boars' exceptional abilities of observation originate from the fact that they are artists; well-liked artists at that. Their forte in the aesthetic arena is social commentary. They find and reveal the weaknesses of society but generally do this in a humorous manner. In addition, they do not mind showing that they are human and deserving of some social irreverence as well. The Sagittarius-Boar appears to be above the fray. They are, after all, also principled and moral. Moral condemnation cannot touch them, and consequently their reputation is excellent. They have fantastic vision when it comes to their surroundings and distance themselves from unsavory issues. Their vision is so acute that the Sagittarius-Boar can see patterns and tendencies when others cannot. They are honest and straightforward as well as trustworthy, and that is the source of their popularity. In addition, they have a true interest in other people. The result is often the brightest star in the galaxy. Their popularity extends far and wide, and no one seems to be paranoid or suspicious of them. They are exceedingly popular even though often they are not the most physically attractive people. It is simply that they are caring and kind individuals, and their moral principles shine through their physical nature.

Romance: The primary motive for marriage in this combination is generally respect, especially respect of the intellect. A partner for the Sagittarius-Boar must have that. In addition, because they are enormously humorous, a partner needs to have a sense of humor to match. The Sagittarius-Boar falls in love and gets married and generally that is for keeps. They are kind and giving to all, especially their families. It is possible they might stray a bit, but that is generally for reasons other than love, and is probably more intellectual than sexual. If they do stray, they are exceptionally careful.

Relationships: To be avoided are Gemini-, Virgo-, and Pisces-Snakes. Further combinations that do not make the list are Gemini-Roosters and Virgo-Monkeys. An excellent low-maintenance selection for love is the Rabbit, who has a peaceful nature. Of the Rabbits, the best selections are the Aries, Leo, Libra, or Aquarius. Additional good choices are Leo- and Aquarius-Rams.

Family Life: Everything in their home has a function, purpose, and place. As parents they are giving, and that is true even of time that is so precious to the Sagittarius-Boar. In addition to love, this combination finds their children fascinating and loves to observe them and their interactions as they do enjoy observing everyone. The Sagittarius-Boar needs a home that is compatible with their work. They are exceptionally busy people. They are not concerned about impressing people with luxury, style, or decor. They do like objects that have meaning for them in their surroundings, but their primary function is working and that means not just at their formal workplace but at home as well. Their desk will be in the place that is the most efficient for them, and that is their byword—*efficiency*.

Livelihood: This combination might be a musician or standup comedian. They have success written all over their persona in this area. They laugh at themselves and make others laugh but are always tasteful in their humor. As a boss they are always just and giving as well as understanding. There is a perfectionist inside this combination though, so those who work for them must be ready to toe the line. The Sagittarius-Boar has many professional choices. It is likely that their choice will be something in the field of art because of their excellent creative aptitude, but that creative aptitude can be located in many different fields of creativity. They could turn to the field of entertainment in its many forms or other spheres where creativity is needed, advertising for example.

Famous Sagittarius-Boars: Hector Berlioz, Noel Coward, Phil Donahue, Woody Allen, Jules Dassin.

Capricorn (Buffalo) Month Combined with Rat Year

"Utilize" Saturn, Earth, Cardinal **"Regulator"** Yin-Positive Water

Characteristics: Meddling, Self-doubt, Sociability, Acquisitiveness, Charisma, Superiority, Intellectual, Epicureanism, Skill, Guile, Influence, Thrift, Loneliness, Generosity, Thirst for Power, Clumsiness, Dependability, Verbosity, Pretension, Resolve, Ambition, Stiffness, Appeal, Nervousness, Wisdom

The Capricorn-Rat courts risks because, as is clear to most everyone, power-hungry individuals are not the most admired and sought-after people on the planet. There are too many negative associations with power, including voracity, greed, and rapaciousness. The Capricorn-Rat is, to be quite blunt about it, a powermonger. They love power and crave it. This trait comes from both sides of the combination; the Rat wants supremacy and the Capricorn wants to influence others. The result is clear and the consequences can, unfortunately, be hazardous. They live a life of constant danger. Of course, the outer appearance of this combination is perfectly reasonable. To put out aggressive waves and vibrations would not work on the road to supremacy. Rather, the Capricorn-Rat must give an air of being trustworthy and helpful. None of this is to say that this combination is bad. It is only to point out the great possibility of being bad. People are aware that those who want power step on and climb over others on their way to influence. The point of life itself for the Rat is to gain power. There is no combination more aggressive than the Capricorn-Rat. There is only one goal in life: to be number one.

Romance: *Romance* is a bit of an odd word relative to the Capricorn-Rat, and even the word *partner* has the wrong ring to it. They need a dependable mate who can be devoted to them. The Capricorn-Rat needs a partner, but it would be misleading to claim she needs love. This is not a Cupid sort of person. Any sort of feeling of love is secondary to expediency or, to put it more kindly, assistance on the road to royalty. That road is, of course, filled with details and chores. Reaching the destination requires support and aid. While they do have energy, it is impossible, for example, to be in two places at once. A mate is needed to take care of the children or take them to the dentist and other such activities.

Relationships: Not especially ideal signs for this combination are the Horse or Rat. Particularly poor choices are Aries-, Cancer-, or Libra-Horses, as are Aries- or Libra-Rabbits. There is a lot going on in the love and romance category for the Capricorn-Ram. Good selections are Taurus, Leo, Virgo, Scorpio, or Pisces. Monkeys combined with these Western signs are good, with the exception of the Virgo-Monkey. Signs that make this combination happy are Taurus-, Virgo-, and Pisces-Dragons.

Family Life: Their decorating inclinations lean toward the refined and urbane. All of this might give the impression that the Capricorn-Rat is not particularly interested in children. That is absolutely not the case at all. This combination loves and cares deeply about the young. They are highly protective and sustaining. The Capricorn-Rat has a strong need to be comfortable at home. They like chores to be easy to do. Combined with the fact that they like to tell the world how important they are, their home will be comfy, convenient, and elegant. Convenience means gadgets of all sorts to make their lives easier. Elegance probably means antiques, which must be highly traditional. They are not in favor, however, of the farmhouse approach to decorating. That is too blue-collar for their taste.

Livelihood: Human nature being what it is, this combination is not the only one on the highway to power—and thus they make enemies. Some of these enemies might be dedicated to the proposition of destroying the Capricorn-Rat. In addition, they create poor losers who are often all around them in their profession. Being in charge is not for sissies. Fortunately for them, the Capricorn-Rat is hardly that. The Capricorn-Rat must win in order to be happy. Winning for them is not a one-time thing. They must win time after time as they reach each rung of the ladder to success and power. Domination is the only thing they will accept. They are huge risk takers because of this compulsion to rule, and consequently live life dangerously.

Famous Capricorn-Rats: Pablo Casals, Rod Sterling, Richard Nixon, John DeLorean, Donna Summer.

Capricorn (Buffalo) Month Combined with Buffalo Year

"Utilize" Saturn, Earth, Cardinal   *"Survivor"* Yin-Negative Water

Characteristics: Vindictiveness, Self-doubt, Stability, Wisdom, Innovation, Bias, Diligence, Superiority, Epicureanism, Dependability, Standoffishness, Eloquence, Generosity, Plodding, Loneliness, Bigotry, Resolve, Clumsiness, Strength of Purpose, Stiffness, Integrity, Stubbornness, Ambition, Pretension

Capricorn-Buffalos' views are unique, and they can be brutal in their approach to other people. They have, to be kind about it, their own view of the Golden

Rule, and being vicious is sometimes fair and in accord with how others should be treated. For that matter, they have their own view about nearly everything, and those views are carved in stone in their front yards. That viciousness does not generally include violence, however. Capricorn-Buffalos are traditionalists in their philosophy and approach to life. They are the type to sit on the front porch and say how good things used to be. They plod on relentlessly but slowly, and changing their minds is pretty much out of the question. It is just that they are powerful and beastly in their willpower and thoroughness. The Capricorn-Buffalo will help their extended family out if need be, but they will not do it happily, and there will be rumblings and grumblings from them about doing it. Friends of friends can take care of themselves. Forget about asking the Capricorn-Buffalo. The antonym for *quitter* is the Capricorn-Buffalo. They never give up, and that is the name of that tune. This combination is a mountain person who says what he means and means what he says. If they say they will be there at 10 a.m. on Tuesday, you can bet your farm on it. They will get out of their hospital bed to do it if necessary.

Romance: This combination is tied too strongly to his family to have a homewrecker seek and destroy. Their commitment to say what they mean includes an attitude that shuns divorce and considers it failure. This combination is, after all, respectable, if not a winner of the good citizenship award. Love, sex, and marriage are important to the Capricorn-Buffalo, and perhaps not in that order. This is a highly sexed individual and downright robust in that department. This combination needs marriage and family. However, it is true that their sex drive might lead to a little dabbling outside of marriage.

Relationships: Moving gently into the realm of negative compatibility for this combination are Aries-Dragons and Cancer-Dragons. Additional poor choices are the Cancer- or Libra-Ram, as are the Libra-Buffalo, -Tiger, and -Monkey. Bringing up the rear is the Cancer-Boar. In terms of excellent selections, the best are Taurus-, Leo-, Virgo-, and Pisces-Snakes. Probably Scorpio-Snakes are not the best of choices. On the other hand, Roosters from those signs are distinct possibilities. Additional good picks are Taurus-, Leo-, Virgo-, or Pisces-Rats. Continuing the list of positive choices are the Leo-Boar or Scorpio-Dragon.

Family Life: The Capricorn-Buffalo lives on the right side of the tracks near the country club. They give home tours and explanations of the furnishing to all visitors. The decor is not only classy, it is famous; or, at least those who designed or built it are famous, even though visitors might not have heard of them. Everything is authentic, regardless of the type of home they have. It could be a farmhouse previously owned by an artist or a church made famous in a song. Farmhouses have real animals and churches have real pews, of course. The Capricorn-Buffalo is an excellent parent and takes care to have children he can be proud of. That means the children will attend good schools and have proper outside interests. Posh and glamorous are words that come to mind describing the home of the Capricorn-Buffalo. That would carry all the way from the inside to the outside of this abode. This home virtually drips with the aristocratic, or, barring this, attempts at it.

Livelihood: Respectability will do just fine for this combination. For what they have and the position they hold, they achieve recognition and admiration. For Capricorn-Buffalos this is a fulfillment of their dreams, and, indeed, most people would be quite satisfied to lead a secure and traditional life with their family as these individuals do. This individual generally attains what he most desires, which is security. They have a good livelihood, and that is what they wanted all along. There never was an interest in being famous.

Famous Capricorn-Buffalos: Chuck Berry, Mary Tyler Moore.

Capricorn (Buffalo) Month Combined with Tiger Year

"Utilize" Saturn, Earth, Cardinal   **"Observe"** Yang-Positive Wood

Characteristics: Authority, Dependability, Self-doubt, Itinerancy, Intemperance, Superiority, Benevolence, Epicureanism, Magnetism, Clumsiness, Disobedience, Loneliness, Generosity, Good Luck, Pretension, Resolve, Bravery, Ambition, Hotheadedness, Stiffness, Fervor, Wisdom, Impetuosity, Swagger

It is true that Capricorn-Tigers are ambitious, but they also happen to be generous in the same way that, perhaps, flower children are generous. This comparison extends to their slightly unconventional lifestyle. It is actually quite amazing that they have the time to get bored, because they are so busy most of the time that they need several calendars as well as an appointment secretary. The hallmarks for the Capricorn-Tiger are speed and kindness toward all. Everything they do, they do quickly: walk, talk, and think. They also happen to be totally authentic without one iota of facade. They do, unfortunately, suffer from boredom from time to time, and this is not a trait that speaks kindly of anyone. They think it is perfectly reasonable to help themselves to the food at a banquet and take some home with them.

They call dignitaries by their first names and might even put their feet on expensive tables or chairs the first time they visit someone. This combination might have been the first on Earth to be known as hyperactive. They make bees and ants look lazy. There is a bit of goofiness circulating through them, and they are terrific at being clumsy, particularly in the social realm. For the most part they do not subscribe to the social graces and think of them as nonsense.

Romance: This combination wants someone who understands and shares their values and someone who can help create a proper home for children, pets, and other animals. It has to be someone special because the Capricorn-Tiger is so active. In spite of their busy schedule, they share their love and want it shared in return: lots of it. This person is, as they say, a keeper. They are worth every bit of effort because they give it all back and then some. Any partner should hang on very tightly and not lose them. The Capricorn-Tiger loves and respects all sentient beings. They love nature. They love children. There is nothing put on about this. It is totally genuine and guides everything they do, including their choice of partners.

Relationships: Combinations that should be avoided in the area of love are Aries-, Cancer-, or Libra-Rams. Additional poor selections are Aries- or Cancer-Rabbits, as well as Aries- or Libra-Monkeys, Aries-Boars, or Cancer-Buffalos or Snakes. Top selections in romance are Taurus-, Leo-, Virgo-, Scorpio-, and Pisces-Dogs. Additional wonderful choices are Leo-, Virgo-, Scorpio-, or Pisces-Horses. The Scorpio-Dragon is not a wise pick, but there is a chance there will be temptation.

Family Life: This combination's abode is relaxed; it's the kind of place where guests can help themselves to anything in the fridge. Of course, that probably will not be necessary, because the Capricorn-Tiger is first-class at taking care of people. This is a freedom-loving and "real," never deceitful, person. As a result their children are free: very free. Love and freedom go hand in hand for Capricorn-Tigers, so their kids often take over the house or yard. The Capricorn-Tiger is a combination that is fond of real estate and holds on to it. This should not be taken to mean that they enjoy working around the house, because they have no interest in that whatsoever. As with the Capricorn-Tiger himself, the home is quite real and there is nothing affected about it. They have as little interest in making a show of their homes as they do in fixing plumbing. Everyone feels comfortable in the home of a Capricorn-Tiger.

Livelihood: The Capricorn-Tiger needs to have some freedom to choose her own approach to life, and she needs to have challenging work to be happy. Capricorn-Tigers are extremely talented at many tasks in many fields, and, in spite of what one might think, they like to have competition. They are also good for problem solving, and, like most things in their lives, they have an unusual ability to solve issues and difficulties quite quickly. Freedom follows Capricorn-Tigers to their professional lives as well. Independence is precisely what they need in their work. They are not exactly anti-authoritarian, because if rules are reasonable they can follow them. They are quite disobedient, however, if they do not see the purpose in something.

Famous Capricorn-Tigers: Jon Voight, Patricia Neal.

Capricorn (Buffalo) Month Combined with Rabbit Year

"Utilize" Saturn, Earth, Cardinal   **"Withdraw"** Yin-Negative Wood

Characteristics: Epicureanism, Self-doubt, Longevity, Complexity, Pedantry, Generosity, Hypochondria, Dependability, Loneliness, Clumsiness, Finesse, Prudence, Dilettantism, Ambition, Resolve, Stiffness, Squeamishness, Retention, Ambition, Virtue, Tact, Wisdom, Secretiveness, Superiority

What is a sure and steady trait for Capricorn-Rabbits, as well as highly meticulous one, is their decision making; this is true particularly on significant issues. That quality, perhaps more than anything else, is what puts financial security firmly within reach. The Capricorn-Rabbit has a lot of dreams and goals. Fortunately for them, they also have the talent and ability to achieve most of them. There might be a Rabbit in the mix here, but the progress is slow and steady. The destination is quite clear, however. There is a very high likelihood that this combination will be successful and prosperous. The ability, for sure, is there. However, this combination is blessed with many more assets to support them on their road to success. They are willing to do the grunt work to make sure that their views are verified. And after the grunt work, they do even more. The Capricorn-Rabbit is self-motivated and energetic. In addition, this individual is well liked. They are a bit on the extroverted side, especially for a Rabbit, and enjoy socializing with friends or family. They like to share their lives and hobnob with their buddies. They do not hold forth in a discussion or try to upstage anyone. Being comfortable and relaxed is important to them. That might include experiments, field studies, data collection, or mock-ups; but it will be done and it will be done correctly. On top of this they are wise and have excellent vision and intuition. They can spot opportunities and dangers from miles away. Their caution runs across the entire spectrum from business to relationships.

Romance: Capricorn-Rabbits like to know a person's inner workings and they like to know them thoroughly. In spite of their reserve and pragmatism, they have a fondness for the unusual and out of the ordinary; it may be for the beatnik or the eccentric poet. They find this something of keen interest and want to have a deeper understanding. That interest is so appealing to this combination that it might last a lifetime. This combination is reserved in the area of displays of affection. The Capricorn-Rabbit is not likely to parade about draped around her partner. They are basically pragmatists and want pragmatic partners.

Relationships: Because the Capricorn-Rabbit has a strong distaste for problems, it is best for compatibility if they stay away from the Gemini-, Cancer-, and Libra-Rooster. Perhaps even worse choices are the Cancer- and Libra-Rat, as well as Tigers or Dragons from these signs. The premium choices in romance for the Capricorn-Rabbit are Taurus-, Leo-, Virgo-, Scorpio-, and Pisces-Dogs. Additional fine selections are Taurus-, Leo-, and Virgo-Boars. For the more creative minded, good picks are the Leo-, Virgo-, and Pisces-Ram.

Family Life: This combination has a need to have the right appearances for those who know them. They do not want things to be unseemly. It would be misleading to say that the Capricorn-Rabbit is banal and middle class. They are a cut above that, but not by much. They love their children and care for them deeply. They must, however, live up to the right image or there will be sparks. Capricorn-Rabbits want a home that is comfortable, but things do not stop there. While this combination can be very modest and down-to-earth in a social situation, they want to impress people. This results in a home that is showy, because they want people to recognize they are ambitious and have standing. Unfortunately there is a bit of arrogance in the Capricorn-Rabbit. Their homes end up being luxurious, albeit in a comfortable manner. It is true that they want people to be at ease, but they also want people to notice their paintings. Their antique vases must be on mahogany shelves, of course.

Livelihood: This combination must have social acceptance and membership in the country club. These are the types of individuals who are precise about their paperwork, their taxes, and their reputations. Searching their files or even hiring a private investigator will produce nothing. They are clean. The type of profession that is best for the Capricorn-Rabbit is one that requires a serious personality and ambition.

Famous Capricorn-Rabbits: Henry Miller, Joseph Stalin, Cary Grant, Fritz Mondale, Judith Krantz.

Capricorn (Buffalo) Month Combined with Dragon Year

"Utilize" Saturn, Earth, Cardinal   **"Take Charge"** Yang-Positive Wood

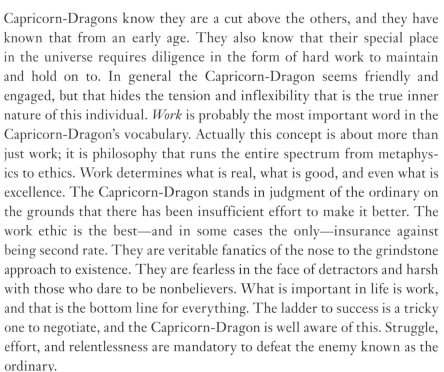

Characteristics: Volubility, Doubt, Epicureanism, Sentimentality, Self-dissatisfaction, Braggadocio, Generosity, Dependability, Clumsiness, Success, Enthusiasm, Infatuation, Loneliness, Mistrust, Resolve, Stiffness, Ambition, Good Health, Pretension, Strength, Rigidity, Superiority, Wisdom, Pluck

Capricorn-Dragons know they are a cut above the others, and they have known that from an early age. They also know that their special place in the universe requires diligence in the form of hard work to maintain and hold on to. In general the Capricorn-Dragon seems friendly and engaged, but that hides the tension and inflexibility that is the true inner nature of this individual. *Work* is probably the most important word in the Capricorn-Dragon's vocabulary. Actually this concept is about more than just work; it is philosophy that runs the entire spectrum from metaphysics to ethics. Work determines what is real, what is good, and even what is excellence. The Capricorn-Dragon stands in judgment of the ordinary on the grounds that there has been insufficient effort to make it better. The work ethic is the best—and in some cases the only—insurance against being second rate. They are veritable fanatics of the nose to the grindstone approach to existence. They are fearless in the face of detractors and harsh with those who dare to be nonbelievers. What is important in life is work, and that is the bottom line for everything. The ladder to success is a tricky one to negotiate, and the Capricorn-Dragon is well aware of this. Struggle, effort, and relentlessness are mandatory to defeat the enemy known as the ordinary.

Romance: Beating in the heart of a Capricorn-Dragon is a wonderful family person. There is, however, one stumbling block, which is that these individuals are extremely appealing and that translates to frequent temptations. Should they succumb to this temptation an exercise in bad faith follows, generally involving excuses for their behavior. These are necessary because the Capricorn-Dragon is a very conservative individual. The Capricorn-

Dragon is, in some ways, a latter-day Puritan. They are of the "Honest Abe" school of truth.

Relationships: In the area of romance, good selections are Rats, especially Rats who are Leo, Virgo, Scorpio, or Pisces. Other good selections here are Taurus- or Leo-Tigers. Continuing the list of positive choices are Taurus-, Leo-, Scorpio-, and Pisces-Roosters or Pisces-Snakes. Both parts of this combination win popularity contests. In fact, they are so popular—there is no need for the contest. In terms of Monkeys, the best picks are Virgo, Scorpio, or Pisces. Bringing up the rear and in the realm of the negative are Gemini-, Cancer-, and Libra-Dogs, and Gemini- and Cancer-Buffalos.

Family Life: This combination's furniture consists of hand-me-downs that do not match. The best thing that can be said about their decor is that it is funky. They prefer fine wine to fine furniture and they like expensive and helpful gadgets more than original works of art. The Capricorn-Dragon is not materialistic. In fact, they are quite a long distance from anything that involves the need to impress others. They approach their house as a pad rather than a home; a place to crash. They are not particularly neat in their housekeeping and not prone to running around picking things up before a visitor arrives. Things often get left where they were set down, the dog sleeps on the couch, the kids' roller skates are in the middle of the living room, and the old and broken computer sits on the dining room table.

Livelihood: Capricorn-Dragons make fine personnel people, especially in areas that require giving directions. As bosses they are generally terrific, because they encourage those who work for them and make suggestions rather than give orders. All this is pleasant enough, but there is one cautionary note. If they feel someone has betrayed them, they have no mercy in dealing out retributive justice. Capricorn-Dragons seek themselves. They want to know who they are, what they are, and where they are in the deepest possible meaning of those questions. They relentlessly partake of self-exploration. A prime mover in this search is the desire to understand others; particularly the needs of others. They are kind and giving, but not to extremes. One of their main aptitudes is managing people.

Famous Capricorn-Dragons: Joan of Arc, Faye Dunaway, Joan Baez.

Capricorn (Buffalo) Month Combined with Snake Year

"Utilize" Saturn, Earth, Cardinal   **"Feel"** Yang-Negative Fire

Characteristics: Exclusiveness, Wisdom, Self-doubt, Compassion, Clairvoyance, Presumption, Superiority, Epicureanism, Dependability, Generosity, Loneliness, Discretion, Laziness, Sagacity, Cupidity, Extravagance, Ambition, Clumsiness, Attractiveness, Pretension, Intuition, Resolve, Stiffness, Dissimulation

Capricorn-Snakes intimidate people just by entering a room; people hide under their beds or get in their bomb shelters if they have one. Capricorn-Snakes move from the bank to the art gallery to the tailor shop before they get on their private jet to do business in Kurdistan. Snakes might not be the brightest stars in the galaxy, but the Capricorn more than makes up for this. The Capricorn-Snake is a nuclear bomb in the conceit and self-possession departments. They blow any competition right out of the water. They thrive on crisis and cash in on it with a capital C for both the cash and the capital. Capricorn-Snakes are not "classy," because they are above and beyond any class and they know it. They love, care for, and help the needy, sick, and homeless. That approach to life extends to all creatures great and small. Feral cats, sick dogs, birds with broken wings, and lizards missing their tails will find help and sympathy with the Capricorn-Snake. Cynics say this combination like the less fortunate because it elevates them all the higher. This may or may not be true, but the fact is they do care and they do help the less fortunate. Consider their clothing for example. A Capricorn-Snake is not a clotheshorse; he is an entire stable. Their wardrobe tells everyone they meet that they are better than the rest. When they are not playing polo, they are driving one of their many cars or navigating their yacht. This should not give the impression that they are selfish.

Romance: The factory setting for this combination is promiscuity driven by the search for the mountaintop of love and romance. This quest, of course, generally results in the loss of one lover after another, because human nature does not take kindly to what they consider debauchery. That is not, however, how Capricorn-Snakes see things, and the fact that they are immensely popular proves to them that they are on the right track. The Capricorn-Snake is in love with love and is the archetypal romantic. They fall in love and then they find someone who is better; at least they will be better after a little tinkering with this and that. There will soon be a new, improved version. The search for Romeo or Juliet is just round the corner.

Relationships: Pretty much out of the running for compatibility are Cancer- or Libra-Boars. Continuing the list of negative matches are Aries- and Gemini-Tigers and Gemini-Monkeys. In last place and out of the running are Aries-Roosters. Excellent choices for romance and love can be found with Taurus-, Leo-, Virgo-, Scorpio-, and Pisces-Buffalos, Pisces-Roosters, and the Leo-Dragon or -Monkey.

Family Life: For this combination there is the country home, the city home, the vacation home, and the home in Paris. They are collectors of homes in the places where people are "supposed" to live, shop, and sunbathe. All of this must come with the right accessories including cars, waterfalls, antiques, artwork, and servants. The purpose of all this is comfort, show, and arrogance, and that does not even include the materialism. It is difficult to find an adjective suitable to describe the elegant, posh, and mansion-type nature of the Capricorn-Snake's home. This is a home that makes the shortlist of those for the rich and famous. There is only one catch to this, and that is the Capricorn-Snake is probably the owner of several, if not numerous, homes.

Livelihood: Capricorn-Snakes attain their goals because they are so certain that they will. They believe so strongly in themselves that others come to believe them. Capricorn-Snakes do not mind being subordinate, however, because they are so sure that they will soon be the boss. This combination is practically destined for success. In the case of the Capricorn-Snake, believing often makes things real. That is to say, because they believe that they are better, superior, and even the greatest at some particular endeavor, they bring that belief into being. That might mean that they become a well-known political leader. Perhaps it is some other field, but whatever it is, they will rise to the pinnacle of success.

Famous Capricorn-Snakes: Edgar Allan Poe, Howard Hughes, Aristotle Onassis, Mao Tse-tung, Mohammed Ali, Martin Luther King.

Capricorn (Buffalo) Month Combined with Horse Year

"Utilize" Saturn, Earth, Cardinal   **"Command"** Yang-Positive Fire

Characteristics: Ambition, Autonomy, Pragmatism, Accomplishment, Anxiety, Dependability, Superiority, Epicureanism, Dexterity, Self-rebellion, Generosity, Doubt, Pretension, Popularity, Loneliness, Unscrupulousness, Style, Haste, Wisdom, Clumsiness, Resolve, Persuasiveness, Stiffness, Selfishness

When other people exclaim that someone is "a good guy," it is the

Capricorn-Horse they are talking about. While Capricorn-Horses might not exactly have bleeding hearts, they care for the less fortunate and act on their beliefs. They take care to see that the details of home, health, and hygiene of the poor and needy are dealt with. They lead by example and show the rich and greedy how things ought to be done. The Capricorn-Horse is the Rock of Gibraltar. Probably no combination in the galaxy is more dependable and steadfast. The Capricorn is solid and has a character that refuses to quit. The Horse, while a bit on the peachy side, is flexible and tuned in. Added to their wonderful and reliable nature is a kind and helpful aspect. They frequently put others ahead of themselves. The Capricorn-Horse works hard and is meticulous. Details are important to them. This combination does not give up. They are relentless in their efforts to complete a task successfully. The Capricorn-Horse can be touchy and judgmental. They can have problems with those who do not understand them or where they are coming from. Fortunately though, they are lovers of peace and acceptance. Their air, which is perhaps a bit on the distant and aloof side, does taint their deportment a bit.

Romance: This combination is profoundly and deeply loyal, and the idea of betrayal is out of the question. The last thing on Earth they are is promiscuous. What they want in life is a partner who has a sense of humor and who is loyal in return. The Capricorn-Horse leaves a lot of suitors behind in a state of unrequited love. This is a combination of love, serenity, and kindness. That is the inner being of the Capricorn-Horse. Not only do they love, they are loved in return; virtually all of them. They are looked up to for their gifts and for their nature. They are chased after by the opposite sex relentlessly. That is fine and interesting. It is also a total waste of time if the Capricorn-Horse is already attached to someone.

Relationships: In the not-recommended group for compatibility are Aries-, Cancer-, or Libra-Horses. In fact, Horses in general are poor selections. Out of the running entirely are Cancer- and Libra-Monkeys. A fine selection in the love category for the Capricorn-Horse is the Ram. Among the Rams the best choices are Taurus, Leo, and Pisces individuals. Continuing with Virgo-, Scorpio-, and Pisces-Tigers. Dogs that are members of the same signs are also excellent.

Family Life: This combination's home will probably have a lot of houseplants, and the outdoors will have a lovely garden with some emphasis on wild flowers. The Capricorn-Horse is an excellent mother or father. They are extremely supportive and demonstrative in their love. They are on the strict side but try to be good examples to their offspring. The Capricorn-Horse is conservative and likes a conservative and traditional environment in the home. The Horse may inject a tiny bit of color, but that will not be overwhelming by any means. This combination is much more interested in the workings of things rather than the appearance of things. They simply are not flashy at all. Earthy or other natural colors are their favorites, and they are somewhat rustic and countrylike in their tastes. Wood is a favorite, as is stone.

Livelihood: This combination likes to help people and see to it that things work for them. They need to see the fruits of their labor. Glamour and fluff are not in this combination's makeup at all. The Capricorn-Horse cares about others and has a keen social awareness. They are humanitarians. Fields that might be of interest to this combination are science, crafts, veterinary medicine, architecture, or nursing. The Capricorn-Horse will find anything in the area of the service professions to her liking. They like routine and situations that involve some creativity and problem solving. They have no interest in being a superstar.

Famous Capricorn-Horses: Isaac Newton, Puccini, Louis Pasteur, Pierre Mendes France, Anwar Sadat, Andy Rooney.

Capricorn (Buffalo) Month Combined with Ram Year

"Utilize" Saturn, Earth, Cardinal   **"Reliance"** Yang-Negative Fire
Characteristics: Worry, Self-doubt, Impracticality, Taste, Wisdom, Dependability, Superiority, Epicureanism, Good Manners, Generosity, Loneliness, Whimsy, Perseverance, Tardiness, Pessimism, Sensitivity, Ambition, Clumsiness, Lack of Foresight, Pretension, Resolve, Invention, Stiffness, Parasitism

This combination is a daydreamer who is sometimes lost in reverie. The more powerful Capricorn portion of this combination refuses to accept this. The result is sometimes internal conflict. There is a general, unpleasant feeling surrounding this clash of opposites. Feelings of anguish are even possible. There is a head-butting dialectic in the Capricorn-Ram combination. The Capricorn brings a lot of ambition to the table. This is in contrast to the lazy and sometimes apathetic Ram. The Capricorn gives the Ram a proper kick in the rear end. The Ram portion of this combination is sensitive. Fortunately for them, both the Capricorn and the Ram have large doses of determination. Dedicated to achieving success, their creative instincts are not allowed to develop as fully as the Capricorn-Ram would like. Still, they remain a bit on the wacky side and lead all Capricorns in that category. The Capricorn-Ram realizes that they must work hard and, above all, be serious about their career. They want power, but often that comes as the result of climbing the ladder from the bottom up.

Romance: This combination is a dreamer and a romantic and believes in frogs turning in to princes and sleeping beauties waking up to kisses. They are extremely affectionate and are the type who throw extravagant surprise birthday parties and give unexpected presents. The Capricorn-Ram is a lover. In fact, in the area of romance they possess a high degree of passion. This shows itself not so much in loquacious statements of eternal love as it does in the bedroom and in the loving way they express their feelings.

Relationships: In the negative department for this combination are Aries-, Cancer-, or Libra-Tigers, as are Aries- and Libra-Dogs. Further combinations that are not recommended are Aries- and Libra-Buffalos. Bringing up the tail end and not recommended at all are Libra-Horses. Superior selections in the area of romance are Taurus-, Leo-, Virgo-, Scorpio-, or Pisces-Boars. Most Boars are positive for the Capricorn-Ram. Additional good choices are Leo-, Virgo-, Scorpio-, or Pisces-Rabbits. Continuing the list of positive picks are Leo-, Scorpio-, or Pisces-Horses.

Family Life: Without warning—not even a moment's notice—this combination might decided to add an entire wing to their home or, barring that, wallpaper the entire house. Costs frequently do not matter to the Capricorn-Ram. They are totally and completely no-holds-barred materialistic and not the least bit ashamed of that fact. Even though Capricorn-Rams do not spend a lot of time at home, they want a showy and tidy abode. This character, as mentioned above, is a bit on the weird side. That eccentricity carries over to the area of home decorating.

Livelihood: Capricorn-Rams can lead people, and they compete with the Pied Piper for followers. Creating that mixture properly can result in a character with mysterious qualities that are much more than the sum of its parts. There is also a fairly good chance that this person will be somewhat insistent on having things their own way. However, because they have achieved such a high level of fame and adulation, that is generally acceptable.

In spite of the Capricorn-Ram's eccentricities and downright craziness, this combination is a human magnet. People love them across the board. If the Capricorn-Ram takes care to nurture and advance their positive qualities, there is nothing stopping them on the road to success.

Famous Capricorn-Rams: Maurice Utrillo, Reverend Moon, John Denver, Ben Kingsley, Maurice Couve de Murville.

Capricorn (Buffalo) Month Combined with Monkey Year

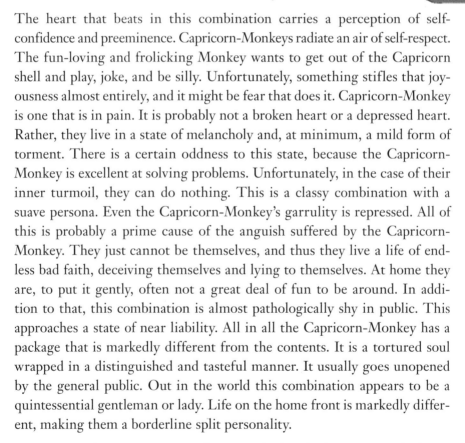

"Utilize" Saturn, Earth, Cardinal   **"Arrange"** Yin-Positive Metal

Characteristics: Loquacity, Zeal, Superiority, Wisdom, Epicureanism, Generosity, Wit, Self-doubt, Clumsiness, Dependability, Loneliness, Opportunism, Self-involvement, Cunning, Leadership, Ruse, Ambition, Improvisation, Pretension, Stability, Silliness, Resolve, Stiffness, Deceit

The heart that beats in this combination carries a perception of self-confidence and preeminence. Capricorn-Monkeys radiate an air of self-respect. The fun-loving and frolicking Monkey wants to get out of the Capricorn shell and play, joke, and be silly. Unfortunately, something stifles that joyousness almost entirely, and it might be fear that does it. Capricorn-Monkey is one that is in pain. It is probably not a broken heart or a depressed heart. Rather, they live in a state of melancholy and, at minimum, a mild form of torment. There is a certain oddness to this state, because the Capricorn-Monkey is excellent at solving problems. Unfortunately, in the case of their inner turmoil, they can do nothing. This is a classy combination with a suave persona. Even the Capricorn-Monkey's garrulity is repressed. All of this is probably a prime cause of the anguish suffered by the Capricorn-Monkey. They just cannot be themselves, and thus they live a life of endless bad faith, deceiving themselves and lying to themselves. At home they are, to put it gently, often not a great deal of fun to be around. In addition to that, this combination is almost pathologically shy in public. This approaches a state of near liability. All in all the Capricorn-Monkey has a package that is markedly different from the contents. It is a tortured soul wrapped in a distinguished and tasteful manner. It usually goes unopened by the general public. Out in the world this combination appears to be a quintessential gentleman or lady. Life on the home front is markedly different, making them a borderline split personality.

Romance: The Capricorn-Monkey sets the bar high in terms of what is acceptable. The person they choose must be very presentable; in fact, more than presentable. They must stand out from the crowd. Complete openness and honesty with a partner is also required. Because of the darker secrets that Capricorn-Monkeys carry in their beings, they must have someone they can open up to, because they certainly will not do this with anyone else. This combination's chosen partner must also be completely trustworthy. After all, the secrets of the Capricorn-Monkey must be in good hands. The combination wants the best in love and romance, and that means an emphasis on quality. They do not want quickies of any kind; sexually or with their hearts. True love comes from real feelings and only the best will do.

Relationships: Moving into the negative realm in this combination are Aries-Tigers. Additional poor selections are Cancer-Horses or Libra-Snakes and -Boars. For the Capricorn-Monkey it is wise to be slow in the selection of a lifetime partner. An excellent place to start the search for love and romance is with Rats. However, it would be best to focus on the Leo, Virgo, Scorpio, or Pisces. Further good selections are Virgo- or Pisces-Dragons. Continuing in this vein are the Taurus-Ram or Scorpio-Tiger.

Family Life: This combination is very handy at fixing and making things, a trait that comes from the Monkey. The home of this combination will probably be very large and well-appointed. Perhaps more important than anything, and the reason for the large home, is the fact that this combination holds that everyone must have space: their own space. Whether it is for work or contemplation, the approach of the Capricorn-Monkey is that people sometimes need to be left alone. The Capricorn-Monkey is tasteful in the selection of decor. Their decorating tastes will be traditional with a preference for unobtrusive colors.

Livelihood: This is a very creative combination, especially in verbal terms. They are terrific storytellers and able to express themselves with a great deal of emotion and feeling. Even though they hold inner secrets that only get shared with those very intimate with them, they can convey suffering and pain in a highly moving manner. Work is critical to the Capricorn-Monkey. They are the antonym to lazy. After they work, they work some more and when they are not working they are pursuing career opportunities.

Famous Capricorn-Monkeys: Federico Fellini, Yousuf Karsh, Rod Stewart, Simone de Beauvoir.

Capricorn (Buffalo) Month Combined with Rooster Year

"Utilize" Saturn, Earth, Cardinal   **"Conqueror"** Yang-Negative Metal

Characteristics: Candor, Epicureanism, Chic, Dissipation, Bossiness, Blind Faith, Generosity, Dependability, Self-doubt, Loneliness, Clumsiness, Enthusiasm, Conservatism, Pedantry, Humor, Resolve, Stiffness, Boastfulness, Pretension, Ambition, Resilience, Wisdom, Cockiness, Superiority

This is a combination that is in harmony with itself: a dialectic without conflict, and a match made in the stars. They are not so much laid-back as they are held back by their personality. There is essentially no internal turmoil in the Capricorn-Rooster, however. This combination is a person of principles. The Capricorn-Rooster presents a distinguished and perfectly groomed individual. They are a tower of strength and as honest as any combination around. They are opinionated, reticent, and traditional. They are also people who place a high value on liberty. This makes them comfortable being on their own, but they do prefer to have other people around them. The Capricorn-Rooster is a person who can be relied on. They are amiable and very well mannered. This is a kind and helpful combination, and they love to make others happy. Smiling and happy, they travel the world, or even their neighborhood, meeting others and learning about customs, cultures, and history. All of this makes them popular, and they are always on people's party lists. They are invited to dinner, asked to the opera, and urged to visit the Taj Mahal with travel friends they made on the Internet. This combination knows the power of words and chooses them carefully. As a result they are both tactful and well spoken. In a way, what one sees and hears from the Capricorn-Rooster is the genuine person. The Capricorn-Rooster racks up the frequent flyer miles because they love to travel. They are intelligent and curious about the world. The new, the novel, and the different fascinate them.

Romance: This combination is standoffish. They are hesitant about hugs and kisses and even touches, particularly if those things are done in public. They do have feelings, and those feelings run deep. They want to be more demonstrative with the person they love because they do care. Perhaps part of the reason for this is that they have so many friends and acquaintances around them all the time. They empathize with others. Nonetheless, if they love someone, that person always comes first. Those in love with the Capricorn-Rooster might need to look a little harder to find the love of the Capricorn-Rooster, but it is there and it is as real as they are. In spite of the wonderful news outlined above, there is an issue with the Capricorn-Rooster, one that pertains to love: this combination can be emotionally distant.

Relationships: Negative matches for this combination are Cancer- and Libra-Rabbits. Furthermore, Aries- and Cancer-Boars are not a good idea at all. Fine selections for romance are those who are Snakes. Among those the best picks are Leo, Scorpio, Sagittarius, or Pisces. Absolutely terrific choices come from those who are Taurus-, Scorpio-, or Pisces-Buffalos, and a good pick is a Taurus-Horse.

Family Life: Capricorn-Roosters want to be comfortable, but when possible they want someone else to take care of the details. Their other pursuits keep them occupied. The Capricorn-Rooster loves her children but is not especially patient with them. Overall, the mind takes the front seat and the emotions take a backseat. The Capricorn-Rooster is not really the sort who cares a lot about their home. They are materialistic and do want to be presentable. They are just not into decorating the home themselves, nor are they into fixing, designing, mending, or building things.

Livelihood: The Capricorn-Rooster is talented and intelligent. They can excel because of their ability to deal with problem-solving issues. Unfortunately there is a difficulty here too. The Capricorn-Rooster can be somewhat insecure and does not assert himself because he is too self-effacing. The Capricorn-Rooster, in professional terms, is very flexible and capable of doing a number of things. This, like life itself, has advantages and disadvantages. The advantages are obvious in that they provide insurance and present options. The disadvantages, while not as obvious, include creating a temptation to move on to something new without finishing the work they are presently involved in. That can mean setbacks. It can also lead to a confused individual in terms of life choices.

Famous Capricorn-Roosters: Rudyard Kipling, Steve Allen, Dolly Parton.

Capricorn (Buffalo) Month Combined with Dog Year

"Utilize" Saturn, Earth, Cardinal   **"Concerned"** Yin-Positive Metal

Characteristics: Dependability, Tastelessness, Self-doubt, Morality, Superiority, Epicureanism, Wisdom, Cynicism, Intelligence, Heroism, Generosity, Loneliness, Respectability, Duty, Self-righteousness, Ambition, Pretension, Clumsiness, Unsociability, Criticism, Resolve, Constancy, Stiffness, Uneasiness

The Capricorn-Dog is a freedom-loving combination. They care about peace, and things that disturb the peace are troubling to them. They have no interest in the theoretical, the formless, or other slippery areas. They are possessive in that they want to keep what they have. This trait symbolizes their extraordinary cautiousness. The Capricorn-Dog can perhaps be summarized as a concrete person who is traditional but caring. This makes pretty short work of the subject, but they are much deeper than that. Where they are not deep is in the area of the conceptual, or perhaps it would be better to say the deeper areas of thinking. They have a very conservative approach to their lives. None of this is to imply any arrogance in association with this individual. They just happen to be people who care about things more than most others. This individual has strong principles and ideals and has the backs of family and friends at all times. They can be counted on to defend those they care about. They demand that the playing field be level. This dog barks, and it is also capable of biting at times. It is a wiry and feisty dog as well. Things need to be neat and orderly for them, and they need to stay that way. There is no lack of courage in the Capricorn-Dog. They are powerful and up for a battle, or even a war, if necessary. They are also capable of being radical when the situation calls for it.

Romance: In the area of romance there are two important things that need to be considered. First is the fact that Capricorn-Dogs are dedicated to the proposition that they will be free. Freedom has intrinsic value for them. Second is the fact that they are clean freaks. They hate messy things. The inevitable result in this is a messiness of a different sort; that is, messy relationships. The independent streak in Capricorn-Dogs is so wide that they have stormy romances that result as much from a sense of obligation as anything else. In many cases, this means that these relationships are broken before they start. Capricorn-Dogs can run and they can hide; what they cannot help themselves from doing frequently is coming out and playing peek-a-boo. The final result is that there may be no relationships at all.

Relationships: The negative choices in this combination are Cancer-Roosters, and very bad picks are Aries-Roosters. Continuing on with the negative are Aries-, Cancer-, and Libra-Rams. Cancer- and Libra-Dragons and Cancer-Monkeys are out of the running. The top choices for love and romance are Horses that are Taurus, Leo, Virgo, and Pisces. Also fine selections are Taurus-, Virgo-, Scorpio-, and Pisces-Rabbits. The good news continues with Leo-, Virgo-, Scorpio-, and Pisces-Tigers.

Family Life: The Capricorn-Dog loves the family, first and foremost. Nothing can compete. Next in line is the intellectual life. They love knowledge, and in that category they enjoying both teaching and learning.

Livelihood: Capricorn-Dogs are not super picky about the kind of home they have or its trappings as long as it works. In this case "work" does include a very functional kitchen. There will be pots and pans of every size as well as jars, bottles, knives, measuring devices, plates, spices, and everything else that is needed. They are, quite obviously, excellent cooks. They also like to be comfortable when they sit down to read. They totally love their children. They are very protective of them but not to a fault. The Capricorn-Dog marches to the beat of his own punk rock band or Brahms Concerto, whichever the case may be. They are, tactfully said, different. They make perfect airheaded professors. Sometimes even that is a little too confining for them, so they decide to move to Fiji and start up a training school for dolphins. They might play right field in the Class C league in the Casper, Wyoming, baseball team or be a designer of alternative energy motorcycles, which they make in their garage. What is for certain is that they will be different. That is not a problem for them either, because they have accepted themselves.

Famous Capricorn-Dogs: Ben Franklin, Moliere, Jann Wenner, David Bowie, Diane von Furstenberg.

Capricorn (Buffalo) Month Combined with Boar Year

"Utilize" Saturn, Earth, Cardinal   **"Cultivator"** Yin-Negative Water
Characteristics: Dependability, Honesty, Self-doubt, Boar-headedness, Epicureanism, Culture, Materialism, Superiority, Gourmandism, Generosity, Loneliness, Sincerity, Hesitation, Voluptuousness, Gallantry, Wrath, Wisdom, Clumsiness, Ambition, Pretension, Resolve, Scrupulousness, Stiffness, Credulity

Capricorn-Boars ride noble steeds and tuck one hand into their shirts knowing that there will be no Waterloo for them. Interestingly though, they have a somehow innocent, though firm, ambition. The Capricorn-Boar shoots for the stars, and usually makes it. This dialectic is gifted to the maximum, and they have a goal and drive that leave others eating their dust. They have always seen themselves as rich, famous, talented, intelligent, and the leader of every dimension, including those as yet undiscovered. They have egos to match the globe, and those are just the ones with limited vision; most Capricorn-Boars have even bigger visions. There has probably never been in the annals of history a Capricorn-Boar that had an inferiority complex. Capricorn-Boars take care of those they love. They join the right organizations and pay their dues on time. They give time and money to the right charities. Capricorn-Boars earn a fair bit of respect because of their deeds and their loyalty. They are respectable citizens in the community, and it would be hard for anyone to criticize them because, in spite of their ambition, they play fair. They are shamelessly ambitious and write it off as healthy because it entails the power of positive thinking. Dale Carnegie probably did not have that in mind, but the Capricorn-Boar does. This combination is law-abiding because of the Boar influence. They are always aware of every section of the civil code.

Romance: To be in a relationship with this combination can, at times, be challenging. They are, however, great to spend time with. They are overprotective not just of their spouses but also, of course, their children. They do not like others to influence those they love. They are even jealous of their friends who have interests other than them. The Capricorn-Boar loves and loves deeply. They are also very romantic. They are generous with their loved ones and very dedicated. No one could ask for a more affectionate partner. All of this paints a good picture, and the picture is true and realistic. There are some things that need to be said, however, as is often the case when things appear so rosy. Perhaps as an offshoot of their ambition, the Capricorn-Boar is extremely possessive. They are too kind to describe their partners as property, but that is the way they often behave. At the very minimum they can be stifling to their lover and essentially give them no room. Among the things that come about in this department is an enormous green monster. Fits of rage are possible—dramatic scenes fit for a soap opera or a tabloid can result.

Relationships: Not recommended are Cancer- or Libra-Snakes. Also bringing up the rear in poor choices are Aries- and Cancer-Horses. Almost surefire choices in the area of love are Taurus-, Leo-, Virgo-, Scorpio-, or Pisces-Rabbits. There is a mutual attraction between the Capricorn-Boar and the Taurus-Tiger. Additional good selections are Leo-, Virgo-, Scorpio-, or Pisces-Rams.

Family Life: There is a kind of geometric feeling to their home, but lacking, perhaps, in the curvy proportions. Black and white are favorite colors or, where more than that is needed, the basic colors. Nothing bright is needed. The Capricorn-Boar is active and as a result does not generally have a large family. There is a very real possibility they will remain single. The Capricorn-Boar is relatively basic in many areas of the home. They do not need to have an overboard amount of comfort, for example. The basics will do just fine.

Livelihood: Capricorn-Boars have a genius at seeing and interpreting the world, and that gives them a special vision and special insights. What they lack in abstract skills they make up for in emotional skills. As a boss this combination would be hardnosed. If an employee betrayed them, there will be hell to pay—several times over. The Capricorn-Boar is a people watcher and learns when observing. They are also usually heavy readers. The result of this is interesting because it brings about a person who is like a mirror of the world, or the individuals in it. They are superb at this. While they are not particularly creative themselves, they can show emotions, speak in public, and generally move people greatly.

Famous Capricorn-Boars: Albert Schweitzer, Humphrey Bogart, Will Rogers, Roland Petit.

Aquarius (Tiger) Month Combined with Rat Year

"Understood" Uranus, Air, Fixed   **"Regulator"** Yin-Positive Water

Characteristics: Cruelty, Charisma, Individuality, Tolerance, Sociability, Thoughtlessness, Meddling, Thrift, Independence, Intellectual, Thirst for Power, Acquisitiveness, Disobedience, Skill, Influence, Verbosity, Separateness, Charity, Guile, Vision, Neurosis, Eccentricity, Appeal, Nervousness, Originality

The Aquarius-Rat tends to be forceful on the one hand but amiable on the other. People are attracted to them because of their charisma. They talk a lot and tend to override others when they want to say something. They have pure desires and feel empathy toward others. The Aquarius-Rat is a walking contradiction of personalities. This combination is a paradigm of dialectics and the end result is a very powerful individual. One can start with the fact that the Aquarius-Rat is an idealist who enjoys exploring new possibilities. Perhaps they begin their journey by seeking material possessions. Oddly, creeping into the mixture is a set of values that is totally nonmaterialistic. They are kind of a yuppie hippie. That is not the only area where there is a clash of values. The Aquarius-Rat wants to be a nonconformist. The balancing act that results from the combination of these two signs produces an individual who is supremely forceful; one who inspires awe. There is a huge desire for freedom that powers their back-to-nature and self-sufficiency side. However, their longing for material possessions is equally as strong and equally as motivating. There are dreams and fantasies of castles as well as stone homes they made themselves. They are, at once, Lord of the Manor and Johnny Appleseed.

Romance: What this combination needs is an anchor in the form of a down-to-earth person. That is a tad difficult to orchestrate because of the Aquarius-Rat's funky, gypsy side. The free bird is always present and attempting to circumnavigate the globe, and anyone attracted to the Aquarius-Rat would be advised not to attempt to cage him. This combination is a lot of things, but being ordinary is not one of them. The Aquarius-Rat is a combination in search of a bridge over troubled water. Attractive and magnetic, the unstable side is not visible to the general public. There are issues in the psyche of the Aquarius-Rat.

Relationships: On the negative side of the coin for this combination are Taurus-, Leo-, and Scorpio-Horses. Also poor selections are Leo-Rabbits and Scorpio-Roosters. Buffalos are an excellent choice in the area of love and romance. The best of the options for the Aquarius-Rat are Buffalos who are Gemini, Libra, or Sagittarius. Dragons that come from these same Western signs are also fine picks. Moving on in the positive area of love matches there are Aries-, Libra-, and Sagittarius-Monkeys.

Family Life: The way the Aquarius-Rat dresses is likely to be the opposite of the simplicity of the home. With their personal dress code they may very well be flamboyant and jazzy. A special note needs to be made regarding the parenting skill of this combination. They are absolutely fantastic parents. Children tend to give the Aquarius-Rat a firm foundation, and this creates a sort of subliminal gratitude in mother or father. They appreciate the sanctuary. The result is a parent who can and will do anything for his or her children. They are very active parents. If a person were to walk into the home of an Aquarius-Rat they would have no idea that a peculiar individual calls that middle-class residence home. Their tastes in decorating are very discerning and their attractive simplicity suggests a traditional Japanese home.

Livelihood: The bird that soars the oceans flies high and has a superior vision of things on the ground. If this vision and unique perception can be focused there is no limit to where they can go. All of this needs to remain somewhat in check, however, or a mad-scientist type will dominate. Once again, a firm grounding is essential for the Aquarius-Rat. Aquarians need to work. It is part and parcel of their emotional health. The Rat is a moody sort. What needs to happen professionally for this combination is a movement toward concentrating on a single profession. Should this come to fruition, mountains can be climbed.

Famous Aquarius-Rats: Wolfgang Amadeus Mozart, Jules Verne, Alan Alda, John Belushi.

Aquarius (Tiger) Month Combined with Buffalo Year

"Understood" Uranus, Air, Fixed   **"Survivor"** Yin-Negative Water

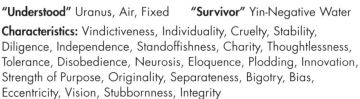

Characteristics: Vindictiveness, Individuality, Cruelty, Stability, Diligence, Independence, Standoffishness, Charity, Thoughtlessness, Tolerance, Disobedience, Neurosis, Eloquence, Plodding, Innovation, Strength of Purpose, Originality, Separateness, Bigotry, Bias, Eccentricity, Vision, Stubbornness, Integrity

This combination likes to intimidate people, but in spite of that the Aquarius-Buffalo has a loving side. The country life far from the madding crowd is the ideal environment in the mind of the Buffalo. They are loners. This does not match the view of the Aquarius at all. That part of their character is sociable and genial. Their approach to life is much more supple and open to variation. The dialectic of this combination is among the more conflicted. The Aquarius-Buffalo has a rough road in life because it has a rebellious side emanating from the Buffalo. There is a battle in the psyche between a worldview that is fairly inflexible and one that is flaky. The life of an Aquarius-Buffalo is very frequently filled with numerous challenges and obstacles that need to be overcome. The Aquarian is cool, calm, and collected, but there is a side that is immovable. Hiding in the psyche of the Aquarian side is a touch of bigotry in spite of them often residing in fantasyland. What all this means in the long run is that the Aquarius-Buffalo has some fairly negative emotions to deal with. These include grouchiness, mood swings, resentment, and acrimony. Added to this is an appearance of indifference that often is not real.

Romance: The odd part of all this is that this combination seems to totally accept this life situation. One reason is success. Once success is accomplished the need for activity, change, and challenge returns. Perhaps they can handle a life with essentially no sex. The intruding problems from the outside world, such as work, are stifled. Regret and disappointment are ignored. The love life of the Aquarius-Buffalo is, predictably, fraught with problems. The Aquarius wants a lot of action because they are prone to ennui. The Buffalo side of this combination is a homebody. They desire the security of home. This push by the Buffalo for home and probably children can generate a yo-yo emotional state. Up and down the Aquarius-Buffalo goes in romance.

Relationships: Heading toward the not recommended category for compatibility in this combination are Taurus-, Leo-, and Scorpio-Dragons. Additional poor choices are Taurus- and Leo-Tigers. Poor selections also include Leo- and Scorpio-Rams. Moving down toward the bottom of the ladder are Scorpio-Monkeys, and Taurus-, Leo-, and Scorpio-Horses. Not recommended at all are Leo-Rabbits and Scorpio-Roosters. In the area of romance Snakes are the best possibility. The very best of these are Aries, Gemini, Libra, or Sagittarius. Additional good selections are Gemini-, Libra-, and Sagittarius-Roosters.

Family Life: This combination is fantastic in the area of parenthood. They have children who are encouraged to be themselves and explore the world with their imagination. This combination enjoys being around children, and children sense this and return the love. Their children are spoiled while at the same time obedient. They do teach their children well. Aquarius-Buffalos have comfortable homes, and this is important to them. The furnishings are conservative but classy. They are art lovers so there will be a fair amount of art house exhibits. They do not want to be flashy or make a huge impression on others. The Aquarius-Buffalo is excellent with finances, and while not stingy, they do know how to save money.

Livelihood: This combination is motivated by money and thus seeks salaries that are upscale. Socially, however, they are not selfish and sometimes work in professions dedicated to making a better world. As a boss it is best to do as one is told and keep the mouth shut. This combination does not want to be opposed. They are the boss and that is that. The Aquarius-Buffalo is excellent with their hands and are great problem solvers. This gives them the ability to repair nearly anything and to make things themselves. They have a wonderful imagination and can create inventions. The Aquarius-Buffalo is very sensible. There is very little they are not capable of.

Famous Aquarius-Buffalos: Charles Lindbergh, Jack Lemmon, Vanessa Redgrave.

Aquarius (Tiger) Month Combined with Tiger Year

"Understood" Uranus, Air, Fixed **"Observe"** Yang-Positive Wood

Characteristics: Originality, Individuality, Authority, Cruelty, Itinerancy, Thoughtlessness, Benevolence, Independence, Intemperance, Disobedience, Good Luck, Tolerance, Swagger, Neurosis, Separateness, Hotheadedness, Bravery, Charity, Magnetism, Vision, Fervor, Eccentricity, Impetuosity

Invention is often the result of this combination's character. They can take something, turn it upside down then inside out, and sure enough, there is a gadget that no one ever dreamed of. The Aquarius-Tiger is an odd mixture. For starters they have a slightly off-center personality. They are a touch on the unpredictable side. The trait that is added by the Tiger side is a lucid mind. The sometimes mixed-up thinking characterized by the Aquarius is straightened out to a degree by the Tiger. For some reason the Aquarius-Tiger wants to remain young. This prevents them from getting attached in a permanent relationship with anyone. It is not exactly due to a desire to sow wild oats, although that can be part of the equation. They can be an adventurer in the sexual realm. They are a kind of a self-contained book of changes, but there is an unpredictability to their movements. They are a ship with no rudder and no anchor. They are the ones who invented that new computer program that everyone thinks leads to instant enlightenment. They took some nuts and bolts and an old treadmill and developed a massage technique that deals with the common headache. Their computer bookmarks are an odd assortment from mathematics to ancient Norse legends. They actually have and read books, but it does not stop there. They read the instruction manuals to the machines, shelving, woodstoves, and kitchen appliances they buy.

Romance: Aquarius-Tigers find themselves in situations where the statement "I am infatuated with you" is more true than "I am in love with you." They are romantic for this reason and generally not for deeper motives. Sometimes they actually tie the knot, and most often that is a mistake and the relationship does not last. Eternal love is not in the metaphysical scheme of the Aquarius-Tiger. There is practically a pathological aversion to commitment in the being of the Aquarius-Tiger. They are not long-haul types. They do not like topics pertaining to rings or gold. Even bringing up sharing an apartment can be risky. They love with a blazing passion sometimes. However, the blaze seems to burn itself out in time.

Relationships: To be avoided for compatibility in this combination are

Taurus- and Leo-Rabbits, Virgo- and Scorpio-Buffalos, and Taurus- and Scorpio-Rams. The worst possible choice for a partner is the Taurus-Snake. In terms of love and romance, Dogs are a fine place to start. The pick of the litter are Aries, Gemini, Libra, and Sagittarius. Another excellent selection is the Horse. While they are not quite as good as Dogs, they have a lot to offer. The best of the Horses are Gemini, Libra, and Sagittarius.

Family Life: Aquarius-Tigers love their children, but they are not the most patient moms or dads on the planet. They are, however, fair. In spite of the tendency to not want to settle down with a partner, the Aquarius-Tiger has a place to call home. Their decorating skills are fairly basic at best, so it is quite ordinary. It is comfortable enough and shows signs of their unusual abilities and interests. They will show their gadgets if possible, so one could find almost anything. There might be a personally designed computer desk or a wall clock based on the Napoleonic calendar. Perhaps they have speakers they made from scratch using a new method they discovered and which they use for playing obscure jazz and modern classical music. Sartre's *Being and Nothingness* might be on their end table.

Livelihood: This is an idea person who works well on his or her own. Aquarius-Tigers simply need a place to work and the appropriate tools to manifest their bizarre ideas. Many of these ideas, after they have been refined to less of a fringe state, prove to be extremely worthwhile. As bosses they can irritate people. As employees they are super if placed in the right position. The highly innovative mind of the Aquarius-Tiger and their mental acuity makes them perfect for those kinds of professions that require new perspectives or inventions. Regardless of what they look at, it is almost guaranteed that they will have a novel point of view at minimum. They are totally out-of-the-box in their mind-sets.

Famous Aquarius-Tigers: Georges Simenon, William Burroughs, Germaine Greer, Judy Blume.

Aquarius (Tiger) Month Combined with Rabbit Year

"**Understood**" Uranus, Air, Fixed   "**Withdraw**" Yin-Negative Wood

Characteristics: Complexity, Originality, Cruelty, Ambition, Longevity, Hypochondria, Independence, Thoughtlessness, Pedantry, Prudence, Dilettantism, Tolerance, Disobedience, Separateness, Charity, Neurosis, Finesse, Virtue, Squeamishness, Individuality, Vision, Tact, Eccentricity, Secretiveness

This combination has an inborn curiosity fit for a cat rather than a Rabbit. They have never encountered an object or a person they did not want to study. These studies are generally not of the superficial, "look it up quickly on the Internet" type. They are deep and detailed. They do not just collect and read books. They collect museums, aquariums, libraries, and universities. The Aquarius-Rabbit sees knowledge, study, learning, and information as ends in themselves. These interests have intrinsic value and are not sought in order to gain anything else. They seek these out for the pure joy of it. They need and look for experience as well as raw facts. They are not cutthroat about this, nor do they force their views on others. They can, with some effort, learn to tame this tendency. However, they will always be prone to making remarks about the stars on a clear night, name classical songs on their friend's stereo, and give the origin of obscure quotations. It is, after all, virtually impossible for a walking encyclopedia not to be a talking encyclopedia as well. They simply want understanding, specifics, data, and knowledge. They are natural scholars. They find enjoyment in discovering facts for themselves. Given their vast sources of information accumulated over time, it is understandable that they have a hint of the know-it-all about them.

Romance: This combination is the family type. They want security, love, and attention. Marriage is in the being of the Aquarius-Rabbit as are children and all the trappings that go with being part of a family unit. They are the hugging and cuddling type, because they want peace and reassurance. They do all they can to avoid problems and are the type whose personalities have no rough edges. They are quite sensitive in their approach to others. The Aquarius-Rabbit, given his or her own intellectual tendencies, wants a partner who is an equal in this regard. Their partner must have a sense of humor, enjoy an amusing chat, and be very open-minded. The partners of Aquarius-Rabbits are never bored or without intellectual stimulation. That, perhaps, can be a bit much for some, because the nonstop PBS radio and TV station that is the Aquarius-Rabbit only shuts down in its sleep. However, this combination is reliable and well thought of.

Relationships: Not recommended for the Aquarius-Rabbit are Taurus-, Leo-, and Scorpio-Rats. Taurus- and Leo-Roosters are also poor choices. Finally, bringing up the rear, are Scorpio-Horses. At the very top of the list for romance and love are Aries-, Gemini-, Libra-, and Sagittarius-Boars. Excellent selections also include Aries-, Gemini-, Libra-, and Sagittarius-Rams.

Family Life: This combination is refined and respectable, and that will be reflected in the home. Given their desire for peace and comfort, their abode must be homey and warm. Of course it needs to be set up so that hobnobbing about the geography of the sub-Sahara is encouraged. There is a mild snobbism in the Aquarius-Rabbit, but it is not over-the-top. As a mom or dad the Aquarius-Rabbit is a tad on the eccentric side. They bombard their children with information and often start when the children are very young. The Aquarius-Rabbit parent is very generous with their time, however. They love to get their children rolling on books early and thus read to and teach them early. The Aquarius-Rabbit is the mother one sees at the supermarket explaining to her two-year-old where rice comes from. The Aquarius-Rabbit has a home that is comfortable and classical. It is not, however, showy or ostentatious.

Livelihood: The Aquarius-Rabbit has a strong desire for money. Finances are very important to them. They want to be rich and they want to keep most of their money for themselves. If they find a great job, they are willing to move on to something else that is bigger and better. It needs to have the concomitant remuneration, however. It is fairly clear that this combination is a brain and not a brawn type of individual. Professionally they do not want to get their hands dirty. That rules out being a farmer or a mechanic. They need a profession that calls forth the intellect. The rule is not written in stone, but repetition is not for them.

Famous Aquarius-Rabbits: Stendhal, James Michener, Tom Brokaw, Juliette Greco.

Aquarius (Tiger) Month Combined with Dragon Year

"Understood" Uranus, Air, Fixed   **"Take Charge"** Yang-Positive Wood

Characteristics: Sentimentality, Individuality, Volubility, Pluck, Cruelty, Braggadocio, Independence, Infatuation, Dissatisfaction, Charity, Thoughtlessness, Enthusiasm, Vision, Tolerance, Separateness, Disobedience, Good Health, Success, Mistrust, Neurosis, Eccentricity, Rigidity, Strength, Originality

If one wants to know who is right, there is no need to look any farther than the Aquarius-Dragon. This combination will, each and every time, virtually without exception, take over. There are reasons for this. The fact is they are so ambitious that what they do is done not only correctly and properly but also beyond the call of duty. The Aquarius-Dragon is a take-charge type of person. They know they are the leader of the pack, and there will be no questioning it. There is a driving ambition that refuses to be deterred, and they know everything. They are the quintessential know-it-alls. This combination is a tough cookie once they have their minds made up. They will not be denied. They are in the ballpark of Attila the Hun in terms of their desire to conquer and the lengths they will go to in that quest. They are willing to step on competitors as if they were annoying insects. They can act and pretend and deceive on their road to power. There is no implication in any of this that the Aquarius-Dragon could be obnoxious. They are not. They are judicious in their approach to everything. They are respectable both in their family life and in their professional life, and this respect is earned. They do not want something for nothing. Aquarius-Dragons are willing to work for what they have; including being the boss.

Romance: Aquarius-Dragons have the green monster of jealousy in their makeup. They are extremely jealous, controlling, and possessive. The Aquarius-Dragon can be charming to the right match, but it is still best to refrain from any hint of interest in a third party. They live in fear of losing their partner to competition, and to betray them, even mentally, is not wise. They are, after all, highly sensitive. The Aquarius-Dragon wants to own and control his or her romantic partner. Their motives are pure even if the idea itself is not. They want to help their partner, and they want to do this because it makes them look better. A happy lover makes an Aquarius-Dragon happy, and, because this combination knows everything, he proceeds to help his partner in the manner of an Aquarius-Dragon: by being dominating.

Relationships: Poor picks for compatibility include Taurus-, Leo-, and Scorpio-Dogs, and at the very bottom of the list are Taurus-Monkeys. A superior choice for love is the Gemini-Tiger. Another terrific selection is the Sagittarius-Rat. Continuing the list of possibly good selections in romance are Gemini-, Libra-, and Sagittarius-Monkeys.

Family Life: The Aquarius-Dragon parent is exceptionally conscientious. They help not only their own children but other people's as well. In parenthood groups they will, of course, want to be in charge. They are prone to want to create their children in their own image. The Aquarius-Dragon is a combination that leans toward the pragmatic over the beautiful. Intellectually they have a good aesthetic sense, but that is not their choice for their personal environment. The most important issue for the Aquarius-Dragon is that things work properly. That means the kitchen must be suitable and completely functional. Their home needs sufficient electrical outlets. Sinks must not drip.

Livelihood: This combination has a realistic philosophy of life and matures at an early age. Their views are well regarded, and they fall in to being the boss in an instinctive manner. The Aquarius-Dragon is naturally tactful. They also have a bit of a nomad in them. As employees they work well, and as bosses they are excellent. They do tend, however, to relocate or change positions. The Aquarius-Dragon has ability for administration and, of course, management. This ability extends from their home to their workplace. They are superb at human resources as well. They do well in positions of leadership and have a calm demeanor. They are knowledgeable about money and know how to use it properly. They take the middle path relative to finances. They have an aptitude for investing and increasing their financial resources.

Famous Aquarius-Dragons: S. J. Perelman, Ayn Rand, Roger Vadim, Roger Mudd, Neil Diamond, Placido Domingo, Stephanie of Monaco, Smokey Robinson, Jeanne Moreau.

Aquarius (Tiger) Month Combined with Snake Year

"Understood" Uranus, Air, Fixed   **"Feel"** Yang-Negative Fire

Characteristics: Compassion, Individuality, Cruelty, Exclusiveness, Thoughtlessness, Clairvoyance, Independence, Presumption, Tolerance, Disobedience, Neurosis, Laziness, Discretion, Sagacity, Attractiveness, Extravagance, Originality, Separateness, Charity, Eccentricity, Dissimulation, Intuition, Vision, Cupidity

In addition to being aware of events, this combination frequently sees them coming ahead of time. The smile that is always on his face is real—with the emphasis on real—because this person is a realist. This combination has desires that are grounded in actuality and never desires items that he knows full well he will never have. That does not prevent the Aquarius-Snake from seriously desiring possessions. Perhaps the best way to summarize Aquarius-Snakes is that they are intelligent optimists. Of course, summaries leave out a lot of details, and in the case of this combination there are some important ones. They are, for example, a bit more than intelligent. They are not only extremely clever intellectually, but they are also intuitive. It is just that they know what they can actually have. They have an amazingly clear-thinking mind and enjoy going after goals. They are excellent at the art of seduction, for example. They love to have an enjoyable game of chess resulting in checkmate. The Aquarius-Snake is not a materialistic person. They are more subliminal than material. Their internal life is far more meaningful to them than objects. They travel the world and have exotic escapades all in the psyche. That is where the smile comes from, and that is why they have magnetic personalities. The Aquarius-Snake has a pretty clear notion in advance, of course, as to what her chances of success are. They are not into losing. They have an inborn self-confidence that is actually attractive. Weaving in and out of the traffic that is called life, they are always playing and seldom losing. They love the new and the novel, and that includes people.

Romance: Aquarius-Snakes have a double standard in that they may be involved with more than one person, yet they are jealous of their partners. The best thing for mates of Aquarius-Snakes to do is to leave them alone. It is not wise to restrict their freedom. Those involved with this combination should be secretive about their comings and goings. This is necessary out of self-defense; not literally, of course. Aquarius-Snakes are in control of their emotions; they are cerebral, not emotional. They are calculating and logical. After a thorough process of thinking things through, they sometimes allow their emotions to show. Their intuition must also approve, however. Their emotions do not override their intellect. Oddly, however, they are often carrying on with multiple people.

Relationships: Pretty much out of the question for compatibility are Taurus-, Leo-, or Scorpio-Boars. Taurus-Tigers and Leo-Monkeys can be tempting but do not work out in the long run. Leading the parade in terms of romance are Gemini-, Libra-, and Sagittarius-Buffalos. Buffalos in general are pretty good choices. In the maybe but not sure category are Aries-, Libra-, and Sagittarius-Roosters. They are worth a try. Aries-Rabbits are also real possibilities.

Family Life: Aquarius-Snakes go the extra mile for their families and happily make adjustments or improvements to their homes if their loved ones will be happier. Their personal appearance is rather dashing. They like to dress in a sexy and brash fashion. The Aquarius-Snake once again emphasizes the intellect in the case of their home environment. They are smart enough to want it to work and be reasonably appointed, but they leave it there. Their psyche is not materialistic, and they actually do not worry much about their home. Of course, they care about those they love, and they certainly want them comfortable and secure.

Livelihood: This combination is free flowing and loves independence. They are at once artistic and mechanical; they feel comfortable in both environments. The Aquarius-Snake is exceedingly inquisitive and highly innovative. They have amazing imaginations coupled with a philosophical thought process. Life is an adventure for them while at the same time approached with logic and care.

Famous Aquarius-Snakes: Abraham Lincoln, Charles Darwin, Chaim Potok, Carole King.

Aquarius (Tiger) Month Combined with Horse Year

"Understood" Uranus, Air, Fixed   **"Command"** Yang-Positive Fire

Characteristics: Accomplishment, Pragmatism, Individuality, Cruelty, Thoughtlessness, Dexterity, Independence, Anxiety, Originality, Style, Tolerance, Disobedience, Popularity, Rebellion, Haste, Autonomy, Charity, Neurosis, Separateness, Unscrupulousness, Vision, Persuasiveness, Eccentricity, Selfishness

This combination is gifted and probably also headed toward success. There is a craving for novelty and originality. After a thorough mixing of these elements, the result is an unconventional and mobile individual. The Aquarius-Horse is quick and does not stay inactive for long. This combination is a bit of a rebel thanks to the Horse. The Aquarius nature brings energy and an alert and watchful character to the table. This Horse probably pushes more than it pulls, and it heads in the direction of places with diversity. Part of the nature of the Aquarius-Horse is an uncanny and highly creative ability with everything involving manual skills. An almost awe-inspiring genius in the area of dexterity rests firmly and literally in the hands of the Aquarius-Horse. Beauty is near the top of the list of things that Aquarius-Horses find meaningful, and they care deeply about the universe and nature. They work for what they care about and what they believe in, no matter how unusual others may think the cause is. This combination has skills with no limit in this department. Continuing with the oddness of these individuals is the fact that they are also gifted with language. Their verbal skills are almost as good as their manual skills. There is a strong likelihood that they will be able to speak several languages because of their superior aptitude. The Aquarius-Horse loves to travel and experience exotic places and cultures. They end up being multicultural as well as multilingual.

Romance: A partner to the Aquarius-Horse has to be flexible and understanding. They do not like problems, and they hate drama. The home life, financial life, and sexual life of any relationship is entirely up to them. If this is not understood and accepted, this combination will simply find someone else and that will be the end of the show. Aquarius-Horses expect to be the boss in any relationship because they know the truth and they know what is right. What they do, in their minds, is enough and no more should be asked for or even desired.

Relationships: Definitely wrong choices are Taurus-, Leo-, and Scorpio-Rats. Also out of the question are Leo-Monkeys. Fine selections, based on intelligence and stability, are Gemini- and Sagittarius-Dogs. The Libra-Ram, while somewhat needy, is appealing to the Aquarius-Horse for that very reason. Reasonably good picks are Sagittarius-Tigers, especially for the second time around.

Family Life: This combination's home blasts people with a cannon of color. The personal dress of this individual is ostentatious and loaded with confidence. From blue suede shoes to top hats, Aquarius-Horses have psychedelic tastes that show they are totally free. The Aquarius-Horse is a good parent, but that is not to say he or she is overly fond of children in general. The idea concerns them relative to their personal liberty. They are movers; literally moving house often. If they do have children, however, they totally devote themselves to parenthood. They are so into it that they can become bores who have little to say not relating to their offspring. The home of the Aquarius-Horse is of the Ripley's Believe It or Not school of decorating. Perhaps a nomadic hoarder designed it. Whatever it is, it is highly unusual and consists of myriad objects collected from around the globe.

Livelihood: This individual is often bright enough to turn her unusual interests and weird character into assets and earn money while being relatively free. They might, for example, be talented at photography. In the unlikely event that they end up as a supervisor, they are not one who leads by example because they want their freedom and their own time. Those working for them, on the other hand, will be expected to work their fingers to the bone. Oddly, in spite of being a marginal character in the area of employment, the Aquarius-Horse has an ample income, sometimes more than ample. They are not particularly interested in finances beyond knowing that money is useful and they need it, especially if they want to travel to exotic places and be involved in lavish projects.

Famous Aquarius-Horses: Franklin D. Roosevelt, Jack Benny, Claire Bloom.

Aquarius (Tiger) Month Combined with Ram Year

"Understood" Uranus, Air, Fixed   **"Reliance"** Yang-Negative Fire

Characteristics: Impracticality, Individuality, Cruelty, Worry, Vision, Parasitism, Originality, Eccentricity, Invention, Pessimism, Taste, Perseverance, Independence, Thoughtlessness, Good Manners, Whimsy, Separateness, Sensitivity, Tardiness, Disobedience, Tolerance, Lack of Foresight, Neurosis, Charity

The Aquarius-Ram is one of those combinations that is balanced relative to its characteristics. The Ram portion of this combination tends to be conflicted, but the Aquarius side brings self-determination to it. This also helps with the Ram's insecurity. The Ram side brings deeper emotions to this individual; this Aquarius has more intense feelings than most. Returning to the contributions of the Aquarius, they add energy and power as well as freedom. What this sign offers the human race is lucidity, compassion, understanding, and assorted castles made of sand. Those traits have vast potential and could open up many options in the life of this combination if directed properly. They are very thick skinned and extraordinarily autonomous. There are some issues relative to the past, present, and future that have a huge impact on their lives. Aquarius-Rams leap before they look. Obviously, some tinkering with this is necessary, and some caution must be added to their approach to life. If they do not learn to have a more mature thought process and reflect on the possible consequences, they run the risk of having a very unhappy life. Their thinking is essentially absent of teleological content. They live a life that is almost totally in the present. The result, of course, is a highly spontaneous individual. This sharpens creativity but brings the risk of lament and even danger.

Romance: For example, in terms of sex there is often a belief that fidelity opposes their autonomy. Aquarius-Rams see no reason for this. There is no implication that this combination is not lovable. They are; at least they are sweet. They just have a rather large mental block that hurts their fundamental need for love. They do not have sufficient amounts of this necessary commodity. There is a reason for this, but it is somewhat complicated for this combination to grasp. The insistence on thinking in the present means when they want pleasure, they want it now. They are certainly happy to give pleasure as well, but that too, resides in the moment. This approach makes others doubtful and even critical of the Aquarius-Ram's intentions.

Relationships: Not recommended for this combination are Taurus- or

Leo-Buffalos. Also very risky are Leo- or Scorpio-Dogs. Absolutely out of the question are Scorpio-Monkeys. Rabbits are fine choices for love and romance. The best selections among the Rabbits are Gemini, Libra, and Sagittarius. Probably the next category that is on the positive side of the scale is the Boar. Those in the same Western signs would be good picks. Also highly recommended are Aries-Horses.

Family Life: These individuals feel home is wherever they happen to be, just as long as they are comfortable and welcome. There are essentially no other considerations. Like most people, Aquarius-Rams appreciate beauty, but they are not very fussy about it in their home. Practically anything will do. They are not going to be found at expensive furniture stores or buying fabric for their curtains. If they have a partner who wants nice decor, that is fine and the Aquarius-Rams appreciate it. As for them, secondhand furniture, towels for curtains, and nothing hanging on the wall but old family portraits are just fine. Aquarius-Rams make for excellent parents. They love to open up the world for their children, and they will happily get down on the floor and play with them.

Livelihood: The mind-set of always living in the present influences everything including this combination's career. They will be only passable employees, and as bosses they probably will not be taken seriously. In the final analysis, a career that allows a great deal of autonomy is the best; perhaps something in the arts. The Aquarius-Ram is neither a particularly strong leader nor a particularly good follower. Neither does their slight tendency toward greed make them terrifically ambitious or driven. They are not people who favor repetition. Plainly put, it is hard to categorize this individual.

Famous Aquarius-Rams: Thomas Edison.

Aquarius (Tiger) Month Combined with Monkey Year

"Understood" Uranus, Air, Fixed   **"Arrange"** Yin-Positive Metal

Characteristics: Thoughtlessness, Loquacity, Originality, Zeal, Wit, Cruelty, Opportunism, Silliness, Individuality, Disobedience, Tolerance, Independence, Separateness, Self-involvement, Leadership, Cunning, Vision, Eccentricity, Ruse, Charity, Neurosis, Stability, Improvisation, Deceit

This combination loves to talk, and words play a vital part in the Aquarius-Monkey's being. Words help this individual think in a lucid fashion. There is a revolutionary hiding in the soul of the Aquarius-Monkey. The

Aquarius-Monkey is a combination that has superior potential and often lives up to that billing. This is an individual with great resourcefulness and strength resulting from a special combination of qualities. The somewhat removed mind-set of the Aquarius sees to it that the Monkey is not overly sentimental nor too emotional. The positive contribution of the Monkey is to provide a sense of reality. A fine equilibrium is the result, and the future looks bright for them. They have a deep concern about society and change. They can be powerful, and they like to be in charge. That does not, however, imply that they are power hungry. What they want is a world that is more peaceful, kind, and caring; and they are happy to lead others toward those goals. Truth and not power is what is they seek. This combination lends clear thinking and intelligence to the world. They work hard and have a lot of strength. They are motivated to make miracles and frequently achieve them. They are people watchers and watch in order to understand. Their observations can lead them to articulate situations in a more understandable manner. Having done this, they can plan and then proceed to lead others toward a common destination. They are incredibly agile at doing this and often take their personal reality and manage it in such a way that others adopt the same frame of mind. Fine areas for them to start on the path to their dreams are literature, history, and writing careers like journalism.

Romance: This combination needs love like most humans, but that does not mean a walk on the beach as the sun sets kind of life. They see love more in terms of a partnership of joy and pain; both of which need another person. Oddly, this does not mean fidelity. They are a combination highly prone to extramarital flings. The reason for this is pure and simple amusement. Aquarius-Monkeys are cautious in the area of romance because they do not want drama or soap operas. Problems are to be avoided at all costs, partly because this person is so clear thinking. They also are ambitious and do not want distractions.

Relationships: Scorpio-Snakes are problematic because the Aquarius-Monkey is attracted to them, but this combination is not suitable for the long haul. Leading the parade in the category of love and romance are Gemini-, Libra-, and Sagittarius-Rats. Right there with these combinations are Aries-, Libra-, Scorpio-, and Sagittarius-Dragons. Lagging behind are Taurus-, Leo-, or even Scorpio-Boars. Even further behind are Taurus- and Leo-Tigers.

Family Life: There is classiness about this combination, but it is not glitzy. Impressing other is not on the Aquarius-Monkey's agenda. The same principles apply to this individual's wardrobe. A parent from this combination is earnest and dedicated to raising children. They have high expectations for them and try to create an environment that encourages them to have meaningful goals. The Aquarius-Monkey is real, and what one sees is what one gets. What is seen in the home of an Aquarius-Monkey is always coherent, functional, and without affectation. This combination is reasonable and so is his home. It is strong but not conservative. There is probably a leaning toward the modern, but there is always the pragmatic.

Livelihood: Aquarius-Monkeys have their own visions and desires and are excellent at bringing them about. On the other hand, they will most likely be fine bosses because of their fundamental respect for others. They care and are friendly and even loving toward those who work for them. The Aquarius-Monkey is a natural intellectual and nonconformist. They are not cut out to be in business, and they are not meant to be bureaucrats stuck in a repetitive job. They are rebels and want freedom not just for themselves but for others as well.

Famous Aquarius-Monkeys: Charles Dickens, Billings Learned Hand, Anton Chekhov, François Truffaut, Milos Foreman, Gay Talese, Carl Bernstein, Angela Davis, Alice Walker.

Aquarius (Tiger) Month Combined with Rooster Year

"Understood" Uranus, Air, Fixed   **"Conqueror"** Yang-Negative Metal

Characteristics: Candor, Dissipation, Humor, Independence, Cruelty, Originality, Blind Faith, Thoughtlessness, Chic, Tolerance, Bossiness, Individuality, Separateness, Disobedience, Conservatism, Enthusiasm, Neurosis, Vision, Boastfulness, Charity, Eccentricity, Resilience, Cockiness, Pedantry

This combination's remote personality helps maintain not only an emotional balance but also a more grounded emotional maturity. The detachment that is part of the mental framework of Aquarians is also useful in assisting them in not clinging and grasping relative to good luck and materialism. They are better able to let go and to realize that what might happen next in the life cycle is ultimately not known to anyone. The Aquarius-Rooster is another roller-coaster combination. One never knows if this individual will end up on the top or the bottom. This yo-yo masquerading as life is eternal. It does not stop. In all of this there is hope, however. The Aquarius is known for its clear vision and sharp mind. The qualities of the Aquarius help to rescue the Rooster from possible ruin and disaster. The standoffish and lucid Aquarius might be an unlikely hero, but that is a distinct possibility. While not stoics, they do not put all their emotional energy into one endeavor. Everyone has emotional and creative enterprises, but the wise person knows enough to have backups, alternatives, and variations. This combination is largely able to pull off that balance. The Aquarius-Rooster knows that happiness is fleeting. They often cover up their true feelings with decorations or distractions. Even though they love appearance, they are aware that it is pretense and with this they have some issues. They also know that it will return if lost. They are human, of course, and do not like failures, but they have a character that refuses to submit. Something always lets them know that cloud nine is not of this universe. Subsequently they have a happy and enthusiastic nature that they show most of the world. Their scars and bad memories are not shared with the public.

Romance: Aquarius-Roosters desire partners who can help them. That is to say, this combination is self-interested. What they want might vary. It could be security, emotional or physical assistance, money, or enlightenment. Primarily they want to be well taken care of on the home front so that they themselves can pursue financial gain. They are wonderful and very desirable individuals and are sought by many but held on by few, and they are not interested in anyone who does not meet their standards.

Relationships: Among those combinations that are not recommended are Taurus-, Leo-, and Scorpio-Rabbits. Strictly out of bounds are Taurus-Boars. Snakes are a top selection for Aquarius-Rooster individuals who are seeking love. The best of the Snakes are Aries, Gemini, Libra, or Sagittarius. Buffalos are also good picks. Fantastic choices are Gemini, Libra, or Sagittarius individuals.

Family Life: Aquarius-Roosters totally and completely love their children. That does not imply that they like dirty diapers or enjoy being the local taxi. Love is there for sure, but the way they show it is not by putting together toys or taking the children to baseball practice. They will attend the games though. Home is terrifically significant to the Aquarius-Rooster. The primary reason for this emphasis is that they hold it up as a portrait of who they are. Consequently it will be in an upscale neighborhood, perhaps a gated community.

It will be safe and secure. Aquarius-Roosters like to make an impression, and their environment will be in accordance with this desire. They are not in the least bit flamboyant and flashy but rather tasteful. They essentially view their home as a refuge and do not like people coming by unannounced.

Livelihood: Aquarius-Roosters' brainpower can take them into virtually any profession they choose, and they will probably succeed there. They work hard for what they have, and for what they accomplish it is virtually guaranteed that it will be plentiful. The Aquarius-Rooster has great verbal skills and will almost certainly ride these skills and other talents to success. They have a wonderful ability to persuade people. In addition, they are kind and bighearted. The Aquarius-Rooster is also very friendly and easy to get along with. With some issues they need to be pushed a little, as they are prone to procrastination with chores like paperwork. They can also overdo things in regard to themselves, resulting in some negativity.

Famous Aquarius-Roosters: Colette, Susan Sontag, Yoko Ono, Costa Gavras.

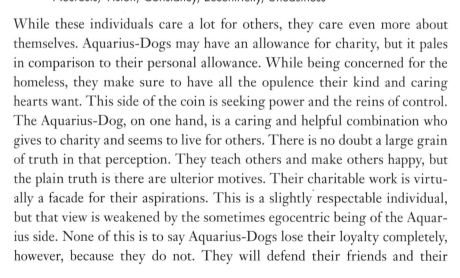

Aquarius (Tiger) Month Combined with Dog Year

"Understood" Uranus, Air, Fixed   **"Concerned"** Yin-Positive Metal

Characteristics: Tastelessness, Individuality, Cruelty, Morality, Thoughtlessness, Intelligence, Cynicism, Independence, Heroism, Tolerance, Disobedience, Respectability, Self-righteousness, Duty, Criticism, Charity, Originality, Unsociability, Separateness, Neurosis, Vision, Constancy, Eccentricity, Uneasiness

While these individuals care a lot for others, they care even more about themselves. Aquarius-Dogs may have an allowance for charity, but it pales in comparison to their personal allowance. While being concerned for the homeless, they make sure to have all the opulence their kind and caring hearts want. This side of the coin is seeking power and the reins of control. The Aquarius-Dog, on one hand, is a caring and helpful combination who gives to charity and seems to live for others. There is no doubt a large grain of truth in that perception. They teach others and make others happy, but the plain truth is there are ulterior motives. Their charitable work is virtually a facade for their aspirations. This is a slightly respectable individual, but that view is weakened by the sometimes egocentric being of the Aquarius side. None of this is to say Aquarius-Dogs lose their loyalty completely, however, because they do not. They will defend their friends and their family every time. They are just not, in the long run, really sincere in what appears to be their genuine humanitarian projects even though they like to associate with those who are, in some sense, needy. The Aquarius-Dog is a mixture of the lucidity of the Aquarius with the loyalty of the helpful Dog. The result is a contradiction. Their verbal skills are pointed and cutting, but their hearts are soft and generous. Their verbal aptitudes win battles, but they treat others well so that others may help them on their quests.

Romance: Aquarius-Dogs are sure they can turn around ex-convicts and lead them to fruitful lives. When none of this works out, they are at a loss to understand why. Their ego-driven side often wins the battle of faithfulness even though they do not have loose morals by character. Unfortunately, the dialectic of the Aquarius-Dog is often an accident waiting to happen in the area of relationships. Aquarius-Dogs have a knack for choosing partners who they think need assistance, thus misplacing entirely that portion of themselves which is truly caring. They are good at marrying alcoholics, for example, because they think they can dry them out. They are good at thinking abusers can be changed.

Relationships: Not recommended for compatibility are Taurus-, Leo-, or Scorpio-Dragons. Also out of the running are Rams and Roosters of the same signs. Leading the pack in terms of love and romance are Aries-, Gemini-, and Sagittarius-Tigers. Gemini-, Libra-, and Sagittarius-Horses are also fantastic in this department. Aries-Rats are a bit on the needy side so the Aquarius-Dog should be careful. They are, however, a possibility. Also in the positive arena are Libra and Sagittarius individuals.

Family Life: This combination has no conception of self-denial. Cooks and butlers and maids occupy the servants' quarters. Aquarius-Dogs are good and responsible parents even though they are sometimes a bit removed. They have a sentimental streak associated with children and, of course, send them to the finest schools. Aquarius-Dogs spare no expense in their homes, and that often means they have more than one abode. Their environment is rich and that is in at least two senses of the word. There may be not only a pool but also a waterfall to go with it. The grounds will more than likely have at least one groundskeeper. The large overstuffed leather chair will be found in the study with the marble desk.

Livelihood: This combination is very good both in social situations and in professions revolving around society and people. They are up to date. They are quite cynical about the world and see it as a large place where people live nasty, brutish, and short lives. They want to change that, and they are willing to push for it. They will take charge at the very first opportunity. They like to give orders and they are good at it. Aquarius individuals are precisely that: individuals. They are solo fliers in their work if they have any choice in the matter. They have no difficulty whatsoever being the boss, especially in a business environment. This combination can grasp essences, make connections, and find hidden meanings.

Famous Aquarius-Dogs: Norman Mailer, Helen Gurley Brown, Zsa Zsa Gabor, Alan Bates.

Aquarius (Tiger) Month Combined with Boar Year

"Understood" Uranus, Air, Fixed   **"Cultivator"** Yin-Negative Water

Characteristics: Boar-headedness, Sincerity, Individuality, Cruelty, Vision, Scrupulousness, Culture, Eccentricity, Credulity, Honesty, Independence, Gourmandism, Wrath, Thoughtlessness, Hesitation, Voluptuousness, Tolerance, Disobedience, Charity, Materialism, Separateness, Originality, Gallantry, Neurosis

The Boar is a country creature, and that alone might lead to a more direct manner of communication. The Aquarius portion of this combination is, like most Aquarius individuals, fairly open. Stir all of this up and the end result can be people who speak before they think, making them, to a degree, mouths waiting to have a foot inserted in them. Part and parcel of this is a sincere individual because, after all, sincerity is a kind of honest and direct form of speech, if nothing else. There is one trait that stands out in Aquarius-Boars more than any other, and that is their sometimes over-the-top tactlessness and belligerence. It sometimes seems as though the mind of this person is totally open to public view. If they think it, they will say it. Why this is the case is a minor mystery. Whatever the case may be, and however the blend is seasoned, it is both audacious and direct. A concomitant aspect of this can be rage and resentment, which they express on a fairly routine basis. That is not to say they are intolerant all of the time. They are not any more interested in conflict than most people. They just happen to be especially quarrelsome and pugnacious. They have a self-image that is blown out of proportion by their self-centered mind-set. They do, however, have a lot of friends in spite of their liabilities. The Boar is powerful and the Aquarius is ambitious. Consequently the Aquarius-Boar is determined. They lead a life of full steam ahead, but they can, at times, be shipwrecks. Besides their tactlessness, they have huge egos that put things out of focus.

Romance: Individuals in this combination want someone with moon-eyes and mouth agape as they tell of how they accomplished this or they did that. The bedroom will not be an especially exciting place, because there the self-centeredness continues. They want someone to carry their bags and to cook their meals and all the while be awestruck about them. Those who are married to the Aquarius-Boar need to be good listeners. The Aquarius-Boar is gifted in the area of displaying affection. They are huggers and kissers. They are the type that hold hands or nuzzle up behind a person and stroke their hair. The show is there. Deep feelings and loyalty are quite another matter. Giving of themselves for the sake of their partner is a bit on the light side at best. This is a person who focuses on himself or herself and expects a partner in life who focuses on him or her as well. They want a cheerleader and a person who listens to them brag.

Relationships: Taurus-, Leo-, or Scorpio-Snakes require some caution because they are not good picks, but they are attractive to the Aquarius-Boar. Taurus-Horses are strictly a no-go. Terrific selections for love can be found with Rabbits and Rams. The elite among those are Aries, Gemini, Libra, and Sagittarius. An additional good choice is the Aries-Tiger.

Family Life: There is a strong likelihood that the Aquarius-Boar will live in the countryside. They have enough taste to make their abodes appropriate for the rural setting. Aquarius-Boars get along fine with children but are somewhat of the seen-but-not-heard school of thought. This mind-set is the result of their concern with advancement. This individual's partner will do most of the child rearing. If one pictures a grand palace they might have some notion relative to the home of an Aquarius-Boar. Start with huge and continue right on down the line to lavish, and that is where this combination reigns. In perfectly chosen locations throughout the home will be computers and other necessary gadgets. The decor of this home is luxurious and pompous. It is, in spite of this, a cultured environment and a place that is comfortable.

Livelihood: They have known from an early age what they wanted and where they were going, and they will not be stopped. At work they are the boss. It does not matter what their job title is or the details of the job description; they will have rank and status. The Aquarius-Boar is driven by the craving for financial gain and control. They are willing to do almost anything in their quest, so clearly this is a primary aspect of the professional life of an Aquarius-Boar. Dangle the prospect of an upward move, and watch their smiles grow.

Famous Aquarius-Boars: Ronald Reagan, John McEnroe, Sonny Bono, Mikhail Baryshnikov.

Pisces (Rabbit) Month Combined with Rat Year

"Faith" Neptune, Water, Mutable   **"Regulator"** Yin-Positive Water

Characteristics: Fearfulness, Charisma, Indecision, Meddling, Rage, Intellectual, Sociability, Skill, Guile, Awareness, Spirituality, Compatibility, Smugness, Thrift, Acquisitiveness, Thirst for Power, Lack of Will, Perception, Diffidence, Influence, Verbosity, Creativity, Understanding, Nervousness, Appeal

This combination is very open and sympathetic on the one hand and very aggressive on the other. Their balancing act in regard to these almost contradictory traits is magical. Working with another person they are essentially guaranteed to win. They are living proof that the sum is more than the total of its parts. The Pisces-Rat is a team player and usually the team is a duo. They work well and win often doing things in tandem. The Pisces, with its fish qualities, has a special relationship to water, which is apparently soft and giving. It can, however, like floods or erosion, be very powerful. The Rat, thanks to the influence of Pisces, gains an awareness of finitude. This awareness helps bring about a wiser and more perceptive individual. Consequently their choices are better. The Pisces-Rat is a dependent person. They do not function singly very well at all. With a partner they can do quite well. This combination does not want to be accountable for things. They would rather stand beside the person who is. In this way they make great assistants or executive secretaries. Awareness of the finite also makes provisions for better planning. Pisces are known for being irresolute, but the Rat quickly puts an end to that issue.

Romance: Pisces-Rats need partners who make them feel wanted. Mushy sentimentalism is an excellent way to keep the relationship with a Pisces-Rat going. Taking a novel approach to romance will be highly effective. The Pisces-Rat sometimes has a fairy-tale love and marriage story, so there is always a chance to fall in love with that prince or princess. A lot of the time this does happen, but they frequently hook up with a good other half and happily play second fiddle to them. Their choice then becomes a pragmatic one and a companionship situation. In this kind of situation there is a good chance their home will be a place to go to after work. Somewhere else, but distinctly not at home, will be their real relationship. The Pisces-Rat is a very sensitive and high-strung individual. They prefer a love on the side, someone who can calm them.

Relationships: For compatibility very poor choices are Gemini-, Virgo-, or Sagittarius-Horses. Buffalos and Dragons are superior selections for love and marriage. The very best selections from these signs are the Taurus, Cancer, Scorpio, and Capricorn. Additionally, Capricorn- and Scorpio-Monkeys are fine picks.

Family Life: The Pisces-Rat who lives alone has a place that is a bit odd but comfy. In relationships of any kind, including groups, this combination goes along with what others decide. As mothers or fathers, the Pisces-Rat is conscientious and trustworthy. They enjoy a good laugh and are happy to play ball with the kids or make the little ones smile. Pisces-Rats allow their partners to decide all matters pertaining to the home, and many other ones as well. In the event that the Pisces-Rat has his or her own personal space at home it will be a bit on the messy side with little regard for decor.

Livelihood: This individual is a worrier and craves security. They are happy to work for the common good, but they expect to be rewarded for their efforts, whether it is monetarily or with increased status. There is absolutely no desire to be the boss, and if they fall into that position they would be unhappy and likely do a poor job. They want control but not the limelight. Their true being will almost never be revealed to others. The Pisces-Rat is very slow to trust others. Somewhat surprisingly, they are critical and somewhat cunning as well as self-righteous. This later trait is exacerbated if they belong to a group that they deem upscale or important.

Famous Pisces-Rats: Lawrence Durrell, Patricia Nixon, Gloria Vanderbilt, Robert Altman, James Taylor.

Pisces (Rabbit) Month Combined with Buffalo Year

"Faith" Neptune, Water, Mutable **"Survivor"** Yin-Negative Water

Characteristics: Vindictiveness, Spirituality, Stability, Indecision, Awareness, Innovation, Standoffishness, Diligence, Bias, Fearfulness, Compatibility, Eloquence, Plodding, Bigotry, Smugness, Lack of Will, Perception, Rage, Strength of Purpose, Creativity, Understanding, Stubbornness, Diffidence, Integrity

The unusual nature of the Pisces-Buffalo lies in the gap between the fundamental sumo wrestler nature of this individual and the real being of the Pisces-Buffalo. This is another one of life's lessons in "what one sees is not always what one gets." They might look like they are in La-la-land, but they are actually a bit on the devious side—and are preparing to hatch new plans. They are not at all, in the final analysis, the Pisces individuals lost in reverie. The Pisces-Buffalo is one of the more unusual characters to be encountered in the galaxy. For starters, they have an appearance of fluff and ruffles. Those who think they have this combination figured out are in for a dramatic and memorable eye-opening. This powerful but seemingly benign entertainer can knock one's socks off. Actually, they are so clever they might remove one's socks, much to the dismay of the now shoeless individual. Furthermore, and as a word of caution, no one should ever run the risk of angering the Pisces-Buffalo. For starters, the quick wit of this individual can cut people down to size with sarcasm. The Pisces-Buffalo continues with the routine, and then waits. After they have waited, they wait some more. In this fashion, they win nearly every time. They cannot be stopped. They generally do not, however, employ that tactic. They are rather more insidious than that. Their tactic for winning is not violence or coercion. The way they win is accomplished more slowly, like chopping down a big tree with a hatchet. They are not abusive, and they are not rude.

Romance: Pisces-Buffalos are very sensitive and intuitive about others, however, and their judgments in this regard are usually spot on. They see weak spots and, in the case of opponents, begin scheming. This individual can be invisible and successful every single, solitary time. It is important to note and be reminded of the fact that success is not a guarantee of happiness, however. This combination is, after all, 50 percent fish, and because of this probably will never attain eternal harmony.

Relationships: On the negative side in the relationship department are Gemini- and Virgo-Dragons. Further poor choices are Sagittarius-Rams or -Monkeys. The Pisces-Buffalo likes Rats. Among them, Cancer, Scorpio, or Capricorn are the top selections for love and romance. Additional excellent possibilities are Snakes and Roosters from the same Western signs. Another good pick is the Scorpio-Dragon.

Family Life: As a parent, the Pisces-Buffalo is loving albeit pushy and stubborn. They love their children so much that it is difficult for them to let the offspring go when they have matured. The family adds balance to this combination. The home of a Pisces-Buffalo is akin to a summer palace. It is grand and, being somewhat castlelike, it is to be defended. That means a kind of concrete and specific approach to decorating. This home, after all, is the vision of the Pisces-Buffalo that the world will have. It is classical as well as traditional and looks like everything has been carefully maintained for a generation or two at least. The colors must not be flashy, and the artwork must be representative and proportioned. There is essentially nothing modern in the decor.

Livelihood: This combination wants luxury and knows how to win through patience. Activating all this guarantees success. They need to come from a family that is guiding and moral. They must be taught principles. Lacking this framework is risky, and being led in the other direction can be disastrous. As bosses they get respect even though they are meticulous and fussy. They are difficult, but they are fair. This combination is steady and brave and assured of success if reared in the proper environment and exposed to the right things in life. They are highly imaginative and inventive as well as having vast stores of energy. They were practically born motivated. There is a wide streak of materialism in their character.

Famous Pisces-Buffalo: George Frideric Handel, John Erlichman, Vincente Minnelli, Edward Gorey.

Pisces (Rabbit) Month Combined with Tiger Year

"Faith" Neptune, Water, Mutable   **"Observe"** Yang-Positive Wood

Characteristics: Indecision, Authority, Spirituality, Itinerancy, Benevolence, Intemperance, Awareness, Rage, Fearfulness, Smugness, Perception, Magnetism, Disobedience, Compatibility, Bravery, Fervor, Lack of Will, Hotheadedness, Good Luck, Creativity, Understanding, Diffidence, Impetuosity, Swagger

This combination loves vast oceans and never-ending space. Boundaries, fences, bars, and shackles bother Pisces-Tigers and have no importance to them. The fish envies the free bird. Their goals and their interests are much more in the area of the spiritual. Illumination. That has a great appeal to them. Pisces-Tigers are more the latter than the former, in spite of the fact that they do not always like it. They search, often in vain, for some kind of self-identity. The Tiger part of their being makes them feel limited even though it is spirited. The unbounded and the limitless appeal to them. Vanity is generally part of the mixture. They have a distaste for borders akin to the Pisces, but they are motivated to move and jump. People are drawn to the Tiger side, and the Tiger loves it. They want to sit under the Bodhi Tree and meditate and discover the mysteries of the universe and the mystery that is within them. Most of this comes from the Pisces who seeks peace and solitude. That is diametrically opposed to the Tiger who loves drama and excitement. The Tiger is hyperactive, brash, and impatient.

Romance: The Pisces-Tiger can become nervous about new loves. Those who want a relationship with the Pisces-Tiger need to play their cards right. Usually keeping Pisces-Tigers on their toes is a good idea. Let them do the chasing and catching. Having a sense of humor also appeals to the Pisces-Tiger. Aggression is not recommended, but tact is. In the area of relationships there is frequently a conflict resulting from the dialectical clash of the two signs. On the one hand, the Pisces-Tiger is affectionate. On the other hand, that loving care sometimes masks a negative sentiment left over from heartbreak. This combination is strong and gets up to start over again after breakups. But all people hurt, and everyone has scars from the past.

Relationships: Negative matches for Pisces-Tigers include Gemini-, Virgo-, and Sagittarius-Snakes and Sagittarius-Rams. These combinations are not recommended. Continuing on the negative side are Virgo- and Sagittarius-Buffalos. Virgo-Monkeys should not be considered at all. In the area of love and relationships, the Pisces-Tiger needs a combination that is pragmatic. Taurus-, Cancer-, Scorpio-, or Capricorn-Horses fit the bill nicely. Additional recommended combinations are Cancer-, Scorpio-, and Capricorn-Dogs. Added to the suggested individuals are Scorpio-Dragons.

Family Life: Pisces-Tiger mothers and fathers are loving and encouraging with their children. What they particularly encourage is creativity. They are, to a degree, easygoing in the discipline department. They will not tolerate, however, back talk or misbehavior. What they say goes. The Pisces-Tiger is the type of person who is at home almost anywhere and everywhere. They are not the least bit materialistic, rather preferring to be comfortable with their friends and family. Doing things around the home appeals to them, and they generally have a project going. They appreciate an abode that is roomy because of their need to be unconstrained. There is a beatnik or hippie in this person even though it may not show all that much. They do appreciate beauty but do not find it essential for their home.

Livelihood: Pisces-Tigers do not make especially good bosses because they have a shy element to their being. That is fine by them, because they do not want to be a boss anyway. The ideal career for the Pisces-Tiger is one where they can work independently, especially if it is something in the arts. Pisces-Tigers are not afraid to move and be aggressive in their professional life. They work harder than most, and overtime in their pursuit of success does not faze them. The Pisces side softens the aggressive Tiger a bit and makes for a friendlier and more tactful individual. They can deal with people nicely and things are essentially bright in their professional life.

Famous Pisces-Tigers: Stephane Mallarme, Nijinsky, John Steinbeck, Jerry Lewis, Rudolf Nureyev.

Pisces (Rabbit) Month Combined with Rabbit Year

"Faith" Neptune, Water, Mutable **"Withdraw"** Yin-Negative Wood

Characteristics: Indecision, Hypochondria, Spirituality, Dilettantism, Rage, Longevity, Ambition, Awareness, Complexity, Fearfulness, Smugness, Prudence, Virtue, Pedantry, Compatibility, Perception, Squeamishness, Lack of Will, Finesse, Understanding, Creativity, Tact, Diffidence, Secretiveness

This combination has a deep and abiding love for the sophisticated and stylish. There is a good chance that this interest will play some role in the Pisces-Rabbit's life; perhaps, for example, as a professional caretaker of meaningful and significant artifacts. Their love for the creative and the artistic will almost certainly be a part of their personal life in the form of, at minimum, having talent in this area. The Pisces-Rabbit is a warm and friendly mixture that works. There is a really wonderful joining together of characteristics. The Rabbit, of course, loves the home and family and is almost certain to be a homebody. They are careful and self-effacing. Their cleverness will make it very possible for them to cash in on their talent in one form or another. The artistic ability of the Pisces-Rabbit will almost certainly be profitable. There is a natural and resolute aversion to conflict from both sides of the Pisces-Rabbit, and Pisces-Rabbits will rarely be found in altercations. Most do not have a vengeful bone in their body and view such feelings as insignificant. Pisces-Rabbits have nothing in their combination to hold them back from accomplishing great things. There is a noble aspect to this combination. The Pisces, of course, has a sponge for a mind and can absorb nearly anything. The homely nature of the Rabbit is put to good use by allowing for time to set goals.

Romance: This combination is old-fashioned. It is true that they are romantic, but they do not sit around waiting for their prince or princess to show up. This individual needs a lot of support and affection. They often need someone to do their talking for them because they are so timorous they are prone to getting tongue-tied. Laying on lots of TLC is necessary to have a successful relationship with this person. One does not find the Pisces-Rabbit as Mr. or Mrs. Personality. They are not sociable and are not back-slappers. Hell would, at the very least, have a coating of frost over it before this combination went dashing around sowing wild oats or any other grains. Pisces-Rabbits stick to themselves, and what they want for a partner is someone they can have breakfast with and exchange comparisons of how well they slept.

Relationships: For compatibility, Scorpio- or Capricorn-Dogs can invest the Pisces-Rabbit's life with plenty of new ideals. Furthermore, a Cancer-Rabbit will make a good marriage partner. Excellent peaceful and quiet combinations for the Pisces-Rabbit are Taurus-, Cancer-, and Scorpio-Boars.

Family Life: At the top of the list in Pisces-Rabbits' lives are their children. They are very protective of them; some would say too protective. They are mildly strict in private, but they are careful never to say anything in public that might soil the image of their family. Pisces-Rabbit mothers and fathers dearly love their kids and do things like read to them and help with their homework, even the mathematics. The Pisces-Rabbit is a family-oriented person with traditional family values. This means, of course, having children. The trappings continue in a snowball fashion. All of the above means that a home is needed to bring up the family. That home will be very tastefully decorated. In addition to being comfortable it will be secure and in the proper sort of neighborhood. These are upward-bound individuals, and how they present themselves is of value and importance. The peace-and-quiet theme must continue because of the Rabbit image, and as a rule this means a home in a small town or the countryside.

Livelihood: Pisces-Rabbits will work hard always, but their timid character may lead them to a job that is routine instead of a high-powered job filled with stress. They are hard bosses to work for because they are highly rigid and strict. They often seem removed from others, but this is generally a defense mechanism to insulate themselves. This combination is easy to get along with and mentally sharp. They are, moreover, shy, and it is this trait that has the potential to hold them back. Their nerves and unwillingness to put themselves forward are liabilities professionally. In the workplace, as nearly everywhere, they are overly conscious of status and how things look.

Famous Pisces-Rabbits: Albert Einstein, Harry Belafonte, Peter Fonda, George Plimpton, Zero Mostel.

Pisces (Rabbit) Month Combined with Dragon Year

"Faith" Neptune, Water, Mutable   **"Take Charge"** Yang-Positive Wood

Characteristics: Sentimentality, Volubility, Indecision, Infatuation, Braggadocio, Spirituality, Awareness, Rage, Pluck, Good Health, Smugness, Enthusiasm, Dissatisfaction, Compatibility, Perception, Creativity, Fearfulness, Lack of Will, Success, Mistrust, Diffidence, Strength, Understanding, Rigidity

This combination is a mover and at times they are a shaker as well. Dragons are not known for being afraid to put themselves forward. What they are known for, more often than not, is bragging. Mixing this with the watery home of the Pisces is a plus. Pisces-Dragons place a significant importance on advancement in their professions and in life. They are a combination of movement. Personal advancement, traveling, jogging, swimming, or career change are used to fend off edginess and nerves. A deeper awareness arises in the combination and lets the Dragon element have a more realistic view of themselves. From the Pisces side of his nature, this subject gains perspective. The Dragon can come back down to earth because of the addition that the Pisces has made. They need to learn how to keep their nose to the grindstone. Practice may not exactly make perfect, but it helps. This combination needs to develop a better understanding of that basic principle of life. Overall, but perhaps in insufficient quantities, this mixture is relatively workable and has some potential. There is a danger, unfortunately, of the combination becoming a free-floating individual adrift in a sea of purposelessness, but this is unlikely. As a way of life there are always some dark clouds present, however.

Romance: There may be some drama in Pisces-Dragons' lives, but they know about love. When they love and when they are loved in return, it is permanent. They know how to forgive the transgressions of their partner as well, because they always remember the wonderful parts of their history. Pisces-Dragons can be fickle and inconsistent in matters of the heart. Part of the cause of this is that they are often quite attractive. This can make them rather conceited because they are so popular. There is some assistance because this combination has rather large doses of sentimentality. However, there is still a strong likelihood that the Pisces-Dragon will go wandering off.

Relationships: Not particularly good choices are Gemini- or Virgo-Rabbits. Virgo- and Sagittarius-Dogs are not good either. The Virgo-Boar and Sagittarius-Buffalo are out of the question. Dragons have a reasonable number of choices for love and romance. Excellent selections are Cancer-, Scorpio-, and Capricorn-Monkeys for a start. Taurus-, Cancer-, Libra-, and Scorpio-Tigers also make the list of excellent picks. Other positive matches include Taurus- and Scorpio-Snakes. And, there are also Scorpio- and Capricorn-Rats to choose from.

Family Life: This combination loves to look at the houses and furnishings in home decoration magazines and dream. Often though, they wait so long that those dreams of a lovely home with a pool and a mountain view but easy distance to the beach will never come about. They are too late for the party. There are never regrets though, so all of this sits okay with the Pisces-Dragon. Pisces-Dragons, of course, love and care for their children. The Pisces-Dragon is not a homebody. They will likely live in an unassuming environment and have somewhat reasonable possessions. It is not that they do not want a nice place to live; it is just that they spend a lot of time either being in other people's homes or traveling.

Livelihood: This combination has a lot of energy. However, Pisces-Dragons often let others run around to assorted seminars, workshops, and continuing-education classes while they spend time in another place in their own minds. The best sort of work for them is totally independent work, perhaps done from the home. As bosses, something they are very unlikely to be mostly because they have no interest, they are very pushy and somewhat aggressive. The Pisces-Dragon is an idealistic dreamer from another world. A large portion of their psyche does not care that most of this particular planet is ambitious and seeking fame and fortune. Many of them are just happy to have a very relaxed attitude in terms of profession. They are not lazy, and they certainly do not lack in intelligence.

Famous Pisces-Dragons: B. F. Skinner, Irving Wallace, Edward Albee.

Pisces (Rabbit) Month Combined with Snake Year

"Faith" Neptune, Water, Mutable   **"Feel"** Yang-Negative Fire

Characteristics: Compassion, Exclusiveness, Indecision, Rage, Clairvoyance, Presumption, Spirituality, Awareness, Creativity, Laziness, Compatibility, Fearfulness, Discretion, Smugness, Attractiveness, Cupidity, Perception, Lack of Will, Extravagance, Intuition, Dissimulation, Understanding, Diffidence, Sagacity

The way this combination sees the world is too deep to share with mere mortals. They are profound and intuitive in addition to being able to focus clearly with a vision of the future. Another way to view this is that the Pisces-Snake has been, through some cosmic error, placed on planet Earth. They are wizards masquerading as simple humans. The Pisces-Snake lives, speaking in psychic terms, on another planet among other enlightened souls who understand them. They simply are not of this Earth. They seem normal enough superficially. However, the Pisces-Snake is a being that is super cerebral and a philosopher at heart. They are not really suited to do things in the fashion of other people, and that leads them to be either unemployed or unhappy. They are not interested in announcing to the world that they are important, special, or different, and they certainly have no axes laying around that need grinding—even though they find mankind in rather dire straits in modern times. They could easily live in a place apart from all the madness. A home with their family would be comfort enough. They could, perhaps be content as a fortune-teller or shaman, but job openings in those categories are rare. This individual avoids trouble and avoids complaining.

Romance: This combination has friends galore, but generally they gather at the home of the Pisces-Snake. This stick-in-mud approach to socialization often turns Pisces-Snakes' mates off, and it is possible their partners will be unfaithful. Pisces-Snakes are a paradigm of being faithful and loving in a relationship. If they get married they perceive it as being forever, and they never stray. They believe that their commitment is for life and that they are bound together with their mate. Because they are loaded with energy, they occasionally need rest and an escape. They prefer to stay at home with their family.

Relationships: To be avoided in this combination are Gemini-, Virgo-, and Sagittarius-Tigers. Not the least bit recommended are Virgo-Monkeys. At the top of the list for love and marriage are Taurus-, Cancer-, and Capricorn-Roosters. Additional fine choices are Cancer- and Capricorn-Buffalos.

Family Life: Pisces-Snakes, for themselves alone, do not need material possessions at all. If they live alone they will be comfortable, but after that not much else matters. They are perfectly capable of living in one very sparsely furnished room. Oddly enough, Pisces-Snakes love clothes, but they are not flamboyant in their choice of attire. They are loving parents but because of their extreme sensitivity find child rearing painful at times. The Pisces-Snake loves the home and essentially stays there. They are quintessential homebodies. This individual is responsible and loving. They recognize the importance of home and family. Their home might be extravagant, but it is worth it because it houses those they love.

Livelihood: Pisces-Snakes are good with people and are capable of hard work. As bosses they are good-hearted but end up being unliked in many cases because such people are frequently taken for granted and used. The Pisces-Snake is multitalented and able to do a vast array of jobs. There is a slight issue in that they do not want to leave their home and family when they turn of age. They are firmly attached to the home of Mom and Dad. If they get a good education the leave-taking is easier, but without it there is a strong resistance.

Famous Pisces-Snakes: Isabelle Huppert, Anthony Burgess, Robert Lowell.

Pisces (Rabbit) Month Combined with Horse Year

"Faith" Neptune, Water, Mutable   *"Command"* Yang-Positive Fire

Characteristics: Accomplishment, Pragmatism, Indecision, Haste, Rage, Dexterity, Awareness, Spirituality, Anxiety, Selfishness, Rebellion, Compatibility, Fearfulness, Popularity, Smugness, Unscrupulousness, Autonomy, Perception, Lack of Will, Creativity, Diffidence, Persuasiveness, Understanding, Style

In this combination the Pisces helps guide the Horse into a more humble individual. In the end, Pisces-Horses are extremely nice; in fact, they are too nice. The reason for this is that the Horse influence intensifies qualities in the Pisces with imagination, sympathy, and acceptance. The problem here is that Pisces-Horses are sometimes too self-sacrificing, and they put their own needs, wants, and desires on the back burner. In the Pisces-Horse combination there is a smoothing and rounding off of issues that come from the generally self-centered Horse. The reason for this is that the Pisces influence makes this combination more aware of its psychic and humanistic qualities. Normally Horses go trotting off looking out for themselves and being terrifically autonomous. They simply overdo it when it comes to helping others. These individuals have terrific potential if they are able to find a partner or friend who can help them reach their destiny. They do, however, need a guide, or in some cases, an easier way to success. They are very gifted individuals who just happen to need someone to help them find their way from darkness to light. This combination is somewhat shy and introverted. What they would like is popularity, and they choose this goal over things like autonomy.

Romance: Partners of the Pisces-Horse should never exploit this incredible adoration and love. Shy Pisces-Horses need their partners to help make them a bit less introverted. To treat them right is to be assured of a lifelong partner who will never stop loving and worshipping them. They are totally reliable and loyal if treated well and not taken for granted. The Pisces-Horse is a fabulous, devoted lover. Their dedication is almost infinite. They know how to love and take care of their partners. Pisces-Horses truly do care and will take care of those they love. Their love is not especially effusive because they are inclined to be shy. But, they do worship their partners and have the highest regard for them.

Relationships: There is a real chance that the Pisces-Horse will not do well with Rats, especially if they are Gemini, Sagittarius, or Virgo. Monkeys born in either Sagittarius or Gemini are not good selections at all. The best choices for love and romance are the Libra-, Scorpio-, and Capricorn-Tiger. Those combinations are superb love partners. More fine choices can be found in Taurus-, Scorpio-, and Capricorn-Dogs. Good news continues with Taurus- or Capricorn-Rams.

Family Life: Pisces-Horses tend to live in their own minds, so what surrounds them is of little consequence. They are excellent, loving mothers and fathers who enjoy doing things with and for their children. They want to understand children in general and realize that being with them is the best way to accomplish that. They are not the stay-at-home type of person who makes brownies and fusses over the style of their drapes. The Pisces-Horse is odd in the home department. They actually like to be at other people's abodes. This individual is not materialistic and has no interest in impressing other people. The Pisces-Horse wants to have a roof over his head and three square meals a day. They could not care less about lounging around on expensive furniture and admiring antique vases or works by famous artists.

Livelihood: There is little chance of this combination ever becoming a boss. At most they might hire some teenagers to mow their lawn or use a word processor to handle the new novel they have written. They are not in the least bit fussy or pushy with other people. The Pisces-Horse is a person from another world and as such does not care much for chasing money. They find the way some people do that, with all the stress in their life, rather humorous. Instead of business, which they are terrible at, they would much rather be involved in the arts in some way. If the gods of the art world, including the written word, are kind to them and they become famous, they can handle admiration with poise. Their shyness and desire to not get involved with trivial pursuits does not detract from their aptitude as a creative thinker.

Famous Pisces-Horses: Frederic Chopin, Mickey Spillane, Patty Hearst, John Irving.

Pisces (Rabbit) Month Combined with Ram Year

"Faith" Neptune, Water, Mutable **"Reliance"** Yang-Negative Fire

Characteristics: Whimsy, Spirituality, Impracticality, Indecision, Worry, Rage, Good Manners, Pessimism, Awareness, Fearfulness, Taste, Smugness, Perception, Perseverance, Tardiness, Compatibility, Lack of Will, Sensitivity, Lack of Foresight, Understanding, Creativity, Invention, Diffidence, Parasitism

Pisces-Rams are extremely bright and have an ability to apply their talents to real situations. They also happen to be quite romantic. It is the hypersensitivity that is the most significant aspect of their personality. Some might think this liability is so great that Pisces-Rams cannot function in the world. Pisces-Rams are doubly sensitive because they acquire sensitivity from both aspects of their combination. However, they do have some other really good and helpful traits. Pisces-Ram is among the strongest of the Pisces signs. That is the case because in the Pisces-Ram, the Ram has a powerful strengthening influence. They need the strength emanating from the Ram in order to deal with more aggressive combinations. There is sensitivity coupled with power, which is a fairly good balance overall. Furthermore, this is necessary because the Pisces-Ram has an astrological geography such that there is a likely connection, in some fashion, to a more powerful combination.

Romance: This combination is generally good at procrastinating with long-term commitments. Eventually, however, they will find the right match and settle down. The right match is probably in the tough-guy category. They need someone like that to give them direction. They also need someone to care for and to help them. These individuals are passionate when they make love. The Earth moves and golden stars fall from the heavens. Pisces-Rams love, and when they do it is written in stone. They tend to be a bit reluctant about falling in love in the first place, but once they do this combination is not about to stop loving. There is no doubt, though, that there is a rather wide spread between the Pisces aspect and the Ram aspect in their combination.

Relationships: Negativity begins to set in with Aries-, Gemini-, and Virgo-Buffalos. Out of the question are Virgo-Dogs, who do not much like Pisces-Rams anyway. In the realm of romance the Taurus-, Cancer-, Scorpio-, or Capricorn-Rabbit are great selections. Horses from the same signs are also fine for love and marriage. Also making the list of positive selections are Taurus-, Scorpio-, or Capricorn-Boars. But that is not all, as Scorpio-Rams are excellent at having fun and perhaps love as well.

Family Life: Pisces-Rams are on the handy side even though they are not practical. They will probably execute some home improvement projects themselves. In the area of children there is no disputing the deep love they feel. This person, however, is somewhat on the impatient side and can get testy when interrupted by the youngsters. Pisces-Rams might actually get to a place where they have a home and family. If they do, the home will be one with opulence in a fabulous environment. This individual will have expensive but uncomfortable furniture. On the other hand, they might simply allow their partner to do the decorating.

Livelihood: There is a chance that Pisces-Rams will be successful, but they must avoid the glass-half-empty syndrome. Negativity will ruin them. As a boss this combination functions as a distant relative to an oracle. The Pisces-Ram's ideal profession would be something necessitating travel and imagination. This individual likes to have freedom of movement. Repetitive routine employment is not for them at all. Obviously, those who want to have a profession in the arts do not find job searching easy. Starting early and associating themselves with a professional is the best way to succeed.

Famous Pisces-Rams: Michelangelo, W. H. Auden, Tom Wolfe, John McPhee, George Washington.

Pisces (Rabbit) Month Combined with Monkey Year

"Faith" Neptune, Water, Mutable   *"Arrange"* Yin-Positive Metal

Characteristics: Leadership, Awareness, Opportunism, Zeal, Rage, Indecision, Stability, Loquacity, Wit, Silliness, Spirituality, Compatibility, Perception, Lack of Will, Smugness, Self-involvement, Cunning, Ruse, Understanding, Diffidence, Creativity, Fearfulness, Improvisation, Deceit

Pisces-Monkeys have no interest in striving for power, yet they are naturals in leadership positions. What the Pisces brings to the table is spirituality and good looks. The Pisces-Monkey is a lover of beauty. The first thing one notices about Pisces-Monkeys is their charisma. This comes about by mixing the happy Monkey characteristics with the uninhibited Pisces. The Monkey is known not just for being happy but also for its problem-solving abilities. They are sensible. They have a great deal of practical judgment. They take the necessary steps to make it a part of their lives. If this combination sets out to get something the odds are that they will get it. The Pisces-Monkey can be counted on to have a clean and stylish appearance without making a show of it. They can be compared, perhaps, to the duke or duchess of the manor yet without a hint of snobbery. Whether that appearance is just a facade is somewhat up for debate. Their popularity and charm, however, is without question. They manage to combine the beauty of nature with class. Much of what they have was given to them by friends and admirers. This includes everything from fashionable clothes to jewelry and mansions. They have a feel of the international about their being. They do not have an arrogant bone in their body, yet they are refined.

Romance: There is a special fascination around Pisces-Monkeys. People fall in love with them in a manner they do not fall in love with others. They fall totally and deeply in love. The vanity of this combination likes that. Because others fall in love and pursue them, they can be perceived as weak. Others might try to use them, and that is a big mistake. It's almost guaranteed to cause problems. Catching the Pisces-Monkey will probably require finances. This combination loves money. They can get it, save it, and use it appropriately. There is a lot of drama surrounding the love life of the Pisces-Monkey. In a manner of speaking, this is to be expected because of the beauty such individuals have. Their beauty is generally more than skin deep, but they are mysterious and charming as well.

Relationships: The Pisces-Monkey should avoid Gemini- as well as

Sagittarius-Snakes and Virgo-Horses and -Boars. At the top of the list for potential love partners are the Taurus-, Cancer-, Scorpio-, and Capricorn-Dragon. Continuing with the positive realm are the Taurus-, Cancer-, and Capricorn-Rat. Another good choice is the Taurus-Monkey.

Family Life: This combination loves pleasure and comfort and well-appointed rooms. They might live in a terrifically upscale apartment in New York or a famous and expensive hotel. This individual is generally not focused on being a parent while young, but with age these feelings change. This is true with the overall picture of their lives as they become more responsible as they mature and experience life. Pisces-Monkeys love opulence in their homes. As lovers of beauty they are very much into decorating their abodes, and it is common to find fancy, expensive, and exotic objects there. The furniture will surely be sturdy and conservative. They will not have tiny cramped rooms but will likely have an impressive fireplace.

Livelihood: This combination has a fine awareness of current events and knows how to put this knowledge to good use. They have mental strength. In addition to everything else, they are imaginative and can grasp things quickly. Should they be a boss they will be loved because of their compassionate nature. They are able to be strict but usually choose to get results via reason and suggestion rather than more directly. Pisces-Monkeys can accomplish nearly anything they seriously set out to do or be. They are talented in most every respect including both the physical and mental. They might be a bit accident prone, but this is usually because they are always on the move.

Famous Pisces-Monkeys: Balthus, Rex Harrison, Ted Kennedy, Liz Taylor, John Updike, Michele Morgan.

Pisces (Rabbit) Month Combined with Rooster Year

"Faith" Neptune, Water, Mutable   **"Conqueror"** Yang-Negative Metal

Characteristics: Pedantry, Awareness, Humor, Dissipation, Rage, Chic, Fearfulness, Candor, Blind Faith, Bossiness, Creativity, Compatibility, Lack of Will, Enthusiasm, Smugness, Perception, Indecision, Understanding, Diffidence, Boastfulness, Spirituality, Resilience, Cockiness, Conservatism

The Pisces-Rooster is an explorer of life. This comes about largely from the Pisces element of their being. The exterior of this combination shows a self-confident and almost smug appearance. The fact is, however, there is a lot of insecurity because they do not trust in their appeal and, indeed, are unaware that they have it on occasions. While there is a certain insecurity in the nature of the Pisces-Rooster, there should not be. They are exceptionally flexible and comfortable in nearly any setting. They can go to the most exotic and otherworldly place on Earth and feel right at home. They are independent and enjoy change. They fear that their love will be one directional, and this makes them sad. Open up this individual and one will discover a modest and self-effacing individual who abhors arrogance. The Rooster is actually an earthy individual with a lot of common sense and the spirit of adventure. This is diametrically opposed to the Pisces side. They have no confidence in their looks and often believe that they are homely. They do, however, put on a good show, choosing some elements they believe in and bragging at times. They will look at a person and proclaim their own wonderful attributes. In this way, and in spite of their insecurity, they are conceited. Their mistake in life is pretending, which, to put it directly, means they are fakes.

Romance: There is a lot of whining involved in the area of romance for the Pisces-Rooster. Partners should not tolerate such behavior. They need to put a stop to it the moment it starts. They need to emphasize the fact that deep inside this combination is a romantic. The Pisces-Rooster is frequently deep in the "nobody loves me" school of thought. No one cares and nothing works. Part of the problem is that this individual gets disheartened too easily. Beating in the heart of a Pisces-Rooster is an idealist who, for some reason, does not stick things out when there is the slightest sign of trouble. This is a consequence, as often as not, of their notion that they are wonderful. Because of this, no one should ever make trouble with them or be ill-mannered, short-tempered, or sarcastic.

Relationships: Not recommended combinations are Gemini-, Virgo-, and Sagittarius-Rabbits. Also Gemini-Roosters are poor selections. Gemini-Boars are out of the question. Terrific choices in the romance department are Taurus-, Cancer-, Scorpio-, and Capricorn-Buffalos. Additionally, Cancer-, Scorpio-, and Capricorn-Snakes are great. Also on a positive note are Taurus- and Capricorn-Dragons.

Family Life: There are enough issues rambling around in these individuals' psyches already, and adding children to the mix is not very appealing to them. In the event they do have children, the responsibility for rearing them will be largely left in the hands of their partner. This combination does not love kids, in general, and is impatient with them. The Pisces-Rooster is prone to being a neat freak. They are particularly so in their home. They will generally choose vivid colors for decorating. They fall into the category of people who want to make an impression with their home and their style. It is therefore important that their choices jump out at people, and their color scheme is used for this purpose. They love earthy and natural objects and probably live in a large country-type home. They also choose the natural and lean toward the traditional.

Livelihood: Pisces-Roosters are good at following orders and do what they are told. They are somewhat lacking in the creativity department and are more by-the-book-type people. They will probably not use much imagination in solving problems or carrying out tasks. As bosses, they are tough and lean toward wanting to do things totally right the first time. The Pisces-Rooster does have empathy regarding others' problems and is flexible in allowing them to carry things out their own way. Pisces-Roosters are filled with both adventure and ability. They want a job that is interesting and challenging. Problem solving is one of their aptitudes, and choosing a profession in that area is a good idea. They can get results and are competent workers. They are particular about doing things right the first time.

Famous Pisces-Roosters: Philip Roth, Lee Radziwill, Gordon Macrae, Michael Caine.

Pisces (Rabbit) Month Combined with Dog Year

"Faith" Neptune, Water, Mutable   **"Concerned"** Yin-Positive Metal

Characteristics: Tastelessness, Morality, Indecision, Awareness, Spirituality, Respectability, Rage, Intelligence, Heroism, Duty, Self-righteousness, Perception, Compatibility, Smugness, Creativity, Fearfulness, Lack of Will, Criticism, Unsociability, Uneasiness, Constancy, Uneasiness, Diffidence, Cynicism

The Pisces is the spiritual side of the Pisces-Dog. They are easily hurt, and often this makes them resentful. In the decision-making department they are wishy-washy and have difficulty making choices. The Dog side of this complex individual is constant. Dogs are loyal and faithful. The Pisces-Dog is a highly sensitive individual. They happen to possess a little more of this quality than the average Pisces. It is best to tip-toe around them and take care of them gently. There is a bit of a difference in the Pisces-Dog's sensitive side in that they do not like to be doubted or disagreed with. They are lacking somewhat in the area of willpower but have a dedicated mind. The Pisces side is accessible but porous. They are dedicated to understanding the world better, and that often comes from personal observation. Many Pisces-Dogs aspire to be heroes and accomplish great feats of daring. They do share some traits that are akin to the Pisces though. It is possible for Dogs to be self-doubting, and, in the Zodiac sense, they can be skeptical. They can even hold forth in a kind of sanctimonious manner. Put this in a pot and stir it up and the result is an anxious person who also is sardonic. They can also be seen as pompous. They can be difficult to be around because they are so crotchety. They love to criticize things and worry about it after they have. Making friends is a challenge for this individual for these very reasons. It takes a rather special person to hang out with the Pisces-Dog because they are always on the defensive. Dogs are devoted, loyal, and trustworthy. Dogs are dutiful and respectable. Pisces-Dogs are just totally bewildered by new people who enter their comfort zone.

Romance: This combination needs a lot of attention, especially in terms of reassurance. They do not like to attempt new projects and need to be urged rather strongly to do them. They need a lot of affection and care because they lack self-assurance. Good-natured tolerance is necessary for those who are married to Pisces-Dogs because they are so high strung and insecure. The Pisces-Dog enjoys the security that marriage provides. They are good and loving partners who tend to remain faithful. They also want their partner to be of high quality and make sure they choose nothing but the best.

Relationships: Not suggested as mates are Gemini-, Virgo-, and Sagittarius-Dragons. Also out are Rams and Roosters from the same signs. Topping the list of recommended romances are Taurus-, Libra-, and Capricorn-Tigers. Additional fine selections can be found among Scorpio- and Capricorn-Rabbits. The good news continues with Scorpio-Horses.

Family Life: This combination makes an excellent mom or dad. They care deeply about their children. Pisces-Dogs support and, indeed, push their children to do well at school. They also promote extracurricular activities. Personal environment is of little consequence to Pisces-Dogs. They are comfortable almost anyplace as long as things are reasonably agreeable. They are not much interested in looking at home-decorating magazines or worrying about whether the curtains match the rug. They do tend

to take good care of those things they have, but
lavishness.

Livelihood: This combination makes a good wor
able. They are prone to having a sharp tongue,
cruel. The Pisces-Dog is a multitalented individual.
people themselves, but they are also capable of taking othe
and expanding them into a new project. They can do this quickly bc
they are sharp intellectually. They are also good-humored. All of this
sounds terrific and is great. There is a fly in the ointment, however, and that
is the oversensitive nature of the Pisces-Dog. If they are criticized, rejected,
or offended, they collapse into a pile of jelly.

Famous Pisces-Dogs: Victor Hugo, Jack Kerouac, David Niven, Sandy
Duncan, Liza Minnelli.

Pisces (Rabbit) Month Combined with Boar Year

"Faith" Neptune, Water, Mutable   **"Cultivator"** Yin-Negative Water

Characteristics: Honesty, Boar-headedness, Indecision, Materialism,
Gourmandism, Spirituality, Awareness, Rage, Culture, Insincerity,
Smugness, Voluptuousness, Hesitation, Compatibility, Perception,
Creativity, Fearfulness, Lack of Will, Gallantry, Wrath,
Understanding, Scrupulousness, Diffidence, Credulity

Pisces-Boars respond to the sensations that they pick up from their environment and other people. These are individuals who live in the past and love
tradition. In this manner it can be said that they were born too late. The
Pisces-Boar is hypersensitive, so much so that it can be a rather large problem. They just seem to have deeper feelings than most other people. This
manifests itself, for starters, as making them very calm and kind individuals.
Somewhat surprisingly, however, is the fact that they are super motivated
to succeed. The problems they encounter in love are frequently the result
of living in the contemporary world, which is, to a degree, a world they do
not fit into and do not understand. They like to have old-fashioned furnishings and accessories, do old-fashioned activities, and be old-fashioned. They
are very fragile. Even if hurt, which can happen easily, they still refuse to
move on in time. They are quite good at making excuses in order to not do
things in a way they dislike or do not understand. They do this to save face.
Unfortunately, because they are sensitive they are probably laughed at or
teased, and this hurts. Doing things the quick, easy, and modern way annoys

ople. They have little interest in technology. This approach to life
s issues for Pisces-Boars necessitating a tougher road to the advance-
t they seek. Clearly an individual who is challenged technologically has
rather serious problem in the modern world. The load and the work that
they must do is heavier, but it is that way because of their own personal
choice. They are immovable in this area and very obstinate about it.

Romance: Pisces-Boars' love is such that they will take almost anything
that is given to them with a smile. Most of all, they cannot handle the idea
of their lover leaving them. There are, like any relationship, plusses and
minuses to having the Pisces-Boar for a mate. They can be hard workers.
What clearly comes to the forefront in a relationship with a Pisces-Boar
is his or her hypersensitivity. They cling to and grasp at those they love.
That is true in romance as well. They will do almost anything to hold on
to a partner. To be happy they need around the clock loving attention and
warmth. One would have to have superhuman powers to fill that need. If a
lover does not measure up, the Pisces-Boar feels deserted.

Relationships: Not recommended in the least are Virgo- or Sagittarius-
Snakes. In fact, Snakes in general are poor choices. Additional negative
picks are the Gemini-Horse or Sagittarius-Monkey; they are not for the
Pisces-Boar at all. Top romantic choices can be found with Rabbits and
Rams. Most of them are good, but the very best come from the Taurus,
Cancer, Scorpio, and Capricorn signs. An additional good selection is the
Cancer-Tiger.

Family Life: The home of the Pisces-Boar is extremely important. They
are not about to live in just any old place. There are constant home improvement projects going on and endless upgrades. As might be expected, Pisces-
Boar moms or dads are doting and nurturing with their children. They will
make absolutely sure that they have the very best and, most of all, that they
are happy. There is no doubt that the Pisces-Boar is a homebody. They love
to find select items for their abode, whether they be antique rugs, special
lamps, or new safety devices for additional security. This combination is
quite handy with projects pertaining to the home and is able to fix and make
all sorts of items. They lead a refined life.

Livelihood: Pisces-Boars make terrific executives, and they are very ethical
in all their dealings with others. Furthermore, they have superb negotiation skills because they have the ability to see every angle and possibility.

Because of their balanced combination they are also creative. They have excellent social skills and are a concerned and caring boss. The Pisces-Boar is a backbone of society and a model citizen. They can perform well in almost any profession. The only thing to be cautious of is that their profession should be selected early, and they need to stay with it. The reason for this is security.

Famous Pisces-Boars: Andrew Jackson, Ed McMahon, Andre Coureges.

CHINESE ANIMALS 2000–2099

Year	Sign	Year Begins	Year Ends	Year	Sign	Year Begins	Year Ends
2000	Dragon	02/05/2000	01/23/2001	2050	Horse	01/23/2050	02/10/2051
2001	Snake	01/24/2001	02/11/2002	2051	Ram	02/11/2051	01/31/2052
2002	Horse	02/12/2002	01/31/2003	2052	Monkey	02/01/2052	02/18/2053
2003	Ram	02/01/2003	01/21/2004	2053	Rooster	02/19/2053	02/07/2054
2004	Monkey	01/22/2004	02/08/2005	2054	Dog	02/08/2054	01/27/2055
2005	Rooster	02/09/2005	01/28/2006	2055	Boar	01/28/2055	02/14/2056
2006	Dog	01/29/2006	02/17/2007	2056	Rat	02/15/2056	02/03/2057
2007	Boar	02/18/2007	02/06/2008	2057	Buffalo	02/04/2057	01/23/2058
2008	Rat	02/07/2008	01/25/2009	2058	Tiger	01/24/2058	02/11/2059
2009	Buffalo	01/26/2009	02/13/2010	2059	Rabbit	02/12/2059	02/01/2060
2010	Tiger	02/14/2010	02/02/2011	2060	Dragon	02/02/2060	01/20/2061
2011	Rabbit	02/03/2011	01/22/2012	2061	Snake	01/21/2061	02/08/2062
2012	Dragon	01/23/2012	02/09/2013	2062	Horse	02/09/2062	01/28/2063
2013	Snake	02/10/2013	01/30/2014	2063	Ram	01/29/2063	02/16/2064
2014	Horse	01/31/2014	02/18/2015	2064	Monkey	02/17/2064	02/04/2065
2015	Ram	02/19/2015	02/07/2016	2065	Rooster	02/05/2065	01/25/2066
2016	Monkey	02/08/2016	01/27/2017	2066	Dog	01/26/2066	02/13/2067
2017	Rooster	01/28/2017	02/18/2018	2067	Boar	02/14/2067	02/02/2068
2018	Dog	02/19/2018	02/04/2019	2068	Rat	02/03/2068	01/22/2069
2019	Boar	02/05/2019	01/24/2020	2069	Buffalo	01/23/2069	02/10/2070
2020	Rat	01/25/2020	02/11/2021	2070	Tiger	02/11/2070	01/30/2071
2021	Buffalo	02/12/2021	01/31/2022	2071	Rabbit	01/31/2071	02/18/2072
2022	Tiger	02/01/2022	01/21/2023	2072	Dragon	02/19/2072	02/06/2073
2023	Rabbit	01/22/2023	02/09/2024	2073	Snake	02/07/2073	01/26/2074
2024	Dragon	02/10/2024	01/28/2025	2074	Horse	01/27/2074	02/14/2075
2025	Snake	01/29/2025	02/16/2026	2075	Ram	02/15/2075	02/04/2076
2026	Horse	02/17/2026	02/05/2027	2076	Monkey	02/05/2076	01/23/2077
2027	Ram	02/06/2027	01/25/2028	2077	Rooster	01/24/2077	02/11/2078

Year	Sign	Year Begins	Year Ends	Year	Sign	Year Begins	Year Ends
2028	Monkey	01/26/2028	02/12/2029	2078	Dog	02/12/2078	02/01/2079
2029	Rooster	02/13/2029	02/02/2030	2079	Boar	02/02/2079	01/21/2080
2030	Dog	02/03/2030	01/22/2031	2080	Rat	01/22/2080	02/08/2081
2031	Boar	01/23/2031	02/10/2032	2081	Buffalo	02/09/2081	01/28/2082
2032	Rat	02/11/2032	01/30/2033	2082	Tiger	01/29/2082	02/16/2083
2033	Buffalo	01/31/2033	02/18/2034	2083	Rabbit	02/17/2083	02/15/2084
2034	Tiger	02/19/2034	02/07/2035	2084	Dragon	02/16/2084	01/25/2085
2035	Rabbit	02/08/2035	01/27/2036	2085	Snake	01/26/2085	02/13/2086
2036	Dragon	01/28/2036	02/14/2037	2086	Horse	02/14/2086	02/02/2087
2037	Snake	02/15/2037	02/03/2038	2087	Ram	02/03/2087	01/23/2088
2038	Horse	02/04/2038	01/23/2039	2088	Monkey	01/24/2088	02/09/2089
2039	Ram	01/24/2039	02/11/2040	2089	Rooster	02/10/2089	01/29/2090
2040	Monkey	02/12/2040	01/31/2041	2090	Dog	01/30/2090	02/17/2091
2041	Rooster	02/01/2041	01/21/2042	2091	Boar	02/18/2091	02/06/2092
2042	Dog	01/22/2042	02/09/2043	2092	Rat	02/07/2092	01/26/2093
2043	Boar	02/10/2043	01/29/2044	2093	Buffalo	01/27/2093	02/14/2094
2044	Rat	01/30/2044	02/16/2045	2094	Tiger	02/15/2094	02/04/2095
2045	Buffalo	02/17/2045	02/05/2046	2095	Rabbit	02/05/2095	01/24/2096
2046	Tiger	02/06/2046	01/25/2047	2096	Dragon	01/25/2096	02/11/2097
2047	Rabbit	01/26/2047	02/13/2048	2097	Snake	02/12/2097	01/31/2098
2048	Dragon	02/14/2048	02/01/2049	2098	Horse	02/01/2098	01/20/2099
2049	Snake	02/02/2049	01/22/2050	2099	Ram	01/21/2099	02/08/2100

1900–1999

Year	Sign	Year Begins	Year Ends	Year	Sign	Year Begins	Year Ends
1900	Rat	01/31/1900	02/18/1901	1950	Tiger	02/17/1950	02/05/1951
1901	Buffalo	02/19/1901	02/07/1902	1951	Rabbit	02/06/1951	01/26/1952
1902	Tiger	02/08/1902	01/28/1903	1952	Dragon	01/27/1952	02/13/1953
1903	Rabbit	01/29/1903	02/15/1904	1953	Snake	02/14/1953	02/02/1954
1904	Dragon	02/16/1904	02/03/1905	1954	Horse	02/03/1954	01/23/1955
1905	Snake	02/04/1905	01/24/1906	1955	Ram	01/24/1955	02/11/1956
1906	Horse	01/25/1906	02/12/1907	1956	Monkey	02/12/1956	01/30/1957
1907	Ram	02/13/1907	02/01/1908	1957	Rooster	01/31/1957	02/17/1958
1908	Monkey	02/02/1908	01/21/1909	1958	Dog	02/18/1958	02/07/1959
1909	Rooster	01/22/1909	02/09/1910	1959	Boar	02/08/1959	01/27/1960
1910	Dog	02/10/1910	01/29/1911	1960	Rat	01/28/1960	02/14/1961
1911	Boar	01/30/1911	02/17/1912	1961	Buffalo	02/15/1961	02/04/1962
1912	Rat	02/18/1912	02/05/1913	1962	Tiger	02/05/1962	01/24/1963
1913	Buffalo	02/06/1913	01/25/1914	1963	Rabbit	01/25/1963	02/12/1964
1914	Tiger	01/26/1914	02/13/1915	1964	Dragon	02/13/1964	02/01/1965

Year	Sign	Year Begins	Year Ends	Year	Sign	Year Begins	Year Ends
1915	Rabbit	02/14/1915	02/02/1916	1965	Snake	02/02/1965	01/20/1966
1916	Dragon	02/03/1916	01/22/1917	1966	Horse	01/21/1966	02/08/1967
1917	Snake	01/23/1917	02/10/1918	1967	Ram	02/09/1967	01/29/1968
1918	Horse	02/11/1918	01/31/1919	1968	Monkey	01/30/1968	02/16/1969
1919	Ram	02/01/1919	02/19/1920	1969	Rooster	02/17/1969	02/05/1970
1920	Monkey	02/20/1920	02/07/1921	1970	Dog	02/06/1970	01/26/1971
1921	Rooster	02/08/1921	01/27/1922	1971	Boar	01/27/1971	02/14/1972
1922	Dog	01/28/1922	02/15/1923	1972	Rat	02/15/1972	02/02/1973
1923	Boar	02/16/1923	02/04/1924	1973	Buffalo	02/03/1973	01/22/1974
1924	Rat	02/05/1924	01/23/1925	1974	Tiger	01/23/1974	02/10/1975
1925	Buffalo	01/24/1925	02/12/1926	1975	Rabbit	02/11/1975	01/30/1976
1926	Tiger	02/13/1926	02/01/1927	1976	Dragon	01/31/1976	02/17/1977
1927	Rabbit	02/02/1927	01/22/1928	1977	Snake	02/18/1977	02/06/1978
1928	Dragon	01/23/1928	02/09/1929	1978	Horse	02/07/1978	01/27/1979
1929	Snake	02/10/1929	01/29/1930	1979	Ram	01/28/1979	02/15/1980
1930	Horse	01/30/1930	02/16/1931	1980	Monkey	02/16/1980	02/04/1981
1931	Ram	02/17/1931	02/05/1932	1981	Rooster	02/05/1981	01/24/1982
1932	Monkey	02/06/1932	01/25/1933	1982	Dog	01/25/1982	02/12/1983
1933	Rooster	01/26/1933	02/13/1934	1983	Boar	02/13/1983	02/01/1984
1934	Dog	02/14/1934	02/03/1935	1984	Rat	02/02/1984	02/19/1985
1935	Boar	02/04/1935	01/23/1936	1985	Buffalo	02/20/1985	02/08/1986
1936	Rat	01/24/1936	02/10/1937	1986	Tiger	02/09/1986	01/28/1987
1937	Buffalo	02/11/1937	01/30/1938	1987	Rabbit	01/29/1987	02/16/1988
1938	Tiger	01/31/1938	02/18/1939	1988	Dragon	02/17/1988	02/05/1989
1939	Rabbit	02/19/1939	02/07/1940	1989	Snake	02/06/1989	01/26/1990
1940	Dragon	02/08/1940	01/26/1941	1990	Horse	01/27/1990	02/14/1991
1941	Snake	01/27/1941	02/14/1942	1991	Ram	02/15/1991	02/03/1992
1942	Horse	02/15/1942	02/04/1943	1992	Monkey	02/04/1992	01/22/1993
1943	Ram	02/05/1943	01/24/1944	1993	Rooster	01/23/1993	02/09/1994
1944	Monkey	01/25/1944	02/12/1945	1994	Dog	02/10/1994	01/30/1995
1945	Rooster	02/13/1945	02/01/1946	1995	Boar	01/31/1995	02/18/1996
1946	Dog	02/02/1946	01/21/1947	1996	Rat	02/19/1996	02/06/1997
1947	Boar	01/22/1947	02/09/1948	1997	Buffalo	02/07/1997	01/27/1998
1948	Rat	02/10/1948	01/28/1949	1998	Tiger	01/28/1998	02/15/1999
1949	Buffalo	01/29/1949	02/16/1950	1999	Rabbit	02/16/1999	02/04/2000

1800–1899

Year	Sign	Year Begins	Year Ends	Year	Sign	Year Begins	Year Ends
1800	Monkey	01/25/1800	02/12/1801	1850	Dog	02/12/1850	01/31/1851
1801	Rooster	02/13/1801	020/2/1802	1851	Boar	02/01/1851	02/19/1852

1802	Dog	02/03/1802	01/22/1803	1852	Rat	02/20/1852	02/07/1853
1803	Boar	01/23/1803	02/10/1804	1853	Buffalo	02/08/1853	01/28/1854
1804	Rat	02/11/1804	01/30/1805	1854	Tiger	01/29/1854	01/16/1855
1805	Buffalo	01/31/1805	02/17/1806	1855	Rabbit	01/17/1855	02/05/1856
1806	Tiger	02/18/1806	02/06/1807	1856	Dragon	02/06/1856	01/25/1857
1807	Rabbit	02/07/1807	01/27/1808	1857	Snake	01/26/1857	02/13/1858
1808	Dragon	01/28/1808	02/13/1809	1858	Horse	01/14/1858	02/02/1859
1809	Snake	02/14/1809	02/03/1810	1859	Ram	02/03/1859	01/22/1860
1810	Horse	02/04/1810	01/24/1811	1860	Monkey	01/23/1860	02/09/1861
1811	Ram	01/25/1811	02/12/1812	1861	Rooster	02/10/1861	01/29/1862
1812	Monkey	02/13/1812	01/31/1813	1862	Dog	01/30/1862	02/17/1863
1813	Rooster	02/01/1813	01/20/1814	1863	Boar	02/18/1863	02/07/1864
1814	Dog	01/21/1814	02/08/1815	1864	Rat	02/08/1864	01/26/1865
1815	Boar	02/09/1815	01/28/1816	1865	Buffalo	01/27/1865	02/14/1866
1816	Rat	01/29/1816	02/15/1817	1866	Tiger	02/15/1866	02/04/1867
1817	Buffalo	02/16/1817	02/04/1818	1867	Rabbit	02/05/1867	01/24/1868
1818	Tiger	02/05/1818	01/25/1819	1868	Dragon	01/25/1868	02/10/1869
1819	Rabbit	01/26/1819	02/13/1820	1869	Snake	02/11/1869	01/30/1870
1820	Dragon	02/14/1820	02/02/1821	1870	Horse	01/31/1870	02/18/1871
1821	Snake	02/03/1821	01/22/1822	1871	Ram	02/19/1871	02/08/1872
1822	Horse	01/23/1822	02/10/1823	1872	Monkey	02/09/1872	01/28/1873
1823	Ram	02/11/1823	01/30/1824	1873	Rooster	01/29/1873	02/16/1874
1824	Monkey	01/31/1824	02/17/1825	1874	Dog	02/17/1874	02/05/1875
1825	Rooster	02/18/1825	02/06/1826	1875	Boar	02/06/1875	01/25/1876
1826	Dog	02/07/1826	01/26/1827	1876	Rat	01/26/1876	02/12/1877
1827	Boar	01/27/1827	02/14/1828	1877	Buffalo	02/13/1877	01/21/1879
1828	Rat	02/15/1828	02/03/1829	1878	Tiger	02/02/1878	02/01/1878
1829	Buffalo	02/04/1829	01/24/1830	1879	Rabbit	01/22/1879	02/09/1880
1830	Tiger	01/25/1830	02/12/1831	1880	Dragon	02/10/1880	01/29/1881
1831	Rabbit	02/13/1831	02/01/1832	1881	Snake	01/30/1881	02/17/1882
1832	Dragon	02/02/1832	02/19/1833	1882	Horse	02/18/1882	02/07/1883
1833	Snake	02/20/1833	02/08/1834	1883	Ram	02/08/1883	01/27/1884
1834	Horse	02/09/1834	01/28/1835	1884	Monkey	01/28/1884	02/14/1885
1835	Ram	01/29/1835	02/16/1836	1885	Rooster	02/15/1885	02/03/1886
1836	Monkey	02/17/1836	02/04/1837	1886	Dog	02/04/1886	01/23/1887
1837	Rooster	02/05/1837	01/25/1838	1887	Boar	01/24/1887	02/11/1888
1838	Dog	01/26/1838	02/13/1839	1888	Rat	02/12/1888	01/30/1889
1839	Boar	02/14/1839	02/02/1840	1889	Buffalo	01/31/1889	01/20/1890
1840	Rat	02/03/1840	01/22/1841	1890	Tiger	01/21/1890	02/08/1891
1841	Buffalo	01/23/1841	02/09/1842	1891	Rabbit	02/09/1891	01/29/1892

1842	Tiger	02/10/1842	01/29/1843	1892	Dragon	01/30/1892	02/16/1893
1843	Rabbit	01/30/1843	02/17/1844	1893	Snake	02/17/1893	02/05/1894
1844	Dragon	02/18/1844	02/06/1845	1894	Horse	02/06/1894	01/25/1895
1845	Snake	02/07/1845	01/26/1846	1895	Ram	01/26/1895	02/12/1896
1846	Horse	01/27/1846	02/14/1847	1896	Monkey	02/13/1896	02/01/1897
1847	Ram	02/15/1847	02/04/1848	1897	Rooster	02/02/1897	01/21/1898
1848	Monkey	02/05/1948	01/23/1849	1898	Dog	01/22/1898	02/09/1899
1849	Rooster	01/24/1849	02/11/1850	1899	Boar	02/10/1899	01/30/1900

1700–1799

Year	Sign	Year Begins	Year Ends	Year	Sign	Year Begins	Year Ends
1700	Dragon	02/19/1700	02/07/1701	1750	Horse	02/07/1750	01/26/1751
1701	Snake	02/08/1701	01/27/1702	1751	Ram	01/27/1751	02/14/1752
1702	Horse	01/28/1702	02/15/1703	1752	Monkey	02/15/1752	02/02/1753
1703	Ram	02/16/1703	02/04/1704	1753	Rooster	02/03/1753	01/22/1754
1704	Monkey	02/05/1704	01/24/1705	1754	Dog	01/23/1754	02/10/1755
1705	Rooster	01/25/1705	02/12/1706	1755	Boar	02/11/1755	01/30/1756
1706	Dog	02/13/1706	02/02/1707	1756	Rat	01/31/1756	02/17/1757
1707	Boar	02/03/1707	01/22/1708	1757	Buffalo	02/18/1757	02/07/1758
1708	Rat	01/23/1708	02/09/1709	1758	Tiger	02/08/1758	01/28/1759
1709	Buffalo	02/10/1709	01/29/1710	1759	Rabbit	01/29/1759	02/16/1760
1710	Tiger	01/30/1710	02/16/1711	1760	Dragon	02/17/1760	02/04/1761
1711	Rabbit	02/17/1711	02/06/1712	1761	Snake	02/05/1761	01/24/1762
1712	Dragon	02/07/1712	01/25/1713	1762	Horse	01/25/1762	02/12/1763
1713	Snake	01/26/1713	02/13/1714	1763	Ram	02/13/1763	02/01/1764
1714	Horse	02/14/1714	02/03/1715	1764	Monkey	02/02/1764	01/20/1765
1715	Ram	02/04/1715	01/23/1716	1765	Rooster	01/21/1765	02/08/1766
1716	Monkey	01/24/1716	02/10/1717	1766	Dog	02/09/1766	01/29/1767
1717	Rooster	02/11/1717	01/30/1718	1767	Boar	01/30/1767	02/17/1768
1718	Dog	01/31/1718	02/18/1719	1768	Rat	02/18/1768	02/06/1769
1719	Boar	02/19/1719	02/07/1720	1769	Buffalo	02/07/1769	01/26/1770
1720	Rat	02/08/1720	01/27/1721	1770	Tiger	01/27/1770	02/14/1771
1721	Buffalo	01/28/1721	02/15/1722	1771	Rabbit	02/15/1771	02/03/1772
1722	Tiger	02/16/1722	02/04/1723	1772	Dragon	02/04/1772	01/22/1773
1723	Rabbit	02/05/1723	01/25/1724	1773	Snake	01/23/1773	02/10/1774
1724	Dragon	01/26/1724	02/12/1725	1774	Horse	02/11/1774	01/30/1775
1725	Snake	02/13/1725	02/01/1726	1775	Ram	01/31/1775	02/18/1776
1726	Horse	02/02/1726	01/21/1727	1776	Monkey	02/19/1776	02/07/1777
1727	Ram	01/22/1727	02/09/1728	1777	Rooster	02/08/1777	01/27/1778
1728	Monkey	02/10/1728	01/28/1729	1778	Dog	01/28/1778	02/15/1779

1729	Rooster	01/29/1729	02/16/1730	1779	Boar	02/16/1779	02/04/1780
1730	Dog	02/17/1730	02/06/1731	1780	Rat	02/05/1780	01/23/1781
1731	Boar	02/07/1731	01/26/1732	1781	Buffalo	01/24/1781	02/11/1782
1732	Rat	01/27/1732	02/13/1733	1782	Tiger	02/12/1782	02/01/1783
1733	Buffalo	02/14/1733	02/03/1734	1783	Rabbit	02/02/1783	01/21/1784
1734	Tiger	02/04/1734	01/23/1735	1784	Dragon	01/22/1784	02/08/1785
1735	Rabbit	01/24/1735	02/11/1736	1785	Snake	02/09/1785	01/29/1786
1736	Dragon	02/12/1736	01/30/1737	1786	Horse	01/30/1786	02/17/1787
1737	Snake	01/31/1737	02/18/1738	1787	Ram	02/18/1787	02/06/1788
1738	Horse	02/19/1738	02/07/1739	1788	Monkey	02/07/1788	01/25/1789
1739	Ram	02/08/1739	01/29/1740	1789	Rooster	01/26/1789	02/13/1790
1740	Monkey	01/30/1740	02/15/1741	1790	Dog	02/14/1790	02/02/1791
1741	Rooster	02/16/1741	02/04/1742	1791	Boar	02/03/1791	01/23/1792
1742	Dog	02/05/1742	01/25/1743	1792	Rat	01/24/1792	02/10/1793
1743	Boar	01/26/1743	02/12/1744	1793	Buffalo	02/11/1793	01/30/1794
1744	Rat	02/13/1744	01/31/1745	1794	Tiger	01/31/1794	01/20/1795
1745	Buffalo	02/01/1745	01/21/1746	1795	Rabbit	01/21/1795	02/08/1796
1746	Tiger	01/22/1746	02/08/1747	1796	Dragon	02/09/1796	01/27/1797
1747	Rabbit	02/09/1747	01/29/1748	1797	Snake	01/28/1797	02/15/1798
1748	Dragon	01/30/1748	02/16/1749	1798	Horse	02/16/1798	02/04/1799
1749	Snake	02/17/1749	02/06/1750	1799	Ram	02/05/1799	01/24/1800

Finding Your Birth Card

THE CONCEPT OF THE BIRTH CARD

In this chapter you will learn how to look up anyone's Birth card and be able to read important and useful information about them, revealing much about their personality and karmic destiny. Our karmic destiny is a path in life that we will take by virtue of choices we made prior to coming in to this life. This phase of your persona will give you unique insight into your personal relationships, particularly your intimate relationships. You will learn even more about yourself as you study the cards of the people with whom you have been intimately involved. After all, our relationships are the clearest mirrors of ourselves. It is like learning a new language, but one that comes fairly easily once you get into it.

In this system, each day of the year is assigned one of the fifty-two cards in the deck. Actually, there are fifty-three, because December 31 belongs to the Joker. For the rest of the birthdays, one card rules each day. It is an uneven distribution. Look at the Birth card Chart at the end of this chapter to quickly find your Birth card. You will also see that there does not seem to be any definable system for determining which card falls upon each day. For example, there are roughly twice as many Diamond and Club birthdays as there are Hearts and Spades. Also, some cards such as the K♠ and A♥ have only one birthday, while others such as the K♣ and A♦ have twelve. In reality there is a very particular system and reasoning behind which cards fall on each day, which was put together centuries ago for our use today. The Birth card can also be called the Sun card, much like our Sun Sign in astrology. It is the card that ruled our planet on the day we were born. People born under a certain card's rulership will all share some distinguishing traits, though there is some variety in the ways these traits may be expressed. We feel that we all choose the day we will be born, which provides the pattern for our lessons to learn in this life. The Birth card is the strongest and most important symbol of who we are in this lifetime. If you studied only people's Birth cards you would have a wealth of information. The Birth card is our soul's essence. It is the card with which we most strongly identify ourselves. All Queens, for example, see themselves as mothers of one sort or another. They will be motherly, nurturing people throughout their entire lives. It is part of their innermost identity.

As you read about your Birth card, see if you can recognize parts of yourself. Each card has a high and low expression. Even though you may be choosing to manifest the highest qualities of your Birth card, you still have the lowest qualities within you. We are the sum total of our Birth card, not just one side of it. It is our choice as to which side of it to present to the world. Later, you may discover that you have had significant relationships with people who are your mirror cardwise. In these cases the partners often manifest opposite qualities of the same card expression. For now, just be open to what may be represented about you in the Birth card description, and reserve judgment until you have had time to see the entire picture. The Birth card descriptions are listed in suit decks starting with the Diamonds, Spades, Hearts, and Clubs from the King through the Ace (One). Each Birth card also has an article or profile that more vividly illustrates the natures of that Birth card.

Each card governs each day of the year, which is very particular and specific. It uses what is known as True Solar Time to determine your time and day of birth. Many people are born on what we call a "cusp date" in which they could be one of two cards. Each month of the year has a couple of days, usually between two and four, where the sun changes from one sign to the next. Because of leap year and other considerations, this can occur within a three- to four-day range each year. If you were born on one of these cusp days you will probably need to have a professional astrological chart in order to determine exactly which sign you are. This information is very important, and you will want to be accurate about this if at all possible.

GENERAL BIRTH CARD PATTERNS

Each person has a specific Birth card identified by rank and suit, such as Nine of Diamonds; however, there are similarities and connections between the cards on a broader scale. This section discusses the cards by rank; that is, King, Queen, Jack, Tens, and so on, to give you a basic idea of the patterns held by each category of cards. Your specific Birth card can be found in the section following this one.

Kings

As the masculine pinnacle of power and leadership, the King has the wisdom of experience. He is the final card in the deck and is thus representative of development's final stage. He is therefore the paradigm of a powerful leader. The temptations of power are the main motive for this potential abuse. (See also the Eights because they share power.) Kings have an awareness of the right thing to do, but unfortunately they do not always carry it out. Such Kings are a disgrace to their symbol. Unfortunately, there will be Kings who are immoral but possess a strong character. On a positive note, the King can learn to not abuse his power as it evolves. Kings are prideful and have an aptitude for leadership. Even those who do not have this characteristic will show some pridefulness and distaste for being told what to do. They often view themselves as special and distinct from others. Some Kings believe they have no power. Many Kings are not aware of their power and the way they are using it. However, a close look shows their stubborn character and persistence. Respect or fear is a common consequence for Kings, but many only need to be aware they are Kings and destined to lead. This is akin to them encountering themselves as Kings. The King of Hearts is very excellent with interpersonal relationships, and the King of Clubs possesses great mental powers. The ninth suit defines a King's foremost power. Their powers can be used in numerous endeavors as well as professions. They have a unique ability to know truths and lies. Materialism often means unhappiness though. The King of Spades has internal strength along with wisdom. Others cannot persuade them because they know the truth. The King of Diamonds is the strong, often amoral, business operator. If it's a takeover they want, they are capable. Kings are not just males. There are female Kings who have a natural ability to lead but possess a woman's body. They are decisive and aggressive. Some well-known female Kings are Jacqueline Kennedy Onassis, Faye Dunaway, Queen Elizabeth II, Janet Jackson, and Bridget Fonda. All are strong leaders. Female Kings must balance the female and male parts pertaining to their personal relationships. Being a King is not easy because of the great responsibility and mastering this can take a lifetime. Being King alone is such a huge responsibility that many do not attain greatness. Some are filled with fear and demote themselves or even abdicate. Not many Kings of Spades, for example, are prepared to reign. They are the King of Kings and consequently are the most powerful. However, they carry the heaviest burden. Most Kings of Spades feel more comfortable as a Jack or a Queen. Most will fail to achieve their full potential as the most powerful card.

Queens

Queens are aware of their power and authority. They are second in command and are very able to rule the kingdom, but in a different fashion from the King. In some cases they are stronger than the King. Queens are more compassionate and helpful. They are wise from the experience in previous lives. Consequently, in some areas, Queens excel. In terms of love karma, Queens often have difficulty, and this is frequently true with the Queen of Diamonds and Queen of Clubs. They sometimes have difficulty in marriage or other personal relationships. Queens want to transcend themselves and help others. Queens fulfill a motherly function and are excellent at helping and nurturing people. They give food and security to assist people. Both male and female Queens are famous for loving children, whether or not they have any themselves. Sometimes they hold on too much to loved ones and do not let them go and develop. One of their biggest challenges is to leave behind the need to nurture. Sometimes they feel like they have no purpose in life, and this is one of their biggest challenges to overcome. Queens are helpful in significant ways. They make excellent doctors, teachers, and counselors. They are especially good at rallying people for a good cause. They radiate love to all. Queens can be victims of those who manipulate them if they have no children. In addition, if childless there can be relationship problems. Numerologically, the Queen is number 12, which becomes Threes and produces the initial cards for the Queen. In addition to Threes, the Queens of Diamonds and Clubs are also in Mars. Unfortunately, it is possible that insecurity and indecision in personal relationships will be prompted by three-energy, particularly in regard to the Queen of Clubs and Queen of Diamonds. All Queens have a creative urge stemming from Threes. Queen of Spades and Queen of Hearts are not as likely to produce tension because they have even-numbered Karma. Insecurity can result in associations and decisions. As the most powerful female card, males and females both display feminine qualities. Queens are romantic and fun loving, but this can produce uncertainty. The Queen of Clubs is an organized businessperson who is smart, temperamental, and usually very active. The Queen of Hearts is akin to Aphrodite, the famous goddess of love and pleasure. She is a man's dream woman.

Jacks

Some people, it seems, do not want to grow up—these are the Jacks. There are several perspectives of the Jack, the royal family's youngest member, and all are meaningful. It is significant, clearly, that someday he will be the King. By their very nature, Princes are young, romantic, creative, humorous, and even charming. As the Prince he does not have the responsibility and power that results from being King. Furthermore, he does not want to accept responsibility. What they want is a life of fun and play. There is another aspect to consider: Jacks want to be treated respectfully and with admiration. Someday, perhaps, they will themselves become Kings. The life of a Jack is one of growing from being young to being responsible. The Jack can also be a counselor to the King. The problem here is that he places his own interests first. Though sitting in the royal court, he nevertheless assumes no actual responsibility for what happens. In general he is a bit dishonest. However, he can be creative and clever at keeping his affairs balanced and not getting caught. Bribery is possible if you desire actions influencing the King. He is supreme at deception, he is sneaky, and he is not trustworthy. These essentially are the two perceptions of Jacks. There is a staggering amount of creativity, but also there is the temptation to abuse that creative energy in hedonism and selfishness. Jacks can also simply avoid situations for which they have a distaste. As Jacks, sometimes they get in trouble. Overall, the Jack is spiritual and directs energy in a saintly manner rather than being manipulative. In actual fact though, many of these people give in to the misuse of their creative forces. On the other hand, Jacks are the initiates of the deck. This normally means ascending to a higher plane. An implication of a new beginning results from past ways. Self-realization helps Jacks release their higher qualities. Many overcome their materialism and become more spiritual and less attached to worldly things. This enables them to become facilitators of spiritual love. Jacks have an innate spiritual component representing higher qualities. They are a paradigm of the spiritual life. A large number of Jacks attain this, but others are not capable. The pinnacle representation of the Jack is a person who has attained true self-expression; this is a prerequisite for releasing lower qualities. Often times these are powerful and difficult to let go. A constant challenge is to let go of their tremendous gifts and sink so low that they may, for example, become criminals. They are also particularly adept at lying and can make others believe almost anything. All in all, the life of a Jack is challenging. The secret is for them to look inside themselves rather than using their intelligence and devious minds to get by. The initiation that all Jacks represent is, therefore, one of turning within.

Tens

You have an indication of the nature of Tens by noticing that they show a One first. This makes them related to Aces, and they share similar qualities with them. This is significant because, like the Aces, Tens have a lot of motivation. They are ambitious. Furthermore, as with Aces, Tens can be very selfish and egotistical. For further evidence note that all Tens have at least one Ace in a significant place in their Life Spread. Aces cause the Tens to be soul searchers for their entire lives. They turn inward to find reasons and answers for the main questions in life. The Ten may not pay much attention to things around them. To some, Tens might appear selfish because they look at their own emotions, concepts, needs, and wants. Tens know they are selfish sometimes, and thus they must come to terms with this. It is the case that they are truly and deeply selfish, but is selfishness immoral? It is possible that selfishness can be good. Perhaps they can balance their needs and the needs of other people. These notions must be answered individually. Let us look at the fact that there is a Zero after the One. What does it represent? The Ten has double Fives just like the Eight has double Fours. Five is the experience number and therefore the Ten person has a large amount of experience they can use to be successful and happy. Zero indicates the experience of completing an important evolutionary cycle; one that runs across the Ace right through the Nine and finally the Ten. Here a new cycle begins, but in the new cycle there will be all of the knowledge that was attained in the earlier cycle. This explains why Tens have such an aptitude for a successful life. There is always a possibility of success for Tens if that is what they want. Their suit will tell us the main area of their wisdom and success in this lifetime. The Ten of Hearts has excellent interpersonal relationship skills. The Ten of Clubs is knowledgeable and wants to share it. The Ten of Diamonds is great with businesses of any size. The Ten of Spades is motivated and can accomplish anything they set their minds to. Tens are hard workers, and unlike the Aces they do not have much to learn to be successful. They do enjoy learning and exploring new ideas but already have a great deal of experience. This is especially true of things they want to apply to their jobs. The Zero portion of the Ten is related to the Joker. It is interesting to note that the Joker has no personal identity and this makes it unique in the deck. A Joker's identity is on loan from other cards and can morph into whatever card it wants to for any period of time. The Ten person is capable of this transformation to a degree. For example, their persona has the One through the Nine already. They are perfectly capable of using these numbers at any time. Being obsessive is the negative aspect of being a Ten if that is something about their suit.

Nines

The nature of the universe is cyclical. This applies to all things including the inanimate. Things come into existence and then they pass on. Cycles apply not just to biology but also to relationships, jobs, things, ideas, and more. The beginning point is the Ace. The ending is the Nine. The flow here is seen as a stage, and the Nine stage is the ending. We might think of it as similar to going through school, grade by grade, with the final grade being Nine. That would be graduation and actually a time of celebration. Attitude, of course, is everything. It determines how we will experience and view what happens. Nines are akin to a person who has a lifetime of experience. The Nine symbolizes the ending of a cycle in the one's evolution. A lot was learned and acquired, but it must fade away to make ready for a new cycle. Good-byes are commonplace for a Nine. In addition, things, lifestyles, ideas, and communication are at their ending. They are no longer useful. How one reacts to this is personal and individual. The Eight precedes the Nine and represents a point of being satiated. It is like the harvest season and, alas, after that there is a time of decay and then death, as shown in the

Nine. The bounty of the harvest has been taken and nothing remains in the field. The suit the Nine is in reveals the place where fulfillment is attained. The Nine of Hearts completes a relationship and love for humanity. There is a letting go with the Nine of Clubs, which involves belief systems and worldviews as well as communication. The Nine of Diamonds will find that things and people they value will be taken away or at least need to be released. The most difficult task is probably done by the Nine of Spades, for they must let go of their ego and give in to the will of God. The Nine of Spades in many ways has the strongest burden. This means ceasing power struggles not just with people but, for example, lifestyle, occupation, and health. Because it is a lifetime of the harvest's bounty, the Nine person gives things away. Furthermore, fulfillment results from giving of themselves. Some actually become saviors of humanity itself, spiritual leaders as well as teachers. Such immense metaphysical undertakings are sometimes the result of big personal disappointments. Nines are, in a way, the opposite of Aces. While Aces actually need to put themselves first and be ego centered, the Nine cannot. Selfish behavior only results in pain and misery for the Nine. It goes against the fundamental nature of their being. Nine is one of the two spiritual numbers, along with the Seven. Fulfillment for Nines is the consequence of following a spiritual path. Many times their path is not what is taught by society. Consequently, the early life of a Nine might be confusing. Following tradition can mean frequent failures. Nines who are aware understand quickly. They come to know that they are different.

Eights

Because the Four symbolizes security, a good supply, and is a cornerstone, the Eight constitutes even more than this because it is double Fours. It has progressed through the challenges faced by the Seven. It is a multiplication of energy because it is Four multiplied by two. This is power that entails the necessary tools to bring about change in any direction. All that is needed is a focus of energy. Eight is the harvest. It is fullness. Eights are shining paradigm cases of production and creation. Eights are producers because they are hard workers. They enjoy seeing the results of power but, alas, like any of the other positives of the Birth card, power can be used for good or it can be twisted. There is a lifetime of facing this challenge. Eights face this choice for their entire life. It is a focal point that many do not perceive. Power emanates not from us but from the highest power. That is God the creator of the universe. Clearly power can be used for good like helping others. It can bring about goodwill and assistance to others. Unfortunately, the flip side of this is addiction to escapism from lack of inner strength and insecurity. If power flows from the creator, we are also given a share of that power. This can lead some to believe they have a right from above to that power. We see this often by some in positions of power. Rather than being grateful for their gift, they distort things. They can believe they are incapable of error and have a right to power. Their view of themselves is that they are some sort of demigod and even immortal. This situation is highly dangerous. It is like giving a child a loaded weapon. Eights who do not recognize that they are God's vessels will make the errors in conjunction with the misuse of power. There is a connection to astrology here. Natal charts of the majority of Eights contain a strong element of Scorpio. They also have Pluto or the Eighth House energy. The action of Eights is similar to Scorpios, without regard to their sun sign. The overall ruler of this element is Pluto. As the planet of death and destruction, the Pluto influence is profoundly significant to the Eights. What comes into play with Pluto and Scorpio is self-transformation. With a strong Pluto or Scorpio influence in a person's character, as in Eights, there will always be some significant alteration in the person's life. This will repeat itself. Changes can pertain to relationships, finances, and work or location. Metaphorically speaking, all Eights pass through several deaths during their lifetime. The death will involve some part of their personality. The Eight is like Phoenix rising. From the very ashes of their own burial it flies again with new, refreshed wings. Powerful people come into their lives, and this can result in a power struggle for the Eight. The Eight must understand that the change is needed within. Turning their power inward in an effort to change can make them even more powerful.

Finding Your Birth Card

Sevens

Nine and Seven are the spiritual numbers. In this regard, Seven is more important. The seven is located perfectly in the center of the deck of cards. Think of this: The number of planets is Seven. By the same token we have seven body charkas, seven seals in the Bible's Book of Revelation. Seven comes up frequently in mathematics and geometry. For ages it has been a meaningful spiritual symbol used in countless religions and cultures. Because it is an odd number, Seven symbolizes imbalance. There is movement away from the static and from balance. Seven is moving away from the stable Six. Since the Six can receive messages from a higher source, the Seven symbolizes stepping into the unknown. This can be frightening. The Seven leaves the security of an organized and harmonious world. However, in the outside world, peace and contentment are the goals. We want these regardless of objective circumstances. A high state of spirituality is needed, and this is very difficult to acquire. It is somewhat related to the difficulty of entering heaven, but it is precisely the Seven that is heaven's gate. The core of the Seven is faith. Sevens are somewhat like a bridge between the everyday world and the spiritual world. During their lifetime they have the opportunity to experience both. True contentment, though, resides in the spiritual. A carefree life full of awe and wonder is what makes them happy and content. The carefree perspective comes from the faith that their needs will be provided for. They are directly connected to a higher power assuring that they will be fine. Worldly concerns are minimized, and they experience a higher state of consciousness: the spiritual. Should a Seven slip back to the material world, they encounter endless difficulties and worries. They worry about their basic needs. They are deeply insecure and are certain they are unloved. Worry is relentless. Therefore, they try manipulative techniques as a defense, but they only sink lower. Depression comes, and sometimes negative attitudes about life worsen the misery.

They become miserly when the Sevens have personalities that are mundane. They never have enough. It becomes critical that Sevens recognize their spiritual side. Sevens simply must live in truth. The name we use does not matter. Sevens, more than others, must walk in the light of truth or be doomed to misery and desperation. It makes sense then, that there are two kinds of Sevens; happy and unattached ones and unhappy and worried ones. There is a magical quality about the unattached ones, because their needs are fulfilled without worry. They give and understand and are carefree about everything. They are service oriented. They can do great things for the world. The other Sevens live in poverty, manipulation, and contempt. They are profoundly unhappy.

Sixes

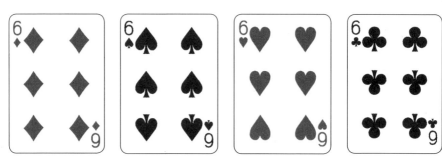

Karma and justice are closely related. Balance, as the Scales in the sign of Libra tell us, is how justice is brought about. The Libra scales of justice are representative of the Law of Karma, or the law of cause and effect. Sixes are very aware of both karma and the law. Their awareness means that these concepts are incorporated into their lives in a number of ways. They are, in fact, integrated into everything. Some Sixes are so aware of them that it knocks their karmic balance off because of the excessive nature of their perceptions. A lot of Sixes worry about money in the form of unpaid debts. Consequently, they meticulously avoid acquiring debts to anyone. Others are acutely aware of laws but feel held back and uncomfortable. Thus they try to move through life on a free ride. Such people are irresponsible freeloaders who believe everyone owes them something. These are exaggerated views of Sixes. The point is that the Law of Karma in an integral part of their lives because it is built into their minds. Because Six is their birth number, it is carried throughout their lives and does not leave until they move on to the next portion of the cycle of life. Destiny and fate are incorporated into Sixes' scheme of knowledge as the number of their fate. They believe in destiny because of past actions in their lives. The relentless Law of Karma is always on their minds as Sixes ponder good and evil and their cause. They often wonder about what sorts of things, both good and bad, will come to them through the inevitable Law of Karma. Holding on to a kind of fatalism, they unfortunately are prone to sitting and waiting for things to unfold. A sense of dread is part of some Sixes lives while others have a more positive viewpoint as they await something good to happen. The wait for good fortune often unfolds slowly for Sixes, but eventually they find themselves in new conditions. These conditions can be good or bad and affect things such as finances and relationships. Complacency sometimes has to be fought before moving on to the next stage. Try as we may, changing them usually does not work. Change comes only when they themselves are ready. The seventh house astrologically is Libra and is associated with Six. The two interlocking triangles of the Star of David are symbols of the Six. Peace, along with harmony, is something they promote always. They may suppress their own feelings and conflicts because it upsets peace and balance. When peace is sought in an escapist manner it can bounce back and result in aggressiveness. Stuffing anger down inside themselves, Sixes can explode. Sixes are often excellent athletes because of not only competitiveness but also balance. This is an integral part of their success both in sports and business. They have a sense of sportsmanship combined with competition that often makes them successful. Finally, Sixes are among the most psychic cards in the deck.

Fives

Five is considered the number of humanity. As such it is highly significant. Its significance is that it is a symbol of our race, of humanity itself. Note that our hands have five fingers. Five planets can be seen in the night sky by the naked eye. One of the only manmade things visible from orbit is the Great Pyramid of Giza and it has five points. The creators wanted to show space travelers how important the Five is. The Five is the adventure number, being a seeker in the dualistic universe. Ever expanding, the Five wants to know what is on the other side of the mountain. They are explorers and seekers of new challenges and discoveries. It is the constant motion of each generation looking to improve on the previous generation. Improvement is important for the planet, and Five people are acutely aware of this. Considering different numbers as the base of a planet is an interesting task. Consider a planet of Fours where security was of prime importance. Simply by being human, without regard to the Birth card, a person has Five characteristics because all Fives are on one level already, and they have a sort of double Five nature. An exaggerated version of Five energy comes about. Extreme examples of Fives are those who are on an endless quest for adventure. They are willing to experience hardships of any manner. Regardless of their station in life and what their motivations appear to be, new experiences are the motive. This is true across the board and includes ideas, relationships, and value systems. They are compelled to look beyond the horizon, always exploring. Clearly then, a vocation involving travel and variety are ideal. Meeting new people and encountering new situations and cultures are things that Fives love. If they are settled in one job for a while, they attempt to take it in new directions. Involvements in some sort of sales are common vocations for Fives. The desire to learn and understand probably contributes to this. In addition, they have an ability to relate to people on their own level. They make others comfortable. These qualities are helpful in sales. The freedom that comes with sales is an appealing factor for Fives. Fives have the wanderlust. Fives are restless. While each person is unique, wandering from place to place is common. Fours are homebodies, and Fives have evolved from them. They seek security in a reverse manner. They are willing, indeed relish, moving from place to place. The concept of staying home is perceived as prison for them. They want to be free as a bird. Anything that gets in the way of their freedom is met with rebellion and leave taking. All of this affects personal relationships too because they involve commitment. Some do get married, but their preference is to keep all options open. They are the type who might live with someone without making a commitment.

Fours

Fours are family oriented. Their priorities are contentment, stability, and security. This is the nature of the life of a Four. Physically, they often appear round or square. Not only does this apply to Four Birth cards but also to their Planetary Ruling card. They appear and seem to be solid, grounded people. They make people feel safe and secure. In astrology Cancer rules the fourth house and represents security and safety. In fact, it is security that is of primary importance to Fours. They create order out of chaos and security out of uncertainty. Another keyword is *protection*. They perceive protection as their birthright. All of this requires work. That and that alone can bring about what they want. Procrastination and avoidance are the biggest enemies of Fours. If they are not willing to exert the effort everything will go wrong to different degrees. Commitment and effort can bring about what they want. Unhappiness comes to Fours who try to avoid the amount of work they have to do. A lot of Fours worry about security too much. This can lead to an overly controlling type of person. Fours who do not measure up to their own commitments become controllers who try to keep everyone and everything in a box. The overly protective parent is probably a Four. Even if they have good intentions, they are stifling the development of their child with their overly controlling approach. Their main fear is one of losing their children, who are a large part of the security network they have created. Micromanaging bosses are cut from the same cloth. They worry so much about details that they cannot see the overall picture. They create problems and limit opportunities. Growth can be seen as a threat. The Four strives mightily to keep things exactly the way they are. They will change, of course, but not on anything pertaining to their security system. Fours who are Diamonds or Clubs can actually be progressive. They enjoy traveling, as do Fives. This could be the result of having Fives as their first Karma cards. The relationship to the Five might also be a cause of frequent unhappiness in work. Conflict can exist in the Four of Diamonds and Four of Clubs because of their work and their wanderlust. Fours establish foundations. They are organized and set boundaries. Generally, they are not leaders. They prefer jobs where they can make a contribution but not be bothered by others. Creativity is not their primary ascent, and they are not farsighted or open-minded. However, they provide security, stability, and a work ethic. After working hard their entire lives, they have the money and freedom to travel and live happy lives. So we can see that the feeling of security coupled with a love of travel are part of the Four's being. Thus a fine balance is required for a happy life; a balance of both movement and stability. Their willingness to work can be used to overcome this challenge.

Threes

Three is an odd-numbered card, and like all such cards the Ace must be understood. The Ace has moved beyond Zero. It is the prime of all the odd-numbered cards. All reflect some qualities of the Ace. As odd, the cards are a step outside stability, which the preceding even-numbered cards have. The Three has stepped away from the Two. This causes dissatisfaction with what they have, which is strong in their personal relationships. It is not a bad thing or a negative. Rather, it is a fact. Everyone, being human, will at one time or another know what it is like to be a Three in this regard. We may have a Three of Hearts Long Range card in one particular year and experience a great deal of variety or indecision about our romantic life. We may have a Three of Diamonds Pluto card one year, and this will transform our worries about money into a positive. Thus, financial ideas can be implemented to reduce stress. Moving on is basically a part of life they must deal with in order to attain peace and contentment. The notion of peace and contentment is difficult for every odd-numbered Birth card. As mentioned, odd numbers are imbalanced and thus seek balance. Odd numbers are seen as masculine, creative, and always moving. Regardless of actual gender, Threes exhibit creativity and self-expression. Peace comes from action or accomplishment in the material arena. This leads them to return to self. Threes are idea people because their thoughts and feelings have to find a suitable outlet or worry and indecision will come about. Threes have a desire for self-expression. Threes are akin to the Gemini and are versatile and often loquacious. They get along with different kinds of people and are interested in different cultures and concepts. They are very inventive and can be good problem solvers. If it is an idea you seek, talk to a Three. They are loaded with ideas but often do not do anything about them. For success in creative areas, the Three has art, music, and writing. These also bring an inner satisfaction. This fulfills their desire for creativity. Should they become bored in one area, they simply move on to the next. For Threes, this works exceedingly well. However, they must be cautious that projects are completed, or they will be failures. Romance is enticing to Threes. The fifth house in astrology has energy pertaining to creativity and self-expression. It also relates to love and romance. There is a strong relationship between Threes and the fifth house relative to fulfillment. It is logical that those with the wonderful creative gifts have the strongest needs for romantic and sexual delight. Looking at the overall picture, you find a deep curiosity and yearning for new experiences and variety. Thus, Threes make wonderful lovers but are, perhaps, not the best marriage partners. Boredom might set in.

Twos

 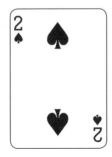  

Twos complement and balance the drive and desire of the Ace. From a sexual perspective, the energy in males and females is balanced by being with a person who complements them. This balance is the primary being of Twos. Our world is dualistic in spite of our limited awareness of this.

The sum of the parts is the combination of opposites mixed together. A look at the blends of life shows colors, emotions, sounds, and thoughts that we call our world. Twos have a special comprehension of balance and harmony. Twos want balance for themselves and those around them. There is a constant search for their counterpart. This is just as strong as the Ace striving to create something new. This is part of a successful relationship for Twos. A poor relationship causes deep suffering for them. They have great difficulty letting go. It is as though they do not want to live alone. That is just one way to see it though, because we could also say that the Aces are afraid of balance or they are afraid not creating something. Twos bond and create relationships. They form a unity, and in the process they feel desired and needed. They make people feel at home and loved. However, they might smother them and be manipulative too. This lack of awareness of their own character can move them to actions that are subconscious. While some come off as lofty or even uncaring, they are not. Some too behave like they do not need anyone. This is absolutely not true. It does not matter how they behave or what the say; a prime mover in their lives is completion. Failure to do this completion openly and honestly can lead to their dysfunctional emotional characteristics. Twos are very intelligent and capable of forming many defenses against people discovering their inner needs and motives. They are sharp at debates and arguments, and it may seem that you will never get through to them. They build walls and push people away sometimes. They can also be extremists, in that one day they may have no one in their life at all, and then overnight they are madly in love with someone. They frequently experience unrequited love. They try to balance things by overdoing it from their side. This is very painful, and cynicism is possible. Pain avoidance is fundamental to people. In addition to intelligence, Twos are often beautiful. On the one hand they have everything, but they need more self-understanding in order to be happy. The battle over whether to have a relationship will continue, and the craving for love and affection will be unfulfilled. Happy Twos fulfill their needs and wants. But they must confess what they are. The acceptance will bring freedom. It will bring peace. It is a huge release that is bound to make for far more happiness. Twos symbolize the dualistic nature of the universe and the necessity of balance. Their quest, therefore, is to complete their being in unification with something or someone else.

Aces

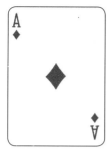

We know from the Book of John that "In the beginning was the Word" (John 1:1). If we deeply understand that, then we understand Aces. The Ace is representative of the primary masculine element. The Ace is the creative principle. From Genesis we know God created heaven and earth. This was done by the Word, "and God said, let it be so" (Gen 1:1–28). The world is both masculine and feminine energy in a matrix; it interacts and evolves but always in balance. Masculine energy is a part of God's creative aspect, but feminine energy is the fertile and receptive force of God. All creation comes, in a sense, from the mind of God. This is clear because our ideas must come from somewhere. Aces have a somewhat masculine nature regardless of their gender. It could be physical or only part of their personality. It is the masculine and creative part of them. The life of an Ace is a constant series of creation after creation. Their creativity results in many new ideas and novel projects. It is as though they receive input from a higher power. Starting new things is wonderful for them. They love to experience what they have created. They are born to create new and novel things. Patience is not an attribute of most Aces. After all, there is a lot to create and time should not be wasted. They want things to happen, and it is not in their nature to wait for them. They have a strong dislike for lines, of any kind. If they are curt, they have something that they want to get accomplished. It is not about disliking you. They also have a charm about them and are kind. The Ace of Diamonds and Ace of Clubs both have a Two as one of their Karma cards. They care about and are concerned about others. Some of this is because they need others in order to complete themselves. The paradox of the Ace is that while it wants to be alone, it also longs for others. Aces are great communicators, and they are forever communicating either on the phone, computer, or directly with others who seem to surround them. But Aces are also loners and can be absorbed with themselves alone.

Think of the Aries, who is self-absorbed. They need some kind of tangible results in order to be content. Relationships that do not give them what they want are ended. The Ace of Hearts is personified in the "search for self" more so than other Aces. While all Aces have undertaken this search, their suit tells us in which area of life they are most interested. Ace of Hearts people search for themselves in their love and friendship relationships. The Ace of Clubs searches for meaning in books read and things they are interested in. The Ace of Diamonds is conflicted. They do not know whether to find fulfillment in their ambition or the need for companionship or marriage. Like the Ace of Hearts, they want perfect love in order to be complete. The Ace is the beginning and the creator. All things stem from it.

Jokers

There is not much to know about the Joker. We have given basically no information for those born on December 31, which is the date of the Birth card of the Joker. We know little about the card. There are no Life Path cards or Yearly Spreads to give us any clue. The Joker is capable of being any card that he or she wants to be. Jokers were Court Jesters in past times. They took the throne on Fool's Day every year and impersonated the King. The Joker's day is December 31, when we celebrate the New Year. That was a time for putting away the serious part of life. The Joker made fun of everyone in order to lighten up things a little. He was excellent at impersonation.

This ability to take on a role is critical to the Joker's personality. Because we do not know which card they are, we cannot make any definite statements pertaining to them. Perhaps a Joker can be thought of as a "Jack of all Jacks." That means they are creative as well as perhaps immature but independent. The Joker is part of the theater. Of course dishonesty is also possible. They probably want to be free and independent.

Spirituality is part of Jokers in the tarot deck. There is the Fool card with the number Zero. Beyond this, the Joker is a mystery. The Joker is the master of disguise in the deck. He is the entertainer who reminds us that life is just a stage. It is the Zero, without which there would be no meaningful number system at all. But, most of all, the Joker is a mystery.

FINDING YOUR BIRTH CARD PERSONA

In this section, you can find your specific Birth card. Again, there is a section for your friends so you can record their personal Birth cards.

King of Diamonds
Big Time Operator

Characteristics: In the realm of the King of Diamonds you will find finances and business. If it pertains to money or business it is taken care of by the King of Diamonds. Utilizing inherited skills pertaining to their work, they can excel in any business pursuit. Rather than working for other people, these individuals succeed at businesses of their own instead. Being aggressive is something they are quite capable of in terms of money and business, but that is not always the case. Due to the fact that the King of Diamonds is one eyed, blindness in some aspects of life and situations is always a possibility. In addition, stubbornness can also be present, because they only see one side of issues. Enemies might come about because of this. Looking at the card you can see a battle-ax. It is possible that the upraised battle-ax on the card represents a fondness for competition. They appear be ruthless and cold up to that point. Making large amounts of money is possible, because their creativity allows this. Positive results from Kings of Diamonds are possible because they are so capable in worldly matters. They embody the phrase "in the world but not of it" to a very high degree. The King of Diamonds has priorities and consequently knows what is really important: to be a respected businessperson. Using knowledge in place of fear, they will come to that logical conclusion and achieve their goal. Selfishness is something they must be very careful with. Because they possess so much innate power, they can disregard other people's feelings, thus creating problems. There are often psychological problems emanating from youth that must be confronted prior to the cards' best results.

Relationships: Relative to peers, domination is a temptation, and some males are unable to deal with a powerful woman. Some women, after a few tries, give up even attempting, and, for that matter, some men do as well.

The King of Diamond's karma is neither good nor bad. There is no compromise in their makeup because of their great power. Unfortunately, this can bring about personal problems. Women, especially, must find ways to balance their strong masculine aspects in the midst of relationships. Most are accustomed to this. Intimacy results from truly honest communication. Kings of Diamonds are attracted to those with a sense of humor and a good education and are often partners with their spouses in a business. For either gender, it is possible to perceive marriage as a financial arrangement. Separation on the business and personal sides of things is best, especially in the beginning. It is good if both sides can learn to reveal their emotions and desires to improve the match.

Personality Connections: Diamond females are exceptionally fond of some King males, and this could make a good marriage. Males often have extreme issues with Spade females and should avoid them for marriage. King of Diamonds women have strong connections with Heart men. It is interesting to note that this is a combination that is powerful but not always easy.

Confrontations: Kings of Diamonds have a widespread reputation with card readers who view them as having essentially more disruptive relationships than any card in the deck. Arsenio Hall is a famous King of Diamonds and has had books written about him detailing the enemies he acquired on his rise to fame. Both Florence Campbell and Edith Randall, authors of *Sacred Symbols of the Ancients*, think that the King of Diamonds is the most materialistic and cruel card of all. Unfortunately, for the ones who operate on the Birth card's lower levels, Kings of Diamonds will stop at nothing in order to acquire what they want or to keep a step ahead. The King of Diamonds is the sole King showing only one eye, though the Jack of Spades and the Jack of Hearts also have one eye. Such cards are inclined to see the world in strictly one way. Among the three cards this trait reveals itself differently in each one. For Kings, however, one-eyed sightedness can be present in many of their professional affairs. In that situation their own ideas are all they can see.

Queen of Diamonds
Benefactor

Characteristics: In the case of the Queen of Diamonds, values are a well-spring of indecisiveness. A result of this, for example, is having problems deciding what is wanted the most. The Queen of Diamonds has a taste limited to the very best. Shopping, according to the Queen of Diamonds, means buying only high quality at a high price. Behaving like this and having such values only exacerbates their financial worries. Even though they are fearful, they are extremely giving. The mixture of the Nine in Jupiter and Nine of Diamonds as second Karma card brings about a natural aptitude toward release and a natural instinct to share their wealth. They are like the grandparent who goes shopping for some new clothes for you and expensive birthday presents. Their asset of creativity can be blocked if they are too worried about money, and, unfortunately, this is not unusual. They are capable, if they choose a spiritual path, of having a special mission and reaching the heights of self-understanding and spiritual awareness. Spiritually they are tied to a lot of the ancient sciences. There is a natural interest in the ancient secret mysteries of knowledge. This initiates studying infinite truths, and, in turn, helps remove a number of ordinary problems. The heights they can reach are unlimited if they dedicate themselves to higher goals. The Queen of Diamonds boasts some of the world's richest people. The best that life has to offer appeals to them. Charm is exuded by the Queen of Diamonds. Challenge is what they seek and at times relationships too. A business mind is inborn in the Queen of Diamonds, and they have an excellent ability for promotion of products or services. They make good leaders and are superb in many fields. Nurturing, of course, is part of a Queens's character. They help others in their work as well as their lives. They have an ability to plan and analyze very well and are naturally critical. Seeing through the deceit of others is something they are blessed with. It is a natural ability. Such a mind, by the same token, can be negatively oriented when things do not come out as planned. They can be quite critical of others and very negative. Pessimism is also sometimes a part of their makeup even though they usually do not know it. For a balance in character, a positive attitude is something they must work on.

Relationships: Relative to the aspect of love, as pointed out, the Queen of Diamonds has major challenges. Starting a new relationship is very easy because they are very charismatic and charming. Keeping a relationship going seems to be the difficult part for them. They need to learn that they will have to live with the consequences of their actions, because they usually get what they want. They can be fearful of being abandoned, stubborn, and proud, and they like variety. A troubling combination can result; they have the power to get what they desire whenever they want it. Even when they seem happily settled, it usually does not last long. Several marriages are very possible for them.

Personality Connections: Difficulties arise with most Heart men as well. An awareness of these personality issues is important. Queen of Diamonds men have fantasies about Spade women. Female Queen of Diamonds are usually passionate for Club males.

Confrontations: Perhaps because of the Three residing in Venus, many Queens of Diamonds have three or more marriages. Clearly there are some who have only been married once, or who never get married at all, but this is an interesting scenario that happens very often with this Birth card. If we look at the Queen of Diamond's Life Path, we see that there is a trinity of very important Threes in it. The first is their Three of Diamonds Karma card, which symbolizes the fundamental uncertainty they maintain about what is the most important part of their lives. Following that is the Venus card, which is the Three. Finally, the third is their Mars card, which is the Three. Due to the fact that the cards found here, more than any others, reflect something about our fundamental being in the world, Venus and Mars are frequently called personal planets. The numbers of cards often have a more profound importance than we think at first. For instance, a lot of Eight individuals have eight children, or, perhaps, they have eight special persons in their life, people that make up their inner circle of loved ones.

 Jack of Diamonds
Seller

Characteristics: Intelligent and shrewd, Jack of Diamonds people are consistently able to make an excellent living using their humor and charming personalities. The Jack of Diamonds, therefore, represents the salesperson's card. Their creativity and independence allows them to operate from instinct as well as their quick and creative minds. Not many listen to the call of their highest ideals and evolve into the King standing close to them. They consistently get by using their inherited financial wisdom. All Jacks are rigid in their minds, and this often stops them from discovering the intuition that is one of their higher gifts. Spiritual realization comes from a natural psychic ability. Some Jacks of Diamonds, however, become professional psychics, but others fear opening up their psychic channel. Regardless, most of them come to use their abilities in later years. The Jack of Diamonds has a unique ability to persuade others. They are skilled in the entertainment or healing fields. Many are inclined to be artists, and some are especially talented. They are unparalleled in the sales area. They are capable of almost anything. Therefore, this is one cause for so many moving toward sales and promotion careers. Because of their great creativity, they get distracted. While they usually mean well, they do not come through on their promises. Jacks in general are capable of being both immature and a bit deceitful. Some Jacks can actually be thief cards. An ongoing deception is often seen being played out in their lives. This is based on their personal definition of the situation. The blind vision can be revealed in their love life. In a nice twist, however, Jacks can do things to help others, because they are often blind to their faults. They enjoy playing and, even when old, retain a youthfulness. They need to find a vocation that gives them an outlet for being creative and recognition for their superior abilities. They are very social, and this makes them the best salespeople of all the cards. They can have a lot of success in a field that puts them in front of groups as well as individuals. It is possible for all Jacks of Diamonds to lead their entire lives just playing around and enjoying themselves. However, they often want to be humanitarians. Because they are a Uranus/Neptune card, Jacks of Diamonds like to keep as many options open in their profession and in their life as possible. Freedom (Uranus) means a great deal to them, and it is seen as almost sacred (Neptune). They will generally want something in self-employment or occupations allowing freedom and the option of setting their own work schedule.

Relationships: There is an idealized concept of their own freedom in the Jacks of Diamonds. Making a commitment in a relationship is frequently difficult for them. They perceive the word *freedom* in such a special way that, whether they admit it or not, it is a strong force keeping them out of permanent commitments. They usually attribute this to their high ideals of personal freedom and independence, but the fact is that often they are truly afraid of the price of real commitment. They usually get their way, but their own indecision and need for freedom often wins out. Being so creative can also make a Jack of Diamonds a playboy or playgirl. However, it is possible for them to have a good relationship once they decide on that and are ready to settle down. They are in the Neptune lineage and each follows the Jack of Diamonds Life Path (from their Mercury to Neptune card). They have the most dreamy love card of all, the Queen of Hearts, as their Neptune card. They have a very idealistic view about love because of so much

Neptune energy relating to their love life. It is possible for them to be the ideal lover or mate. They are often creative with their romantic fantasies but suffer a lot when people do not match the wonderful potential the Jack of Diamonds perceives in them.

Personality Connections: Male Clubs find the female Jack of Diamonds very appealing, although sometimes very difficult. The male Jack of Diamonds fantasizes about female Heart cards.

Confrontations: July 4 is a Jack of Diamonds, and, as mentioned, this is often referred to as the salesman's card. Jack of Diamonds people are usually gifted in promoting what they believe in, and many have had a great deal of success in sales. Being irresponsible and crafty, on the other hand, are qualities of some. When we look at our country from this point of view, it reveals a great deal pertaining to us both as a culture and as a political body. This is interesting because people usually do not think of their country as having a Sun Sign or Birth card.

 **Ten of Diamonds**
Anointed One

Characteristics: The Ten of Diamonds is protected by Jupiter's blessings on each side. It is in the center of the Life Spread. While only a few of these individuals actually reach this in real life, it is the card of material luxury. This card will always be lucky to a degree, and all these cards have financial protection. Tens of Diamonds prefer their own businesses as opposed to working for someone else, and this is where they are best suited. Regardless of the size, they are knowledgeable about running a business. Inherited wealth is often the case in their lives. They want to be at the center of things. Being at the midpoint of the Life Spread is the reason for this. Many are not as generous as you might think, however. The acquisition of additional money is where some direct these gifts, and there are those who actually become ruthless in these terms. Their Queen of Diamonds Karma card can be listened to, and this symbolizes intuition and service through learning. Rewards can be found in artistic avenues for creativity in their later years. Doubt and indecision can be removed if their spiritual awareness develops, which can happen in their later years if they expand their minds and souls. Talents and resources for helping others can actually be devoted in this manner. An obsession with accumulating things is a temptation for some. Selfishness is a quality of some Tens of Diamonds, but they invariably succeed in whatever they do because of their creativity and intelligence. Monetary gain is usually where this aptitude points. They can deal with businesses or financial enterprises of any size.

Relationships: There must be a discharge of karma from past lives relating, perhaps, to a difficult divorce or separation. Love and relationships are the cravings of Tens of Diamonds. A person who left unfairly and in a less than loving way is the karma brought into this life. The same person from the previous life often reappears in this life. They most often initiate a new relationship in their search for love. There are frequent sacrifices of personal needs for affection because of a higher priority, or in order to assist others who need help. Because of the Five of Diamonds in Saturn and the fact that the Personality card for the feminine aspect is the notorious Queen of Diamonds, things can result in indecision romantically and heavy burdens associated with romance and marriage. Before they can have a successful marriage, they must address the fact that they are restless emotionally. Finding their inner child is a process of them learning to love themselves. This helps them find other relationships too. The female Ten of Diamonds should avoid letting relationships come before her work or career, unless there is extraordinary rapport.

Personality Connections: Although sometimes challenging, the female Ten of Diamonds finds cordial relations with male Hearts. The females are very compatible with most Club males. Blessings from other Diamond women attract both male and female Tens of Diamonds, especially business-minded ones.

Confrontations: There is always conflict between wanting things for themselves and giving to others, despite wanting to be loved by others. In relationships, compromise and adjustment are necessary. Tens of Diamonds can see it as a sacrifice as opposed to compromise, because it is taking away from them. Some must choose between self-love or love of a mate or partner at some point. Sometimes quite selfish and self-centered, the Ten of Diamonds can be very humanitarian and giving as well. They can believe that the entire world belongs to them and that they are worthy of the constant attention of everyone, again because they are positioned at the exact center of the Life Spread. They think they do not really have to be concerned so much about being taken care of. They have a high opinion of themselves in many cases and believe they are truly the most blessed cards. Search for self is what this card symbolizes.

Nine of Diamonds
Patron

Characteristics: Nine of Diamond individuals are here to complete a significant chapter in the evolution of their soul and being. When the time is right, there is a lot of giving to others along with a willingness to release people and material items from their lives. They may have a life of disappointment and remorse if they have not listened to the call to give and release others as well as materialism, relationships, and love. On the positive side, there is a tendency for these individuals to be philanthropic; those who take this path are happy and productive. Living a universal life, each one has the opportunity to directly experience a heightened consciousness. Regardless of occasional losses, such people can do quite well in business terms, in particular when it involves selling or other creative pursuits. They are superb at promoting activities they believe in. Communication is something at which they excel. Counseling others, even if not professionally, is something they will likely do. Those who do not are, nevertheless, excellent friends and family members. It is possible for them to achieve affluence if they have the ability to keep their own values in proper perspective. When taking any kind of risks at all, even driving, caution should be maintained. Bad luck and misery will result from failure to realize that we must give in order to receive. The King in their Mars palace is the reason for this. Sales or promotional work is something the Nine of Diamonds is unusually talented at. In addition, legal matters and disputes are also areas this card is more successful at than most other Birth cards. While most choose a line of work intellectually stimulating to them, they are likely to make money doing this. Improving and utilizing their charm and power for good work is a challenge for Nines of Diamonds. They frequently bring others to a higher knowledge and understanding, and thus many are fated to make great contributions to humanity. Nines of Diamonds, fortunately, are not prone to recklessness. Many are attracted to the legal professions, thus allowing use of their intellectual abilities, which are well developed. Attorneys or members of assorted communications fields are often Nines of Diamonds.

Relationships: Normally marriage is perceived as a job involving numerous duties by the Nine of Diamonds. In this lifetime, their families are often the main area of their accomplishments. Talking with others is something the Nine of Diamonds enjoys doing. Good wit and intelligence are their qualities. In terms of karma, many have had challenging lives. Responsibilities associated with parenting and being spouses or offspring are usually a part of their lives. Their karma is involved in their marriage, and this is long lasting. Relative to marriage, they approach things in a traditional manner, and they are generally easy to get along with and very generous.

Personality Connections: A good match for Diamond men is the female Nine of Diamonds. With the exception of the Jack, the male Nines of Diamonds should be careful with female Clubs, who are potential marriage partners. Caution should be brought to bear. This is true of both males and females. Unexpected challenges frequently are the result in such cases. Men who are Clubs are seen as attractive to female Nines of Diamonds. Good marriage or business partnership can result. Even though they are a challenge for Diamond females, female Spades love Nine of Diamonds men.

Confrontations: An unlucky area for the Nine of Diamonds is gambling. Even though they give to others, they take advantage of them. Nines of Diamonds experience these things more than most, to the point where they sometimes feel they have been cursed. They feel they are victims of the cosmos and almost persecuted by financial loss. For Nines of Diamonds, this is their nature. When it comes to money or even their lives, many Nine of Diamonds individuals believe they are treated unfairly. Often they are not repaid money they loaned a person. The majority of the profits in business partnerships appear to go to their partners. Their entire investment is lost in the partnership when it fails. Illegal activities can victimize them and there can be losses in their lives because of this.

Eight of Diamonds
Solar Star

Characteristics: Leadership is one of the aptitudes of the Eight of Diamonds. An addiction to power is possible in powerful people, and they can be dominating. The Sun card has the opportunity to go to great heights in this life span, and this is the Eight of Diamonds. People look up to them and respect them and their work, whether or not they are famous. Standing out from the crowd and being noticed is something they enjoy. Power and control issues with other people and the way they work out their karma are significant. Being controlled is something they do not like, and they try to maintain the superior position in relationships. Occasionally they have a pushy personality because they occupy the eighth position in the Crown Line and are very independent. For the Queen of Spades Karma card these are keywords. They have a strong desire to learn and explore and are sharp mentally. There is not much they cannot achieve and very few issues they cannot overcome if they elect to work for something. If not abused they are able to conquer and rule, and this power brings them satisfaction. Because they have power, some Eights of Diamonds are fearful or have a distaste for the responsibility that comes with it. Much of their natural talent and potential is forfeited in this case. They are good negotiators and are aware of the value of things. Power pertains to money for many Eights of Diamonds. They may become addicted to spending money, and both genders are capable of quickly spending huge sums. They are extreme shoppers. They deal with stress by shopping, it seems. They can achieve anything by using their excellent intuition and hard work. They are capable of both inner peace and inner power, thus allowing for self-mastery if they learn to direct power back inwardly toward personal transformation and resist trying to change the world.

Relationships: Generally speaking, Eights of Diamonds go after what they desire because they know what it is. Sadly, eventually what they want changes. Their relationships should be placed behind careers in most cases. When they attempt to have a relationship more significant than their work, they often lose a bit of their power. Individuals of the Club suit are better for both genders. Many blessings come from being less attached in the realm of love. They lean toward indecision and are fickle as far as love relationships go. Change can happen because of an independent nature, but the Eight of Diamonds resists. Others who cannot make a commitment either can be attracted to them. Many Eights of Diamonds have one monogamous relationship after another. Multiple marriages are possible. One person often cannot satisfy their desire for variety in love. They should express themselves without trying to reinvent others and learn to give others freedom. Furthermore, they need give themselves the love they want from others and to accept themselves as they actually are. Abandonment is a fear they must let go. They must not push loved ones with their abundance of power. Challenges like these are some of their greatest obstacles.

Personality Connections: Female Hearts often want the Eight of Diamonds male, and he receives blessings from female Clubs. Spade females have the greatest compatibility, although it is important to check the Birth card relationships individually before drawing any firm conclusions. A Spade man, particularly if he is powerful and well respected, is good for Eight of Diamonds females, and they have a good disposition for married life too. Lifelong friends can be found in Heart men.

Confrontations: A big, happy, sunny face is present in most Eight of Diamond individuals. That sunny appearance radiates from their faces. Tammy Faye Bakker, Dolly Parton, and Loni Anderson are Eight of Diamonds women. These Eight of Diamonds women share some physical attributes. A somewhat similar appearance is even shared. It is easier to see why these women share basically the same look if we keep in mind that the Eight of Diamonds is the Sun card.

Seven of Diamonds
Holy Virtues

Characteristics: Money is always connected to the suit of Diamonds. Seven of Diamond individuals will experience continuing problems in this area, so they must maintain a detached attitude about finances, because they are spiritual in nature. Either they have as much as they want and never worry, or they worry about it all the time because they do not have enough. Nevertheless, through this area many of their lessons in life come. We call the Seven of Diamonds Semi-Fixed, and this is one of the unique cards that has this quality. Such folks fall into a different category and possess a particular mark on their lives because they are part of a special family of seven distinctly different cards. They are also extremely creative, and some are destined to become super rich by accessing the higher side of this spiritual-finance card. But most are quite stubborn. Their close relationships such as family, lovers, and even friends are all very meaningful to Seven of Diamonds people. They are close with family and share in their trials and tribulations for good or bad. They love nature and are spiritual. That often entails making sacrifices for people close to them and that includes their spouses. For their parents or other family members, there is little they would not do. Their success stems from dealing with life in ways other than traditional or materialistic, so they are highly spiritual. The successful ones live in the faith that all their needs will be met. Frequent changes in, for example, occupation or location, show they are mostly restless. In their spiritual quest they find satisfaction internally and validation for their own intuitive nature. Having begun a spiritual path, everything in their lives is put into the right perspective, and they can do well in any chosen field. Unfortunately, they are usually confronted with sacrifice and disappointment prior to learning to let others go in romance.

Relationships: For Seven of Diamond individuals, ideals such as "letting loved ones go" are tested every step along the way. They will learn important lessons from the fact that they are stubborn and independent. In life they attract strong relationships. Problems in relationships center around letting go of personal attachments and developing a renewed spiritual approach to love; they are, after all, such a spiritual card. They are willing to sacrifice for those they love, and by nature these individuals are very loving people. They will be challenged to raise their level of love to a spiritual plane and have to have at least one karmic love involvement. Similar to other cards regarding love and relationships, they maintain high ideals.

Personality Connections: Most men who are Hearts attract Seven of Diamond females. There is often marriage. Female Sevens of Diamonds are challenges for Club males. In addition, a female Spade attracts the male Seven of Diamonds, and males usually have many Club women as friends and coworkers.

Confrontations: There seems to be a rapport with the special Family of Seven cards, while the rest of us just stare and wonder what is happening. They are responsible about keeping their word, and they work hard. They are all a bit strong willed and inflexible. It is next to impossible to get them to change course, because they are stuck in their ways. These individuals are quite different from most people, but it is difficult to describe just how they are different. Getting to know one is the only way that a person can understand them. While there are many, they include George Carlin, Andy Warhol, Geena Davis, and Frederico Fellini. These people march to the beat of a different drummer. The "person on the street" of our society and culture does not have the viewpoints and ideas about life that they do. There is no match in their priorities. For some reason they are cut from a different cloth like all the Fixed and Semi-Fixed cards seem to be. Being unlike the other forty-five cards in the deck is something all of them seem to share. As a result, they often gravitate toward each other. Sevens of Diamonds or Jacks of Diamonds have friends or relatives who are Eights.

Six of Diamonds
Monetary Accountability

Characteristics: Like all Sixes, during their lives they receive exactly what they give to others. In their past lives there might have been huge financial losses or gains. Accounts might need to be settled. They seem to fall into two types. There are those who go out of their way to remain debt free. However, some must learn to be independent, and, unfortunately, there are those who are not responsible when it comes to money. In some cases they are owed. The suit of Diamonds maintains a strong financial relationship. The Six signifies responsibility and karma. Six of Diamonds individuals are very aware of debt and financial issues. A kind of suspicion about being in debt is the usual characteristic often showing itself. So they will not have to think about finances later. For example, a Six of Diamonds might pay the bills early. Six of Diamonds males and females share this common quality. It is sure that Sixes of Diamonds will get exactly what they deserve, and it does not matter what their situation. They may need to push themselves into the fray once in a while because they are a bit down on occasions. They can achieve almost anything they want once motivated. Both in work and action they are protected. On a more significant level, they may be here to understand values in a deeper way and to assist others. They will always be content if intuition guides them from deep inside, regardless of the situation in their lives. They will not be concerned about finances if they have found their special purpose in life. Excellent teachers often are Sixes of Diamonds. An awareness of the law is also present. They can be trusted with great responsibility and are generous. They are capable of giving informed personal choices, clear knowledge of superior values, and the ability to do more.

Relationships: In the Six of Diamonds there are people struggling to meet their needs for affection beneath the serious external parts of them. There can be an impact on their personal relationships because they often fear abandonment. They can have a difficult time understanding that, and repeated failures that constitute their love life result until that is dealt with directly. Their approach to love is highly cerebral. They need to work at being not only with others but also with themselves. They should not slip in to fooling themselves by avoiding their real feelings. A transformation in the lives of Sixes of Diamonds, according to their karmic pattern, often means one breakup of a significant relationship that teaches a lesson to them about themselves. There is a fear of disappointment for some, but others think they can orchestrate everything. First they have to learn to give themselves the love they seek from others. They need to make better determinations of their relationship issues stemming from frankness about their own emotions, which can give them the knowledge they need.

Personality Connections: Six of Diamond females are a large challenge for Spade males and create issues for them. Other Diamonds are attractive to both genders, although the females may also be interested in male Hearts.

Confrontations: There is a need to be appreciated and liked that is almost impossible to fill. Emotionally, a highly intense drive for achievement can result from this. Therefore, the Six of Diamonds is often introverted on a personal level and quite touchy. They seem content and well adjusted on the outside. Sixes avoid seeming engaged with the world around them, or even emotional. A huge drive for being successful is found in such people, and they can operate under high-powered pressure even at the professional level. Many Sixes find sports an outlet and that includes the Six of Diamonds. Joe Louis, Joe Montana, Fred Couples, Jack Nicklaus, and O. J. Simpson are all famous sports figures who are Sixes of Diamonds. Obviously their sports abilities have achieved fame for them. Deep emotional wounds in Six of Diamonds cards are frequently the case for making them successful individuals. Their kind exterior hides the internal wounds. Their life is in the Saturn position so we can see this in their lives.

Five of Diamonds
Inquirer of Value

Characteristics: There is an internal sensation of not being satisfied in all Five of Diamonds individuals. However, value and acquiring stable lives are what they desire to achieve. It is not easy for them to discover a vocation that gives both these two notions, because they are frequently in conflict. Sales is an excellent choice for many. They can achieve great success in this arena because they are able to relate to all kinds of people. Both obstacles and blessings are the possessions of this card. There is a distaste for routine and hatred for anything that tries to limit their freedom or push them in any way; that is the nature of the Five of Diamonds card. They may never settle down for anything long enough to make something worthwhile, and they have the wanderlust. They are capable, however, of bringing about security in an uncertain life and even discovering a relationship or profession they can stick to. Jobs and relationships are the main reasons for restlessness. Their kindness is, unfortunately, costly too, and they will probably experience financial loss during their lives. They have debts to pay from a previous life that must be paid in this card, much the same as the Nine. These people love sharing resources with family and close associates because they are givers. However, sometimes they can be bitter about it because others take advantage of them. Their giving is a lesson as well a gift. They need to do the task without evading responsibility, by practicing their knowledge and doing what is necessary. As a portion of their life's work, the strong Neptune influence brings about a desire to assist others. They will then acquire more success and fulfillment in life. This allows them to become the masters of their destiny and aligns them with a higher purpose. Because they are located in the Neptune column, they are naturally spiritual. True value is something they know. Psychic knowledge is even something they are aware of. Their knowledge branches out to the psychic, and some have a great aptitude in this area. Many Fives of Diamonds have great aptitude in this area. Putting into practice what they know is where the difficulty comes in. That frequently takes a lot of hard work to eliminate because of the karma they bring to this life. There will be numerous problems if they are lazy.

Relationships: Charm is frequently one of their qualities; however, there can be a sneaky and calculating way about them when it comes to romance. In many cases they lose awareness of their feelings as they get more enamored with analysis of the concept of love. Romance is a mind game for them. With romance, the Five of Diamonds is restless and fickle. Commitments are frequently avoided. Many have a hard time making a relationship work for very long because of this. They are viewed as some of the best lovers because they are quite romantic, charming, and have a sexual aura. A huge challenge for them is the entire notion of marriage and longing for intimacy in love; this challenge is one that they will surely be faced with often in the course of their lives. As Fives they do not want to return to the limitation that marriage can represent in some cases. Exploration and new journeys are what they are interested in. Those with humor and creativity are the kinds of people they are drawn to. If they decide to, they can even be dishonest in this aspect of life. Educational sources such as books, which pertain to love and relationships, always take them up to a higher plane and increased happiness. Books have a big influence on them.

Personality Connections: Fives of Diamonds want someone who does not infringe on their lifestyles. Male Clubs are whom Five of Diamond women are attracted to, and they can also be fascinated with Diamond males. Spade females strongly attract Five of Diamonds males.

Confrontations: Ask them if they want to travel across the entire country tomorrow and they will be ready to go the minute you call them. This Five is a paradigm of this. Their love of freedom and their desire to maintain security and a mark for themselves in this life cause internal conflicts. Traveling is a favorite, and they are the type that might just take off anywhere.

Four of Diamonds
Backbone in Virtues

Characteristics: Responsibilities will always be involved in all money Four of Diamonds individuals have or will get. They have the ability to be successful managers of a business, an area where they are skilled. The fact is, even though some people think they are stubborn, they realize that maintaining structure and having clear goals is most important for being successful and content. They are not about to change it, regardless of what others say, if something is working well for them. Taking care of finances is what the Four of Diamonds card symbolizes. Hard work is required for such a task to be accomplished. More than most other cards, diligent work is required to earn their rewards. There are definitely rewards. Failure and frustration will result if they try to get something for nothing. They know what is good for them even when young. Nevertheless, because they do not have roots in a single area, there is an inner restlessness that must be dealt with. This comes from not being satisfied. Fortunately, to get additional happiness all that is required is work. All things run smoothly, and their fears are put to rest once they get busy. They can enjoy traveling the world and experiencing the things they wanted while young. They often have the most freedom, happiness, and security in the twilight of their lives. They often need to work on their closest friends and relatives or marriage. These individuals meet a lot of people and usually have numerous friends because they are very sociable. They have to watch a tendency to get into a pattern they are unable to get out of, because they face difficulties they have to deal with.

Relationships: For both men and women, in the case of Four of Diamonds people, relationships require a lot of work. A life of ease and luxury is not achieved until later in life in many cases. If they view their relationships as a way of escape from life's challenges, problems creep in. Confusion in actual romantic involvement for both Four of Diamonds males and females is possible, because they are idealistic relative to love. They can most often acquire what they want in a romance because they are exceedingly charming. That power should be used with caution. If they are not careful, there will be swift and painful consequences, to the point where it might even affect their health. In relationships in order to avoid some very challenging problems, integrity is the key. The Four of Diamonds is a very uneasy person, while being secure and able to handle things externally. This applies to their love lives to a degree; consequently, some are challenged to settle down with one individual. Furthermore, one or multiple marriages are difficult because of their karmic pattern. The result is divorce. You have people who really desire a good relationship who must first pass some tests.

Personality Connections: Four of Diamonds women find Club men fascinating. Spade men are good partners for Four of Diamond women. With women of the Hearts suit, caution is necessary for Four of Diamond men, who should avoid them. The difficulty in karmic ties is the reason for this.

Confrontations: Many Fours, and the Four of Diamonds in particular, have a strong ability to deal with a struggle. The key to happiness for them is to acknowledge this portion of their being and to take a good hard look at it. There is kind of a strong and heavy-duty quality about these people. They seem to be able to take abuse because they are often built strong. There are challenges to meet in their lives, and this is not surprising. An example of this is Roseanne Barr, the comedienne, who has had a life of challenges. She is a Four of Diamonds Scorpio. Four of Diamonds individuals seem to be able to handle more abuse than others. They do a lot of work and many of them become bitter about this because it is so hard to get anything without it. There are some strings attached even to those things most would think of as blessings. That leads to a life that would make most people bitter.

Three of Diamonds
Monetary Inventiveness

Characteristics: These individuals can see the secrets of this world and beyond with their minds. This includes an understanding of the karma they are here for in this lifetime. Much peace will come into their lives with this understanding. Although sometimes they try to dismiss what they know, they are acutely aware of right and wrong. Because they operate out of the high side of this card and they are quite creative as well as productive, not all Threes of Diamonds suffer from these problems. The Three of Diamonds maybe has the hardest life path of all. Because the Six of Diamonds is the Karma card, this is especially true of females. Particularly, relative to relationships Three of Diamonds females are in for a lot of difficulty. A constant threat is worrying about their finances. Frequently they must sacrifice for someone younger and often this is one or more of their children. Their later years can be less than they hope for because of the two Nines in their Life Path, unless they have worked on their spiritual side. Peace and wisdom come from this. They should pursue a career that gives them freedom in these areas and benefit from variety and travel. Experimenting with ideas and then to settling on the truth is why such individuals are here. Threes have to find constructive releases for their highly active minds because in general they are guilty of worry and indecision. Finding some outlet for their creativity is the best solution, and expressing themselves is important. If they are to achieve tranquillity in their lives and jump the hurdles and difficulties they will face, they should develop their natural aptitude for metaphysics. Many useful ways can be found to express themselves. Super entertainers and speakers are things they can be, because their minds and their voices are powerful. They can be very effective promoters once they have found something they can believe in. Those who have a Three of Diamonds promoting their business are lucky. Traveling or doing an assortment of tasks is where they get more satisfaction in business.

Relationships: As with the Queen of Diamonds, multiple marriages often are the case with this card. They are learning to let people go their own way and to heal their fears as the Seven of Diamonds in Venus shows. They come into this life with the disposition to be somewhat uncaring about other people's emotions. Their first Karma card lets us know that. Other people can be uncertain about their affection because of their carefree nature. The Queen of Diamonds runs in sync with the Three of Diamonds card as being the most difficult in terms of relationships. This card comes into life feeling as though there are endless kingdoms to explore and experience because of their enormous creativity. They realize that they too have big fear of abandonment and disloyalty that has to be dealt with somewhere along the line. This often results in frequent indecision regarding matters of the heart, as well as marriage, and possibly multiple relationships. Generally, most of their happiness in love comes later in their lives, because usually it takes time. They will elect impermanent relationships if they are unable to deal with their own insecurities. They will learn the importance of being consistent in the areas of romance in this incarnation. Because the romantic forces for relationships will usually sustain themselves well into the last years of their life, that can be fine for Threes of Diamonds.

Personality Connections: Club women are very attracted to Three of Diamonds men. Three of Diamonds men have an attraction to Spade women. No suit is particularly strong though. Male Hearts and Spades are often attractive for female Threes of Diamonds, but they mix well with Clubs, too.

Confrontations: The Sevens and Nines are always thought to be the most difficult cards to have in one's Life Path. There are many obstacles in the Life Path of the Three of Diamonds. We notice that Threes of Diamonds have two Sevens and two Nines, so we can understand better what their lives might be like.

Two of Diamonds
Entrepreneur

Characteristics: With their closest relationships, their ambition is no problem, because it keeps them from difficulties. They will find a way for them that is interesting and provides rewards if they tap in to their inner mind. They do well in a single business by setting it up themselves and sticking with it. In the deck, this is a highly successful card. Any blame is their own for not being happy and productive. The Two of Diamonds will consistently be shown the right path to proceed on and, if permitted, has a natural intuition for that. Built in to this is a lofty set of values, and that frequently includes a mission in life which every time involves partners and other people as part of it. There frequently is a monetary motivation and a bit of ambition that motivates them. Because they love business and finance deeply, they are the wheeler-dealer card, especially with friends and partners. Rather than work alone, this card usually chooses to work with others in a partnership. The Two of Diamonds has a mind that is quick at categorizing and evaluating, because the Two is the logical number. They can move toward working with computers and are good at it. Two of Diamonds individuals can lose that and their capable mind and lean toward becoming pessimistic and argumentative if they are emotionally unfulfilled. This is a very fortunate card in terms of money. They can live to one hundred if they take care of themselves. Making deals and mixing with others is their first love. They bring a message of light. Twos of Diamonds have something that takes them to a higher knowledge of some kind, and they have a special purpose. Especially beginning in middle age, most of them have high incomes. Caution should be used pertaining to social obligations so as not to tax their health and well-being, even though they are blessed. They do not take care of themselves if they are too compulsive about money. In later life, real estate is a good source of money.

Relationships: A Two of Diamonds male will avoid divorce at all costs, but in a marriage that is emotionally trying he will frequently have affairs, even numerous ones. Before marrying, they should all examine for truth the conviction that it is forever. Because they are so involved in the cerebral side of things, their Ace of Diamond Pluto card shows a strong, but often unrevealed, craving for affection that can go unseen or unfelt. The Two of Diamonds has fixed and strong feelings in romance terms: views and values about love that are excellent in most ways. For romantic and emotional well-being, however, this is their greatest obstacle. Love and marriage are more than their fixed ideas about them, and this is something many of them must learn. Because of these fixed principles, once starting a relationship, good or bad, they are often there to stay. Even if happiness is not there, this can make them stick around. They can become bitter and prone to negativity resulting in the mean side of this card coming out. At the heart of most of their relationship issues and problems is this inner need for affection and self-respect. This serves them well in their careers but can be a stumbling block to success in personal relationships, because it inhibits their ability to feel. This inhibition can be overcome, and with work they can learn to communicate the intimate feelings that are necessary for a healthy relationship. A very intellectual person is usually found in the Two of Diamonds.

Personality Connections: A Spade man is a good marriage for a Two of Diamonds woman. Many Diamond women friends are common with both genders. Women of the Hearts suit are better with Two of Diamonds men.

Confrontations: It is clear that these two Aces are important if we examine the Life Spreads of Two of Diamonds people. Romance is a significant pattern with the Two of Diamonds and Ace of Diamonds. This pattern comes from the two Aces standing right beside each other in the Life Spread in both cases.

♦ ## Ace of Diamonds
   Longing for Adoration and Funding

Characteristics: The Ace of Diamonds can be extremely generous and kind or, oddly enough, impatient, selfish, and aggressive. Jupiter leans toward expanding the Neptunian notion of charity to great extremes at times, and their makeup has the Jupiter/Neptune card in their Life Spread. All of them tend to help those in need and are kindhearted on one level. They hate to see not just humans, but any animals suffering. Many make significant contributions to worthy causes because of the influence of Neptune making them want to reach high ideals. Rescuers of some kind are the way most Ace of Diamonds individuals think of themselves. Neptune can lead us on a path of great deception and wrong ideals, because they are sometimes an illusion, even if they save friends, family, associates, partners, or spouses. This depends on an ability for discrimination. The Ace of Diamonds can manifest itself in numerous fashions and is inherently passionate. Having money (or security) and love at the same time is one main issue for them. They tend to focus all of their being toward one place and exclude all others, maybe because this is their nature. This aspect is at the forefront of both men and women regardless of the cause. One Ace of Diamonds was Paul Newman, who did a lot for charities. However, another Ace of Diamonds was Adolf Hitler. Believing he was right caused him to be responsible for the deaths of millions of innocent people. In Neptune's idealism these are opposites. Ace of Diamonds people have a lot of diversity in their dreamlike and optimistic natures. It is always there, regardless. These individuals can easily work two jobs at the same time and are capable and creative. All are naturally attracted to the metaphysical side of existence and have a psychic ability. They can lead lives of superior satisfaction and accomplishment if they are not fixated on money as their main value. A lot of their good luck comes from the new people they meet every day. While having artistic ability they are also ambitious. They love to travel, and it is a significant part of their lives. An integral part of their lives is communication of every kind, and they are usually active. They believe they are here to assist the world and make important contributions in the process, no matter what they do.

Relationships: Ace of Diamonds men should refrain from marrying, according to many. They seem better suited to affairs and not long-term commitments because of restlessness about them. But if they can find a perfect partner who will take the journey of life with them they are able come to terms with this restlessness. The identical energy that often results in love affairs can be satisfied this way. Again, whether they will have to sacrifice their career to experience the love they want is the primary challenge for Ace of Diamonds people. They frequently see their partner irregularly because they have a long-distance relationship. Their vocation is thus permitted enough time, which is usually of prime importance to them. Occasionally the partner does not live up to their end of the agreement even though they have a positive view of them and are good providers and supporters. Disappointment and anger can result. Their needs must be spoken about, and they need to have a more realistic view of other people. The door is opened by communication. They spend a lot of time traveling with their partner in some cases. Many find out the importance of having a partner with them instead of being separated by long distances at one time in their life. There is an influence in their relationships with others due to the powerful Neptune/Pisces element in the Ace of Diamonds.

Personality Connections: Men who are Clubs, particularly those who have a more mature side in their personality, are invariably better with Ace of Diamonds women. While a lot of Diamond women are friends of both genders, they are not usually recommended for marriage. A Heart woman is better for an Ace of Diamonds man. A close look at the specific card should be done in order to avoid problems, however.

Confrontations: A Five in Venus may explain their romantic side, in these terms. There is a great distance created, for some reason, between Ace of Diamonds people and others.

King of Spades
Skilled

Characteristics: The King of Spades is ready to undertake great responsibility. Some become our greatest leaders because they are the most powerful of the Kings. King of Spades people must be prepared and willing to take on the huge responsibility that leadership requires in order to release this great power. To be an example for the others to see, they must overcome restlessness in order to succeed in their chosen field. In any case, the King of Spades is the wisest and most powerful card in the deck. Kings of Spades will surely rise to the top of any profession they desire, providing the men do not decide to remain Jacks. Being a master of anything they choose is a quality of Kings of Spades. Many men give up most of the power they possess and choose the arts or entertainment arenas. Acting more like a Queen is usually a quality of the female King of Spades. To avoid becoming stuck in the commonplace, caution is necessary. However, this is not representative of the pinnacle that is available to every King. They are frequently dissatisfied in spite of all their ability. Progressiveness is also another way to see this. They are able to comprehend the secrets of the universe easily when they enter their spiritual realms. They master our physical and spiritual universes. Everyone benefits from their contributions when they accept the burden of responsibility as King. They are willing to do anything to acquire success and recognition. In addition, they respect the wisdom and love the learned. While it is not always their choice for work, they can manage huge organizations. There is a stubbornness about King of Spades people, and no matter who it is they will not change their minds. Inner fortitude and resolve is something they have in abundance. Unfortunately, this makes most changes in their life very difficult to handle because of these same qualities. They often never get married and are indecisive relative to love and close friendships. They are always go-getters and are ambitious. This never fails. It is very rare for one to be lazy. While all do have a basic wisdom and seldom sink to lowly acts, not all reach the heights.

Relationships: The King of Spades has a lifetime goal to conquer fears of being abandoned and betrayed, because of the Pluto card. Negativity can result when they experience both at stages in their lives. This possibility motivates them in a positive way in issues about love or personal growth and other significant areas. Changes and uncertainties are certain to result, because the King of Spades tends to take a very cerebral approach to love. Insecurity can often result, and sexual areas can be influenced by this uncertainty. They have betrayals at times in their lives according to the karmic system. Learning to let others be themselves and letting go of emotional attachments to loved ones are blessings in life. We find many will rarely allow others to get very close because of their strong will.

Personality Connections: King of Spades females frequently have difficulty with Diamond males, although they do share a strong attraction for each other. For the King of Spades women, Heart men are a difficulty, as are Club women. King of Spades men, when they do mate, frequently select a Club or Heart woman because they share a physical attraction.

Confrontations: When we examine the lives of King of Spades individuals, we can see a definite pattern that shows something about what it feels like to have such enormous power and all that responsibility. Many prefer doing work that would normally be associated with Jacks, the card of actors. Sales, artists, musicians, or even gamblers are some occupations of many Kings of Spades. One might think that all Kings of Spades are super successful and hold powerful positions in society, because it is the most powerful card in the deck, but this is not the case. The majority of Kings of Spades do not seem to live up to that perception.

Queen of Spades
Self-Cultivation

Characteristics: Among Queen of Spades individuals we find some that are the actual mothers of the Earth and others who are the most bitter and driven people there are. Some are people who selflessly share and convey their wisdom. They must activate their own destiny to show they are born rulers. How things turn out in their lives depends on their personal approach to values. For some reason, Queens of Spades are not in positions of authority or even importance, even though they have so much power and authority. They object bitterly about their situation in life and do not amount to anything when they end up in low positions. Wrapped in the battle mentality and doing hard work to see it clearly can distract them. However, they sit in a quite high position in the Spiritual Spread, and they can master themselves. They can lift themselves to the heights they want if they recognize their tremendous powers and assume responsibility for their lives. Their power and potential dissipate being interested only in material gain, which is frequently so. Listening to their intuition and inner self is how their highest state can be achieved. While they enjoy spending money and they despise getting the short end of the stick in legal issues, sadly, they usually do. Their best is achieved when they are aware of their position in the royal family, thus connecting with their internal wisdom, which they are entitled to. They are elevated in the perception of God. They have all the necessary assets to carry out whatever they want to. The King of Spades is the Ruling card for all Queens of Spades. They are capable leaders and have a lot of success in school or writing because they are very bright. They have a strong independent aspect and a lot of intuition. Becoming teachers and leaders is possible if they tap their highest potential. There is certain trouble when legal issues come up. Mixing love and money is not a good idea. Arguing with powerful men is not wise for them.

Relationships: If Queens of Spades do not give up on their desire for happiness, love for them may come later in life. Making true commitments, like marriage, is something they shun because many are extremely independent. The Queens of Spades hold lofty ideals about romance and marriage; they are so positive that they almost border on fantasyland. Fulfilling their tendency to have affairs usually causes loss for them. Lost money usually follows lost love in addition to heartbreak. They like to have a wealthy partner and to have the appearance of wealth too, but this generally does not take place.

Personality Connections: Queens of Spades have a strong physical attraction to Diamond men, as well as good communication. Diamond women feel quite close to male Queens of Spades because of a mystical fascination. A Club man is often the spouse of the Queen of Spades woman, although the relationship can be difficult at times.

Confrontations: Never at rest, the male energy is always moving and always performing from the creative desire of the word. At peace, the female energy receives. Rather than running after the things that they desire, people with a strong female energy will attract them and get energy. The Queen is a representative for self-sufficiency. Spades represent spiritual progress. Work, service, and health, however, are also strongly connected. Change and development of the soul itself is on the highest plane and in the suit of Spades. Both masculine and feminine energy make up the world. All that exists is a mixture of both in everything. Both masculine as well as feminine energy are equally significant. There is a dependence on balance by the universe, as we know it. The four Queens in the deck personify feminine energy. There is still a lot of the feminine and receptive energy no matter the physical gender of the person who has the Queen Birth card.

Jack of Spades
Headliner

Characteristics: Jack of Spades individuals have talent for doing anything involving the mind, and it is certain they are strong in creative endeavors. Whether this strength will be utilized in a knowledgeable and patient way without deception is the question. Falling into the negative aspects of the Jack of Spades is a possibility for individuals if they are not cautious. Their status can either take them in the direction of goodness and value, or fool them and take a downward spiral toward lies and deception. This card has an easier Life Path than most of the deck in material terms, and a lot simply comes easily for them. A lot of their difficulties, however, can originate here: individuals may not appreciate the significance of what they possess if life is too easy. There is a broad range of things about a Jack of Spades ranging from a visionary to a spiritual guide to a criminal. A combination of creativity and oversupply of mental power is the cause of this. It has been referred to as the Thief's card even while representing a spiritual novice. It is up to the individuals to channel their superb creativity with dignity and knowledge, because most Jacks of Spades have some of both of these characteristics in them. They lose their way and sometimes believe the falsehoods they invent to avoid a difficult life. These individuals are capable of being successful artists, actors, and actresses consistently, and do well with others. In spite of the fact that they can make enough themselves, frequently they inherit money. They usually have a successful life in most cases and are often driven. What gives them their direction and final success is their fundamental value system, learned in their youth. The fine things they possess are exactly those things they may be more apt to neglect or be unaware of. It is often that way for Jacks of Spades who follow the way of the thief, because of their false reasoning. Challenges for them are found in the extreme boundaries of experience. The remedy for this can be ending up in jail, because it is a challenge that holds a powerful lesson. The spiritual aspect residing in this card often does not reveal itself until these individuals get caught and look at themselves in the mirror. It is never wise to play with fire; however, it is the fire that purifies the Jack of Spades.

Relationships: Jacks of Spades fantasize about the perfect lover or partner more than most other cards, but it is precisely this that often causes them to keep looking. In a lot of their romantic lives this might also be the cause of the turnover rate being so high. Their idea of romance is so idealized that no single person could ever achieve it. There is no one but themselves who are responsible if they are not happy in this area. Whether or not they succeed, their success in love is always up to them. In the present lifetime the Jack of Spades must disperse some karma pertaining to love. People make commitments in relationships that teach the importance of truth and the right use of their strong sexuality. Qualities capable of getting them in trouble are their very creative, romantic, and independent natures. They must be combined with knowledge and purpose.

Personality Connections: Two things should be remembered: Jack of Spades women are as strong-minded as the males and royal cards, including the King, Queen, and Jack. Female Jacks of Spades find the Heart suit difficult and most often too much to handle. Generally speaking, Diamonds of both sexes do great with other people. There is a high attraction to Club males for Jack of Spades females, especially those who are more experienced and have power.

Confrontations: Their natural creative talents to deceive others and use them, with no regard for how their actions are affecting those they are stealing from, are emphasized in this case. Frankly every one of them has this nature within them. Getting so mixed up with the bad side of their card's expression is perhaps the reason for this. A big change, however, is always possible in their lives. Regardless of whether they elect to express this or not, a lot of Jack of Spades people are using mostly this side of their card: in one form or the other, every Jack symbolizes initiations. The strongest representation of initiation though is the spiritual foundation. One of the aspects in the Jack of Spades person's lifetime is the transition from the lower essence of the Jack to a higher. We can almost be sure of this, so sure that there is practically an extreme of these aspects. The Jack of Spades' lowest nature is not trustworthy and always pursuing the more base side of things.

Ten of Spades
Striving Accomplishment

Characteristics: The spiritual essence of the Ten of Spades can provide the option to go beyond materialism. A fear of being poor can lead to difficulties for Ten of Spades individuals in making up their minds about love, which can introduce problems in marriage. They can cause a lot of problems in their personal situations if they abuse the power they have been given. On the other hand, unattached spiritual love is available to these individuals. Seeing their higher aspects in the area of direction and guidance, they can have anything they desire. There can be a tendency in the direction of addictive behavior due to both Karma cards residing in the Neptune line of the Life cards. Materialistic and compulsive worker types are often found among Ten of Spades people. Suffering in their home life always results, and this is painful because home and family are very significant to them. Many will have battles between these two fundamental desires. This largely depends on their individual concentrations in life. Pursuing a profession is particularly difficult for Tens of Spades who have trouble keeping a satisfying family life while working. Dramatic ups and downs are possible for some. Learning the value of releasing personal attachments to concepts and personal styles is what the Ten of Spades was intended to learn in this life. They can have a life experiencing the heights of spiritual knowledge and wisdom, which is a part of their fate if they meet the challenge. Such individuals can master their fate and go soaring to heights helping other people. They can be blinded to their ascent, however, and limit their growth because there is also an attraction to material gains. There is a natural move toward doing everything all out, and therefore you find a personality that frequently overdoes things, both good and bad. They experience events to their fullest and learn a great deal this way.

Relationships: Fulfillment is most possible at a later point in life. Before they can go ahead with such a significant commitment, they need to get answers to a great many questions. There is no reason they cannot have a good married life, because their fundamental karma in terms of love is excellent. They must only find a means to reconcile their desire for family life with their basic intensity and ambitious being, because ultimately they are very giving and loving. They are both strongly devoted to work as well as family, and they often have inner conflicts pertaining to these two parts of life. They can become uncertain in love, which can bring about problems resulting from their ambitious and creative natures. Tens of Spades do not do well with the financial matters that are usually involved with separations. Their proximity with Venus reveals some uncertainty relative to the romantic side of life, and they must deal with it before a successful, meaningful relationship is brought about. They continually have partners who are unable to make a commitment, and, in addition, they are often not sure of what they actually want in romance. Change and up-and-down periods in love are the results regardless.

Personality Connections: On the level of romance, other Spade men are also fine for Ten of Spades women. Heart men are a weakness for the Ten of Spades women and have good emotional connections with Diamond men. Generally speaking, the female Club cards and Ten of Spades men can make good marriages.

Confrontations: The fourth house in astrology is the residence of security, emotions, and nourishment, while the tenth house sits exactly opposite. It is peculiar that the two main cards for marriage and family life have such strong internal relationships with the Ten of Spades. The Ten of Spades individuals, having dual Heart cards for their Karma cards, the Four and the Queen, are totally work oriented and driven for success. Being closely related to family and home, these cards are somewhat opposites of the Ten of Spades. Big ambitions in careers are often a part of Ten of Spades. The tenth house is motivated for success and recognition, because as the Ten of Tens they personify the Capricorn. Many of them reach their desires due to being very practical and motivated pertaining to their drive for success. Their need for a home with love and family is the single thing that can stop this determined drive for recognition. That such an extraordinary radical opposite tendency resides within the personality of a single person is fascinating.

Nine of Spades
All-Embracing Vitality

Characteristics: Being inherently spiritual or psychic can never be totally dismissed. Nine of Spades individuals are led to a life of universal giving and releasing of that which does not serve higher concepts, if they recognize this significant portion of themselves. In this regard, some of them can make a great contribution to the world. A lot of Nines of Spades are successful, creative individuals including artists, teachers, and performers. They are also givers. Friends in high places help them through some of the difficult emotional periods they are sure to encounter; these friends give them the wise nature necessary to conquer their feelings and fears. The Nine of Spades has the most powerful internal desires of the universal cards. They range from people who have had lives that are almost total losses to those who have a complete and wonderful life, including the gift of giving to others. As this is the "Nine of Nines" Birth card, the aspect of the remaining three Nines is there as well. Interestingly, a few important characteristics of their personalities must be permitted to fade away so that they can be reborn. This is because in some way there is a significant release that must happen for them. This issue could be anything from the way they handle relationships or money to as basic as a personal hygiene habit or work function. It might, at times, involve each of these simultaneously. A good business ability is also present in these individuals, and that can bring financial success if put to use. Nevertheless, their mission is one of love, and they find their fulfillment there. Their inborn power radiates. The further they ascend to importance on their path to the divine, the more the result of the wide scope of their work, and concentrating on giving to large groups, can develop.

Relationships: When they desire one, the Nine of Spades has every charm as well as the emotional strength to have a mate. There can be a slight fear that if they find themselves in love they might lose that person, because even though they are the Nine of Nines, there are sure to be losses in their lives. In addition, emotional trauma early in life means many Nines of Spades have scars that prevent personal relationships. At any rate, the Nine of Spades woman longs for a relationship—the exception being one where, for example, she is stuck with codependent activity and trying to rescue her partner. She will not accept nonsense from any man. They love groups just as they do individuals, and they are truly loving, generous, and wonderful people. There will be key people in their lives who give emotional endings and completions, but these may not necessarily be viewed as losses. It is clear that a Nine of Spades with no partner is keeping potential mates away for some reason, because we know that with all the charm the Nine of Spades can have a partner easily. Otherwise, they can have anything they want romantically. Their Karma card makes the Nine of Spades woman strong-minded and freethinking. Personal relationships can be challenging. Such power from a woman cannot be dealt with by all men. From the same perspective, any female who is a King can be both father as well as mother to her offspring; this card can readily be a single parent.

Personality Connections: Spade males are also a possibility for Nine of Spades females, and there is a similar type of bonding. There is a strong love compatibility with Nine of Spades females and Heart males. Heart females and Nine of Spades males have a special connection for friendship that can reach matrimony. Diamond males are seen as attractive by Nine of Spades women.

Confrontations: Some Nine of Spades individuals believe this is their last incarnation. This is actually quite odd because it would seem that a person who is in their final incarnation would be a very happy individual who has experienced all of their dreams, desires, and wishes. Most people do not know a person who is undergoing their final lifetime. One ought to approach people who believe that with caution; this the wisdom of Nine of Spades.

Eight of Spades
Effectiveness in Labor

Characteristics: Eight of Spades individuals enforce their actions through their strong wills. Abuse of power would seem to follow those who have the greatest power to use. Using such power any way they want is one way they might react to this gift. A person might automatically believe that because they have such power they must be right. All Eights are hurt from the consequence of actions based on this conception, because it is so far from the truth. As an extremely powerful card and the Eight of Eights, the Eight of Spades has the heaviest weight to carry and a major obligation to use power for good. There is a temptation to take this power and apply it, or to run away from fears and deny looking at themselves. In the final analysis their work must take priority over their love life because they are to make a contribution to society. They are hard workers and even, in some cases, workaholics. The majority of Spade individuals cannot free their focus from materialism. Actually, Spades should guide us to the spiritual realm. If they are motivated to work then success is almost guaranteed for them. Their tremendous power is something of which they are aware. Frequently, challenges highlight their real abilities. They can change the lives of others because of a profound healing power. Having a less negative attitude about life during the changes that come with it will be a challenge for their development. Healing and more individual autonomy come from the study of the spiritual. However, the question is how it will be applied. Self-destruction is possible if they work from a lower plane, or if they are motivated by fear. However, admiration and respect are also results that can motivate them. They frequently try to marry individuals who are well off financially, but they do make good providers themselves. If their marriages should end, they are the exception who always seem to come out on top financially.

Relationships: Eights of Spades seem to have thought of love more than we might suspect, even though their work is generally the primary part in their lives. They respect people who are very intelligent and are drawn to those with whom they can communicate well. They learn that this same power can destroy the delicate balance that is necessary in a meaningful relationship, especially when they have so much power that they can use. They have success in relationships if they are aware of their personal fears. Their job is often the place they find the individual they are seeking. Their mates often work with them in business partnerships. With their choice of mates, finances appear to be an important factor. There is a distinct emotional foundation in the Eight of Spades, and there is usually no restlessness or indecision emanating from them as there is with a lot of the cards in the deck. In a committed relationship, including marriage, they have a better chance than most at success. Due to an emotionally immature aspect, how-ever, it frequently takes awhile for them to comprehend the concept of love as well as they do their vocation. Learning through trial and error, they often take a conceptual or intellectual approach to love, romance, and mat-rimony itself. They often follow a practical rule in their choices and choose someone who has more money and is well off.

Personality Connections: Diamond females are found to be attractive by Eight of Spades males, but they can also disagree a great deal. There will be control problems with people born as a Jack or higher of any suit, because the Eight of Spades is a power card. Both men and women enjoy the friend-ship of other Spades. The Eights of both genders are very challenging for Diamond men.

Confrontations: Their knack to bring about things by a sheer sense of will and determination means the Eights of Spades surpass the other Eights in this regard. This can create confrontations with others, and they have to be carefully aware of these qualities in their interactions with others.

 **Seven of Spades**
Belief

Characteristics: Having a positive attitude when health issues arise is a difficult obstacle, but that is precisely what Seven of Spades individuals have to do. They must live the higher values they are aware of if they are to keep the power and blessings inherently residing within them. There is a tendency to stress at times, but they have a lot of internal strength. They are on the line as the Seven of Spades. They suffer countless problems, often physically oriented, if they do not talk and behave from a higher perspec-tive. Sickness, accidents, or other physical difficulties make up most of their problems. Because this is one of the most spiritual in the deck, these indi-viduals can generally have a lot of success as long as they do not waste the wisdom that is meant to lead them through life. Seven of Spades members are present here on Earth to learn to trust as well as keep their faith despite their environment. Challenges in their lives come in from work and physi-cal health. Their Life Path is one of the better ones in the deck. They will have a lot of their personal desires come true in this lifetime, because their Birth card sits in the Jupiter area of the Life Spread. Many become well-known and successful because they have so many abilities they can use to be prominent and satisfied in their lives. They need to follow their intuition and live according to their knowledge. A high, spiritual force is the source of their protection, but this must be realized and honed through their actions with the highest level of truth and pure motives. Their lives take on a magical quality once this is accomplished. Being almost unlimited in their ability to do good, many accept a special goal of helping the world. Selfish notions and goals are sure to lead to suffering to some extent for those who are attached to them. Romantic associations or marriage often lead to receiving monetary support. If they are hard workers and stay honest, they will always do fine. Only they can stop themselves. A symbol of protection and security is found even in their Saturn card, and this symbolizes that almost nothing can actually harm them except their own fears or self-doubt.

Relationships: Much like their Karma card, Seven of Spades women are generally strong-willed. They have trouble filling the role of a passive, subservient female because of their fundamental strength. Any man in her life must be confident to get along in a relationship, because she can stand up for herself. In spite of their good marriage karma, they still cannot get away from the obstacles of their Birth card, which infringe in every area of their lives, including their romantic relationships. Even if they have everything they desire, they may be overwhelmed by fear or a negativity about life. To maintain positive energy between each other, they need to have faith and remain positive. The advantage of marriage can carry over into both the financial as well as spiritual realms. They must watch an inclination to place too much importance on financial aspects, because a lack of higher values will bring them more difficulties than good. However, they are drawn to people of means as well as mental power.

Personality Connections: Spade females are attracted to Seven of Spades males, but Diamond females experience them negatively. Both Diamond and Club males draw in Seven of Spades women, and there is an affection felt by Club males. Heart females find that Seven of Spades males are a challenge.

Confrontations: The Seven of Spades frequently have had a major accident in their lives, and, surprisingly, it is often recently. Auto accidents seem to be common, and a lot of them appear to have experienced a series of them. If you see someone who appears to have been in an accident, odds are that person is a Seven of Spades. If you should meet a Seven of Spades individual, try this experiment: prior to them telling you anything about their life, ask them whether they have ever been in a serious accident.

 **Six of Spades**
Fate

Characteristics: It is true that we cannot amend actions once they are in motion, and this is one of the big lessons for the Six of Spades. The Six of Spades is the most powerful representation of the law of cause and effect and is seen as the card of Fate. Indeed, it is so much so that a lot of Sixes of Spades start to believe that in life they have limited choices and little power to influence the outcome. There are still a lot of events in life over which we have a huge responsibility, and our options in this life are always important in this regard. Regardless of whether it is done for good or ill, we reap what we sow. Six of Spades people can expect there to be events that seem to be fated at different points in their lives. Our actions or things we have said in earlier lifetimes set events into motion for events experienced later, when situations are correct to create a balancing of those actions. Some of these events can be negative and harmful and show what it is like to receive such negativity; others are positive and rewarding. This is a person who is here to learn the responsibility of such power. These people either have their power turned on them for their own destruction, or line up with a higher purpose and vision and achieve great success. A strong Neptune influence can mislead a lot of them to go down the highway of escapism and waste time in fantasy and delusion, but, in general, they are very responsible for their actions. Falling into a comfortable or even uncomfortable rut is something they should be alert to. There is a stubbornness about them. Many Six of Spades individuals are destined for supreme achievement, as this card has some of the highest possibility for success and fame of any card. There are glimmers of the big possibility for monetary gain. There needs to be action and a willingness to carry great responsibility, of course, if this is to come to fruition. They find a lot of fulfillment, reason, meaning, and friendship through gaining knowledge. Love and romance are their biggest obstacles in this area. Indecision is against them. As dreamers they must be cautious to keep their dreams in sync with higher ideals and morals, otherwise they will become nightmares. Their power can be used to grab the highest dream and utilize it. Completion on each level is guaranteed, and if their vision is clear, they are unstoppable.

Relationships: True intimacy in a relationship with another person is very difficult if one is fearful of something; once the feared thing is seen and admitted, intimacy improves. Intelligence and wit attract both genders. Wealth, authority, or prominence are things Six of Spades women like. In matters of love they can be sneaky or dishonest and need to avoid catching themselves in their own fantasies and ideas. Thinking about love and romance is something the Six of Spades cannot halt. They have many experiences, both positive and negative, while they collect experience to fortify their notions and ideas at the same time. This causes them to tend to have a somewhat mental approach to the whole situation. They usually have negative results from being drawn into several relationships. Underlying these attempts at relationships is usually a hidden fear of not getting ample affection.

Personality Connections: Women who are Sixes are quite alluring to Club men and Diamond men. The Six of Spades would have to assume the backseat in the relationship with a Heart for it to really work, but they do have great connections with them.

Confrontations: In the late 1800s, according to many published stories and interviews in newspapers, a Six of Spades could prove that his life was totally fated with a specific destiny. He had, so it was claimed, an ability to foretell without error what cards would be picked from a deck by any person after he knew the time of day and birthday of the person. Hindu astrologers hold the same notion. Fixed principles and laws of mathematics, they claimed again and again, could tell us how the world operates.

Five of Spades
Roamer

Characteristics: The Five of Spades represents changes and travel. And, to be sure, there is a kind of restlessness that shows itself in certain ways. Occupations that offer some variation are helpful to most Fives of Spades, because they find routine uncomfortable. Many of them relocate to a new place often or are frequent travelers. Their mission for truth and the expansion of their inner being frequently affects their spiritual journey. There is a degree of personal sacrifice made in the area of education, or for those they love. This is particularly the case in their early lives. It is after this time that satisfaction in love and finances usually arrives, and their desire for travel slowly fades as they find more meaning and appreciation in their home and family life. They are lucky to have much social success because of their Karma card; however, on occasions their social life can be difficult, especially when they partake in excess. They have good organizational skills and a fundamental sense of value. Many of them are financial experts or highly successful in sales. Their life gets better, especially after age thirty-nine, and with age they go through a transformation for improvement. The spiritual Nine in Venus in their relationship connection causes many personal disappointments, particularly with friends and those they love. Therefore, they are usually more successful in groups rather than one on one. They have to learn to show unconditional love in their nearest relationships so that they can tap the higher side of the spiritual cards that are located in the personal areas (Venus and Mars) of the Life Path. Usually the Five of Spades is one of the luckier cards in the deck in material terms, because the cards in Five of Spades' Life Path are the more successful ones.

Relationships: The pair of Nines in Venus and Mars inform us of the challenges Fives of Spades face in intimate relationships. However, with the soul's development and with the right attitude, such finalities can be turned in to graduations, ultimate achievements, and profound completions. Their friends and peers like these individuals; they are very popular, and there is an enjoyment of travel, love, and romance. There are sure to be some disappointments due to being here to finalize some relationships they began in previous lives and let them go. Therefore, disappointments in love from time to time will exist. There will be some important relationships in their lives that appear to be what they want, but these will not work out as hoped for. They are able to permit their partners the freedom to be their best, as well as sacrifice for those they love. When Jupiter is brought into the picture, we note that this card at the minimum will bring a friendship lasting a lifetime that is both special and rewarding. After they have comprehended the lessons of the pair of Nines, it can also bring a lot of love into their lives. Their biggest love experience frequently comes later in their lives for this very reason. They develop an awareness that what is taken from them is probably not good for them anyway and is best left forgotten. It is something the Five of Spades person needs to learn. Two Nines are clearly in their personal lives and are very strong. We think we will see our own personal and romantic progress with Venus and Mars present, but that can mean letting go of what we desire. This can be a great challenge for some Fives of Spades, but for others it brings about the existence of a tremendous nature entailing spiritual love.

Personality Connections: Heart males are a good choice for marriage with Five of Spades females, but it will have some obstacles and problems. Even though there are sure to be a few lessons given in the relationship, Club females can get along with Spade males. Good friends come from Diamond males.

Confrontations: Five symbolizes the number of the human race, so Fives represent those who are here to experience what life is all about. We can see more clear examples of this in the Five of Spades. Fives of Spades are best known for the degree to which they will go in order to have new experiences in their lives. This is partly because they are the strongest of the Five cards. While this is the case with all Fives, the Spade remains the strongest.

Four of Spades
Bliss in Labor

Characteristics: Four of Spades individuals have the right to be stubborn, and they most certainly are. They must live by truths they discover, but fortunately the Karma card provides ample knowledge. Being restrained in any manner is something they hate. Thanks to Venus they are intuitive and intelligent, as well as liked by others. They seem to attract friends with money, but they themselves should resist the temptation to emphasize money regarding their choice of associates or lovers. Their health should be taken care of by natural means, but they normally have good health. Gratification through work is symbolized by the Four of Spades. If we consider all the cards in the deck, this one is the most substantial. A square or even a boulder comes to mind relative to these individuals. They are reliable and are there for you when needed. They work hard and always maintain their balance. In regard to finances and success, they have one of the luckiest life paths and most often enjoy their work. However, some can interfere with their success if they are not careful. Their Saturn card informs us that even though they are lucky, they often worry about finances anyway. At social activities, they make excellent communicators or lecturers because Mercury usually allows them immediate credence. The literary arts are ideal for them and they can be well-known writers, promoters, or even performers. They provide their own true peace and meaning in life because the Four of Spades is a worker card. To find satisfaction they will frequently align themselves with a humanitarian cause. Traveling the world is usually something they do not get to do while young, but they can fulfill this dream in their later years.

Relationships: While they can be difficult and even stubborn, Fours of Spades will normally give you anything because of their extraordinary generosity. They need to be careful, though, because they are attracted to those with money and can get wrapped up in trying to keep up with the Joneses in their relationships. Confusion and fears about finances will frequently cause too much stress in their romantic life. Their karma for marriage is better than most, and they particularly appreciate someone who can travel with them. Business and personal relationships are usually not wise to mix, nor are money and pleasure.

Personality Connections: Diamond females are good friends for the Four of Spades. Fours of Spades of both genders find males of the Clubs suit a problem, and therefore caution is required. There is a unique fascination for Diamond males, and Spade males and Four of Spades women find them very good looking.

Confrontations: There is a desire for money related to the Four of Spades, or the fear of not having it, and this is an area of difficulty. It is usually unconscious in most cases, but is a deep-seated fear. If they want to liberate themselves from a life of difficulty, they need to deal with this because it is one of the most important driving forces in their existence. Fear that necessities and resources will not be there when needed comes from Saturn. Their entire life could be wasted trying to fill emptiness if they are not conscious of such feelings and cannot see them for what they are. Being a workaholic is a common characteristic for Four of Spades people. There are other cards that have this dynamic, but for the Four of Spades this quality can often be the result of a deep need to have material security. There is a strong drive for a secure life as well as a materialism, and that is sometimes the cause of a serious and arrogant exterior to a Four of Spades. The Four of Spades might be the most security-conscious of all the Fours. Security in their work is always a goal, and consequently they are wonderful workers whose lives are improved by working. Four of Spades people are more motivated than other cards in the deck. This is due to the relationship of Saturn's position in their Life Path. The area where things are difficult in an individual's life is often related to the card he or she has in Saturn. Things that are almost impossible to fulfill are represented by the Saturn card.

Three of Spades
Artisan

Characteristics: While they have a heavy burden as can be seen in their Saturn line, with hard work huge success is possible for the Three of

Spades. Hard work, as we see in the Jupiter spread, will bring them good results. A karmic debt must be paid on either a financial or value basis. Their Karma card tells us that. A Six individual often is involved, and they, of course, are the debt collectors. Learning responsibility and fairness with finances is the main lesson they must learn. Passing through something where they believe they were treated unjustly on a monetary level is something a Three of Spades individual will often have to do. Payments being made from past lives explains this. Indecision about work or wellness can be present, and they should be careful about their health. Worrying about their health, however, only makes their condition worse. Everything they desire and need will be available if they only get focused about what is most significant to them in life. Although it is not as satisfying on the creative level as artistic pursuits, they can be excellent at sales and marketing. They must be cautious and not take on a heavy load even though they are able to have several occupations. The temptation to tell only part of the truth or make up stories to make their lives easier is there for a Three because of a large amount of creativity. Their Jack Karma card means this is especially true. Threes of Spades must watch their thoughts and feelings as related to health issues. Their health concerns can be rooted in emotional problems in their lives; excessive work and career moves often interfere with body awareness and emotional issues. They can get highly stressed because of powerful creative urges. Furthermore, they can spread themselves too thin. Through the knowledge of their inner principles they are blessed with the opportunity for fantastic business success. As far as satisfaction in life goes, this can be one of their best routes for them. They create some wonderful expressions and inspiring works in the artistic area of their choice.

Relationships: Threes of Spades frequently have high goals for their marriage, and love can be a strongly spiritual thing for them, but this idealism can blind them to the negative aspect of individuals they attract. It is possible that because of this they will end up with people who do not really align with their dreams. They must deal with emotional issues that began in childhood before Threes of Spades can have happy marriages or meaningful romance. If they are to overcome some of the obstacles in this department, they need to maintain positive mental habits about love itself. Their romantic lives are restless, a quality stemming from their personality. It is possible, although it might be time consuming, to find the mixture of qualities in someone else that aligns with their own diversity. Because they are so creative and possess a romantic personality, the Three of Spades requires a partner with whom they can share their interests. In general they have good marriage possibilities, even though hurdles exist in love due to inner fears concerning abandonment or rejection. These must be dealt with first. Extramarital affairs can result by not allowing themselves a meaningful creative outlet, because their essence requires this. A partner with a pessimistic nature is often a part of their lives. Such a mate, however, often has an excellent income, and they like that portion of the relationship. It should be noted too that overlapping into their romantic life there is a good deal of idealism in this card.

Personality Connections: Club males are often present in the lives of both genders, though they are a mixed blessing at best. Diamond women seek Three of Diamonds men because they find them very attractive in general. Diamond males, as well, can be somewhat challenging at times.

Confrontations: Jacks in this suit, interestingly, are very similar to Threes. They exhibit many of the same qualities of the Three of their suit even while the Jack seems to be such a different number.

Two of Spades
Rapport

Characteristics: Generally speaking, rapport has the potential to plague Twos of Spades for their entire lives. They are very friendly but should not let themselves be self-indulgent or docile. They enjoy, overall, an easier life path than most. Money is often something they marry in to. Recognition or fame is sometimes their destiny. They are excellent at most things they do and usually get promoted to levels of leadership at work. This is particularly true of the males. Their second Karma card tells us that higher abilities are present in all of them, and naturally when the opportunity arrives they grab it. If they turn to their spiritual side they can be highly progressive, dynamic, and move to shape the world in to a harmonious and cooperative place. Partnership in work and friendship is what the Two of Spades represents. A fear of being alone shows us why Twos are also called fear cards, and the Two of Spades fits this pattern. All of them are personally hurt if others abuse their friendship or trust, but many will go out of their way to be in the company of other people. The Six is the Karma card of the Two of Spades, and it is one of the more powerful Karma cards. It states that the Two of Spades has an increased fated quality about it compared to other cards. In addition, their lives get in a rut from time to time, as dictated by the Karma card. This results in challenges in their health and their over-all constitution. They totally avoid their emotions and situations that try them in this realm, because they are so involved with their work and let-ting logic dominate over feelings. Sometimes this means the avoidance of marriage and commitments in romantic relationships. They do experience success in social situations, but the Pluto card shows some skepticism and indecisiveness romantically. For most of them, active good health habits are critical. The Uranus/Uranus position of the Spiritual Spread is the location of the Two of Spades, and this informs us that they all have a strong gift of intuition. They must hone a sincere interest in the spiritual aspect of life, however, to utilize this, something that a lot of Spades tend to not do, rather favoring their strong work and career activities. Logic does not help them, unfortunately, in personal relationships. But they possess a strong, logical mind, which helps them make a good living.

Relationships: Twos of Spades do have good karma from past lives, and they will receive good returns at some point in their lives. They are the kind that are steady and true and make excellent husbands and wives. Their uncertainty about love and romance comes primarily from the Pluto card. Long periods of inactivity in romance are brought on by themselves. The fears or doubts that prevent them from starting new partnerships or romantic commitments are frequently the cause of this. It is very helpful to get work done in this emo-tional area. Some of the better marriage karma of all the cards is in the Two of Spades. However, they need to resolve some of the uncertainty and fear related to being with another person before they can experience a quality mar-riage. This usually comes later in life. Push-pull relationships are what they have. They push their partner away after wanting them to get closer, appar-ently afraid of what closer intimacy might bring. Their approach to love often reflects their highly logical nature. They will often analyze endlessly the con-cept of marriage and of being together. They try to develop truths and draw conclusions about love and relationships so that they can quantify it. They, however, often neglect these areas because they are in the emotional realm.

Personality Connections: Two of Spades females hold vivid fantasies about other Spade males, but Diamond men find them especially attractive. Heart females give Two of Spades men blessings. Club women are friends and companions of both genders. They are a challenge for Club men.

Confrontations: An individual who we might call the classic Two of Spades might have his birthday on May 4th. He would be logically minded and hardworking. A computer programmer would be a likely occupation, and he is highly successful at what he does. The hottest computer company in the Silicon Valley would be his place of work.

♠ Ace of Spades
Burden of Goals and Hidden Treasures

Characteristics: The Ace of Spades is either very materialistic or driven by work and career, or extremely spiritual with an esoteric mind. They give to others even if materialistic, because they have special places and means. It comes naturally for them to give. It is suggested by their Karma card that their most challenging issues lie in the area of relationships, family, and friends. Counseling their friends is a gift, and they share it freely with others. It is even a career for some. Letting others be themselves is something they are learning to do, as is loving them unconditionally. Painful lessons are sometimes necessary. The supreme spiritual card, the Ace of Spades, is the ancient representation of secret mysteries, and it is most ambitious and materialistic. The Magi card, as it was and still is known, is the symbol used by many of the esoteric schools of wisdom. The members of the Order of the Magi are responsible for the conservation and dispersion of the card system itself. The Ace of Spades person frequently has deep, previous-life spiritual roots, but a lifelong battle with their material, worldly urges is present also. Trials and challenges on the material plane are a part of a Life Path represented with two Sevens and two Nines. Happiness can only be found by adopting a spiritual attitude relative to their life. Finding satisfaction in that area is something the Ace of Spades individual needs to learn. The four spiritual cards, in the case of this card, are sending this message directly. Because of their spiritual nature, many doors that are not options to most other cards in the deck open up for the Ace of Spades, because they have more aptitude and resources. The challenge is realizing this. There is an extreme aspect here. In the end the Ace of Spades is a very loving and considerate person. Inner contentment that results from a life of service and loyalty to higher principles is their goal in life. They become aware of this and learn to abide by the unwritten law that tells us we harvest what we sow. This happens as a consequence of their karma from previous lives being released. There is, in many ways, a supreme sacrifice. They seem to be unjustly punished if they stray from the law or ignore their spiritual side.

Relationships: Aces of Spades are seeking a perfect union with someone, so an individual who is spiritual in nature is the best choice. Bringing great expectations to relationships results from a sense of the possibilities of a divine union in love. Their relationships improve, along with their odds of finding their true love, after they set aside this dream and start working on their emotions as well as the communication of feelings. Their path, while not impossible, is a difficult one in the area of relationships. They have beautiful dreams of love that wait to be fulfilled, and at the core of an Ace of Spades is a very kind and giving individual. It is not beyond their ability to have their perfect relationship. Whether or not they are using a more spiritual direction in their life largely determines whether their relationships fail or succeed. Difficulties come up again and again in the arena of romance for Ace of Spades people who are more materialistic. Emotional attachment, for materialistic cards, brings repeated pain. Betrayal by people they love, family, and disenchantment again and again take place until they become aware that it is their own subtle attachments that cause these problems. Holding true love on such a pedestal of idealism is another factor that is at the forefront for them.

Personality Connections: Diamond men find it difficult to be with Aces of Spades. Spade males often like Ace of Spades women, and women like Diamond men. Heart males are a benefit for Ace of Spades women, and they always benefit from Heart males. They normally give blessings to Club women.

Confrontations: A good example of the Ace of Spades' romantic life is Princess Diana. Everything appeared almost like a fairy tale with this young woman who married a prince. Surely there would be a fairy-tale ending where they married and lived happily ever after. Everything seemed to be going right for them. We know, though, that in real life that is not what happened. Such a life is possible for the Ace of Spades.

King of Hearts
Caring Patriarch

Characteristics: Love is the pinnacle of power and atop the Love suit is the King of Hearts. Often the focus of these individuals' love is moved from their spouse to their children. While not always the best husbands or wives, the Kings of Hearts are superb and loving parents. They are also devoted to their profession. On occasion they make the wrong friends and that causes problems, but they do love everyone, forever. They should, therefore, be mindful of their associations, especially those with a poor character, as all Kings can be overbearing but generally only with traitors among those who are close to their hearts. They bring with them from previous lives the wisdom and mastery of their own emotions as well as their family lives. If they think of you as one of their family you are truly blessed. As a dealer or advisor in the finances of other people, the King of Hearts excels in the area of business. Association with others or partnerships are better than a solo undertaking. In legal areas they are luckier than average too. Arguing with them is not advised, because their sharp minds can always find an adequate response. Unfortunately, there are sure to be personal and tragic losses, but they have the ability to let go, though they still feel the pain of loss we all do. Many of them have mental gifts and psychic abilities. They seem to ascend to the top of their careers, because it seems that knowledge just flows to them.

Relationships: It is often said that Kings of Hearts make poor husbands but great lovers as well as fathers. Power can, as we all know, be used or abused and this is particularly true of all the Kings. As with the Eights there are many playboys among them, and they are the Kings of Charm as well. Many male Kings of Hearts are unmarried but manage to have a circle of women around them most of the time. The paradigm of the King of Hearts is something like the sultan who has a harem. The women themselves could possibly be his lovers, but they could instead be his family members, students, or just casual acquaintances. We often find, whatever the situation, some sort of group of admirers surrounding the King of Hearts. Female Kings of Hearts are so strong and willful that they have a problem simply because they are women. They usually want to be the head of the household, and, furthermore, they can generally stand up to any man. There is a difficulty inherent for some male partners. They have a nature that can be difficult for a person to handle, because all Kings of Hearts are very argumentative. In terms of love and relationships they have a particularly strong sense of justice. They may play the role of peacemaker at work or with their family, and they often stick up for others who have been treated unfairly. If they believe others have treated them wrongly, they may strive for some form of retributive justice. There will be a reflection back on them: indecisiveness and the consequences will result in some fated relationships.

Personality Connections: Diamonds make good marriages with King of Hearts women, particularly if they are a bit more mature and responsible.

Avoiding Spade males is wise for King of Hearts women. Male Kings of Hearts should be cautious of Diamond females.

Confrontations: Jacqueline Kennedy is known for how she handled herself with class. She was widely admired around the world for many things, including her charm and artistic awareness. She handled everyone in her King of Hearts manner, and we were enthralled with the way she dressed and her makeover of the White House. John Kennedy was the perfect match for her. Especially if we keep in mind that the King of Hearts is a master of relationships. The love triangle that was apparently part of the lives of the president, Jackie, and Marilyn Monroe was fated by their cards, their karma, and the location of the planet. We can see in Jackie then a sort of paradigm of power as well as the difficulties involved in being a King of Hearts.

Queen of Hearts
Caring Matriarch

Characteristics: The Queen of Hearts has a dose of idealism because of the double Neptune card. There is a special charm and charisma that each of these individuals has that attracts others. They share this motherly love with everyone they meet, and they are, in this sense, a maternal card. Queens of Hearts either go into some white collar career or get married and devote their lives to their family. Regardless of their gender, they have an above-average ability to be a success in numerous professions, and there is particularly good fortune in professions that are mostly male. A great deal of them will have a lot of success throughout their lives, as we can see by their King in Mars, which is a terrifically strong card. The role as mother or father is taken seriously by both genders. Some of them are more devoted to their children than their spouses are. There is a sweetness as well as attractiveness about such people who are fundamentally loving and sociable. They all have a taste for the arts and aesthetics, making them successful in these fields in many cases. There is a lot of psychic and even musical aptitude, and some of them make use of this as well. They are able to live a life of love and care that is part of their being, as long as they have an idealism guided by truth. The more love they can share the better. This is their calling in life: to love others. They can overindulge themselves, be lazy, airheaded, and basically hedonistic if they are operating on a lower level. Enjoyment of the senses and exciting experiences is what this card is about. If they turn to their higher ideals and leave behind laziness and boredom, there is no limit to the heights they can reach in their work and career. However, the Queen of Hearts also includes many codependents and people escaping through alcohol or other means.

Relationships: Power and finances attract Queen of Hearts individuals. In the deck there is a sense that they are the darlings. They are the women of all men's dreams. Aphrodite is symbolized by the Queen of Hearts. The perfect wife or lover, she naturally has all the feminine qualities a woman can have. They are the ideal of love, have charm, and are dedicated to their families. We think twice before ever criticizing them, and there is a fun-loving innocence in their personality. Occasionally they attract someone who brings them a heavy dose of reality regarding their lofty ideals. They fall, but from varying heights. Charm and grace are found in the men as well. Frequently they become stay-at-home dads who watch the children while their spouse is the breadwinner. Sensitivity is more common in them than most men. On occasions they are attracted to an individual who is unfaithful, but they can play the field exceptionally well. People who have power and are financially successful attract both genders, and many of them marry individuals like this. A certain awareness of the feelings of others sometimes results from charm turning toward the self.

Personality Connections: Club women are friends with both genders, but the Queen of Hearts males find Club women somewhat unpredictable and hard to comprehend. Powerful men, especially the Spades suit, attract the Queen of Hearts women. Queen women attract Diamond men, and Club men find them very difficult.

Confrontations: Sexuality, romance, and mothering are the realms of the Queen of Hearts. On the other hand, there can be someone who is too idealistic as well as overly sensuous. Occasionally there is one who is too easygoing and lazy. What appears to be laziness though can also be seen as a relaxed view of life and a person who enjoys luxuries and comfort. Frequently both genders are charming as well as attractive.

Jack of Hearts
Enduring through Devotion

Characteristics: The Jack of Hearts has a powerful vision of love and is a Fixed card along with two others. There is a spirit of Christ and sacrifice through love that surrounds these individuals. Because of the influence and wisdom of the Christ spirit, they generally have higher guidance and higher motives in spite of being Jacks. As we know, sometimes Jacks are immature and sneaky, but the Jack of Hearts has characteristics that mitigate against this. They must be careful, however, not to acquire a martyr complex, which can happen if this gets out of control. It is possible for them to seek escape and be misguided, but this is not all that common. They have come to share their love and to guide us on their way by their example, because love is their strength and birthright. After they recognize that they have a mission of love, they do accept the responsibility, because they know how to love with the good heart of a King. Their personal dreams may be given up for a higher vision or viewpoint, and they frequently make sacrifices in their lives. They are usually successful in their own field and are born leaders. These individuals are focused and lead by a strong sense of fairness and duty. Unless they fall to the lower side of the sneaky Jack, they are dependable and follow through on promises. Bringing higher energy to their occupation and lives in general is where they are fulfilled, and this is on a spiritual path. All those they associate with are to some degree uplifted by their presence, because they carry the spirit of Christ within them.

Relationships: Jack characteristics are there even though the Jack of Hearts is a spiritual card. The young, playful playboy or playgirl characteristics of this card can trap them too. Being the most romantic card in the deck, they too can be led into affairs and romantic liaisons. Depending on the individual, the sacrificial character of this card can work for or against them in relationships. A degree of immaturity may prove to be their downfall at times in their life, but these persons have the power and are strong enough, in their love character, to deal with it with resolve. They have their own philosophy of love that is immutable and usually they are devoted to higher ideals. You may be involved in their plan to save the universe, and they sacrifice for you if they love you. By the same token the Jack of Hearts can employ their savior mentality to do odd things in love such as selecting a partner who is totally unworthy or damaged so that they can use their love to heal someone. Bad consequences can result with this victim and savior situation, or codependent relationships can result. They begin to understand the pain love can bring and start to be an understanding and loving partner after a few losses in love. They are the most highly devoted and loyal companions of the cards when they seek their higher purpose, which many of them do. They are prepared to make sacrifices for their loved ones if they need to, and they are paragons of love that is profound and immovable.

Personality Connections: For the Jack of Hearts woman, Diamond men are generally not a good choice for love or marriage. The Jack of Hearts usually proves a great difficulty for Club females. Other Heart men are good, however. The King and Eight have strong pulls because of karmic bonds. Sometimes, though, it is too powerful.

Confrontations: Jesus Christ, the savior and messiah of the Age of Pisces, is often mentioned in association with the Jack of Hearts. The Age of Pisces, however, is now concluding. In terms of the ordinary human experience he was a teacher who exemplified transcending love, or agape. Venus in Pisces is a profound symbol of his love through sacrifice of the highest kind. Depending on what use it is put to, such a Neptunian quality can do wonderful good or terrible bad. At this point some consider such sacrifice to be codependent and even an addiction. This is because, perhaps, we are entering the Age of Aquarius. Sadly, in the name of helping others, we have seen endless cases of people and groups misusing their spiritual power and, indeed, other powers as well. What Pisces teaches us does not matter and is useless in Aquarius. Exhaustion from giving so much afflicts many Jack of Hearts individuals. They become empty and spent unless they give something to themselves. If this happens, they are less able to give because there is less of themselves to do it.

Ten of Hearts
Triumph with Congregations

Characteristics: Ten of Hearts people can go astray from the truth because they have a lot of ambition in this world. Actually, they have this awareness as an innate ability to guide them every step of the journey, because they have already become aware of the truth. Frequently they are artistic as a result of their creativity. They are not followers, but rather they were born to lead. They love an audience and therefore love children and gatherings of people. They are either surrounded by many relatives and social issues or in an area where they can be in front of others. Regardless, their Birth card dictates that they are surrounded by Hearts. Because the two Aces in their Life Path and are part Aces themselves (the One in the Ten), Tens of Hearts have a strong requirement to question themselves in order to decide what is most important to them as individuals. Others may view them as selfish or even self-centered, because a lot of them are so concerned with this process. However, only those who have a fundamental goal that is selfish and exclude all others' needs will suffer consequences. Generally, they are considerate and caring people who value their relationships more than most other priorities. An important concept with the Ten of Hearts is honesty. It could be just to be more truthful to themselves, or to work out a philosophy that overcomes all the highs and lows that are a temptation to be less than honest in their communications with others. Their lives can be a difficult mixture of one fiction after another until they commit themselves to personal truth. A great deal of energy will be wasted with that commitment. Personal expression and leadership are better and more productive uses for this energy. They can make a huge contribution in their field of choice in the event that they exercise clear judgment. The fact is that they are innovators. They can act from either humanitarian or selfish motives, and this generally has a great deal to do with their final destination. They are normally gentle and wise. Their guardian and guiding light is wisdom. Their wisdom keeps them in balance even though they are independent and frequently act on impulse. Because they have inborn gifts it is possible that they will make a special mark on the world.

Relationships: Tens of Hearts are attracted to those who are powerful. They have the power of love as well and consequently are not fearful of working for the love they desire in their lives. They are popular and have a lot of charm. They are not shy about making the initial overture to get a relationship going, and, having done so, they are willing to work for it. For success in love as well as marriage, this can be the winning ticket. While there can be some indecision that can lead to issues, they have fundamentally good karma in romance. Relationships with Diamond women can be a struggle due to indecision and fickleness carried over from their karma. While Ten of Hearts individuals are highly intelligent, when they use their intelligence and creativity in the area of romance they can get in to trouble. The may try too hard to force things to turn out according to plan. Planning a daily schedule is one thing, but love is not something to be planned and adjusted in that way. Rather than thinking things out, there is the necessity to learn feelings in matters of romance.

Personality Connections: Both genders should avoid Diamond women. Club women attract Ten of Hearts men. Ten of Hearts of both genders are a benefit to Spade males. Some Spade women can make a good partnership with Ten of Hearts men. Queen of Diamonds women are difficult for the men. The Ten of Hearts woman is a large issue for Diamond males, too.

Confrontations: Children and big groups of individuals draw in many Tens of Hearts in the area of work. Hearts represents young people and the very early years of life. An obsession or preoccupation with that aspect of that suit is a possibility. Many Ten of Hearts individuals can overdo groups, students, family members, or youngsters. A paradigm of the Ten of Hearts would be Michael Jackson. Notice how he gave so much of his life to his performing for audiences and to the children around the globe. Building an amusement park for children on the grounds of his home topped this off.

Nine of Hearts
Cosmic Delight

Characteristics: The Nine of Hearts is a spiritual card, and the fulfillment that these individuals experience is rarely lasting until their personal desires are put in their proper place. Fulfillment, major loss, or both of these are a portion of the Nine of Hearts. No straying from what is right, wise, and true is permitted because of the double Saturn in this card. If they do stray there is an immediate and often a painful rebuke. All Nines are here to settle what is owed and proceed after settling issues and debts from the past. For the Nine of Hearts key relationships might end and thus complete certain cycles. They represent graduations; if these climaxes are resisted, they will seem to be disappointing and even tragic. Spiritual lessons fill their life paths. Those who give in to their fears and allow in escapist tendencies will experience suffering, while those who listen to their calling and stick to higher principles will experience seemingly blessed lives. Payment of obligations from the past might mean experiencing financial losses at certain periods in their lives. They have excellent minds and good hearts allowing them to share with the world. Because of their innate wish to give to others, many are found in the field of counseling. The Nine of Hearts is either a person who has been disappointed frequently in life or an exceedingly happy, generous person. Manifesting their higher attributes is always an individual choice, even when dealing with highly spiritual challenges and patterns. They must keep things on a business basis and be cautious not to be the martyr. Any field of science or business will be successful because of their intelligence and creativity, which is unsurpassed. Part of their challenge is not to go to the lower path and low morals but rather to use this creativity in a mature manner and not cheat.

Relationships: Nines of Hearts can have some of the most challenging personal relationships of all the cards in the deck unless they operate on a higher and moral side of the card. Attitude is critical in turning sure losses into completions and fulfillments. They will probably either change their perspective about what kind of relationship they would like or attract individuals who cannot make the commitment that is necessary for true love. There is an emotional restlessness about them. They can get to the truth quicker and discover the satisfaction they are looking for if they stop telling themselves that they are doing all they can to help their partners. There can be a highly codependent aspect to a Nine of Hearts. Adopting a victim-savior attitude in their personal relationships is a possibility. This creates numerous problems and makes it more difficult to sort through obstacles when they appear.

Personality Connections: Heart males and Nine of Spades women are often found together, although a Club man can also prove interesting and worthwhile. Men have an attraction to women of the Spades suit. Certain Fives could make for a good partnership.

Confrontations: Among the special Birth cards are those we call the Semi-Fixed cards; the Nine of Hearts is one of only four. There are two pairs of cards in this four; each of the pairs in this small group share a special relationship with their other half. There is kind of a magic about them, and they have their own special place in the deck. Pleasantness, beauty, abundance of material comforts, and pleasure are in the Nine of Hearts, because it sits in the Venus/Venus position relative to the Life Spread. Their Birth card moves, though in a highly unique way, because each New Year they relocate to the opposite spot in the Life Spread. We can picture a life that is the pinnacle of pleasure and relaxation, maybe even too much so if we double this. If this is doubled, we can only imagine how potentially difficult their life may be. Clearly there are opposites at work here across the spectrum, and this shows up in their position in the Life Spread.

Eight of Hearts
Ecstatic Strength

Characteristics: Caution and responsibility are needed for Eight of Hearts individuals because of the power they wield in love. Actually, all Eights need to be careful here. Some become addicted to the power they have by virtue of their supreme charm and magnetism. If used unwisely at the expense of others they can cause pain. Sevens are both Karma cards of the Eight of Hearts. This tells us that they have a great deal of spiritual knowledge that helps lead their actions. Unfortunately they will see almost instant results when they abuse their power over others. They realize that they can go to great heights if they follow the truth and share their love and healing with others. Because they can really give people the love that is necessary for healing themselves, this is seen as the healer's card. Many will become well-known teachers, artists, statesmen, and performers. The Ten, Eight, and King are in their Life Paths, and all are in the Crown Line. They will lead very lucky lives. They have superior potential for being recognized and being successful. There will be obstacles in the area of health unless the Eight of Hearts is attentive to it. Their work and relations will be neglected and their bodies pushed to the point of breaking down if they are not careful. Neglecting this will bring about the first Karma card demanding payment in full. You might think that they would just relax and enjoy such a good life, because things go so well for them. However, they frequently go at such a fast pace that they end up physically ill. Exactly eight, it is interesting to note, is often the number of their immediate family or close friends. Eight of Hearts represent the people that they love. Eight can come up with eight children, eight spouses, eight pets, or other things. In any occupation where a good mind will make a difference—and they have great minds—they can be exceptional. They do not have to worry about money, but they will work hard for that which they make. Many Eights of Hearts will become famous in their lifetimes. This is particularly true after the age of thirty-six, when their power and achievements increase. They are powerful and can succeed at anything.

Relationships: Eights of Hearts need, in some sense, to be good administrators because of the power they have. They have the charm and attractiveness to get what they desire, and they do go after who they want as well. As a result they can be playboys and playgirls. Eight of Hearts women must be aware of their actions and at least realize that some men would prefer a woman who is not so forceful. The fastest karmic rebounds come to them more than any other cards. Maturity and wisdom must be in place if their power is to bring about true happiness. Making others know they are loved also makes them feel they are special. They usually retain the upper hand in all of their relationships because they are less needy than most and consequently find it difficult to maintain someone who is. If they feel uncomfortable they usually just move on to another partner. Aggression can be present.

Some suitors of Eight of Hearts women are scared away by their aggression.

Personality Connections: The Hearts suit attracts Eight of Hearts men, and they are usually compatible. The Jacks can be a problem for them. In general, Eight of Hearts individuals are found to be difficult by Club men, especially the women. They are liked by Diamond men.

Confrontations: In the emotional arena, being an Eight of Hearts allows a person a lot of power. They can easily acquire what they want from most individuals in their life with such power. They are really able to practically blast someone with this power by giving them attention and sometimes flattery. If they choose to, they can make a person feel like the most admired and desirable person on the face of the Earth. This is a powerful tool, and they can use it in any way they choose. There are many celebrities and others with this power among the Eight of Hearts. Joe DiMaggio, John F. Kennedy Jr., and Richard Gere are all Eights of Hearts.

Seven of Hearts
Metaphysical Rapture

Characteristics: It is easy for Sevens of Hearts to get what they desire from most people in life. Metaphysically they are old and here to reach the peaks. They are here to complete a grand circle in their work on their soul and to let go of a lot of things in order to progress to the next level. This is shown by the Nines in their Life Path. Letting go of their attachments and giving to others and not expecting return or reward is what they must learn. Their karma often brings with it health issues, so their health should be monitored carefully to avoid serious challenges. There is a need for a change of lifestyle or a need to let go of some part of it if there is a problem. They might, for instance, have to resign from a job because it is just too much stress. Carried over from previous lives are sometimes certain physical habits that are hard to break, like smoking. It is their destiny, though, to deal with these issues, and that includes the unhealthy patterns, even though they will be difficult to let go of. Some highly successful finance managers and owners of businesses are Sevens of Hearts. Many Seven of Hearts men, interestingly, are involved in the world of finance. Their desire for financial success and their inclinations for justice in all their friendships and relationships are a challenge that needs to be balanced. The desire to have harmonious relationships and strong ambitions often is in conflict.

Suffering great pain and disappointment will be the result for the Seven or Nine who has not learned to give and let go. They can experience the pinnacle of unconditional love as the givers of wisdom and love. They can be preoccupied with many suspicions and jealousies on the lower side, but this is often just a reflection of their own insecurity. We also find, on the higher side, counselors and others who make huge personal sacrifices to help others and who are capable of giving so much to the world. Sevens of Hearts are always there for understanding and to be a sounding board. To acquire peace and satisfaction they all have to find a way to give something to the world. Teaching, counseling, or consulting are often paths they choose.

Relationships: The best area for personal growth and well-being is in relationships. They care for their loved ones so much that Sevens of Hearts will frequently attempt to dominate or push their loved ones, and this generally does not work out well for them. The reverse can happen when a dominating person is attached to them. They will find the best companion in someone who is a friend first and will become their real true mate. The most satisfaction resides in this approach to love. Once they stop being so self-controlling it will work out for them. Social ability and charm are part of their character. They meet these challenges only in their closest relationships. There is an aggressive quality in the male Seven of Hearts when meeting new people or potential lovers. Their mates are invariably powerful. Because of their staggering spiritual power, something less than the truth and nonattachment will cause more suffering than it is worth every time. They can be a bit restless emotionally and this carries over into a bit of the wanderlust. Sudden love affairs are possible, just as are sudden endings.

Personality Connections: Both genders benefit from Diamond females. Diamond men challenge all Sevens of Hearts. Upon meeting a King, Sevens of Hearts know they have met their match, a person who can deal with them yet not restrict them.

Confrontations: The essence of the Seven of Hearts is an exceedingly loving person who longs for a life without fears about love and affection. They are a beacon of unconditional love and want to love all for who they are. Previous incarnations, however, mean they also have a profound inner conflict. They had a great emotional power in a previous life, according to their Karma card, and this was possibly abused. They got used to doing things their own way and permitted themselves a lot of slack in the their sexuality, or their character, in that former lifetime.

Six of Hearts
Problem Solver

Characteristics: Peaceful, harmonious, and stable is the nature of the Six of Hearts. It is a card of family love. They strive to maintain stability in relationships and have a keen awareness of the Law of Love. Such stability can make for a life of monotony and boredom, or one of contentment. How it is handled is the determining factor. These individuals do not like changes and upsets and are a bit fixed. As they organize their desires and motives it is possible to stay in a relationship longer than necessary. They are able to apply their intelligence to most any areas successfully, even though there are occasional fears about not having enough. They can rise to high levels of spiritual awareness via their actions. They are here to settle karma pertaining to love debts, as well as to forgive and forget. Injuring others is not something they get away with and they know it. Their lives are meant to be plentiful; giving or sharing their bounty of love with those near them is their purpose. Their highest fulfillment and happiness can be in that area. We can see this in the fact that they are the same card as governs Christmas day. Six children, interestingly, is fairly common, or there are six close friends in their circle. Other Heart cards have this situation too. We see the strength of their competitive side come out if a Six feels that they have been the victim of injustice or that someone in their care has been wronged. If provoked in this way they are capable of being very forceful. Business dealings or sports can be approached with this competitive nature as well. They have a cool demeanor even in heated battles. The knowledge or communications areas are where success often lies. Through developing a single area and staying with it, they most often do better. Learning practically anything is one of their abilities, and they have an inherited gift of creativity. From financial planners to designers or artists, a lot of them find success. They always have good ideas on how to improve income, and they can be very business minded.

Relationships: Some Six of Hearts individuals have personal relationships to deal with stemming from a past life; this is part of the process of understanding the responsibility involved with love. Depending on their exact karma, these can be either positive or negative in nature, but such relationships always seem destined. For this same reason, many Sixes of Hearts believe that somewhere in the world is their special soul mate. They can have an excellent marriage, and their basic love karma is fine. They expect those they marry to live up to their part of the bargain, and they prefer to be with people they are able to do business with. As long as they have a responsible attitude and hearken the call of the higher love nature in them, they usually get what they desire in the area of love. Magically they feel and believe that special person will come into their life someday to make everything good for them. Many hold on to this dream for their entire lives, regardless of whether it happens.

Personality Connections: Males of the Spades suit are attracted to Six of Hearts females, and an irresponsible or dishonest person will probably be among them. For a Six of Hearts woman, the Four is a strong marriage because of a karmic bond. Six of Hearts females should avoid men of the Hearts suit. Club females are enjoyed by both genders, especially the Four, Eight, and Ten.

Confrontations: Relationships seem to have a more predominant importance in today's world, and the Law of Karma extends into all-important areas of our lives. It is not surprising that this has become the number one area for personal development, because we learn a great deal about ourselves from our personal relationships. They are the last and highest steps in personal growth. The Six of Hearts card carries with it a lot that is important for every one of us. We really are not prepared to go on in any way with personal or spiritual progress until we have become truly aware of a loving relationship.

Five of Hearts
Passionate Experiences

Characteristics: If they ever want to bring about any long-term success in their lives, all Fives must settle down some, and the Five of Hearts is not an exception. These individuals have, according to their Karma card, an issue with security that will remain in their lives until they consciously deal with it. Finances are usually the nature of their security fear. Sticking with a single goal and working hard brings success every time. Whether they are able to remain in one location long enough to enjoy the rewards is the question. It is often not easy for them, but a lot of them do. Some Fives of Hearts are incapable of making commitments at all and are promiscuous. Traveling and visiting foreign lands sometimes fills their need for new experiences. The Hearts suit is also related to home and family, in addition to symbolizing relationships. To fulfill their need for new and novel experiences, the Five of Hearts may establish new homes and friendships in foreign countries. The

Five of Hearts Saturn card in the Life Path makes these individuals restless beyond the degree of the other Fives. Their Life Path has few even-numbered cards. This tells us that there is a creativity and usually a restlessness in the Five of Hearts. They frequently express an artistic talent in the things they do around the home with loved ones, or even professionally. Fives of Hearts want to experience everything that love and money have to offer. If one is stuck in one place at the same job for long periods, then a job that means travel is often the solution to this boredom. It is just fine with them if they are traveling all the time. They are willing to travel extensively and go almost anywhere. Because they are in search of fresh and different relationships, the Five of Hearts is on a mission of a kind. Their present relationship is most often just another experience for them. They want to know and experience something if they actually stay married for any duration of time. There is something of importance in the relationship. They may just continue on without any hesitation; they have received what they have of something. This could be an individual or the emotions they experience from them.

Relationships: The Life Path of the Five of Hearts also contains a powerful Venus card, which also tends toward variety in personal relationships. They also have a love of creativity and artistic expression and an attraction to those who are similar. Many just feel a need for more than a single partner, and the grass will always seem greener on the other side of the fence. Ending relationships for the Five of Hearts is often bitter and hard. It is frequently scarred by rage and resentment. Represented by Mars, it is rare that they are the winners in divorce unless they release all of their personal wishes. Many elect to never take that gamble again and remain single for the rest of their lives. At some point in their life they become aware that they need some autonomy in their love life due to their restless nature in matters of romance. Other cards that appreciate the same individuality that they do can lead to a successful relationship. The Five of Hearts, like other Fives, frequently has an internal fear of commitment, believing it is something that will take away their freedom of movement. The majority are happiest remaining single or minimally in a relationship that provides them lots of room and freedom. They can be happily married in some cases if the basics are met for them.

Personality Connections: Younger Club men attract Five of Hearts women, but these women can probably have a better relationship with a Diamond man. A Diamond woman and a Five of Hearts man can make a good marriage. Spade females can be friends.

Confrontations: Any student of the cards can think of what some of the manifestations of the Five of Hearts challenges might be. For example, a sign of a divorce is the Five of Hearts in a Yearly Spread. This does not necessarily mean that the Five of Hearts individual is always headed for a divorce. There is more than one way to unfold the cards found in Yearly Spreads. The energies of our Birth cards and the Five of Hearts individual are not an exception.

Four of Hearts
Matrimony and Kind Folk

Characteristics: The Fours of Hearts have stability in relationships, whether intimate ones or with friends and family. The first Four in the deck is the first card to strive for stability and foundation. The pain resulting from failure to reach their very high ideals about love and family can be so great that they need to escape to ease their personal and emotional pain. There is a strong, psychic side in the Four of Hearts that can bring them a lot of success, if they develop it. Whether they are conscious of it or not, they all use it in their work. By developing one thing and staying with it they are generally highly successful. Some are destined to be important leaders. They become prominent in their special field and a part of the road to that success forces them to face things pertaining to money and power. Holding on to their foundation of love and support is an important part in this process, while at the same time finding their own power. These individuals can be fulfilled with their family and romance if their ideals are mixed with truth and objectivity. They put away some of their personal desire and heed the inner call to assist others. If they do that, they have fewer dreams that become nightmares, and far more satisfaction. These people, more than most, never get away with overdoing things—either physical or emotional—so they must have good health habits. All Fours of Hearts will often try to control their relatives in order to keep focusing on what they consider to be the most important aspects of their lives. All Fours, for that matter, can be controlling. If done to extremes, there will be suffering when it comes time to let their children have their own lives. They will frequently attempt to keep some people in their lives for their own security, even among friends. Codependent behavior needs to be watched out for. Regardless of what the Four of Hearts might believe, not everyone on Earth needs to be saved or nurtured. Healers and protectors are what many Fours of Hearts are. Others come to them for guidance, love, and support in difficult times. Giving to others and caring for them provides satisfaction. They all do well with clubs and organizations, as teachers and planners, and they also have a need to express themselves. Great scientific intellects are found in some. They have only themselves to blame if they are unhappy and unproductive in their lives. They are excellent with finances.

Relationships: In the realm of love and family, the Four of Hearts has high ideals, frequently too high for the real world to match. A lot of pain can result if their idealistic vision of love forms into fantasies that clash with reality. They are, however, devoted to their relatives, loved ones, and people in general. They are called to let others be who they are, but there are sure to be a number of challenges pertaining to love along the way. If they find a more spiritual vision of their love lives they can come close to attaining their high ideals. They possess a certain strength as well as charm if they apply themselves.

Personality Connections: Club males are good matches for Four of Hearts females. They are excellent friends with Diamond men and Heart women. Spade female hearts are stolen by Four of Hearts men. Frequently, however, there is a better relationship with Diamond females.

Confrontations: Fours of Hearts are the nurturers of their children. Furthermore they are the protectors of home and family. They will treat everyone like they would their child. You will be taken good care of, regardless of your gender. If you are a good friend or even a coworker of a Four of Hearts individual, that is especially true. As nurturing is a quite feminine trait, the Four of Hearts individual is a lot like a Queen, who is also known for her nurturing aspects. Nurturing like this, of course, also can be difficult at times. Fours of Hearts will usually seek to have a small circle of Hearts individuals around them. The astrological sign of Cancer has very similar characteristics to the Four of Hearts, which represents the home and family. The fourth house is governed by the sign of Cancer. Residing here are security, home, relatives, and, just as important, nurturing. The Four of Hearts person has all of these things as a prominent part of their makeup. The strong Cancer, Moon, or fourth house in the natal charts of Four of Hearts people is always there.

Three of Hearts
Assortment of Affections

Characteristics: The Three of Hearts symbolizes the departure of Man and Woman from the Garden of Eden, and it is the initial card in the Life

Spread. The cause for their departure was temptation on many levels. Furthermore, we might think of this card as the entrance into a dualistic world of confusion, because it is the first card in the Life Spread. Somewhat like landing on an alien planet, the Three of Hearts experience might be like having to figure out everything from scratch. Threes of Hearts, in this respect, are endlessly questioning but mentally prepared to evaluate and analyze what they observe. They are unclear about what is most important to them in life, and this results in concern about their own financial lack, whether real or imagined. In this case their own natural creativity becomes a burden of indecision. They never feel financially secure, partly because they can develop so many ideas of what to do and what they might want to do that they never complete things. This indecisiveness can be the cause of some very challenging relationships in terms of karma. They may meet a person who shares these same qualities but leaves them not knowing whether they are loved. Their creativity becomes a great talent that guides them in the direction of their goals after the Three of Hearts has learned the value of foundation and stability. Three of Hearts women do better than most women when working in male-ruled organizations and associations, and both genders have good success working with men. Their life and finances are often improved through travel or making changes, and they are progressive in their work. They are successful at whatever work they do, and they are very hard workers. To be happy they need some change or travel in their jobs. There is artistic and creative potential in the Three of Hearts. Their very souls are expressive. Two of their most important lessons in life are learning to transform value-based indecisiveness into creativity in their work or business and overcoming their worry about poverty. Faith is something they are learning to develop in order to understand that the necessary materials will always be there for them when needed.

Relationships: Sexual uncertainty and experimentation is sometimes the result of Three of Hearts energy. Many Three of Hearts individuals choose to explore sexuality in their quest for wisdom, and bisexuality and homosexuality are concepts they may be curious about. What is most required by the Three of Hearts individual is to spend time with themselves so that they can learn to become more emotionally self-sufficient and self-reliant. The first Karma card informs us of that. They can feel less needy and less stressed about finding love from others if they learn to give some of their boundless energy to themselves. At that point their love life starts being much more fun and enjoyable. That is how they want it to be in any case. Lightheartedness and cheerfulness is their favorite way of being. They have no trouble getting others to love them and have a charm and attractiveness. After they find someone the challenge begins. Wit and high intelligence often attract them, but frequently it is to someone who is just as indecisive as they are. The Three of Hearts can become the most mixed mentally and emotionally of the Threes. All of them demand the freedom to explore various possibilities. They can frequently become unsure or dissatisfied in search of what and whom they love, even if they see the perfect individual standing right in front of them. Emotional uncertainty, on a deeper level, is represented by the Three of Hearts. Asking themselves whether they will be loved is often foremost in their minds. Emotionally challenging experiences in childhood are often the cause of this.

Personality Connections: Three of Hearts females are attractive to Three of Hearts men. Spade men see them as very attractive but a challenge in other ways. Club females are found attractive by Three of Hearts males, as are Diamond women. The Three of Hearts female will have problems with a lot of the Club and Heart males.

Confrontations: Errors associated with youth and learning from the school of hard knocks is something the Three of Hearts will experience. Their creative side is something all the Threes strongly identify with.

Two of Hearts
Romantic Courtship

Characteristics: The Two of Hearts possesses the Karmic Soul Twin in the Ace and shares many of that card's traits. It is in the unique family of Semi-Fixed cards and thus also brings with it a certainty of its direction. These individuals will not listen to anyone else. They have a natural curiosity that leads to terrific mental development, and they have great minds. However, as the meaning of the card is lovers, they never stray far from this essence of themselves. Their ideals about love and marriage are high, sometimes too much so. Rather than be alone, they always prefer being with someone. They will wait as long as needed for the correct person to come along; a person to whom they can give their complete and dedicated love. Unfortunately, in some cases these ideals can topple when they shy away from exactly what they desired so much; their vision comes crashing ashore in reality. Luckily

Twos of Hearts end up as those with finances or power, and they prefer this kind of company. They must handle financial fears that come up from time to time very carefully so that they do not impact their health and well-being. A positive thought process and fulfillment can result from a study of metaphysics. The psychic abilities that many have can be used for fun or even profit. They will have, as Capricorns, an inclination to be too practical and serious with themselves as well as others. There is often a conflict resulting from the gentle dreams of love that the Two of Hearts has. They have to find a way to strike a balance between wanting this high, spiritual love and the real world around them. Developing the more practical way to love can bring true benefits. There is a somewhat fortunate life path that the Two of Hearts has, especially related to the areas of money and business. Caution, however, is necessary in all of their business deals. Clear financial agreements should be spelled out and discussed to avoid difficulties. They need to exercise care in partnerships. When they mix love and business, care is necessary because of a tendency to leave significant expectations unspoken.

Relationships: They absolutely must have, because of their nature, someone in their life. That is probably because it is the card of the love affair. They have to learn to balance their logic with their passion because they tend to have an intellectual approach to love. Learning to express their passion is something they must also be careful of, because they are required to go through tests pertaining to the pursuit of personal pleasure, particularly if it is at the expense of others. Rather than having no one in their life, they will generally choose to have anyone in their life. If, however, they have been emotionally hurt or had their dreams damaged, they may possibly deny themselves a love.

Personality Connections: Spade males as friends are also common for Twos of Hearts. Two of Hearts men often make good friends with Club women. Males of the Diamond suit are often attracted to Two of Hearts women, particularly if they possess money or success. Heart males also make good marriage partners, and Heart females are very attracted to them.

Confrontations: The special family of four Semi-Fixed cards includes the Two of Hearts. The entire story, however, of these special relationships among the cards is more significant. The Semi-Fixed cards are two pairs of cards that are special. They move from one place in the Grand Solar Spread to another place every other year in their lives. The Ace and the Two of Hearts exchange places with each other each year just as the Sevens and

Nines do. No other cards do this, and that makes them unique. But how these two pairs of cards are joined to one another is most interesting. The Ace and the Two of Hearts are so similar that it is hard to differentiate their qualities from each other. What is a relevant Life Path for one is also for the other. The other pair of Karmic Twins also has the same characteristics. They are practically soul mates when viewed from this perspective. However, this does not mean anything with regard to marriage and romance.

Ace of Hearts
Compulsion for Adoration

Characteristics: As the first card in the deck, the Ace of Hearts is the desire for love. Because of its Karma card, however, the desire for finances is present too. It might be assumed that like Aries, being the first card in the deck and the first sign in the zodiac, these are young souls, prone to make a lot of errors and selfishness. With some this is true, but it is by no means the majority. Lives as writers or in other creative occupations might bring success. They can be impulsive because they have a double Ace influence. Their last years will be the most meaningful of their entire lives if they focus their attention on finding spiritual meaning. Changing values will be one of the biggest burdens to carry, and they are often restless individuals. Fickleness and promiscuity should be avoided if they are ever to hope to discover the peace of mind they seek. High rewards come from finding an outlet for compassionate giving. Along with the two Threes in their Life Path, their Karma card gives them tremendous creative potential. However, the downside of this is indecision, worry, and stress, because every gift can be a negative at times. Relaxation time away from their job is a healing remedy. These same Threes create the need for variety in work and a better structuring of their life and work. Allowing some flexibility helps them. All are Capricorns, so their work is important, as is the recognition it brings. Many of them, according to the Planetary Ruling card, tell us that they will gain reputations as artists or creative persons. If they turn their pursuits in the direction of metaphysics and self-understanding, a lot of difficulty in later life, both emotional and psychological, can be avoided. One of their main traits, courage, actually has this as a symbol. Combined with this courage is wisdom that is often misleading, but it does direct their actions toward success. Learning to look before they leap, the successful ones practice patience. Strong spiritual inclinations are part of people with this Birth card, but they are frequently led astray by indecision and buried desires. They need to deal with a fear of not having sufficient funds in particular so that they can have more success and peace of mind. According to the Ace of Hearts Karma card, there is a need to develop a sense of gratitude and successfulness, but with this Ace of Hearts having a Mercury card in their Life Path, acquiring money or material goods will be a prominent refrain in life anyway. Great financial success often comes to these individuals, who are natural achievers. Great stress and physical issues can result if they are not careful and let themselves get stretched too thin or in too many directions.

Relationships: The Ace of Hearts embarks on a search for love experiences at every corner for a new adventure. They are changing values that bring about consequential changes in their romantic lives, and they are sometimes emotionally restless. Women of means are a favorite and are generally well liked by all. It would be smart to keep in mind that unless the Ace of Hearts is aware of his inclination toward indecision and restlessness in love, he will probably not be around for long. A selfishness can exist in an Ace of Hearts and a concern only with her own needs. Interfering with the romantic life are fears about not having enough financially and being materialistic. A relationship that had some variation of shared experiences, coupled with communication and opportunities to travel, would be best to be happy as an Ace of Hearts. Restless urges that are part of the Ace of Hearts character, if met through healthy outlets, would help satisfy all of this card's creativity.

Personality Connections: Club men and Ace of Hearts women get along well in general, and Spade men find them enticing and hard to resist. Diamond women and Ace of Hearts men get along well.

Confrontations: This card represents entering into the world with our soul and character more than any other. It is a masculine and creative force, because it is a One. Potential that has not yet been released is the Zero. Counting from the Natural or Spiritual Spread, the Ace of Hearts card is the deck's first card.

King of Clubs
Adept of Doctrine

Characteristics: Escapism for a lot of Kings of Clubs centers around substance abuse in the form of drugs, alcohol, or something else. They perhaps had a childhood that had many challenges such that they are often very emotionally sensitive. They are often pulled in the opposite of their highest potential. In a journey to understand and deal with inner conflicts, the King of Clubs can go through many trials and tribulations in life. They usually have an awakening sometime in their thirties and go on to acquire the recognition, power, and responsibility that is their birthright. The King of Clubs can be an expert in any field they choose because they sit at the peak of the suit symbolizing knowledge and communication. Previous lives provide this knowledge, and they have direct access to it. Their own philosophy and values are almost always respected, and they live life on their own terms. They seem to be able to tap knowledge from a higher source any time they want to. Living by their own truth they are found in many types of occupations. Very frequently they occupy positions of responsibility. They are highly intuitive in their approach to life, and this makes them the most psychic card in the deck. Marriage can be a big challenge, as can their periodic habit of getting into a rut of comfort and not motivating themselves to their highest potential. Regret in their later years can take place if they do not realize their full potential of giving to the world. Regardless of what they do, they are respected for their work. Some highly successful artists, leaders, and other creative individuals in the world are Kings of Clubs. They are clever and personable in character, meaning they are usually popular and well thought of. The majority of Kings of Clubs will be in partnerships because they seem to do their best job with a partner. One of their greatest assets is the ability to logically analyze things and categorize well.

Relationships: For male and female Kings of Clubs alike, there is a need to make minute distinctions between subjective truths and their dreams of romantic or marital happiness. They have an internal fortitude and are powerful people who make fine mental distinctions. Those who are involved with these individuals have to be able to handle this strength and power without becoming defensive, which is quite difficult in many instances. For this reason the women are, therefore, likely to be more masculine in their approach and sometimes domineering. Finding a partner can consequently be difficult at times; particularly one with whom they can be themselves. Other cards have issues around the notion of freedom, but it does not prevent them from getting married or settling down. In terms of marriage, sex, or children, they sometimes face challenges. As far as the King of Clubs goes, the Pluto card can show itself in many ways, but there is always some obstacle related to it in the lives of the female Kings of Clubs. A lifelong transformation and its rami-fications are important to them. King of Clubs men generally attract women who personify some of the negative traits of the Queen, in particular the escapist, indolent, or self-indulgent ones. The feeling of being emotionally close is something the King of Clubs possesses. In addition, their marriage karma is basically good. There are, however, portions of matrimony that are very difficult for them. Fear of losing their personal autonomy is definitely one of the major challenges in a marriage. Freedom treasured above every-thing is obviously an important concept for the King of Clubs. Sometimes it is more important than anything, including a happy relationship.

Personality Connections: Clubs are generally friends with Kings of Clubs, and there is often a mentoring relationship involved here. Diamonds get along with King of Clubs men and women but have challenges with Hearts, with the exception being the King. They are always a good connection.

Confrontations: Regardless of how small their complaint is, Kings of Clubs are not satisfied unless there is perfection. They can be a stickler for details, and, in their mind, there has to be a reason for everything. There is, therefore, an endless quest for perfection. All Kings of Clubs make distinc-tions about everything. They are extremely sensitive to things that others hardly think about. They are, in essence, perfectionists and are not at ease until every small detail has been done to perfection.

Queen of Clubs
Matriarch of Clairvoyance

Characteristics: Mentally, Clubs are inclined in the direction of a publishing or administrative vocation. If they are more tuned in, this could be a psychic vocation. Being Queens, their place in the royal court is always something they are aware of and thus rebel against trying to be molded in any manner. Receptive by nature, all Queens are oriented toward service. Uncertainty and indecisiveness about love and relationships make it hard for them to find lasting happiness in these regards; this might be because their displaced card is the Three of Hearts and their Five of Hearts is in the Venus position. They are constantly receiving wisdom from their natural psychic gifts, and their intelligence is abundant even if they do not realize it. Their minds are incredibly organized. However, they live at such a fast pace that they often overdo things and are stressed out. If they elect to follow a spiritual or psychic type of work, Jupiter promises great rewards. Knowledge from previous lives is always available as a result of a heritage steeped in it. Sacrificing for one or more children, whether literal or not, is not uncommon. They often have multiple jobs and Queens of Clubs are quite creative and innovative. They have numerous interests. Freedom of movement in their careers and expression are where they thrive. Doing a job well makes them proud. Great things for society are possible for the Queen of Clubs. Work that assists countless people is a natural inclination along with nurturing others.

Relationships: Queens of Clubs are very high strung, and therefore they must have some mental agility and communication talents for things to be workable. Their emotional indecisiveness, to a certain degree, adds to the barriers they must deal with every time they fall in love. Of all the cards, sadly, this card brings some of the most difficult emotional and relationship karma of them all. Their Karma and Saturn cards both reveal this. Emotional needs with these cards require care if they are to be dealt with effectively. Any Queen of Clubs, however, with determination and effort, can apply herself with great success. Whether the effort will be made is the issue. Open relationships, long-term but not monogamous, are sometimes the solution for them. Their first priority is frequently their job, thus the necessary time and emotional price to make true intimacy possible is not as important to them. However, they should remember that with all the love they can give, they have some of the largest potential for satisfaction in a relationship of any card. This card can be the Princess who finds Prince Charming and ends up marrying him. Though many Queens of Clubs get married, not all are happy about it or make a success of it. Their powerful intellects and will mean not all partners can deal with them. Sometime during their lives they will bring to fruition some challenging relationship that is a result of their karma. A total renunciation of marriage may take place if it does not work out the first time. An inability to make up their minds is also a very real possibility. Insecurity with their partners can result, and their marriage can sometimes end in divorce.

Personality Connections: Diamond women are often attractive to Queen of Clubs men. Heart men often have problems with Queen of Clubs women, although there are some exceptions. The Queen of Clubs is often found to be attractive to Spade men.

Confrontations: The Queen of Clubs is terrifically creative and energetic. These individuals are the Indy 500 drivers of the world. Driving the Mercury card in our Life Path often shows something about our driving habits.

Often, Queens of Clubs are pushy and arrogant with people they consider beneath them, dumb, or lazy. They are quite high-strung. Most would be stressed operating on a high plane such as they do. Sometimes it appears that they are on some sort of energy drink. There are practically countless Threes involved with their Birth card and Life Path.

Jack of Clubs
Cerebral Producer

Characteristics: Jacks of Clubs can make a lot of money doing what they truly like if they find their calling. Males, more than the females, frequently find themselves as entrepreneurs. Mentally astute, they are frequently prone to arguing but usually unable to see that it is their love of debate that precipitates many of their disagreements with others. Practically as though they want some mental exercise, they will debate you whenever the opportunity presents itself. However, their minds are often made up, and this on occasions gets in the way of their striving for the truth. On the other hand, it can give them the chance to stand up for what they believe in and give them the opportunity to conclude what they start. Pettiness, because they are royal, is disliked, and they tend to be a bit impatient with the shortcomings of others. They need a position that permits their intelligence the freedom to create and explore. Jack of Clubs individuals are an odd mixture of the most creative and the most dishonest. So, in the end, when we confront the issue of what they are, the answer is both. Intellectual and monetary creativity is the realm of the Jack of Clubs. Their sharp minds are way ahead of the average person and society. They are productive and highly energetic. They are neither entirely feminine nor masculine in their traits because they are individuals of the Aquarian Age. In the evolution of our society and even the world, they are the progressives and the pathfinders. Their great mental facilities can always make an excellent livelihood for them. They have a constant reminder from Saturn's hand of the boundaries that keep them attuned and just. Believing their own fictions is where the trouble begins, because they drift away from reality a bit too much and create a lot of problems before resuming course. Being good and giving is their fundamental nature despite being argumentative at times. Finally, they are friendly and loving to everyone they encounter. For some there are large financial gains, because they can always come up with new and novel ideas. However, the Jack of Clubs, unfortunately, can lack responsibility and on occasion not be honest. They have such a loose framework of mental constructs that one perspective is just another way of perceiving things. They can rationalize away almost anything because they can make up an event so quickly and believably. Generally it is hard for them to get away with much in that respect though.

Relationships: The Jack of Clubs' Love Karma, however, is not particularly bad. Friendship first is what they need: a person who will let them have the freedom to be themselves. They are faithful and devoted if they have this. The males are superb lovers, and the females are wonderful companions. The poor health of someone they love can be something they have to deal with, be it a family member, friend, or loved one. Another possibility is their own health issues. Such issues in the case of Jack of Clubs usually pertain to something emotional related to a family member or lover. Obstacles for the Jack of Clubs result from a strong and inflexible mental concept of life. Particularly in the area of love, a mental approach does not always work.

Personality Connections: Heart women are a weakness for Jack of Clubs men. Jack of Clubs men are challenging for Diamond women. Diamond men are a karmic ally connecting to Jack of Clubs women, although some are more difficult than others. The men of the Clubs suit are easier.

Confrontations: Jack of Clubs individuals have a look of intelligence about them. Outspokenness combined with this mental approach means they are a match. Their love life as well as most things is taken intellectually. This cerebral approach includes those they love and have feelings for. Love is present, but everything is a mental construct. Their strong mind is there even though they have the feelings. Such a mind draws conclusions even about love. There is a hard to describe and unusual aspect about Jacks of Clubs that manifests itself in all of them. The men and women are very different. There is a peaceful manner to the women and a calmness in their appearance.

Ten of Clubs
Imaginative Proficiency

Characteristics: An independent character is the nature of the Ten of Clubs. They behave as if they are a King or Queen, regardless of their gender. All of them want total and unfettered freedom to do what they choose at the time they choose it. Ten of Clubs women have masculine mentalities and characters. Coming full circle, the Ten of Clubs finally arrives at knowledge. They are still driven in a quest for more knowledge that makes them highly successful and strengthens their already powerful minds. In a profound twist, their minds are so strong they must determine how to get back in control, because their minds develop lives of their own. Loss of sleep is even sometimes possible for them because their thoughts refuse to quiet down. Inspiring groups and individuals can come into their lives, through spiritual wisdom and interest in spiritual philosophies. It will increase their quality of life. Work that is most fulfilling will result from that which allows them freedom of expression and creativity. Deciding which way to go or what it is that will truly fulfill them is their greatest challenge. Higher principles, hard work, and honest motives can guide them in a return to self-mastery. Staying busy and working hard are things they must do. There is an emotional restlessness in their souls, because the Three of Hearts in their spread represents indecisiveness in terms of their choice of vocations. This can be a difficult pressure on relationships and can restrain them from attaining their highest goals. They will try many fields of work to find out what truly satisfies them. The Three of Hearts challenge card also tells us this very clearly. Either a blessing or curse comes from the Jack of Clubs Karma card. It depends on how it is revealed by them. Indirectly, it is the card of the Thief and the Spiritual Initiate or the Actor. Consequently, there is a potential for fame in the arts, or heavy interest in spiritual subjects and study. Unfortunately, using their gifts in a dishonest way is also possible.

Relationships: Frequently a satisfactory marriage means that they work while their spouse manages the domestic responsibilities. The ones that do find satisfaction in marriage manage to maintain their careers while their husbands or wives take care of the domestic responsibilities. There are emotional difficulties for the female Ten of Clubs due to the Queen of Clubs in the Saturn position of her Life Path, making it difficult to develop any true intimacy with her partners. Ten of Clubs women's willful natures, together with their very independent spirits, often exclude marriage and meaningful relationships. Often the Ten of Clubs cannot pay attention for long in personal relationships. Frequent change and a desire for variety are things they lean toward. There is a bit of difficulty in maintaining a long-term relationship because they are so independent, strong, and creative. Shirley MacLaine, Madonna, and Barbara Streisand are excellent examples of the Ten of Clubs. For some it might just be better to remain single in order to realize their success. Unquestionably though, there is a deep thirst for love, and love has a kind of truth about it that they must deal with. Union of one kind or another is what Love always wants more of, and this includes intimacy, which brings more pleasure. Because of this there is the challenge of commitment for everyone including the Ten of Clubs. A strong reluctance to make a choice is either a part of them or of the partner. Most Tens of Clubs, regardless of their gender, have such a powerful vocational motivation that few sacrifice this in the name of a personal relationship.

Personality Connections: Other Club women and Ten of Clubs females do not get along. Most Heart men and Ten of Clubs females have difficulty, although Diamond males get blessings from these individuals. There is an attraction to powerful men of high standing for Ten of Clubs women, especially men who are Spades. Women of their own suit should be avoided by the men, because there is a strong likelihood of a great price or burden.

Confrontations: There are characteristics about Tens of Clubs that mean they have an additional restlessness. For example, the Three of Hearts is in Mars and the Three of Hearts is a Pluto card. Furthermore, their card resides in the Crown Line of the Grand Solar. Both in their romantic life and their vocational ambitions, most Ten of Clubs individuals have a restlessness about them. Tens, it may be recalled, are much like Aces, with the Ace being a One and the Ten being a One with a Zero.

Nine of Clubs
Cosmic Consciousness

Characteristics: If Nine of Clubs people do not let greed spoil their spiritual characters, they do well in business, especially their own. Successful Diamond suit businesspeople often help in their business and financial goals. Honesty and moral values are their life challenges. They are frequently mixed up with others who are lacking in these areas, and this can drag them down. They are here to remain true to a philosophy that will guide them on the difficulties in life and to comprehend and focus their own mental power. Those who have this Birth card know connections and revelations about life itself and the truth behind the appearances on Earth. Expanded consciousness is the nature of the Nine of Clubs. Their revelations emanate occasionally when Nine of Clubs people let go of their attachment to some of their biases, ideas, and concepts. Individuals of this Birth card need to let go of a lot of negative mental habits collected from previous lives if they are to contact their inherent power. It can be a card of negative thoughts. Some reach the very highest form of recognition via their work and provide knowledge to the world. There are those, however, who are unable to do this. Sexuality is a part of this card's nature too. A highly sensuous aspect with strong love drives is created by the Queen of Clubs Karma card and Two of Hearts in Venus. Their great accomplishments could be wasted if their sensuality is allowed to take over. To end a major cycle in their soul's development is why Nine of Clubs individuals are here. This is a completion that ought to see them sharing their store of knowledge with the world. Debts are to be paid, particularly to Queen of Clubs people as well to their own relatives, but upon paying these debts they can continue with their cosmic assignment of enlightening others.

Relationships: Husbands of the Diamond suit frequently give lots of money to the Clubs women who have a special karma with them. A lot of them marry such a man at some time in their lives, and this can be seen in their King in Jupiter, which is a symbol for him. Many men and women alike are fated to be with the Six of Hearts Birth card, which has a particular karmic connection with the Nine of Clubs. They have high ideals of love and can be extremely romantic. Reality, however, frequently dashes this fantasy of love and their misplaced desires and dreams. Suffering is the result. Loving and sexual people are found among Nines of Clubs. Love affairs with Nines of Clubs are attractive to the Two of Hearts, as Venus tells us, and they actually favor romance over marriage. Nines of Clubs view marriage more as a responsibility and obligation than something to desire for its own sake. Extramarital affairs might result from this, or some choose to just be single in order to freely pursue their own goals. They are also very devoted to their children. As they become aware of responsibilities, they are fated to experience one or more very difficult relationships involving a true partnership. One significant love separation or divorce will likely alter their lives.

Personality Connections: Heart women are attracted to Nine of Clubs men. Diamond and Spade men often marry Nine of Clubs women. Spade males are a constant problem, but Diamond men often have something to give them.

Confrontations: The cards in their Life Path and their Karma cards reveal their secret even though nothing else does. Primary is the Two of Hearts in Venus. The significance of the Two of Hearts helps us realize some of this. Highly significant is the Venus-Neptune card residing in the Life Spread. The highest expression of Venus is in the sign of Pisces. Venus represents love, marriage, and sensuality. It is almost worshiped by astrologers. Piscean love is the highest expression of love symbolizing selflessness and universality. Leonardo DiCaprio, Demi Moore, Jack Nicholson, Al Pacino, and other stars have this special card, and some Nine of Clubs celebrities are among the sexiest actors and actresses in Hollywood.

Eight of Clubs
Psychic Prowess

Characteristics: The Eight of Clubs has powerful mental power and is not easily influenced by others' views and opinions. It is also one of only three Fixed cards. Eights of Clubs frequently make successful attorneys. They can conquer mental fields of any kind with great success. Scientists, physicists, doctors, and other challenging fields are fine for Eights of Clubs. They are capable of learning anything. One of the most successful life paths in the deck belongs to them. Wealth and fame are in their grasp, because they can achieve almost anything they are determined to do if they make certain their life is in balance. Maintaining success along with both psychological and emotional peace is important. They can be great healers and have a lot of psychic energy. They just need to truly know their real goals to be successful. A Jack of Clubs or King as a workmate brings excellent success, especially if they are dedicated to doing some great work for the world. To be most successful and in order to bring about happiness, they should keep their work and personal lives separate. It is hard for them to handle changes because they are so fixed; consequently, this has its drawbacks. Their mental approach, including concepts, ideas, and principles is what is so fixed. They often live their entire lives with the same principles they are born with. It is not possible, however, for a person to grow without changing some mental aspects of their lives. They must and will change on occasion. These are challenging, but a part of the Eight of Clubs karmic path. There is a kind of death and rebirth event when old ways of thinking change. After changes, they are invariably more healthy and alive.

Relationships: Their fixed nature makes Eight of Clubs individuals difficult to get along with at times. They do not find it easy to deal with changes of any kind. A young Diamond man is often the one who introduces them to a very spiritual or romantic love. Often this romance occurs when they are in their forties, and, having discovered there is more experience than just their rigid psychological concepts, they realize their need for adventure and a variation in romance. Their divorce, therefore, helps them move to a new stage in their lives and to escape their fixed concepts. Secret affairs can take place at any time during this stage. They have more freedom to pursue whatever sorts of relationships they need after this change takes place. The female Eight of Clubs should not let the personal and work get entwined, because only a disaster in both can result. There is good marriage karma with the Eight of Clubs essentially because they are a Fixed card and do not have a lot of emotional changes like other cards. In addition, they enjoy the stability of domestic and family life enough to avoid changes in love life that affect others. This is because of their Four in Venus. At one point in their life, unfortunately, many go through a difficult divorce. Someone of the Diamond suit is usually involved in this. Previous lives and karma are, like most things, the reason for this.

Personality Connections: Diamond women attract Eight of Clubs men, who never fail to bring challenges to their lives. Divorce for these men is frequently from a Diamond woman. Diamond males are not as bad for the women. There is often an attraction for Heart females by the Eight of Clubs man. Both genders get along fine with Club men.

Confrontations: As one of the three Fixed cards, Eight of Clubs individuals are particularly fixed in their psychological makeup. Changing their minds is not common. Once it is fixed they are usually unable to remove it. This can, at times, result in a very stubborn individual who is totally inflexible about some issues.

 Seven of Clubs
Cosmic Observation

Characteristics: As highly spiritual cards, Sevens need to turn this spirituality from a negative into accomplishment and personal autonomy. One trouble following another in their lives come about until they do this, because of the Seven's influence. Always resting in the negative areas of the mind, namely worry, pessimism, and doubt, is the Sevens of Clubs' challenge. If they do not follow their very high-level inborn inspirations and insights, Saturn's bearing brings despair and even depression. Their thoughts cause almost all of the issues they experience. More than the other cards in the deck, the Seven of Clubs has a major duty to keep positive as well as healthy thoughts. Spiritual thought of any kind is sure to be a positive force, as are strong ideals. The Seven of Clubs challenge, among other things, is developing honesty and integrity. This is the result of their Jack of Clubs Karma card, which is often nicknamed the Thief. Love and family will pay a price in the event that they let their need for success overcome their character. They have to apply themselves in a good fashion so they have the power to deal with their issues and to gain the fame and respect they secretly desire. Frequently they spend the large amounts of money they will probably acquire as fast as it comes in. Managing money is not something they are good at. As a result of their Karma card, they look for those who have power in other areas. They are good at getting a bargain but bad at holding on to money.

Relationships: Sevens of Clubs are more successful financially and always function better if they are married, and they will eventually make that commitment. Issues for the men come from the Jack of Clubs Karma card. A kind of flamboyant self-perception of an actor or great romantic person is how many of them see themselves. Promiscuity and deceit can result from this. Anything that will help them feel special, including extramarital affairs, is what many Sevens of Clubs desire most. They are more tempted with indecision in their personal lives and choosing a partner if they actually do become famous. Multiple marriages frequently result. The karma of the Seven of Clubs individual is neither bad nor good as far as love is concerned. It is how their life in general is dealt with that determines their personal love story. If they are diligent, the positive news is that they have more opportunities than any other card to acquire mastery of their emotional and romantic involvements. Determining how to release personal attachments to others or create a positive perspective about their partner, as well as the remainder of their lives, is an aspect of their karma.

Personality Connections: Seven of Clubs females tend to hold fantasies about other Club men and are greatly challenged by Diamond males, represented by their Jack of Clubs Pluto card. A male Spade might be the perfect match for a female Seven of Clubs. The Seven of Clubs has a special connection with Spade women or women who are hardworking and determined, regardless of suit.

Confrontations: There are sometimes major mood swings in Seven of Clubs individuals; they can first be jovial and not long later worried and depressed. Perhaps we can use a famous couple to illustrate some of this. Bill and Hillary Clinton seemed like the ideal couple. In the Ordinary Spread the Seven of Clubs and Nine of Clubs are located right next to each other. Already we can see a good marriage connection, but there is even more. Sitting right in front of the Seven of Clubs is the Nine of Clubs. This translates as the Nine of Clubs being the Moon card to the Seven of Clubs, and the Seven of Clubs the Mercury card to the Nine of Clubs. If the individual in the rear allows the person in the front to be the leader in a relationship, this can be a good combination. During Bill Clinton's presidency, Hillary was perfectly happy supporting him and allowing him, apparently, to take the leadership role. Those who support them can provide the necessary items they need to do their jobs. This is extremely important. Hillary gives Bill a feeling of structure and foundation coming from her Semi-Fixed Scorpio. Bill is Leo, Seven of Clubs, and destined to go through the positives and negatives in terms of confidence.

Six of Clubs
Revivalist

Characteristics: Sixes of Clubs always have problems with what they say and do because they are the cards that are responsible for the spoken word. While inwardly holding on to their own lies, some will proclaim their truthfulness for years. Dire results take place when their lies catch up with them, which they most certainly will. Of course, those who are on the high side of the card do what they say they will and are responsible. Abusing power seems to have some kind of connection with them though, and Six of Clubs individuals will usually have to confront that at some time in their lives. Power plays a role in their lives. They will either attract a person with power who brings about some struggles for them or receive some position with power and learn about it in that fashion. They are fated to learn the true meaning of power, however, and how it can corrupt people. It is odd how few of the individuals of these birth dates are aware of their psychic gifts because it is also known as the psychic card. Responsibility and truth are also meanings of the Six of Clubs. These individuals must learn to find a mechanism of truth in which they can have faith and formulate a method of life values. There is no limit, after attaining this, to the amount of good these individuals can accomplish in the world. People who fret, worry, and procrastinate are those in the deck who have not yet discovered their path. Helping others come to a special spiritual and mystical place is the special project that some Sixes of Clubs have in their lives. These are the keepers and carriers of the light. After tapping their inborn intuition and their hidden reserves, they will note that they are led and protected from on high. They are responsible for maintaining inner equilibrium and peace in communications with other people in their lives. They often have built-in protection in their lives and may achieve financial affluence. The most material or spiritual success attainable is by this card. There is always another side to the coin, however. In this case, they can get wrapped up in their self-satisfaction and amount to nothing.

Relationships: The Eight of Clubs Karma card is the connection here. Many pleasurable things come to the Six of Clubs. Romantic and sexual pleasure is something they will experience a significant amount of during the course of their lives, because the Queen of Clubs is in their Venus position. Watching out for the sexual side of life is something they would be wise to do. They have good marriage karma, and they generally have at least one fine marriage in their lives. There is kind of an idealized and romantic vision about love and marriage. Choosing a partner is something they need to do carefully, because at times their perfect mate may not turn out to be what they thought them to be. Being in love is something Six of Clubs loves as well. However, often there exists some childhood problems that interfere with their ability to make wise choices. Running from their feelings and emotions is something they have a tendency to do, and this causes them to appear emotional or upset. Such feelings, though, are paramount if Six of Clubs individuals are to actually comprehend themselves and discover the issues that drive them in their choice of relationships. While the men are often dominated by some females in their circle, the females make excellent wives and mothers.

Personality Connections: Spade men are difficult for both genders, particularly Spades more than thirty-six years old. Six of Clubs women and Diamond men have problems even though there is the attraction there. Club men and Six of Clubs are good friends. Heart women and Six of Clubs men are often found together because they hold a lot of affection for each other.

Confrontations: There is a huge acceleration of energy when we discover our purpose. It even increases enthusiasm for our work. At this point it stops being a job and transforms to a mission due to a loss of petty self-directed identity. We then unite with a purpose much greater than our ego. A power and ability we thought was impossible is the result. There is a deep-seated expression that is internal to every card in the deck, and this is found in the suit, number, and location in the Life Spread. We could speed up our journey of satisfaction and peace of mind if we just comprehended the nature of that highest expression.

Five of Clubs
Crusade for Legitimacy

Characteristics: Five of Clubs people are always on the go, because they have a lot of things they are curious about. These individuals change and have a mental restlessness about them. Changes in their romantic lives are there as well, as we can see in their Karma card. Thus, marriage is not usually suitable for them. They love adventure and research and exploring new things. Those interested in commitments, for this reason, are usually seriously avoided. The Five of Hearts is highly restless and practically nomadic. They are so changeable it actually borders on the extreme. Due to the fact that they can relate to a great many individuals on their own level, they are great in sales and promotion. These areas are especially good for the Virgo and Gemini birthdays because of their powerful presence and ways of expression that can bring good. They have a natural curiosity with a lot of potential for knowledge; however, they do not often utilize it. In addition, they have difficulty sticking to something. Skepticism is often the result, because they do not even get satisfaction from their own categories of belief. They can be disagreeable in debates just to try out the opposite side of a position. A more satisfactory approach is studies in spiritual material, because this can result in satisfaction in their later lives and give answers that allow more peace into their beings. In that respect a spiritual teacher would be useful. Moving to a new home or job means a change in lifestyle and thus responsibility. Being flexible helps, but there are still challenges with it. Clandestine love affairs and an inability to make up one's mind about which to choose is in the Ace of Hearts in Venus. A sexy and rich voice tone also comes from the same Ace. A lot of Fives of Clubs have large financial resources from the Seven of Clubs in Jupiter, which is a millionaire's card. Frequently they spend it or lose it as quickly as it is received. There should be an avoidance of speculation and gambling. Their tendency for spending money, even with their luck, means they are poor gamblers because they simply do no know when to quit.

Relationships: Values and their attitudes about them are the center of the matter, especially because there will be emotional losses in their life no matter what they do. The restless nature of Fives of Clubs means that they are, perhaps, the least marriageable card in the deck. Commitment is avoided any way they can. The sneaky ones often try to pin the problem on their spouse or partner. But, as a matter of fact, they are profoundly fearful of any relationship because of freedom issues. Clandestine affairs, sometimes even with married people, can come about because of this fear coupled with their Ace of Hearts in Venus. Privacy is also something they value highly. In general, they are best off single. Relative to relationships, sometimes it seems that being a Five of Clubs can be a blessing, depending on the individual. They can, on the positive side, relate to almost anyone on their own level. They are also very progressive individuals. As a result they are popular, sociable individuals, but there is an issue with commitments, which they fear. This can be so overwhelming that they are like magnets for sometime bizarre situations. This can prevent them from having the inner peace necessary for a real relationship.

Personality Connections: Fives of Clubs of both genders like to be with Club women. Diamond men and Five of Clubs women often have a good marriage. Heart men are friends of both genders, who seem attracted to them. A difficulty can arise because of a karmic connection.

Confrontations: Some, however, are able to accept this restlessness and inquisitive nature and utilize it in their lives positively. Doing so can bring about a measure of financial success and satisfaction at work. There is an unhappiness with themselves for Fives of Hearts. Being unable to accomplish things of significance or worry about finances plagues them.

Four of Clubs
Psychic Contentment

Characteristics: Four of Clubs individuals want to be accepted by people as the result of their motivation and drive. But they hide their desire to accept themselves behind wanting acceptance from others. Work can, for some, take the place of the desire to be loved. Financial success and protection often arrive for them late in life. This card shows that happiness and success can be applied to what we already have. It means they are practical. An invisible restlessness can reveal itself in several fashions even though the Four of Clubs is a stable card in general. This is because of the underlying Five of Hearts. It is possible for them to use their progressive approach to initiate new ideas in the field instead of allowing something to block success. They are not likely to change their minds, because they are confident in their own knowledge. Frequently they are thought of as stubborn. They generally win in arguments, which they enjoy, and they are also good at legal issues. Hard work does not bother them because of their excellent health and stamina. They are successful and particularly excellent at sales because of the ease with which they talk with other people. They also like to talk about their beliefs. If they do not let their love of debating get the best of them, they are popular and do fine with groups of people. Their reputations are generally stellar, but they also desire a successful love life, and this is their biggest challenge in life.

Relationships: Their basic karma in love is good. A partner who enjoys some space can help provide happiness. Venus informs us that they must be cautious about their choice of peers because they might seek out those of ill repute. Dishonest but romantic lovers result from choosing this lower aspect, and they will attract those of similar values. Questionable associates are often artistic types, who they are frequently attracted to. On the high side they can also seek out those of a spiritual nature and have relationships that are more satisfying. A significant issue in their lives is their desire for affection. This can reveal itself several ways. Unfortunately, painful relationships can come about if this need is mixed with their restlessness and fear of commitment. However, this does not apply to them all.

Personality Connections: Club women are a weakness for Four of Clubs men, as are Spade women. This is particularly the case if they are under twenty-four years old. Fast friends are made with Spade men and Four of Clubs women, but Diamond and Heart men see Four of Clubs women as particularly appealing. There is a big challenge with other Club men.

Confrontations: Happily married people as well should be careful of their mates. Cases of deception and infidelity are common, and, in some cases, this is very long lasting. They can be quite clever in their deceptions, such that no one suspects it. There is great potential for using their assets in negative ways and being liars and manipulators. The Jack of Clubs shows us that the Four of Clubs can behave dishonestly in romantic life, attract others, or a combination of both. Possible negatives are lying about their real intentions in order to get sexual pleasure or money. Sometimes they simply do not mean what they say. In the Venus position the Four of Clubs indicates that the Jack of Clubs is set up to have relationships with dishonest and immoral individuals. The actor and the thief is what they represent. Consequently, Four of Clubs people can be with musicians, actors, and artists in addition to those with dubious values and belief systems.

Three of Clubs
Essayist

Characteristics: Once Three of Clubs individuals decide on a single philosophy and stick with it, they can be excellent salespeople or even propagandists. Business is definitely the forte of this card. They have an aptitude for business because of the second Karma card. Big business and big finances are what moves them and they can, under the right circumstances, be great leaders. An issue can develop as the result of their first Karma card, which leans them toward vocations that limit their freedom too much. Freelance work or other areas that permit more autonomy call them for this reason. Because the Three of Clubs is very creative, some good things in that area are possible. They include being successful writers, actors, or teachers. They can, on the negative side, be worriers and let indecisiveness get in their way; they may waste time on the frivolous. Repeatedly, even with successful individuals, there is a strong tendency to worry, fret, and have difficulty deciding things. This can be lifelong. How God-given abilities and blessings are applied in life is what determines success. Sadness will come into their live through emotional loss in relationships that seemed eternal but, as it turns out, are not. These graduations or completions, as they are best viewed, can lift them to a higher plane such that they limit their disappointment. Universal love is a potential in their lives if they activate their spiritual knowledge and inheritance. Changing worry into something creative and transforming energy in this manner is why they are here. Faith is the operative word. This could result in them being great examples for others. They can be tempted to use their creativity in dubious fashions, because this card gives them a fear of poverty motivating them at times. They generally get caught if they try to involve themselves in immoral activities. Something pertaining to entertainment is a possibility for this card, because they can use their creativity to be writers, speakers, or producers.

Relationships: Playing the field, dating, and enjoying the variety that life has to offer makes the most sense in terms of happiness for Threes of Clubs. A lover in addition to their spouse is possible for these individuals. Losses come into their lives, but happiness is possible once they decide to refuse anything less than what they desire. These are very kind people with very good hearts, and they will do almost anything for others. Plainly put, they have to deal with a lot prior to having a meaningful relationship. Commitments are the issue for this fundamentally indecisive person. But they do try to experience the essence of life and the variety of things it has to offer; this is a positive. Relationships are often a come-and-go situation. Continuing to move toward those who do not make commitments themselves is a big drawback for them.

Personality Connections: Threes of Clubs of both genders can be good friends with Clubs men, but there is little marriage potential there. Spades women should be avoided by both genders. Diamond women are a weakness for Three of Clubs men, and there is a possible love connection there. A possibility for a meaningful relationship exists. Diamond men are enjoyed by Three of Clubs women, and there is a positive mysterious aspect there.

Confrontations: Threes are fond of keeping options open in their lives so they can go in different directions. Allowing for every possibility, though, can be hard work. All of these choices can become annoying and can become the cause of problems in addition to being enjoyable. The Three of Clubs knows this. A sort of panic attack can be precipitated. There can be quick shifts in mood as the result of this nervous tension. Three of Clubs individuals are happy. They are loquacious and enjoyable to be with. Distress can pop into their lives, however, and they begin to question every detail. Variety is something all Three of Clubs people value.

Two of Clubs
Conversationalist

Characteristics: Interestingly, the Two of Clubs has many gifts and aptitudes. They can be excellent at business, particularly in partnerships, and usually are good with others. The life path is a lucky one. This card is protected, and these individuals need to feel gratitude for their good fortune. They just need to look around at their lives and they should realize that they are blessed and their fear will be released. They are able to think clearly most of the time and are highly intelligent. If they avoid fear, which can negatively impact their mood, they are clever and charming. Their challenge in life is to accept themselves, their situation, and their close relationships. There is a huge variety of personality types in this card. They often need to be around others because of fear of being by themselves. They want people to talk to and make them feel good about themselves. In spite of this, they are good conversationalists and very sociable for the most part. However, they can be recluses, too, and need absolutely no one. Attachment is the issue and they are afraid of this. Internal fear, especially of change and death, comes from their Karma card and explains their personality.

Relationships: The Queen of Clubs is often an indication of the sort of relationship they might have. Primarily it is one of learning the meaning of responsibility. The Pluto card needs to be looked at carefully, because it is often associated with difficulties standing in the way of a satisfactory love life. The Two of Clubs are often attractive or even beautiful people in addition to having a good intellect. They appear to be the type who can choose their partner at will. Oddly, they often choose the least likely person of all. Women generally do this more than men. Their love of self and emotional well-being are prime movers in their love relationships. They can, unfortunately, settle for just anyone, including abusive or otherwise sick individuals, just to be with another person. Codependence and a totally disappointing relationship can result. A partner who is beneath them is not unusual, and at that point they commence criticizing even superficial things and paying attention to the negative. Backing off a bit on this tendency not only will help the relationship but also brings out a better side of their partner. If they let their idealism reign they are both happier. Being careful about who they choose as a partner can help a lot. A very sexual partner is often the choice, according to Mars, but that person can be difficult to get along with and aggressive as well. Two of Clubs people can also be the one to start arguments. Their mental set is such that they like to pick at others and be a faultfinder. This, of course, does not help in relationships.

Personality Connections: As for Diamond men and Two of Clubs women, there is a powerful love connection that brings pleasure but is probably not lasting. Two of Clubs males should be careful with Heart females. That connection is very challenging. Clubs and Diamonds men get along well with Two of Clubs females. If she is a homebody, she would be an excellent choice for a spouse.

Confrontations: *Sacred Symbols of the Ancients* by Florence Campbell takes a hard stand regarding Two of Clubs. She claims that the Two of Clubs is highly fearful and mentally challenging. However, in our experience that is most often not the case.

♣ Ace of Clubs
Passion for Consciousness

Characteristics: As Aces they need travel and change in their lives and perhaps their work, too. This is necessary to take care of their need for knowledge. Things associated with the arts or groups, particularly women, are possible sources of income for them. They can turn most things into a profit. The main influence for the Ace of Clubs is wanting knowledge and love. This comes from their Karma card. Oftentimes the result is a student of romance and love, perhaps as much or more than a desire for love itself. There is a strong notion of promiscuity associated with Aces of Clubs, but not once they have found their soul mates. Being with any person is, for them, preferable to being alone. They do not, however, truly give themselves until they have found the right person. As is the case with all Aces, there is a restlessness about them as well as impatience. They frequently have a large library and other collections of learning materials because they are such dedicated students. Their wide spectrum of interests keeps them young at heart. New ideas, fashion, controversies, discoveries, and ideas are always of their interest. Spirituality is important for their later years because they need it for guidance. The latter portion of their lives are influenced by the two Sevens in Uranus and Neptune, and this means they will either have financial problems or spiritual awakenings. A lifelong journey in search of knowledge is what brings them happiness, as does discovering themselves. Their personality is very friendly and kind and this allows them to easily make friends in any situation. They are excellent communicators. They make people feel comfortable, special, and included in what is happening. They tend to be loquacious but quick and sharp in their mental abilities. Frequently these individuals' mothers are important figures in their lives. They are powerful and intelligent as well as intuitive. The mothers can have such strong effect that they influence everything in these individuals' lives, including love and romance.

Relationships: The Aces of Clubs are lovers and have an eternal search for the perfect love, which does not necessarily translate into a perfect marriage. In the event we find them, we can marry our perfect lover, but that that does not mean it is necessary—at least for the Ace of Clubs. The Ace of Clubs is searching for a relationship that transcends time and space. As with the Two of Hearts, they can be promiscuous. But again, this generally does not take place with one who has found their perfect soul mate. Should they find that individual they are almost sure to be monogamous as well as devoted. This is a Semi-Fixed card, one of just four. There is a special connection with the Two of Hearts because it is a Karmic Soul Twin. These cards are, in some sense, reproductions of each other; mirror images, if you will. Their personalities are almost identical relative to their traits as well as their characteristics.

Personality Connections: Ace of Clubs men have trouble with Heart women. Clubs women are friends with Ace of Clubs men and occasionally lovers. Other Clubs are attractive to the Ace of Clubs women, and they can be friends or lovers. Problems usually result from Diamonds, particularly the Jack and King. Ace of Clubs women are loved by Spade men.

Confrontations: There are two types of Ace of Clubs individuals. They seem to fall into the categories of those who have long periods with no relationships and those who flit from one relationship to another. Neither type lets someone get close to them. Analyzing this helps us realize that both types are being too fussy about their lovers.

BIRTH CARD DATES

January

1. K♠	17. 10♦		
2. Q♠	18. 9♦		
3. J♠	19. 8♦		
4. 10♠	20. 7♦		
5. 9♠	21. 6♦		
6. 8♠	22. 5♦		
7. 7♠	23. 4♦		
8. 6♠	24. 3♦		
9. 5♠	25. 2♦		
10. 4♠	26. A♦		
11. 3♠	27. K♣		
12. 2♠	28. Q♣		
13. A♠	29. J♣		
14. K♦	30. 10♣		
15. Q♦	31. 9♣		
16. J♦			

February

1. J♠	17. 8♦
2. 10♠	18. 7♦
3. 9♠	19. 6♦
4. 8♠	20. 5♦
5. 7♠	21. 4♦
6. 6♠	22. 3♦
7. 5♠	23. 2♦
8. 4♠	24. A♦
9. 3♠	25. K♣
10. 2♠	26. Q♣
11. A♠	27. J♣
12. K♦	28. 10♣
13. Q♦	29. 9♣
14. J♦	
15. 10♦	
16. 9♦	

March

1. 9♠	17. 6♦
2. 8♠	18. 5♦
3. 7♠	19. 4♦
4. 6♠	20. 3♦
5. 5♠	21. 2♦
6. 4♠	22. A♦
7. 3♠	23. K♣
8. 2♠	24. Q♣
9. A♠	25. J♣
10. K♦	26. 10♣
11. Q♦	27. 9♣
12. J♦	28. 8♣
13. 10♦	29. 7♣
14. 9♦	30. 6♣
15. 8♦	31. 5♣
16. 7♦	

April

1. 7♠	17. 4♦
2. 6♠	18. 3♦
3. 5♠	19. 2♦
4. 4♠	20. A♦
5. 3♠	21. K♣
6. 2♠	22. Q♣
7. A♠	23. J♣
8. K♦	24. 10♣
9. Q♦	25. 9♣
10. J♦	26. 8♣
11. 10♦	27. 7♣
12. 9♦	28. 6♣
13. 8♦	29. 5♣
14. 7♦	30. 4♣
15. 6♦	
16. 5♦	

May

1. 5♠	17. 2♦
2. 4♠	18. A♦
3. 3♠	19. K♣
4. 2♠	20. Q♣
5. A♠	21. J♣
6. K♦	22. 10♣
7. Q♦	23. 9♣
8. J♦	24. 8♣
9. 10♦	25. 7♣
10. 9♦	26. 6♣
11. 8♦	27. 5♣
12. 7♦	28. 4♣
13. 6♦	29. 3♣
14. 5♦	30. 2♣
15. 4♦	31. A♣
16. 3♦	

June

1. 3♠	17. K♣
2. 2♠	18. Q♣
3. A♠	19. J♣
4. K♦	20. 10♣
5. Q♦	21. 9♣
6. J♦	22. 8♣
7. 10♦	23. 7♣
8. 9♦	24. 6♣
9. 8♦	25. 5♣
10. 7♦	26. 4♣
11. 6♦	27. 3♣
12. 5♦	28. 2♣
13. 4♦	29. A♣
14. 3♦	30. K♥
15. 2♦	
16. A♦	

July

1. A♠	17. J♣
2. K♦	18. 10♣
3. Q♦	19. 9♣
4. J♦	20. 8♣
5. 10♦	21. 7♣
6. 9♦	22. 6♣
7. 8♦	23. 5♣
8. 7♦	24. 4♣
9. 6♦	25. 3♣
10. 5♦	26. 2♣
11. 4♦	27. A♣
12. 3♦	28. K♥
13. 2♦	29. Q♥
14. A♦	30. J♥
15. K♣	31. 10♥
16. Q♣	

August

1. Q♦	17. 9♣
2. J♦	18. 8♣
3. 10♦	19. 7♣
4. 9♦	20. 6♣
5. 8♦	21. 5♣
6. 7♦	22. 4♣
7. 6♦	23. 3♣
8. 5♦	24. 2♣
9. 4♦	25. A♣
10. 3♦	26. K♥
11. 2♦	27. Q♥
12. A♦	28. J♥
13. K♣	29. 10♥
14. Q♣	30. 9♥
15. J♣	31. 8♥
16. 10♣	

September

1. 10♦	17. 7♣
2. 9♦	18. 6♣
3. 8♦	19. 5♣
4. 7♦	20. 4♣
5. 6♦	21. 3♣
6. 5♦	22. 2♣
7. 4♦	23. A♣
8. 3♦	24. K♥
9. 2♦	25. Q♥
10. A♦	26. J♥
11. K♣	27. 10♥
12. Q♣	28. 9♥
13. J♣	29. 8♥
14. 10♣	30. 7♥
15. 9♣	
16. 8♣	

October

1. 8♦	17. 5♣
2. 7♦	18. 4♣
3. 6♦	19. 3♣
4. 5♦	20. 2♣
5. 4♦	21. A♣
6. 3♦	22. K♥
7. 2♦	23. Q♥
8. A♦	24. J♥
9. K♣	25. 10♥
10. Q♣	26. 9♥
11. J♣	27. 8♥
12. 10♣	28. 7♥
13. 9♣	29. 6♥
14. 8♣	30. 5♥
15. 7♣	31. 4♥
16. 6♣	

November

1. 6♦	17. 3♣
2. 5♦	18. 2♣
3. 4♦	19. A♣
4. 3♦	20. K♥
5. 2♦	21. Q♥
6. A♦	22. J♥
7. K♣	23. 10♥
8. Q♣	24. 9♥
9. J♣	25. 8♥
10. 10♣	26. 7♥
11. 9♣	27. 6♥
12. 8♣	28. 5♥
13. 7♣	29. 4♥
14. 6♣	30. 3♥
15. 5♣	
16. 4♣	

December

1. 4♦	17. A♣
2. 3♦	18. K♥
3. 2♦	19. Q♥
4. A♦	20. J♥
5. K♣	21. 10♥
6. Q♣	22. 9♥
7. J♣	23. 8♥
8. 10♣	24. 7♥
9. 9♣	25. 6♥
10. 8♣	26. 5♥
11. 7♣	27. 4♥
12. 6♣	28. 3♥
13. 5♣	29. 2♥
14. 4♣	30. A♥
15. 3♣	31. *Joker*
16. 2♣	

Famous Birthdays

We trust that you have enjoyed your journey creating your own persona from five different angles—Chinese twelve animals, Western zodiac, Sun and Moon Sign combinations, Chinese and Western combinations, and your Birth card personality and destiny.

Now let us have some fun with some heroes or stars of the past as you discover their personas and why they did the things they did or are currently doing.

To review how to determine someone's persona, if you were born, for example, on June 6, 1956, then you would use the charts at the end of chapters 2, 3, and 4 to determine your persona (year, element, combinations, and Birth card) as follows:

You were born the Year of the	Fire/Monkey
Month of the	Horse (Gemini)
Animal (Monkey) and Zodiac (Gemini) combination of the	Gemini-Monkey
Sun (Gemini) and Moon (Taurus) Sign of the	Instigator
Jack of Diamonds Birth card of the	Seller

This would give you the persona of the Fire Monkey, Horse, Gemini-Monkey, Instigator, and Seller. After reading the analyses from chapters 1, 2, 3, and 4 of your complete persona, you will have a clear understanding of yourself and how you interact with the people around you. Also, you will understand why they react to you the way they do.

EXAMPLES OF PERSONAS OF FAMOUS PEOPLE

Michelangleo Buonarroti was born March 6, 1475:

The Year of the	Wood/Ram
Month of the	Rabbit (Pisces)
Animal (Ram) and Zodiac (Pisces) Combination of the	Pisces-Ram
Zodiac Sun (Pisces) and Moon (Virgo) Combination of the	Complusive Purist
Birth card of Four of Spades, or	Bliss in Labor

George Washington was born February 22, 1732:

The Year of the	Water/Rat
Month of the	Rabbit (Pisces)
Animal (Rat) and Zodiac (Pisces) Combination of the	Pisces-Rat
Zodiac Sun (Pisces) and Moon (Sagittarius) Combination of the	Sophist
Birth card of the Three of Diamonds, or	Monetary Inventiveness

Marie Antoinette was born November 2, 1755:

The Year of the	Wood/Boar
Month of the	Boar (Scorpio)
Animal (Boar) and Zodiac (Scorpio) Combination of the	Scorpio-Boar
Zodiac Sun (Scorpio) and Moon (Virgo) Combination of the	Bloodhound
Birth card of the Five of Diamonds, or	Inquirer of Value

Henry David Thoreau was born July 12, 1817:

The Year of the	Fire/Buffalo
Month of the	Ram (Cancer)
Animal (Buffalo) and Zodiac (Cancer) Combination of the	Cancer-Buffalo
Zodiac Sun (Cancer) and Moon (Gemini) Combination of the	Sky Wire
Birth card of Three of Diamonds, or	Monetary Inventiveness

Nicola Tesla was born July 9, 1856:

The Year of the	Fire/Dragon
Month of the	Ram (Cancer)
Animal (Dragon) and Zodiac (Cancer) Combination of the	Cancer-Dragon
Zodiac Sun (Cancer) and Moon (Libra) Combination of the	Yes Man
Birth card of the Eight of Diamonds, or	Solar Star

Marilyn Monroe was born June 1, 1926:

The Year of the	Fire/Tiger
Month of the	Horse (Gemini)
Animal (Tiger) and Zodiac (Gemini) Combination of the	Gemini-Tiger
Zodiac Sun (Gemini) and Moon (Aquarius) Combination of the	Originator
Birth card of the Three of Spades, or	Artisan

John Lennon was born October 9, 1940:

The Year of the	Metal/Dragon
Month of the	Dog (Libra)
Animal (Dragon) and Zodiac (Libra) Combination of the	Libra-Dragon
Zodiac Sun (Libra) and Moon (Aquarius) Combination of the	Altruist
Birth card of the King of Clubs, or	Master of Knowledge

Bill Gates was born October 28, 1955:

The Year of the	Wood/Ram
Month of the	Boar (Scorpio)
Animal (Ram) and Zodiac (Scorpio) Combination of the	Scorpio-Ram
Zodiac Sun (Scorpio) and Moon (Aries) Combination of the	Dude
Birth card of the Seven of Hearts, or	Metaphysical Rapture

Tiger Woods was born December 30, 1975:

The Year of the	Wood/Rabbit
Month of the	Buffalo (Capricorn)
Animal (Rabbit) and Zodiac (Capricorn) Combination of the	Capricorn-Rabbit
Zodiac Sun (Capricorn) and Moon (Leo) Combination of the	Absolute Ruler
Birth card of Ace of Hearts, or	Complusion for Adoration

You can find the persona of admired people throughout history in all the arts, business, government, and sports with this book. If you study history, these energy patterns keep reappearing. So, remember the key to life from a Taoist perspective is to enjoy the ride, and trust that with a clear understanding of your complete persona it will become easier to deal with yourself and others as you achieve your own divinity in your life.

# Bibliography

Andersen, Jefferson. *Sun Sign Moon Sign*. Los Angeles: International Books, 1967.

Camp, Robert Lee. *Love Cards*. Concord, Calif.: Seven Thunders Pubishing, 2004.

Chia, Mantak, and W. U. Wei. *Sexual Reflexology: The Tao of Love and Sex*. Thailand: Universal Tao Publications, 2002.

Ende, Michael. *The Neverending Story*. New York: Penguin, 1984.

Grahame, Kenneth. *The Wind in the Willows*. New York: Aladdin Publishing, 1989.

Koh, Vincent. *Hsia Calendar: 1924–2024*. Singapore: Asiapac Books Pte. Ltd, 1998.

Lao-tsu. *Tao Te Ching*. Translated by Gia-Fu Feng and Jane English. New York: Random House, 1972.

"Moon Sign Calendar." http://Moonsigncalendar.net/moonphase.asp (accessed February 12, 2012).

Randall, Edith L., and Florence Evylinn Campbell. *Sacred Symbols of the Ancients: The Mystical Significance of Our Fifty-Two "Playing" Cards and Their Amazing Connection with Our Individual Birthdays*. Camarillo, Calif.: DeVorss and Company, 1974.

Sewell, Anna. *Black Beauty*. New York: HarperCollins, 1998. First published in 1877.

Tolkien, J. R. R. *The Hobbit: Or, There and Back Again*. New York: Houghton Mifflin Books, 1966.

White, Suzanne. *Chinese Astrology Plain and Simple*. New York: St. Martin's Press, 1998.

———. *The New Astrology: The Chinese and Western*. New York: St. Martin's Press 1988.

Wu, Cheng'en. *Monkey: Folk Novel of China*. Translated by Arthur Waley. Auckland, New Zealand: Evergreen Books, 1994.

About the Authors

MANTAK CHIA

Mantak Chia has been studying the Taoist approach to life since childhood. His mastery of this ancient knowledge, enhanced by his study of other disciplines, has resulted in the development of the Universal Healing Tao system, which is now being taught throughout the world.

Mantak Chia was born in Thailand to Chinese parents in 1944. When he was six years old he learned from Buddhist monks how to sit and "still the mind." While in grammar school he learned traditional Thai boxing, and he soon went on to acquire considerable skill in aikido, yoga, and Tai Chi. His studies of the Taoist way of life began in earnest when he was a student in Hong Kong, ultimately leading to his mastery of a wide variety of esoteric disciplines, with the guidance of several masters, including Master I Yun, Master Meugi, Master Cheng Yao Lun, and Master Pan Yu. To better understand the mechanisms behind healing energy, he also studied Western anatomy and medical sciences.

Master Chia has taught his system of healing and energizing practices to tens of thousands of students and trained more than two thousand instructors and practitioners throughout the world. He has established centers for Taoist study and training in many countries around the globe. In June of 1990 he was honored by the International Congress of Chinese Medicine and Qi Gong (Chi Kung), which named him the Qi Gong Master of the Year.

WILLIAM U. WEI

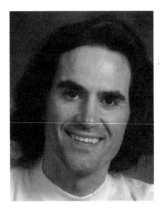

Born after World War II, growing up in the Midwest area of the United States, and trained in Catholicism, William Wei became a student of the Tao started studying under Master Mantak Chia in the early 1980s. In the later 1980s he became a senior instructor of the Universal Healing Tao, specializing in one-on-one training. In the early 1990s William Wei moved to Tao Garden, Thailand, and assisted Master Mantak Chia in building Tao Garden Taoist Training Center. For six years William traveled to more than thirty countries, teaching with Master Mantak Chia and serving as marketing and construction coordinator for the Tao Garden. Upon completion of Tao Garden in December 2000, he became project manager for all the Universal Tao Publications and products. With the purchase of a mountain with four waterfalls in southern Oregon, USA, in the late 1990s, William Wei is presently completing a Taoist Mountain Sanctuary for personal cultivation, higher-level practices, and ascension. William Wei is the coauthor with Master Chia of *Sexual Reflexology*, *Living in the Tao*, and the Taoist poetry book of 366 daily poems, *Emerald River*, which expresses the feeling, essence, and stillness of the Tao. He is also the co-creator with Master Mantak Chia of the Universal Healing Tao formula cards, Chi Cards (six sets of over 240 formulas) under the pen name The Professor—Master of Nothingness, the Myth that takes the Mystery out of Mysticism. William U. Wei, also known as Wei Tzu, is a pen name for this instructor so the instructor can remain anonymous and can continue to become a blade of grass in a field of grass.

The Universal Tao System and Training Center

THE UNIVERSAL TAO SYSTEM

The ultimate goal of Taoist practice is to transcend physical boundaries through the development of the soul and the spirit within the human. That is also the guiding principle behind the Universal Tao, a practical system of self-development that enables individuals to complete the harmonious evolution of their physical, mental, and spiritual bodies. Through a series of ancient Chinese meditative and internal energy exercises, the practitioner learns to increase physical energy, release tension, improve health, practice self-defense, and gain the ability to heal him- or herself and others. In the process of creating a solid foundation of health and well-being in the physical body, the practitioner also creates the basis for developing his or her spiritual potential by learning to tap into the natural energies of the sun, moon, earth, stars, and other environmental forces.

The Universal Tao practices are derived from ancient techniques rooted in the processes of nature. They have been gathered and integrated into a coherent, accessible system for well-being that works directly with the life force, or chi, that flows through the meridian system of the body.

Master Chia has spent years developing and perfecting techniques for teaching these traditional practices to students around the world through ongoing classes, workshops, private instruction, and healing sessions, as well as books and video and audio products. Further information can be obtained at www.universal-tao.com.

THE UNIVERSAL TAO TRAINING CENTER

The Tao Garden Resort and Training Center in northern Thailand is the home of Master Chia and serves as the worldwide headquarters for Universal Tao activities. This integrated wellness, holistic health, and training center is situated on eighty acres surrounded by the beautiful Himalayan foothills near the historic walled city of Chiang Mai. The serene setting includes flower and herb gardens ideal for meditation, open-air pavilions for practicing Chi Kung, and a health and fitness spa.

The center offers classes year round, as well as summer and winter retreats. It can accommodate two hundred students, and group leasing can be arranged. For information worldwide on courses, books, products, and other resources, see below.

RESOURCES

Universal Healing Tao Center
274 Moo 7, Luang Nua, Doi Saket, Chiang Mai, 50220 Thailand
Tel: (66)(53) 495-596 Fax: (66)(53) 495-852
E-mail: universaltao@universal-tao.com
Web site: www.universal-tao.com

For information on retreats and the health spa, contact:
Tao Garden Health Spa & Resort
E-mail: info@tao-garden.com, taogarden@hotmail.com
Web site: www.tao-garden.com

Good Chi • Good Heart • Good Intention